The Sociology of Sports

Third Edition

The Sociology of Sports

An Introduction

THIRD EDITION

TIM DELANEY *and*
TIM MADIGAN

McFarland & Company, Inc., Publishers
Jefferson, North Carolina

All photographs were provided by Tim Delaney
unless otherwise noted.

LIBRARY OF CONGRESS CATALOGUING-IN-PUBLICATION DATA

Names: Delaney, Tim, author. | Madigan, Tim, author.
Title: The sociology of sports : an introduction / Tim Delaney, Tim Madigan.
Description: Third Edition. | Jefferson, North Carolina :
McFarland & Company, Inc., Publishers, 2021 | Revised edition of the authors'
The sociology of sports, 2015 | Includes bibliographical references and index.
Identifiers: LCCN 2021037503 | ISBN 9781476682372 (paperback : acid free paper) ∞
ISBN 9781476644097 (ebook)
Subjects: LCSH: Sports—Sociological aspects.
Classification: LCC GV706.5 .D463 2021 | DDC 306.4/83—dc23
LC record available at https://lccn.loc.gov/2021037503

BRITISH LIBRARY CATALOGUING DATA ARE AVAILABLE

ISBN (print) 978-1-4766-8237-2
ISBN (ebook) 978-1-4766-4409-7

Front cover images © 2021 Shutterstock

Printed in the United States of America

*McFarland & Company, Inc., Publishers
Box 611, Jefferson, North Carolina 28640
www.mcfarlandpub.com*

Tim Delaney dedicates this text to two
early founders of the sociology of sport
who had a great influence on him—
James H. Frey and Hal Charnofsky.

While Hal passed away years ago sadly,
Jim remains as a steady confidant
and that is greatly appreciated.

Tim Madigan dedicates the book
to two other stalwarts in the sociology
of sports—Don Sabo and Merrill Melnick.

Table of Contents

Preface

Sports are a universal phenomenon. There is no known culture which has not engaged in some sort of sporting activity, and participating in and being a fan of various sports is an important aspect of billions of people's lives. From early childhood, individuals start the process of taking part in organized games, and it is a rare person who has no interest at all in rooting for (or against) particular organized (including national) teams. The study of sport, therefore, is of value, both for its own sake and for what it can tell us about individuals, cultures, and societies.

In this, the third edition of *The Sociology of Sports: An Introduction*, the authors have significantly updated statistics/data and information found in each chapter, and many of the "Connecting Sports and Popular Culture" boxes have also been revised or replaced. That the information and statistics found in each chapter has been updated is an expectation of a new edition; it is the state of affairs in which the book was updated that is especially noteworthy. These circumstances include a global pandemic (COVID-19) that wreaked havoc around the world, especially in the United States, and impacted sports at all levels and in all sorts of ways including the cancellation, postponement, or drastic modification under which sports were played in 2020 (this pandemic would influence the authors as they penned this new edition throughout 2020). At the time of this writing, it was too soon to know if sports in 2021 were also affected, although many winter 2020–21 sports were negatively impacted. The pandemic served as a figurative "slap in the face" that reminded us that we cannot take anything for granted, not even annual sporting seasons and events. In addition to the global pandemic were social movements such as Black Lives Matter and Me Too that impacted sports and became of paramount importance from a sociological perspective. The Black Lives Matter movement was especially impactful as it involved a large cross-section of Americans protesting daily over a period of consecutive months for racial and social justice. The impact of the BLM movement led to demands to "defund" the police; racist statues being knocked down; musical acts changing their names; product brands changing their names; and the demise (finally) of both the NFL's Washington franchise's and MLB's Cleveland franchise's racist nicknames. The BLM movement also contributed to an increasing number of athletes protesting during the playing of the national anthem, resulting in a further polarization between certain socio-ideological groups of people.

Another topic that came to the forefront in recent years is the "pay for play" concept wherein college athletes demanded greater compensation and, at the very least, the right to profit from their own names, images, and likenesses (NIL). The issue of NIL is in its infancy and will surely have a dramatic impact on collegiate sports and likely high school sports as well. As schools have come to realize, it has become increasing difficult to distinguish between a student capitalizing on their athletic fame and being a social influencer. The economic importance of football to colleges became very clear when many great efforts were made in an attempt to assure that college football would be played in 2020 and athletes were initially asked to sign health waivers amidst a global pandemic. In September, many of the major college (FBS) programs did start playing football, including three of the Power Five conferences (ACC, Big 12, and SEC) along with the American Athletic Conference, Conference USA, the Sun Belt Conference, and some independents. After first stating they would not play football in 2020 due to concerns with the pandemic, the remaining FBS conferences decided to delay the start of their football season and play a reduced number of games: Big 10, late October, 10 games; Pac-12, early November, 7 games; Mountain West, late October, 8 games; and the Mid–American Conference, early November, 6 games. The 2020 season was concluded and a limited number of bowl games were played and a national champion crowned. With the pandemic still not eradicated prior to the start of the 2021 season the COVID-19 concerns continued.

As with the earlier editions of *The Sociology of Sports*, this third edition maintains a commitment to a straightforward, student-friendly presentation of key sociological concepts and issues that pertain to the sociological study and analysis of sport in contemporary society. That is to say we describe the institution of sport, present theories that explain why sports are so important to people and societies, present a historical look at sports, and describe the cultural aspects of sports. The importance of the socialization process is demonstrated through sport. We also reveal the interplay between major sport and social institutions (e.g., education, gender, race and ethnicity, economics, politics, religion and the media). Other important subject areas discussed include youth sports, deviance, and violence. Each chapter contains key material on the topic at hand, a popular culture box, summary, key terms listing, and discussion questions. Chapter tables have been updated with the most current data and, in some cases, new tables created, including in Chapter 2 where we introduce a new concept, "Basking in Another's Failure" (BIAF), and present our preliminary research on this topic. We continued to update our tables on our research on heroes (Chapter 4) and the role of prayer (Chapter 14) in sports.

In Chapter 16, the final chapter, we describe some of the many reasons people love sports other than the games and sporting events themselves. Among these reasons are fantasy sports; video gaming; the desire and need for physical activity; sports for people with special needs and physical disabilities; new and unusual sports that attract new sports fans; a discussion on the creations of sports studies programs; and our continued emphasis on the value of sportsmanship.

This third edition of *The Sociology of Sports* covers all of the major topics of the sports world and we firmly believe that it represents the best sociology of sport text on the market. The text was certainly written during a historic point in sports. Little did we anticipate when we began working on this new edition of the book that the sports world would turn upside down when we had finished it. For the first time, a worldwide pandemic temporarily caused the suspension of almost all sporting activities across the globe, including the postponement of the 2020 Summer Olympic Games. Athletes and sports fans were blindsided by this completely unexpected chain of events (including the authors of this book, two ardent sports enthusiasts who had looked forward to supporting their favorite sports teams and athletes). This was followed by another unprecedented situation, as all four of the major North American team sports (baseball, basketball, football, and hockey) as well as several other major sports were played at the same time. Sports fans went from being deprived of all sporting activities throughout the spring and most of the summer of 2020, to being overwhelmed by the end of summer and the beginning of the fall. While this was a truly unique period of time, we fervently hope it will not happen again. As it turned out, the 2020 Tokyo Summer Games were held in July 2021 but sans fans in the stands as Japan was experiencing high numbers of COVID-19 cases. A number of athletes tested positive for COVID but the Olympic glory was experienced by many athletes, their families and friends and supporters.

The authors encourage all sports fans to engage in and promote good sportsmanship as they cheer on their favorite teams and athletes.

CHAPTER 1

The Sociology of Sport

Sport is a pervasive social institution in nearly every society around the world. In the United States, sport is as much a part of American society and culture as such other major social institutions as the family, religion, politics, economics and education. To ignore sport is to overlook a phenomenon that extends into a multitude of social arenas, including the arts, mass media, the economy, the community, and international diplomacy. In this book we will use the term "sport" to signify its role as a social institution and we will use "sports" to signify specific activities such as football, baseball, or cycling.

Sport reflects the norms and values of the general culture of a society. In American culture, as in most world cultures, winning and success are highly valued commodities. Sport can serve as an excellent exemplar of the cherished "win-at-all-costs" philosophy. This prevailing attitude often leads to elitism, sexism, racism, nationalism, extreme competitiveness, abuse of drugs (including performance-enhancing drugs), gambling, and a number of other deviant behaviors. However, the true spirit of sport often reveals itself as well. The notions of cooperation and team work, fair play, sportsmanship, hard work, dedication, reaching to achieve personal excellence, obedience to rules, commitment and loyalty are also revered values of American society, and that is, perhaps, the primary reason that Americans love sports so much. Despite the highly publicized negative sport stories that are often sensationalized by the mass media, including social media, there are far more positive sport-related stories which help to reaffirm that our support of our favorite teams and athletes is not a wasted endeavor.

The institution of sport is very important, useful, and beneficial to American society. Sports adherents share the emotional roller coaster of the fortunes that their favorite teams' experience. Both fans and participants find in sport a reaffirmation of central values and myths of the larger society that help give meaning and direction to their own lives. Athletic contests are important to the socialization of youth, to the integration of disparate groups and social classes, to physical and mental well-being, and to the enhancement of community pride.

The Sociological Perspective

The term "perspective" refers to a particular attitude toward something; it is a point of view. Since this book is written from a sociological perspective it is important to clarify a number of fundamental sociological concepts and constructs relevant to the sociological study of sport. Let's begin with the sociological perspective. Among the core tenets of the sociological perspective are the following basic assumptions:

1. *Individuals are, by their nature, social beings.* There are two main reasons for this. First, newborn babies are completely dependent on others for their survival. Second, in order to survive as a species, humans have formed groups as a defense mechanism against the other animals and the environment.
2. *Individuals are, for the most part, socially determined.* As social beings, we are products of our social environments. Trial and error, reinforcement, and modeling account for the primary methods of learning.
3. *Individuals create, sustain, and change the social forms within which they conduct their lives.* Humans are both "puppets of their society" and "also puppeteers" (Eitzen and Sage 1989: 5). Our lives are not biologically predetermined; we are capable (within certain social limitations) of making decisions to alter our life courses. "Through collective action individuals are capable of changing the structure of society and even the course of history" (Eitzen and Sage 1989: 4–6). Adding to this core tenet is the idea that individuals are not passive bystanders in the social world. "Rather, they actively shape social life by adapting to, negotiating with, and changing social structure. This process, too, illustrates *human agency*" (Sage and Eitzen 2013: 6). *Agency* refers to the thoughts and actions taken by people that allows them to express and shape their individual power and their own life course.

The sociological perspective teaches us to look beyond the limitations of so-called "common sense" and shows that things are not always as they seem. Utilizing the sociological perspective involves analyzing the underlying structures and forces at work by questioning things that are presented to us as facts by authority figures. Utilizing the sociological perspective helps us to better understand how society operates, highlights diversity in thought, and reminds us that people with different life experiences often develop different outlooks on life.

Sociology is an extensive field with many different theories, methodologies and areas of interest. Sociology is a member of the social sciences; it involves the study of groups, institutions, organizations, cultures, societies and human interaction. The social sciences, which also include anthropology, economics, education, psychology, and political science, concentrate their study on the various aspects of human society. In contrast, the natural sciences, such as astronomy, biology, chemistry, geology, and physics, focus their studies on the physical features of nature and the manner in which they interact and change. The social scientist is concerned with furthering knowledge for its own sake.

Sociology is nearly always defined as a science that engages in rigorous research guided by theory. The authors define sociology as the systematic study of groups, organizations, social institutions, societies, and the social interaction among people. The word "systematic" is used because sociology is committed to applying both theoretical perspectives and research methods to the examination of social behavior and also because sociologists generally study regularly occurring behaviors. By definition, sociology is a science. A science possesses such characteristics as theory guided by empirical observations, measurement of variables, analysis, synthesis, and replication/ public verification. Definitions of the term *science* usually include such criteria as having knowledge and knowledge obtained and tested through the scientific method. The scientific method itself is defined as the pursuit of knowledge involving the stating of a problem, the collection of facts through observation and experiment, and the testing of ideas to determine whether they are right or wrong. As we shall see throughout this book, sociology has a strong commitment to research and to the testing (through statistical analysis) of its theories.

The roots of sociology are firmly entrenched within the scientific tradition. Auguste Comte (1798–1857), one of the earliest sociologists, and the person who coined the term "sociology," was a strong proponent of positivism. Positivism is a way of understanding the world based on science. Positivists believe that the social world can be studied in the same manner as the natural sciences and believe that "laws" exist that apply to the human species; they merely have to be discovered by social scientists. Comte was an early positivist and his concept of positivism is based on the idea that everything in society is observable and subject to patterns or laws. These laws help to explain human behavior. The role of the sociologist is to reveal these patterns, or laws, of human behavior. "Comte believed positivism would create sound theories based on sufficient factual evidence and historical comparisons to predict future events. The discovery of the basic laws of human behavior will allow for deliberate courses of action on the part of both individuals and society" (Delaney 2005: 25).

In an attempt to understand the laws of society, sociologists often utilize the *sociological imagination*. The American sociologist C. Wright Mills coined the term "the sociological imagination" to show how our private lives are influenced by the social environment and the existing social forces. The sociologist gains insights into human behavior by utilizing the sociological imagination. "The sociological imagination enables its possessor to understand the larger historical scene in terms of its meanings for the inner life and the external career of a variety of individuals. It enables him to take into account how individuals, in the welter of their daily experience, often become falsely conscious of their social positions" (Mills 1959: 5).

The sociological imagination stresses the importance of the historical social context in which an individual is found. Mills emphasized that it is important to understand the personal biography (life history) along with the current actions of an individual to truly understand the meaning of his or her behavior. To underscore the importance of this point, Mills made distinctions between personal troubles and public issues. This distinction is critical to fully understand the manner in which the sociological imagination operates. Personal troubles "occur with the character of the individual and within the range of her or his immediate relations with others. They have to do with the self and with those limited areas of social life of which the person is directly and personally aware" (1959: 8). An example of personal trouble would be an athlete who gets "cut" from the team because his or her performance was not good enough to make the team. Public issues "transcend these local environments of the individual and the range of her or his inner life. They have to do with the organization of many milieus into the institutions of a historical society as a whole and form the larger structure of social and historical life" (1959: 8). From this standpoint, "the sociologist acknowledges that social forces, often out of the control of the individual, affect the individual's life for both the good and the bad" (Delaney 2005: 88). For example, let's say an athlete is good enough to make a team's roster but then the league folds due to financial shortcomings (e.g., the former XFL football league). Such an athlete was not "cut" from the team due to a personal shortcoming (personal troubles), but rather because of reasons beyond her or his control (public issues).

Another example of the application of the sociological imagination to the sports world is provided by Nixon and Frey's (1996) example of steroid use. They argue that when one individual out of hundreds of professional athletes uses steroids, that is an example of a personal trouble. However, when it becomes known that a relatively large number of athletes are using steroids, the problem becomes a public issue. (As we shall see in Chapter 8, steroid use in American society as well as in many other societies is as much a public issue as it is a personal trouble.)

The Sociology of Sport

The sociology of sport is a subdiscipline of sociology that focuses on the relationship between sport and society. Sport sociology is concerned with the behavior of individuals and groups within sport and the rules and processes that exist within the formal and informal design and makeup of sport. With a commitment toward objective analysis the sport sociologist places a great deal of emphasis on the *evidence*. It is the role of the sport sociologist to keep his or her own biases under control and to refrain from making value judgments while conducting research and presenting findings. In other words, as with any social scientist, sport sociologists are to remain objective and present facts. However, offering suggestions and courses of actions to correct the "wrongs" and injustices found within the institution of sport is within the reform tradition of sociology.

The objective sociological perspective represents a more viable alternative to biological and psychological attempts to explain sport. Sport psychology focuses on the mental processes and behavioral characteristics (e.g., motivation, perception, cognition, self-confidence, self-esteem and personality) of the individual almost to the point where it ignores the importance of social forces. As Eitzen and Sage (1989) explain, biological and psychological explanations of sport focus exclusively on the individual and not the social forces and processes that affect behavior. The sociological approach, in contrast, examines social conditions in the community or society (e.g., varying degrees of unemployment, leisure time, urban blight, restricted opportunities for minority groups, or distribution of power to a ruling class) that may affect individual decision-making and behavior.

As a discipline, sport sociology has been in existence for at least four decades. When people consider the early sport sociologists, most point to Kenyon and Loy's 1965 article "Toward a Sociology of Sport" and Harry Edwards' 1973 publication *Sociology of Sport*. In 1965, Kenyon and Loy had already declared that sport had "become a cultural phenomenon of great magnitude and complexity" and was "fast becoming a social institution" (24). They also noted that "despite the magnitude of the public's commitment to sport, as a social phenomenon it has received little serious study" (24). This pattern holds true today as sports play an even bigger role in society (than in 1965) and yet is still ignored (or considered somewhat frivolous) by some in academia. Kenyon and Loy (1965: 24) advocated the scientific-sociological approach to the study of sports: If sociology is the study of social order—the underlying regularity of human social behavior—including efforts to attain it and departures from it, then the sociology of sport becomes the study of the regularity, and departures from it, of human social behavior in a sports context. Sport sociology, as Kenyon and Loy see it, is a value-free social science. "It is not an effort to influence public opinion or behavior, not is it an attempt to find support for the

More than 35,000 orange-clad fans pack the Carrier Dome on the campus of Syracuse University to watch a men's college basketball game.

'social development' objective of physical education…. The sport sociologist is neither a spreader of gospel nor an evangelist for exercise. His function is not to shape attitudes and values but rather to describe and explain them" (25).

There are many sport sociologists who disagree with Kenyon and Loy's assertion that the sport sociologist should remain neutral. In fact, they argue that it is the job of the sport sociologist to spearhead change where there are flaws in the system. Snyder and Spreitzer (1978) were among the early sport sociologists who advocated the need for an *applied* sociology of sport. "If the policy implications of sport sociology are not brought out in the research of social scientists, this burgeoning field will die on the vine of academic trivia" (8). Many examples of applied sport sociology will be presented throughout this book.

Conflict theorists (see Chapter 2 for a review of Conflict Theory) have also questioned the commitment to the value-free approach. As Jack Scott stated in his introduction to *Rip Off the Big Game: The Exploitation of Sports by the Power Elite,* "Any serious social scientist must admit, however, that the value-free approach to social science has always had its critics both within and without the social-science movement…. It should go without saying that Marxist social scientists have never accepted the legitimacy of a value-neutral orientation" (Hoch 1972: 3–4). Critics of the value-free approach to sport sociology claim that such an ideology is one of non-involvement and an attempt to free oneself from social responsibility. There remains a great debate among sport sociologists today as to whether the field should maintain a commitment to the roots of sociology as a value-free, scientific approach to the study of sport in society or whether it should be a critical field that concentrates on negative issues. This text will provide a scientific approach while pointing out many of the problems of sport.

Edwards' publication of *Sociology of Sport* (1973) represents a major turning point in the discipline. Edwards compiled an extensive amount of research material and established a leading textbook for the field. He also established the basic properties of sport sociology: "In its broadest sense, this field should be concerned with the descriptions and explanation of the interrelations between sport and other societal components. More specifically, these fragmentary writings have been concerned with the functions of athletics in relation to basic social institutions and processes. The unique feature of the sociological approach to sport, as distinct from that of psychology, has been a focus upon sport in its function as a component of social organization" (10–11).

Kenyon and Loy (1965) reference a work entitled *Soziologie des Sports* (published in Germany in 1921) as one of the first isolated works on sport sociology, but they do not elaborate on its contents. We believe that Thorstein Veblen's *The Theory of the Leisure Class* (1899) establishes Veblen as an early pioneer of sport sociology. Of particular importance are his descriptions and analyses of conspicuous consumption and conspicuous leisure, as they represent early theoretical explanations of the growing role of sport consumerism in the United States specifically and of Western societies in general. Veblen used the term conspicuous consumption to describe the *nouveau riche* (first generation wealthy people), who purchased luxury items as a means to convey to others their social position. In this regard, the nouveau riche were looking for approval from the upper socio-economic classes and envy from the lower socio-economic classes. Conspicuous leisure refers to living a lifestyle where the pursuit of leisure and the appearance of privilege are instrumental in one's behavior. In other words, it involves participating in non-productive activities.

THE SOCIOLOGY OF SPORT DEFINED

The academic and scholarly interest in sport has grown tremendously over the years. And, although the interest in sport comes from a varied array of sources, "sport sociology has been defined to a great extent by the topics that have been investigated, both by those formally trained in the area, and by those who identify with the area in order to legitimate their own work" (McPherson 1981: 10). As a subdiscipline of sociology, sport sociology has a focus on the processes and patterns found within the institution of sport and how these social forces impact human behavior. The authors define the sociology of sport as the systematic study of the processes, patterns, issues, values, and behaviors found in the institution of sport.

As we shall see throughout this book, the social institution of sport has a relationship with all the other social institutions found within a society. Sport affects billions of people around the world either directly or indirectly.

Why Do We Study Sports?

Sport is one of the most significant and influential social institutions found in societies around the world. Sports are a major part of people's lives. Sport participation provides opportunities for intrinsic and extrinsic rewards and is an excellent way to help develop a physically fit body. The sports world also provides us with opportunities to gain insight on racism, sexism, labor struggles, structured inequality, and so forth.

SPORT IS SOCIOLOGICAL

Nearly every element of sport has sociological significance. The truth of this statement will be demonstrated throughout the text as entire chapters dealing with specific social institutions and their relation to sports are provided. In brief, sport participation provides personal health benefits for individuals. Sports play a significant role in the culture of a given society. Sports help to provide historical continuity (e.g., through record keeping and maintaining allegiances to a favorite team over a lifetime) and more important, sports have existed throughout recorded history. Sports help to provide continuity in life as sports allegiances formed in childhood generally persevere throughout adulthood. Sport often serves as a positive diversion from the negative aspects of life by providing people a temporary "escape" from the mundane, sometimes monotonous and painful elements in one's personal or social life. Years ago, ESPN ran a commercial featuring a female jogger in an urban environment followed by numerous people who have demands on her life (e.g., husband, son, daughter, boss, women's group, etc.) with the catch-phrase "Without Sports, How Would We Escape?" In short, sport is sociological because it is interconnected with all the other social institutions found in society.

SPORT IS PERVASIVE

The institution of sport has become increasingly important and dominant throughout a large portion of the world. To ignore sport is to ignore a significant aspect of any society and its culture. Add to this the realization that most people have a great deal of leisure time which, for many, involves sports—either as a participant, observer, or consumer. Although the pervasiveness of sport will be detailed throughout the text in a variety of fashions, for now, let's consider the following as samples of the pervasiveness of sport in society:

- Newspapers in most cities devote entire sections of their daily editions to the coverage of sport. There are many very popular sport magazines such as *Baseball Preview, Runners World, Bicycling, Golf Digest, Fantasy Baseball, Golf Magazine, Tennis, The Hockey News, Powder,* and *Slam.*
- There are hundreds of "sports talk" radio stations and sports podcasts available from different sources such as AM, FM, Digital Radio, Satellite, or Internet (streaming).
- Many sport contests are global events (for example, the World Cup, the Olympic Games, the Tour de France, Wimbledon, and the Super Bowl). Children around the world are exposed to these sport events.
- Sports venues continue to draw large crowds. College football stadiums continue to expand as universities hope to brag about the size of their stadiums with Michigan Stadium (109,901) currently the largest followed by Ohio State's Ohio Stadium (104,944), Penn State's Beaver Stadium (106,572), University of Texas

A&M's Kyle Field (102,512), and Neyland Stadium (102,455) at the University of Tennessee as the five largest (The TV Shield 2020).
- The pervasiveness of sport is also revealed through Internet sites. In May 2020, the authors typed the word "sport" (on a Google search) and found that there were over 15 billion results for "sports" and more than 17 billion results for "sport."

As these few examples indicate, sport is quite pervasive in society. (For a closer look at sport pervasiveness in society see "Connecting Sport and Popular Culture" Box 1 at the end of the chapter.)

Sport as a Social Institution

As stated earlier in this chapter, sport is a social institution. Social institutions represent the means (e.g., a set of organized beliefs and rules) that each society develops to meet its fundamental needs. The original social institutions discussed in sociology were the family, religion, education, the economy, and the government or politics. Today, the mass media, sports, science and technology, medicine, and the military are also considered to be social institutions.

Functionalists argue that each social institution is designed to meet specific needs. The family, for example, is responsible for, among other things, the replacement of members of society and teaching the next generation cultural expectations; the government is responsible for maintaining and preserving social order. Conflict theorists argue that social institutions exist to maintain the status quo and therefore disadvantage those without socioeconomic or political power. The interactionist perspective, with a micro focus, emphasizes that human behavior is influenced by the roles and statuses that we possess, the groups to which we belong, and the institutions within which we function. (See Chapter 2 for a more comprehensive review of theoretical perspectives on sports.)

Edwards (1973) describes sport as a "secular, quasi-religious institution" (90). As a secular institution, sport takes on a functional, non-religious role in society by upholding and reaffirming basic values and norms found in that culture. It can serve as the functional equivalent of a religious ceremony that brings a community together under a coherent system of beliefs.

Sociologists are generally concerned with how a social system works; specifically, the norms, roles and structures that hold the system together. The institution of sport provides an excellent system for analysis by sociologists. It is characterized by regulation, formalization, ideological justification and the transmission of culture. Sport as a social institution possesses many general characteristics of all social institutions. The following is a brief review of six key characteristics of sport as a social institution:

1. *A Ranking System (Stratification).* Within all institutions, groups and societies, a hierarchy (a ranking system) exists. This hierarchy is often based on something of value. In business, seniority and position are valued (e.g., a senior vice president has higher value than an entry-level clerk). In sport, a hierarchy exists based on such things as "skilled" positions, star performers, and, to a lesser degree, seniority.
2. *Roles and Statuses (the Organizational/Structural Aspect).* One's role is determined by one's position in the hierarchy. Star players are expected to perform at peak

levels at all times. Secondary players do not experience such demands. One's status reflects one's social position in the hierarchy (e.g., head coach, trainer, athlete, team manager, water boy).

3. *Social Control (The Ability to Provide Rewards and Levy Punishments/Sanctions).* Social control is a mechanism designed to maintain conforming behavior. Sport channels human actions so that they abide with predefined expectations. For example, a coach may have a team rule that if an athlete is late for a film session, team practice, or curfew, that athlete will not be allowed to start (or play) in the next game. Sport itself is filled with rules. There are rules that apply during the game and outside of the game. When rules are violated during the game, a referee will punish the violator with a foul or some other type of sanction. For example, the National Football League has a rule against "excessive" or preplanned celebrations. (Social control and deviance will be discussed in further detail in Chapter 8.)

4. *Social in design.* Social institutions are created, maintained, and modified by humans to meet human social needs.

5. *Social institutions are interrelated.* Every institution is unique and designed to meet specific social needs but they are also intertwined. For example, when youths play organized sports it automatically involves the family, the economics of the family, and a number of other social institutions.

6. *Rules (Norms and Expectations of Behavior).* The need for social control is the result of the large number of rules in sport. All organizations have formal (written) rules as well as informal rules (how things are *really* done). An example of a formal rule is the NCAA's ban on college athletes from gambling and taking illegal drugs. All groups have informal norms as well, such as making a teammate pay a "fine" for inappropriate behavior, or for making a bonehead play.

In sum, sport has the same characteristics as all other social institutions and is therefore accepted as a social institution in its own right.

What Is Sport?

We have discussed many aspects of sport, but what exactly *is* sport? We could list the vast array of sports from "A" (anvil shooting) to "Z" (zebra hunting). Listing categories of sport is relatively easy. Classifying sport as indoors or outdoors; professional or amateur; and so on; is only slightly more difficult. Nearly everyone believes that they know what a sport is; however, if one is asked to define "sport" that usually causes some difficulty. Formulating a definition that draws clear and clean parameters around what activities should be included and excluded is relatively difficult to do. For example, is the backyard leisure activity of badminton a sport? Years ago, the notion of badminton as a sport would have caused great laughter. Today, badminton is not only considered a sport by some people, but it has also been an Olympic sport since its debut in 1992 at the Summer Barcelona Games with four separate medals for the men's and women's singles and doubles champions. Mixed doubles was added at the 1996 Atlanta Games as a fifth medal. Through the 2016 Rio Games (the 2020 Tokyo Games were postponed a year due to the novel Coronavirus global pandemic) China, Indonesia and South Korea have dominated the total medal count. Kickball is another youth activity that has been

transformed into a sport. The World Adult Kickball Association is the largest sanctioning body to oversee the official rules of the sport. Now that badminton and kickball are,
more or less, viewed as legitimate sports what about such activities as anvil shooting,
playing bridge, cup stacking, playing in a marching band, and zebra hunting; are these
activities sports?

In rural areas of the South anvil shoots have become an increasingly popular sporting activity. An anvil shoot involves participants blowing up the blacksmith's tool (anvil)
as high as possible in the air. According to a spokesperson for the National Anvil Shoot-
ers Association, anvil shooting is "a guy thing" (Hoffman 1996). "Anvil shooting involves
placing one large blacksmith anvil upside down on the ground and filling its cavity with
a fine grade of black powder. A second anvil weighing up to 150 pounds is then placed
upright on top of the bottom one. The powder is ignited and the top anvil is thrust as
high as 125 feet into the air. The earth literally shakes; and the deafening boom, it is said,
can be heard from as far away as 15 miles" (Museum of Appalachia 2005). According to
the Museum of Appalachia, anvil shoots have a long history in the United States with
"accounts that the shooting of the anvil was employed to celebrate the nation's independence, Christmas, and even Davy Crockett's election to the United States Congress."

What about playing bridge, is that a sport? A number of bridge players petitioned
the English Bridge Union (EBU) requesting that the popular card game be recognized as
a sport and the case went to the European Court of Justice where it ruled in October 2015
that bridge is not a sport because it did not involve physical activity (*BBC* 2015). The idea
of physical activity, as we shall see shortly, is a key aspect of the definition of sport; that,
and the requirement that the activity involve athletic activity. The EBU was very disappointed in the ruling.

Have you been to a good elephant race lately? Elephant races occur at various locations throughout the world. A Google search for elephant racing will reveal a tourist site
listing various elephant races, generally found in Asia, that directs you to elephant racing careers and employment. A well-publicized elephant race occurred in Germany in
2000. More than 40,000 spectators watched the event. The idea for the race came from
the Indian-born mayor (Ravindra Gujjula) of the town of Altlandsberg, just east of Berlin. Elephant racing is a tradition in India, but only two states currently hold such events.
(The International Elephant Race began in Nepal in 2005.) Despite the large turnout in
Berlin's Hoppegarten, elephant racing is very controversial. Elephants have protected status in India, since the pachyderm is revered by many Hindus because of its resemblance
to the elephant-headed god Ganesh. *BBC News* (2000) reported that "members of the
Animal Peace group objected to the race and were supported by French film star Bri-
gitte Bardot, German rock singer Nina Hagen and India's Social Affairs Minister Maneka
Gandhi" (1). The event featured 14 circus elephants, half of them African and half Asian,
and six races. Promoters of the race insist that the elephants enjoy racing. After crossing
the finishing line, the elephants were rewarded with treats of fruits and vegetables (*BBC
News* 2000).

What about competitive marching band, is this activity a sport? Participants practice regularly just like athletes, they generally perform on a football field, it involves competition, competitors do possess skill (musical), and the participants engage in physical
exertion. On the other hand, the activity does not involve a sporting activity, competitors are not engaged in activity requiring athletic skill, and the participants would not be
described as athletes with specific athletic skills.

Zebra hunting rounds out our epigrammatic look at the "A to Z" description of sport, or not a sport, assessment. As the name implies, "zebra hunting" entails hunting zebras, generally while on safari on conservation sites. Zebra hunts, condemned by many people, generally take place in Africa but there are areas of Texas where the activity also takes place. One company, African Sky, provides trophy hunting opportunities. Their website, African Sky (2014), describes the weapons necessary to kill a zebra and informs those interested how to become involved in a zebra hunt. The Texas Hunt Lodge (2014) website provides information for a variety of hunting packages open to wild gamers. Zebra hunting does not involve athletic skills and the ability to hunt and kill does not make one an athlete.

Will any of these quasi-sporting activities become labeled as legitimate sports and find their way in such international competitions as the Olympics? What do you think?

Defining Sport

Labeling activities such as anvil shooting, playing bridge, marching in a band, and elephant and zebra racing as sports is contingent on one's definition of sport. The word "sport" has its origins rooted in the idea that it is an activity designed to divert people from the routines of everyday life. "Sport derives its root from 'disport,' meaning 'to divert oneself.' It carried the original implication of people diverting their attention from the rigors and pressures of daily life by participating in the mirth and whimsy of frolic—some physical activity" (Edwards 1973: 55).

There is a lack of consensus among most people, sport sociologists included, on how to define sport. John Phillips (1993) even suggests that "in one sense the word *sport* need not be analyzed. Anyone who speaks English knows what sport is and is not" (30). As a sport sociologist, Phillips takes a unique stand as sociologists are known for establishing standardized and operational definitions of key concepts. Phillips reflects the mentality of most students and followers of sport that we all unconsciously *know* which activities our culture defines as a sport and we therefore take for granted what is and is not sport. Snyder and Spreitzer (1978: 11) state that it is important for social scientists to have "workable analytical handles" on the meaning of sport. We agree. Simply being able to list sport will not help the social scientist understand sport sociologically.

Among the earliest social scientists to define sport was Günther Luschen. Luschen (1967, 1970) defines sport as an institutionalized type of competitive physical activity located on a continuum between play and world. He felt that it was particularly important to emphasize the fact that sport is a physical activity which would therefore automatically eliminate such activities as playing cards as being considered a sport—an important point to make as there are some members of the contemporary media (especially ESPN) that would have us believe that playing poker is a sport. Poker is not a sport as it does not involve athletic activities. Edwards (1973) states, "One of the most salient features of sports is that they always involve physical exertion. This physical exertion is an imperative characteristic that cannot be overstressed. Without it there simply is no sport activity" (55). In his own definition of sport, Edwards emphasizes the physical aspect, as well as the organizational, rule-making, and goal-directedness of sport. Edwards goes on to define sport as "involving activities having formally recorded histories and traditions, stressing physical exertion through competition within limits set in explicit and formal rules governing role and position relationships, and carried out by actors who represent or who are part of formally organized associations having the goal of achieving valued tangibles or intangibles through defeating opposing groups" (57–58).

Nixon and Frey (1996) adapted Edwards and Luschen's definition and define sport "as institutionalized physical competition occurring in a formally organized or corporate structure" (3). Describing sport as institutionalized reflects the earlier discussion in this chapter of sport as a social institution possessing such key elements as norms, statuses, roles and social relationships. The second significant element of this definition of sport is physical competition. Physical competition mandates that physical activity and skills are involved in order to determine a winner or loser.

Curry and Jiobu (1984) believe that sports are physical actions but also nondeviant activities: "*Sport* is a physical activity that is fair, competitive, nondeviant, and that is guided by rules, organizations, and/or tradition" (8). Once again, the idea that sport is a physical activity is a part of this definition of sport. The idea that sports are fair is an idealistic view of sport that we all like to believe is true but realize is not. The most unusual aspect of the Curry and Jiobu definition of sport is the stipulation that sport is nondeviant activity. "In general, deviant activity does not fit our cultural ideas about what sport is or should be. Sport has moral overtones about it. It's supposed to represent the ideals and high goals of our society, something deviance does not do. We therefore find it advisable to keep deviance separate from sport" (11). Idealism should no longer be confused as a primary element of sport. Deviance not only occurs in sport (as Curry and Jiobu do acknowledge) it is sometimes taught and engaged in freely by athletes, trainers, league officials, referees, and owners.

Jay Coakley (2006) defines sports as "institutionalized competitive activities that involve rigorous physical exertion or the use of relatively complex physical skills by participants motivated by internal and external rewards" (21). Note once again the idea that sports are physical activities (in this case rigorous) is included in this definition. However, there is a very critical addition to this definition of sport: "*or the use of relatively complex physical skills.*" The importance of this amendment is that it allows many other forms of recreation to be included as sports. For example, Delaney has had many students comment to him in his sociology of sport classes, "How can golf be listed as a sport when there is little physical activity involved; especially if golfers use a golf cart?" As anyone who has ever played golf can attest, there most certainly is an element of skill involved; whether it is "complex" or not is debatable. Coakley also includes motivational factors in his definition of sport. Internal or intrinsic rewards are those which come from "inside" the person, a feeling of accomplishment for having achieved some sort of athletic goal (e.g., finishing a marathon regardless of "place" or climbing a mountain and reaching the highest peak). Extrinsic rewards refer to "outside" accolades that one may receive for successful sport participation (e.g., monetary rewards, trophies, cheering and adoring fans).

While we acknowledge that the designation of an activity as a sport may be, to some degree, up to the participants themselves, and while recognizing that different cultures have different perspectives on what constitutes as a sport, we provide a definition that includes certain and precise parameters. *Sports* are institutionalized, structured, and sanctioned competitive athletic activities (e.g., competitive running, jumping, and throwing) that go beyond the realm of play that involve physical exertion and/or the use of relatively complex athletic skills. We maintain the consistent perspective that sports must involve physical athletic activity and the ability to use athletic skill to gain an advantage over an opponent and we want to make it clear that there is a distinction between play and sports. (This point will be elaborated on later in this chapter.) Thus, although neighborhood kids may play football in backyards across the United States, it is a far different game than when professional or highly skilled high school and college athletes play football as a sport.

UNIVERSAL AND REGIONAL SPORTS

We will discuss a wide variety of sports in diverse settings throughout this book, but the authors feel it is necessary to briefly distinguish between universal and regional sports here. Remember that sport reflects culture. The great diversity of sport is a result of the diverse world we live in. Specific sports have appeal in particular regions of the world, while other sports, because of their mass popularity, enjoy a universal following. In the United States, football is the runaway favorite American sport. Around the world, however, *futbol,* or what Americans call "soccer," is the most popular of all sports. It would appear that Americans prefer the hard-hitting violence, strategic planning and offensive scoring of *their* football over the world's obsession with the "beautiful game" (*o jogo bonito,* a Portuguese phrase) low-scoring, wide-open artistry of kicking the ball player to player, defense-minded *futbol* (soccer).

Universal sports (e.g., running, swimming, throwing things, soccer) are those sports which appear throughout most of the world. Some sports, such as archery and wrestling, are indigenous to nearly all cultures in the ancient world (Craig 2002). Running and throwing things, such as big rocks, spears and disk-shaped items, are also universal sports. As mentioned above, the world's most popular sport is *futbol.* Soccer's World Cup—played every four years—garners an audience that is rivaled only by the Olympics.

Regional sports are those sports which are not played universally. They may be isolated to specific countries or regions (e.g., Afghanistan's *buzkashi*) or specific areas within a society (e.g., lacrosse has greater appeal in the Northeast than in the Southwest regions of the United States). In light of continuing world events, Americans have learned a great deal about Afghanistan's culture, including sports. Under the rule of the Taliban, most Afghan sports were banned. Many national sports have returned to the forefront in Afghanistan since the U.S.-led forces removed the Taliban from power. These sports include cockfighting, kite fighting and buzkashi. Cockfighting is controversial throughout the world and yet it appears in many "back alleys" across the United States. According to the American Society for the Prevention of Cruelty to Animals (ASPCA), cockfighting is illegal in all 50 U.S. states and the District of Columbia; 42 states and Washington, D.C., list this blood sport as a felony (ASPCA 2020). In organized cockfights, the roosters' natural fighting instincts are exaggerated through breeding, feeding, training, steroids, vitamins, and several months of training before a fight for the main purposes of gambling and entertainment (ASPCA 2020). Although still popular in countries such as France, Mexico, Belgium, Spain, Haiti, Italy, and Malaysia, in the United States the simple possession of birds for fighting purposes is prohibited in 39 states and the District of Columbia, and being a spectator at a cockfighting event is illegal in 43 states and the District of Columbia (ASPCA 2020).

Kite fighting (or *Gudiparan Bazi*) is another Afghan sport that is popular in many Asian countries including Bangladesh, Pakistan, India, Nepal, Korea, and of course,

Afghanistan. Banned by the Taliban, kite fighting is once again very popular in Afghanistan. This addicting outdoor sport involves kites of different designs and sizes wherein participants hold onto a string of wire laced with unbreakable tar and extremely sharp razors. The idea is to cut the string of your opponent's kite while it is in the air before he cuts yours. Competition and pride are key aspects of kite fighting but so too are many injuries for the competitors and spectators as the cut kite strings crash downward to the ground, cutting people and sometimes causing death. Many people are also injured when they chase after dismantled kites and they fall from rooftops (Afghanistan Culture 2020). A best-selling novel, *The Kite Runner*, by Khaled Hosseini, describes in great detail this potentially bloody sport.

The most popular sport in Afghanistan is the traditional game of buzkashi—jostling on horseback with other riders trying to grab a decapitated goat.

> Buzkashi is a contest between two teams of horsemen over the possession of a dead calf or goat carcass, with the object being for one talented and fearless rider to gain control of the slippery carcass and then separate from the pack of horsemen vying for the same prize. "Buzkashi" means goat, but a calf carcass is often used because it reportedly stays intact longer. The animal is beheaded, bled, and behooved [*sic*] before being used. It can be either gutted or not [Craig 2002: 154–155].

In the movie *Rambo III* Sylvester Stallone's character, Rambo (in an ironic U.S. political misfortune), is in Afghanistan to help rebel forces against Russian "aggressors." Rambo plays the Afghan sport of buzkashi and quickly dominates, earning the praise of the Afghan rebels.

Buzkashi was spread by the Mongol hordes that swept out of China and across central Asia. Today, the sport is played mostly by Turkic people, including the Uzbek, Turkomen, Kazakh, and Kirghiz. Interestingly, the Navajo of North America played a game similar to buzkashi called "the chick pull," with a live rooster replacing a four-legged carcass (Craig 2002).

Among the most entertaining and demanding regional sports in the United States is lacrosse (lax for short). Fans of lacrosse realize immediately that the hotbed for lacrosse is New York State. New York has the highest number of total high school athletes (over 26,000) participating in lacrosse, as well as the highest number of male high school lacrosse players and, the greatest number of female high school lacrosse players; it also has the largest number of high schools that play boys and girls lacrosse with 314 (2018–2019 survey) (Anderson 2019). Illinois, Ohio and California are three states that are witnessing significant growth in participation rates and California has the second-most number of lacrosse players with just over 20,000 athletes in 273 boys and 279 girls high school teams (Anderson 2019). As recently as 2015, lacrosse was touted as the fastest growing sport in college athletics as well. In 2015, there were 470 Women's lacrosse programs (D-1, D-2, and D-3) and 350 Men's lacrosse programs (D-1, D-2, and D-3) (Piscotty 2015). There are multiple reasons for the appeal of lacrosse. It is a fast-paced game that combines elements of soccer (constant running), hockey (play behind the net), and football (wearing pads, violent, controlled collisions, one-on-one defenses, zone defenses, set plays). It is an imaginative and wide-open game where most of the participants are not huge, hulking athletes. Youth sport leagues and high schools like lacrosse because it is much cheaper to fund than sports such as football and hockey. With roots in Native American culture, it could be argued that lacrosse is the *true* American sport. (There will be more on lacrosse in Chapter 11.)

Defining an Athlete

Have you ever heard someone say, "I used to be an athlete?" Such a statement generally implies that when that individual was younger they played a sport (most likely a traditional sport such as football, baseball, tennis, track and field, etc.), but now that they is older, they do not. In other words, many people agree with Nixon and Frey (1996) that athletics is a synonym for sport played in school or college settings. But what if an individual, who is in his or her 40s, works out for 75 minutes a day, including a three mile run—is he or she an athlete? Or, do you have to play an organized sport in order to be considered an athlete? A lot of people play golf but we would not refer to all of them as athletes. On the other hand, there are athletes who play golf. Where do we draw the line of distinction between someone who is "physically active" and "athlete?"

A *physically active* person is someone who puts forth physical energy while engaged in some sort of activity that involves exertion. This may include walking, gardening, hiking, sightseeing, and so on. A physically active person engages in such activity simply for the enjoyment or benefit it provides. Thus, one may walk on a regular basis for health purposes as opposed to training for some athletic event. An *athlete*, on the other hand, is in training for some specific sports event or participates in a sport while competing against other athletes or previously set records. According to the *Merriam-Webster Dictionary*, an athlete is someone who trains to compete in athletics. Athletics is defined as exercises and games that requiring physical skill, strength and endurance. Note that sport is not specifically mentioned as part of the definition of athletics. Most sport sociologists believe that an athlete is someone who is involved in a sports activity. For Harry Edwards, the distinction is clear. "It is only in sports that the participant can accurately be termed an 'athlete'" (55). Thus, Tiger Woods, a professional golfer, is an athlete, whereas the typical weekend golfer is not. Michael Jordan, now that he is retired, is among the millions of people who "used to be an athlete" but would now be labeled as a "physically active" person.

The idea of Michael Jordan, one of the greatest basketball players of all time, not being labeled as a current athlete is difficult for many people to accept. There is also a heated debate over whether or not a race car driver should be labeled as an athlete. Detractors will claim that race car drivers, NASCAR in particular, simply drive a car in circles, and that, they believe, is something anyone can do. On the other hand, there are those who support the idea that race car drivers are athletes because they meet the criteria. Let's take a look and see. Auto racers do certainly compete against others and do attempt to break established records; and fans of auto racing certainly believe that it is a "real" sport (something detractors find hard to believe). So now, we have to look at auto racing: Is that a real sport like football, basketball and baseball? We put forth the definition of sport as institutionalized, structured and sanctioned competitive activities beyond the realm of play, and auto racing meets that criteria. The definition also calls for participants who exert physical energy and relatively complex athletic skills. Anyone who has driven for 4–6 consecutive hours, or more, at a given time will agree that it can at the very least be tedious, but is also complex and physically challenging. Consider the track at Charlotte Motor Speedway with "its corners, which slope upward from a lush green infield to the wall at an angle of 24 degrees. The setup offers a terrific calf workout for a pedestrian climbing the track, but it's punishing to a body in the driver's seat. Taken at 192mph ... the banked curves subject the driver to almost four times the force of gravity"

(Lawrence 2014: 52). To put this in perspective, NASA has serious concerns for the safety of its astronauts being exposed to 3 g's for the nine minutes of liftoff (Lawrence 2014). This strenuous activity would seem to be enough to meet the criteria of physically challenging. What do you think?

Distinctions Between Leisure, Play and Sports

As stipulated in our definition, sports go beyond the realm of play. Consequently, it is important to make distinctions between a number of related terms, including leisure, play and sports.

Leisure

Most economists and sociologists generally regard *leisure* as unobligated time that is free of work or maintenance responsibilities. The term leisure suggests fun, distraction, and pleasure. "Leisure came to use through the Latin word *licere* by way of the French, *leisir*, the Middle English *leisere* and finally to its present spelling, leisure. The root word, *licere*, meaning to be permitted, evolved into another word—license. The word leisure literally meant exemption or permission as applied to opportunity afforded that was free from legal occupation" (Arnold 1980: 13).

Leisure provides time and opportunity for personal and creative growth, self-actualization, and intrinsically motivated goals. Obviously, most of us look forward to our leisure time and we feel that we deserve some time off from work and other obligations so that we can "recharge our battery." The idea that we "deserve" leisure time is a relatively new notion as historically, most people had little time to pursue leisure because they were too busy trying to meet primary needs (food, clothing and shelter). Leisure was reserved for the upper class, the privileged members of society. All of this would change with the rise of industrialization and the resulting formation of a middle class. Industrialization afforded an opportunity for the masses to enjoy leisure. Among the most notable economists/sociologists to examine the relationship between industrialization and rise of leisure prospects was the sociologist Thorstein Veblen (1857–1929).

More than a century ago, Veblen defined leisure as non-productive consumption of time. "Time is consumed non-productively (1) from a sense of the unworthiness of productive work, and (2) as an evidence of pecuniary ability to afford a life of idleness" (1934: 43). The primary concept of Veblen's theory of the leisure class is *conspicuous consumption*, "according to which the consumption of goods from the very early 'predatory' stage of history to the present, has served not so much to satisfy men's true needs or to provide what Veblen chooses to call the 'fullness of life' as to maintain social prestige—status" (Adorno 1981: 75). Thus, Veblen noted that when people acquired an economic surplus they did not purchase necessity items; instead, in an attempt to build their self-esteem, they purchased products that conveyed to others their increased socio-economic position.

Veblen believed that individuals participated in "wasteful" behaviors as a means of attaining self-esteem. Sport participation (even as spectators) allows members of the lower economic classes to engage in some of the same activities as the wealthier members of society. Clearly, this can be very meaningful to people. As for the wealthy, Veblen theorized that merely possessing wealth and power is never enough. Instead, wealth or power must be put into evidence for esteem to be awarded. Veblen stated, "Not only does the evidence of wealth serve to impress one's importance on others and to keep their sense of importance alive and alert, but it is of scarcely less use in building up and preserving one's self-complacency. In all but the lowest stages of culture the normally constituted man is comforted and upheld in his self-respect by 'decent surrounding' and the exemption from 'menial offices'" (Mitchell 1964: 230). Thus, Veblen understood why some people participated in leisure activities; however, he felt that leading a good productive life should be enough for one's positive self-image. Outside verification from others should be unnecessary. Clearly, Veblen's upbringing is reflected in his view of the leisure class. His parents worked hard so that their children had an opportunity to pursue advanced education. Their frugality afforded this opportunity. As a result, Veblen learned to appreciate and value hard work.

Many people disagree with Veblen's conclusion about leisure. Beginning with industrialization and continuing in contemporary society, individuals who work hard feel "entitled" to leisure time. They also feel a need to remove themselves, at least temporarily, from their work environments and enter preferred leisure domains. "The very development of capitalist society has thus produced forms of physical leisure pursuit … for getting away from it all, for escapism and ecstasy" (Brohm 1976: 88). Many sport sociologists believe that leisure is important to so many people because these activities often reflect one's social identity—they define who people really are, more so than other labels (e.g., occupation).

Americans are generally hard workers and people who enjoy their leisure time. According to 2018 data compiled by the Organization for Economic Co-operation and Development (OECD), Americans work slightly more annual hours (1,786) than the average annual hours of OECD countries (1,734) but far less than the hardest working nation, Mexico (2,148) (OECD.Stat 2020). Data compiled by World Atlas (2017 data) reveals the next leading nations (after Mexico) in the number of annual hours worked: South Korea (2,113), Greece (2,042), Chile (1,988), Poland (1,963), Latvia (1,903), Iceland (1,880), Portugal (1,868), Israel (1,858), Estonia (1853), Turkey (1,832), Ireland (1,82) and coming in 13th place, the United States (1,790, 4 hours more than in 2018) (Gilbert 2017). As a point of reference, Germany is ranked 35th at 1,371 annual hours worked (Gilbert 2017).

On the other hand, Americans aged 15 and over also enjoy their leisure time, nearly five hours (4 hours and 59 minutes) of it on an average day. Watching TV (2 hours and 47 minutes) is the most favorite form of leisure for Americans (Bureau of Labor Statistics 2017). Other leading leisure activities include: socializing and communicating (41 minutes); playing games/using computers for leisure (25 minutes); reading (19 minutes); participating in exercising, recreation, sports (18 minutes); relaxing and thinking (17 minutes); and other leisure activities (BLS 2017). Younger people are more likely to spend their leisure time exercising and playing video games while older people are more likely to watch television, read and think. Men are more likely than women to participate in sports, exercise, or recreation—23 percent compared with 18 percent (BLS 2017).

Play

Play is a universal concept. It is as old as culture itself. Play, like leisure, represents an absence of obligated time. Play is an activity that is performed voluntarily during leisure.

Play, however, is less organized than most leisure pursuits and is unstructured and open to fluidity in behavior. "Play is an enjoyable experience deriving from behavior which is self-initiated in accordance with personal goals or expressive impulses; it tolerates all ranges of movement abilities; its rules are spontaneous; it has a temporal sequence but no predetermined ending; it results in no tangible outcome, victory or reward" (Snyder and Spreitzer 1978: 12). For example, two girls wander toward the swing set and begin to swing aimlessly. Next, they pick up a basketball and haphazardly take shots at the hoop. When they are bored they drop the ball and walk away. This type of behavior is the direct opposite of seriousness—it is play. "Play provides an opportunity to temporarily shelve reality and thus find one's inner self again" (Hellendoorn, van der Koolj, and Sutton-Smith 1994: 25). Children are far more likely to play than adults.

Guttmann (1988) describes two types of play: spontaneous play and organized play (games). Spontaneous play is voluntary, flexible, and uncertain with latitude for innovation. For example, at family picnic baseball games, youths may be allowed four or five strikes (instead of the customary three) and adults may be required to bat from their "opposite" side (left-handed for natural right-handed batters). Adaptations to rules are allowed, such as "do-overs"—repeating the play for some reason (e.g., the batter wasn't paying attention when a called "strike" pitch was made). In sports, there are no do-overs; you must comply with the rules and be ready to play. Recreation is a type of spontaneous play. As Nixon and Frey (1996) explain, it is a leisure activity designed to refresh the mind or body. Arnold (1980) explains the origins of recreation:

> In Latin, *recreatio* carried a connotation of restoration or recovery from something. Its root is in the word *re-creo* (to create again) to refresh, invigorate, or revive. Further references include such inferences as to amuse oneself after obligation: *laxandi levandique animi gratia*, having to do with which we are dealing has a metaphysical quality. If we are to accept the various synonyms given, we would need to substantiate activity as a means for attaining relaxation or rest. The assumption indicated would produce a dichotomy: rest from activity or a cessation of movement on the one hand and diverting activity on the other hand [9–10].

Thus, recreation has a strong component of leisure. It is meant to be a refreshing activity, and it is playful. It may, or may not, be productive.

As play becomes more serious, more organized, we have the beginnings of competitive contests and sports. According to Guttmann (1988), organized play, or games, involves both noncompetitive games (e.g., kicking a ball with friends) and competitive games (contests). Competitive games can be divided into two categories: intellectual contests (e.g., chess) and physical contests (sports). With organized play, games tend to have less freedom, they are bound by rules. There are designated time limits and boundaries (e.g., organized baseball has a set number of innings, bowling has 10 frames a game) and there is nearly always a clear winner (and loser) at the end of organized games. "Since games imply winners and losers, there may be a degree or emotion or ego investment involved, although such investment tends to be small compared to that found in sports and athletics" (Figler and Whitaker 1991: 14). Incorporating the elements of games described above, Snyder and Spreitzer (1978) define games as "activities with an agreed-on organization of time, space, and terrain, with rules that define the objective and limit the pattern of human behavior; the outcome, which is to determine a winner and a loser, is achieved by totaling or accumulating objectively scored points or successes" (12).

Contests may be between two individuals, between two teams, between an individual and a group, between an individual or team and inanimate nature (such as mountain climbing, white water rafting), between a person or group and animate nature (e.g., hunting, fishing, or bull fighting), or between an individual or team and an ideal standard (e.g., a home run–hitting contest). A number of "competitive eating" contests have sprung to life in the twenty-first century. The International Federation of Competitive Eating (IFOCE), which overseas competitive eating contests, believes that competitive eating is a survival technique and argues that "30 hungry Neanderthals in a cave" fighting over a rabbit constitutes the first instance of competitive eating (Grabianowski 2020). The IFOCE requires that all competitive eaters must be at least 18 years old. Contestants who throw up during competition are disqualified.

Contests may also involve a struggle between animals (e.g., dog racing or horse racing) or between a real and an artificial animal (as in a greyhound race against a mechanical rabbit) (Calhoun 1987). Games and contests are rule-bound, earnest and organized. As our definition of sport implies, the more institutionalized and structured competitive games and contests become, the more sport-like they turn out to be. This is not meant to imply that we consider competitive eating a sport, or competitive eaters as athletes. Furthermore, considering that numerous people around the world starve to death every day, the concept of competitive eating hardly seems sporting.

Sports

We defined the term "sports" earlier in this chapter. Sports, by their very design, are highly structured, they involve institutionally defined rules, give rise to a hierarchical authority pattern, and are often so over-regulated that they seem only nominally related to play. Although it is commonly said that athletes "play" sports, the rules and customs that control the behaviors of athletes often distances sports from the realm of play. Sports represent the formalization of play, with every move scrutinized and subjected to rules and rules-interpretation by game officials and league administrators. The participants of sports (athletes, owners, trainers, etc.) have an investment with the games they play. Their very livelihoods are dependent upon success in the sports world. Generally, the investment aspect of sport outweighs the recreational, playful aspect of the game itself. Thus, as Edwards (1973) notes decades ago, sport is often "anything but a diversion to its participants. In fact, for many participants it is sport that produces the primary stresses and strains in their lives" (55).

The Most Popular Sports in the United States

It is well understood that sports are very popular in the United States and around the world. Any discussion of the popularity of sport in society presupposes the necessity to clarify what is meant by "most popular." Put another way, if you are asked, "What is America's favorite sport?" you must realize that there are two different ways to answer this question, depending on whether the question refers to America's favorite participatory sport or America's favorite sport to follow. The authors examined numerous studies, including their own previous research, and organizational websites. Sifting through it all we found that the most popular participatory sports in the United States (in 2017) are: Running/jogging (60 million) (110 million Americans participate in walking for fitness but it is competitive speed walking that would be considered a sport, not walking for fitness); bowling (45.5 million); basketball (30 million); golf (24 million); tennis (18 million); and inline skating (17 million) (Gough 2018; Gough 2019c; Lock 2020). Americans also participate in a number of popular recreational activities including treadmill exercise (53 million); stretching (50 million); freshwater fishing (49 million); and horseback riding (38 million).

The most popular sport for Americans to follow is professional football (NFL) and it has been the clear most popular sport in the United States for nearly the past 40 years. Regardless of the poll cited, professional football always turns up as the most popular, generally with 25–38 percent of respondents choosing the NFL as their most favorite. Major League Baseball (MLB) is consistently ranked as the second most popular sport to follow in the U.S. It becomes more complicated choosing the third most popular sport as some polls only list professional teams in their rankings and other polls only use the venue attendance as the criterion. Sifting through the complicated quagmire of "most popular sports to follow" leaves us to stick with college football as the third most popular sport followed by professional basketball (NBA); professional ice hockey (NHL); college basketball (NCAA); professional soccer (MLS), professional golf (PGA); professional tennis (ATP), motor sports (auto, truck and motorcycle), primarily NASCAR; and ultimate fighting (UFC)/mixed martial arts (MMA).

The Most Popular Sports in the World

Americans love *their* sports. We like our football and we do not call it "American football" like the rest of the world. The rest of the world loves their *futbol*, which Americans call soccer. One of our fastest growing sports is lacrosse and yet most of the world does not play it. We do not play cricket and yet, for the rest of the world, this is the most popular sport in many highly populous nations. Americans like auto racing, but we like NASCAR; the rest of the world prefers open-wheel (especially Formula One).

Once again, we updated our own research and examined the research of others and found that determining a ranking of the world's most popular sports presents a more daunting challenge than examining the most popular sports in the United States. With more than 3.5 billion followers, it is universally accepted that soccer is the most popular sport in the world. The sport is played in more than 200 countries across the globe but is especially big in South America, Europe, Central America, China, and Africa. The World Cup, the pinnacle of soccer's top-tier global competition which is played every four years, is rivaled only by the Olympics for top television viewership. Based on data accumulated by Statista, roughly 3.6 billion people watched at least part of each of the 2012 and 2016 Summer Olympics while both the 2010 and 2014 Men's World Cups drew a television audience of approximately 3.2 billion (Jackman 2018). FIFA (2018) reports that nearly half of the world's population (3.57 billion) watched the 2018 Men's World Cup. The 2019 Women's World Cup held in France had a viewership less than one-third of the Men's global viewership but still exceeded one billion (1.12 billion) for the first time. The 2019 viewership was an increase of 56 percent over the 2015 Women's World Cup (Glass 2019). When comparing the Olympics to the World Cup we have to realize that the Olympics include multiple events from a wide variety of sports and participants from far more countries than the World Cup and that the World Cup consists of just one sport. Clearly, the global appeal of soccer is quite evident. The winning nation in World Cup competition receives the highly coveted FIFA World Cup Trophy—the most cherished of all championships trophies. (In North America the most coveted trophy, arguably, would be the Vince Lombardi trophy awarded to the Super Bowl champions, or the Stanley Cup awarded to the NHL champion.) The second most popular sport in the world is cricket (2.5 billion followers). Few Americans have played cricket or even watched a match, let alone understand it. And yet, it is the number one sport in the populous country of India, as well as in many other nations such as Pakistan, Bangladesh, Nepal, Australia and parts of the Caribbean and Africa. The growing popularity of basketball in China has led this sport to climb to the third most popular sport (2.2 billion followers); it remains very popular in the United States, Canada, the Philippines, and throughout Europe and South America. Field hockey (2 billion followers, primarily in Europe, Africa, Asia, and Australia) and tennis (1 billion followers, primarily in Europe, the Americas, and Asia) round out the top five (Das 2020). The remaining sports to make the top ten lists of most followed sports in the world are: volleyball (900 million), table tennis (850m), baseball (500m), American football (410m), and rugby (410m) (Das 2020). Golf is just outside the top ten with 390 million followers.

When it comes to the most popular sports by participation it becomes nearly impossible to determine a definitive number. Once again, it is generally accepted that soccer/futbol is the most popular participatory sport with an estimated 1.3 billion participants. The remaining top ten participatory sports worldwide are: volleyball (800m); basketball (475m); table tennis (300m); cycling (250m); badminton (220m); tennis (75m); baseball/softball (65m); cricket (62m); and golf (60m) (Listerious.com 2019). We looked at several other lists and they all had the same ten sports and mostly in the same order.

As we will demonstrate throughout this book, for many people, sport is so important to them, it is like a religion. Sport is not a religion in the same sense as Christianity or Islam, for example, but rather, in terms of the secular meaning and self-identification that sport allegiances provide. There are members of society who do not closely follow sports. They will have a hard time understanding how sport can provide such significant meaning to their lives. This same rationale is applied by those who do not adhere to a particular religion and have a hard time understanding another's devotion to a creed.

Connecting Sports and Popular Culture

Box 1: Sports Pervasiveness in Popular Culture: Bobbleheads, Candy Bars and More!

As demonstrated throughout this chapter, sports are a vital aspect of billions of people's lives across the globe. It was pointed out that many newspapers devote an entire section of their news coverage to sports, generally surpassing the space allocated to any other specific social institution such as politics, economics, religion, or the environment. In addition to newspaper coverage, there are literally hundreds of sports talk radio stations and radio programs dedicated to the single topic of sport. We can add to this the great amount of sports programming on television. The ESPN Network is so popular that they have numerous spin-off networks such as ESPN2, ESPN3, ESPNews, ESPN Classic, ESPNU, and ESPN Deportes. ESPN3, once known as ESPN360, is an online streaming service that provides live action and replays of sports from around the world as well as major college football and basketball. ESPN3 is just one source of sports on the Internet. In brief, sports are so pervasive they are available for our consumption 24 hours a day, 7 days a week. This was particularly evident during the COVID-19 crisis of 2020, when major and minor sporting events throughout the world were cancelled, and viewers had to make do with reruns of previous games and sports analysts desperately trying to fill the time with endless top ten lists of best athletes and speculations about when things would likely get back to normal.

That so much news coverage is allocated to sport compared to other social institutions and news issues that are, arguably, more important is a clear indicator of the importance placed on the sports world by so many people. (It also helps to justify the field of sport sociology and texts on the sociology of sport.) On occasions when news events of the day are so dramatic sports do take a back seat. And yet, during "states of emergency" (e.g., terrorist attacks, natural disasters, and social unrest) the resumption of sporting events is often viewed as a beacon of light that the immediate danger has waned and it's time to try and resume a sense of normalcy. Certainly this is the hope of many for when the COVID-19 pandemic finally comes to an end, or is believed to "under control."

The media attention given to sport is just one indicator of the pervasiveness of sport in society. As we pointed out in this chapter, not only do billions of people view sports, millions of people attend live sporting events (at least when there is no pandemic going on). Attending a sporting event is much more than simply going to a ballgame, it is often a social event that entails planning and arranging one's daily/weekly schedule. Sports such as football and auto racing also imply all-day tailgate parties (see Chapter 4 for a discussion on tailgating). In contemporary society, media attention is also measured in terms of the social media presence of athletes and ball teams. As we shall see in Chapter 15, athletes have a strong presence on Facebook, Twitter, and other media outlets.

The pervasiveness of sport is revealed through sport-related movies and videos. The 2004 Academy Award for best film went to a boxing movie, *Million Dollar Baby*. It was about a female boxer (played by Hilary Swank) and a trainer (played by Clint Eastwood). The film has grossed over $100 million and also garnered Academy Awards for best actress (Swank), best supporting actor (Morgan Freeman) and best director (Eastwood). And Sondra Bullock won the 2010 Academy Award for Best Actress for her depiction of the real-life Leigh Anne Tuohy, the foster mother of football star Michael Oher. An ESPN poll of the top 20 sports films of all time lists the following: *Bull Durham, Rocky, Raging Bull, Hoosiers, Slap Shot, The Natural, Field of Dreams, Caddyshack, The Hustler, The Longest Yard, North Dallas Forty, Jerry Maguire, Hoop Dreams, Breaking Away, White Men Can't Jump, The Bad News Bears* (the original version), *Chariots of Fire, Brian's Song, Eight Men Out,* and *When We Were Kings*. All of these are among the most popular films ever made. Students have informed the authors that they really like *Coach Carter, The Way Back, Creed, 42, The Express,* and *McFarland, USA,* among other films not on this older list.

The pervasiveness of sport is also demonstrated in many other ways including the oddity of parents naming their children in honor of sports-related themes and no we are not simply talking about naming a child after a favorite athlete (e.g., fans of Peyton Manning naming their son Peyton or fans of Abby Wambach naming their daughter Abby). Believe it or not, a number of parents have named their children in honor of ESPN! Variations include: ESPN, Espn, and Espen. In 2006, Leann and Rusty Real named their son ESPN Montana Real after the sports network and former football great Joe Montana (*Associated Press* 2006). Leann had promised her husband that if they ever had a son, he could name him. A young boy showed up at a Baltimore Orioles game on a summer's night in 2014 with a sign that read, "My name is really Camden Yards." The Orioles play at Camden Yards Stadium. Camden's parents confirmed that the boy, a fan of the O's, is named after the park. Parents have also named their children Wrigley Field (Chicago Cubs Stadium) and Crimson Tide (University of Alabama nickname). Michael Dow and first wife, Crystal, named their child "Cuse," the shortened nickname for his favorite college team Syracuse. They were going to name their daughter Sarah Cuse Dow, which would have been very clever, but named her Cuse Flynn Dow instead (the middle name is in honor of former Syracuse basketball star, Jonny Flynn) (*The Post-Standard* 2015: C-2).

It is common for popular athletes to have food items, such as sandwiches and drinks, named after them. For example, Reggie Jackson ("Reggie!" bars) and Ken Griffey, Jr., have candy bars named for them and former Buffalo Bills quarterback Doug Flutie had corn flakes ("Flutie Flakes") named after him. A number of athletes have sandwiches named after them that appear in local delis; they usually remain on the menu for as long as the athlete remains popular, such as the Carnegie Deli's Melo Sandwich, named for Carmelo Anthony in 2011 when he played for the Knicks (which he ceased to do in 2017, the year after the Carnegie Deli itself closed for good). Some athletes have barbeque sauce named after them, such as former NFL player William "the Refrigerator" Perry and his "The Fridge BBQ Sauce." Golfer Arnold Palmer was known to enjoy combining lemonade with iced tea and now the drink is commonly known as "the Arnold Palmer." There are countless other examples of athletes being named after food items.

Sports franchises commonly give away a wide variety of promotional items to induce fans to attend live sporting events. Among the more common give-away items are beach towels, team ball caps, team t-shirts, key chains, hockey pucks, baseballs, miniature baseball bats, magnets, posters, water bottles, and so on. Many spectators look forward to "Bobblehead night" when they are given a free promo Bobblehead. Sport fans (including the authors of this book) really enjoy Bobbleheads of their favorite athletes. In turn, athletes realize that it is an honor to have their face on a Bobblehead. The authors, like most sports fans of their generation, complain however that today's Bobbleheads do not really bobble, especially compared to Bobbleheads of the past that used a giant spring to assure that the head of the figurine actually bobbles with a slight touch. Today's Bobbleheads rarely actually move up and down. Nonetheless, they make for a great collection item for die-hard sports fans.

Sport itself is a hugely popular social institution. Sport's connection with popular culture all but assures that the people cannot ignore the pervasiveness of sports in society.

SUMMARY

Sport is one of the most pervasive social institutions in the world. Sports are played in nearly every society and are intertwined with cultural values, mores, norms, and expectations of behavior. The sociological perspective of sport teaches us to analyze the underlying structures and forces that influence sports in a given society and to look beyond the limitations of so-called "common sense" knowledge. Sociology is an extensive field and relies on the systematic study of society. The scientific study of sport helps to provide great insights regarding human behavior in their various cultures. The sociology of sport refers to the systematic study of the processes, patterns, issues, values, and behaviors found within the institution of sport. The systematic study of sport provides a metaphoric mirror into such negative issues as elitism, racism, sexism, nationalism, competitiveness, the abuse of drugs, and other deviant behaviors. More importantly, though, it can help one understand the positive aspects of societies such as cooperation, hard work, dedication, loyalty, understanding rules, and ethical norms.

Most people think they know what "sports" are but providing clear parameters around activities that some label as a "sport" may come in conflict with what others think is meant by sports. The definition of sports to be used in this text is: *Sports* are institutionalized, structured, and sanctioned competitive activities that go beyond the realm of play that involve physical athletic exertion and the use of relatively complex athletic skills. Many other important terms were also defined, including: athlete, physically active persons, leisure, and play.

An analysis of the most popular sports—both in terms of participation and following—in the United States and globally was provided.

KEY TERMS

Athlete A person who is in training for some specific sports event or participates in a sport while competing against other athletes or previously set records.

Athletics Exercises and games that require physical skill, strength and endurance.

Conspicuous Consumption A term coined by Thorstein Veblen; it refers to spending money, time and effort quite uselessly in the pleasurable business of inflating the ego.

Conspicuous Leisure A term coined by Thorstein Veblen; it refers to living a lifestyle where the pursuit of leisure and the appearance of privilege are used instrumental in one's behavior. In other words, it involves participating in nonproductive activities.

Contest An organized competition. It may be between two individuals, between two teams, between an individual and a group, between an individual or team and inanimate nature, between a person or group and animate nature, or between an individual or team and an ideal standard.

Culture The shared knowledge, beliefs, values, and rules about behavior that exist within a society.

Leisure Unobligated time that is free of work or maintenance responsibilities.

Organized Play Activities which are bound by rules, in which there are designated time limits and boundaries and nearly always a clear winner and loser.

Play An activity that is performed voluntarily during leisure.

Recreation A leisure activity designed to refresh the mind and/or body.

Scientific Method The pursuit of knowledge involving the stating of a problem, the collection of facts through observation and experiment, and the testing of ideas to determine whether they are right or wrong.

Social Institutions A set of organized beliefs and rules that establishes how a society will attempt to meet its basic social needs.

Social Sciences Academic disciplines such as sociology, anthropology, economics, education, psychology, and political science, which focus their study on the various aspects of human society and interaction.

Social Structure The organization of society—its social positions and the ongoing relationships among these social positions, the different resources allocated to these social positions, and the social groups that make up the society.

Society A group of persons who interact with one another as members of a collectivity within a defined territory and a highly structured system of human organization.

Sociological Imagination A term coined by C. Wright Mills. Sociological imagination stresses the importance of the historical social context in which an individual is found, and the ways in which our private lives are influenced by our social environment and existing social forces.

Sociology The systematic study of groups, organizations, social institutions, societies, and the social interaction among people.

Sociology of Sport A subdiscipline of sociology that focuses on the relationship between sport and society with a focus on the behavior of individuals and groups within sport and the rules, processes, and patterns found within the institution of sport and how these social forces impact human behavior.

Spontaneous Play A type of play which is voluntary, flexible, and uncertain with latitude for innovation.

Sports Institutionalized, structured, and sanctioned competitive athletic activities (e.g., competitive running, jumping, and throwing) that go beyond the realm of play; involve physical exertion and/or the use of relatively complex athletic skills.

DISCUSSION QUESTIONS

- Provide at least five examples of the pervasiveness of sports in contemporary society.
- What do you think of the definitions of "sports" and "athlete" provided in the text? Do these definitions reflect how you would define sports and athletes?
- Do you think playing bridge constitutes a sport? Are members of a competitive marching band athletes?
- Why are sports so important in American culture? What social institutions do you think are the most important for a society?
- Why do so many popular films deal with issues of sport? Do you think this is a good or bad thing? Think of some recent examples of films that have sport as their central theme.
- Describe the differences and similarities between leisure, play and sports. Provide examples of each. Which activity—leisure, play or sports—consumes more of your time?

CHAPTER 2

Social Theory and Sport

Two friends are cheering for their beloved hometown college football team, a team that competes in one of the five power conferences (FBS) that make up the NCAA's elite teams. (The five power conferences are: ACC, SEC, Big 10, Big 12 and the Pac-12.) Their school, however, has a current talent level that keeps them in the lower half of the super teams. The two friends reminisce over past glory days and wonder what it will take for their team to reach the level of national championship-caliber.

One friend suggests, "We need to schedule non-conference games against the best schools we can play." (Note: Every school that plays at the elite five conferences only has a few non-conference games that they can schedule.) "We should play the teams that are already competing for a national title every year." He believes that playing "big-time" teams will attract big time recruits. These recruits will eventually lead the team to the promise land.

His friend disagrees and states, "We need to play teams we can beat so that we can get victories." She adds, "Top recruits want to play at schools that win. Once we get the top recruits and double-digit victories for a season on a regular basis we can start to play the top-tier non-conference teams. And then, we can start to compete for a national championship."

Each of these two friends has the same ultimate goal—for their team to win the championship. But they have different viewpoints on the best method to achieve this goal. What each of these friends has expressed, essentially, is a theory about how to gain top recruits with the goal of winning a national title.

Social theory involves expressing ideas about human behavior and the social world. As demonstrated in the story above, every one of us is capable of formulating a theory about social life. Unlike most amateur theorists, a social theorist seeks to understand the social world by means of reason and rational thought. These scientifically driven theorists seek validity for their theories through empirical research and data analysis and interpretation. Sport sociologists use theory as a "guide" in their attempt to understand the institution of sport. Sport sociologists, like other sociologists grounded in the scientific tradition, incorporate research, the use of statistical data, and analysis to support their theories about the sports world. As for the best way to recruit top football players, data will have to be collected in an effort to determine which theory seems the most plausible.

The Importance of Social Theory

Sociology attempts to provide insights and explanations as to why people behave the way that they do and why social institutions exist the way they do. Social theory, then, focuses on interactions, patterns and events found in the social environment and attempts to explain such observed phenomena. A theory on social reality reflects one's perspective on the nature of society. There are numerous perspectives and theories within the sociological tradition. A sociologist's preference for one theory over another often reflects his or her own values and possible biases. Preference for a particular theory or perspective is also impacted by current, in vogue, and fashionable trends found within sociology. "Theories about society are shaped by people's past experiences, current needs, and future hopes, and it is more likely that at given points in history one perspective may be more popular or more reflective of current events than others, rather than one being 'true' and the others 'false'" (Figler and Whitaker 1991: 25). All social thinkers—at least to a certain degree—are influenced by the ideas of people who preceded them; in this manner, we all benefit from the knowledge of others. Relying on previous knowledge allows social thinkers to treat certain bits of information as "givens." The discoveries of today will be treated as "givens" in the future. This is all a part of the theoretical "chain of knowledge."

What exactly is social theory? "The word *theory* is often misunderstood. It seems to imply speculation or uncertainty because it is viewed *merely* as a theory, not a statement of 'truth.' Theories are generally contrasted with 'facts.' It is usually believed that facts are established truths, whereas theories are speculations about what might be true" (Delaney 2005: 1). However, to social scientists, the word "theory" does not imply mere speculation as theories may already be established as true. Theories provide explanations or accounts concerning social events or phenomena. As Gabriel Abend (2008) explains, a theory is "a general proposition, or logically-connected system of general propositions, which establishes a relationship between two or more variables" (177). The authors define theory as a statement that proposes to explain or relate observed phenomena or a set of concepts through a logically-based system of general propositions. Theory involves a set of inter-related arguments that seek to describe and explain cause-effect relationships. Portraying ideas (theories) in the form of statements allows for empirical testing. Thus, any theory that can be tested for empirical verifiability is considered a "good" theory.

Although sociological theory has existed since the time Auguste Comte coined the term "sociology" more than 180 years ago, most sociologists ignored sport as an academic study. George Herbert Mead represents one of the earliest sociologists to examine critical aspects of play and games—essential elements of sport.

GEORGE HERBERT MEAD AND PLAY

George H. Mead (1863–1931) was an American pragmatist, philosopher, social scientist and the primary founder of symbolic interactionism and the "Chicago School" approach in the study of human behavior. Mead established a developmental theory (of self) centered primarily on the play of children. Mead (1934) argues that the "development of self" begins with the "imitation stage" wherein infants acquire an emerging awareness of other people and physical objects. Babies learn to grasp, hold and use simple objects like spoons, bottles and blankets. As their physical skills further develop, they learn to play with objects by observing and imitating their parents (Delaney 2004). For example, the parent or guardian may pick up a ball and throw it, then encourage the child to do the same thing. Mead (1934) described the second stage of development as the "play stage." At this stage, the child, among other things, learns to "play" (act out) the roles and attitudes of other persons. This is an important stage of development as other animals play but only humans are capable of playing the role of others. Learning to play the roles of others helps the child to take on the different roles that people in society perform. "To learn the role of others, the child must come to understand the meanings of symbols and language. Much of this learning takes place through various forms of play" (Delaney 2004: 181). It is the third stage of development, the "game stage," that children learn how multiple roles take place at the same time, as in teamwork. Children also learn that games, like life itself, consists of multiple rules, norms, values, and social expectations. The importance of learning makes it clear that Mead's theory is not biologically-based, but socially-based. The final stage of development, according to Mead, is the "generalized other" stage. At this stage, individuals have learned to do what is best for the community or, in the case of sports, to do what is best for the team (e.g., take a pay cut so that the team can sign free agents and stay under the "salary cap") and the community (e.g., athletes will work within the community to help the less fortunate or to take part in charities such as the "Make-a-Wish" Foundation). Mead's developmental theory has four stages.

1. *The Imitation Stage.* During this preparatory stage, infants develop an emerging awareness of other people and physical objects found in the environment. Babies learn to grasp, hold and use simple objects like spoons, dolls, bottles, and blankets. As their physical skills continue to develop, they learn to play with objects by imitating the people around them. The infant may observe an older sibling playing and may try throwing a ball like the other, older children. A parent might pick up a ball and toss it, in an attempt to coax the child to do the same thing. Imitation implies learning, as infants find out that some behaviors are positively rewarded and other behaviors bring punishments. Interactions with significant others are especially important for the infant's development of self. Significant others are those specific individuals with whom a child interacts with on a regular basis, generally the child's immediate family members and friends.

2. *The Play Stage.* Mead was among the first theorists to emphasize the importance of symbols in the socialization process. In the play stage, the child has learned to use language and understands the meanings of some symbols. Language allows the child an opportunity to adopt the role or attitude of other persons—they can speak with the mannerisms of the other. They not only act out the roles of others, but their imaginations allow them to pretend to be that person (Pampel 2000). Although lower animals also play, only humans "play at being someone else" (Aboulafia 1986: 9). Through role-playing, the child learns to become both subject and object, a critical step in the development of self (Ritzer 2000). It is important to note that children are also developing their own personalities at this stage. "In play, the child takes on and acts out roles which exist in his immediate, but larger, social world. By acting out such roles he organizes particular attitudes about them. Moreover, the child in the course of role playing becomes cognitively capable of 'standing outside himself' and formulating a reflected view of himself as a social object separate from but related to others" (Loy and Ingham 1981: 197).

3. *The Game Stage.* At this stage, the child is capable of putting herself in the role of several others at the same time, and of understanding the relationship between those roles (e.g., teammates). "If we contrast play with the situation in an organized game, we note the essential difference that the child who plays in a game

must be ready to take the attitude of everyone else involved in that game, and that these different roles must have a definite relationship to each other" (Mead 1934: 151). Mead, who taught at the University of Chicago, was a fan of the Chicago Cubs and enjoyed watching baseball. He used the game of baseball to illustrate his "game stage" theory. For example, when the ball is hit into play, the fielder must make the play, but must also know the role of his teammates and the complexities of the game—such as, where to throw the ball if there are already runners on base, and so forth.

> Understanding the roles of others is not enough in the game stage; participants must also know and understand the rules of the game (Miller 1973). As Mead explained, abiding by the rules involves the ability to exercise self-control and implies that the child has learned to function in the organized whole. Mead insisted that children take a great interest in rules. "They make rules on the spot in order to help themselves out of difficulties. Part of the enjoyment of the game is to get these rules. Now, the rules are the set of responses which a particular attitude calls out. You can demand a certain response in others if you take a certain attitude" (1934: 152). Thus, games teach children to take multiple roles but also teach them to abide by rules. "The game is viewed as a sort of passage in the life of a child from taking the role of others in play to the organized part that is essential to self-consciousness" [Delaney 2004: 182].

4. *The Generalized Other.* This marks the final stage of development. The generalized other refers to the attitude of the community, a specific group, or society in general. It is the universalization of the role-taking process (Pfuetz 1954). The generalized other is not a person; it is a person's conscious awareness of the society that she or he is a part of (Cockerham 1995). Such associations occur with multiple, diverse others in the community (e.g., geographic community, church-group, sport-booster team, the greater society). As mentioned previously, athletes (as well as sport organizations) often give of their time and money to help out others that are less fortunate. For example, Houston Texans defensive end J.J. Watt, one of the NFL's most famous philanthropists, has his own foundation—the Justin J. Watt Foundation—that has given generously to local communities, including coming to the rescue in the wake of Hurricane Harvey in 2017, when he raised $37 million to build more than 1,100 new homes and nearly 1,000 new child care and after-school programs in and around the devastated Houston area (Lisa 2020). Steph Curry (NBA player) donated $118,000 of his own money to Hurricane Harvey relief and Tom Brady (NFL player) donated $100,000 to the Justin J. Watt Foundation. LeBron James (NBA player) created the LeBron James Family Foundation which has raised $40 million for the After-School All-Stars and I Promise program, among other donations. Professional wrestler John Cena holds the Make-a-Wish foundation record for having fulfilled more than 600 wishes (as of early 2020) and has given millions of dollars to a variety of causes including his 2019 donation of $500,000 to firefighters battling historic wildfires in California (Lisa 2020). These are just a few of the countless examples of athletes who understand the meaning of taking on the perspective of the greater community and its needs.

The development of self is dependent on interactions with others within the community. These interactions help to shape and determine the individual's personality. Whereas the play stage requires only pieces of selves, the game stage requires a coherent self (Ritzer 2000). Mead's development of self theory is very sociological. It considers interactional patterns, past experiences, and the impact of "outside" social forces on the individual. The impact of social forces on sport participants and the creation and maintenance of the institution of sport is the central theme of contemporary theory.

In the following pages a number of contemporary sociological theories are applied to the study of sport. The first theory to be examined is functionalism.

Functionalism

Functionalism, or structural functionalism as some sociologists prefer to call it, was the one-time dominant theory of sociology (especially during the 1950s and early 1960s). Functionalism is a macrosociological theory that explores the characteristics of social patterns, structures, social systems, and institutions. Functionalism views society as an organized system of interrelated parts that seeks equilibrium or balance. These interrelated parts work in cooperation with one another so that the entire social system functions properly.

Functionalism has two basic postulates. The first is the concept of interdependent parts, where all of society's social institutions (e.g., sports, religion, politics, economics, and the media) are linked together. "Functionalism begins with the idea that any stable system (such as the human body) consists of a number of different, but interrelated, parts that operate together to create an overall order" (Levin 1991: 76). With this reasoning, a change in one institution inevitably leads to changes in other institutions; additionally, a change within one aspect of the system will affect the system itself. For example, if the NCAA were to mandate that all athletes must maintain a 2.5 (4.0 grading system) GPA, member institutions would be forced to enact many changes; especially with regards to recruitment and retention. (Note: Academic requirements will be discussed in Chapter 7.)

Because social systems wish to run smoothly, they constantly seek equilibrium, or stability. Functionalists recognize that certain behaviors cause a disruption in the system—they are labeled dysfunctional acts. Robert Merton (1910–2003) was the first sociologist to articulate the potential dysfunctional features of certain aspects of the social system. Merton stated that dysfunctional aspects are those which disturb the normally functioning social system. Furthermore, Merton argued that aspects of the social system may be functional for some, but not for others. For example, it is common for sporting events to be held during national holidays. This is convenient for the fans who wish to watch the games, but not so convenient for the athletes who may have preferred to spend time with their families. Functionalists prefer the status quo over change (especially rapid change); and any change in the system is generally introduced in such a manner that allows ample time for a smooth transition. Thus, if the NCAA did mandate higher grade requirements among its athletes, it would undoubtedly provide ample time for a smooth transition.

The second postulate of functionalism is centered on the idea that individual members of the social system (e.g., society, sports league or team) generally endorse the same basic values and beliefs. A common agreement on issues of right and wrong, basic values, and morality allows for the system to function appropriately. On sports teams, players are expected to follow the rules and norms dictated by league rules, governing bodies, coaches, athletic directors, and school administrators in addition to NCAA guidelines. If members of a social system lose faith in their society (the system) they will seek change. In professional sports it is often coaches or someone in the front office who lose their jobs when the team is losing and dissent takes place. There are also occasions where individual players are singled out as the violator of the prevailing culture and they may find themselves traded to another team, released from the team, have playing time dramatically reduced, or lose their scholarship. Rapid social change within the system is something the functionalist approach is not geared to handle.

Among the leading structural functionalists of the twentieth century was Talcott Parsons (1902–1979), a major sociologist at Harvard University. Parsons's analysis of social systems and social action remains as the cornerstone of the functionalist perspective. As with most social thought, Parsons's ideas were a reflection of the era in which he lived. The post–World War II era was highlighted by great prosperity among many Americans. The 1950s was a decade of relative social calm and stability. Parsons reasoned that social systems strive for stability in order to function at peak levels, and "argued that the overall system and subsystems of which it is composed work together to form a balanced, stable whole and that the system naturally tends toward stability rather than toward disorder" (Levin 1991: 77). Systems have parts, or subsystems. The social system also includes the interaction of a plurality of individual actors oriented to a situation (e.g., a sports team). "Reduced to the simplest possible terms, then, a social system consists in a plurality of individual actors interacting with each other in a situation which has at least a physical or environmental aspect" (Parsons 1951: 5). Importantly, the social system is designed to continue to exist even when some individual members leave. For example, as members of a college sports team graduate, transfer, or drop out, they are replaced by other individuals. This cycle of individuals coming and going continues year after year and yet the social system (the team, the league) manages to maintain itself (with varying degrees of success).

Although social systems are quite diverse (some are small, some large; some are complex, others relatively simplistic) a number of general assumptions about social systems can be made:

1. Systems are orderly and made of the interdependence of parts.
2. The system and all the subsystems strive for equilibrium (normal activity, a self-maintaining order).
3. Systems are generally static or move in a progressively deliberate manner.
4. A disruption in the "normal flow" of one subsystem can cause a disturbance throughout the whole system.
5. Systems have boundaries, which may involve actual physical space, or time and distance [Delaney 2005: 48–49].

By the late 1960s and early 1970s, there were many criticisms of functionalism. One criticism is that functionalism is too conservative and fails to explain social change. Functionalism's focus on systems equilibrium leads functionalists to ignore conflict. People do not agree on all the values and beliefs of the dominant society and, as a result, functionalism is criticized for failing to acknowledge socioeconomic inequalities that lead to different perspectives of the social system. Because of its conservative nature and focus on the status quo, functionalism is also criticized for ignoring such social patterns as "discrimination, exploitation, and political dominations by elites or ruling classes who have a vested interest in maintaining their power and prestige" (Nixon and Frey 1996: 10).

Despite these criticisms, the staying power of functionalism as a dominant sociological theory cannot be denied. The relevancy of this perspective is demonstrated in the sports world as well.

FUNCTIONALISM APPLIED TO SPORT

The functionalist perspective has great relevance to sport. Sport, as a social institution, may be viewed as a social system with interrelated parts and a plurality of individual actors interacting with one another. All social institutions are evaluated in terms of their functionality and that's true whether we are talking about economics, politics, the government, and so on. Sports teams are also evaluated in terms of functionality. "Team owners evaluate everyone in their organizations based on their functionality. Sports fans and spectators evaluate players, managers, and even owners on their ability to field a winning team. Many fans prefer a certain style (e.g., defensive-minded, offensive-minded, entertaining performances, 'flair players') from their favorite team" (Delaney 2018:19). Ultimately, an evaluation of athletes, sports teams, coaches and managers, and sports leagues are evaluated based on their functionality and ability to reach its goal—success on the playing field/court. A winning team is deemed functional if it wins and dysfunctional if it loses, this is true even if the winning team has many dysfunctional aspects. As the authors shall demonstrate throughout the text, sport possesses both functional and dysfunctional aspects.

Sport provides many societal functions, some of them manifest and others latent. Merton (1949/1968) described manifest functions as those consequences that are expected, or intended; they are conscious motivations for social behavior. For example, the manifest function of two friends attending a baseball game is to watch the athletes perform or to cheer for a favorite team. Merton described latent functions as consequences that are neither recognized nor intended; they are by-products of the original intended behavior. Thus, friends who attend ballgames together are also afforded an opportunity to reaffirm their friendship by spending time together. Parents and children may also bond over sports activities. Individuals bond with the community of the sports team they support. Eitzen (1989) adds:

> Most people view society and the role of sport in terms very similar to those used by functionalists. They look for the ways in which sport contributes to the communities in which they live. They see sport providing valuable lessons for their children and opportunities for themselves to release the tensions generated by a job or other life events. Sport gives them something to talk with strangers as well as friends and it provides occasions for outings and get-togethers. Many people believe that sport can serve as a model of the goals we should strive for and the means we should use in trying to achieve those goals [28].

During the 1970s many sport sociologists (for example, Allardt 1970; Wohl 1970; Luschen 1970b; Gruneau 1975; and Sage 1979) embraced the functionalist perspective by describing sport "in functionalist terms as supportive of the social order" (Figler and Whitaker 1991: 28). Stevenson and Nixon (1972) detailed five general functions by which sport helps the social system maintain equilibrium and operate smoothly and efficiently:

1. *Socioemotional Function.* Sport provides opportunities for conflict and tension management, camaraderie and community bonding, and ritualistic behaviors that people find comforting.

2. *Socialization.* All people learn society's expectations through the socialization process (see Chapter 5). Of primary concern to functionalists is the transmission of cultural values from one generation to the next.
3. *Social Integration.* A commonly cited function, sport, it is argued, provides opportunities for diverse groups and individuals to interact with one another.
4. *Political Functions.* The role of politics and sport is both functional and dysfunctional (see Chapter 13). The singing of the national anthem before sporting events is among the more obvious manifest functions of politics in action within the sports world.
5. *Social Mobility.* A recurring theme in contemporary society as well, it has long been argued that sport provides individuals with opportunities to improve their socio-economic status (SES). Sport does provide both direct (through professional sport participation) social mobility and indirect (through college scholarships with afford athletes an opportunity to earn a valuable education needed in the job market) social mobility.

Vogler and Schwartz (1993) argue that sport is so strongly endorsed by most people in American society that it has been given nearly "sacred status" and that the majority of people feel that sport is "compatible with American values" (6); and thus is congruent with the functionalist perspective. As a result, sport is viewed as having a positive function in society. Among other things, sport transmits cultural values; is educational; provides a release for physical and psychological pressures; provides a feeling of group membership; provides a means of social mobility; and generates a sense of personal competition (Vogler and Schwartz 1993: 6). Functionalists acknowledge that there are many people who do not follow sport. In his "theory of social action" Parsons (1949/1937) acknowledged the role of the subjective aspect of human activity. Thus, while it is true that some people in society do not share the value of sports, the same can be true for all social institutions. For example, religion and spiritual belief are very important for many people, but not for all; and while many people take part in the institution of marriage, a number of people will never marry.

Functionalists, in the tradition of Parsons and his conception of functional imperatives (adaptation, goal attainment, integration, and latency; or AGIL), argue that there are four basic "system needs" in order for any society (club, organization, team, etc.) to run smoothly and effectively. This principle can be applied to the sports world as well.

1. *Adaptation.* Members of society must learn to adapt to changes in the social structure and culture in order to survive. The adaptation aspect is very relevant to the sports world, for example, the emphasis on being physically fit (a requirement for most sports) is an important element in survival. The ability to adapt to changes in coaching philosophies is often critical for athletes when a new coach or system is introduced to the team. Sports leagues and franchises and colleges and universities alike must generate more revenue than they spend if they are to survive. And players and coaches must learn to adapt to rule changes.
2. *Goal Attainment.* Individual societal members are expected to seek society's goals. The predominant goal in Western societies is to be successful. Sport teaches participants that working hard leads to victory, and, therefore, success. Sport is preoccupied with tracking the successes and failures of its participants. Statistics are used in an attempt to provide empirical evidence of success and failure. As

former Green Bay Packer coach Vince Lombardi is reputed to have said, "Show me a good loser, and I'll show you a loser."

3. *Integration*. This functional imperative involves the regulation and coordination of actors and subsystems within the greater social system in order to keep it functioning properly (Delaney 2014). Sport leagues must regulate and coordinate all of the participating franchises or teams, coaches and managers, sport participants, and spectators and fans. Sports bring people together. Sport provides people an opportunity to bond with a group and a community. It provides a sense of social identification as well as a source of personal identity.

4. *Latency*. Latency consists of two related issues: tension maintenance (internal tensions and actors' sense of strain) and pattern maintenance (displaying "appropriate" behavior). Proper socialization is supposed to address the issue of latency. Sport provides many forms of pattern maintenance—primarily through participation where participants are taught to accept a well-defined authority structure (e.g., athletes know they must abide by their coaches' rules and the authority of referees, etc.). Sport also provides spectators and participants a socially approved outlet for their aggressive energy. Very few work environments involve workers being booed, or cheered, as they perform their duties, but this is life in the sports world.

It is perhaps, the social systems-approach that gives functionalism the most relevancy to the sports world. Parsons (1949) described the "social system" as a network of inter-related parts, or subsystems, arranged in such a way as to accommodate the interaction of a plurality of individual actors who are oriented to a given situation and striving to achieve goals. The social system concept is commonly hyped in the sports world especially by players and coaches alike who use some variation of the cliché, "we have to play within the system." (Note: A Google search of "Sports: Buy into the System" yields more than 3.2 billion results.) "Coaches routinely attempt to implement a system. This system is generally the one they feel most confident in, although there are times when a coach may change his or her system to fit the particular talent on the team. The coach will introduce the system to players and then proceed to teach the system to the team" (Delaney 2018:24). Often, there are times when if just one person steps outside the system it can become ineffective, dysfunctional. Team players are likely to see more playing time and greater success when they buy into a coach's system and if there is an injury it's simply a matter of next player up (to take the place of the injured player). If that player plays within the system, success is still possible even with a back-up. Team players are likely to see more playing time and greater success when they buy into their coach's system. However, if the team players lose faith in the system, the team is more likely to experience failure. There are countless examples about the importance of playing within the system. If any one aspect of the functionalist perspective stands above the rest to highlight the relevancy of this theoretical approach it is the social system component.

There are a number of criticisms of the functionalist approach, including: (1) it fails to explain social change and it stresses structure over process; (2) functionalism is better suited to deal with static structures; (3) the conservative nature of functionalism is often criticized as an inefficient way to study a society that is fluid; and (4) while functionalism stresses the importance of shared societal values, it ignores the *interests* of people

(Delaney 2014). Despite any such criticisms of functionalism, this theoretical perspective, especially its system's analysis, is still relevant to the sports world.

Structural functionalism represents just one outlook on sport. Among the leading challenges to the functionalist approach is the conflict perspective.

Conflict Theory

Functional theory is centered on the idea that there is a general consensus in values and norms of society and that the social institutions found within a society are integrated into a functioning whole. In contrast, conflict theorists argue that society is composed of competing parts (e.g., social institutions and special interest groups) that are in competition with one another over scarce resources. The competing parts possess different levels of power. Consequently, conflict theory examines the role of power and the inequality found methodically throughout society. The conflict perspective also puts forth the notion that there is no true consensus of values found in society and that, instead, society's primary norms and values are those of the dominant group. Dominant groups, because of their power, are in a position to dictate to others rules and procedures that must be adhered. In sports, there are a number of dominant groups, including governing bodies, league commissioners, owners (in professional sports), university presidents and athletic directors (in collegiate sports), and to a lesser degree, coaches and game day officials.

Conflict theory is based primarily on the ideas of Karl Marx (1818–1883) and rose to prominence during the late 1960s and early 1970s because of growing disillusionment with structural functionalism. As Turner (1975) explains, "The growing disenchantment with structural-functional theory has been marked by the rise of alternative theoretical perspectives over the last two decades. One of the most conspicuous of these alternatives has been 'conflict theory' which has presumably rediscovered for the discipline such phenomena as power, force, coercion, constraint, and change in social systems" (443).

Marx did not "create" conflict theory; rather, it was his ideas on such subjects as human potential, the historical method, class conflict, economic inequalities, class consciousness, and communism that influenced future social thinkers. Marx noted that all of human history was highlighted primarily by a class struggle between those with power (the elites, or owners of the means of production) and those without power (the masses, or workers). The result is predictable: the people who possess power will want to keep it, while those without power will want to gain it. People may react to class differences in a number of ways including open hostility and revolt against the existing social system (and those who benefit from it) to simple acceptance of how things are in society. Marx referred to this latter response as *false consciousness*—the inability to clearly see where one's own best interests lie.

Marx viewed religion as an example of false consciousness and as a weapon of the power elite to keep the masses in their place. He recognized that the power elites encouraged the masses to embrace afterlife considerations because it diverted people from taking action against social inequalities on earth. (For example, *Psalms* 37: 11 states that "the meek shall inherit the earth.") Religious institutions, therefore, are useful to the power elites as means of keeping the powerless from questioning their status. Marx suggested that "religion is the opiate of the masses" (McLellan 1987; Hadden 1997). An opiate is a drug used to dull the senses; if one is not thinking clearly, one is likely to believe almost anything. Likewise, religions can help dull the pain of reality by encouraging a feeling that, no matter how oppressed or unfulfilled a person may be, there will be a joyous and exciting afterlife for those who endure such inequalities on earth. Using this Marxist perspective, Paul Hoch (1972) argued that sport has replaced religion as the opiate of the masses. "Five generations ago, Karl Marx called religion the opiate of the masses. Today that role has been taken over by sports" (Hoch 1972: 19). At the time Hoch made this statement he suggested that perhaps the word "opiate" was a little strong, but he felt it was the best possible answer to the climate of the time. Hoch noted that people were more concerned with baseball and football scores than with the Vietnam War. Additionally, people appeared more concerned with whether Muhammad Ali would defeat Joe Frazier than the possibility of the Vietnam War extending into Laos. "To many, sports are such an escape from reality that the political economy is too mundane to be mentioned in the same breath" (Hoch 1972: 11).

The idea that sport is the opiate of the masses is reinforced by the realization that sports are in an "age of the spectator" and the "age of the sport consumer." This is evident by high attendance and spectatorship figures, the large number of hours fans spend watching televised sporting events, the growing popularity of sports fantasy leagues, sports gambling, the amount of space dedicated to sports in most newspapers and social media, and the everyday casual conversations centered on sports among the populace. As Yiannakis and associates (1978) argued four decades ago, sport has taken on the quality of a secular religion because it provides the "followers" an escape from the mundane (as other opiates provide) and provides a sense of belonging. In addition, many sports fans say they follow their favorite teams "religiously" and pray for favorable outcomes. These are truly "devout" fans. (See Chapter 14 for a further discussion on the relationship between sport and religion.) Such terminology, sociologists argue, is not merely ironic but is in fact descriptive.

The conflict perspective remains relevant in the contemporary era as there exist great social conflicts among a variety of special interest groups, politicians, and groups and categories of people. The validity of the conflict theory is also very evident by the continuous waging of war throughout this century. That war and conflict have dominated every century in human history also attests to the validity of the conflict perspective. That sport serves a diversionary role in society also reflects the conflict perspective on power. This means the polity is afforded an opportunity to continue "business as is" because so many people have become "fed up" with the socio-economic reality of society and rather than concentrate their collective efforts to bring about change; they turn to sports for a diversion.

Conflict Theory Applied to Sports

Although Marx did not write much about sports, a Marxist perspective proves to be quite enlightening, as well as relevant. Marxist interpretations of the rise of modern sports are related to the organization of ownership over the means of production. Sport sociologists who utilize the Marxist point of view analyze the rise of modern sports from a materialistic perspective. Today, many elite sport teams and events are controlled by corporations, corporate sponsors, and those whom could be labeled as "power elites." Even the individualistic sports, such as tennis, golf and surfing, are controlled by

Members of the 2014 Stanley Cup champion Los Angeles Kings ride in a parade in Redondo Beach, California (courtesy of William "Bear" Konopka).

corporate sponsors. Although most fans are aware of this corporate domination, few find it overly threatening. Marx would most likely identify this behavior as a form of false consciousness. Conflict theorists in general and Marxists in particular, are concerned about the role of power and domination found in sport. The role of power and domination in sport is evident in many ways, including the efforts of professional sports leagues to bust unions and, in effect, strengthen their position over the workers. Those who control the means of production will attempt to maintain their advantageous position. The players, who represent the workers, are in competition with the owners over the control of the means of production. Players' unions work to guarantee as many benefits as possible for the workforce while the owners attempt to break player unions and guarantee themselves a disproportionate amount of the profits—profits earned via the labor of the workers.

Owner lockouts and player holdouts are examples of this power struggle. As with any business, professional sports are subject to unforeseen and unusual circumstances such as the virus Severe Acute Respiratory Syndrome Coronavirus 2 (SARS-CoV-2) which caused the COVID-19 epidemic of 2020. In mid–March, all American sports were cancelled, and most sports leagues across the globe. Months later, the sports leagues (i.e., National Basketball Association and National Hockey League) were contemplating how to resume their schedules. Major League Baseball (MLB), which would have begun a couple of weeks after the national shutdown, pondered when they could start their season and how to adjust their schedule to something feasible (as a full schedule was not practical). During the shutdown, both the owners and the players union attempted to flex their muscles to negotiate the best deal possible. Eventually a deal was worked out and a scheduled 60-game season started in July. Major League Baseball also announced that the postseason would be part of a bubble designed to minimize exposure to the corona-virus. The World Series would be played entirely in Arlington, Texas. Because sports fans want games to resume, they tend to side with ownership who portray the players as being greedy. In this manner, the owners exercise power.

Marxists also argue that the power elite promote sports as a means of keeping the masses preoccupied with more mundane things than matters of the state (e.g., social problems). Those who participate in sport are taught to accept authority (e.g., from coaches, administrators, and officials). From this perspective, sports are not only viewed as an opiate of society, but the power elites of society may also be viewed as the ones "pushing" or "selling" the opiate to the masses. Furthermore, the power elites use sport to help socialize the masses into accepting rules. The power elites, it is argued, determine the rules and laws of the land, and individuals have little or no say in their formation and modification. Likewise, athletes have no chance of changing a rule while the game is being played; and, aside from sports with "instant replay," the decision of the referee/offi-cial is final. (Have you ever seen a home plate umpire change his mind after a called third strike is disputed by the batter? It doesn't happen.)

The idea that power elites control society is underscored by the conflict perspective's central tenet that power is differentiated unequally, resulting in oppressive and coercive relationships that are manifested in the social system of sport. According to Gruneau (1975) this includes the following:

1. Sport is wedded to material gain and must be seen in this light [not simply as recreation and entertainment].
2. Sport is intimately associated with differences in wealth and power.
3. Competitive sport reflects bourgeois (i.e., middle class, upwardly mobile) ideology; as a meritocratic, mobility-oriented institution, it fosters a false consciousness and false hopes for the lower class.
4. Sport, particularly the professional variety, alienates the athlete-workers from each other and, in fact, pits them against each other (e.g., many athletes vying for few positions), thus undermining social revolution.
5. "Competitive sport" cannot exist in a classless society because competitive sport is not, by its nature, egalitarian. [Its outcome draws a clear line of distinction between participants—rewarded winners and nonrewarded losers.]

Many of today's "holdouts" and "strikes" are based on a demonstration of power. The owners, in an attempt to maintain their power position, attempt to weaken the power of player unions, and use holdouts as a sign of their power (e.g., the NHL's cancellation of the 2004–05 season). Players, on the other hand, will often go on strike in an attempt to demonstrate their power—they are, after all, the product that owners promote to the fans in an attempt to generate revenue. Player strikes may also come about as a result of frustration directed at the social system and its power structure. Consider for exam-ple the unprecedented player strikes that began August 26, 2020, following the police shooting (by a white police officer) of Jacob Blake, a Black man, in Kenosha, Wiscon-sin. Blake was shot seven times in the back (he did not die but was expected to be para-lyzed for the rest of his life) as he leaned into his SUV with three of his children seated inside. With tensions already extremely high in the U.S. between police action directed toward unarmed black motorists (and pedestrians), the NBA's Milwaukee Bucks players refused to come on to the court for their playoff game versus the Orlando Magic. Two other NBA playoff games scheduled for that same day were also postponed as the players refused to play. (Note: Some people referred to this action as a "boycott" but labor experts called it a strike.) Athletes in other sports also refused to play including those from the WNBA, MLB, NHL, MLS, MLB, and tennis star Naomi Osaka pulled out of her semi-final at the Western & Southern Open. NFL and college players refused to practice (their seasons had not yet started). This collective action among the athletes was a part of the greater Black Lives Matter social movement (to be discussed throughout this text) and threatened the continuation of sports; however, a few days later, the players for all the respective sports decided to resume play. Nonetheless, the athletes had demonstrated their power and resolve to seek social change and never before had athletes from so many diverse sports gone on strike at the same time.

The owner-player relationship in a classic example of the Marxist analysis of a two-class society—although this two-class system has become distorted in the contemporary era because of the high salaries earned by athletes. The result is the masses (the fans) viewing the players as a part of the ruling, or elite, class. Conflict theorists also believe that:

1. *Sport Generates and Intensifies Alienation.* Standardized rules and a rigid structure destroy the spontaneous freedom characteristic of play.
2. *Sport Is Used by the State and the Economically Powerful as a Tool for Coercion and Social Control.* Sport, as an opiate, provides a temporary "high" (for both fans and participants); it diverts attention from political and economic realities; it masks the problems of everyday life; and it emphasizes success through hard work, leading to people to disparage "losers"—often failing to acknowledge the unequal opportunities to succeed.
3. *Sport Promotes Commercialism and Materialism.* Sport is viewed as a product to be consumed; athletes are commodities to be exploited; and advertising makes consumers believe that they must have certain products.
4. *Sport Encourages Nationalism, Militarism and Sexism.* Many powerful countries use sport as a showplace for displaying their national symbols and military strength (e.g., Germany's Adolf Hitler attempted to use the 1936 Berlin Olympics to showcase his Aryan "superior" athletes, the East German government tried to legitimize its Communist regime through the medal winnings of its athletes, and most major U.S. sporting events include military "fly-overs" just prior to the start of the game—especially in the NFL). Nationalism and militarism will be discussed in further detail in Chapter 13 and sexism in Chapter 10.

Among the criticisms of the conflict perspective on sport is the fact that many sports fans and sport participants are concerned about matters outside of sport but they love sports because it provides them with moments of thrills, hours of entertainment and a lifetime of cherished memories. In short, many people do not feel alienated or exploited by sport. They enjoy the recreational aspect of sporting events and find the release that sports provides as invigorating. Because of its concentration on power differentials, conflict theorists often ignore the many areas in which most people arrive at an uncoerced consensus about the important values of life. Conflict theorists fail to acknowledge the numerous elements of shared morality, values and beliefs held by citizens of a society. Furthermore, sports can be sites for positive experiences that individuals find rewarding and fulfilling. The fact that many people have found alternatives to corporate sports underscores the truth that sport still provides meaning—free from coercion—in many people's lives. The conflict perspective's focus on materialism, and economic issues, shields its discovery of the quasi-spiritual experience that many athletes and sport and leisure participants enjoy. Both conflict theory and functionalism are subject to criticism because of their macrosociological orientation. The major sociological theory that addresses micro concerns is symbolic interactionism.

Symbolic Interactionism

As essentially a social-psychological perspective, symbolic interactionism focuses on how people interact with one another through the use of symbols (something that represents something else). Symbolic interactionism is based on the idea that social reality is constructed in each human interaction through the use of symbols. The human ability to communicate via spoken and written language, gestures, and symbols becomes the primary method of symbolic interaction. Language is especially important as it allows individuals to discuss and comprehend ideas and events that transcend the immediate environment, both in terms of place and time.

Herbert Blumer (1900–1987) coined the term "symbolic interactionism" in 1937. According to Blumer (1969):

> Symbolic interactionism rests in the last analysis on three simple premises. The first premise is that human beings act toward things on the basis of the meanings that the things have for them. Such things would include everything that the human being may note in his world—physical objects, such as trees or chairs; other human beings, such as a mother or a store clerk; categories of human beings, such as friends or enemies; institutions, as a school or a government; guiding ideals, such as individual independence or honesty; activities of others, such as their commands or requests; and such situations as an individual encounters in his daily life. The second premise is that the meaning of such things is derived from, or arises out of, the social interaction that one has with one's fellows. The third premise is that these meanings are handled in, and modified through, an interpretative process used by the person in dealing with the things he encounters [2].

Symbolic interactionists presume that human behavior involves choices and that choices are made based on *meanings*, or *definitions of the situation*. Because objects found in human environments often carry no intrinsic meaning, humans are capable of constructing meanings for them. Sports are filled with symbolic meanings. Examples are found through its rituals, rhetoric, culture, emotion, "coach talk," and trophies. The Stanley Cup, awarded to the National Hockey League's champion, is among the most cherished championship trophies in all of sport. The Stanley Cup is treasured because it is so hard to earn. The NHL title is the most difficult of all professional sports to earn because the championship team has to win four best-of seven playoff series resulting in a minimum of sixteen games played and the possibility of 28 games. During the NHL playoffs it is common for hockey fans to bring homemade replicas of the Stanley Cup to hockey games. Fans will wait in line for hours to have their photo taken next to the Cup whenever it is on tour.

The interactionist approach maintains a belief in the ability of actors (individuals) to modify their behaviors to meet the needs of the present and immediate environment. Additionally, during interaction, social acts and events come to be defined in some manner by participating interactants. Thus, perception of events also affects interaction. Perception refers to the ways in which organisms respond to the stimuli acknowledged by their sense organs. Perception is selective; that is, people often see what they want to see. Perceptions can be distorted because of the perceiver's needs and motives. Consider, for example, a controversial call made by a referee. Fans of one team will see the call favorably while fans of the other team will see the call unfavorably. Perception plays a huge role in sports.

Symbolic interactionism is a micro theory with a focus on individuals and group behavior. "Symbolic interactionism takes as a fundamental concern the relationship between individual conduct the relationship between individual conduct and forms of social organization. This perspective asks how selves emerge out of social structure and social situations.... The interactionist assumes that human beings are capable of making their own thoughts and activities objects of analysis, that is, they can routinely, and even habitually, manipulate symbols and orient their own actions towards other objects" (Denzin 1969: 922–923). The interactionist perspective maintains a belief in the ability of individuals to alter their behaviors to meet the needs of the present and the immediate environment. Humans come to define their acts and the social environment during interaction. Additionally, human interaction involves both covert and overt elements, both of which are capable of being modified to meet the actor's expectations and needs. For example, players and fans alike are capable of adding extra meaning to a game that pits two bitter rivals competing against one another (even if each team has a losing record at the time of the game).

Symbolic Interactionism Applied to Sports

As symbolic interactionism is defined within the context of people interacting with one another through the use of symbols, it is clear that symbolic communication is the key to this micro theory. The letters of any alphabet are merely symbols and, when put together in a coherent fashion, form words and language. It is language that allows for "story-telling" of past events as those listening to the story can create images and perceptions in their mind about the details being told. Sports fans tend to enjoy hearing stories regarding the past exploits of favorite sports teams and athletes. We also like to hear broadcast announcers describe the sports event—even while we are watching it on television or as a streaming video—as the commentary adds to our overall experience. When we listen to a game on the radio we are completely dependent on the vocal commentary of the announcers. It is fascinating to listen to games on the radio because the announcer is telling us about the sporting event from his or her perspective and perception of events. Many times the authors have listened to a game broadcast by one team's announcers and switch the dial to the other team's announcers and noted how the events are described differently. You can do this quite easily with Sirius radio and their NFL broadcasts as they provide coverage from both the home team and the visiting team. The radio announcers are paid by a particular team and almost always the meanings or definitions of the situation are modified by their allegiance to the organization paying their salaries.

It is the nonverbal aspect of communication, however, that provides us with the full picture of an event. Nonverbal communication comes about through the interpretation of gestures and symbols. The use of symbolic communication is ever-present in sports. In baseball, for example, the catcher flashes signs to the pitcher to indicate what type of pitch (e.g., fastball, curve, or breaking ball) the catcher thinks will work best in a given situation. Sometimes, the pitcher will shake his head "no" to indicate he does not want to throw that type of pitch. If the pitcher and catcher cannot reach an agreement, they may have to meet on the mound and discuss it verbally. The first base coach and the third base coach will flash a multiple of gestures to runners on base to indicate what action or inaction they should take (e.g., to try and steal a base or to wait until the ball is put into play). The coaches generally receive signals from another coach inside the dugout. For knowledgeable baseball fans, the nonverbal aspect of communication is like a game within the game.

All team sports rely on nonverbal forms of communication. In football, the coaches on the sidelines often send messages for the play or formation that the players on-the-field are supposed to run. Sometimes they use a series of images with only one image as the actual play to run (the location, such as upper right, is pre-determined) and other times, like baseball coaches, they will use a series of hand signals with only one of them to designate which play to run. Often, the crowd noise can be so loud at a stadium that the visiting team cannot hear the quarterback (QB) yell formations and audibles. When this happens the QB will rely on a series of gestures and hand signs to communicate. In some instances, the offense may want to run a "hurry-up" offense which means the players on-the-field do not huddle to hear the play call but instead, the players completely rely on hand signs and gestures. The referees use a number of different signals to illustrate a violation or penalty. Knowing the meaning behind such signals helps players on the field, players and coaches on the sidelines, and spectators in the stands to know what infraction was called even when it is too loud to hear them speak verbally.

In hockey, the fast pace of play would make it seem like players do not have time to communicate with the bench or with each other but, in fact, both things do happen. The precision of most "line changes" (when players on the ice are replaced by players on the bench simultaneously) is dependent upon symbolic (and verbal) forms of communications. One of the many cool aspects of hockey is the "hat trick"—when a player scores his or her third goal of the game and spectators that support that player's team throw their own hats onto the ice. This is a symbolic gesture of respect for the player and for the game.

These are examples from just three sports; essentially all sports utilize nonverbal forms of communication in addition to verbal forms.

There are a variety of symbolic interactionist approaches (those with a micro focus). The phenomenological approach to sport examines "sport through the senses and emotions of the player. A crunching tackle or a dive into water are intrinsically rewarding and satisfying experiences for the tackler and the diver. Some of these specific experiences are remembered for a lifetime, as though they had happened the day before" (Vogler and Schwartz 1993: 8). In fact, most people who participated in sports can think back to a sporting event that has significant meaning to them. The old story of the fisherman who retells the story (defining the situation) of catching a prize fish, only to have the length of the fish grow over the years of storytelling, reflects the phenomenological approach.

Because of its micro orientation, symbolic interactionism has great cross-over appeal to psychological theories; especially those which examine personality traits and relaxation techniques. This should not surprise too many people as sport psychology, oddly, has enjoyed greater success than sport sociology. "The primary goals of sport psychology are to describe, to explain, and to predict the attitudes, feelings, and behaviors of sport participants—including athletes, coaches and even crowd members" (Anshel 1994: 16). However, as will be demonstrated throughout this text, most problems, issues, and events encountered by sport participants are sociological in nature.

Psychological theories that examine personality traits of athletes have found that successful athletes differ markedly from their less successful counterparts in several ways.

> Despite flaws in personality research, studies have shown that successful participants tend to be self-confident, have a high need to achieve, maintain a relatively high self-image, at least in the sport environment, and score low on personality inventories in trait and state anxiety, tension, depression, mental fatigue, confusion, and anger. They often score relatively high in mental toughness, intelligence, sociability, creativity, stability, dominance, aggression, and extroversion. Still, personality scales should not be used to predict the level of an athlete's future success, the type of sport for which a person is best suited, or any other sport-related measure [Anshel 1994: 51–52].

The simple reason why individual psychological personality theorizing alone cannot predict future success in sport is because of all the social factors (e.g., opportunities to play, grades in school, family support, coaching, school funding) involved between an athlete and the sports world (thus reaffirming the importance of the sociological analysis of sport).

Relaxation theory teaches athletes how to handle tense situations so that they do not "choke" when the pressure is on to perform. Relaxation, as defined by theorist Bud Winter (1981), "involves getting the tension out of muscles not directly involved in the task at hand. Relaxation also involves getting rid of mental tensions so that you can have peace of mind to think or not to think, as you choose" (27). Winter is convinced that anyone can learn to relax physically and/or mentally at a high level of proficiency. An athlete learning how to relax so that he can perform basic tasks is perhaps the most legitimate area of psychological study in the field of sports. Relaxation theory teaches the need for repetition of behavior to the point where it becomes so routine that one can visualize in their minds before it happens (e.g., making a free-throw in basketball). However, at times, some athletes have trouble performing basic tasks; why is this the case? For example, many basketball fans marvel at Shaquille O'Neal's dismal free-throw shooting percentage (just over 50 percent for his career). Many "professionals" have worked with O'Neal, but to no avail. Despite being one of the most dominant "big men" in NBA history, O'Neal fails at the easiest task in basketball—an uncontested set shot from relatively close distance. O'Neal appears to be relaxed, and his gentle demeanor off-court would seem to imply that he is a mellow fellow and therefore casts doubt on the idea that he is not relaxed at the free-throw line.

Among the criticisms of symbolic interactionism is its overly individualistic approach and reliance on personal definitions of events—thus ignoring social process. Psychologists interested in the same topics as symbolic interactionists tend to criticize the perceived lack of scientific rigor utilized in their methodology. Because of its commitment to, and overemphasis on, everyday life and the social formation of self, symbolic interactionists tend to ignore social structure, especially structured forms of inequality.

One of the leading sociological perspectives to study structured forms of inequality is feminist theory.

Feminist Theory

Feminist theory attempts to highlight the importance of women in society while providing evidence that gender differences are socially created rather than inherent to any sexual classification system. Historically, and cross-culturally, women have fallen victim to discrimination and oppression in nearly all spheres of social life. This includes sports. Mary Wollstonecraft (1759–1797), author of *A Vindication of the Rights of Woman* (1792), was one of the first to argue that this state of affairs was unacceptable and immoral. Patricia Altenbernd Johnson writes,

> In a *Vindication of the Rights of Woman*, Wollstonecraft advocated an education for women based on the principle of independence rather than obedience. In addition, she advocated changes in social practices that would enable women to actualize this independence. She was optimistic about the political changes that were possible and about the speed at which changes could take place [Johnson 2000: 81–82].

While Wollstonecraft (whose daughter, Mary Shelley, would write the bestselling novel *Frankenstein*) might have been optimistic that such social changes would occur quickly, such was not to be the case. Although a number of social thinkers (both men and women) promoted the idea of equality for both sexes, it was not until the early 1800s that any significant women's rights movement took place. In the United States, the origins of feminism can be traced to the abolitionist movement of the 1830s. Seneca Falls, New York, lays claim as the birth place of American feminism. A small group of women led by Elizabeth Cady Stanton spearheaded the first Women's Rights Convention, in Seneca Falls, in 1848. More than 300 people attended the convention that was held in the Wesleyan Methodist Chapel. The convention highlighted the many ways social institutions were designed to keep women subordinate to men. For example, "once a woman married, she forfeited her legal existence. She couldn't sign a contract, make a will, or sue in court of law. If she received property from her father or some other source, her husband could sell it and keep the money for himself" (Gurko 1978: 8).

Feminism is as much a social movement to empower women worldwide as it is a theory. As a social movement, feminism is an ideology in support of the idea that a larger share of scarce resources (e.g., funding for women's athletics, equal pay for coaches) should be distributed to women. In short, feminists fight for the equality of women. As a social theory, feminism is a women-centered, broad-based theoretical perspective designed to reveal how sexual discrimination is a result of historic man-made conditions and not biological inferiority. "Through analysis of gender roles and gender appropriateness, feminist theory demonstrates how women have historically been subjected to a double standard in both their treatment and in the evaluation of their worth" (Delaney 2005: 202). It is important to note that there are a variety of feminist theories (for example, liberal feminism, Marxist feminism, radical feminism, critical feminism, socialist feminism, and postmodern feminism) that advocate different approaches and solutions to end the male supremacy that dominates most cultures of the world. With this precaution in mind, feminism can be defined as "a recognition and critique of male supremacy combined with efforts to change it" (Hartmann 1998: 41). Feminists argue that women should enjoy the same rights in society as men and that they should share equally in society's opportunities and resources.

FEMINIST THEORY APPLIED TO SPORTS

The women's rights movement reached new heights during the 1960s—a decade of unprecedented social change in the United States. The feminists of the 1960s ignored inequality found in the sports world. They were more concerned with socio-political issues designed to empower women in the workplace and in the home. This would change in the 1970s—a decade that would forever alter the role of women in sports. In 1972, the United States passed Title IX of the *Education Amendments to the Civil Rights Act of 1964* (see Chapter 10 for a further elaboration of Title IX). Title IX is perhaps the single most important event that ever occurred in regard to women's participation in sport. In brief, Title IX declared, "No person in the United States shall, on the basis of sex, be excluded from participation in, be denied the benefits of, or be subjected to discrimination under any educational program or activity receiving federal financial assistance." Initially, this piece of legislation was overlooked in the sports world. In 1971, there were nearly 3.7 million boys playing varsity high school sports, but just 295,000 girls (a 12.5:1 ratio). A number of lawsuits followed, and women's participation rates soared in the 1980s and 1990s (see Chapter 10 for current participation statistics).

In the 1970s, feminists realized that with sport, they had a social institution that provided a clear arena to document and measure sexual inequality. Feminists critiqued sport as "a fundamentally sexist institution that is male dominated and masculine in orientation" (Theberge 1981: 342). As Messner and Sabo (1990) describe feminism of the 1970s and 1980s:

> Feminist analyses uncovered a hidden history of female athleticism, examined sex differences in patterns of athletic socialization, and demonstrated how the dominant institutional forms of sport have naturalized men's power and privilege over women. The marginalization and trivialization of female athletes, it was demonstrated, serve to reproduce the structural and ideological domination of women by men. In the decade that has followed, the feminist critique both of the institution of sport and of the androcentric biases in sport studies has had a profound impact. Feminism now makes a major contribution to defining terrain of scholarly discourse in sport studies [2].

Feminists and equality minded theorists and professionals have so successfully increased the role of women in sport (both in terms of perception and participation) that many young female athletes today take for granted their opportunity to play sports and have seldom faced outright discrimination like their female predecessors had experienced. This is not to imply that full gender equality is found in sport today. As we shall see in Chapter 10, gender issues are still relevant in the sports world.

Among the criticisms of feminist theory is its primary focus on just half of the population—women. As the role of women in society (and sport) has changed so too has the role of men. The issues facing men must also be addressed, especially if feminists hope to change the once-dominant view held by men against women's increased participation in sports. Focusing a theory on just one issue—gender—leaves the feminist approach open to objections that it ignores other critical variables (e.g., social class, race, and willingness and desire of individuals to play sports). There are feminists, such as Sandra Harding, who have noted that gender, class, and race are interlocking variables and cannot be separated. In addition, Carol Gilligan, author of *In a Different Voice* (1993), raises the possibility that women, in general, may have a different concept of competitiveness than men do, rooted in their moral concerns. She writes: "Sensitivity to the needs of others and the assumption of responsibility for taking care lead women to attend to voices other than their own and to include in their judgment other points of view" (16). Such an "ethics of care" could mean that men and women fundamentally differ over the importance of competitiveness and the need for a hierarchical structure in sports contests.

Thus, the wide variety of approaches to feminist thought demonstrates that feminists lack a clear and comprehensive agreed-upon theory to explain human behavior and gender differences in sport.

Functionalism, conflict, symbolic interactionism, and feminism represent four of the more "traditional" theories of sociology that may be applied to the sports world. We now address a pair of related theories that has been mostly applied to the sports world and not to other social institutions. The first concept is "basking in reflected glory" (BIRG) and the second is "cutting off reflective failure" (CORF).

Attachment, BIRG, CORF, and BIAF Theories

There's a tendency among humans to attach themselves to successful others while distancing themselves from persons who have been stigmatized in some manner. For example, if you win a multi-million-dollar lottery, chances are, many people will suddenly claim to be your best friend or closest relative! A kid from a poor neighborhood who makes it big as a professional athlete will have all sorts of people trying to attach themselves to the successful person. However, if you are accused of doing something wrong (e.g., committing a serious crime or immoral behavior) chances are many of your so-called friends, or even your employer, will suddenly distance themselves from you. There's a song by John Lennon, "Nobody Loves You (When You're Down and Out)," that expresses this sentiment. Lennon wrote the song during a time of depression and loneliness. The idea being that when you are depressed and shut yourself off from others, the attachment you once had is broken. Conversely, individuals who are cheerful and happy will attract others.

That we attempt to associate with successful others is rooted in a branch of human study known as "attachment theory." Attachment theory itself is quite complex and multifaceted (Mooney 2009). Essentially, attachment theory centers on the idea that infants, from the moment they are born, are completely dependent upon primary caregivers providing nourishment and safety in order to survive and therefore become attached to primary caregivers because they represent survival.

Attachments take on meanings beyond basic survival; they become emotional. Humans are often very emotional and form strong attachments with a number of select others as they grow and age. Following primary socialization (provided by parents, guardians or caregivers), we form bonds with peers and develop friendships. Some friendships last a lifetime while others fade. Most people date and eventually mate and form a strong attachment to each other. Having one's own child leads to the "circle of attachment" wherein a new caregiver role is established.

We become attached to many other entities as well, including the community we are raised in, the schools we attend, and the activities that give us a visceral stimulation. For some, belonging to a musical band, choir, dance troupe, or ball team stimulates feelings of attachment. Sports fans, especially passionate ones, develop a strong emotional attachment to their favorite athletes and teams. When the attachment level is particularly high, the emotions of sports fans become interconnected to the fortunes of the team's performance. Thus, when the team wins, we feel better. And when the team loses, we feel pain.

When highly attached sports fans feel better about themselves because of the success of their favorite team, they are said to be "basking in the reflected glory" (BIRG) of their team. On the other hand, when people try to distance themselves (emotionally or otherwise) from the disappointment brought on by their favorite team's poor performance they are said to be "cutting off reflective failure" (CORF).

BIRG, CORF, and BIAF Theories Applied to Sports

In 1976, Cialdini and associates uncovered a phenomenon which they called "Basking in Reflected Glory" (BIRG). In their study of "big-time" college football programs, they noticed that students had an increased tendency to wear their schools' logo (e.g., on items of clothing) on Mondays following Saturday victories. Additionally, Cialdini and associates note that students are more likely to use "we" in discussing wins but use "they" when describing losses. The BIRG theory is based on the premise that individuals purposely manipulate the visibility of their connections with winners and losers in order to make themselves look good to others. Individuals showcase positive associations and try to bury negative ones, thus encouraging observers to think more highly of them and to like them more.

Subsequent research (Snyder, Lassegard, and Ford 1986; Wann and Branscombe 1990) reveals that in additions to increasing their association with successful others (BIRGing), people also tend to increase the distance between themselves and unsuccessful others. This phenomenon is called "Cutting Off Reflective Failure" (CORF).

Wann and Branscombe (1990) theorize that the extent to which allegiance to a group or team that a person has will modify the effects of BIRGing and CORFing. They suspect that individuals high in identification would demonstrate a stronger tendency to BIRG in their team's success when compared to persons low in identification. The reverse was anticipated for CORFing; persons high in identification should CORF less than those low in identification. The results of their study support their hypotheses. Persons high in identification did show an increased tendency to BIRG following the team's victory, relative to persons moderate or low in allegiance. In addition, persons highly identified with the team appeared to maintain their association with the team even when faced with defeat, thereby showing a reduction in the tendency to CORF when compared to those lower in identification. Consequently, Wann and Branscombe show that the effects of BIRGing and CORFing are affected by one's identification level to the group or team.

The pervasive nature of group identification has shown that fans identify not only with sport teams but with the institutions represented by sport teams they support. In fact, fans who maintain high levels of identification with a sports team also show feelings of bonding with other fans of that same team (Wann and Branscombe 1993). Throughout time people have derived much of their identity and self-worth from groups to which they have membership (Baumeister 1991).

In an attempt to replicate Wann and Branscombe's (1990) findings, Delaney (1999) conducted research on a sports booster group (the Southern California Browns Backers Association) in 1993. Delaney's research analyzed BIRG and CORF techniques based on respondent's identification and self-esteem levels. (Note: Earlier editions of this text include tables of Delaney's 1993 data.) Delaney found that highly identified fans exhibit many signs of BIRGing but not of CORFing. Additionally, the moderately identified fans are less likely to BIRG, but also less likely to CORF. The highly identified fans utilize BIR-Ging techniques as a means of identification-enhancement when the team wins, but do not utilize CORFing techniques to distance themselves from the team following a defeat. Thus, the tendency to BIRG is consistent with past research but the tendencies to CORF were not consistent with past research; that is to say, in Delaney's study, respondents were not so quick to CORF. One explanation for this could be the fact that the entire group under study by Delaney may have been more highly identified fans than Wann and Branscombe's non-booster participants.

The examination of BIRG and CORF techniques based on levels of self-esteem (using Rosenberg's Self Esteem Scale) indicate that those with high self-esteem have a slightly increased tendency to BIRG when compared to those with low self-esteem. The tendency to CORF is nearly identical for members of both the high and low levels of self-esteem. Based on Delaney's data, the argument that BIRG and CORF are techniques used in the maintenance of self-esteem is questionable. The data from the in-group/out-group analysis was not consistent with past research where it was shown that people low in self-esteem were more likely to have negative feelings toward out-group members than those with high self-esteem. In Delaney's study, the higher the level of self-esteem the higher the percentage of those who strongly disliked rival teams (out-groups).

In the earlier editions of this text we did not explore another BIRG/CORF related concept that Wann and Branscombe (1990, 1993) discussed, blasting. "Blasting" is a strategy used to reestablish or reinstate lost self-esteem. That is, when individuals have suffered a blow to their social identity (e.g., their favorite team loses a game), they would try to regain their positive social identify by blasting a member of an out-group (a rival team and its fans). The idea behind blasting theory is that one can feel better about themselves by putting down others or finding joy in others' defeats and misfortunes. We took the concept of "blasting" and modified it to fit within the parameters of BIRG and CORF to come up with the idea of BIAF (Basking in Another's Failure). (Note: We did an extensive search to see if anyone else has used the BIAF acronym in this context but could not find any such research having been published.)

BIAF is a blasting technique that consists of concepts similar to *schadenfreude* (taking joy or pleasure in the misfortune of others) and *epicaricacy* (rejoicing at or deriving pleasure from the misfortunes of others). This technique is often a diversionary tactic to draw someone's attention away from your own shortcomings, perceived or real, by pointing to another target as a scapegoat. There may be elements of amusement (finding entertainment value, humor or satisfaction in the misfortune of others) and sadism (taking a certain sadistic pleasure in the misfortunes of others) involved with BIAF as well. The authors are at the early stages of developing their BIAF theory and have shared their preliminary results in Table 2.1.

Table 2.1. BIAF (in percent [N=105])

BIAF Variables	Yes	No
Have you taken joy in the failure of others?	68	32
Have you watched a sporting event just to cheer against a team you do not like?	56	44
Do you find joy in the failure of a team you do not like?	75	25
Are there fan bases of sports teams that you really hope that their team losses?	72	28

Based on our research, we found that respondents were fascinated by the BIAF theory. As the data in Table 2.1 reveals, respondents by a margin of more than two-to-one (68 percent yes, 32 percent no) have taken joy in the failure of others; a majority (56 percent) of respondents have watched a sporting even just to cheer against a team they did not like; by a three-to-one margin (75 percent yes, 25 percent no) respondents found joy in the failure of team they did not like; and, 72 percent of respondents report that there are fan bases of sports teams that they really hope their team losses. This preliminary data indicates that the BIAF theory is indeed worthy of further research. Respondents found pleasure in reporting their explanations as to why they enjoy to BIAF. In response to Question #1, a student reported that they believed karma was giving back what the other had given out. Variations of karma or payback dominated the explanations to this question.

Students seemed fascinated by the BIAF theory. It dawned on them, as it did with us, that within this context of sports people were able to say things like, "I hate Patriots fans, they are all so arrogant" and yet, if you said that about an ethnic or racial category of people one would be chastised as culturally insensitive. In turn, Patriots fans would refer to fans of the Bills and Dolphins as "losers." This is an interesting proposition about why people might like to BIAF and the authors plan to explore this in far greater detail in future publications.

It should be noted that other researchers have also established variants of the BIRG/CORF concepts. Campbell, Aiken, and Kent (2004) created "Cutting Off Reflected Success" (CORS)—which occurs when fans distance themselves from successful favorite teams because of other reasons (e.g., they become angry when they learn that the owner donates money to a disliked politician)—and "Basking in Reflected Failure" (BIRF)—which occurs when fans BIRG even when the team is unsuccessful.

Connecting Sports and Popular Culture

Box 2: "It's Gonna Be a Good Year": BIRGing and Big Fan

BIRGing (Basking in Reflected Glory) is something all true fans can relate to. But sometimes BIRGing can get out of hand, especially when one's entire life becomes invested in the experiences of one's favorite team. Such is the case for the lead character in the 2009 dramatic movie *Big Fan*, written and directed by Robert D. Siegel.

In *Big Fan,* the comedian Patton Oswalt (in a decidedly very serious role) plays Paul Aufiero, a diehard New York Giants fan living in Staten Island who avidly follows the team's exploits. Like many other fans, he reads all he can about their latest statistics, he constantly wears clothing with the team's logo (and on game day paints his face with the team colors), and he and his friend Sal go to every Giants' home game, where they gleefully take part in tailgating activities in the stadium parking lot. (See Chapter 4 for a further discussion on the joys of tailgating.)

However, all is not quite right with Paul. For instance, instead of entering the stadium to watch the game, he and Sal plug in a TV attached to his car and as an alternative watch the game *outside* of the stadium, since they can't afford the price of a ticket. Paul's daily life is also, to put it mildly, rather dismal. He works a dead-end job as a parking lot attendant, is a 35-year-old bachelor with no girlfriend (and no prospect of ever having one), and still lives at home with his mother, who constantly compares him unfavorably with his two siblings even while being dependent upon him for transportation and companionship.

The bleakness of Paul's existence is considerably brightened, though, by his deep feelings for the Giants. In fact, he takes on a new persona as a blustery, opinionated know-it-all called "Paul from Staten Island" as a constant caller to a late-night talk radio sports show hosted by a guy called "Sports Dogg." During his job at the parking lot, while waiting for car owners to pay their fees, he jots down on a yellow legal pad the thoughts he will later relay (seemingly spontaneously) on Sports Dogg's call-in show. His dedication to the team, his deep knowledge of the game, and his disparaging comments about the Giants' rivals, makes him a hero of sorts to other Giants fans listening. And, as is the case with many sports teams, he even has a hated rival—"Philadelphia Phil"—a fanatical Eagles fan and his on-air archenemy. The two—who have never met, and don't know each other's true identities—engage in nonstop battle on the show, to the delight of the listeners (but not to Paul's mother, whose bedroom is next to his, and who frequently yells at him through the wall to get off the phone and go to bed).

Much to Paul and Sal's surprise, one day they see the Giants' quarterback (the fictional Quantrell Bishop) driving through their borough of Staten Island. While they know as much about him as any true fans could, they have never seen him up close before, and impetuously decide to follow him in hopes of getting an autograph. Unbeknownst to them, Bishop's reason for being on Staten Island is to illegally buy drugs. Paul and Sal end up following him into Manhattan (Paul, who seldom ventures into "The Big Apple," is shocked by how difficult it is to find parking, a problem he never has in Staten Island). When Bishop enters a strip club, they go in as well. Uninterested in watching the strippers, all Paul wants to do is introduce himself to his hero and get his autograph, which he finally gets up the nerve to do. Bishop is at first polite, in the way many professional athletes are when meeting their fans, even in such an unorthodox setting. But when Sal blurts out that they'd followed him all the way from Staten Island, the drug-impaired quarterback—thinking they witnessed his buying illegal drugs and are trying to shake him down—brutally beats up Paul, who passes out from a concussion, only to wake up days later in a hospital room.

When Paul awakens and is told he'd been in a coma for a few days (and therefore missed watching that Sunday's Giants game), his first words to the visiting Sal are, "How did we do?" He's particularly interested in hearing about Bishop's statistics, only to learn that the quarterback had been suspended due to the beating that occurred in the strip club. A detective investigating the incident (who suspects that illegal drugs were involved) tells Paul that, should he testify against him, Bishop would likely not only be kicked off the team for good but would serve time in jail as well. Being the "Big Fan" he is, however, Paul feigns amnesia, and since no one else who witnessed the beating—including Sal—is willing to say what happens, the charges against Bishop are dismissed and he is reinstated to the team.

However, Paul's sleazy lawyer brother Jeff then files a multi-million dollar claim against Bishop on his brother's behalf, saying that due to the beating Paul is no longer mentally capable of making rational decisions. When he discovers this by hearing about it on the radio, the usually meek Paul angrily confronts his brother and has the charges dropped. But due to the claim's initial publicity, "Philadelphia Phil" is able to piece together the true identity of "Paul from Staten Island" and gleefully "outs him" on the Sports Dogg show.

Ashamed and angered by losing the one thing that gave his life any sense of meaning—his alter ego role as the blustery radio hero—Paul (whose mental stability seems to be on increasingly shaky grounds) tracks down "Philadelphia Phil" and at first gets into his good graces by pretending to be a fellow Eagles' fan. The two join a group of other Eagles supporters at a Philly sports bar to watch them play the Giants. But when his beloved team loses to their hated rival, Paul finally loses it as well. He follows *his* rival into the men's room and pulls out a gun, and reveals to the frightened Phil his true identity, yelling out "The Eagles *suck*" after firing the gun several times.

Luckily for Phil, it was a *paint* gun, and he is unharmed (except for the damage done to his Eagles' logo-filled attire). But Paul is arrested for assault, and ends up in prison—ironically, given his shielding of Bishop from having to undergo the same experience. The movie ends with Sal visiting his friend in the prison, where he delights the otherwise deeply depressed Paul by telling him that next year's Giants season has just been published. An excited Paul eagerly reads the schedule and predicts a 12–4 season at the very least. And, when he realizes that he will be released in time to attend next year's home game against New England, Paul exuberantly exclaims to his buddy, "It's gonna be a good year…. No way we're losing with us in the parking lot!"

Big Fan is a melancholy look at BIRGing gone bad. Patton Oswalt—otherwise known for his brilliant standup comedy routines and also for being the voice of Remy the Rat in the children's classic film *Ratatouille*—is outstanding as a man whose love for his team has overridden every other aspect of his life. *Big Fan* is a cautionary tale about the extremes of BIRGing and the need to "get a life" outside of being a sports fan.

Summary

Social theory involves expressing ideas about human behavior and the social world through the formulation of theories about social life. A theory is a statement that proposes to explain or relate observed phenomena or a set of concepts through a logically-based system of general propositions. "Good" theories are those which can be tested empirically. A social theorist seeks to understand the social world by means of reason and rational thought. These scientifically driven theorists seek validity for their theories through empirical research and data analysis and interpretation.

George Herbert Mead established a developmental theory (of self) consisting of four stages including the "play stage" wherein children learn to play (act out) the roles and attitudes of other persons and a "a game stage" wherein children learn how multiple roles take place at the same time (as in teamwork) and that games (like life itself) have rules, norms, values, and social expectations.

Contemporary sociological theories are applicable to the sports world and to that end, a number of theories including functionalism, conflict, symbolic interactionism, feminist, attachment, and BIRG and CORF theories were used as exemplars. Systems analysis is the most relevant aspect of functionalism as athletes, sports teams, coaches and managers, and sports leagues are subject to evaluation based on their functionality. Conflict theorists examine the role of power and inequalities found within society. For them, the sports world often exemplifies such power inequities. Owner lockouts and player holdouts are examples of this power struggle.

Both functionalist and conflict theories are subject to criticism because of their macrosociological orientation. Symbolic internationalism takes a micro approach, by focusing on how people interact with one another through the use of symbolic communication. The sports world is filled with symbolic communication, both verbal (spoken language) and nonverbal (the use of gestures, signs, and symbols). Symbolic internationalism has connections with psychological theories; especially those which examine personality traits and relaxation techniques; phenomenology; and relaxation theory. Critics of symbolic internationalism claim that the theory is overly individualistic and ignores social processes and structures.

Feminist theory attempts to highlight the importance of women in society while providing evidence that gender differences are socially created rather than inherent to any sexual classification system. It is one of the leading sociological perspectives which focuses on the discrimination and oppression that women have undergone in all societies throughout history.

Attachment theory serves as a basis for two other theories—BIRG and CORF—that can be applied to the understanding of sports. BIRG stands for "Basking in Reflected Glory" and is based on the premise that individuals purposely manipulate the visibility of their attachment with winners to make themselves look good to others. CORF stands for "Cutting Off Reflective Failure" and is based on the premise that individuals distance themselves from perceived losers. These theories help to explain the allegiance which persons have to sports teams and individuals. The authors introduced a new variation of attachment theory—BIAF (Basking in Another's Failure).

KEY TERMS

Attachment Theory The emotional bond we form with others that helps to provide personal identity.

BIAF ("Basking in Another's Failure") A variation of "blasting" theory and a self-esteem enhancement technique wherein individuals find joy in another's failure.

BIRG ("Basking in Reflected Glory") Individuals reflect positively about themselves through a bond and identification with successful people and teams.

Conflict Theory A sociological theory that examines the role of power and the inequality found within society.

CORF ("Cutting Off Reflective Failure") Individuals distance themselves from perceived losers.

False Consciousness A term used by Marxists to signify the inability to clearly see where one's own best interests lie.

Feminist Theory An attempt to highlight the importance of women in society while providing evidence that gender differences are socially created rather than inherent to any sexual classification system.

Functional Imperatives A term coined by Talcott Parsons, who argued that there are four basic "system needs" (adaptation, goal attainment, integration, and latency; or AGIL) necessary in order for any society (club, organization, team, etc.) to run smoothly.

Functional Theory The idea that there is a general consensus in values and norms of society and that the social institutions found within a society are integrated into a functioning whole.

Phenomenological Approach A type of symbolic interactionism which examines sport through the senses and emotions of the player.

Social Theory Perspectives on human behavior that attempt to explain or relate observed phenomena or a set of concepts with a focus on social interactions, patterns and events found in the social environment.

Symbolic Interactionism A micro theoretical perspective that examines human behavior in the context of symbolic communication and the viewpoint that human behavior involves choices and that choices are made based on *meanings*, or *definitions of the situation*.

Theory A statement that proposes to explain or relate observed phenomena or a set of concepts through a logically-based system of general propositions; involving a set of inter-related arguments that seek to describe and explain cause-effect relationships.

DISCUSSION QUESTIONS

- Explain the importance of social theory and its application to sports.
- Apply Mead's developmental theory to your own life and determine whether or not his theory has merit.
- Do you agree or disagree with the statement "Sports are the opiate of the people"? Why or why not?
- A number of theories were discussed in this chapter that are applicable to sports. Which one to you find to be most useful? Explain.
- Do you think that men and women have different views on the nature of competition? Explain.
- Have you ever watched a sporting event just to cheer against one of the athletes or teams?
- Have you noticed that you noticed you BIRG, CORF and/or BIAF? Describe examples of when you have BIRG, CORF and/or BIAF.

CHAPTER 3

A Brief History of Sport

The rudiments of sports can be traced back thousands of years. Based on cave paintings found in Lascaux, France, dating back more than 15,000–17,000 years ago, it would appear that wrestling is the oldest "sport." Historians inform us that yes cave drawings are legitimate sources of information but the depiction of "wrestling" on the walls of caves is not what we would today refer to as "sports." Cave paintings of wrestling in the Bayankhongor Province of Mongolia date back to the Neolithic age of 7,000 BCE. In Japan, prehistoric cave paintings evoke familiarity to traditional sumo wrestling practiced in the country. However, as we will learn in this chapter, distinguishing between "sport-like" activities and what we consider sports today are two different things.

Nonetheless, the roots of sports date back to ancient times and as a result, our review of the history of sport begins with the "ancient" societies.

Ancient Sports (Circa 1400 BCE–800 BCE)

The word "history," when applied to humanity, refers to the period of time when humans first provided a formal written account of events and, thus, not the entire scope of our civilization. This realization helps us to realize that while drawings on a wall provide information, it is still art and therefore open to interpretation.

SPORTS IN ANCIENT AFRICA

The first variations of sports and games of the ancient world would reveal a pattern that held consistent until the time of the Romans; namely, that early sport reflected religious significance combined with activities associated with physical survival. For example, Africans participated in archery because it was valued as a warring skill and dance because it held religious value.

Sports in ancient Africa are divided into two uneven categories: Egypt and the rest of the continent. Egypt, because of its geographical location (at the crossroads of Africa, Asia, and Europe), has always been different from the rest of Africa. The ancient Egyptians were a highly advanced society that had a written language and left behind visual biographies in the form of wall paintings, thereby providing archaeologists with a wealth of information on their sporting activities. A number of identifiable sports were played in Egypt, including archery, stick fighting, wrestling, dance, running, swimming (especially in the Nile River), *mancala* (a counting strategy game), and *senet*, also called *senat* (one of the world's oldest recorded tabletop games) (Craig 2002). Poliakoff (1987) also mentions boxing and pankration as sports played in ancient Egypt. "Pankration (or in Latin spelling, pancratium) is a Greek word that means 'complete strength' or 'complete victory.' … These terms reveal a lot about the sport: pankration allowed boxing, kicking, wrestling throws, strangleholds, and pressure locks. The bout ended when a competitor signaled unwillingness or inability to continue the fight" (Poliakoff 1987: 54). The ancient sport of pankration is actually much like today's "ultimate fighting." (This helps to explain why some people consider ultimate fighting as an ancient, barbaric sport.)

Stick fighting is a particularly interesting sport in Egypt as it was a minor sport elsewhere in antiquity. The Egyptians held formal stick fighting contests and their artwork shows crowds of spectators watching the fighters. Some stick fights involved combatants wearing a shield on the left arm, keeping the right arm free to swing. As Mandell (1984) explains, "The sticks, which are about a meter long, were swung with the right hand, the left arm being shielded. Some stick fighters wore a light helmet to protect their faces and ears" (21). It remains unclear, unfortunately, how a winner was determined, although most believe a record of "hits" was recorded and perhaps a knockout blow also determined a winner.

Sport in the rest of Africa remains more mysterious. We know that archery and dance were popular throughout Africa, as were a wide variety of games that required dexterity and skill. One of the oldest documented games in North Africa, however, was a traditional board game called Zamma. Archeologists found some boards dating back to 1400 BCE. The square-shaped playing board was 9x9 or 8x8, consisting of lines that intersected. Each player had 40 playing pieces, black or white. Zamma resembles checkers (Alcantara 2017). Like wrestling, variations of boxing are one of the oldest known sports. In northern Nigeria, the Hausa people traveled from village to village to find opponents for Dambe boxing. The ancient sport took place during harvest season and a result it became a form of entertainment. Instead of wearing gloves, a fighter's dominant arm was wrapped with rope and dipped in resin and shards of glass. The combatants would fight for three rounds or until the first boxer tapped out or dropped to the floor (Alcantara 2017). Ancient Africans also played *ta kurt el mahag* literally translated to "the ball of the pilgrim's mother" (Alcantara 2017). The game was discovered in the 1930s in a remote village in Libya, where the Berber tribesmen lived. It is said to have very similar rules and goals as baseball and involved the concepts of batting, fielding, and base running, although there were just two bases, home and a resting base, and the pitcher stood just a few feet from the batter and served the ball in a gentle arc (Alcantara 2017; Block and Wiles 2006). Stick fighting, which resembles a type of martial art, was popular among the Nguni herders in South Africa. The stick fight could last up to five hours where opponents take turns playing offense and defense scoring points based on which part of the body is struck; this bloody sport often led to death (Dream Africa 2017).

Sports in Ancient Asia

As in other parts of the world, sports in ancient Asia were tied to physical survival. Participation in Asian sport also possessed a philosophical quality. There is great diversity in the Asian continent, and as a result, sports varied from one society to the next. Ancient Chinese culture was relatively advanced and served as "the major civilization of the Far East" (Freeman 1997: 62). Chinese culture is rich in sport and game participation. The Chinese played many board games including chess. Early versions of soccer (called *t'su chu*, a regimented game involving a foot striking a ball is traced back to 770 BCE), polo and competitions in archery and wrestling were practiced by the Chinese people. Polo, or *pula*, is believed to have begun in Tibet and then spread throughout Asia; recognizable evidence exists in Persia dating from 525 BCE (Bell 1987). In addition, "A program of mild exercises, similar to gymnastics-oriented calisthenics, was developed and called *cong fu*. The objective was to prevent disease, which the Chinese believed could result from a lack of physical activity. Dancing was also popular. Although it was primarily ceremonial, there were both religious and popular forms. The popular forms were informal recreational dances" (Freeman 1997: 63). Martial arts, of course, were also popular in China, and throughout Asia. "In Mongolia, the men have participated for centuries in what they consider the 'three manly sports' of archery, equestrian races, and wrestling" (Craig 2002: 58).

Japanese ancient sports are similar to the Chinese and include board games, archery, and sumo wrestling. The Japanese had their own version of chess called *shio-ghi*, played chiefly by the intellectual classes (Falkener 1961). Sports were not as predominant in Indian society. There were some recreational sports and games dances that were used for ceremonial purposes and religious observances.

The review of ancient sports in Africa and Asia represents a mere sampling of sports and games played in the ancient world. As Craig (2002) summarizes, there are some sports, such as archery and wrestling that are indigenous to nearly all cultures of the ancient world. Throwing objects (e.g., spears), dancing, and running are also common sports activities shared by all ancient people.

Sport and Ancient Greek Culture (800 BCE–100 BCE)

According to Bell (1987), the only non–Western game to influence the Greeks was *pula*, or polo, which (as stated earlier) originated in Tibet and spread throughout Asia. The Greeks were concerned with the use of the horse in sport, more than the sport of polo itself. "The combination of the horse and chariot in Asia soon evolved into a chariot race that would fascinate both the Greeks and Romans.... The first horse race as an Olympic event came at the twenty-third games in 624 BCE—one of the first visible signs of cultural cross-pollination, the Greeks playing the Asian game, which would lead to the Hellenistic world: everyone playing the Greek games" (Bell 1987: 92–93).

The Minoan civilization had participated in two primary sports games, boxing and bull vaulting (Bell 1987). Of historical note, the boxers wore boxing gloves. (The significance of this will be explained later in the chapter.) Bull vaulting involved an individual standing in front of a charging bull, catching it by the horns, and leaping over the back of the animal. The fascination of the Minoans with bulls did not appeal to the Hellenic world. Boxing, on the other hand, held such great appeal that certain matches were described in Homeric poems when the sport was adopted by the early Greeks. Poems were written to honor heroes. The most heroic quality in the era of ancient Greece, just as it was in ancient times, was one's ability to demonstrate physical strength and survival techniques. "A general and persistent feature of Homer's poems is emphasis on physical prowess, whether this be manifested in armed combat, in organized athletic contests, in acrobatic dancing, in erotic adventures or in the sheer capacity for survival displayed by Odysseus on his way home to Ithaca from Troy" (McIntosh 1993: 20).

The Egyptian sport of pankration found its way to Greek society as well. "The object was, as in boxing, to force the opponent to acknowledge defeat, and to this end almost any means was allowed" (Gardiner 1930: 212). Serious injuries occurred often. The Spartans used pankration as a means of training warriors. Eventually, rules prohibiting biting and gouging were introduced to the sport. As with ultimate fighting, or street fighting, participants work with their strengths. Generally, taller athletes, with a longer reach, rely on hitting; while short, stocky athletes rely on wrestling.

The ancient Greeks loved their sports; this characteristic reflected the highly competitive character of the Greeks, "who were not only avid participants in athletic contests but also regularly held competitions in, for example, dancing, lyre playing and drinking…. In a society as competitive as that of the ancient Greeks, it is not surprising that sports, particularly competitive sports, were very popular" (Sansone 1988: 76–77). Homer's poems describe how sporting events were social gathering events. However, it was also clear that the "contests also reveal a near obsession with winning. The stratagems employed to win offend our sense of 'fair play' as, for example, in the case of the goddess who blithely trips the superior runner, Aias" (Mandell 1984: 39). Greek society valued physical excellence and cities glorified athletic victories of their citizens, rewarded victors materially and honored them in legend in the form of statues and poems/stories. Every Greek city had athletic facilities (similar to the stadiums found in most major world cities today).

Greek sport was such a serious endeavor that it took on cultural and religious significance. The Greek culture, heavily influenced by mythology, infused religious rituals and significance with athletics. Many city-states throughout Greece participated in religious games and festivals. As Freeman (1997) explained, these religious events and festivals "were generally celebrated by athletic contests, dances, and music. Some of the festivals were celebrated within a single city-state and by only one sex, as in the case of honoring local gods. Other festivals, however, were broader in appeal and sometimes were celebrated by all of the Greek people" (69). Freeman also acknowledges that there is some debate over the origins of the religious games. Some scholars trace religious games to the great Irish funeral festival, Aonach Tailteann, which may be older than the Olympics games. Thus, "the Irish claim that it was the inspiration for the Greek games" (Freeman 1997: 69).

Clearly, the most significant of the Greek festivals was the Olympic Games. The Olympic Games are the oldest of the four panhellenic festivals. The other three panhellenic Games were the Pythian Games at Delphi, held in honor of Apollo; the Isthmian Games held in Corinth for Poseidon; and the Games at Nemea, which, like the Olympics, were held in honor of Zeus (Swaddling 1980). Bell (1987) argues that the Olympics did not reflect any high ideals of the Hellenes, but rather served as a way to keep the Hellenistic world unified. As we shall learn, it is common for competition, sport or otherwise, to divide rather than unite people.

The Olympics

The Olympics were held in honor of Zeus, the most revered and powerful of all mythical Greek gods. The first recorded Olympic Games took place in 776 BCE. We know

that many festivals were held before this first recorded Olympic Games and there is speculation that the games "may have been held originally to honor Herakles (Hercules in
Roman culture), an early traditional hero, with the worship of Zeus appearing in the
sixth century. Women were banned, perhaps because Herakles was a warriors' hero, and
because the presence of women was thought to diminish the warriors' power" (Freeman
1997: 69). The Olympics were greatly modified over centuries but every four years, from
776 BCE to 395 CE, the games continued. People flocked to Olympia, originally a small village existing for the purpose of hosting the most prestigious of all Greek sport spectacles.
"There is no modern parallel for Olympia; it would have to be a site combining a sports
complex and a centre for religious devotion, something like a combination of Wembley
Stadium and Westminster Abbey" (Swaddling 1980: 7).

The timing of the Games was sacred to the Greeks. They took place every four years,
on the second or third full moon alternately after the summer solstice, in the months of
August or September (Gardiner 1930). Months before the Games began "Truce Bearers
of Zeus" would set out from Olympia wearing crowns of olive and bearing heralds' staves
to proclaim a month-long peace. This truce was always honored, as the Games took precedence over war. The city-states leaders did not want war to interrupt the training of
the athletes or the eventual five-day competition. Originally, women were not allowed to
compete or view the Games. (The women would eventually create their own games and
dedicate them to the Goddess Hera, sister-wife of Zeus. These games were held at a time
separate from the male Olympics.) The athletes competed in the nude and were often
beaten for violating rules (e.g., a false start in a race led to a whipping from a referee). The
athletes prepared themselves (trained) for a month before the Games began. Only those
of pure Greek birth were allowed to compete (Gardiner 1930). Many of the athletes spent
their time exclusively on training for the Games (like professional athletes); they had
coaches and received medical advice and assistance. As this special treatment implies,
Olympic athletes were generally privileged males from well-to-do families.

There are some romantic revisionists who look at the ancient Olympics as something the modern Olympics should strive to be. Ironically, perhaps the modern Games
are already like the ancient ones. Consider, the ancient Olympics were sexist (did not
allow women), elitist (only those from wealthy families could participate), racist (Greeks
only), politically corrupt and full of displays of poor sportsmanship (poor sports, cheaters, and enviousness of winners). Students may want to examine other ways that the
ancient and modern Olympics mirror one another.

Regardless of any criticism of the original Olympics, they stand alone as a monumental testament to the value of sport in ancient Greece. They also represent an idealistic
view of how sport could/should be organized.

Sport and Roman Culture (100 BCE–500 CE)

The Olympics stand alone as the longest running sporting event in human history.
The Games survived early Roman occupation, but eventually disappeared after it lost
Roman financial support due to a Roman public that preferred bloody gladiator sports.

Before the infamous gladiator games dominated Roman culture, citizens participated in a number of games. The Romans, especially the wealthy, loved to play ball games.
Playing ball afforded participants an opportunity to increase coordination and provided

a measure of physical fitness. Although harpastum (interpreted in a variety of ways, including as an early form of rugby, "keepaway," or "monkey in the middle," was played by of a group of players) and trigon were never major spectator sports, there was a following for these athletes and games. Roman children and adults participated in hoop bowling, loosely described as a game that entailed participants throwing a spear, or stick, or stone through a rolling hoop. The hoop was pushed to keep it rolling through the streets. The Roman hoops generally had jingling rings attached to forewarn oncoming traffic to clear a path (Craig 2002).

Initially, the Romans had a different perspective on sport than the Greeks. They did not consider sport to be a philosophical activity but were more interested in military development and popular entertainment. The Romans, unlike the Greeks, had no interest in the balanced development of the individual. For the Romans, sport was merely a practical activity.

As a predatorial regime, the early Roman Empire placed a great deal of importance on military training. General physical education and training for boys was directed almost exclusively toward military goals. Military training involved pace training in marching, weapons proficiency, and weight training. Swordsmanship was a valued trait for Roman soldiers. It should be noted that professional athletes, along with coaches and trainers, were also expected to maintain a strict physical training program.

Over the centuries, the Roman Empire continued to grow. During the later centuries of the Empire, the Romans no longer felt the need to train. The Empire paid armies to fight for it, and other armies to defend Rome from potential invaders. Slaves did most of the day-to-day work previously performed by poorer citizens. Romans no longer had to work to survive; the state even provided free food. Political corruption abounded. Roman societal morals and ideals of patriotism and self-sacrifice continued to deteriorate. Roman citizens became increasingly bored and restless. They needed a diversion. What they got was entertainment spectacles, especially in the form of the brutal gladiator games.

GLADIATOR GAMES

Rome's citizens had become lazy; they had transformed themselves into a nation of spectators more content with watching other people play sports and athletics than performing such activities themselves. (It could be argued that the United States has become a nation of spectators, much like Ancient Rome.) Greek festivals and the pursuit of athletic excellence was not enough for the Romans. Instead, the Romans wanted a show, a spectacle, and the bigger the better. Winning was everything, and the more decisive the victory, the better. After a few centuries, the Romans had completely transformed the Greek ideal of athletics and sports. As Dunning (1999) indicates, the ancient Roman gladiator "sports" represent a regression into barbarism. The Romans ignored the decay of sport and sportsmanship. The level of cruelty and violence in Roman gladiator sport, the massacres and the blood thirst of the crowds, were very different from the contests engaged in by the ancient Greeks.

The gladiators of the Roman spectacles entered the arena with the intent to kill each other; the spectators were fully aware of this. Romans developed a great appreciation for the "art" of killing. The gladiators were fed three meals a day, received relatively good medical care, and if they performed well enough, they could gain their freedom. They were not allowed to become citizens, however. Females were allowed to be gladiators and the practice was rather widespread, until women were forbidden to participate by the Emperor Septimius Severus in the early third century CE. The gladiator games pitted "undesirable" people (e.g., criminals, captured soldiers, slaves, and Christians) against heavily armed and trained gladiators. Generations later, gladiators would be matched against such animals as lions, crocodiles, bears, and elephants. Beyond human death, it was common for hundreds of wildlife deaths to occur during a gladiator spectacle. During a "half-time," or lunch break, executions would be performed against those convicted of capital offenses. Burning at the stake or crucifixion was a common method of execution. These also served to entertain the Roman spectators.

As Zeev Weiss (2014) points out, Herod the Great built theaters, amphitheaters, and hippodromes at great expense in ancient Palestine in an attempt to ingratiate himself with Rome. While rabbinic and clerical elites tried to convince their respective populations not to participate in pagan form of entertainment such as the Romans, Jews, Christians and Romans all intermixed in the Palestinian gladiator games from first century BCE to the sixth century CE.

Sport in the Middle Ages (500 CE–1500 CE)

The secularization of sport that started during the Roman Empire continued during the Middle Ages. This was a transitional period between a time when a large, unified nation or civilization (the Roman Empire) had disappeared and a later time when nations regained strength and stability (the Renaissance). Greek festivals and Roman spectacles were replaced by a variety of tournaments, hunts, and folk games. Sport participation during this era tended to be class specific.

Participation in tournaments was restricted to the upper class, although all classes were allowed to be spectators of the knights who displayed their prowess. The tournaments actually have chariot racing as their roots. During the early Middle Ages, chariot racing was quite common in Eastern Europe and the events staged were similar to what the Greeks had done a thousand years earlier (e.g., two- or four-horse teams driven by professionals on a roughly 900 meter course, generally running 7 laps) (Mandell 1984). The medieval tournaments conducted by knights served the dual purpose of providing entertainment but also served a military purpose: training for fighting. The tournaments lasted for centuries (11th–16th) until the invention of gunpowder would make such an activity inane. (King Henry II of France died from jousting injuries in 1599, ending the tournament games there.) Performed primarily in France, England, Germany, and southern Europe, tournaments featured armed horsemen in simulated battle. They were held with great pageantry at the invitation of royalty or the nobility and were meant to display the ideals of chivalry (e.g., a knight fighting for "a fair maiden's hand"). Jousting (two knights in full armor ride at high speed directly toward one another with the object to unhorse one's opponent with a long tilting spear) was the most famous activity of the knights during the tournaments, but tourneys featuring two opposing factions of knights were also held. Death was common. The dead knights often had their possessions stolen from them. Those knights who lived but lost in battle were potential victims of hostage demands (the kingdom of the losing knight might pay a ransom for the safe return of the knight).

The medieval sport of jousting is reenacted at a Renaissance Faire.

Jousting became obsolete as gunpowder became increasingly prominent in warfare. Today, interestingly, jousting is popular at medieval reenactment faires and became the official sport of the state of Maryland in 1962, becoming the first state to adopt an official sport. Instead of two combatants riding at each other in full gallop and wearing armor, a solitary rider, without armor, attempts to place his or her spear through a small ring that is suspended roughly in the same position that an ongoing rider would be. In subsequent rounds the ring keeps getting smaller.

Hunts and other activities that lead to the death of animals are viewed by some as barbaric, and yet most of these same activities exist today. Cock-fighting and dog-fighting, for example, occur in many places of the world, including the contemporary United States. Hunting was not restricted to the poorer classes, as "leisured Europeans hunted with horses, dogs, hawks, and falcons" (Mandell 1984: 112). Mandell also points out that there are almost no literary records of fishing. He assumes, therefore, that either fishing was viewed as a degrading trade, or if it was pursued strictly for leisurely purposes, it would have been done only by illiterate, lower-class persons. We disagree with Mandell, however, as our research finds that the consumption of fish was an important part of diet and nourishment during Medieval times and, therefore, the catching, preparation, storage, and cooking of fish would be a respectable skill (Green 2003). It is understandable that perhaps fishing was not conducted competitively for sporting purposes.

During the Dark Ages, archery remained as a popular activity (as it had been in ancient Egypt and Greece). Archery had been popular in war for thousands of years, but now, a bull's eye target was established for sporting purposes—although, as Bell (1987) points out, the target could just as easily be a barbarian or a rival lord. The invention of the crossbow, a later development, proved to be a status symbol among archers, and because it was an expensive instrument, tended to identify people of a higher social status.

Because the peasants were not allowed to be participants in the upper class tournaments, they played a number of folk games, some with ancient origins. Dance, for example, remained popular during the Middle Ages just as it had for thousands of years prior. All social classes participated in dance, although their venues were quite different. The peasants, for example would dance at local festivals, while the wealthy would enjoy facilities equipped with stages and other conveniences of the time. Boxing, with its roots in the ancient world, was still common during the Middle Ages. The game soule, a French game (called *la soule*) similar to rugby, served to unite members of all classes (e.g., farmers, clergymen, and noblemen) from one city or town who teamed together against another city or town. After the game, it was common for members of both teams to share a communal meal, thus encouraging a sense of equality and fellowship.

In Medieval Ireland, the Irish played a game called "fives" (five fingers to the hand) that is the forerunner to handball. They players bounced a ball off a single wall, alternated turns, and kept score. Field hockey, or simply hockey, was also played in Ireland. The Celts played with a curved stick and a rough style of play that was very physical; it is believed by some sport historians that the origins of the term "fighting Irish" originated from hockey (Bell 1987). Other Irish historians focus on the style of the stick rather than the hockey reference. The curved stick, or shillelagh, was popular in Irish culture as a walking stick that had a large knob at the top that could easily be used as a weapon. Thus, the everyday Irish person with a shillelagh could be a "fighting Irish." Fighting with a shillelagh was the Irish variation of the sport, stick fighting. Stick fighting as a martial art was once common throughout Europe and the world (Farrell 2019). Bell also claims that hockey has its roots in medieval Ireland, but that is not completely true as hockey can be traced back to the ancient Arabs, Greeks, Persians, and Romans, all of whom had their own version of this stick game (*Encyclopædia Britannica* 2020). In Greece, images reveal people playing with a curved stick dating back to 600 BCE. In medieval Ireland, the Irish played a more refined version of hockey, which in turn would be modified again in English schools in the late nineteenth century.

Bowling has its roots in the Middle Ages. It was so popular that in 1366 King Edward III of England outlawed bowling to keep his troops focused on archery. Bowling lanes were roofed over for the first time during the mid-fifteenth century in Germany and it became an indoor game after that. The Dutch would bring bowling to North America. In Connecticut in the 1840s, a tenth pin was added; this became the standard in the twentieth century.

The high price of bows led many peasants to ignore archery and pursue games, most of which were prohibited. Football (soccer) was a popular sport in England during the Middle Ages and although its true roots are hard to determine, the first certain reference dates to 1314 from an edict of Nicholas de Farndon (Magoun 1966). From this edict it is clear that football was regularly played in London and was regarded as a dangerous nuisance. The first recorded football fatality occurred in 1321. There were no recorded rules of the game during this era (although there is evidence that the playing fields may have been marked out), and it is, therefore, not known whether the ball was only kicked, or whether carrying the ball was allowed. Medieval English football was certainly viewed as an undesirable alternative to archery, however. King Edward IV specifically forbade football and urged archery instead. In 1477, he made playing football a punishable offense which led to imprisonment. In 1477 the king proclaimed that no person shall participate in any unlawful games such as dice or football and that every strong and able-bodied person shall practice archery for the purpose of the national defense of England (Magoun 1966). By the 1700s, football was very common in England and still quite a violent game.

During the Middle Ages, the English also played a game called *stoolball*, in which a batter hit a ball pitched toward an upside-down milk stool and ran around three other stools before coming home safely. This game would be transformed into a game called *rounders* in the seventeenth century. Rounders, a game much like stoolball but with a diamond shaped field, would be brought over to colonial America, where it would eventually evolve into *town ball* (the rules varied from town to town). This game would eventually evolve into baseball.

Clearly, a couple of patterns of sport were established during the Middle Ages. First, many sports played in this era were also played in ancient times. Second, many sports played during the Middle Ages would evolve into sports played today.

Sport in the Pre-industrial Age (1500 CE–1750 CE)

After the Protestant Reformation, Calvinism and Puritanism took hold as dominant cultural influences in both Europe and colonial America. The ideals proclaimed by these social forces were in stark contrast to that previously represented in sport. "Sports were seen as frivolous, profane, useless distractions from religious observance, hard work, family devotion, and expressions of good character that Puritans associated with good, virtuous, godly lives" (Nixon and Frey 1996: 20). These restrictive measures were aimed primarily at the peasants. The Puritans detested the English tradition of playing sport on the Sabbath. James I had proclaimed in a royal decree, published as the *Book of Sports*, that his subjects had the legal right, after religious services, to engage in lawful recreation (e.g., dancing, archery, vaulting, etc.). When the Puritans briefly took power in England, "they ordered the state executioner to publicly burn the *Book of Sports*" (Curry and Jiobu 1984: 27).

In colonial America, the Puritans forbade sports on Sundays. They also sought to discourage horse racing (Radar 2004). The occasional farm festival was allowed, but such activities were restricted to post-barn raising celebrations, quilting bees and cornhusking contests (Eitzen and Sage 1989). The New England Puritans "permitted fishing and hunting if those activities were pursued for food, to refresh the body, or to rid the colony of vermin. Towns even paid bounties to those killing foxes, wolves, and bears" (Radar 2004: 7–8). The Puritan influence was not so strong in frontier America, though there was seldom time for recreational activities on the frontier.

As time moved on, the Puritan influence would diminish in colonial America. The wealthy would enjoy more opportunities for sports and leisure than most others. Horse racing and yacht racing (not as we know yachts today) was fairly common. Yacht racing, or sailing, a sport where one yacht chases another, first became popular among the upper classes in Holland and then England in the seventeenth century. The first yacht club, the Walter Club of Cork Harbor, was founded in Ireland in 1720. Competitive sailing continued to gain popularity in England and the United States through the modern era. The less wealthy people enjoyed many sports, but especially bowling. At times colonial gatherings would feature a variety of games and contests on large open fields. Hunting and other contests that led to the killing of animals (e.g., cockfighting) were common. Because these contests involved the spilling of blood, the contemporary term used to describe these contests is "blood sports" (Radar 2004). It was also common to gamble on sports and contests in colonial America.

In Europe, sports had become popular at the universities, although the amount of time students were allowed to participate in such activities was limited. University officials limited the amount of time students played sports because they did not want it to interfere with academics. (This is something that colleges and universities struggle with today.) Taking the Athenian approach—the need to balance mind and body—the Renaissance era encouraged the idea of an all-around person (i.e., a Renaissance Man). The sports played in colleges during the Renaissance were similar to student intramural sports today. As with education, sport was generally limited to the elite. They enjoyed such activities as swimming, running, horseback riding, acrobatics, archery, swordsmanship, and wrestling (Freeman 1997).

Archery remained important for military purposes and became mandatory for English soldiers. The elites also enjoyed the skill of archery. The Finsbury Archers of London, who held tournaments in the seventeenth and eighteenth centuries, had their origins with Henry VIII, who provided a grant for the association in 1537. The world's oldest continuous archery tournament, the Ancient Scorton Arrow Contest, was commissioned by England's Charles II in 1673. Charles II viewed archery as a sport as much as a military and hunting technique. Settlers in the United States would also take up archery. The native people were already experienced with bow and arrow. The first archery club in the United States, the United Bowman of Philadelphia, was organized in 1828.

Modern bowling can trace its roots to mid-fifteenth-century Germany and other European countries. The Dutch brought the game to North America in the seventeenth century where it gained an immediate and immense popularity. A section of lower Manhattan and towns in Kentucky and Ohio were named Bowling Green in honor of this sport. In the 1840s, players in Connecticut added a 10th pin to the traditional ninepin game. As we learned in Chapter 1, bowling is the most popular participant sport in the U.S. today.

Sport During the Early Industrial Era (1750 CE–1900 CE)

The rather archaic versions of sports activities that had developed throughout the previous centuries were evolving to modern versions during the Industrial era. Industrialization was the process of transforming an agricultural (farming) economy into an industrial one, through an increase in large factories, rapid population growth, and urbanization. Standardized, written rules are a sure sign of the impending modern version of sports. Heavy bureaucratization would be one of the last developments to finish this transition from loosely-organized games to highly structured sports leagues. "Old traditions, customs, and rituals, as well as the folk groups of family and friends, were being replaced with such radically different social inventions as standardization, centralization, division of labor, impersonal authority, and rational planning. Bureaucracy and formal organization were proving to be effective ways to organize the emerging social order. This included recreation-sport" (Leonard 1988: 33).

Golf, a sport that is likely derived from a Dutch game called "kolf" (meaning "club"), was first played in Scotland dating back to the mid-fifteenth century. The formalization of golf dates to 1754 when the basic rules of the game (e.g., playing 18 holes) were established at the Royal and Ancient Golf Club (Everard 2011). The first true golf club in the United States was founded in Foxburg, Pennsylvania, in 1884.

In the 1860s, the Marquis of Queensbury endorsed a set of rules, including requiring boxers to wear padded gloves and three-minute rounds that would become the standard of modern boxing. The American John L. Sullivan, "the Boston Strongboy," won the last bare-knuckles heavyweight championship in 1889.

In Germany, Friedrich Ludwig Jahn (1778–1852), who is often considered the "Father of Gymnastics," and someone who was an ardent Prussian patriot (he was against the provincialism of Germany), introduced gymnastics in an outdoor setting. Jahn described this outdoor exercise activity area as *turnplatz*, or "exercise group," which was basically a playground with various apparatuses for exercises. Adolf Spiess (1810–1858), another German, would later develop a system of "free exercises"—no apparatuses were needed.

During the late 1700s and early 1800s, Americans participated mostly in the same games and sports as they had during the colonial era. Furthermore, the Puritan ethic still surrounded American sport. Playing sports on Sunday was still forbidden and made officially taboo by the blue laws. *Blue laws* were given this name because they were printed on blue paper in New Haven, Connecticut, in 1781. These statutes restricted sports and recreation but did not forbid utilitarian activities such as hunting and fishing (Leonard 1988). The slow transformation of American sport was primarily attributed to the fact that the urbanization of American cities did not take place until the mid–1800s. Urbanization is the process by which a country's population changes from primarily rural to urban. It is caused by the migration of people from the countryside to the city in search of better jobs and living conditions.

So what social factors occurred during the mid–1850s that would lead to a new outlook on sports in the United States? For one, massive Irish and German immigration to American cities such as New York and Boston led to a huge urban development in the United States and also created ethnic diversity. Traditional values were challenged and crime sky-rocketed. Overcrowded, unsanitary conditions characterized America's growing cities. Numerous reform efforts were spearheaded to alleviate social problems that plagued the cities. Although urbanization was in full bloom in the United States at this time, social critics condemned city life and looked idealistically at rural society. Farmers, especially, were portrayed as healthy, honest, self-reliant people (Riess 1995). Now, physical fitness programs were promoted by social reformers as instruments of positive social change. It was argued that sport participation would benefit society by instilling traditional American values upon immigrants, lower- and middle-class persons.

The increased importance placed on sport participation hit a snag each winter in the northern U.S. states. As a result, a number of sports clubs emerged toward the end of the 1800s. Sports such as basketball and volleyball were created as a result of these sports clubs. By the late 1800s a number of sports clubs, including religious based groups such as the Young Men's Christian Association (YMCA), an evangelical organization founded in London in 1844, emerged throughout the United States. James Naismith invented basketball as a class YMCA project in 1891 in Springfield, Massachusetts. He had his players shoot a ball into half-bushel peach baskets attached to the gym balcony 10 feet off the ground. The peach basket hoop was replaced by a metal rim and netting about a decade after the sport was invented but the netting at the bottom of the basket remained closed. It was not until 1906 that the bottom of the net was cut out to allow the ball to fall through the hoop (Eitel 2018). In men's basketball, the number of players on a side dropped from nine to five in 1895, a year before Chicago and Iowa played the first college game. Women started playing basketball in 1892. A few years after the YMCA opened, the Young Women's Christian Association (YWCA) was formed and encouraged women to participate in "feminine" sports such as swimming, golf and tennis (Riess 1995). Volleyball, created by William G. Morgan while he served as physical director of the YMCA at Holyoke, Massachusetts, was designed for older men who found basketball too demanding (Rader 2004).

During the early industrial era, a number of sports were popular in the United States. Most of these sports have their roots with the colonial period. However, as society became urbanized, many sports changed as well. Horse racing, for example, became both a sporting enterprise and a business. Race tracks built in cities helped to transform horse racing from strictly a rural sport to an urban sport. The entrepreneurs that founded race tracks may have loved horses and horse racing, but they also loved the economic benefits associated with owning such a business. Betting on horse races was also very common and led to both opportunities to make money and corruption (e.g., fixing races, bribery) (Curry and Jiobu 1984). Horse racing was also quite popular in Canada at this time as well. By the 1850s, there were horse races in forty towns and villages throughout the Quebec province (Eitzen and Sage 1989). Rowing developed as the first "big-time" college sport and regularly attracted huge crowds (Curry and Jiobu 1984). Cricket, an English sport, was quite popular at this time and was organized under the guidance of the American Cricket Club (1855). In the 1850s, cricket was a very popular American sport. Bicycle riding, although not as physically demanding as running, was viewed as an excellent form of physical activity. Kirkpatrick Macmillan (1812–1878), a blacksmith, invented the first completely self-propelled (with foot pedals) bicycle. Macmillan never bothered to patent his invention, but others were quick to realize that a great deal of money could be made in the manufacturing and sale of bicycles. The earliest recorded bicycle race was held in Paris in the late 1860s. As the bikes became lighter and safer, racing became fashionable in Europe and the United States. In 1891, the first international bicycle race was held at Madison Square Garden in New York City. Cycling events were held at the 1896 Olympics. The first Tour de France, the world's premier bicycle race, was held in 1903.

In brief, there was no shortage of sporting activities during early industrialization. It would be fruitless to try and provide a discussion of all the variations of sports and recreation endeavors during this time. However, baseball deserves special attention.

Baseball

By the Civil War, a number of baseball clubs were competing against one another in the United States. Baseball was especially big in the Northeast, with New York City leading the way in the number of teams. By 1858, there were ninety-six baseball clubs in the New York metropolitan area. There exists a great controversy over the origins of baseball. As mentioned earlier in this chapter, baseball is similar to the English game of rounders, but the modern version played in the United States is not nearly the same sport. The popular belief is that Abner Doubleday (1819–1893) is the founder of modern baseball.

In 1905, the A.G. Mills commission, headed by Al Spalding, wrongly credited Doubleday with inventing the game of baseball in Cooperstown, New York, in 1839. In actuality, Doubleday was a cadet at West Point when he was supposed to have founded baseball. The commission made its ruling based primarily on a single, unsubstantiated letter from an elderly man named Abner Graves, who claimed to be a friend of Doubleday and present at the time when he allegedly invented baseball. The discovery of an old baseball in an attic of a farmhouse in Fly Creek, a village three miles from Cooperstown, was said to have substantiated the story. The stitched cover had been torn open, revealing stuffing of cloth instead of wool and cotton yarn, which comprise the interior of the modern baseball. The ball became known as the "Doubleday Baseball" and is still on display at Major League Baseball's Hall of Fame in Cooperstown.

The rules established by Alexander Cartwright include nine contestants at a time for each team during the play of the game and the use of a diamond field with ninety feet in between the bases. Thus, it is generally accepted that Cartwright and not Doubleday established the modern game of baseball. However, Cooperstown's claim to be host to the first game of baseball is a different argument.

After three years of unorganized play, Cartwright established a permanent site for his baseball club at Elysian Fields in Hoboken, New Jersey (1845). This is one reason why Hoboken claims to be the birthplace of modern baseball (Hoboken disputes Cooperstown's claim to have hosted baseball in 1839). Furthermore, as Adelman (1997) states, a report in the *Herald* mentioned that the New York Club played a baseball game versus the Brooklyn Club at Elysian Field as early as 1843. Despite the controversy over the exact origins of baseball, Adelman (1997) declares that "historians universally accept the Knickerbockers as baseball's pioneer club even as many of them recognize the existence of earlier teams" (59). A number of New York Knickerbocker Club members claimed to have played a "bat-and-ball" game as early as 1842, in the Murray Hill section of New York at Twenty-seventh Street and Fourth Avenue before the club team moved to Elysian Fields in Hoboken (Riess 1989).

Adding to the baseball origin controversy, city officials and historians in Pittsfield, Massachusetts, claimed to have evidence proving that baseball originated in their hometown in the late 1700s. A 1791 bylaw was passed to protect windows in Pittsfield's new meeting house by banning anyone from playing baseball within 80 yards of the building. Baseball was so common that it was necessary to pass the law, officials claimed. A librarian found the original Pittsfield document in a library vault and its age was authenticated by researchers at the Williamstown Art Conservation Center (*The Post-Standard* 2004).

Claiming to be the first professional baseball club and the site of the birthplace of baseball depends on how people define *professional* baseball. For example, if baseball was indeed played in Cooperstown in 1839 (and Pittsfield, for that matter), but not by professional baseball players, was that really a baseball game? Most sport historians say it may be impossible to ever pinpoint the exact time and place that baseball was invented. As is often the case, according to the conflict perspective, those in power (in this case, Major League Baseball) generally dictate the official answer—which is, as of now, baseball was founded in Cooperstown by Abner Doubleday.

The story of baseball is far more important than a debate over its origins. Baseball attracted huge crowds; in many cases, people were turned away from the small stadiums of the 1800s. "Even before the Civil War, a crowd of 5,000 was not unusual for a baseball game in Brooklyn, and after the war, crowds of 10,000 to 15,000 were attracted to the more popular games" (Szymanski and Zimbalist 2005: 16). Baseball and Brooklyn would go hand-in-hand for another 100 years (until the beloved Dodgers were moved to Los Angeles, breaking the hearts of Brooklyn Dodgers fans). Baseball games were usually followed by elaborate postgame festivities where food and spirits abounded (somewhat like pregame tailgating at American football games). Baseball was quickly on its way to becoming the "national pastime." And for most people, this meant being socialized into the role of spectator and consumer of a sports culture.

The Formation of the Modern Olympics

Another critical development during the industrial era was the reintroduction of the Olympics. In brief, the Games were revived by a Frenchman, Baron de Coubertin (1863–1937) in 1896. Paris-born Coubertin was an aristocrat, a well-versed intellectual and talented sportsman who took part in boxing, fencing, horseback riding, and rowing. His passion for education extended to sports education. After visiting organized sports organizations in England and the United States, Coubertin returned to France to persuade officials to introduce physical education in schools. Coubertin did not promote physical education simply for sports purposes but rather, as a means of keeping his countrymen in shape. He was convinced that the humiliating French defeat in the Franco-German War (1870–71) was tied to the fact that the Germans were physically superior. Furthermore, in the spirit of French democracy, Coubertin viewed sports as a way to bring the social classes together (Hill 1992).

Coubertin was convinced that sports education was an important part of the personal development of young people. He believed that sports education presented opportunities to develop what he called "moral energy." To publicize his plans to revive the Olympic Games, Coubertin established the International Olympic Committee (IOC) during a meeting held at the University of Sorbonne in Paris on June 23, 1894. Among the ideals that Coubertin hoped the Olympics would inspire was the concept of amateurism. Coubertin embraced this ideal when it was suggested to him by Professor William Milligan Stone during his 1893 visit to Princeton University. Sloan promoted what he called "clean sport" (Mandell 1984). The IOC decided that the first modern Olympics would be held in Athens, Greece, and that they would be held every four years at a site to be determined by the IOC. The Athens Games were a huge success. Unfortunately, the Paris Games of 1900 and 1904 were not so successful and were overshadowed by international fairs. The 1906 Paris Summer Olympics was a success and the momentum carried on. Coubertin served as IOC president for 29 years and died of a heart attack in Geneva on September 2, 1937.

Thanks to the efforts of Pierre de Coubertin, the modern Olympics are now played on a regular basis, with the Summer and Winter Games alternating every two years. There have been some exceptions to the regularity of the modern Games. They were cancelled three times (1916, 1940 and 1944 due to World War I and World War II) and the 2020 Tokyo Games were postponed for a year (as of this writing) due to the SARS-CoV-2 pandemic. As with the original Olympics, new sports are regularly added, and old ones are dropped. For instance, in 1992 badminton and in 1996 beach volleyball became Olympic sports, whereas baseball and softball were eliminated from the Olympics beginning in 2012. The 2020 Gamers were supposed to feature the return of baseball and (shortboard) surfing and the introduction of karate, skateboarding, and sport climbing. Also, as with the ancient Olympics, the modern Games are filled with political controversy (see Chapter 13).

Sport in the Twentieth Century

A number of general aspects characterize sports in the twentieth century. According to Riess (1995), sport is used "to engender pride in one's hometown (boosterism) and country (nationalism). According to conventional wisdom, people could more easily identify with their neighborhood, city, region, or nation when they cheered for athletes or teams who represented them in sporting competition" (26). Having a major league sports franchise, or a minor league sports franchise in smaller cities, became a way to express boosterism, to show pride in one's hometown. Sport provided a tangible comparison between cities that symphonies, for example, could not. Nationalism grew throughout the twentieth century. Once again, sport provided a tangible measurement through which comparisons between nations would be possible. Americans were especially eager to show the British and other European powers that their athletes were able to successfully compete in sports. Reiss also points out that technological improvements, especially in communications, helped to fuel the interest and importance that sport commands in the twentieth century.

Allen Guttmann (1978) suggests that there are seven characteristics of modern sports:

1. *Secularism*. Secularism means nonreligious. The sports of the Greeks were quasi-religious ceremonies. Modern sports are more like Roman sport with an emphasis on show and spectacle.
2. *Equality*. Modern sports are, more or less, equality driven. Women, minorities, and lower-class persons all have, at least theoretically, an equal chance to achieve in the sporting world. Equality is assured because of the standardization of rules and passage of laws that ensure egalitarianism. Of course, participants who lack athletic ability are less likely to seeing playing time as the level of competition increases; thus, there is always some form of inequality in sport.
3. *Specialization*. In an attempt to keep an edge over competitors, many advanced athletes practice their primary sport almost exclusively. Furthermore, there is great specialty in sport. For example, in baseball, there are starting pitchers, middle-relievers, "set-up pitchers" and "closers." Baseball's designated hitter position (which did not exist in 1978 when Guttmann established these characteristics) is the ultimate example of over-specialization and a clear example of diluting the quality of baseball.
4. *Rationalization*. Rationalization, a product of the scientific, lucid outlook on social life that characterizes modern society, is exhibited in the development of standardized rules.
5. *Bureaucracy*. As German sociologist Max Weber (1864–1920) articulated, bureaucracies are goal-oriented organizations designed to meet rational goals. As sports evolved, the bureaucracy that oversees it also continued to grow (mirror-effect). Guttmann used the IOC as an exemplar of an overly bureaucratic sports organization. The modern world is so overly bureaucratic that it often

seems impersonal. Realizing this, Weber viewed future society as an "Iron Cage" (inescapable from bureaucracy and rationalization) rather than paradise (Delaney 2004).

6. *Quantification.* The rationalistic approach to social life involves documenting everything. Measurement and keeping performance records is a critical aspect of modern sport. The beauty of quantification (numbers and statistics) is that it provides something tangible for the athlete and participant. A bowler realizes the significance of a 300 game. A golfer wants to shoot below par. Major League Baseball hitters want to reach the 762 number (Barry Bonds' career record). Quantification is equated to precision. It provides a specific goal to strive for.

7. *Records.* Directly tied to quantification, the concept of keeping records is mirrored by society's idea of progress. As long as records are being broken, progress is being made. Thus the cliché, "Every record was made to be broken." Fans and athletes alike love the chase of famed records; it reflects our continuous desire to improve, to be "the best ever."

The characteristics of sport described in this section are meant to provide a highlight of the primary features of modern sport. In the proceeding chapters, the review of a number of specific topics (e.g., gender, race, politics, and economics) will focus on a number of specific characteristics (both positive and negative) that characterize sports today.

Sports Played

Most of the same sports played since industrialization still exist today. Among the more popular sports *played* is billiards (or pool). The ancient activity of lawn game (dating back to ancient Persia) is most likely the forerunner of billiards. A similar table game developed in England and France in the fourteenth century, although it is unknown if this game evolved into billiards. Pocket billiards, or pool, originated in the 1800s. In the twentieth century billiards became hugely popular. Tables were found in pool halls and saloons. In the mid–1920s there were about 42,000 poolrooms, over 4,000 in New York City alone (Riess 1989). Poolrooms also had a bad public image, as they were viewed as places where young males went to gamble and drink and otherwise engage in deviant behavior. In the early 1900s poolrooms outnumbered bowling alleys, but this would change by the end of the century, as bowling is the number one participatory sport in the United States.

Tennis and golf are two relatively popular participant sports; both have often been viewed as semi-elitist sports, played mostly by upper-class persons. Dwight Davis, for whom the "Davis Cup" in tennis is named, attempted to make tennis accessible for all—not just the country club crowd—early in the twentieth century. Davis was a world class tennis player and a World War I hero who served as President Coolidge's secretary of war and as President Hoover's governor general of the Philippines. Davis realized that most inner city children did not have adequate places to run and play. He promoted building playgroups where people from all social classes could enjoy recreational activities such as tennis. As park commissioner of St. Louis, Davis was responsible for a boom in parks development. By late spring 1913 there were tennis courts at four parks (including 32 new courts at Forest Park alone) in St. Louis. Many other cities followed suit and before long parks across the country had tennis court facilities. Today, tennis is played at most public high schools, but overall, it has remained primarily a sport for upper-class white persons.

Throughout most of the twentieth century, golf was played on private country club courses. These private clubs restricted play to a mostly upper-class, male, white clientele. Although the multiracial Tiger Woods is a household name, when he first joined the professional tour (PGA), he was confronted with the reality that some golf courses still did not allow blacks to play. Today, many public courses have extended the participation of golf to middle-class persons.

As mentioned earlier, baseball evolved from the English sport rounders. Throughout most of the twentieth century, baseball was known as the "national pastime" because it was the most popular sport in the United States. Youth played baseball, followed professional baseball, collected baseball cards, and dreamed of playing for their favorite Major League team. For many, baseball is a simple game to understand, but filled with chess-like strategic moves and displays of physical excellence. Baseball is both a rural and urban game. And many of today's Major League Baseball (MLB) players are from economically-depressed Central American countries.

Football is a game derived from English football (soccer) and rugby. Toward the end of the twentieth century, football replaced baseball as America's favorite sport. American football is controlled violence and it is poetry in motion. It is chaotic and it is planned precision. In many respects it is very primal and yet quite evolved in sophistication and technology. While football remains as the most popular sport to follow, it was just recently surpassed by outdoor track and field as the most popular played sport in high school (see Chapter 7).

The Post-Modern Era: An Interest in "Extreme" Sports

Traditional sports remain hugely popular throughout the world. However, the increasingly prominent role of sport in society has led to a nontraditional backlash. Many people, especially the younger generation, have become frustrated with the overly specialized, overly competitive and highly selective character of most traditional sports. Many sports have become so rule-oriented that people have sought alternatives to traditional sports. Collectively, these "nontraditional" sports are known as "alternative sports" and characterized by: participant controlled and directed; emphasis on personal achievement and fulfillment; and, possessing a subcultural context (which, ironically, makes it selective). The most prevalent version of alternative sports is known as "extreme sports." In this section, we will discuss the development of extreme sports and provide a brief review of some of the more prevalent extreme sports. As we shall see, ironically, or maybe predictably, many of these extreme sports are becoming as bureaucratized as the sports these participants shunned.

Extreme Sports

The term extreme sports (sometimes called action or adventure sports) is a collective idiom used to describe a number of relatively newer sporting activities that involve risky, adrenaline-inducing action. Adrenaline junkies are susceptible to all kinds of dangerous activities not limited to sports. Many behaviors that attract such people are often dangerous and risky, defying common sense.

The longer any sport is in existence, the more likely it is to become standardized and commercialized; many extreme sports have been unable to escape this inevitability. For example, in 1995, ESPN created the "X Games." The X Games are a made-for-television phenomenon that features a number of extreme sports. The popularity of the X Games led ESPN to create annual Winter X Games and Summer X Games. Some of the Summer events include: Moto (motorcycle) racing; skateboarding; BMX freestyle; real video series (video competition); Red Bull Phenom; and Esports. Among the most recent Winter X Game sports are: skiing; snowboarding; snowboarding; and real video series. Advertisers who covet the audience drawn to the X Games have been eager to join the extreme bandwagon. Sponsorships have guaranteed the success of the Games for both ESPN and the participants.

As with any discussion of traditional sports, it would not be practical to try and provide a complete analysis of all extreme sports. Consequently, our review will be brief and begins with surfing and its post-modern variations. Surfing is an extreme sport that entails the possibility of wiping out in waves 50 feet or higher and the constant threat of shark attacks just adds to the exhilaration. If traditional water surfers want to avoid sharks they can try Arctic surfing in Iceland or Norway's Lofoten islands. The Nordic terrain inspired Disney's film *Frozen* but these remote islands have become an unlikely Eden for some of the world's most adventurous spirits who battle frostbite and fierce currents (*CBS This Morning* 2017). Improvements in wet suits help surfers brave waters too cold for sharks, and summer surfing where the sun never sets leads to quite a day of surfing.

The thrill enjoyed by water surfers is shared by land-lovers who transformed traditional surfing into such sports as skateboarding, snowboarding, sky surfing and elevator surfing. Skateboarding represents one of the first activities to be classified as an "alternative" or "extreme" sport. Skateboarding has actually been in existence for generations dating back to its California origin during the 1950s. Skateboarding started as a dry land hobby for surfers while they weren't in the ocean. By the 1960s, skateboarding was so popular that a number of competitions with various styles (e.g., downhill slalom and freestyle) of competition were judged (Cave 2006). Skateboarding is so popular today that it enjoys subcultural status and has been immortalized by skating movies and long-time television rebel Bart Simpson. There are estimated 6–7 million skateboarders in the U.S.

Snowboarding is another extension of surfing. Adopting a similar stance to the surfer and skateboarder, the snowboarder seeks gravity free moments of excitement and adrenaline rushes. Snowboarders first appeared at ski slopes in the early 1980s. They quickly earned the reputation as "bad boys" which only fueled the initial attraction of this sport to nontraditional sport enthusiasts. The number of snowboarders in the U.S. continues to dwindle. According to data provided by Statista there were approximately 7.6 million participants in snowboarding in the U.S. (Gough 2020a). The data also shows that snowboarders are overwhelming male (nearly 75 percent); young (51.7 percent are under the age of 25); and tend to come from wealthy families or are wealthy themselves.

Sky surfing is an extreme sport that combines "getting air" with attempts to make "turns" on waves or slopes prior to parachuting to safety. Elevator surfing is one of the newest extreme sports. It involves daredevils riding, or "surfing," on the top of elevators. The inherent danger of elevator surfing includes being crushed between the elevator and the top of the elevator shaft or simply falling off the elevator top and falling to one's death. Elevator surfing typically takes place in skyscrapers and college campuses with tall buildings. Participants generally enter the building early or late in the day or whenever there are few people around. They pry the doors open and use emergency hatches to enter the elevator shafts. Another variation of surfing is volcano boarding, or volcano surfing, which involves boarding down volcano slopes that are covered in cool cinders or ash (consisting mostly of particles of rock, mineral, and glass that were expelled from a volcano during a volcanic eruption). Surfers must first hike up the volcano with their boards strapped to their backs and generally reach speeds of 30 mph. Volcano surfing advocates report that Cerro Negro (Black Hill), an active volcano outside of Leon, Nicaragua is the best place to engage in this extreme sport (Karsten 2019).

Another example of an extreme sport is street luge. Street luge, as with most extreme sports, evolved from existing traditional sports, in this case from a combination of ice luge and skateboarding. Street luge races may be conducted legally (sanctioned events) or illegally (a hill in any neighborhood). Street lugers lie down on a skateboard-like apparatus that is equipped with four large urethane wheels and no brakes. The luges are generally made with aluminum frames. Steering is accomplished by leaning the body weight from side to side. Starting from the top of a hill (this could be in any neighborhood) lugers allow gravity to take them on their thrilling joy ride. One variation of illegal street luging involves the rider grabbing a hold of a moving vehicle for a "free ride."

One of the most dangerous extreme sports is BASE jumping. BASE jumping is defined as parachuting from stationary objects (e.g., buildings, bridges, steep mountains). BASE is an acronym for building, antenna (an uninhabited tower such as an aerial mast), span (bridge, arch, or dome) and earth (cliffs or other natural formation). Unlike skydiving, no aircraft is involved with BASE jumping. BASE jumping is a very dangerous sport and has a high fatality rate. There have been isolated examples of BASE jumping since the early 1900s (e.g., Frederick Law jumped from the Statue of Liberty in 1912), but these were usually done for publicity purposes. BASE jumping is somewhat like parachuting except BASE jumping is done from lower heights and at lower airspeed than a skydiver. Furthermore, an off-heading landing is most likely to lead to fatal consequences for BASE jumpers, whereas skydivers have some time to maneuver. Most BASE jumpers already know how to skydive. It is advisable that BASE jumpers learn skydiving first so that they know how to safely fly and land a parachute (there is more room for error when learning how to sky dive than when learning how to BASE jump).

Unlike skydiving, the FAA has no jurisdiction over BASE jumping. However, to legally BASE jump, the jumper must secure necessary permissions to use the object that is being jumped and the area used for landing. Obviously, due to risk concerns, there is great reluctance among most owners of jumpable objects to allow BASE jumping. However, there is one bridge in the United States where it is legal to BASE jump—the Perine Bridge in Twin Falls, Idaho. The bridge is a perfect site for jumping. It sits 487 feet above the canyon and Snake River below. There is a flat area to land.

One of the more brutal extreme sports is ultimate fighting. Ultimate fighting has grown in popularity during the early 2000s. Ultimate fighting combines such traditional sports as karate, wrestling, boxing, kickboxing, and a variety of marital arts. Ultimate fighting generally involves participants beating up one another where the rules are flexible enough to allow for a number of fighting styles. This sport has become standardized already under the Ultimate Fighting Championship (UFC). The UFC is a series of international competitions televised internationally several times a year. Ultimate fighting is little more than sanctioned gang warfare or a bully who beats someone for the sheer enjoyment of harming another human being. Despite the brutality of this sport and its challenge to the premise of a civilizing movement in the premodern era, the popularity of ultimate fighting has not yet reached its peak.

It is important to reiterate the point that many sports classified as extreme have existed in the past. For example, many people climbed rocks, mountains and ice glaciers before these activities became labeled as extreme sports. Surfing is sometimes classified as an extreme sport, and yet it has a relatively long history in the United States. Running with the bulls in Pamplona, Spain, is certainly an extreme way to get one's kicks in life, and yet this event dates back to the thirteenth century. The annual running with bulls became popular in the late 1800s. Numerous people are gored each year and fatalities are common in this action activity.

There are so many examples of extreme sports that lists exceed 100. Some other noteworthy examples include: abseiling (rappelling); barefooting (water skiing without skis); canyon swinging (participants lower themselves down a cliff and swing horizontally and vertically); caving; flowriding (surfing waves created by a wave machine; surfing legend Kelly Slater created an artificial wave machine that could revolutionize surfing); hang gliding; ice canoeing; paragliding; parkour; roof topping (scaling and walking atop roofs and dangerous ledges; hanging from cranes without a harness, etc.); skydiving; and zorbing (rolling down a hill in a giant inflatable ball/orb) (Lockwood 2020).

Participation in extreme sports is steadily growing. However, participation rates for females in extreme sports remain distant to that of males. As with traditional sports, males generally control access to participation and the processes by which females could become accepted as fellow extreme athletes. Boys generally control the local parks and high school parking lots often used by extreme sport enthusiasts, thus depriving girls of the opportunity to develop their skills. Nonetheless, the popularity of extreme sports has increased so quickly that some of these sporting activities have become so standardized that they are included in such international sporting contests as the Olympics. Snowboarding, for example was included in the 2002 Winter Olympic Games.

Sports in the Future

In this chapter, a brief review of the history of sports was provided. It was not intended to be an exhaustive listing of sports and games played throughout history, as that would take volumes of published works. Rather, it was our intention to provide an accurate glimpse of sports throughout human history. As we have demonstrated, a number of specific sports and activities have existed for thousands of years. One other thing should be quite clear as well: sports have existed for so long and are such a pervasive aspect of humanity; they will certainly remain popular in the foreseeable future.

Connecting Sports and Popular Culture

Box 3: "It's Like Fight Club with Swords": Modern Medieval Combat

As described in this chapter, jousting was a popular form of entertainment, as well as a means of preparing future soldiers in the art of warfare, throughout the Middle Ages.

While the practice died out long ago, in recent years it has seen a revival of sorts. Richard W. Kaueper, a History professor at the University of Rochester, is one of the leading experts on the topic of chivalry in medieval times. He notes that "a revival of jousting has become a feature of the medieval or Renaissance fairs that now dot the summer landscape of the United States, drawing large crowds especially to watch colorful combats between fully armored knights while enjoying a roast turkey leg and quaffing mead. Usually the jousting is sadly false and scripted to ensure victory by the obvious hero, but the sheer physicality of armored men atop snorting, stamping horses remains impressive enough" (Kaueper 2016: 208). Kaueper told one of the two authors that he once took his young granddaughter to such a fair to witness a jousting contest. When it ended, he revealed to her in confidence how inauthentic the whole thing was, and that it was a mishmash of different techniques from various centuries, carefully choreographed to make sure ahead of time who would be the winner. After the match he brought her over to say hello to the jousters, and they courteously asked him who he was. When he told them his name the men insisted on shaking his hand, and said they were honored to meet him. They had read and admired his many books on medieval warfare. And they were proud to let him know that they were meticulously following the jousting rules he had written about. Kaueper was glad that his granddaughter didn't tell them what he had told her a few minutes before.

While it is true that most such "contests" at Renaissance fairs are scripted and meticulously rehearsed, that does not mean that there is no such thing as actual unscripted "modern medieval combat." In fact, there are many people throughout the world who participate in genuine tournaments using historically accurate (albeit blunted) weapons and following as closely as possible the rules used in medieval contests. Participants— both men and women—train long and hard, wielding swords, maces, cleavers, scythes, and shields while donned in protective armor. "Team members have suffered broken bones and dislocated shoulders, and a patchwork of bruises is worn as a coat of arms," writes Tim Chester of a match in South Wales. "I overhear one particularly worrying account from a fighter talking about receiving a head blow from a pole axe: 'My right vision completely went; there were sparkly lights and stuff. I spent a week in a brain-fog haze, walking around like a zombie'" (Chester 2020).

This fast-growing sport began in Eastern Europe in the early 2000s and has since spread across the globe. It's especially popular in areas identified with actual medieval tournaments, and appeals to mixed martial arts fighters, role-players, ancient weapon experts, history buffs, and *Game of Thrones* enthusiasts. In addition to learning the complicated rules of medieval combat, participants must also abide by stringent conditions, including wearing armor that can weigh up to 100 pounds. And it must be completely made of metal—no plastic or other non-time specific materials allowed. Like the Renaissance fair Professor Kaueper and his granddaughter attended, spectators are welcome, but unlike the situation those two experienced, no one knows ahead of time who the victors will be.

The Armored Combat League of New Hampshire is one such group of modern medieval athletes. "Fighters train in The Knights Hall, located in an old warehouse in Nashua, New Hampshire, where they dive into the art of medieval style combat. The armor is real, the weapons they use are made of actual steel, and the training to use it all is intense. 'We are basically Fight Club with swords,' says fighter Cat Brooks" (Michaelson 2017). The Armored Combat League, in addition to its local contests, is training to compete in the annual International Medieval Combat Federation (IMCF) World Championship.

According to the IMCF website, there are 25 countries represented in the World Championship contests, which are held in actual medieval castles. "Our combatants hold themselves to the highest knightly standards, and treat their opponents with respect, and many are friends off the field. They fight their hardest, then help each other up, and congratulate the winner" (www.medievalcombat.org). Now that's real chivalry.

The next IMCF Medieval Combat World Championship is scheduled for September 10–12, 2021, in Malbork Castle, Poland. This gives new meaning to the expression "Get medieval…!"

SUMMARY

It is difficult to trace when sports were first played; but, the rudiments of sports can be traced back thousands of years. The ancient Africans, and especially the ancient Egyptians, played a number of identifiable sports, including archery, wrestling, running, swimming, and tabletop games. This is also true in Ancient Asia as many board games, early versions of sports (e.g., soccer, polo, archery, and Sumo wrestling), and martial arts were engaged in throughout Asia.

The ancient Greeks loved their sports, which characterized their highly competitive nature. This was reflected in the Olympic Games, which combined cultural and religious aspects and helped to produce unity throughout the Hellenistic world. The Roman Empire continued the traditions begun by the Greeks, but during this period sports became increasingly professional and secularized. Eventually, the Roman Empire became dominated by the infamous gladiator games, which led to a debasement of the culture.

In the Middle Ages, the secularization of sport that started during the Roman Empire continued with the rise of tournaments. These were held with great pageantry at the invitation of royalty and displayed the ideals of chivalry. Such tournaments were limited to the upper classes, but folk games were popular with the lower classes. The Pre-industrial age (incorporating the Renaissance, Reformation and Enlightenment) marked a major period of transition where religious and philosophical debates had an impact upon the sports being played. Calvinism and Puritanism, for instance, became dominant cultural influences in both Europe and America, and looked upon sports as frivolous, profane distractions from religious observances. Sports did become popular in universities, which had risen during the Middle Ages, although officials limited the time students played because they did not want it to interfere with academics.

In the mid–1700s the Industrial Revolution radically changed the Western world, through the introduction of machinery and mass production. With the rise of a middle class, there was an increase in the number of people with disposable income and the time to spend on leisure and sport pursuits. Urbanization also had an important influence on the rise of spectator sports. This transition marked a development of higher-level organization and standardized rules.

The modern Olympics were founded in 1896 by Baron de Coubertin as a way of bringing social classes together and encouraging international cooperation. As the twentieth century began, sports and leisure activities enjoyed a valued status in the Western world.

Today, sport is such a well-established social institution that it is as much a part of the character of a nation as are its politics, economics, and religion. Sport has been seen as a vital part of the civilizing process. However, due in part to increasing frustration with over-specialized, rule-oriented sports, the late twentieth and early twenty-first centuries have seen the rise of extreme and alternative sports.

Key Terms

Blue Laws So-called because they were once printed on blue paper, these are laws restricting activities or sales of goods on Sundays or holy days.

Boosterism Efforts to engender pride in one's hometown. Having a major league sports franchise can be a means to show pride in one's hometown.

Chivalry The qualities idealized by knighthood in the Middle Ages, such as bravery, courtesy, honor, and gallantry toward women.

Extreme Sports A collective idiom used to describe a number of relatively newer sporting activities that involve risky, adrenaline-inducing action. Features of extreme sports may include speed, height, danger, peril, stunts, and illegality.

Folk Games Popular and traditional games, primarily played in rural areas and passed along from one generation to another.

Industrialization The process of transforming an agricultural (farming) economy into an industrial one, through an increase in large factories, rapid population growth, and urbanization.

Jousting Competition between two knights in full armor who ride at high speed directly toward one another with the object to unhorse one's opponent with a long tilting spear.

Marquis of Queensbury Rules Set of rules agreed upon in the 1860s which became the standard of modern boxing, including requiring boxers to wear padded gloves and limiting rounds to three minutes.

Pankration A Greek word that means "complete strength" or "complete victory."

Secularism The process of moving from a religious orientation toward one that is focused on the world.

Senet One of the world's oldest recorded tabletop games.

Tournaments Public contests held in the Middle Ages between armed horsemen in simulation of real battle; these were restricted to the upper classes.

Urbanization The process by which a country's population changes from primarily rural to urban. It is caused by the migration of people from the countryside to the city in search of better jobs and living conditions.

Discussion Questions

- How would you compare and contrast sports in Ancient Africa with Ancient Asia?
- What is "Pankration" and how does it relate to contemporary "ultimate fighting" events?
- Why was the ancient Olympics started by the Greeks? What is the idealized view of the ancient Olympics, and how does this differ from the reality of the Games?

- How did the Romans differ with the Greeks on the role of sport in society? How did gladiator fighting originate, and what were its effects on the Roman character?
- How was jousting both a sport and a preparation for war?
- What is a shillelagh and how is it connected to sports?
- In what ways did the Industrial Revolution impact upon the development of modern sport? Why have sports become more rule-oriented and bureaucratized? Is this a good or a bad thing, in your opinion?
- What are "extreme sports" and how are they a reaction to the civilization process?
- What is the most extreme sport you have participated in? Describe that experience.

CHAPTER 4

The Impact of Sport on Culture

Once upon a time, there was a legend of a man who could "walk on water." Imagine that, walking on water. How could that be possible? This man resided in the tropical paradise of Honolulu, Hawaii, but word of his accomplishments reached faraway lands. The legend grew so big that people in the United States wanted to see for themselves someone perform such an extraordinary feat. And so, this mysterious fellow left his tropical homeland for America so that he could showcase his talent. Tens of thousands of people descended upon the beautiful Redondo Beach, California, shoreline to witness this miracle. The curious wanted to know who was this "man who could walk on water." His name was George Freeth, and although he was descended from Hawaiian royalty, he was no god. Freeth was a surfer. Henry Huntington, a wealthy Californian entrepreneur, had witnessed Freeth surfing while he was on vacation in Hawaii in the early 1900s. Huntington convinced the part royal Hawaiian and part Irish beach boy to come to Redondo Beach in 1907 to promote Redondo Beach tourism. Freeth was advertised as the "Man who can walk on water."

George Freeth did much more than simply bring surfing to the United States; he helped to transform the Southern California culture. For many, surfing is not just a sport, it is a lifestyle with a spiritual feel to it. Beach communities throughout the United States have developed a highly identifiable subculture centered on surfing and the beach way of life. Surfing as a subculture will be discussed later in this chapter.

Defining Culture

No review of the sociology of sport is complete without a chapter on the role of culture within the sports world. The study of culture is one of the most important things sociologists do because of the impact of culture on individuals, groups, organizations, social institutions and society. *Culture* is defined as the shared knowledge, values, language, norms, and behavioral patterns (customs) of a given society that are handed down from one generation to the next and form a way of life for its members. The prevailing culture of a society will dictate what is "proper" and "improper" behavior based on a number of variables, including the context and circumstances of a situation. For example, a child who throws a temper tantrum in a store is engaging in unruly behavior and is the cause of onlookers' scorn, but such behavior is discounted by the fact that the child is immature and has not learned to control his or her own behavior. An adult throwing a temper tantrum is not acceptable and deemed odd or peculiar.

Oddly, a number of professional athletes, managers and coaches feel that it is okay to throw a temper tantrum in public view of spectators and a television audience. Lou Piniella, for example, a former long-time MLB manager, is known for his emotional outbursts in dugouts and on the playing field. (Piniella has been known for kicking dirt on umpires, picking up bases and throwing them, making a number of strange gestures, and in short, "blowing a fuse!") His antics would lead to ejection, of course, but only after he finished his childish outbursts. Piniella is hardly alone when it comes to baseball managers displaying poor sportsmanship, in fact, he does not even crack the top ten list of MLB ejections (his 63 ejections place him in 11th place) (Goldman 2018). The top ten list of MLB manager ejections consists of: Joe Torre, who ironically, currently (as of 2020) serves as MLB's senior vice president who decides punishments for on-field incidents (66 total ejections); Jim Leyland (68 total ejections); Ron Gardenhire (73); Frankie Frisch (80); Paul Richards (80); Tony La Russa (87); Leo Durocher (94); Earl Weaver (94); John McGraw (132); and the leader of this pack, Bobby Cox, with an embarrassing 161 ejections (Goldman 2018). Somehow, this boorish behavior has been tolerated as a part of baseball. Fans seem to enjoy this clownish behavior and cheer the manager as he leaves the field following ejection. The sports media will replay over and over again these comical and pathetic antics as a form of entertainment even though such behavior would not be tolerated in any other profession. In many cases, such temper tantrums would likely be subject to a psychological evaluation. And yet, this behavior serves some important cultural lessons. For example, some societies will tolerate this behavior and others will not and it reveals that context is a critical aspect in determining which social acts are deemed in violation of cultural norms, values, and social expectations.

It is culture that influences members of society. A *society* refers to a group of people who interact with one another as members of a collectivity within a defined boundary and a highly structured system of human organization that helps to form the social structure.

Sociologists generally identify two components of culture: material and nonmaterial. Material culture refers to the physical, tangible creations of a society (e.g., clothing, merchandise, football stadiums, sporting equipment, automobiles, art, and so on). In societies obsessed by conspicuous consumption, the material culture plays a prominent role. A preoccupation with conspicuous consumption and conspicuous leisure leads to a consumer culture. The possession of material goods is, in essence, "social communicators" of cultural values. In this manner, a season ticket holder of a particular sports team is "socially communicating" to others that he or she has the time and money to support the team on a full-time basis.

Nonmaterial culture includes the more abstract creations of society, such as beliefs, values, ideology, and norms. To illustrate how these two components of culture work, let's examine the merits of building a new stadium. Most fans, owners and players value a new stadium with all the modern amenities over an old and deteriorating stadium. However, Boston Red Sox and Chicago Cubs fans love the character of their respective old stadiums and value the sentimentality of the stadium over the idea of a new luxury one. The point is, no matter what type of stadium one prefers, culture has played a role in that fan's preference.

There are other aspects of culture that sociologists examine. We will limit our examination to a few key aspects of culture that are of particular interest to the sociology of sport; specifically, symbols, language, cultural diversity, and subcultures. (Social norms, the rules that govern behavior, will be examined in Chapter 8, when we discuss the role of deviance in sport.)

SYMBOLS

The use of symbols is another important aspect of culture. *Symbols* are items that possess meaning and represent something else by association, resemblance, or convention to a people in a society. We come in contact with a large number of symbols on a daily basis, including road signs, parking instructions, male and female bathroom indicators, and so on. Members of a society generally share an understanding of the meaning behind symbolic representations. Emojis, often used with electronic forms of communication (especially when texting), are another example of symbols that have meaning for people who use them.

Sport, as an institution of society, is also consumed with symbolic gestures. For example, in baseball, it is common for a catcher to flash signals to the pitcher. Elementary signals include the index finger as symbolic of a fastball, two fingers for a curveball, and three fingers for change-up pitch. If a catcher flashes a sign for a fastball "down the middle" (directly over home plate) but the pitcher "reads" the sign as a pitch-out (throwing outside and away from the batter) the ball is going to sail away from the catcher's reach. The third base coach is responsible for flashing signs to the batter. If a "run and hit" (the base runner takes off immediately for the next base and the batter is supposed to "protect" the runner by swinging at the pitch—no matter what) is called by the third-base coach but the batter fails to recognize the symbolic meaning of the signs that the coach is flashing and does not swing at the pitch, the runner is "hung out to dry." Referees in sports use symbolic gestures. One of the most common referee symbolic gestures in football involves the ref raising both arms straight in the air signaling a touchdown. A soccer referee may pull out a yellow (warning) or red (suspension) card from his or her pocket and flash it toward a player indicating a violation has occurred. All soccer fans understand the significance of the red or yellow card symbolism. Trophies and championship rings become the ultimate symbols of achievement in sport. There is a cliché in certain sports that athletes play for "the ring." "It's all about the ring." Of course, it's not really the ring itself the player wants, even though it has monetary value, it's the symbolic meaning of being a champion that the ring represents. Anyone can order a "championship" ring (and some are available on eBay); it's the symbolic nature of the ring that is important to athletes.

LANGUAGE

Among the most important symbols used by a society are those that make up a language. Language is an abstract set of symbols that make up a body of words and provides systems for their common use by people who are of the same culture or society. The words you are reading right now consist of a number of symbols that have meaning for those who comprehend the English language. If we wrote this book in Russian (which consists of a different set of symbols) most Americans would not be able to read this text. Language is used to describe events, to express feelings and beliefs, and to convey the importance of specific values and norms. The language developed by a society reveals the aspects of culture that are deemed most important.

Just as language tells us a good deal about what is important and relevant to a culture, subcultural groups modify language to fit their needs. This is especially true in the world of sports, as all sports utilize language in a symbolic manner relevant to their domain. Tennis uses the term "love" instead of the number "zero." Thus, after an opening point has been won, the score is 15-Love. Soccer uses the word "nil" instead of "zero." Thus, after the first goal of a soccer match is made, the score becomes "one" to "nil." Baseball uses such expressions as: "Texas Leaguer" (a weak hit to the outfield), "can of corn" (a type of catch made in the field), "sacrifice bunt" (attempt to hit the ball in play to move a runner, rather than going for a "hit"), "grand slam" (a bases loaded homerun) and "infield fly rule" (a rule used with runners on base and less than two outs). Football uses such phrases as "blitz" (when the defense sends extra players to rush after the quarterback), "post pattern" (the receiver runs a pattern that ends near the goal post), and "going deep" (the receiver runs a long distance down the field).

Language is used to emphasize important aspects of the sport. It is also a method of introducing the basics of the sport to novice fans. As Extreme sports become increasingly commercialized, a language that reflects the events being played has developed correspondingly. The media (especially ESPN) encourages the use of subcultural language to convey the uniqueness of extreme sports. Examples include "no hander lander" (ending the trick ride without hands on handlebar), "back flip no handlebar" (doing a back flip without holding onto the handle bar), "360-tail flip" (a complete circle spin while shaking the back of the bike), and "double tail whip" (shaking the back of the bike twice while airborne). The colorful language used to describe extreme sports leads to judging based on subjective and aesthetic criteria (similar to such sports and figure skating and gymnastics) rather than objective and measurable criteria such as time, distance and score (e.g., track and field and the major team sports).

Sport language emerges from the obvious elements of sport (as described above), and terms and expressions developed over time by sport participants, fans, and clever announcers. One of the most colorful sports announcers of all time is the late voice of the Los Angeles Lakers, Francis Dayle "Chick" Hearn (1916–2002). Hearn, who "was instrumental in introducing professional basketball to Southern California sports fans when the team moved from Minneapolis in 1960," coined unique phrases that became known as Chickisms (Stewart 2002: D3). *Los Angeles Times* writer Larry Stewart compiled a list that included the following:

- *Slam dunk.* A shot that is thrust down hard into the basket
- *Airball.* A shot that badly misses the rim
- *Dribble drive.* A player is driving hard toward the basket
- *"No harm, no foul."* A player might have been fouled, but no damage was done, so no foul was called
- *Ticky-tack.* A foul not worth calling
- *Frozen rope.* A line-drive shot
- *"You can put this one in the refrigerator. The door's closed, the lights are out, the eggs are cooling, the butter's getting hard and the Jell-O is jiggling."* The game has been decided [Stewart 2002: D3].

Although sport language is vibrant, curse words remain the most colorful and troublesome. There are times when people find it necessary, no matter how inappropriate, to curse. Cursing is so common in English soccer that one British educator called for the games to be banned from television during daytime hours. English soccer officials have proposed a ban on cursing. Politicians have called for civility in English soccer. Martin Ward, deputy general secretary of the Secondary Heads Association, called the behavior of many English soccer players "very childish." England's Premier League players' union has even joined in for the call of proper language in soccer by printing posters urging its members to straighten up. Sports leagues and venues across the United States have also attempted to thwart the use of curse words. Spectators, especially in "family-friendly" sections of venues, can be kicked out of games if fellow spectators complain or if venue officials deem certain instances of cursing overly offensive. Many people involved in sports, including spectators, feel that they have the right to vent their displeasure at sporting events and this includes the right to use profanity. What do you think?

DIVERSITY OF CULTURE

Every culture found around the world possesses aspects that are unique when compared to others. The diversity of culture is the result of each society's adaptation to its specific natural environment (e.g., climate and geography) and a number of traditions, customs, routines, values and norms that develop over time a form a way of life for people. Some nations, such as Japan and South Korea, are referred to as homogeneous societies because they mostly consist of people who share a common culture, language, religion, ideology, customs, norms, and values. Conversely, some nations, such as the United States and Canada, are heterogeneous societies because they consist of people who do not universally share key social characteristics such as language, religion, race, ethnicity, politics, and economic backgrounds. Heterogeneous societies are likely to be characterized by conflict and tension, as behaviors that may have been acceptable in one's old culture are not acceptable in the host society. Each unique group tends to view their culture as the "best" and the others as inferior. Such an attitude is referred to as ethnocentric thinking. Ethnocentrism is the belief that one's own culture is superior to all others and is the standard by which all other cultures should be judged.

Cultural differences are often reflected in sport. This may include styles of play, the level of deference shown to authority figures, the willingness to "win at all costs" philosophy versus ideals of sportsmanship, and so on. As Luschen (1981) explains, "Games of strategy are found in societies where obedience [is stressed], games of physical skill in those where achievement is stressed. Individual sports would mainly qualify as games of physical skill and again show achievement as their basic cultural value. Team sports as well are games of strategy. Their relation to training of obedience would support exactly what we called earlier the value of collectivity" (291). The prevailing cultural value of the United States, as with other nations of the West, is winning and achievement. These cultural values are reflected in America's most popular sports.

SUBCULTURES

A subculture refers to a distinctive category of people within a greater culture that possesses its own cultural values, behavioral patterns, and other traits distinctive enough to distinguish it from the dominant group. Members of a subculture generally abide by the prevailing norms and values of the greater society, but distinguish themselves on a specific criterion that provides them with a sense of identity. There are many examples of subcultural groups, including athletes, gang members, drug users, students, and surfers. Members of a subculture identify one another in a number of ways, including greeting styles, outlooks on life, priorities in life, mannerisms, clothing, and language. It is their language, or jargon, that really helps to differentiate subcultural members. Surfers for example get "stoked" about "duck-diving" and executing an "alley-oop. "They don't want to "wipeout" or look like a "barney" in front of a "nugget" (Quintanilla 1998). Surfers understand this language, but others may not. Quintanilla (1998: D1) has compiled a list of surfer terms. Below is a sampling:

- *Air.* When the surfer and board take off into the air and land on the wave again
- *Alley-oop.* When a surfer rotates 360 degrees backward above the wave
- *Barney.* A clueless surfer
- *Duck-dive.* While paddling out, the technique of submerging the surfboard under oncoming waves
- *Filthy.* Flawless waves
- *Lineup.* The area where surfers linger for waves
- *Nugget.* An attractive member of the opposite sex
- *Stoked.* Excited
- *Wipeout.* Crash

In the United States, surfing is mostly a subcultural sport restricted, obviously, to beach communities. Thus, logic dictates that surfing will enjoy greater subcultural participation in California and Florida as compared to Nebraska and Iowa.

An interesting aspect about subcultural language and its usage is that as the popularity of a subculture increases, it begins to become mainstreamed in the greater society. From the list above, most people understand the expression, "I was stoked about my grade in class" or, "She was so out-of-control riding her bike down that hill so fast that it was inevitable she would wipeout."

Professional Sports and Their Relation to the Community

Community members generally have a strong emotional commitment toward their home professional sports team. They care a great deal about the outcome of a game, perhaps caring too much in some cases. Sports fans rejoice together in victory and console one another in defeat. They invest a great deal of leisure time following the fortunes and tribulations of their favorite teams. They believe in the old adage, "We'll get 'em next year." Year after year fans show up at the start of the season and support their team. They give freely of their time and energy because they have a feeling of loyalty and commitment to the team. But what if there is no next year? What if the fans are willing to show up, but the team is no longer there? Does professional sport have the same level of commitment and loyalty to its fans as the fans have for the professional franchise? Often, sadly, they do not.

The owners of professional sports expect the fans and taxpayers of the community to support them (frequently) unconditionally. The owners are motivated by greed and when they feel that they are not making enough revenue they threaten to relocate the franchise, hold the community "hostage" for better stadium deals and revenue sharing agreements, or use any number of other tactics to maintain their profit margin. What can the average fan do about such power moves? In short, nothing. They are powerless. The undying loyalty to the team does not guarantee permanence of the franchise. The shared history between a franchise and its community does not promise a continued relationship. Fans want to know that their team will be there next year, and the year afterwards. The problem with supporting a professional sports team in the United States and Canada is the realization that they may not be there next year. Stadium public address announcers excitedly yell at the start of a game, "And now, your…" But, let's realize that it's "your" team only as long as the owner wants "your" money. The following season the owner may want some other community's money. Consider, for example, the NFL, which celebrated its 100th anniversary on September 17, 2020. There have been 78 franchises in 60 cities that have played at 187 different venues throughout the history of the NFL. The growth of American cities and westward and southward expansion of the nation accounts for many new franchise locations; conversely, European nations with much longer histories have not experienced franchise relocation as the United States has.

Even when a team has a long history of support from the community, such as Brooklyn had with their beloved Dodgers that alone does not guarantee the stability of the franchise in a community. It was inevitable, of course, that the future most populous state would have MLB franchises but that did not make the fans of Brooklyn feel any better about losing their franchise. The Brooklyn Dodgers abandoned New York for California in 1958 because of civic inducement factors offered by the city of Los Angeles, even though Brooklyn fans were among the most loyal of all baseball fans. Although lacking in the mystique of the Dodgers, the cross town rival Giants would also leave New York City in the same year for California. New York City still has two MLB franchises so community members still have teams to cheer for but this is not the case for all cities that lose their franchises. Two New York State cities—Syracuse and Buffalo—lost NBA franchises and are still without such franchises. The Syracuse Nationals, an NBA championship team, lost their franchise to Philadelphia (76ers) and Buffalo lost the Braves to San Diego (the Clippers), who in turn, lost their franchise to Los Angeles. San Diego also lost its beloved NFL franchise (the Chargers) to Los Angeles in 2017. All across the mainland, one city after another has lost major professional franchises despite the loyalty of their respective fan bases.

Cities across the nation play host to countless professional sports teams at levels below the top tier and they too are subjected to the prospect and/or realization of relocation or elimination. Baseball has long claimed to be "America's pastime" and this declaration is not simply the result of its one-time status as America's favorite sport but rather, because the game is played at the professional level across the country in small and midsize cities. Baseball may be cutting its own throat if it follows through with its 2019 announcement that it would eliminate 42 minor league baseball teams, most of whom were either at the rookie level or short-season Class-A ball. Make no mistake about this, when these cities (and Delaney's hometown is one such city) lose their baseball teams there will be a huge void felt within the local communities. And sooner or later, that void will be filled, by a different sport or activity. The public was expected to learn of the fate of these sports franchises in early 2020 but the COVID-19 pandemic put all sports on hold beginning in mid–March and the minor league baseball season never did materialize that season. In late 2020, MLB made a new proposal that involved turning short-season (developmental leagues) minor leagues (i.e., the New York-Penn League) into short-season pro leagues that would use wood bats for college players adjusting from aluminum bats used in college baseball. The important thing to consider is that any scenario that involves decreasing the number of host professional minor league baseball cities results in fewer people following baseball and that means that both baseball and local communities lose out.

Assuming the community wants the franchise to stay, there is very little they can do to stop the owner from relocating a franchise. The city that put up the biggest fight to save a franchise was Cleveland. In 1996, Art Modell, the owner of the Cleveland football team, broke the hearts of tens of millions of Browns fans when he moved his franchise to Baltimore and named the team the Ravens. The city of Cleveland managed to secure the Browns' franchise name, colors, and history, and was awarded a new franchise in 1999, but it certainly wasn't the same thing. And die-hard Browns fans never did forgive Modell or the NFL (for allowing the move in the first place). To add salt to the wound, the Ravens, with many of the same players that played in Cleveland, would win a Super Bowl a few years later and they have gone on to become a successful franchise, much like the Browns once were. The "new" Browns have yet to enjoy success, making the playoffs just once in their first 20 years of rebirth. There is little wonder why the name Art Modell lives in infamy in Cleveland and why Browns fans despise the Ravens even more than their long-time rival the Steelers. Such are the repercussions of professional sports and their relation to the community.

Interestingly, franchise relocation is mostly a North American phenomenon. However, global soccer/futbol communities have a different worry, relegation. In most futbol leagues, the bottom teams of any particular division are demoted to the next lower division. In the English Premier League, for example, the bottom three teams of the 20-team league are relegated in any given season to the Football League Championship. In turn, three teams are promoted, the top two teams of the Football League Championship as well as the third place finisher. Relegation is devastating for the players, clubs, owner, and to the host city as a whole, as their collective self-esteem takes a hit, and the overall financial well-being of clubs is compromised. A soccer franchise may go bankrupt, but the new owner will keep the team in the same city.

Back in the United States, no community is safe from the realization that their beloved franchise may relocate. Fan groups, which come and go, and legislative attempts have failed to stop owners from moving their team from one community to another. The Professional Sports Community Protection Act of 1982, for example, has failed to stop franchise relocation (Johnson 1983). A number of municipalities have attempted to gain ownership of franchises through the laws of eminent domain, which enable municipalities and states to acquire private property, so long as the owner is compensated for the value of the property. This strategy has been tried and failed on a number of occasions: A Massachusetts lawmaker introduced legislation to seize the Boston Red Sox during the 1994 baseball strike; the city of Oakland attempted to stop the Raiders' move to Los Angeles; and the city of Baltimore challenged when the Colts fled to Indianapolis (Katz 1994; Euchiner 1993).

In 2008, Seattle went to court to stop the NBA's Super Sonics franchise from leaving the city. Seattle used the same legal principle—specific performance—that Cleveland used in 1996 to ultimately secure a replacement NFL team. The "specific performance" clause used by Cleveland against Art Modell stemmed from exact language in Cleveland's lease requiring that the Browns must occupy the stadium until the lease expired, and that a lease buyout was not an option. In 2008, the Sonics still had two years remaining on their contract. As it turned out, Seattle and Sonics fans shared the same fate as Cleveland and its fans—the franchise moved (in the case of the Sonics, to Oklahoma City) but the city retained the nickname, colors and records of the team. As of 2020, Seattle was still without an NBA franchise, however. (Note: Seattle was awarded a new NHL franchise starting in 2021 however and it is reported to have the nickname of the Kraken.)

Other team owners seldom speak out against franchise relocation because they realize they may want to move their own team someday if a better deal comes along. There are two possible solutions to ending franchise relocations, however. The first involves empowering the league commissioner with the authority to refuse to schedule games for the team that relocates. This will never happen because the owners pay the commissioner's salary; and they certainly are not going to give the commissioner power to supersede their wants and desires.

The best solution to keeping franchises in the communities that support them is to allow the community itself to own the franchise; not an individual or corporate ownership, but community ownership. If the team is really a representation of the community, let the community own it. The Green Bay Packers (NFL) have enjoyed this type of relationship within their community for several decades. In a city of just under 105,000 residents (in 2019), the business of football is secondary to the game of football, thanks mainly to the structure of Green Bay Packers, Inc., a publicly held nonprofit corporation with over 360,000 shareholders (no one is allowed to hold more than 200,000 of the more than 5 million shares). The Packers have a management team to run the franchise. Fans know that the team will not be relocating, and stadium concerns become public concerns because the money going in is shared through the revenue generated by tenants. All fans should be as lucky as Packers fans. The time has come for communities and fans to own the sport franchises that they cheer. Unfortunately for communities, the owners do not want to give up this type of power and it is not likely that many communities will own franchises in the near future.

Followers of college sports do not have to worry about their team relocating—although occasionally, sport teams are dropped from the program. This helps to explain why so many U.S. sports fans prefer to align themselves with college sports over professional sports.

The World Cup as a Global Community

The World Cup represents the pinnacle of achievement in the sport of *futbol*, forming a global community of highly invested fans from around the world. The WC is overseen by the Federation International Football Association (FIFA), the governing body. There is both a Men's and Women's WC. The popularity of "soccer," as Americans call it, rests primarily with its relative simplicity, a game that needs just a ball, a field (called a "pitch" in *futbol*) and any sort of makeshift goal that is played primarily by kicking a ball to teammates while avoiding defenders in attempt to score a goal. Unless you are a goalie, players may not use their hands while the ball is in play. American football, representing an advancement of technique and skill, allows players to kick, throw and run with the ball, thus increasing dramatically the level of complexity of the sport. Soccer, then, can be played around the globe by people from developed and developing nations alike and nearly any nation can assemble a reputable soccer team (in contrast, no other nation has mastered American football).

The Men's World Cup is an event that is held every four years and draws the attention of more than half of all the people on the planet. As described in Chapter 1, nearly 3.6 billion people watched the Men's World Cup on television in 2018. The Women's World Cup is also held every four years, one year after the men's and in 2019 enjoyed a viewership that surpassed one billion (1.12 billion) for the first time ever. The viewership of the 2019 Women's World Cup represents an increase of over 56 percent when compared to the 2015 Women's World Cup. The data reveals a great deal about the soccer's global popularity and the strides that women have made in the global sports world. We pointed out already (see Chapter 1) that the World Cup is rivaled only by the Olympics and acknowledged that while the Olympics consists of many sports with far more participating nations to draw from, the World Cup is a solidarity sport played by a limited number of national teams. The Men's WC includes 32 national teams (the host nation and 31 qualifying nations), while the Women's WC consists of just 24 national teams (the host nation and 23 qualifying national teams). The winning nation in World Cup competition receives the highly coveted FIFA World Cup Trophy—the most cherished of all championships trophies.

The World Cup brings with it some outstanding competitive matches and some of the most passionate fans imaginable. For soccer fans, a 0–0 draw can be as exciting as a 28–27 football game is for Americans. Americans tend to enjoy sports that lead to scoring and often find low-scoring soccer matches to be boring. But true soccer fans realize that the game is much more complex than scoring alone. They find a fascination with precision passing and great defense even if it does not lead to a score.

The first Men's WC was held in Uruguay in 1930. After the 1934 (Italy) and 1938 (France) World Cups, the games were interrupted by World War II. They resumed in Brazil in 1950 and have continued every four years since then. In the Foreword of *The Official History of the FIFA World Cup* (2019), FIFA president Gianni Infantino states, "There is simply nothing like the FIFA World Cup. There is certainly no other sporting competition—and arguably no single event in any area of society—with the power to trigger the passion of so many different people around the whole planet." Infantino also points out that the global importance placed on the World Cup is the cumulation of futbol passion found around the world. He adds to his comments in the Foreword, "I am not referring only to those four weeks during which the tournament is staged, when the convergence of passion and excitement overflows at once. The magic lies in how the outcome of that handful of matches somehow determines what millions of human beings will feel for years to come. It is a testament that creates archetypes and hones characters. It defines images and, eventually writes true history" (p. 7).

The 2018 FIFA Men's World Cup marked the 88th anniversary of this global sporting event but the history of FIFA dates back to 1904. Much like American football, which now places emphasis on the Super Bowl, there were championships held before these more publicized events. The first *futbol* championship was actually held in 1908 (FIFA World Football Museum 2019).

The FIFA Women's World Cup began its competition in China in 1991. Twenty-four national teams participate in the tournament under the current format and, like the Men's WC, the host nation is awarded an automatic slot and nations around the world compete for the 23 qualifying slots. As of 2021, the FIFA WC has taken place eight times in six countries, including the United States and China twice (Kiprop 2019). The U.S. Women's team is dominant, having won the first WC and the most recent, for a total of four titles followed by Germany with two titles and Norway and Japan as the only other two Cup winners. Japan's championship in 2011 (they beat the U.S.) represents the first Asian team to win a FIFA World Cup (men's or women's).

By all accounts, soccer is the most universally popular sport. The World Cup is the event that draws the attention of more than half of the planet's population. With the increased participation and interest in women's soccer, the World Cup represents the closest thing we have to a global community.

Tailgating as Community

While the World Cup stimulates gatherings of sports fans across the globe at local pubs, bars and house and office parties, American football games are highlighted by the very unique social gathering of sports fans at tailgate parties. The camaraderie experienced by tailgaters represents a true community marked by interpersonal relationships, conversations, games, tossing a football, and especially the consumption of food and drink. Ah, the tailgate.

Tailgating is mostly exclusive to football but also occurs at auto races and lacrosse games. For football fans especially, it is a near necessity to plan a pre-game tailgate, and this is true at college games and professional games (as well as many high school football games). And with all the football games played in the United States, there are literally thousands of tailgating venues throughout the season. While the vast majority of college football games are played on Saturday, is it common for some college teams to play one another on weekdays, especially Friday nights. The NFL has football every Sunday but also on Mondays and Thursdays. Occasionally, there is a football game being played at the collegiate or professional level every day of the week. High school football is generally played on Friday nights or Saturdays. The common thread among all these football games, especially collegiate and professional, is the realization that tailgate parties, spread across stadium and other nearby parking lots, will precede them all. It should also be noted that many spectators tailgate after the games are played as well.

While there are hundreds of football games played each week, hometown fans have limited opportunities to see their beloved local teams play. In the NFL, each team is only guaranteed eight regular season games spread across four months. Most major college teams have six to eight home games during the four-month regular season. Thus, football spectators treat each home game as a social event.

Tailgating at sporting events represents a type of secular sentiment that helps to bond fans together in collective action where ritualistic behaviors are the norm. As with the staging of any social event, there is a relative amount of planning involved, especially for the host of the tailgate. The first order of business is to secure a regular or predesignated spot for everyone to convene. Regular tailgaters often have a special lot they go to and are likely to have season parking passes to assure a regular spot. Organized tailgates (as opposed to the haphazard simple gatherings of folks with a beverage cooler and some simple food items) employ the "controlled menu" format of planning (this assures that the tailgate does not consist simply of chips and beer). While both of the authors of this text have tailgated often, Delaney has tailgated and played host at tailgate parties for nearly 40 years. He likes to have a list, and at the top of the list are the most crucial items to remember to bring: the grill and propane tanks for the grill (yes, we recognize that some people instead prefer charcoal grilling) and food to be grilled (people love hot food, especially when the weather cools).

A true American tailgate party must involve the grilling of some combination of meat (e.g., hot dogs, burgers, sausage, chicken, steaks, and/or ribs); conscientious tailgate hosts will make sure there is something for vegetarians and vegans to eat. The host must make sure there is "plastic-ware" (plates, eating utensils, red Solo cups!), napkins, paper towels, and trash bags. The host knows that regular attendees to the tailgate party can be counted on to bring their "signature" side dishes, desserts and special drinks. The host and regular guests will also bring tables to set up the food and anyone who needs a chair to sit in generally is expected to bring their own. Some tailgates necessitate a protective covering, like an Easy-up tent, to protect tailgaters from inclement weather and they may also bring portable heaters to keep folks warm. (Note: At Ole Miss, some tailgaters bring tents so that they can hang chandeliers over the tailgating tables covered in fine linen.) Other invited friends tend to bring their own beverage and snacks (e.g., chips, pretzels, and peanuts). Alcohol and other beverages for the tailgate are generally taken care of by the hosts and regular guests. By the time the tailgate begins, there is enough food and drink to embarrass most Thanksgiving meals. The feast will last for hours prior to kickoff.

Tailgate parties are social events intended for fun and will include a number of behaviors designed to form a community among fellow tailgaters. Tailgaters can be counted on to wear the team's colors and replica jerseys. Face painters and tailgaters who dress up with a certain "gimmick" (some type of "costume" that has special meaning to fellow fans) are often praised for their team loyalty. Some fans will fly the flag of their team high above the tailgate party as a sign to all of their allegiance to the team. Music serves as background white noise. Tailgaters may also participate in good-natured ribbing of nearby tailgaters who are supporters of the opposing team.

While the vast majority of tailgaters know how to party within reasonable limits of alcohol consumption, there are certainly those who get carried away and drink way too much and cause a ruckus. As is generally the case in any social arena, younger people are more likely to over-consume alcohol than older people. Lawrence and associates (2012), predictably, found that those university students who drank excessive amounts of alcohol while tailgating were more likely to engage in high-risk behaviors than students who did not drink. We would expect that college students who drank excessively at college parties would be more likely to engage in high risk activities than students who did not drink. The common thread associated with high risk activities is alcohol and not tailgate parties. College students tend to consider drinking alcohol during their college years as a type of cultural rite of passage; combine this cultural norm with peer pressure and it becomes unsurprising that high risk behaviors will occur. It is also foreseeable that males are more likely than females to engage in risky behaviors (CDC 2020; Alcohol.org 2019; Gerbi et al 2009). At NFL games, most tailgate parties are fun and "under control." However, it seems that many fan bases have that infamous group of tailgaters that draw the attention of the outside world. This is especially true of Buffalo's "Bills Mafia." Tailgaters among this group of hundreds engage in all sorts of high risk behaviors including jumping from the tops of RVs onto tables and running through fire pits. Nearly all media outlets, including

ESPN, have chronicled the exploits of this rowdy group (Grossman 2019). (It should be pointed out that while the Bills Mafia is known for its excessive partying, they have also raised huge amounts of money for various charities.)

Tailgating represents a community formed on bonds of friendship and family and for fans of a football team that generally losses, the tailgate may be the best part of the day, weekend, and even the week. Tailgating, essentially, represents the pinnacle of sports spectatorship. It is a crowning achievement of American sports culture. Beebe and associates (2010) go so far as to suggest that tailgating is itself a "sport." But, before tailgaters start thinking they are now athletes, remember the criteria we spelt out in Chapter 1. (Note: See "Connecting Sports and Popular Culture" Box 4 as we examine tailgating from the perspective of Homer Simpson.)

Sport Heroes

Who is a hero? A hero is usually someone who is admired for his or her achievement, courage, skill, dedication, or integrity. Heroes are recognized for feats of courage or notability of purpose, especially when one has sacrificed his or her own life for the betterment of others. But must one save another's life in order to qualify as a hero? Kirk Gibson is a hero to Dodgers fans. He did not save anyone's life to become a hero, but he did hit a dramatic walk-off homerun in his one and only plate appearance during the 1988 World Series and spearheaded Los Angeles to a World Series championship. Patrick Mahomes leading the Kansas City Chiefs to a dramatic fourth quarter victory over the San Francisco 49ers in Super Bowl LIV, played on February 2, 2020, will increasingly gain in legendary status as the years go on and most assuredly will secure his place as a hero. Should athletes even be considered heroes? Shaquille O'Neal once said that the only hero is a sandwich. Charles Barkley feels that a child's parents should be heroes, not athletes. Perhaps the word "hero" is used too freely in our culture. Just doing the right thing should not qualify someone as a hero, and yet, that is often the case. What if someone's job *is* to save lives (e.g., firefighters and police officers) and they do indeed save a life of another, is this person a hero, or doing what they are paid and trained to do?

The ancient Greeks, who coined the word, had a precise meaning and limits for "hero." A hero was a person who was descended from a god or goddess on one side of the family, and from a mortal on the other side. This definition is flawed, as the Greek gods never actually existed. But there are common themes in the various stories about heroes. Psychologist Otto Rank, in his influential 1909 book *The Myth of the Birth of the Hero,* argued that all cultures have heroic figures who share a similar story: they are fathered by supernatural beings and born to queens or goddesses but the birth is kept hidden; they are raised by either animals or people from a low status; they eventually discover their true origins and finally receive the proper honors due them after engaging in some significant courageous activity.

According to Webster's dictionary, a hero is a mythological or legendary figure endowed with great strength, courage, or ability, and favored by the gods. It also says a hero is a man admired for his achievements and noble qualities and considered in a literary or dramatic work. A heroine is a woman admired for her achievements and qualities, or the leading female character in a literary or dramatic work.

Baseball fans head into the National Baseball Hall of Fame and Museum in Cooperstown, New York.

Representatives of Culture

Heroes have existed in society since ancient times. The study of heroes in any given culture is very revealing, as the people proclaimed as heroes gain such a status because they reflect cultural ideals and values. As Leonard (1988) explains, "Cultural heroes or heroic archetypes typically manifest the major value orientations and symbols that a society holds in high regard.... Values provide directives and motivation for action; hence, it is predictable that cultural heroes, individuals who personify such values, become objects of admiration and emulation" (72). Heroes, then, reflect the character traits most desired by members of a society. In this regard, heroes help to reaffirm and maintain the social structure of a society by perpetuating cultural values and norms. As Crepeau (1985) elaborates, "The hero shows us what we ought to be, and we make him a hero because we wish to be what he is. He calls us beyond ourselves, toward the ideal" (76). Brown (2019) states that the world needs heroes who are just like us but yet possess the extraordinary capacity to make a profound difference. A hero is someone that we admire. Consequently, heroes are chosen whether they want to be or not. Conversely, someone cannot claim to be a hero. Such status needs to be conferred by others.

One difficult issue is the role which heroes play in a democratic society. Traditionally, heroes were either godlike figures or members of royalty who rise above the common crowd. How might heroes fit into a society which places emphasis on equality rather than superiority? In his book *The Hero in History,* philosopher Sidney Hook (1943) noted that "a democratic society has its 'heroes' and 'great men,' too. It is no more exempt from sharp political crisis than other societies, and rarely lacks candidates for the heroic role. It selects them, however, on the basis of its own criteria. Where a democracy is wise, it will wholeheartedly co-operate with its leaders and at the same time be suspicious of the powers delegated to them—a difficult task but one which must be solved if democracy is not to become, as often in the past, a school for tyrants" (14).

Contemporary American society views someone as a hero based on such criteria as achievement, courage and skill. Heroism also involves the ability to overcome extreme adversity, requires dedication and integrity, and involves a willingness to accept responsibility. With these qualities in mind, the authors define a *hero* as a person of distinguished courage or ability who is admired for brave deeds, noble qualities, outstanding achievement, dedication, integrity, or skill. Certainly, many athletes demonstrate these qualities. Sports heroes are admired and idolized figures in American society. The sports hero has become the central role model of young children and has gained enormous adoration from his or her fans. "Hero worship in sport is common and its manifestations are multitudinous.... The nature of the sport hero is the United States has changed throughout the present century and these changes mirror significant alterations in dominant cultural values" (Leonard 1988: 72). In the first half of the twentieth century sports heroes such as Jack Dempsey, Babe Ruth, Knute Rockne, Joe Louis, Lou Gehrig, and Joe DiMaggio "were all portrayed as embodying various positive qualities of the American character" (Crepeau 1985: 76). In the years following World War II, most sports heroes were clean-cut, modest, all–American boys like Johnny Unitas of the Baltimore Colts (Carroll 1999). By the end of the century, flamboyant, brash, and often boastful athletes (i.e., Joe Namath, who played in the NFL from 1965 to 1977; boxer Muhammad Ali, who became heavyweight champion in 1964 and referred to himself as "the Greatest"; and tennis player Andre Agassi who led the charge for athletes to promote a "style" as much as demonstrate athletic substance) became heroes. Many of today's athletes are brash and boastful and are fueled by a desire to achieve while drawing attention to themselves via flashy means.

There is a great deal of evidence to support the claim that athletes are among society's leading heroes. Children and young adults play video games (e.g., *Madden NFL 20, FIFA 18, NBA 2K18, UFC 3, Rocket League,* and *MLB The Show 18*) that include their favorite sports stars; sports enthusiasts seek autographs (sometimes to be sold at high prices on a variety of online sites and auctions); sports fans memorize statistics, read box scores, newspapers and sports features; attend publicity events; visit sport Halls of Fame (e.g., the NFL in Canton, Ohio, and MLB in Cooperstown, New York); watch sports videos on YouTube; fans collect trading cards; and many fans play "fantasy" sports. Fantasy sports are quite fascinating. (Note: Fantasy Sports will be discussed further in Chapter 16.) Fans will draft and trade "players" like real sports owners, belong to a fantasy league where records are kept, and compete against others. It's just a matter of time before someone creates a "Fantasy Hall of Fame"—one that can be visited only in cyberspace.

FUNCTIONS OF HEROES

Sociologically speaking, heroes represent culture and value components. By understanding a country's heroes, one has an idea of what is culturally important in that society. Heroes become representatives or symbols of a given culture. Thus, heroes serve many functions in society.

First, sport heroes help to perform a pattern maintenance function in society. Key beliefs and values such as hard work, achievement and success are essential in society and sport. Sport heroes are shining examples of these cultural beliefs. They shape our lives with lessons of their fervor and follies, their tragedies and triumphs (Chua-Eoan 1999). Second, heroes serve as agents of social control. Behaviors of heroes help to control, or at the very least, influence, other members of sport, as well as citizens of a society. Young athletes hear their coaches, parents and teammates say, "Why aren't you more like _____?" This particular person shows up for practice early, doesn't complain, accepts his or her role, and so on. In the film *Rudy*, high school and college teammates of Rudy constantly heard from their respective coaches about the heart and determination of Rudy, despite his overall lack of athletic talent. In this real-life–based story, Rudy served as an agent of social control because the coaches were able to use him as an example of how others should behave. Likewise, in the famous film version of the life of Notre Dame football coach Knute Rockne, Rockne inspires his team to victory by reminding them of their late teammate George Gip (played by future U.S. president Ronald Reagan), whose inspirational words were to "go in there with all they've got and win just one for the Gipper."

A third function of heroes is that they help to provide for social integration. It is often said that sports serve a valuable function to society by helping to bring disparate groups together. At ball games we will see spectators of all ages, races, ethnicities and social classes joined together while cheering for their shared favorite player or team. The social integration function is not limited to fans. In many ways sports was ahead of society in the integration of African Americans into mainstream society. Athletes such as Jackie Robinson, Larry Dolby, Jack Johnson, and Jesse Owens helped to change the course of sport and society and helped to shape the future of sports. These athletes are known as "political-social-athletic leaders" (Dorison 1997). The African American sport hero served as role models for black youth. Guidance from identifiable role models is imperative if the greater culture is to be assimilated.

Jack Johnson (1878–1946) is considered a sports hero because of his efforts to overcome white supremacy by defeating white boxers. Johnson inspired black youth to think that they too could attain success in a white dominated society. Johnson became the heavyweight champion of Negro boxing in the early 1900s. Jim Jeffries, the white champ at the time, refused to fight Johnson. After Jeffries retired, Johnson became heavyweight champion of the world when he defeated Tommy Burns in Australia in 1908. Johnson officially received the title in 1910 after he defeated Jeffries, who came out of retirement. Race rioting was sparked after the Johnson-Jeffries fight. Johnson was clearly a trailblazer in the attempt to integrate sport in the United States. He gave hope to all blacks that they might find an equal place in American society.

The Brooklyn Dodgers broke the color barrier in Major League Baseball by signing Jackie Robinson in 1947. But it was Harold "Pee Wee" Reese, Robinson's teammate, who showed the game and a nation how the integration process would be possible. Reese did this with a simple gesture of purposely putting his arm around Robinson's shoulders while he was enduring a high degree of harassment from Cincinnati Reds fans during a game at Crosley Field early in his career (Smith 1999). Reese, the Dodgers' captain, endured the wrath of some bigots for his thoughtful embrace, but he became a hero to others by taking a stand against racial injustices. At Reese's funeral (August 18, 1999) Rachel Robinson, widow of Jackie, said that she was not sure whether the integration of baseball would have worked without Reese (Whitmire 1999).

That athletes such as Jack Johnson and Jackie Robinson served as inspirations to many young African Americans leads us to the fourth function of heroes—they can serve as agents of social change. Colin Kaepernick is a contemporary example of a sports star that has influenced social change in sports and in the United States. During a home preseason game in August 2016, the San Francisco 49ers quarterback remained seated on the bench during the national anthem. When asked about it, he explained that he could not "show pride in a flag for a country that oppresses black people and people of color" and added that this concern was of greater importance than football (Boren 2020). The several shootings of unarmed black men that summer led to his decision. Kaepernick's demonstration would continue the following week in a preseason game in San Diego where he was joined by teammate Eric Reid and both players took a knee in silent protest. They decided to take a knee following a conversation with Nate Boyer, a former Green Beret and NFL player who thought taking a knee alongside his teammates was a better idea as soldiers take a knee in front of a fallen brother's grave to show respect (Boren 2020). Kaepernick received push-back from the NFL, most politicians and most fans. President Obama supported Kaepernick. Kaepernick would continue to protest peacefully throughout the season but eventually lost his starting position and was blackballed by NFL owners. He has not played professionally since the 49ers final game of that season, on January 1, 2017. However, with the rise of the Black Lives Matter massive social protests of 2020, the perception of Kaepernick switched from that of "un–American" to that of "an inspiration to others" (sans the negative conservative reaction held by some fans and politicians, including Donald Trump). (More on Kaepernick in Chapter 11.)

Serving as a source of identity is a fifth function of heroes. The once popular "Be like Mike" (Jordan) media campaign is an extreme example of heroes serving as a source of identity—the ad flat out said, *Be* like Mike. Athletes often serve as role models for youth. This is especially true among minority or discriminated persons. Former MLB player Roberto Clemente (1934–1972) instilled great hope to young Puerto Ricans. Clemente played for the Pittsburgh Pirates from 1955 to 1972. During the off season, Clemente would travel around his home island of Puerto Rico and conduct baseball clinics as a way of reaching out to youngsters. He spoke about the importance of sports, the importance of being a good citizen, and the importance of respecting parents (Feldman 1993). The economically poor Puerto Ricans were able to identify with Clemente because he was one of them.

Categories of Heroes

There are a number of categories of heroes. We will briefly review some of the more common types and offer suggestions of athletes that fit each category (you can decide for yourself who best fits each category). Perhaps the most identifiable category of sports hero is the *winner*. This type of hero is determined by outcome assessment—did he or she win a championship or individual honor of achievement? If yes, this athlete is winner. The emphasis is on outcome and not the processes that were involved to achieve such a winning performance. Some athletes are not always the most graceful while performing, or they may appear not to be the most physically talented, and yet, they find a way to win. Generally, such heroes become winners because of good old-fashioned hard work and dedication. Eli Manning, Drew Brees and Robert Horry are examples of this type of hero. Not all winners are necessarily heroes, however. Baseball legend Ty Cobb, for instance, was one of the greatest players in the history of the game, but it is usually noted that he was also violent, ungracious to other players and a bigot, and his own teammates often refused to associate with him.

Skilled performers are a second category of heroes. These athletes do possess exceptional skill. They give off an aura of invincibility and have usually psyched out the opposition by their mere presence. Surfer Kelly Slater, USA National Team; soccer goalie Tim Howard; tennis players Roger Federer and Serena Williams; NBA stars Kobe Bryant and LeBron James; soccer players Lionel Messi and Cristiano Ronaldo; and MLB star pitcher Clayton Kershaw and Angels outfielder Mike Trout are examples of skilled performers. The skilled performers generally perform exceptionally well every time they step on to the field/court and rise to the occasion of key events and big games. They are show persons for their sport and shine before an audience.

The hero of *social acceptability*, a third category, is admired because he or she upholds the values of society. Through their efforts on the playing field these athletes instill and uphold such beliefs as good sportsmanship and dedication. The hero of social acceptability often transcends the sport they participate in. Jesse Owens, at the 1936 Berlin Olympics, not only shattered Adolf Hitler's concept of Aryan superiority, but he also helped to unite whites and blacks in the United States. All Americans cheered for Owens because of his athletic prowess and his virtues. Heroes of social acceptability demonstrate great character and become excellent role models. Athletes that overcome personal tragedies and hardships and still perform admirably are especially admired. Athletes who give generously to charities, often without great fanfare, fall into this category of hero. Examples of athletes that give generously to charities were provided in Chapter 2 and included such players as J.J. Watt; LeBron James; Steph Curry, and John Cena.

The *group servant*, similar to a martyr, represents a fourth category of hero. The group servant is willing to put the needs of the team above individual needs, wants and desires. The group servant wants to do what is best for the team even if it means sacrificing individual statistics. Tim Duncan of the San Antonio Spurs (NBA) is an example of a group servant. He sacrificed his own numbers (e.g., points, rebounds, assists) early in his career while David Robinson was still on the team, and continued to do so with later stars like Manu Ginobili and Tony Parker, and through it all, he continued to win NBA championships. Many star athletes (i.e., Russell Wilson, LeBron James, Tom Brady, and Tim Duncan) take pay cuts (in the short term) to restructure their salaries so that the team can sign other players. Pat Tillman (former NFL player with the Arizona Cardinals) is an example of a group servant, for he gave up his own career, and ultimately his life, to serve the U.S. Army team, and thus, all of the United States. This is one of many reasons why a large number of Americans consider Tillman a hero.

Most people will not take life-threatening risks in their everyday lives; they do however, admire the risk takers. The *risk taker* category of hero is reserved for athletes who are inclined to place themselves in peril—and thus, become the object of fans' affection. Risk takers are found in many sports, especially in contact and extreme sports. For example, in football, a wide receiver who is willing to run a pattern across the middle of the field; in baseball, a catcher who will dive into the opponent's dugout for foul ball; and in basketball, a player who will drive the middle of the paint. Athletes who thrive on the action and danger of the game they play are risk takers. They give their all and they have no fear. Most extreme sport athletes are risk takers; snowboarder and skateboarder Shawn White is a perfect example of a risk taker. Examples of extreme sports athletes that fit the risk take category include: Ryan Doyle (parkour); Chris McDougall (BASE jumper); Xavier De Le Rue (big mountain snowboarder); William (Bill) Stone (extreme caver); Alex Honnold (free solo rock climber); and, Chris Sharma (rock climber). All professional race car drivers take huge risks every time they race. Passionate NASCAR fans have made heroes out of such drivers as Dale Earnhardt, Jr., Jeff Gordon, and Jimmy Johnson. Jackie Robinson took a huge risk, of a different type (especially in terms of the abuse he would take from fans), when he signed with the Brooklyn Dodgers and Colin Kaepernick is a risk taker by taking a very public stand (in this case, a knee) against police brutality. Cuban-born MLB star Yasiel Puig took a huge risk when he defected from Cuba and had to pay black-market smugglers to help him enter the United States (Eden 2014).

A sixth category of hero is the reluctant hero. The *reluctant hero* would rather lead by example (on the playing field) than by trying to motivate teammates with an inspiring speech, pep talk, or some other indirect method of leadership. These athletes are usually unselfish and assuming. They may, in fact, be shy individuals. Among the many examples of reluctant sports heroes are: Albert Pujols (MLB); Joe Thomas (NFL); J.J. Watts (NFL); and Alex Morgan (U.S. soccer). Road and track racing cyclist Bradley Wiggins is described by *The Telegraph* as an example of a British reluctant hero. So revered is this unassuming sports hero that he was knighted as Sir Bradley Wiggins (Hayward 2012). *The Guardian* described South African Caster Semenya, who won the world 800m title in 2009, as a reluctant hero because of the attention she drew as an intersex athlete. Semenya became a spokesperson of sorts for intersex persons when it was revealed that she was made to undergo gender testing to determine whether she was a "woman" or a "man" (Kessel 2011). Decades ago, baseball great Lou Gehrig, the "iron man" and "the Pride of the Yankees," was also known for his quiet competence and dedication to the game.

The *charismatic hero* represents a seventh category. The charismatic hero is "viewed as exceptional, autonomous and unique, as endowed with super-human powers, and commanding a divine violence…. The triumphant moment of charisma is the moment of effervescence on the part of the community of followers. They hail, cheer, cry and try desperately to touch or be close to the heroes" (Giesen 2005: 276–277). The charismatic sports hero possesses unique qualities that distinguish him or her from the rest of the group. This person need not be the most talented on the team, but is likely to be the team captain, or clubhouse leader. The charismatic hero is often the fan favorite and media darling. Examples include: Lindsey Vonn (skier); LeBron James (NBA); Baker Mayfield, Odell Beckham, and Patrick Mahomes (NFL); Tiger Woods (PGA); and Vladimir Guerrero, Jr., Bryce Harper, Miguel Cabrera, and Mike Trout (MLB).

Perhaps the most fascinating category of hero is the *anti-hero*. What makes the anti-hero such an enigma is the fact that he or she does not demonstrate the desired values or norms of society and yet still possesses a fan following. Traditionally, heroes have been noted for outstanding achievements, bravery, nobility of actions, moral and intellectual qualities, or some other contribution to society that has improved the quality of life for others. But hero identification is specific rather than diffused, and in most instances the hero is not a model of behavior in other spheres of social life. The anti-hero is the opposite of the group servant. The anti-hero thinks of him or herself first and the team second. The anti-hero is "someone who says that he does not need other people" (Crepeau 1985: 77).

The sports world has had its share of anti-heroes dating back at least as far as Ty Cobb and continuing on with such colorful characters as Pete Rose, Billy Martin, John

McEnroe, Tonya Harding and former Chicago Bulls player Dennis Rodman who was noted for his bizarre behavior, including multiple body-piercings and numerous tattoos (before they became fashionable), and general unprofessional conduct. Yet this "bad boy" of basketball was a hero to many people because of his insubordination and colorful antics. Even in retirement, Rodman remains in the spotlight because of his odd friendship with North Korean Supreme Leader Kim Jong-un. There is a seemingly growing list of anti-heroes in contemporary sports, including Floyd Mayweather, Kyrie Irving, Conor McGregor, Colin Kaepernick, Kobe Bryant, Kyle Busch, Hope Solo, Tony Stewart, and Uruguay soccer player Luis Suarez who has been known to literally bite opponents during play (including the 2014 World Cup). As we can see from these examples, some athletes that might be considered anti-heroes to some people, such as Kobe Bryant and Colin Kaepernick, may be seen as examples of skilled performers (Kobe Bryant) and risk takers (Colin Kaepernick) by others.

Heroes Survey Data

In 2020, Delaney and Madigan replicated their 2005 and 2014 research and the 1994 and 1999 research conducted by Delaney (1999) on college students and whether they have heroes. Students were asked whether they had a sports hero when they were younger and if they had one currently. Respondents were also asked whether they presently have a hero of any kind, other than a family member or religious figure. In addition, students were asked whether or not they believe that there are as many heroes in this country today as in the past. Due to the 2020 SARS-CoV-2 pandemic, we could not conduct as many surveys as in the past.

The data in Table 4.1 reveals that a higher percentage of males report having had a hero when they were young compared to females in each of the five sample years. Only in the 1994 survey did more than half (62 percent) of all females report having a sports hero in childhood; and 2014 represents the lowest percentage (28 percent) in the four years.

Table 4.1. Did You Have a Sports Hero in Childhood?
(in percent. 1994 N = 199 [82 males, 117 females];
1999 N = 201 [97 males, 104 females]; 2005 N = 239 [110 males, 129 females];
2014 N = 199 [83 males, 116 females]; 2020 N = 124 [60 males, 84 females]

	1994		1999		2005		2014		2020	
	Yes	No	Yes	No	Yes	No	Yes	No	Yes	No
Males	79	21	64	36	69	31	72	28	73	27
Females	62	38	36	64	35	65	28	72	40	60

As people age, they are less likely to view sport athletes as heroes. The data in Table 4.2 reveals that the percentage of respondents, both males and females, who report currently having a sports hero drops significantly compared to childhood. In each of the sample years the pattern holds true that males still are more likely to report having a sports hero than are females.

In past years, respondents were also asked to indicate who their sport hero was, if they had one. (We did not ask this question in 2020 due to time constraints as our respective colleges were closing due to the pandemic.) The list of all these different athletes is not provided here, but a startling and sociologically significant pattern, first noted in

1999, has continued in 2005–100 percent of all male respondents who indicated having a hero named a male hero. In contrast, only 50 percent of females in the 1994 study had a same-sex hero. In 1999, this figure rose only slightly to 53 percent. Consequently, not a single male reported having a female hero, while one-half of females had males for a sport hero. Delaney (1999) had anticipated that the number of women who report having a female sports hero would increase throughout the 2000s with the continued growth of girls and women's sports. The 2005 results were surprising, as only 40 percent of reporting females identified a female as their sports hero. Among the questions raised by this data are: do males really not see females as hero-material, or are they worried about a possible negative label from male cohorts if they identify with a female as a sports hero? Further, why do so many females report male athletes as heroes? In 2014, respondents were simply asked whether they currently had a sports hero, but not to identify any specific hero. This survey resulted in the largest percentage (62 percent) of males reporting that they currently had a sports hero. The numbers of females reporting to have a current sports hero was nearly identical to the 2005 survey with just 25 percent saying that they did have a sports hero.

Table 4.2. Do You Have a Sports Hero Currently?
(in percent. 1994 N = 199 [82 males, 117 females];
1999 N = 201 [97 males, 104 females]; 2005 N = 239 [110 males, 129 females];
2014 N = 199 [83 males, 116 females]; 2020 N = 124 [60 males, 84 females]

	1994		1999		2005		2014		2020	
	Yes	No	Yes	No	Yes	No	Yes	No	Yes	No
Males	54	46	35	65	40	60	62	38	60	40
Females	38	62	14	85	24	76	25	75	32	68

In Table 4.3, male and female responses were combined to answer the question, "Do you currently have a hero (other than a family member or religious leader)?" We had speculated, following the 2005 survey that since the events of September 11, 2001, there was a groundswell of support for people who act admirably in the light of terrorist events since 1999. The 2014 and 2020 survey results indicate that an even greater percentage of respondents report currently having a hero other than a family member or religious leader. In light of the Black Lives Matter social movement we expect to see this trend continue in the future.

Table 4.3. Do You Currently Have a Hero
(other than a family member or religious leader)?
(in percent. 1999 N = 201; 2005 N = 239; 2014 N = 199; 2020 N = 124)

	Yes	No
1999	24	76
2005	51	49
2014	58	42
2020	60	40

Respondents were asked whether they believe people have as many heroes in this country today as in the past. The data in Table 4.4 reveals a consistent pattern that far fewer believe we do have as many heroes today as in the past. This is an interesting development as Table 4.3 reveals that in 2005, 2014, and 2020 a significant higher number of respondents reported to having a current hero (especially compared to 1999) even though in Table 4.4 they indicated we do not have as many heroes as in the past.

Table 4.4. Do We Have as Many Heroes Today as In the Past?
(in percent. 1999 N = 201; 2005 N = 239; 2014 N = 199; 2020 N = 124)

	Yes	No
1999	30	70
2005	41	59
2014	39	61
2020	40	60

ARE WE WITNESSING THE DEMISE OF THE SPORTS HERO?

Heroes have existed for a long time. Flattering stories and generous embellishment of the facts over any given period of time eases the accession of mortal beings to hero status. Often, these tales of accomplishments were unchallenged, further enhancing heroes to legendary proportions. Heroic behaviors in one sphere of life were assumed to carry over to all other spheres as well. When a person displayed an admirable trait in one field, it was assumed (or ignored) that this person must demonstrate the same qualities consistently in all endeavors. Newspaper writers wrote heroic stories of such icons as Babe Ruth and Mickey Mantle, leaving their personal shortcomings out of print and away from the public's knowledge. Mickey Mantle, for example, admitted in 1985, years after his retirement that most players can look back on their career and say that they gave it their best; he could not do that. He admitted that he never worked out or trained as he should have. He went boozing regularly. The general public was unaware of this. Mantle was a hero for many kids growing up in the 1960s. The truth was revealed in 2005, in an HBO 60-minute presentation on Mickey Mantle, titled *Mantle*. Bob Costas stated, "On the ball field there was something very dignified and heroic about the way he carried himself. But Mickey's life overall was not always a study of dignity" (Poliquin 2005).

Today's heroes (in all fields) have a higher risk of having their private lives become public than heroes of the past did because of the ever-growing presence of the social media and the athletes themselves often creating controversies because of the posts they make on social media platforms. As a result, their star status is in constant risk of burning out. For example, if a hero does something deviant (e.g., gets drunk at a bar and does something foolish) he or she is likely to have it revealed by the traditional or social media outlets. No athlete is immune from media coverage and the sports hero (or any other type of hero) seldom holds the mythical status once enjoyed. We know about the private aspects of public persons, and consequently they do not stand apart from us anymore. Thus, the media, especially social media, has as much impact in the potential demise of a hero as it does in creating and expressing the existence of one. On the one hand the media may help to create an image of a sports star as some type of larger-than-life character that we should admire because of their athletic ability; on the other hand, the media cannot wait to air dirty laundry capable of crushing the once positive image they created of an athlete for their audience's consumption. Sport stars are treated like any other celebrity, a life to be consumed. As a result, many athletes see themselves as celebrities that need to entertain the public. And while athletes want to be celebrities, celebrities want to be athletes. ESPN found a way to combine them both with their annual production of the

ESPYs. This award ceremony combines celebrities—who hand out the awards—with athletes. It seems that each group wishes to be the other!

Earlier in this chapter, the authors offered examples for each of the categories of heroes; and while it is true that readers may have their own ideas as to which athletes best fit each category, there is one thing we all have to consider—their potential fall from grace. For instance, at one time, the authors, along with most Americans, considered Lance Armstrong a hero (i.e., the hero of social acceptability). After all, his achievements both on the bike (he won an unprecedented seven straight Tour de France bicycle races only to later have them stripped away) and off (he became an inspiration to those with cancer because he successfully won his battle against life-threatening testicular cancer that had spread to his lungs, abdomen, and brain) earned him acknowledgment as a hero. However, once we learned that he had indeed cheated (he admitted to taking performance-enhancing drugs) throughout his famed career he fell off his pedestal as if he had crashed down a mountain cliff in Col du Tourmalet. He has yet to fully recover from his fall from grace because of his dismissive attitude. Another example of a seemingly obvious sport hero is swimmer Michael Phelps, the most decorated Olympian of all time (currently at 22 total medals). However, in 2014 he was arrested for speeding, crossing double lane lines and suspicion of DUI after failing a field sobriety test. His 2014 arrest for DUI added to his list of unacceptable behaviors, a list that includes a previous drunken-driving arrest a decade earlier, and a published photograph of him in a British tabloid smoking marijuana from a bong (pipe) (*The Citizen* 2014a). These two stories should serve as an alarm that just because someone (e.g., an athlete) performs heroic in athletics does not mean they are a true hero in life. Of course, the same thing can be said about a hero from any walk of life. A firefighter, police officer, military personnel, religious and political leader, teacher or individual from any other background may act heroically in one sphere of life, but that does not guarantee they act heroically in all spheres.

It sounds as though we are proclaiming the demise of the hero, but that is not completely true. We *are* sounding the alarm that we have to be careful about who we choose to treat as heroes while also pointing out that heroic deeds performed as an athlete do not imply immunity from poor behaviors in other areas. However, we are also supporting the idea that there are indeed many people in society acting heroically, and this includes athletes. Sports fans seem to want a hero, a person that can burden the expectations of a fan base that dreams, desires or demands a championship and thus justifies the time, effort and passion fans exert.

Cleveland Cavaliers fans, for example, so desperate and so deserving of a professional sports team championship from their hometown city, placed their collective hopes on hometown favorite LeBron James to bring them an NBA Championship. (James is actually from nearby Akron, Ohio.) James was selected number one in the 2003 NBA draft straight out of high school. He played with the Cavs until 2010 when, after bringing many exciting playoff appearances but no titles, he announced, in a very public manner, that he was leaving Cleveland to "bring his talents" to Miami. Cavs fans specifically, and all Cleveland sports fans in general, were devastated by the announcement. They felt betrayed. They burned their James jerseys. They tore down his banners. They cried. They cursed James. They begged him to say it wasn't true. Every emotion you can think of, the Cavs fans experienced. Their beloved hero had purposely broken the hearts of fan base that idolized the man. It seemed like the person you loved had broken up with you for another lover. James as a hero, the idea of anyone as a hero, had demised.

Then the unthinkable happened. Like a long-lost beloved pet, or the love of your life coming back to you, James announced, again very publicly (James's letter, titled "I'm Coming Home," was published in *Sports Illustrated* on July 21, 2014), that he was returning to Cleveland, the city he spurned years earlier. He had been in sunny Miami and won two titles, but now he promised to move back to the snow and cold and win titles there. The fans very eagerly accepted him back. All was forgiven, or mostly, forgiven. After all, the hero had returned to save the day. James did help the Cavs win a title in 2016. The king was reborn. And then, he left again, this time for the glamour and glitz of the Los Angeles Lakers. Cavs fans were left to decide whether the glass was half empty or half full; but the city of Cleveland did finally have a NBA championship. As for James, he did lead the Lakers to their franchise's 17th NBA title (tying them with the Boston Celtics for the most titles in NBA history) at the conclusion of the 2019–20 season. It was a season like no other in that it was the longest season ever (356 days from start to finish) as a result of the COVID-19 pandemic and it was played in a "bubble" format that lasted over three months for the two Finals teams (Lakers and Miami Heat). James also became the third NBA player (Robert Horry and John Salley were the other two) to lead three different franchises to NBA titles and he won his NBA Finals fourth MVP award.

The study of a society's heroes is indeed quite revealing, as the attributes possessed by a hero reflect the values and norms of the greater culture. We often judge a society by the individuals it holds up as its own exemplars, so learning about those individuals granted heroic status by their own fellow citizens can be highly educating and a cause for further reflection.

Connecting Sports and Popular Culture

Box 4: Tailgating with *The Simpsons*

Early in this chapter we discussed tailgating and its ability to help form a sense of community among tailgating participants. Tailgating is a time-honored tradition in the United States that combines fandom, celebration, and bonding over two behaviors that Americans love to do—eating large amounts of food and consuming large sums of alcohol. People may paint their faces, wear team colors and boast of their favorite team's upcoming victory.

No one knows for sure when the first sports tailgate party began, but it's a good bet that tailgating was involved at the very first collegiate football game between Princeton and Rutgers played at New Brunswick, New Jersey, on November 6, 1869. According to the American Tailgater Association (2014), Rutgers fans showed up at the game wearing scarlet-colored scarves (converted into turbans). However, these fans did not grill and drink in nearby paved-parking lots.

Contemporary tailgaters drive to the football game with their vehicle filled with food and drink and seek out their favorite tailgating spot in a parking lot near the stadium. Tailgating at football games is like picnicking but instead of a comfy blanket on a grassy field, tailgaters cook up a feast on a parking lot. This may seem like an odd thing to do; after all, who picnics at a parking lot under any other circumstances? Football tailgating, however, is not like any other circumstance or experience, for that matter.

America's favorite animated family, the Simpsons, also like to tailgate; or at least, father Homer likes to tailgate. In *The Simpsons* (2008) "Any Given Sundance" episode, we see Homer Simpson preparing to take his family to Springfield Stadium where arch-rivals Springfield University and Springfield A&M will meet on the gridiron. (*Futbol* may be played on a pitch, but American football is played on a gridiron; advantage, American football!) Homer is very excited and eager to get an early start on tailgating. He hustles his family out of their early morning sleep and packs them in the car already full of food and beverage. Speaking aloud what his other family members, other than Homer, are privately thinking, Bart says, "Why are we arriving so early? The game doesn't start for hours." Homer laughs at his son's complaint and proudly proclaims, "We're not here for the *game*. The game is nothing. The real reason we Americans put up with sports is for this. Behold the tailgate party! The pinnacle of human achievement. Since the dawn of parking lots man has sought to stuff his guts with food and alcohol in anticipation of watching others exercise." Homer goes on to proclaim the gloriousness of eating "trunk meat"—a very interesting term of endearment for the food about to be grilled because it was packed away in the trunk of people's cars.

Homer, perhaps representing the sentiment of tailgaters everywhere, proclaims, "What could be greater than eating and drinking for hours in a drizzly parking lot?" The authors toast you, Homer Simpson, and all the other tailgaters eating trunk meat on a parking lot. And if you ever get the chance to join either of us, we put on great tailgates!

SUMMARY

Culture refers to the shared knowledge, values, language, norms, and behavioral patterns (customs) of a given society that are passed down from one generation to the next and form a way of life for its members. The institution of sport contains all of these same elements and is firmly ingrained into a society's culture. Each society across the globe possesses its own unique culture and these cultural differences are often reflected in sport.

Sports also play an important role in local communities and in this chapter, we paid particular attention to professional sports. In North America, primarily the United States and Canada, local communities often have to worry about franchise relocation. Franchise relocation occurs mainly because greedy owners seek higher profits and are willing to sever the communal bonds between a sports franchise and the loyalty of local fans. Seemingly, any franchise, but especially in smaller markets, is ripe for relocation if owners receive financial enticements to move their teams.

There are some sporting events, such as the Olympics and the World Cup, that help to form a global community. The World Cup draws the largest global audience for any single sports event, soccer (*futbol*). The Men's World Cup drew nearly 3.6 billion viewers in 2018 and the Women's World Cup surpassed the one billion mark for the first time ever.

A characteristic of American football, and many race events, is the tailgate party. Tailgating occurs for hours before the kickoff of a football game and often is resumed following the game. It involves groups of fans who get together in parking lots outside the stadium and is centered on plenty of food, beverages, games, and great conversations.

While some tailgating parties may get rowdy because of the over-consumption of alcohol among those who would have drank in excess elsewhere anyway, the vast majority of tail-gate parties are good-humored, communal events.

The study of heroes is very enlightening as those labeled as a "hero" reaffirm the cultural values and social expectations of society. Heroes then, are representatives of culture. Heroes serve many functions including, helping to perform pattern maintenance; agents of social control; social integration; social change; and as a source of cultural identity. The authors have been collecting data on sports heroes for more than 25 years and shared their data in this chapter. They have identified eight different categories of heroes: the winner; skilled performers; social acceptability; group servant; risk takers; the reluctant hero; charismatic hero; and, the very intriguing anti-hero.

KEY TERMS

Culture The shared knowledge, values, language, norms, and behavioral patterns of a given society that are handed down from one generation to the next and form a way of life for its members.

Diversity of Culture The result of each society's adaptation to their specific natural environments (e.g., climate and geography) and a number of traditional customs, habits, values and norms that develop over time to form a way of life for people.

Hero A person of distinguished courage or ability who is admired for brave deeds, noble qualities, outstanding achievement, dedication, integrity, or skill.

Heterogeneous Societies Consist of people who are dissimilar in regard to social characteristics such as religion, race, ethnicity, politics, and economic backgrounds.

Homogeneous Societies Consist of people who share a common culture and are generally from similar social, religious, political and economic backgrounds.

Language A set of symbols that can be strung together in an infinite number of ways that expresses ideas and abstract thoughts and enables people to think and communicate with one another.

Material Culture The physical, tangible creations of a society, such as clothing, merchandise, football stadiums, sporting equipment, automobiles, and art.

Nonmaterial Culture The more abstract creations of society, such as beliefs, values, ideology, and norms.

Social Norms The cultural rules and expectations that govern behavior of a particular group of people.

Society A group of people who interact with one another as members of a collectivity within a defined boundary and a highly structured system of human organization that helps to form the social structure.

Subculture A distinctive group within a greater culture that possesses its own cultural values, behavioral patterns, and other traits distinctive enough to distinguish it from the dominant group.

Symbols Items that possess meaning and represent something else by association, resemblance, or convention to a people in a society.

Tailgating A time-honored tradition that combines fandom, celebration, and bonding among a gathering of people, usually in parking lots outside of a stadium prior to a sporting event where large amounts of food and beverage are consumed.

DISCUSSION QUESTIONS

- How would you describe the culture of your society?
- What are some of the differences between material and nonmaterial cultures? Think of some examples relating to a specific sports team—what would be the material and nonmaterial aspects of the team?
- Identify some of the symbolism used in the sports world.
- How does language help members of a subculture identify one another?
- List some recent examples where sport has helped to unify a community, and where it has divided a community.
- Why are sport franchises important to communities? Should owners be allowed to move their franchise to another city? Do the owners owe the loyal fans of a franchise the same sense of loyalty?
- Do you think that athletes should be considered as "heroes" in modern-day societies? What do you think are the characteristics of a hero?
- Why are so many "anti-heroes" in sports admired by the general public?
- Provide an example of a contemporary athlete that best fits each of the categories of heroes discussed in this chapter.
- Do you feel that sports heroes are as important today as in the past? Why or why not?
- Have you ever tailgated? If so, how would you describe the experience?

CHAPTER 5

Socialization and Sport

A father is telling a story to his young children about his favorite football player, and hero, Jim Brown. As he tells of the legendary running skills of Brown the father becomes increasingly excited reminiscing about past glory. His enthusiasm is contagious. The children eagerly pry their father for more details, as if listening to a favorite bedtime story. The heroic tale told by the father will influence his children for some time. As they grow older, whenever these children hear the name "Jim Brown" they will think of him as a hero based primarily on the testimony of their father. Soon, these youth will search for their own "bigger than life" person to admire, just as their father did.

If you are a true fan of football it is likely that you have heard of Jim Brown and know him as a former great NFL running back. And yet, it is highly unlikely that any of you remember seeing him play. Many young Cleveland Browns fans know of Jim Brown but they will choose their own contemporary player (i.e., Baker Mayfield or Nick Chubb) to admire just as young Green Bay Packers fans admire Aaron Rodgers, Kansas City Chief fans admire Patrick Mahomes, and Houston Texans fans admire J.J. Watt. Those who admire athletes were socialized into this social realm and have learned to admire the exploits of their favorite players.

The Socialization Process

Despite the focus on early childhood development favored by psychologists, sociology teaches us that the developmental process is actually a life-long (from infancy to old age) progression of learning via the socialization process. Consequently, *socialization* is defined as a continuing process of social development and learning that occurs as individuals interact with one another and learn about society's expectations of proper behavior so that they can participate and function within their societies. At the micro level, the socialization process also enables an individual an opportunity to acquire a personal identity wherein he or she learns the norms, values, behavioral expectations, and social skills appropriate to his or her social position. Thus, an athlete is expected to conform to certain expectations that correspond to her role, just as a coach is expected to conform to specific expectations attached to his role.

Every person we come in contact with, either directly (face-to-face) or indirectly (e.g., mass media), has influence over our behavior. However, socialization is most effective when enforced by significant others—family, peer groups, schools, the mass media, and so on. We learn *directly* through socialization, trial and error, and behavioral reinforcement, and we learn *indirectly* by observing others (modeling). All of these aspects of learning are components of socialization wherein we learn about cultural norms, values, and societal expectations.

At the macro level, socialization is critical for the survival and stability of society, as it is critical that members of a society are socialized to support and maintain the existing social structure. Furthermore, it is through the socialization process that members of a society learn about culture. Thus, just as children learn about culture from their parents (or other primary caregivers), these same children will some day grow up to become adults who must teach the next generation. In this manner, culture reproduces itself.

But what if the culture that is reproducing itself is dysfunctional to some members of society? In such situations, people may rise up to challenge the status quo, and they may teach the next generation that change is necessary. Those who are upset with current societal inequalities will attempt to educate others why change is necessary. Such is the case with the global "Black Lives Matter" social movement. Those who were disadvantaged by an old system decided to claim the power that comes with collective action.

Whether we are talking about accepting old customs, values and norms or new ones, the effectiveness of the socialization process is predicated by the need for individuals to internalize the messages being sent to them. Messages become internalized when people react automatically to certain stimuli. For example, when teaching the fundamentals of running the bases in baseball, young (or new) players are taught that they must "tag" before advancing from one base to the next following a fly ball out. Players are also taught that when there are two outs they run as soon as the ball is hit into play. Before long, players do not need to be reminded of such fundamentals because they have internalized the norms of base running. This is why it is so frustrating to others when an experienced player forgets (or makes a mental error) the fundamentals of the game.

The Nature-Nurture Continuum

How does the socialization process work? That is, are we born (the nature perspective) with the knowledge of a culture's norms and values? And, is our behavior predestined? If this were true, there would be no need for a learning process, as a society's social expectations would be innate and so too would our behavior. Or, must we learn (the nurture perspective) about the demands and expectations of society? And, consequently, is our behavior a matter of free will that others will attempt to shape and modify? Sociologists lean heavily on the nurture end of the continuum. While it is true that biology dictates a number of physical attributes of an individual (e.g., skin color, hair color, eye color, ancestry and potential hand size) and plays a role as to whether or not an individual is mentally capable of learning, it does not dictate behavior. The nurture perspective states that socialization and reinforcement, experience (trial and error), modeling, and motives—in short, the social environment—determines human behavior. Sociologists argue that humans are free to make their own decisions and therefore our behavior is not predetermined by biology.

As a point of illustration, let's say a child wants to become a professional athlete. Will they become a professional athlete because they were born to be an athlete or will they become an athlete because they work hard at attaining this goal? All athletes, even Michael Jordan (who was once cut from his high school basketball team), rely on individual effort, good coaching and encouragement, and not some natural biological or

Tailgating at football games is a great way to socialize the next generation into sports.

genetic predisposition to play ball. "The notion of a natural or 'born' athlete is mislead-ing because it belies the fact that individuals must learn a host of social, psychological, and kinetic movements associated with a particular activity. Typically, an individual is referred to as a 'natural' if he or she possesses the 'tools' or motor skills (i.e., coordination, agility, speed, strength, power, and stamina) enabling one to perform sport feats with rel-ative ease" (Leonard 1988: 112). Clearly, possessing certain physical attributes (e.g., in bas-ketball, having significant height and large hands to palm a ball) are important, but so too are socio-psychological skills such as desire, opportunity, coaching and encouragement, to mention just a few. Being tall is not much of an asset in basketball if the individual is not willing to run up and down the court to play ball. (The topic of genetics will be dis-cussed in further detail in Chapter 11.)

Primary and Secondary Groups

What if someone tells you, "I am very disappointed in your behavior?" Does such a statement bother you more if expressed by someone close, like a parent, sibling, significant other, or best friend, or if it is expressed by a complete stranger? Most of us are more concerned about the sentiments and opinions of someone close rather than someone who hardly knows us. This is because the people closest to us are supposed to know us the best. The people closest to us are known as significant others and primary groups consist of these significant others. Because primary groups have the greatest effect on us, socialization is most effective when taught by significant others. A *primary group* may be defined as a relatively small group of significant others with whom members share a sense of "we-ness," intimacy, and mutual identification.

Charles Cooley (1909), an early symbolic interactionist, described primary groups as "those characterized by intimate face-to-face association and cooperation.... The result of intimate association, psychologically, is a certain fusion of individualities in a common whole, so that one's very self, for many purposes at least, is the common life and purpose of the group" (23). It is the face-to-face association between group members and the high degree of intimacy (especially when compared to non-primary individuals) that leads to a sense of "we-ness." Every one of us uses various expressions with "we" in it. For example, "We went to the game last night"; "We won our game today"; or "We wished my brother a happy birthday." Think about how many times you have used the word "we" in a conversation as a means of identifying yourself with a group of significant others. Chances are it is far more common than you might suspect.

As of point of clarification, Cooley (1909) highlighted five fundamental properties of a primary group: face-to-face association, unspecified nature of associations, relative permanence, a small number of persons involved, and relative intimacy of participants. As social beings, humans are prone toward forming groups. For most of us, the first primary group in our lives is our family. As a child grows older, she will seek friends of her same age (peers) in an attempt to form a bond of friendship. Ideally, individuals will also learn to form a number of other relationships that involves forming a bond with their school, neighborhood, community, and eventually, with society as a whole.

Cooley also acknowledged that individuals often have interactions with others that are, more or less, impersonal. That is, we associate with a number of people on a fairly regular basis but our relationships are not very deep. For example, many of us shop at a favorite grocery store and see the same clerks time and time again. We say hello to each other, but other than that, we do not spend any time with each other. Most of us do not know our postal carrier on a personal basis, and yet, he or she comes to our homes six times a week. As a result, of the impersonal nature of secondary relationships we can define a *secondary group* as a collectivity whose members interact with one another in a relatively formal and impersonal manner.

Agents of Socialization

A sports team may be viewed as a primary group because it consists of a number of significant others. This is one reason why athletes generally value the opinions of teammates, coaches and other team-related personnel. Symbolic interactionist George Herbert Mead used the term significant others to refer to those who play a major role in shaping a person's sense of self. Significant others may also be viewed as agents of socialization. In brief, agents of socialization are sources of culture. They are the people, groups or institutions that teach us what we need to know in order to function properly in society. The most important agents of socialization for any individual are the ones that are most highly revered and trusted.

The agents of socialization include:

1. *Parents and close family members.* They provide the early preparation for life; primary socialization. The role of parents and the family will be explored in Chapter 6 with our discussion of youth sports.
2. *Schools (and day care).* Raised within the family structure, the young child receives mostly consistent messages about social expectations from an extended number of significant family members. However, once children start going to day care and then school they begin to interact with other children and adults with potentially different outlooks on what constitutes proper behavior (Delaney 2012). Parental influence usually declines as the child progresses through school. This period marks the beginning of the secondary socialization process.
3. *Best friends and peer groups.* As the young child grows older, the opinions, values and norms of best friends and peers become increasingly influential. Best friends are the friends we are very close to; they are our confidants; they are the people we count on the most (Delaney and Madigan 2017). Peer groups are people who are of the same approximate age, status and interests. The opinions, values and norms of peers are especially significant to school-age children.
4. *The mass media.* Providing news, information, and entertainment is the cornerstone of contemporary mass media. The media includes television, radio, magazines, motion pictures, newspapers, video games, musicians and music, Internet (e.g., social networking and news and entertainment), and the like. Most people, especially sports fans, are heavily influenced by the mass media (see Chapter 15).
5. *Religion.* The importance of religion varies a great deal from one individual to another. Many athletes attribute their success to a divine source, while others attribute success to hard work, determination, and sometimes, luck. (See Chapter 14 for a review on the relationship between sports and religion.)
6. *Employment.* Many people's lives are dictated by their work environment; it either hampers or allows for opportunities for individuals to pursue sports and leisure activities.
7. *The government.* The type of socio-political structure found in a society will have a great deal of influence on individuals and the sports world. (See Chapter 13 for a further discussion.)

These are the principal examples of the agents of socialization. They impact individuals in varying degrees, but collectively, the agents of socialization are responsible for the transmission of culture from one generation to the next.

Development of Self

Although the socialization process continues throughout one's lifetime, early childhood is a critical time in the initial development of self. Consequently, primary group participation is very important for children. It is within the primary group that children develop a sense of self. "The self develops in a group context, and the group that Cooley called the primary group is the real seat of self-development" (Reynolds 1993: 36). The development of self is the result of a number of interactions with others over a period of time in a variety of social and cultural contexts.

Throughout time people have derived much of their identity and sense of self from groups to which they have membership. Identity involves those aspects of one's life that are deemed as essential to the character and maintenance of self. A sense of self, which develops in a social group context, provides an individual with an identity. Thus, individual identities are socially constructed. Correspondingly, if such an identity is to sustain, it must be worked on and maintained in a group context (Berger 1963). For example, someone may claim an identity as the team captain, but that identity can only be sustained in the context of a group (team) setting. As individuals come to see themselves by a particular identity they must meet the expectations of that role (e.g., the team captain must take on a leadership role and be an exemplar of expected behavior). Loy and Ingham (1981) elaborate: "As the individual takes a position (status) in a group, he learns to define himself in response to the expectations which the group has of a person occupying that status. That is, the person attempts to interject a group-defined identity into his own identity. The more congruent the projected self is with the group-defined self, the more social sustenance (reinforcement) one expects. Once having established one's claim to an identity, one works to preserve it, and if possible to enhance it" (190).

While engaging others, individuals attempt to present themselves according to their identity constructs. "The 'self label' is an identity that one presents to others in an attempt to manage their impression of him or her" (Delaney 2005: 122). Individuals are secure in their identities for as long as they interact within their primary group. As college freshmen learn, the identities held in high school do not necessarily remain attached in college. The "big man" on campus in high school, who once basked in all the glory that comes with that identity, finds himself a mere freshman in college where people are rarely impressed with high school achievements. Athletes that dominated in high school sports are often shocked by the decreased identity they possess in college. Whenever someone joins a new group they encounter new people who come to define them with a new identity. Modifications to self-identity are often necessary with new involvements. The individual must know how to adjust his or her role to meet the new group's requirements.

In team sports it is critical for everyone to play their role and accept the responsibilities that come with that role. The new person to the group will be accepted as long as they perform their role up to preconceived expectations.

Acceptance into the group is also dependent upon the actor's willingness to take on and internalize the communicated values and norms of the group. In turn, it is the responsibility of the group to socialize the neophyte within the idealized ideology. When the individual shares the perspective of a reference group, she has, in Mead's (1934) terms, taken on the attitudes of the generalized other (the community). At this stage of development the individual not only identifies with significant others (specific people) but also with the attitudes of the group or community as a whole. The generalized other is not a person; instead, it is a person's conscious awareness of the society that he or she is a part of. The ability to adopt the attitude of the reference group is what allows for diverse and unique persons to share a sense of community.

Thus, every team is composed of individuals who maintain their own sense of individuality while working cooperatively as a functioning whole. In a team context, any individual member has the power to disrupt the functioning operation of the whole by inappropriate conduct. Thus, the group influences the development of individual self and, individuals influence the group. For example, when a college football player wins the Heisman Memorial Trophy (considered the most prestigious award in American college football, awarded annually to the top NCAA football player of the year), the whole team, coaches and the university benefits because of the prestige involved and the fact that football is a sport where individual achievement is accomplished only through teamwork.

Sports Identity

Participation in sport is generally recognized as a positive endeavor for at least two crucial reasons: sports provide valuable opportunities to develop physical skills, competency and proper conditioning, and sports are a powerful socializing agent that promotes the values and norms of the prevailing culture. Because of the cultural importance of sport in society, many people have their identities directly, or indirectly, tied to sports. Sport participants have a generic identity as an "athlete." Within the athlete identity label are a number of subcategories based on such criteria as success (elite versus marginal); professional status (amateur or paid professional); team sport or individual sport; team leader (or captain) or backup player; and so on. Clearly, an elite athlete has a higher status than a marginal athlete. Non-athletes with a sports identity include sport consumers (e.g., fans and spectators) and sport producers (the media).

An elite athlete is someone who has reached a top performance level of competition. Most elite athletes begin their sports involvement at an early age and generally enjoy success in their chosen sport. Elite athletes generally have a strong support system from significant others, and often a parent may have been the elite athlete's youth coach. As Kenyon and McPherson (1981) explain, "The elite athlete emerges from an environment which was highly supportive; that is, he was exposed from an early age to an abundant opportunity set (middle-class values and ample facilities, equipment, and leadership) and much encouragement, reward, and reinforcement from a variety of meaningful others" (234). A team leader or team captain enjoys an elevated sense of self, as generally these labels are bestowed upon individuals because they have displayed character traits deemed most desirable in a team context. Team captains lead by example. They are especially significant to younger team members who look up to and admire team leaders. Possessing an identity such as an elite athlete or team leader comes with great responsibility and a conscious effort by such individuals to maintain such a status.

The effects of sports on self-identity and self-image are not fully understood. However, we know that boys learn at an early age that masculinity is related to achievement in sports and the more successful a boy is in sports, the more masculine he appears and the more likely he will be accepted by his peers. Furthermore, all boys are judged according to their ability, or lack of ability, in competitive sports. Because they equate a positive sense of self through becoming a successful athlete, boys learn to develop instrumental relationships—those based on pragmatic principles that assist individuals in their pursuit of goals (Messner 2002). Understandably, young males who are successful in sports benefit from such an identity. Boys who are not good at sports, or shun sports, will have to find another way to attain an identity. Some find identities through becoming waterboys, scouts or other related roles connected with sports while not actually involved in active participation. Considering how important sports are for boys, alternative identities seldom have the same level of status as that of an athlete.

Research on the effects of sports on girls is not as extensive as it is with boys. (The effects of sport participation on female sense of self will be examined in Chapter 10.) As more girls and women participate in sport, it would stand to reason that females will also benefit from a sports identity. For instance, a popular photo exhibit called "Game Face: What Does a Female Athlete Look Like?" opened in the Smithsonian Institution's Arts and Industry Building in 2001 to celebrate the increasing role of women in sport. It focused on the revision of beliefs about womanly and feminine behavior, and the positive ways in which women use athletics to enhance their sense of self.

The sport consumer (anyone who purchases sport-related products, including game tickets and sports merchandize) is an identity embraced by millions, and thus, far outnumbers the athlete as a sports identity. The pervasive nature of group identification has shown that sport consumers identify not only with teams but often with the institutions represented by the teams they support. In fact, fans who maintain high levels of identification with a sports team also show feelings of bonding with other fans of that same team (Wann and Branscombe 1993). Research indicates that discriminating between groups can increase self-esteem (Lemyre and Smith 1985; Oakes and Turner 1980). As a result, sport consumers who have formed an identity by pledging an allegiance to one team (an in-group) view fans of another team (an out-group) as rivals. (See Chapter 2 for a review of our research on BIAF.) Rival teams are also viewed as out-groups. As described earlier, identity involves those aspects of one's life that are deemed necessary to the character and maintenance of self. For many sport consumers a fan identity to a particular team or favorite athlete is in fact deemed as a critical identifier of self.

Agents of Sport Socialization

Why is it that some people love sports and others ignore them completely? How is it possible within the same home environment that siblings do not share the same level of passion for sports, and why they don't always cheer for the same teams? Socialization, life experiences, opportunities, and individual motives are among the explanations to these complicated questions.

American society provides ample opportunities for youth sport participation. Most schools have sports programs, a number of community centers provide safe venues for those interested in sport, and organized youth leagues such as Little League and Pop Warner Football abound throughout the United States. Children form informal playgroups in their neighborhoods and engage in sports. In short, if a child is motivated enough, there are plenty of sporting options available in every community.

Not every child is motivated to play sports. Some children played sports, had initial bad experiences and never returned to the sports world. Others never were interested in playing sports, and did so only under duress. As Turner (2006) explains, we need motives to occupy positions in life. We need to be energized to play certain roles in life. Some people simply never possessed a motive or desire to play sports when they were young. The motivation for sports participation is affected by a number of variables, including:

1. *Individual ability.* Possessing skill in a sport is a prime motivator to continue participation. Youth who lack skill in certain sports (or all sports) are less motivated to play when compared to those who demonstrate sporting skills.
2. *The availability of opportunities to play sports.* Sports programs and teams must be available for youth to try out. Unfortunately, an increasing number of school districts face budget constraints that sometimes lead to the elimination of sport programs. Geography plays an important role as well. For example, youth in Los Angeles have far more opportunities to surf than youth in Montana do.
3. *Socioeconomic factors.* A number of sports (e.g., club hockey, polo, tennis, and golf) are too expensive to participate in and thus limit participation. On the other hand, other sports (e.g., soccer and basketball) are less expensive to play and therefore are accessible to youth of all socio-economic backgrounds.
4. *The influence of family and friends.* Youths who are encouraged to play sports and who are positively reinforced for their efforts by friends and family are more likely to start and continue their sport participation.
5. *The prestige and power of the socializing agents.* Possessing a sports identity is a great motivator for youth and provides them with an edge in the social world. Conversely, when sport participation loses its appeal, the prestige attached also decreases.

Individual motivation toward sport participation, or away from it, is greatly influenced by the agents of socialization. While the agents of socialization prepare individuals "for many roles in life that have little or nothing to do with sport, they also play a significant part in the individual's sport socialization" (Vogler and Schwartz 1993: 15). Research indicates that parents and peers are fundamental contributors to motivational outcomes of young athletes (Smith and Ullrich-French 2006).

The Family and Sport

It should not come as a surprise that parents, as the primary agent of socialization, especially the father, and other immediate family members have the greatest impact on a child's socialization into sport. As Phillips (1993) states, "Children are more interested in sports when they receive encouragement from parents" (86). Over the past few decades many mothers have become actively involved in encouraging their children to play sports, especially soccer—leading to the popular expression of "soccer moms." Nearly all parents engage in ball playing with infants as a means of developing coordination, balance and basic motor skills. Rolling a ball to a baby and encouraging active participation in such an activity provides the child its first introduction into sport. It is also a non-threatening and fun way of developing a bond between a guardian and child. American boys are almost always encouraged to play catch or bat a baseball. Sports equipment (e.g., ball, glove) is a common gift for a newborn baby boy. Messner's (2002) research on male former athletes revealed that their earliest experiences in sports came in childhood from male family members, including uncles and older brothers, who served as "athletic role models as well as sources of competition for attention and status within the family" (128). Messner (2002) also found that in some cases, attempts by younger aspiring athletes to meet the standards of older siblings was too much pressure and was difficult to contend with. Still, as adult males, these aspiring athletes looked back upon their childhood relationships with their athletic older male family members in a positive light.

Many parents also encourage their children's participation in board games and other fun activities as a way of providing entertainment but also as a way of introducing the child to the world of rules and clear-cut winners and losers. Children who learn to enjoy competition will become increasingly drawn to sports and other contests. Some children may be turned off by the physical activity or the competition and will begin to turn away from sports. Additionally, parents who encourage their children to engage in more passive activities such as reading and starting a coin or stamp collection are more likely to have children who shun sports.

The age and physical condition of the parents can affect a child's socialization into or away from sport. A father or mother who is physically fit and active will be more likely to encourage sport participation in the child. Conversely, if the parents are physically incapable of sport participation, their children may not be exposed to as many sport opportunities. The age of the parents in relation to the child can have an effect as well—many older parents are less able or willing to play sports with their children. A family's economic status and geographic residence are two additional factors that influence a child's socialization into sport. Families with limited disposable income will generally be limited to sports that they can afford to register their children into. Thus, the wealthy have opportunities to play the vast array of sports, including polo and golf, while the poor are more likely to play street basketball, soccer, or stickball.

The ethnicity of the family has also been cited as a variable in sport participation. Phillips (1993) examines the "ethnic influence" from the standpoint (and tradition of Harry Edwards) that certain ethnic and racial groups that are discriminated against are more likely to participate in sport. Blacks have valued sports excellence for decades and view it as a way of getting ahead and therefore have a higher percentage participating than whites (Edwards 1973). This trend has continued into the early twenty-first century and explains, in part, why blacks dominate many American sports. Today, many other minority ethnic groups are beginning to use sport as a means of getting ahead and have begun to re-shape the elite strata of sport. (This topic will be discussed in further detail in Chapter 11.) Phillips (1993) notes that whites have a higher participation rate in sport than Asians and that this difference holds across all income and social class levels. Vogler and Schwartz (1993) examine the ethnic influence as a socializer in sport from a different perspective. Their focus is on ethnic neighborhoods that have a fondness for a specific sport (e.g., a Brazilian neighborhood would encourage soccer participation among its youth) that leads to a greater interest and participation in such sports. Furthermore, parents who are highly identified by their ethnicity and active in the community are more likely to encourage their children's participation in the ethnically preferred sport.

Peers and Sport

A child's playmates will also have an influence on sport participation. In simplest terms, if a child's friends play ball, the child is more likely to play ball. As the level of importance in ball playing increases among peers, so too will the commitment level to participate in sport increase. As the child plays with others, talent levels are compared. A child that receives praise for his or her sports propensity is more likely to continue participation. Conversely, if a child's performance level is sub-par he or she may be subject to ridicule from peers. This will result in a negative self-concept and a negative outlook on sports, thus decreasing the likelihood of continued participation. Most children are somewhere in between the elite and inept extremes of athleticism. These children will continue to play sports for as long as it remains fun and relatively fulfilling. They will most likely remain fans, or consumers, of sports after their playing days have ended. The bond shared among peers who cheer for the same team or individual athlete is a very strong and important one.

Kenyon and McPherson (1981) summarize the peer-induced factors related to sport socialization:

1. The greater the peer involvement in sport, the greater the propensity for sport involvement.
2. The greater the positive sanctions from peers, the greater the propensity for sport involvement.
3. The greater the amount of sport-oriented face-to-face interaction with peers, the greater the propensity for sport involvement.
4. The higher sport is placed in the peer group's hierarchy of values, the greater the degree of sport role socialization [235].

SCHOOL AND SPORT

Obviously, children need opportunities to participate in sports and to develop a passion for sport and physical play. Ideally, all schools would mandate physical education. Unfortunately, and as hard as it is to believe, some school districts have cut back on physical education (due to budget cuts) and do not require regular physical activity among their pupils. For most children, however, physical education is provided in school. Before long it becomes clear who has athletic ability and who does not. Physical education instructors, who often serve dual roles as coaches, will identify those kids with potential for school sports and encourage more advanced and specialized training. Since most junior high and middle schools have interscholastic teams and intramural leagues, children with sports ability are given a platform to showcase their skills. Success, to any degree, will most likely lead to a continuation in sport participation. Accolades from classmates, teachers and school personnel will enhance the ego of these young athletes and will, in turn, generally lead to a further commitment to sport. Schools with a winning tradition in sports will especially value athletic excellence, leading to both more pressure to succeed among elite athletes, but also providing an even bigger stage from which to shine when successful.

Socialization into Sport

The agents of socialization pave the way for the socialization into sport. Socialization into sport is a process whereby an individual is encouraged by the agents of socialization to partake in sport either as a participant or as a spectator and consumer. Generally speaking, individuals are socialized "into" sport by significant others (agents of socialization) because of the perceived positive attributes of sport. As stated earlier, parents introduce games to children because they are rule-bound and encourage conforming behavior. A game that involves multiple players means that each participant must know the role of others. Behaviors must be adjusted to conform to group or team needs and game rules. Once a child learns how to play games, he or she is mature enough to be socialized into sport.

Socialization into sport is most effective when it begins in early childhood. This is especially true if a father shows an interest in sport and encourages his son or daughter to play sports. A highly identified fan and parent may try to "force" socialize a son or daughter into sport by dressing him or her in baby clothing of a favorite team, including pajamas, t-shirts or baby bibs; giving the child a stuffed animal that is either a replica of the mascot of a favorite team or one that is simply wearing clothing that supports a favorite team; watching the favorite team on television with the child in hopes that the excitement and passion will carry over; and so on. Clearly, children who are raised in a family where the parents, or older siblings, already demonstrate an interest in sport (either directly as participants, or indirectly as consumers) are more likely to embrace sports as well. Some parents want to live vicariously through their children's sport participation. These parents encourage their sons and daughters into sport either to recapture (indirectly) their loss athletic glory and the attention that sport participation garnered, or they hope to experience the glory that sport can provide and that they never enjoyed themselves when they were younger. The level of parental vicarious attachment and encouragement of sport participation increases as the level of competition (e.g., from intramurals to interscholastic sports) and corresponding prestige increases (Nixon and Frey 1996).

It is interesting to note that regardless of the sex of the child, the father typically has the most influence over whether a child will be socialized into sport. Fathers are also more likely to "type" sport activities that are gender "appropriate." For example, fathers are more likely to tell their sons that sports such as football and baseball are more appropriate than ballet and dance to participate in. Because of socialization influences, boys are more concerned than girls about sports that are deemed "gender appropriate." A child's ordinal position in the family is also a factor in socialization into sport. First born children do not have the same opportunity to imitate siblings and lack older sibling role models to shape their behaviors.

Historically, boys, especially in American culture, have been encouraged to play sports. Girls have not. As we shall see in Chapter 10, women have had to overcome a great number of obstacles in their attempt to reach gender equity in the sports world. Socialization into sport is the first barrier that women had to shatter. Sports were believed to be a male's domain and most parents, fathers and mothers, socialized their children into this gendered view of sport. For instance, as J.C. Reeser (2005) notes: "Historically, female athletes have been subjected to a variety of discriminatory and prejudicial practices that have affected their access to sport. For example, women were not permitted to compete in the ancient Olympics, nor were they included when the modern Games were first organized in 1896" (695).

With the rise of the women's rights movement in the 1960s and the passage of legislation in the 1970s, a number of sporting opportunities became available for girls and women. Initial inroads made by women seeking gender equity in sport were met by a variety of challenges. For example, in 1980, Iris Marion Young questioned whether women should participate in sport and utilized the sexist putdown in baseball, "You throw like a girl" as her central theme (Wedgwood 2004). In a later version of her 1980 article, Young (1998) suggested that women underestimate their physical power and skills and approach tasks with timidity, doubt and hesitancy because they are afraid of getting hurt. Conversely, boys and men are not afraid of getting hurt. People get hurt playing sports; ergo, boys are more suited for sports. Twenty-five years later, few people in sport share this sentiment.

Nikki Wedgwood turned the phrase "throwing like a girl" around to "kicking like a boy" in her study of a schoolgirl Australian Rules football team. Wedgwood's (2004) research centered on why the girls played football; whether they played football as a means of consciously resisting male domination; whether they felt empowered by playing football; and how they handled gender role conflicts. Among Wedgwood's (2004) findings:

- Because some of the women on the team felt physically strong and confident before playing football, it is hard to conclude that they felt more empowered after playing football.
- However, for the women who had not previously felt strong and confident, football encouraged them to come out of their shells and "playfully experiment with their bodies" (159).
- The exhilaration of physical play and assertiveness boosted their overall confidence.

Wedgwood concludes that these young women benefited by their socialization into a male-dominated sport and that their participation in football provided them "the opportunity to resist the traditional ideal of women as fragile, defenseless, weak sexual objects" (159). Furthermore, Wedgwood found that most of the women were not inspired by tenets of feminism to play football; rather, just like boys, the inspiration to play football was attributed to a love for the game. More than a decade prior to Wedgwood's study, Ryckman and Hamel (1992) concluded that adolescent girls participated in sport to maintain and prolong friendships more than any desire to develop and improve their athletic skills or nurture a love for the game.

The social characteristics of race, ethnicity and social class are also factors involved in the socialization into sport. Wealthy people are often socialized into sports that reflect their status and perceived dignity (e.g., fox hunts in England, rowing at Oxford and Ivy League schools, polo "at the club," golf in private country clubs). People from lower socio-economic classes and those who are discriminated against are generally attracted to sports (e.g., basketball, baseball, football, and soccer) that provide accessibility and enjoyment, and also a chance for economic success.

Geographic location plays a role with the socialization into sport. Children raised in Syracuse, New York, are more likely to play lacrosse than children in Los Angeles. Conversely, children living in the beach cities outside of Los Angeles are more likely to surf than kids in Syracuse. This is despite the fact that someone from one geographic area may have a greater ability to play a sport popular in another area. Certain geographical areas are known for their sports: basketball in New York City; hockey throughout Canada; football in Texas, Florida and Alabama. Whether someone resides in a city, the suburbs, or a rural community can also affect the socialization into sport (e.g., what sports will be made available, funding, coaching, interest from the community to finance a specific sports team).

Socialization Via Sport

Once an individual has entered the sports world, what keeps him or her interested? From the functionalist perspective, continued participation is related to individual ability, the influence of family and friends on the individual, the continued availability of resources, and whether one experienced success, or a positive experience, while playing sport. Developing a commitment to sport participation involves a number of factors, including:

1. A willingness to accept a sports role and the corresponding relationships and networks affiliated with it. This includes a willingness to abide by the rules.
2. The continued development of the web of personal relationships connected to sport participation.
3. Assessed potential for achieving success.
4. Degree of involvement in the sport. Those who play a lot have a vested interest in continuing their participation. Those who primarily sit on the bench are likely to lose interest.
5. Whether participation is voluntary or involuntary. Youths who are pushed into a sport (involuntary) by a parent, coach, or some other significant person are less likely to *want* to keep playing, compared to someone who participates voluntarily.
6. The prestige and power associated with playing the sport and how rewarding an individual finds sport participation will affect one's willingness to continue playing.
7. Gradually accepting the established personal reputation and identity as an athlete; in other words, seeing oneself as an athlete.

As athletes increasingly accept their role and position within the sports world, they acquire a number of character traits. Proponents of sport love to point out the positive attributes of participation, such as working hard, dedication, loyalty, teamwork (where applicable), and commitment. Detractors point to the undesirable attributes, such as athletes who cheat, take drugs, or employ a "win-at-all-costs" mentality instead of fair play and cooperation among all participants.

Socialization via sport involves the social processes and significant others that influence an individual's decision to remain in sport. This process can only occur through participation. Individuals who decide to continue their athletic careers do so at many costs. They must give up free time to practice. They may need to diet and exercise. Strength and conditioning programs are often a part of an athlete's "off season" training. Some athletes, such as football players, often need to bulk up. Other athletes, such as wrestlers, must meet a weight limit before each match. Athletes learn that they must abide by their coaches' rules, team rules, school rules, and league rules. They must also accept any negative sanctions for non-conforming behavior.

Ideally, all participants learn good sportsmanship. Poor sportsmanship, according to John Rosemond, a family psychologist, is a show of self-centered disrespect for others. Children should develop positive sportsmanship by age 10. To instill good sportsmanship, Rosemond (2000) recommends that a child (at age 7) who begins to gloat or get upset during a game should be immediately removed and not allowed to continue unless he or she apologizes to everyone—the coaches, teammates, and the other team members. If the child refuses, then he or she should be removed from the game. Rosemond recognizes that the disciplined child will feel embarrassed and believes that's the point in properly socializing a child. "He must be required to experience a negative emotional consequence powerful enough to cause him to begin controlling his anti-social behavior on the field" (2000: C3). Most likely, readers will find Rosemond's approach a little extreme, but imagine if all of today's professional athletes had been required to meet such criteria in sportsmanship. (Note: We will discuss sportsmanship in greater detail in Chapters 6 and 16.)

Athletes on teams often retreat to their own social worlds. It is here that they feel most comfortable. Peer pressure is a powerful form of "socialization via sport" technique. Not only is there pressure to follow the formal rules (e.g., meet curfew, no gambling) there is pressure to follow the informal rules of the team. Some of these rules are harmless forms of socialization. For example, baseball players may have a "donation" cup for every time a player makes an error. This mild form of sanction serves to bond teammates. Players begin to regret and fear making an error as much for the informal ridicule they will receive (along with the "donation" sanction) from teammates, as the fact that the error could cost the team the game.

An important element of the "socialization via sport" process is the fraternal bond. The fraternal bond is a process whereby members of a group foster and reinforce team camaraderie and a commitment to group goals. Curry (1991) describes the fraternal bond as a force, link, or affectionate tie that unites men. It provides bonding opportunities among teammates. The fraternal bond is a crucial element of fraternities, sports teams and other subcultural groups. The fraternal bond is not inherently negative or positive. Cooperation among team members who work hard to achieve a goal is one of many positive examples of the fraternal bond. However, the fraternal bond may also promote negative character traits. Curry (1991) suggests that "doing gender" in the locker room (e.g., communication among team members that involves putting down women, treating women as sexual conquests, mocking gays and bragging about sexual conquests) is a means of strengthening the fraternal bond. More recently, we think of the term "locker room talk" as when Donald Trump downplayed his boasting about physically forcing himself on women as merely "locker room talk" (he uttered this phrase in 2005 while conversing with *Access Hollywood* host Billy Bush and laughed it off during his 2016 presidential campaign after the video resurfaced) (Dickerson 2016; Mathis-Lilley 2016). Trump's inference was that his boasting about an act of sexual assault—he said, "…And when you're a star, they let you do it. You can do anything. Grab them by the p***y. You can do anything"—was just similar to athletes talking about sexual conquest as a means to establish in-group solidarity by establishing dominance over another. His supporters, including female supporters, did brush aside such talk as "boys being boys" bravado, while his detractors considered such behavior as the same thing as taking pride in rape, and especially so as no one looks at Trump as an athlete. It is especially important to point out that "locker room talk" is not condoned in most locker rooms.

Socialization Out of Sport

Eventually, sport participants are socialized out of sport. This can be voluntary (e.g., retirement, quit) or involuntary (e.g., being cut from the team, career ending injury). Socialization out of sport involves a desocialization process where an individual leaves sport and experiences a modification of sense of self. For professional athletes, exiting can be very difficult. (Think of all the tearful retirement speeches shown on television.) Drahota and Eitzen (1998) describe the role transition of athletes out of sport as a difficult one because: "They *lose* what has been the focus of their being for most of their lives, the primary source of their identities, the physical prowess, the adulation bordering on worship from others, the money and the perquisites of fame, the camaraderie with team-mates, and the intense 'highs' of competition. All of these are lost to professional athletes who are in their twenties and thirties when they exit sport" (263).

"Big-time" athletes have heard deafening crowds chant their names and have had adoring fans nearly worshipping them throughout their playing days. But when the career ends, so to does the cheering. Many professional athletes miss this type of attention after retirement. This is especially true if the person's primary identity was tied to sport participation. Many athletes stay close to sport by becoming coaches or sports media personnel.

EXITING SPORT VOLUNTARILY

There are a variety of ways for individuals to leave sport voluntarily. One simple reason for leaving is because participation has merely lost its appeal—it is no longer viewed as a rewarding endeavor. The sport participant may come to a realization that the personal time allocated (e.g., practice, training, game day) is taking away from the time needed to pursue other interests (e.g., dating, school work, family). In other words, at some point in time, usually during childhood, most people stop playing sports because it has lost its appeal. But how does sport lose its appeal? Most young children play sports because they are fun. However, as the level of competition increases and becomes more structured and the emphasis on skill and success becomes paramount, the lesser talent participants simply turn away. These young athletes desire that their sporting activities remain fun and do not like the intrusion of seriousness (e.g., emphasis on improving skills, utilizing techniques that attempt to maximize the chances of winning versus a commitment to playing everyone) creeping into their leisure activity.

From the participant's point of view a lost appeal in sport is one of the easiest ways to exit. However, the individual may find that significant others have objections to this decision. Friends, teammates and coaches may try to assert pressure on the individual to remain. Many parents become upset when their children quit sports because they had an emotional, communal and financial (e.g., purchased specific equipment that now will now go unused) attachment and involvement with their children's sport participation. Parents and family members that made a number of sacrifices so that their child could play sports may try to influence or coerce the young athlete back into sport. Parents who were living vicariously through their children's participation will especially be upset when their kids quit. However, it is also true that some athletes will quit or retire voluntarily to spend more time with their families. Professional athletes who retire voluntarily (especially those with seemingly more years of playing time ahead of them) often cite the desire to be with their families as their primary reason for leaving.

Many athletes are also pressured by friends, spouses and business associates who have a financial as well as emotional interest in their remaining in the game. This is often the case, for instance, with professional boxers, who have significant entourages and who find it difficult to voluntarily break away from the perks and privileges their status provides them in their community. Quite often, even after retiring, such athletes will find themselves returning to the sport they had voluntarily left, due to such financial, emotional and status pressures.

Another reason participants exit sport is because of burnout. Burnout occurs when individuals feel overwhelmed by their sport participation; to the point where they feel (or fear) that they have lost control over their lives and believe that their identity is too closely tied to sports. These young athletes come to believe that they may be missing out on other opportunities and identities apart from sports.

Retirement represents an exit strategy out of sport for the professional athlete. Voluntary retirement is different for professional athletes than it is for "other retirees who, typically, are elderly and leaving the occupational world altogether" (Drahota and Eitzen 1998: 264). Although common sense alone should serve as a reminder to athletes that when they retire (even if it is after a long and successful career) they will have decades remaining in their lifespan, many are not prepared for life after sports. This is usually because of their single focus on their sport and the failure to plan ahead. Drahota and Eitzen (1998) believe that many athletes know but do not necessarily accept the fact that playing sports is a temporary role to be performed for a relatively short period of their lives. Often this failure to realize that a career will come to an end is tied to denial. Most athletes view retirement as the only acceptable way of exiting sport because it implies they left on their terms—ready, or not, for life after sports. And there does seem to be a special status for athletes who retire on their own accord, often at the top of their game or at least before inevitable decline in their skills sets in. Rocky Marciano, "The Brockton Blockbuster," retired as Heavyweight Champion in 1956, after holding the title for four years, and remains the only undefeated champion. He was noted for his courage, dignity and sense of grace, and managed his money and career well after leaving the ring, unlike many other athletes who find it difficult to adjust to life after sports.

EXITING SPORT INVOLUNTARILY

The two primary ways that sport participants exit sports involuntarily is through a career-ending injury and being cut (or /kicked off) from the team. Injuries are a common occurrence as the playing field can be a violent, risky, and hazardous environment. In the time period of 2011–2014, the CDC reported that there were an annual estimated 8.6 million sports- and recreation-related injury episodes reported, with an age-adjusted rate of 34.1 per 1,000 population. Males (61.3 percent) and persons aged 5–24 years (64.9 percent) accounted for more than one-half of injury episodes (Sheu, Chen and Hedegaard 2016). The CDC (2019a) reports that in 2018 more than 2.6 million children 0–19 years old were treated in emergency departments each year for sports and recreational-related injuries. The Insurance Information Institute (III) (2020) reports that in 2017 personal exercise, with or without exercise equipment, accounted for some 526,000 injuries, the most of any category of sports and recreation. This was also the leading category of sport activity to cause injury to those 65 and older. The III provides great charts and data with a breakdown of all the leading sporting and recreational injuries in total but also breaks it down by age category. Here, we will limit the leading sporting and recreational injuries to overall totals. Following exercise, with or without sporting equipment, the top ten leading sporting activities to cause injury are: basketball (500,085 injuries); bicycles and accessories (457,266); football (341,150); playground equipment (242,359); soccer (218,926); ATVs, mopeds, minibikes, etc. (214,761); swimming, pools, equipment (199,246); baseball, softball (187,447); and trampolines (145,207) (III 2020). While all of the injuries enumerated here do not lead to the end of an athletic career, the data does provide a glimpse into how common injuries are in sports and recreation.

Being cut from or kicked off a team is the other major way of exiting a sport involuntarily. There are a variety of reasons that someone might be cut from a team: skills level is not high enough to successfully compete; diminished skills; increased competition; poor attitude; off-the-field problems; and so on. Lately, there has been an increase in the number of veteran professional players being cut because they carry too high of a salary. For example, in the National Football League (NFL) salary contracts are not fully guaranteed (although some players can get some guaranteed money in their deals, including via signing bonuses) and as a result, if a player is earning a high salary and a younger player is available for less money, a number of franchises have decided to cut the veteran as a cost-saving mechanism. This veteran must now decide whether to take a playing offer for substantially less income (and "lose face" in the process), hope that some other team will sign him, or her, or retire.

Every year, in the NFL alone, nearly 420 players leave the league involuntarily. When we consider all the professional sports and all the sports played at youth, high school and college levels, the number of athletes that leave sport involuntarily would be well over one million annually.

In Chapter 6 we will learn about the odds of making it to the professional level of sports. Suffice it to say, they are slim. When athletes do make it to the professional level most of them will have short careers. Citing data from Statista, Gough (2019a) found that the average length of a player's career in the NFL is just 3.3 years. At 4.87 years, kickers have the longest average career. Quarterbacks average 4.44 years, cornerbacks 2.94 years, wide receivers 2.81 and running backs just 2.57 years. The NFL counters that, first-round draft picks average a 9.3-year career and that the high number of players who only last one year negatively skews the overall average. The average MLB career is 5.6 years, and the average NBA career is 4.71 years.

Resocialization

Just as we are socialized into new roles, we are also socialized out of existing ones. Being socialized out of a role means being re-socialized into yet another new role. Socialization "out of" sport involves a re-socialization process, as one's sense of self changes when the athlete stops playing sports. This is true whether a participant exits voluntarily or involuntarily. Some athletes handle the transition quite well. They find jobs in the professional workforce or start their own companies. A number of former athletes will find jobs in the sports world (e.g., coaching, administration, the sports media). As we shall see in Chapter 13, some athletes even make a successful transition into the world of politics.

The NFLPA claims that upon retirement, 66 percent of NFL players report having emotional problems, 50 percent report personal problems, and 1 of 6 were divorced within 6 months. The NFLPA compares the experiences that professional jocks have after leaving sport to that of war veterans—the transition into civilian life is difficult, almost shocking (Leitch 2005). This difficulty in transition of roles is partly explained by the realization that the athlete can no longer perform his or her role successfully—he or she has been replaced. The truth of this reality can be painful both physically and psychologically. Resocialization out of sport will be especially difficult and stressful under these conditions:

1. The athlete's level of intensity of involvement in the sport was high.
2. Retirement from sport was involuntary.
3. Retirement will result in a loss of income and prestige (celebrity).
4. The athlete has not come up with a substitute career to fill the void that sport once filled.
5. The athlete's self-concept and sense of self were directly tied to sport participation.
6. The athlete does not seek counseling or assistance during the resocialization process [Figler and Whitaker 1981].

The successful transition from sport athlete to non-athlete involves a process known as role exit. "Role exit is depicted as a process of disengagement, disidentification, and resocialization. Disengagement involves the actual means of withdrawing from the type of behavior associated with a role. Disidentification refers to the time when individuals stop associating their self-identity with the role being exited. The process of leaving a role means that one also is being socialized into a new role" (Drahota and Eitzen 1998: 266). The key to resocialization for the athlete is to re-identify one's sense of self. Many athletes have a difficult time with this. Identifying with the "ex-athlete" role identity is something that takes years for many athletes. Tim Green (a first-round draft pick), the former defensive lineman with the Atlanta Falcons and an athlete who has made a successful transition, believes that "it's hard for pro players to retire—regardless of how long or successful their careers were—after dedicating their lives to going pro" (Gifford 2004: A-5). Green, who became a lawyer and best-selling author, ended his eight-year career in 1994. His book *The Dark Side of the Game: My Life in the NFL* chronicles some of the problems that players face after exiting sport. Green (1996) reports that many players have problems with alcohol, other drugs, and marital relationships, and engage in reckless behavior. Green now suffers from ALS, Lou Gehrig's disease (a link between the disease and playing football has not been established).

Research conducted by David Frith (2001) on cricket players reveals that they have the highest suicide rates of all ex-athletes. Since the early 1900s there have been 143 documented cricket player suicides worldwide. The largest percentage of cricket suicides occurs in South Africa. Frith reports that cricket athletes do not seek professional counseling for their emotional problems after exiting sports. Frith believes the high suicide rate is related to the pressure of the game. The most important matches take 6 to 8 hours a day for 5 days. As with other athletes that dedicate their lives to sport, the loss of night and day involvement in sport and the idea of being a "has been"—despite a relatively young age—is too much to handle for many athletes. Frith (2001) insists that it is not cricket that causes personal problems for its players; rather, it is the loss of cricket that is responsible. Frith's conclusion seems plausible. After all, golf matches often take 6 to 8 hours and last for four days, and Major League Baseball players play 162 games in less than six months. Consequently, the high suicide rate for cricket players cannot be attributed to being over-stressed due to the demands of the sport.

As we shall see in Chapter 9, there is growing evidence that many former athletes face serious physical ailments such as chronic traumatic encephalopathy (CTE), a degenerative condition many scientists say is caused by head trauma and linked to depression and dementia. CTE is the term used to describe brain degeneration likely caused by repeated head traumas (Mayo Clinic 2019).

Successful transition into the "ex-athlete" mode is a difficult for many athletes. As

Drahota and Eitzen (1998) found, some professional athletes never completely exit the role of professional athlete.

Connecting Sports and Popular Culture

Box 5: Tim Green Is Unstoppable

For an athlete, knowing when to retire is always a difficult decision. Of course, for many this decision is made for them, when they are let go by their team. But for those who are fortunate enough to decide on their own when to leave the game, there is another crucial concern (discussed above in the section on "Resocialization")—what to do next? As previously stated, the key to resocialization for the athlete is to re-identify one's sense of self.

One former athlete who seemingly had no trouble re-identifying with his sense of self is Tim Green (1963—). As stated on his personal website, www.timgreenbooks.com, "As a boy, Tim had two dreams: playing in the NFL and becoming a best-selling author. Both of those dreams have come true."

Before playing in the NFL, Green, born in Liverpool in Central New York, was a star defensive tackle at Syracuse University from 1982 to 1985, where he majored in English and studied writing when not practicing football or playing on the field. His defensive skills made him a first round draft pick in 1986. He played eight years with the Atlanta Falcons as a linebacker and defensive end, retiring in 1993 with 24 career sacks.

Unlike many ex-athletes, Green had planned out his next moves well ahead of time. In fact, he has had more successful post-football careers than most people have careers period. Green returned to his native Central New York to live, and also returned to his alma mater Syracuse University where he completed a law degree and became a practicing attorney with the Law Firm Barclay Damon LLP. Making good use of his communications skills, he was a legal commentator on ABC's *Good Morning America* and a regular sports commentator on NPR. And for 11 years Green was an analyst on *NFL on Fox*. In addition, he toured the country as a motivational speaker, promoting adolescent literacy.

Perhaps most importantly, Green realized his second great dream, becoming a successful author. He wrote more than a dozen books for adults, including 1996's *The Dark Side of the Game: My Life in the NFL* and 1997's *A Man and His Mother: An Adopted Son's Search,* where he describes in moving detail finding and then meeting both his natural mother and father, as well as the deep love he holds for his adoptive parents. He also wrote a series of suspense novels, drawing upon his experiences as a lawyer.

In 2007 Green published *Football Genius,* his first of many novels for young readers. Like his previous books for adults, it sold thousands of copies. One of his most poignant novels is the 2012 *Unstoppable,* the story of Harrison, a foster child adopted into a loving home whose new father is a football coach who becomes a star running-back at his junior high school, only to come down with cancer. As described on the timgreenbooks.com website, "In his most dramatic and hard-hitting story yet, NFL defensive end Tim Green writes about what it takes to be a winner, even when it seems like fate has dealt an impossible hand." It debuted at Number 2 on the *New York Times* bestseller list.

Sadly, the fictional story became all too real for Green himself. In 2018 he revealed on *60 Minutes* the awful truth—he had contracted Amyotrophic lateral sclerosis (ALS), popularly known as "Lou Gehrig's Disease." By the time of the interview, Green's speech had been severely affected, as were his motor skills. This was an unspeakable tragedy for an athlete noted for his physical prowess and an author proud of his gift for words.

But Green is never one to admit defeat. He has helped raise millions of dollars for his Tackle ALS campaign, whose slogan best expresses his overall approach to adversity: "Don't be sorry. Let's beat this" (tackleals.com).

On September 15, 2019, Green's number 72 jersey was retired at a special ceremony held in the Syracuse Carrier Dome during halftime at a Syracuse vs. Clemson game. The two authors of this text were there, along with 50,000 other fans in the sold-out stadium, former teammates, coaches, and members of Green's family. Unable to speak, Tim had his son Troy read his moving words, thanking everyone for their support.

Like the title of his best-selling book, Tim Green is unstoppable (at least for the time being).

SUMMARY

Sports are not just physical activities and games; they serve as focal points for the formation of social worlds. In order to fit into a social world, group members will adjust their behavior and mindsets to revolve around a particular set of activities. People are socialized into sport worlds by the agents of socialization.

The socialization process is a continuing process of social development and learning that occurs as individuals interact with one another and learn about society's expectations of popular behavior so that they can participate and function within their societies. The sociological perspective leans heavily toward environmental factors as the key to learning. Socialization takes place most effectively in primary groups—intimate associates who play a direct role in shaping one's sense of self. Significant others are those who play the most major role in such developments. Primary and secondary socialization comes about via interaction with the agents of socialization—parents and family; schools (and day care); best friends and peer groups; mass media; religion; employment; and the government.

Sport is instrumental in creating self-identity for many individuals, through their interactions with primary groups involved in sport activities, and through their identification with specific teams and players as well. In team sports, it is critical for all members to play their role and accept the responsibilities which come with it. The values and norms of the group are internalized and new members must learn these rules. Many achieve identity in sport through participation as an athlete. Some reach elite status or become team leaders, while others are primarily followers or sport consumers. The latter form an identity through practicing allegiance to a team and often through rooting against the chief rivals of that team.

The socialization into sport is the result of individual motivations to participate in sport; influence from the agents of socialization and significant others, especially parents; and initial successes and failures in sporting activities. Socialization via sport will help to determine whether sport participants will continue playing sports. Among the deciding factors of continued participation are individual ability; the influence of family and friends; the continued availability of resources; whether or not sport participation was rewarding; and determining whether the time and effort is worth the loss of time that could be spent on non-sporting activities. An important aspect of socialization via sport is the bonding and camaraderie opportunities provided by sporting competition.

Socialization out of sport can be difficult and essentially comes down to whether such exiting is done voluntarily or involuntarily. Reasons that athletes leave voluntarily include the realization that participation has lost its appeal; the time commitment comes at too great of a cost; and, the acknowledgment of diminished skills. Exiting involuntarily may include a career-ending injury or being cut (or kicked off) from the team.

Once a sport participant has exited the sports world, they face the resocialization process. Re-socializing can become an issue, as one's sense of self must change in light of the new situations. Such a transition from sport athlete to non-athlete is known as "role exit." The transition can be a difficult one for those whose personal identities are interwoven with the sport participation.

KEY TERMS

Agents of Socialization The people, groups or institutions that are sources of culture that teach us what we need to know in order to function properly in society.

Development of Self The result of a number of interactions with others over a period of time in a variety of social and cultural contexts.

Elite Athlete Someone who has reached a level of competition at or near a national standard.

Generalized Other A person's conscious awareness of the society that he or she is a part of; the community or communities one belongs to.

Identity Involves those aspects of one's life that are deemed as essential to the character and maintenance of self.

Instrumental Relationships Those relationships based on pragmatic principles that assist individuals in their pursuit of goals.

Primary Group An intimate association where members share a sense of "we-ness"—a sort of sympathy and mutual identification for which "we" is a natural expression. The primary group is relatively small, often informal, involves close personal relationships, and has an important role in shaping an individual's sense of self.

Role Exit A process of disengagement, disidentification, and resocialization.

Secondary Group A collectivity whose members interact with one another formally and impersonally.

Significant Others Those who play a major role in shaping a person's self.

Socialization A continuing process of social development and learning that occurs as individuals interact with one another and learn about society's expectations of acceptable behavior.

Socialization into Sport A process whereby an individual is encouraged by the agents of socialization to partake in sport either as a participant or as a spectator or consumer.

Socialization Out of Sport A desocialization process where an individual leaves sport and experiences a modification of sense of self.

Socialization via Sport The social processes and significant others that influence an individual's decision to remain in sport.

DISCUSSION QUESTIONS

- Do you admire any athletes whom you never actually saw play? If so, how did you learn about their careers, and what is it you admire about them?
- How does the socialization process influence an individual's decision to participate in sports? Give some examples, based upon the role which the following agents play: parents, peers, the school, the community, and the media.
- Why does sociology lean heavily toward nurture in the nature-nurture continuum?
- Why is the notion of a "natural born athlete" misleading?
- How does sport participation influence the development of self?
- How does one develop a sports identity?
- Why do parents usually encourage children's participation in sporting activities and games?
- Do you think that schools should support physical activity and sports involvement? Why or why not?
- Do you think that sport participation is beneficial for children?
- What are the processes involved in socialization via sport?
- Based on your own experiences does "locker room talk" regarding sexual conquests still exist? Is this type of behavior okay within the context of the locker room?
- Have you ever tailgated? If so, how would you describe the experience?

CHAPTER 6

Youth Sports

It is only natural for children to play. Participating in organized sport, however, is different. The highly structured design of formal sports is not attractive to all youth. Children should be allowed to make their own decisions as to whether they want to play organized sports. Encouraging children to participate in sport is certainly acceptable; however, pressuring a child is not. Marv Marinovich, co-captain of the undefeated 1962 football national champion University of Southern California (USC) Trojans and former offensive lineman for the Oakland Raiders, was obsessed with the idea that his son, Todd, would become a quarterback for USC and then the Raiders. Marv trained his son with the assistance of over 20 specialists while Todd grew up. They were designing a quarterback, a "Robo-quarterback," as Todd was known. Todd's youth was totally regimented. He slept and woke at his father's direction and worked out in between. He was not allowed to eat any junk food while he grew up; cake at his friends' birthday parties was also banned. Marv Marinovich would make Todd run several miles home after a poor performance (Weiner 1999). Todd Marinovich did become the quarterback for both USC and the Raiders (he also played for the Arena Football League and the Canadian Football League).

But, his NFL career was short-lived and his off-the-field problems include 30-plus-years of drug addiction and numerous arrests (Weiner 1999; *USA Today* 1999; *USA Today* 2000; Dowd 2016; Powers 2018). At the time of his 2018 arrest he was playing football for the SoCal Coyotes, a developmental football team. As a youth, Todd Marinovich was physically prepared to play football; but, all this training did not prepare him for life as an adult. Would Todd have had as many problems if his father had not pushed him so hard? We will never know. Child-rearing experts do say, however, that "hot housing," or the forced maturing of young children, has become a frightening national trend among upper- and middle-class parents and that this over-programming of their children deprives them of childhood (Smith 2011). "Hot-housing" is applied to academics, social life, and sports pursuits, experts say.

Did Marv Marinovich learn his lesson, that you cannot force someone to be an athlete and not let them grow as an individual? Well, the answer is "no." Marv has another son, Mikhail (Todd's half-brother), who was also subjected to the same regimen that his father devised for Todd. Mikhail was once described as the "greatest 6-year-old athlete" his American Youth Soccer Organization team coach had ever seen (Fernas 1994). Should six year olds be described in terms of "greatest athlete" ever? Is this too much pressure for a child to handle? These are among the concerns of youth sport participation that will be discussed in this chapter.

After starring in football at JSerra Catholic High School in San Juan Capistrano, California, Mikhail signed with Syracuse University to further his football career. He wanted to get as far away from his father and the USC legacy that father Marv planned for him. He chose to be a defensive end instead of trying his hand as a quarterback. Mikhail's Syracuse career did not start off too well as before playing a single down with the Orange, Marinovich was arrested and charged with misdemeanor criminal mischief following an alleged break-in of a sports equipment room at Manley Field House. Marinovich was also a partner in a controversial hookah bar near campus, which he later gave up at the suggestion of his coaches (Heisler 2011). From that point on, Mikhail settled down quite nicely and had a good career with Syracuse. He married his high school sweetheart and claims to have never taken any drugs (Heisler 2011). When asked if his father was the worst parent in sports history, Mikhail laughed and said that his father was only second, behind the father of tennis player Mary Pierce (Heisler 2011). (As a point of interest, Mary Pierce, as a young teenager, successfully filed for a restraining order against her father who was known to be verbally abusive to his daughter and her opponents.)

Should Children Play Sports?

Should children play sports? And if so, when and what sports should children be allowed to participate in? Are organized sports worth all the time, money and effort put into them? These are questions that confront parents, and to a lesser extent, society in general. In most countries, organized youth sports are a luxury. They cost money and time that many people cannot afford. This is true even in the United States and Canada. The authors believe that it is important to indicate that youth sports benefit the vast majority of participants, including youths and parents. Furthermore, most parents have the best intentions when they encourage their children to play sports and certainly do not go to the "hot housing" extremes of Marv Marinovich.

Below, we will describe some of the many benefits of youth sport participation; later in the chapter we will describe some of the negative aspects.

Benefits of Youth Sport Participation

It has long been argued that sport participation helps to develop motor skills and physical fitness in youths. Play and sport are healthy behaviors that should be encouraged; and, that is exactly what medical professionals argue. There are many reasons why youth should participate in sporting activities beginning with the most obvious, to help fight off the growing possibility of becoming obese. The Heart Foundation reports that about one in three American kids and teens are overweight or obese; nearly triple the rate in 1963 (Erlinger 2018). Childhood obesity causes a broad range of health problems including high blood pressure, Type 2 diabetes, elevated blood cholesterol levels, asthma, sleep disorders, and nonalcoholic fatty liver disease (NAFLD). The Heart Foundation also states that there are psychological effects associated with obesity, including low self-esteem, negative body image, behavior and learning problems, and depression (Erlinger 2018). Causes of childhood obesity include poor diet, lack of exercise, family factors, psychological factors, and socioeconomic factors. To prevent obesity, the Heart

A young boy reaches first baseball after getting a hit.

Foundation recommends the encouragement of healthy eating habits, regular exercise, making it a family issue, reduce sedentary time, and schedule yearly doctor visits (Erlinger 2018).

In addition to promoting weight loss, other benefits of youth sport participation include: the development of hand-eye coordination; reduced risk of osteoporosis; improved stamina and endurance; improved flexibility; and long-term benefits (e.g., children who follow a healthy diet and exercise regularly are more likely than kids who are sedentary to stay active as adults) (Ashe-Edmunds 2017; Baca 2017).

All research on the topic of the benefits of youth sport will tout the healthy aspects of active exercise as a means of combating obesity and a sedentary lifestyle and the idea that sports activities help to develop hand-eye coordination. Some other benefits include: physical development (stronger muscles and bones, which helps to reduce the likelihood of suffering from physical injury); improved cardiovascular endurance (which helps to decrease the risk for heart disease); boosting self-esteem (being a part of a team with similar goals will increase the child's value of their self); strengthening perseverance (learning to cope with adverse situations via practices and game day activities); developing teamwork sills; teaching discipline; promoting healthy competition; providing guidance; and, helping to build character (learning to work with others, teamwork, leadership and responsibility) (Fitness Revolution 2015).

Proponents of youth sport participation often point to the idea that sport builds character. In the United States, the "sport builds character" concept can be traced back to the post–Civil War era. It should be noted, however, that this character development concept was applied primarily to boys. As Rader (2004) explains, a number of social leaders were concerned that modern life had become too soft and effeminate:

> Frontiers and battlefields no longer existed to test manly courage and perseverance. Henry W. Williams observed that the 'struggle for existence, though becoming harder and harder, is less and less a physical struggle, more and more a battle of minds.' Apart from sports, men no longer had arenas for testing their manliness. Theodore Roosevelt worried lest prolonged periods of peace would encourage 'effeminate tendencies in young men.' Only aggressive sports, Roosevelt argued, could create the 'brawn, the spirit, the self confidence, and quickness of men' that was essential for the existence of a strong nation [105]. [For the Williams quote reference see Williams 1895; see Dubbert 1979 for the Roosevelt quotes.]

The post–Civil War period marks a point in history where the traditional expression of manliness took on new meanings. Rapid industrial and technological advancements were making life increasingly "easy" (less dependent on physical brawn as a means for survival) for those in Western societies, especially the United States. Sports, especially aggressive ones, were viewed as a way for males to express their manliness.

Although this bit of historical information provides a framework for when advocates first touted sport as a means of building character, it does not inform us as to what character is, and whether sport can provide it. "Character" has a different meaning for people. Generally, it is assumed that "good" character is displayed when someone abides by the rules and acts according to social expectations. "Aristotle said that character is the composite of good moral qualities, whereby one shows firmness of belief, resolution, and practice about such moral values as honesty, justice, and respect. He also said that character is right conduct in relation to other persons and to self. Our humanness, he continues, resides in our ability and capacity to reason, and virtue results when we use our reasoning ability to control and moderate our self" (Stoll and Beller 2000: 18). Others would argue that reasoning alone is not enough to determine good character; instead, one must have a strong value system as well. As Stoll and Beller (2000) explain, "To say, 'Cheating is wrong,' is inadequate. One must know why it is wrong and put into action what one values, knows, and reasons is right. It is easy to say that one does not cheat but another thing not to cheat when surrounded by others who are cheating" (19).

There are a number of personal qualities associated with "character." "They include responsibility, persistence, courage, self-discipline, honesty, integrity, the willingness to work hard, compassion for others, generosity, independence, and tolerance" (Griffin 1998: 27). The authors define *character* as individual personality and behavioral traits, both good and bad, which define who a person is. Those who abide by societal rules are said to have good character; whereas those who flaunt society's rules or become overly self-absorbed do not.

Griffin (1998) states that "good character" comprises four traits:

1. *Responsibility*. Someone who can be depended upon to get the task or job done. This person works hard and is self-disciplined and persistent. Furthermore, a responsible person does not blame others for his or her own shortcomings or failures.
2. *Integrity*. A person with integrity "lives according to personal values" and possess deep conviction for his or her conduct in the social world.
3. *Decency*. "This person is directed by a firm sense of what is just and fair.... They respect the rights and dignity of others."
4. *Independence*. A free thinker who "is not the tool of someone else" [56].

Childhood and adolescence is a critical time in character formation and social development. "Social development comprises such things as friendship, social ranking, status, power, rejection and acceptance, inclusion and exclusion, dominance and submission, leadership, connection to the group, cooperativeness, aggression and passivity and withdrawal, and conflict" (Griffin 1998: 27). The ability to get along cooperatively with others and a willingness to accept society's rules are signs of good character and proper social development. Sports provide a good mechanism to develop character, and it does so under the watchful public eye. Because of this, youth receive immediate feedback regarding their behavior. At the same time, they become increasingly aware of their sense of self and role in the community.

Stoll and Beller believe that sports can build positive character traits in participants if the athletic programs themselves are designed to contribute positively to the ethical and moral development of athletes. "While teaching the will to win does not have to be eliminated, coaches, athletic administrators, and others in sport leadership positions must re-evaluate their philosophy regarding the importance of winning as it relates to character development, particularly when the participants are children and young adults. Without this fundamental shift in philosophy, sport will never fulfill its potential as a tool to educate and build positive character traits in our nation's youth" (2000: 27).

Schreiber (1990) argues that sport *does* build character. "Perhaps more important, sports *reveals* character—in kids and adults. Just watch a group of kids play basketball, and see if you can't immediately discern who looks to pass, who looks to shoot, who hollers at teammates when they make a mistake, who berates herself for the slightest error, who's the leader, who's eager to take the ball during crunch time, and so on. Sports is an uncanny truth-detector" (Schreiber 1990: 9). Schreiber makes a good point about sport revealing character. It is quite enlightening watching children play, as many of their character traits are revealed. However, it is important to note that some people transform themselves when playing sport in order to perform at a maximum level. Thus, a youth who plays football very aggressively is not necessarily an aggressive person off the field. In short, it is difficult to make general statements regarding sport participation and the building of character.

Griffin (1998) concludes, "No matter how one wants to define character, athletes very likely have no more of it than members of any other group" (67). Some athletes display very positive character traits; in some cases these values were learned in conjunction with sport participation and in other cases these values were learned by other agents of socialization. Unfortunately, all athletes do not display positive character traits. Throughout the remainder of this book a great number of negative character traits displayed by athletes will be detailed (see, for example, Chapter 8, Deviance; and Chapter 9, Violence).

Another benefit of sport participation is tied to the idea of personal identity. For many youths, being an athlete is a big part of who they are. For girls of all grades, 34 percent report that sports are a major aspect of their identity (35 percent for girls grades 3–4; 40 percent for girls grade 6 to 8; and 28 percent for girls grades 9 to 12). A much higher percentage of boys have their identity tied to sport participation, 61 percent for all grades (70 percent for boys' grades 3 to 5; 63 percent for grades 6 to 8; and 53 percent for grades 9 to 12). As both boys and girls age, a small, but still significant, percentage report that sports are a big part of who they are (Kelley and Carchia 2013). Regardless of age, boys find sports far more important than girls when it comes to personal identity.

Malm, Jakobsson, and Isaksson (2019) summarize the positive effects from sports

High school football played under the lights on a Friday night.

participation as achieved primarily through physical activity, but secondary effects of health benefits include psychosocial and personal development and less alcohol consumption. The researchers found a correlation between high daily physical activity in children and a low risk for obesity, improved development of motor and cognitive skills, as well as a stronger skeleton. "Positive effects on lipidemia, blood pressure, oxygen consumption, body composition, metabolic syndrome, bone density and depression, increased muscle strength, and reduced damage to the skeleton and muscles" (Malm et al 2019). Summarizing the positive aspects of sport participation Malm and associates state, "If many aspects are merged in a multidimensional analysis, the factors important for future good health are shown to be training in sports, broad exposure to different sports, high school grades, cultural capital, and that one takes part in sport throughout childhood."

Another interesting finding cited by Malm et al (2019) is that sport builds bridges between generations. This is especially true when parents are actively involved in supporting, encouraging, and in some cases participating alongside their children as they engage in sporting activities. For example, many parents will exercise with their children, play ball, ride bikes, and participate in 5k races with their children. This is a great healthy way for parents to forge bonds with their children. In many cases, other family members will join in with sporting activities with their grandchildren or nieces and nephews. The holiday family kickball or softball game is a good example of this. One thing that all generations seem to remember fondly were the times they spent engaged with one another in sporting activities, whether it was at holiday gatherings or regular days.

Research has also found that youth sport participation serves a positive function for the 1.5 million children and youth experiencing homelessness in the 2017–18 school year (School House Connection 2020). These young athletes, lacking a stable place to live and often going hungry, found structure, support and joy in their lives through sport participation. Wertheim and Rodriguez (2014) found that virtually every homeless athlete interviewed found sports to be a positive force in their lives. "Coaches often become mentors and even surrogate parents; pregame and postgame meals provide essential nourishment; [and] kids benefit from the exercise and structure" (Wertheim and Rodriguez 2014: 56). Sports also provide academic benefits as well. While homeless youths are 87 percent more likely to stop going to school than their non-homeless classmates, homeless youth who play sports are far more likely to stay in school, graduate from high school and attend college. These same homeless youths may not find a career in sport, but they have better life chances because of their sports play. (See "Connecting Sports and Popular Culture" Box 6 for a discussion of Michael Oher, a former homeless youth who was adopted by foster parents and went on to play in the NFL, as depicted in the movie *Blind Side.*)

WHEN SHOULD YOUTHS BEGIN SPORT PARTICIPATION?

Infants, from birth until about eighteen months, are just beginning to learn to interact with their environment. A physically active infant is an important foundation for a healthy life. Infants learn to play through interaction with caregivers (e.g., family members) and by self-exploration. There are very few "skills" that can be encouraged at this age. However, playful slapping, smacking, and pounding a ball can be encouraged by placing a ball in the baby's crib. When the infant can sit up, rolling a ball is a good way to develop motor skills. Infants can kick a ball before they can walk, so parents should encourage this activity as well. Parents who take their young children on walks and bike rides provide another way to encourage early active participation. When toddlers begin to walk, it is important to encourage the activity, so that the child will feel proud of his or her accomplishment. From around eighteen months to 2 and a half years of age, children develop a well-organized autonomous achievement orientation that evolves from increasing mastery of competence motivation. Around age two or three, children learn to throw items; if not a ball, then a doll, or food. At this age, the child throws only with his or her arms and does not use any body motion. Catching a ball is more difficult than throwing one. Playing catch with toddlers is an excellent motor skill development activity. Learning how to run backwards is another example of a motor skill that children learn around age 7 or 8. Running backwards combined with another skill such as catching a ball is more complicated. Many team sports emphasize such motor skill developments as being able to run backwards.

In short, it is never too early for physical play, as infants can be encouraged to roll a ball or kick one. When a toddler has learned to walk, running is the next type of development, and this activity should be encouraged. Caroline Silby (2000) argues that at young ages, it is very important for children to discover the numerous ways their body can move. Relying a great deal on imitation and trial and error, youngsters will develop most of their complex motor skills by age six or seven. At this age of maturation, children are beginning to develop self-perceptions of physical, social, and cognitive competency. As a result it is very important for adult care-givers to emphasize a positive social environment (Silby 2000).

The early school years of a child mark an important stage in development, and thus, athletic competencies. Around age seven, most children experience a growth spurt; including the size of the brain, which increases to 90 percent of its total weight (compared to 25 percent at birth). Along with body growth comes an increase in ability to handle more challenging physical activities. Children tend to cling to rules and organization at this age.

Early elementary age children have learned the basic skills necessary to play any sport of their choosing. "It is crucial for youngsters to practice their newfound skills in order to gain proficiency in sports" (Small and Spear 2002: 14). At this age it is advisable for youths not to specialize in one sport, as they are still developing and may enjoy or excel at another sport. From ages 10 to 13, children generally undergo their adolescent growth spurt as they reach puberty. During this growth spurt, many children are often physically awkward. As these children become comfortable with their new physiques, they may find that they have new athletic grace and ability (Schreiber 1990).

Sports become increasingly competitive with each succeeding year. Selection for team sports comes to the forefront. "By age eleven, more than half of children have quit organized sports. Kids cite several common reasons for quitting: sports cease to be fun; sports become too competitive; she does not receive enough playing time" (Small and Spear 2002: 17). Kids who drop out of organized sports have the option to participate in informal sports such as hiking, skateboarding, skating, snowboarding, bicycle riding, and walking.

In short, by age 7 or 8, children have developed a capacity for reason and an understanding for rules and are therefore ready for organized physical activities. At the very least, children at this age are capable of participating in physical education classes in school. Organized sports before the age of 7 should be matched with that child's needs and abilities. As for contact sports, Martens and Seefeldt (1979) believe that youth at age 6 are ready for noncontact sports (e.g., swimming, tennis, track and field); 8 year olds are ready for contact sports (e.g., basketball, soccer, wrestling); and 10 year olds are ready for collision sports (e.g., ice hockey, tackle football).

Origin and Development of Organized Youth Sports

One of the outcomes of industrialization and urbanization of the United States and Canada midway through the nineteenth century was the emergence of leisure time for many children, especially urban youth. The large number of children roaming the streets convinced social policy makers and citizens alike to find a way to organize children's lives through a combination of sport and education. The linking of sport with formal education began in the United States around the time of the Civil War. This idea was influenced by European sports programs of early nineteenth century.

Toward the end of the nineteenth century, advocates of youth sports were proclaiming the moral value of participation. Combining sport and morality with education was accomplished through an ideology known as "Muscular Christianity." Muscular Christianity, then, refers to the religious philosophy of teaching morals and values through sport. The idealism of Muscular Christianity had a great impact on the development of sport in English and American society. Muscular Christianity triggered the development of sports in American schools; especially for boys. Sport activities were organized for boys in schools, on playgrounds, and in church groups. Team sports were supposed to teach boys how to cooperate and work productively together with others. It was believed that boys would become strong, assertive, competitive men.

Ideas of Muscular Christianity and boys acting manly influenced the establishment of the Young Men's Christian Association (YMCA). The "Y" as it is most commonly known was started in 1844 in industrialized London, a place of great turmoil and despair. George Williams and 11 friends organized the first YMCA, a refuge of Bible study and prayer for young men seeking escape from the hazards of life on the streets (YMCA 2020). The first U.S. YMCA opened at Old South Church in Boston on December 29, 1851. After the Civil War, the YMCA broadened its sports programs but maintained a commitment to developing a spiritual "physical culture."

The development of organized youth sports was not limited to the schools or a religious realm. A "play movement" developed outside the schools and gained momentum toward the end of the nineteenth century. Massive immigration during the nineteenth century had led to overcrowded cities and youth with no place to play. "In an effort to provide suitable play space for children in this environment, sand piles were first erected in Boston in 1885. In 1888, New York passed the first state legislation that led to an organized play area for children. By 1899, the Massachusetts Emergency and Hygiene Association sponsored 21 playgrounds" (Lumpkin 1994: 213). Jane Addams' Hull House in Chicago also had a playground. As the twentieth century began, a large number of political and community leaders worked to ensure that children had a place to play, either at parks, playgrounds, or indoor facilities.

With the development of sports in and out of school it became necessary to train people to teach physical education courses and to coach sports. By the end of the nineteenth century many colleges offered degrees in physical education. It became a recognized subject by the National Education Association in 1891. As the twentieth century progressed, schools across the nation provided competitive sports for youth. Slowly the number of sporting opportunities for girls would increase. Summer sport programs ensured that children had an opportunity to remain active in sports year-round. During the 1950s, general fitness programs were established in schools. And although the popularity of sport has continued to grow in the United States since the 1950s, American school children have tested poorly on fitness (Lumpkin 1994). The 1950s also marked the beginning of the "Baby Boomer" generation. For the first time in history, a large number of children had a great deal of leisure time on their hands, with families that had the means to provide for their children's athletic pursuits. Sports were funded by a combination of public, private and commercial sponsors. Parents were active. Some fathers would serve as coaches, managers and league administrators and mothers became chauffeurs and short-order cooks so that their kids could be on time for practices and games and still have time to eat. During the late 1970s, girls' participation in sport began to grow in earnest.

In the following pages we will take a closer look at youth sports in the twentieth and twenty-first centuries in our analysis of formal and informal youth sports.

Formal Youth Sports

It should be fairly well established by this point that sport plays an integral role in American culture and is a major social institution in society. Furthermore, because of the free time afforded children (because they are not expected to work full-time) and a general concern that idleness leads to delinquency, it comes as little surprise that formal sports are strongly encouraged.

The main objective of organized youth sports was to provide opportunities for all youths to participate in sport in a wholesome character-building environment as they made the transition from childhood to adulthood (Berryman 1988). The concept of character development has always been associated with youth sport. As described earlier in this chapter, sport is promoted as a setting where youth can develop good character traits such as positive attitudes about competition, sportsmanship, authority, and discipline. Martens and Seefeldt (1979: 11) identify a number of objectives for youth sport programs that hold true today:

1. To develop motoric competencies.
2. To develop physical fitness.
3. To teach children how to cooperate.
4. To develop a sense of achievement, leading to a positive self-concept.
5. To develop interest in, and a desire to, continue participation in sports in later years.
6. To develop healthy, strong identities.
7. To help develop independence through interdependent activities.
8. To promote and convey the values of society.
9. To contribute to moral development.
10. To have fun.
11. To develop social competencies.
12. To help bring the family together.
13. To provide opportunities for physical-affective learning, including learning to understand and express emotion, imagination, and appreciation for what the body can do.
14. To develop speed, strength, endurance, coordination, flexibility, and agility.
15. To develop leadership skills.
16. To develop self-reliance and emotional stability by learning to make decisions and accept responsibilities.
17. To teach sportsmanship.
18. To develop initiative.
19. To teach children how to compete.
20. To help children learn about their capabilities through comparisons with others.

Formal youth sport leagues were formed to help keep the idealized view of sport as a character-building activity for youths. Children would develop positive character traits and their idle time would be minimized. There are a number of organized youth leagues in the United States (as well as Canada and other Western nations) and in most cases all those involved, especially the coaches, have the best intention of the athletes in mind. It is refreshing to know, especially for sports fans that have to listen to, and acknowledge, the many negative aspects of sport portrayed in the media, that many people, including former professional athletes willingly give freely of their time. During the summer of 2014, one of the authors, Tim Delaney, had the pleasure to speak with Preston Shumpert, a former Syracuse University basketball star (1998–2002), who went to star in European leagues for over a decade (for 11 years he played on teams in France, Italy or Turkey).

Shumpert had returned to the Syracuse, New York, area to raise his two sons with his wife Ashley. He turned down an offer to play in Turkey to be near his family and watch his boys play ball. As of early 2020, Preston's sons, Payton and Preston, were starring at basketball at Jamesville-DeWitt High School in Syracuse.

Shumpert wants to help other youths too, so he decided to serve as a coach at the Bellucci Basketball Academy (BBA) in Syracuse. The BBA is named after Ben Bellucci, a Syracuse kid who went on to star at SUNY Brockport and then play professional basketball in Europe (2006–2008). While the BBA teaches youth fundamental basketball skills such as shooting, dribbling, defense, improving speed and agility, and reacting to play on the court, it also stresses building confidence, self-esteem and a wide range of skills that transcend the court and will be beneficial throughout life (Bellucci Basketball Academy 2014). Shumpert always appeared to be a good-natured young man on the playing court and having spoken with him one cannot help but be drawn in by his positive attitude. He loves to encourage youth to be positive. Shumpert shared our belief that nurturing and teaching basketball skills is far more important than relying on any natural attributes that might help an athlete (e.g., having big hands is helpful in basketball but does little good if one does not understand how to use them to catch, pass and shoot the ball).

In the following pages we will examine a few examples of organized youth leagues beginning with, perhaps the most famous of them all, Little League Baseball.

Baseball

One of the biggest formal youth baseball leagues is Little League Baseball (LLB). LLB was founded in 1939 in Williamsport, Pennsylvania, by Carl E. Stotz and Bert and George Bebble. Carl, Bert, and George would become the managers of the first three teams formed. The mission statement of LLB is a belief "in the power of youth baseball and softball to teach life lessons that build stronger individuals and communities" (Little League 2020a). There are many divisions (decided by age) in Little League Baseball: players (boys and girls) who age 4–7 are eligible to be selected to Tee Ball team; 7–12 are eligible for the Minor League Division; players 9–12 are eligible for the most popular Major Division, this is the division that receives the most media attention during its annual World Series (Note: A 2006 rule change now allows 13 year olds to play in the World Series as long as they turned 13 after May 1.); players who are 12–14 are eligible for the Junior League; and players 13–16 are eligible for the Senior League Division (Little League 2020b).

There are nearly three million youths world-wide play Little League ball, making it the world's largest organized youth sports program. Little League baseball teaches sportsmanship and promotes the ideals of character building. One of the characteristics that makes Little League Baseball (Major Division) so special is its annual World Series. Little League baseball teams from all 50 U.S. states, more than 80 countries, and six continents (understandably, Antarctica is the lone continent which does not have Little League Baseball) compete against one another for the opportunity to play in the Little League World Series (LLWS), held in Williamsport annually in August. The top 16 qualifying teams from around the world are invited to the 6 week tournament. A local league has the option to choose a "Tournament Team" (or "All Stars") of 11 and 12 year olds from within its division and enter the International Tournament leading to the series. As of 2019, Taiwan had won the most titles (17). All expenses for the teams advancing to the

LLWS (travel, meals, housing) are paid by Little League Baseball. The LLWS is broadcast live in the United States and in many other countries around the world, adding to the overall formal, organized nature of the game. Little League Baseball also has its own Hall of Fame Museum located in Williamsport. While the annual LLWS brings with it many storylines the 2020 storyline was the most unusual of all as the tournament was cancelled due to the SARS-CoV-2 global pandemic.

Some of the best young baseball players do not play in Little League but instead play with the Amateur Athletic Union (AAU). The AAU sponsors baseball tournaments throughout the country. The AAU develops players "physically, mentally and morally and engage in good sportsmanship and citizenship on and off the field. Being able to participate in challenging situations through AAU baseball tournaments and other competitions also helps these developments occur" (Next College Student Athlete 2020).

Another formal baseball league is the Babe Ruth League, founded in 1951 for boys between 12 and 15 years of age. The organization recognizes Marius D. Bonacci as the founder of the program. At present there are well over one million players on some 60,000+ teams in more than 11,000 leagues that now include girls on the rosters and over 1.9 million volunteers (Babe Ruth League 2020). The League is made of divisions: Cal Ripken Baseball (for ages 4–12); Babe Ruth Baseball (13–18); Babe Ruth Softball (with different age categories); Bambino Buddy Ball (for players ages 5–20 who are physically and/ or mentally challenged and who may use a "buddy" to help the player swing a bat, round the bases, and catch a ball); and, Extreme Fastpitch. The Extreme Fastpitch division was added in 2013 to meet the needs of "those who wish to play on a recreational level to those who seek a higher degree of competition to hone their skills with the goal of continuing play into high school and beyond" (Babe Ruth League 2020). The Cal Ripken division was named after Cal Ripken, Jr., the former Baltimore Orioles great and a graduate of the Babe Ruth program, who is often cited as an example of someone who played the game the "right way"—"The Ripken Way." Ripken is also an example of a hero of "social acceptability" because he upholds the values of society, especially those of sportsmanship and hard work.

Little League and Babe Ruth League baseball are highly organized youth sport programs. They are adult-centered, meaning adults run the operation and children follow the standardized rules. Many people support these organized youth sport programs for those very reasons. Others, however, complain that a formal and rational organization deprives young people of playlike experiences. Nixon and Frey (1996) use the term *little leaguism* to describe youth sports that have become bureaucratic, standardized, efficiency-driven, rationalized, calculated, and predictable. It is worth noting that many times when sport sociologists describe the institution of sport in a critical manner people conclude that they must not like sports; but this is not the case. Jim Frey, for example (and referenced above), coached his 13-year-old son's team to the Little League World Series for that age group. His Henderson's Green Valley (NV) team lost a best-of-three championship series. Of the nine starters on the Green Valley team three signed major league contracts, five had college baseball scholarships, and the other went to jail. Five of the players were members of four straight high school state championships for the baseball factory program (Frey 2020). Frey also points out that once kids reached the 12-year-old level there was little attempt to develop less-talented players and the emphasis was placed on the all-stars.

Another major youth club organization is the United States Specialty Sports

Association (USSSA). Originally USSSA stood for United States Slowpitch Softball Association but its expansion into other youth sports (e.g., girls fastpitch, boys baseball, youth basketball, martial arts and more) led to the name change. The organization's primary focus is the development of programs that allow teams of all skill levels to compete against one another. In baseball, USSSA offers programs for four levels of play: Major and AAA programs are national programs that culminate in a World Series; the AA program, a regional program that culminates at a National tournament; and the A level that is for recreational teams and is at a state level only (USSSA 2020).

FOOTBALL

The most recognized formal and organized youth football program is Pop Warner Football. (Another program is USA Football.) The history of Pop Warner Football can be traced to Philadelphia in the late 1920s and a group of factory owners who were tired of having youth throw rocks through their factory's windows. They attributed this delinquent behavior to the idleness of children with nothing better to do (Powell 2003). As a result, they formed an athletic program for kids. They also assumed that football would be best sport to keep idle kids occupied and out of trouble. The league was called the Junior Football Conference and operated for the first time in 1929.

Pop Warner is the oldest national youth football and cheerleading organization in the world, with over 120 leagues and over 325,000 participants (Pop Warner 2020). Pop Warner hosts an annual Pop Warner Super Bowl and National Cheer and Dance Championship which takes place at ESPN's Wide World of Sports Complex at Disney World. (Note: This is the same facility where the NBA resumed its postponed 2019–20 season under a "bubble" format—meaning no one could leave or enter the facility while their respective teams were still playing.) More than 300 cheer and dance squads and 72 football teams compete for the respective titles (Pop Warner 2020). The 2020 Pop Warner football and cheer season was cancelled due to the SARS-CoV-2 global pandemic.

Over the past few years the number of youth playing organized youth football has decreased somewhat due to parental fear that their children may suffer from a concussion. Researchers have found that the single factor that best determines whether players develop CTE was not how many concussions they suffered, but instead the number of years they played tackle football (Dobnik 2019). As a result, over the past few years a number of states, including New York, have discussed banning youth tackling. The Pop Warner association has addressed this fear by establishing a stringent concussion prevention and treatment protocol in addition to increased hydration awareness, establishing proper nutrition guidelines, and adhering to general health and safety issues. Pop Warner football has also established a Little Scholars Program (that rewards its members for their outstanding performance in the classroom); a National Scholar Banquet; and a college scholarships program (Pop Warner 2020).

The concern over possible concussions and later-life CTE has led to a dramatic increase in the popularity of flag football. Flag football is the fastest growing youth sport and participation increased 44 percent in 2018 from 2014 (Geist 2019). Flag football is similar to football in nearly all ways sans the tackling. Drew Brees, quarterback for the New Orleans Saints, didn't play tackle football until high school and is a proponent of youth flag football. As a result, he helped to form Football 'N' America (FNA) a non-contact youth co-ed flag football league for children in grades K-10, in a coed format (Football 'N' America 2020). FNA is just one example of the emerging flag football craze.

Tennis

Tennis is a sport that historically has been linked to the wealthy socio-economic classes. At private clubs, the girls wore white skirts and boys wore hip-hugging white shorts and swung wooden rackets while adults often drank cocktails courtside (McKibben 2006). Many public schools offered tennis in the 1950s and 1960s and baby boomers began to embrace the sport as way to stay fit. The interest in tennis reached its peak in the 1970s when an estimated 36 million boys and girls played tennis (McKibben 2006). Court time was coveted. Private clubs and public tennis courts were rapidly built to meet the growing demand. "During the sport's peak in the mid–1970s, developers couldn't build private clubs fast enough to satisfy the public's urge to whack a fuzzy yellow ball. The building boom continued through the 1980s, even as the number of recreational tennis players fell by more than half and cheap-to-build suburban public courts flooded the landscape" (McKibben 2006: A21). Today, many of the private clubs have closed their doors.

There is a formal youth tennis association, the United States Tennis Association (USTA) Juniors, which hosts local competition at all levels: entry-level, intermediate, and advanced. Competitors that advance may qualify to compete at regional- and national-level tournaments. Competitors can participate as individuals, teams, and wheelchair (USTA 2020).

Soccer

Soccer has gained popularity in the United States over the past few decades. Many youth soccer leagues have developed across the nation. Soccer is often a preferred sport because it is an inexpensive sport to fund (all that is really needed is a ball and an empty field with a goal at each end) and smaller children can compete more evenly than in contact sports such as football, rugby, and basketball. Soccer is appealing because it is a simple game to comprehend and youth can easily pick up the few critical rules. Today's youth also prefer soccer over baseball because they get to run around in soccer, whereas in baseball there is a great deal of inactivity—especially for outfielders. The recent success of the men's and primarily the women's U.S. National Soccer teams has led to many American youth idolizing soccer stars.

Among the more popular formal youth soccer associations are the American Youth Soccer Organization (AYSO), which helps to support and manage youth soccer leagues, and the U.S. Youth Soccer, association which assists those who wish to organize youth soccer leagues. AYSO (2020) mandates that every player on every team must play at least 50 percent of every game, an appealing aspect of this formal activity; creates balanced teams for more equal competition; positive coaching; good sportsmanship; and player development. AYSO has roughly 650,000 participants. Far more youth play soccer outside of the AYSO, creating a "soccer mom" phenomenon. A soccer mom is someone who drives her children to soccer games and watches them compete. Since the parents were probably never soccer players, the children get to play a sport for which parents are not "armchair quarterbacks"—constantly suggesting better playing techniques based on their own overstated knowledge of the game.

Hockey

In certain areas of the United States, especially in areas close to the Canadian border, youth hockey is very popular. The fees associated with formal youth hockey are quite expensive due to high organizational registration fees; travel and hotels for out-of-town tournaments (a regular occurrence); hockey equipment; and ice arena fees. One of the author's nephews are heavily involved in youth hockey in Upstate New York and the parents and families involved semi-jokingly refer to youth hockey as cult-like because of the dedication and hours put into the sport by the entire family. When the youth hockey teams travel, they travel in caravans of families and stay in the same hotels, forming a tight-knit bond centered on their kids playing hockey. Many parents go through a type of withdrawal when the season is over and some have a very hard time when their children no longer play youth hockey.

There are a wide variety of leagues and associations and formal organizations such as USA Hockey and Youth Hockey. The Youth Hockey association helps leagues with online scheduling; round robin matchups; online team declaration processes; and results and standings (Youth Hockey 2019). USAA Hockey also organizes youth hockey leagues, assists in player, coaching and official's development. During the 2020 COVID-19 pandemic, the league was involved in a variety of virtual training activities until it was deemed safe to host large group gatherings. Coaches could maintain their certification via virtual coaching clinics.

Special Olympics

The Special Olympics is a global movement of people creating a new world of inclusion and community, where every single person is accepted and welcomed, regardless of ability or disability (Special Olympics 2020). As of 2018, there were nearly 5.5 million participating athletes from 193 countries competing in over 106,000 competitions assisted by over 1.1 million volunteers (Special Olympics 2020).

The Special Olympics has helped to create a global community of inclusion, helping to change stigmatizing attitudes while fostering acceptance and understanding. Since the start of the twenty-first century, there exists a general acceptance of the idea that youth and adults with disabilities should no longer be excluded from sports, as they once were. We will look at the Special Olympics (and the Invictus Games) again in Chapter 16.

Most Popular Youth Sports

As our brief review of formal youth sports reveals, there are a number of opportunities for youth to play a variety of sports in an organized fashion and most of these organizations tend to promote inclusion, fair play, and good sportsmanship. In addition to such organizations as Little League, Babe Ruth, Pop Warner, AYSO, and so on, there are a large number of club sport organizations for kids as young as 9 and through high school. Club competition in certain sports, such as swimming, soccer, baseball, and hockey, attract elite athletes. These clubs include high participation fees ($3–5k annually to belong) (Frey 2020). Add it all up and there are approximately 45–50 million youth (19 and under) participating in organized youth sports. No wonder, as an industry, youth sports represents a \$15.3 billion market, according to WinterGreen Research, a private firm that tracks the industry (Gregory 2017).

What are the most popular youth sports in America? According to EngageSports, there are more than 45 million children ages 6–17 who currently participate in at least one sport, and the most popular sport, with 9.5 million participants, is basketball (In Sports 2018). The top ten most popular youth sports in 2018 are shown in Table 6.1.

Table 6.1: Most Popular Participant Youth Sports in the U.S. (in Millions)

Activity	Participants (in millions)
1. Basketball	9.5
2. Soccer (outdoor)	7.5
3. Baseball	6.5
4. Football (tackle)	3.5
5. Gymnastics	3.0
6. Volleyball (court)	2.5
7. Track & Field	2.5
8. Soccer (indoor)	2.0
9. Football (touch)	2.0
10. Softball	1.5

(Source: In Sports 2018)

There are a lot of reasons why participating in team sports is attractive including: they provide opportunities for youth to create friendships, reaffirm established friendships, have fun, get exercise, develop skills, learn of the benefits of a nutritional diet, and engage in parental-approved activities. The vast majority of children (75 percent of boys and 69 percent of girls) in the United States participate in organized and team sports in any given year, and just 15 percent have never participated in sports (Uzoma 2018). Participation in sports by youths tends to be higher among those living in suburban areas compared to those living in urban and rural areas. For example, 81 percent of girls in grades three to five in suburban areas participate in at least one organized sport compared to 73 percent for rural girls and only 59 percent for urban girls (Uzoma 2018). Across all grade levels (3 to 12), boys participate in sports at a higher percentage than girls, and boys tend to start playing organized sports earlier than girls.

Criticisms of Organized Youth Sports

There are detractors of organized youth sport sports that point out the negative aspects of participation, beginning with the realization that as youth age competition and winning often supersede the playful character of sport (Nixon and Frey 1996; Devereaux 1976; Horn 1977). According to a poll from the National Alliance for Youth Sports, around 70 percent of youth in the United States stop playing organized sports by the age of 13 because "it's just not fun anymore" (Miner 2016). The idea that sport participation is no longer fun is the first criticism of youth sports.

Sport participation stops being fun when the focus shifts from play-centered to performance-centered which is accompanied by a corresponding overemphasis on winning occurs (the second criticism of youth sports). A "win at all costs" approach is not appropriate for youth sport. Most parents find it very important that their children win at the sports they play. Winning is a high priority to most parents. However, when children are asked why they play sports, they overwhelmingly indicate that winning is a low priority (until around high school age). Kids play primarily to have fun, develop skills, get exercise and to hangout with friends.

The overemphasis on winning is often encouraged by over-zealous coaches, the third criticism of youth sports. In his research of Pop Warner football, Powell (2003) found that coaches at the elite 95-pound division conduct drills and practices like a "boot camp. "These practices consisted of sprints, rope-netting skip drills and agility tests. After an hour of conditioning drills, the team breaks down into groups to run drills and plays. Powell (2003) quotes one coach barking commands to one of his young players, "Get mean! Wipe that smile off your face. Get ready to hurt somebody. Get mean! Come on, get mean!" (3). In addition, the play aspect is compromised in formal youth sports because of the regimentation of organized sport programs. As sports become increasingly regulated, the spontaneity of the game is greatly compromised. Many youth turn to informal sport because it is less structured and offers greater freedom and creativity. Thus, when formal sport stops being fun, youth are likely to quit playing organized sports and search out other fun activities.

The over-emphasis on youths specializing in one sport is the fourth criticism of youth sport. It has become increasingly common for coaches and parents of elite youth athletes to steer participants toward concentrating on the one sport that they excel at. This push for youth to specialize and achieve at the highest possible level in one sport can lead to social isolation (because they are missing out on a lot of other activities); overdependence (schedules dictate the lives of the participants planned for them by parents and coaches); burnout (especially when the young athlete feels as though they cannot live up to the demands and expectations placed on them); injuries (young athletes' bones, muscles, and ligaments are still developing and repetitive overuse, as participating in one sport can do, can cause harm) (Curtis 2017). In order to reduce the stress on the development of youth's bones, muscles, and ligaments, sufficient recovery periods for restoration of physiological balance are very important (Malm et al 2019).

A fifth criticism is the big business aspect of organized youth sports that has led many league officials and coaches to over-emphasize winning and sport specialization (the sixth criticism) and failing to concentrate on the physical (motor skills), cognitive, emotional and developmental stage of their youth athletes (Chalip and Green 1998; Nixon and Frey 1996; Hellison 1995; Hutslar 1985; and Martens 1988). The case described by Powell (2003) regarding "boot camp" practices may be applied here as well. In her book *Little Girls in Pretty Boxes* (2000), sports columnist Joan Ryan describes the often harrowing experiences which young female gymnasts and figure skaters undergo in their training. Many of them end up suffering from eating disorders such as bulimia and anorexia all because coaches push them too hard. Ryan writes:

> Coaches push because they are paid to produce great gymnasts. They are relentless about weight because physically round gymnasts and skaters don't win. Coaches are intolerant of injuries because in the race against puberty, time off is death. Their job is not to turn out happy, well-adjusted young women; it is to turn out champions. If they scream, belittle or ignore, if they prod an injured girl to forget her pain, if they push her to drop out of school, they are only doing what the parents have paid them to do. So, sorting out the blame when a girl falls apart is a messy proposition; everyone claims he was just doing his job [Ryan 2000: 11].

Many youth find organized, formal sport as not only too restrictive, but filled with anxiety and angst. They are turned off by adults who bark orders and league officials who impose standardized rules. Formal youth sport participants may also be turned off by experiences with their teammates and in other cases they may feel like they were not a good enough player to continuing playing.

These negative aspects of sports lead many youth athletes to experience stress, the seventh criticism of youth sports. Athletic stress can be defined as forces that cause bodily or mental strain. Bodily strain is caused by excessive physical demands on the body, such as fatigue as a result of a strenuous workout. Mental strain can be caused by internal pressure that the youth places on self-performance. The source of this stress is not sport participation itself; rather, it is often caused by youth athletes' parents, coaches and league officials. The authors have attended numerous youth sports events over the years and have heard a number of parents yelling at their children by calling them "bums" and "useless" (and far worse) when they make a bad play. The children who are screamed at not only feel bad about themselves, but they are also embarrassed by their parent's behavior, and experience a great deal of stress. The consequences of experiencing such stress may be both immediate and delayed. Youths who no longer value sport participation because of stress will most likely quit and find some other activity free from parental involvement. For other youths, years of stress caused by fanatical parental interference may boil over in early adulthood when the young athlete becomes free from direct parental supervision. The case of Todd Marinovich, described at the beginning of this chapter, serves as an exemplar of behavior of youth who have experienced harmful stress. When Marinovich was old enough to go to college and live on his own, he finally allowed himself the opportunity to express his newfound freedom. Some of these youthful transgressions had harmful results. Although few parents go to the extremes of pushing their children into sports as Marv Marinovich, there are parents who do push their children toward unrealistic goals of college sport scholarships and professional sports contracts. These slightly-delusional parents hear and read about all the money professional athletes earn and believe that their children can also be as accomplished.

The odds, of course, are strongly against any youth making it to the professional level. It has already been stated that 70 percent of youth athletes quit formal sports by age 13. Add to this, that of the estimated 7.3 million high school athletes competing in the major team sports (men's and women's basketball, football, baseball, men's ice hockey, and men's soccer) just 6 percent (492,000) will become NCAA student-athletes, and just 2 percent of NCAA athletes turn pro, and we can see that it is highly unlikely that any youth athlete will earn a paycheck as a professional athlete in any of the major team sports (NCAA 2018). (We will look at the odds of becoming an NCAA and professional athlete again in Chapter 7.)

In an effort to achieve, whether to please others, or themselves, some youth athletes will turn to performance-enhancing drugs, especially anabolic steroids (the eighth criticism). (See Chapter 8 for a full definition and explanation of how anabolic steroids work.) Anabolic steroids are classified as Schedule III Controlled Substances by the U.S. Drug Enforcement Administration, meaning that only the medical profession can prescribe them. Athletes learn that professional athletes take steroids and wonder if it will work for them too. As the Food and Drug Administration (FDA) (2017) warns, "The abuse of anabolic steroids can cause both temporary and permanent injury to anyone using them. Teenagers, whose bodies are still developing, are at heightened risk. An alarming number of them are trying steroids in hopes of improving their athletic prowess or their appearance." The FDA (2017) reports that among U.S. high school students an estimated 4.9 percent of males and 2.4 percent of females have used anabolic steroids at least once in their lives. High school students generally report that it is relatively easy to obtain steroids. The Mayo Clinic (2020) reports that among teens, the most common performance-enhancing drugs and supplements include: Creatine, anabolic steroids, steroid precursors (e.g., androstenedione and DHEA), amphetamines and other stimulants, and caffeine. Possible red flags that parents should be on the lookout for include: behavioral, emotional or psychological changes—particularly increased aggressiveness (so-called "roid rage"); changes in body build, including muscle growth, rapid weight gain and development of the upper body; increased acne; needle marks in the buttocks or thighs; enlarged breasts, male-pattern baldness and shrinking of the testicles in boys; and smaller breasts, voice deepening and excessive growth of body hair in girls (The Mayo Clinic 2020).

Noting yet again that the importance of stressing having fun in youth sport works to help prevent youths from turning to performance-enhancing drugs. It also helps to remind parents that children are initially attracted to sports because they want to have fun, develop motor skills, and hang out with their friends. And yet, violence has become a trademark of many youth sports. This violence is not between participants but instead includes parents fighting parents, parents attacking youth participants, parents attacking referees, coaches attacking referees, youths attacking referees, and referees attacking coaches (the ninth criticism of sport). In the earlier editions of this text we have chronicled a number of examples of escalating violence in youth sport to help illustrate the point. However, it seems pointless now as nearly everyone is aware of such forms of violence. If you want to see videos of youth sport violence you can find plenty on YouTube.

Most parents and league officials do their best to assure that injuries in youth sport are minimized. As a result, most children who play sports will not be seriously injured. Nonetheless, sports injuries are fairly common for young athletes (tenth criticism). More than half of all youth sport injuries occur at practice rather than during competition (National Center for Sport Safety 2006). The two most common types of sports injury for youth athletes are sprains (in injury to a ligament such as tearing or stretching) and strains (an injury to a tendon or muscle). Growth plate injuries (the growth plate is at the end of the long bones in developing children before it is replaced by solid bone) are also common for youngsters. Immature bones (growth plate), insufficient rest after an injury, and poor training or conditioning contribute to a large number of sport injuries for youngsters (National Center for Sport Safety 2006).

The eleventh criticism of youth sport is the growing concern over a particular form of sport injury, concussions. We usually hear about concussions at the professional level especially with regard to football, hockey, and soccer, but thousands of youth sport participants also suffer from them. Ice hockey accounts for the highest percentage of concussions (12 percent) followed by snowboarding (10 percent), water tubing (9 percent), football and lacrosse (8 percent for each sport) (Insurance Information Institute 2020). The CDC reported in 2016 that over 273,000 children (17 or younger) were treated in U.S. emergency departments for nonfatal traumatic brain injuries (TBI) related to sports and recreation (III 2020). There were also 199,000 swimming injuries treated in emergency rooms in 2017, with children between ages five and 14 suffering the most injuries (III 2020). (See Chapter 9 for a further discussion on concussions.)

As we can see, there are many potential reasons why a youth may turn away from formal youth sports. One viable alternative for youth who wish to remain physically active is to participate in informal youth sports.

Informal Youth Sports

It is very important for everyone to exercise and especially youth. Earlier in the chapter we pointed out all the health, physical development, and psychological bene-fits of an active lifestyle. While most youth will play sports in a formal setting, this is not a requirement for sports and recreational activities as they can be accomplished in an informal setting as well. Children are to be encouraged, and need to, live a healthy life-style. One of the simplest activities that nearly all youth can participate in is running and basic exercising (e.g., doing 100 sit-ups and push-ups a day). Research indicates that youth are much slower runners today than their parents or grandparents were when they were children and this is due primary to obesity and a sedentary lifestyle. "Worldwide, children are 15% less aerobically fit than we were at their age (however, in the U.S., the cross-generational fitness disparity is over 18%). In more understandable terms, today's kids take 90 seconds more to run a mile than kids the same age did just 30 to 40 years ago. Running speed, as it turns out, is a good indicator of overall fitness" (Brott 2019). The consequences of a generation that is so much more out-of-shape than past gener-ations will result in dramatic increases in diabetes, heart disease, obesity, and osteoar-thritis (Brott 2019). Brott, a former U.S. Marine, author of two syndicated columns and a number of books on fatherhood (i.e., *Father for Life*; *The Expectant Father: Facts, Tips, and Advice for Dads-to-Be*; *The New Father: A Dad's Guide to the First Year*, and others), and referred to by *Time* magazine as "the superdad's superdad" points out the irony of fit-ness levels going down while participation in formal sports has increased. Touting the value of informal sports and an active lifestyle, Brott (2019) points out that organized, highly structured sports may build individual skills, but they don't encourage endurance. Other problems, according to Brott, that have resulted in slower kids: the use of elec-tronic devices is taking up a lot of free time that kids used to actively spend outside, and parents that are so worried (often unnecessarily) about their kids' safety they don't let them walk or bike to school. To these last two points it should be noted that prior genera-tions that did not have access to electronic devices to distract them kids would not simply be outside playing; instead, they might be reading comic books, trading baseball cards, or watching television. In other words, kids have always found some sort of passive activity to entertain themselves. And it is not as safe for kids to be walking or biking alone with-out any sort of supervision as it seemingly was in the past.

So, what are informal sports? Informal sports are those which are player-controlled, free from governing bodies and adult supervision, and which allow the participant an opportunity to have fun in a self-expressing format. Informal sports include running/ jogging, biking, dancing, ultimate Frisbee, weight-lifting, skate boarding, bicycle riding, jogging, and so on. They also include most of the extreme sports described in Chapter 3. (As noted in Chapter 3, some of these extreme sports have become formalized in some settings.) Informal sport participation can still involve the sports more typically associ-ated with formal sports as kids across the country will have pick-up games with neigh-borhood youth and best friends.

The Aspen Institute (2020) reports that 17.1 percent of kids ages 6 to 12 were physically inactive in 2018 and that there is an inverse correlation between household income and physically inactive children. As the data in Table 6.2 indicates, as household income goes down, the percentage of physically inactive children goes up (see Table 6.2).

Table 6.2: Physically Inactive Children and Household Income

Household Income	Inactive Children (in percent)
Under $25,000	33.4
$25,000 to $49,999	24.5
$50,000 to $74,999	17.4
$75,000 to $99,999	15.0
$100,000+	9.9

(Source: The Aspen Institute 2020)

The Aspen Institute (2020) also reports that 31.3 percent of youth ages 6 to 12 regularly participate in high-calorie-burning sports. The Sports & Fitness Industry Association (SFIA) considers high-calorie burning activities as: bicycling (BMX, mountain, road); running/jogging; basketball; field hockey; football (tackle, touch); ice hockey; roller-hockey; lacrosse; rugby; soccer (indoor, outdoor); swimming (on a team or for fitness); track and field; badminton; racquetball; squash; tennis, cross-country skiing; martial arts; wrestling; stand-up paddling; climbing (sport, traditional); trail running; triathlon; boxing; dance; step; and other choreographed exercise to music (The Aspen Institute 2020). In 2012, 37.6 percent of kids ages 6 to 12 were regularly involved in high-calorie-burning sports.

Informal youth sport participation can be done on a solitary basis but usually involves family members such as siblings and cousins, along with friends and neighborhood peers. These youths get together, without the help or interference of adults, and ascertain for themselves what sporting activities to engage in. There must be a general agreement on what to play, and how to play it, in order for team play to occur. Whether kids are playing stickball on city streets (where they must determine what serves as "bases") or football in an open field (where boundaries may be determined by corn fields or hedgerows) they must work out for themselves how the game will proceed. When cooperation fails, kids go off to do their own thing.

There are a number of characteristics that distinguish informal sports from formal ones. The significant characteristics of informal sports include:

- Activity that is player-controlled
- Activity that involves action, especially that which leads to scoring opportunities
- Activity that maximizes personal involvement in the sport
- Spontaneity of play; that is, the plays do not come from a pre-written "playbook"
- No referees, the youth work out disputes for themselves
- A close score and relatively even teams, which lead to a competitive sporting activity
- Activity can end at any time; even if it's just because the kids are bored of playing or they are called to dinner
- Opportunities to reaffirm friendships through participation in the sporting activity
- Seldom impacts the total family life; family schedules are not adjusted so that youths can participate in informal play.

These are just generalizations of informal play. Nowhere should it be implied that informal play is problem-free. For example, disputes between participants may be settled by the bigger kids imposing their will on the smaller ones. As we all know, kids can be very cruel to one another. Because of the lack of adult supervision, the informal setting allows unrestricted opportunities for the dominant kids to pick on others.

The Need for Physical Education in Schools

We have discussed the importance of youth participating in sports and their need to be physically active for health and fitness sakes while also pointing out that an increasing number of youth are not physically active and are becoming less aerobically fit than previous generations. If youth are not a part of formal youth sports teams or are not motivated on their own to stay active, it is up to the schools to meet the challenge via physical educations (PE) programs and regularly scheduled physical activity that involves exercising (e.g., stretching and calisthenics) and playing sports.

While most schools provide PE programs for students, especially pre–K through 8th grade, the quality of the instruction may vary a great deal. Until kids reach high school it is also common for schools to provide a recess period; in high school, recess is replaced by a study hall. High-quality physical education programs will include instruction by certified physical education teachers and set tangible standards for student achievement and for high school graduation.

As established in this chapter, physical activity is necessary for a person's overall conditioning and well-being. PE helps the physical and emotional development of children who are positively affected by the benefits of activity. While the schools cannot control the amount of exercise youths get under home supervision they can influence eating habits (nutrition) and physical activity (via PE). Michelle Obama created an initiative called "Let's Move!" in 2010 in response to the large number of U.S. children (one-third) that are overweight or obese. She had hoped that this generation of youth could improve their overall health. Obama's initiative was directed at parents, kids, and schools. Schools were to take five simple steps to success: (1) Create a school health advisor council; (2) Join the Healthier U.S. Schools Challenge (HUSSC), which combines nutrition education programs and physical activity opportunities; (3) Set a good example; make your school a healthy workplace; (4) Incorporate nutrition education and physical education into the school day, such as teaching young children their colors using fruits and vegetables; and (5) Plant a school garden (Let's Move! 2017).

Physical education programs in schools directly impact students' physical health in a positive manner. As we have emphasized a number of times in this chapter, good physical health helps to combat obesity which in turn reduces the risk for diabetes, heart disease, asthma, and other disorders. Students who exercise regular become physically drained by the end of the day in a positive manner and thus generally sleep better at night.

Emphasizing Sportsmanship

In our review of formal youth sports we learned that emphasizing sportsmanship is of particular importance, especially for younger children. This changes somewhat as youths age and by the time they reach high school it becomes clear that winning is generally more important than having fun and emphasizing sportsmanship. It is not a coincidence that kids begin to burnout or start to turn away from organized sports around age 13 as this coincides with a focus on skills development and elitism that will be prevalent in high school.

Sportsmanship, which will be discussed again in Chapter 16, involves fair play, decency, and respect—for oneself, the competitor, fellow fans, game officials, and the sport itself. Sportsmanship involves adhering to proper forms of moral conduct. With these criteria in mind, the authors define *sportsmanship* as conduct and attitudes considered as benefiting participants, especially in regards to a sense of fair play, courtesy toward teammates and opponents, game officials, and others involved in sporting contests, as well as grace in losing.

Those of us who played sports as youths recognize the benefit of having coaches that stress that having fun is as important as winning. Coaches, and parents, that create PE and PA (physical activity) experiences that involve fun, enjoyment, skill development and mastery of skills over ego-centered activities, establish activities as part of a social opportunity to bond with peers and coaches, and create challenging but attainable sport goals, will help to develop youth participants who are more likely to adapt to prosocial behaviors, including sportsmanship (Mobley 2016). "Therefore, when coaches and adults create a motivational climate that focuses on personal improvement and cooperative learning, they will have greater influence over an athletes' sportsperson-like behavior and cultivate a positive behavioral culture for their team" (Mobley 2016: 83). PE teachers and coaches have this same opportunity to foster a nurturing environment that maintains a commitment to PA while promoting the ideals of sportsmanship. The ideals of sportsmanship are more likely to be embraced if coaches, parents and PE instructors first model good sportsmanship, as this provides an observational learning arena which youth can aspire to replicate. Coaches, parents and PE instructors must then reward good sportsmanship as this serves as a type of positive reinforcement. In turn, poor sportsmanship behavior must be addressed with positive punishment.

Reinforcing positive sportsmanship behavior is an aspect of character development discussed earlier in this chapter. Shields and Bredemeier (1995) promote the idea that the role of sport in character development lies with the development of moral character. Moral character includes four virtues: compassion, fairness, sportspersonship, and integrity (Shields and Bredemeier 1995; Harrison 2016). The manner in which coaches and PE instructors teach sports to youth will influence youth character development and whether or not they embrace sportsmanship. (Note: Some people do not like the word "sportsmanship" because they believe it contains a sexist connotation because "man" is a part of the concept; as a result, they may use the term "sportspersonship." As an astute person can ascertain, the word "son" is in the term "sportspersonship" and thus, is not any less "sexist." By no means does the word "sportsmanship" imply a gender specific description of character ideals.)

Does sport participation help to build good character and sportsmanship? Koc (2017) conducted research on the relationship between PE courses and sportsmanship behaviors, tendency to violence, and empathetic ability for elementary school students. Among the interesting findings: students that participate in physical non-contact sports (e.g., volleyball) displayed a higher level of sportsmanship and empathetic ability as well as a lower tendency to violence compared to students interested in other types of sports (e.g., football); sportsmanship levels of people engaged in individual sports are lower; team sports without physical contact are less aggressive than those interested in other sports; those engaged in individual sports have a more negative ethical decision-making attitude compared to those engaged in team sports; students engaged in sports with contact displayed a higher level of general aggression and toughness; levels of physical contact in sports adversely affect the players' ethical judgment; and, those engage in contact sports are much more likely to legitimize aggression in sports than those who played non-contact sports. Koc (2017) believes that the social environment and the manner in which sporting activities are taught and reinforced influences character development and sportsmanship.

Connecting Sports and Popular Culture

Box 6: Blindsided by Homelessness, Saved by Foster Parents: The Semi-biographical Story of Michael Oher as Depicted in *The Blind Side*

Federal education data provided by the National Center for Homeless Education (the U.S. Department of Education's technical assistance center) show that public schools identified 1.5 million children and youth experiencing homelessness in the 2017–18 school year—an 11 percent increase over the previous school year and the highest number ever recorded (School House Connection 2020). Youth are considered homeless if they are staying in shelters, cars, motels, or with other people temporarily. Everyday life experiences are consumed with trying to find a place to sleep from one night to the next, a place to wash, and food to eat. Schoolchildren try to hide their situation from their classmates in order to avoid stigmatization. Working on homework presents a challenge, especially when access to a computer and the Internet is necessary. Without a proper diet and lacking health care coverage, maintaining good physical and mental health presents additional challenges. Many homeless children feel compelled to quit school during their teen years in order to help their family or to take care of themselves. If the homeless youth is living on the street, or even with family members or caregivers, victimization via sexual and physical abuse is also a possibility. For the homeless youth who possesses sports skills, a formal sports program may provide structure and a temporary release from the nightmare of a life they live, but it does not guarantee food to eat. Consequently, many homeless youths who play sports are distracted by thoughts of where they would sleep that night and where, or if, they will eat that night. While they are distracted, their sports performance is compromised. Some of these homeless youths will find success in life; others will disappear into the cracks of a broken social system.

From time to time, a well-meaning coach or teacher may take in a homeless, abandoned youth under his or her wing. In some other instances, a member, or family, from the community may intervene and make sure the homeless youth has a better life. Such is the case with Michael Oher, a former NFL player with the Tennessee Titans and one-time homeless youth from Memphis, Tennessee. Michael Oher is the subject of Michael Lewis's book *The Blind Side*, and the 2009 film of the same name (Oher 2014; Tennessee Titans 2014).

Oher was born on May 28, 1986, in Memphis as Michael Jerome Williams, Jr.; he came from a "broken home," with his estranged father murdered while Michael was in high school and his crack-addicted mother seldom to be found (Oher 2014). Michael was one of twelve children born to Michael Jerome Williams, Sr., and Denise Oher, who provided their children very little support. Michael Sr. was often in prison, and with a crack-addicted mother, Michael Jr., and his siblings found themselves in and out of different foster homes and frequently homeless. Michael rarely saw his siblings, let alone his parents. He was forced to fend for himself. Without love and support, his school grades suffered tremendously. Michael repeated first and second grade and attended 11 different schools during his first nine years as a student (Oher 2014). Most likely, we never would have heard of Michael Oher if not for the kindness of Leigh Anne Tuohy and her family.

Michael Oher joined the ranks of popular culture via Lewis's book and highly-acclaimed 2009 feature film, both of the same title, *The Blind Side*. The movie grossed nearly $310 million worldwide, a hefty sum for any film but especially for a sports film. The film was adored by filmgoers and critics alike and won Sandra Bullock, who played Leigh Anne Tuohy, the Academy Award for Best Actress, as well as the Golden Globe Award for Best Actress and the Screen Actors Guild Award for Outstanding Performance by a Female in a Leading Role. The film was also nominated for an Academy Award for Best Picture. There were a number of cameos from current and past college coaching legends including Lou Holtz, Nick Saban, Phillip Fulmer, Houston Nutt, Ed Orgeron, and Tommy Tuberville.

The film does a great job of depicting the life of a homeless, loner student. Michael alternates washing his one extra shirt at the local laundromat and sometimes sleeps there. He also sometimes sleeps on the couch of a friend of his. Near the beginning of the film, Michael's friend's father is shown talking to Burt Cotton (Ray McKinnon), the football coach of Briarcrest Christian, to help enroll his son and Mike. Cotton is immediately impressed by the size of Oher and despite his poor grades, helps to get Michael admitted into the school. Michael is quickly befriended by a boy named Sean Jr. (SJ) (Jae Head), the son of Leigh Anne Tuohy. SJ notices how all the other kids run away from Michael because they are intimidated by his size and are a little afraid of him because he is black (nearly all the other kids at the Christian school are white) and suggests to him that he smile. As a homeless youth, Oher has had little to smile about, but his life is about to change. Sean Tuohy (Tim McGraw) and Leigh Anne notice Michael and ask SJ who he is and SJ replies, "He's big Mike." Not knowing who he really is, everyone calls Michael "Big Mike" simply because he *is* so big.

When Michael is informed by a school staff member that his father has died, he has little reaction. That same night, Michael seeks shelter from the pouring rain at the Laundromat. Later on, the Tuohy family is watching SJ's sister Collins (Lily Collins) play volleyball in the school gym. Sean notices Michael going through all the discarded boxes looking for food. Such is life for a homeless athlete, scrounging through popcorn boxes and the like, in search of anything to eat. Sean arranges to have a meal ticket paid for Michael so that he can eat at school. On a rainy night, the Tuohy family drives by Michael, who is walking on the road shivering in the cold. Leigh makes Sean pull over and learns that he hasn't a place to go for the night. She asks him to get in the car and offers Michael a place to stay on their couch. The next morning, Leigh Anne goes downstairs and finds that Michael has neatly packed up the blankets and pillow and has left the house. She asks Michael to join them for Thanksgiving dinner. Leigh Ann invites Michael to live with the family. She asks about his family and requests that he tell her one thing about himself.

Michael replies that he does not like being called "Big Mike." Leigh Anne states that he will only be addressed as Michael from that point on.

Over a period of time, Michael becomes very close to the family and Leigh Anne starts the procedure to become his legal guardian. The Tuohys are very wealthy, as Sean owns a chain of fast food restaurants. Leigh Anne learns that although his grades are low, he is actually a pretty smart kid and that he scored in the 98th percentile (top 2 percent) in "protective instincts." Knowing little about the game of football, Leigh Anne instructs Michael to think of the team as his family and his job is to protect his players and as an offensive lineman, he is especially to protect the quarterback so that no one hits him from the "blind side"—football terminology for the vulnerable point of attack by defenses from the quarterback's back, or blind, side. From that point on, Michael begins to excel at football. The Tuohys hire a private tutor to help Michael raise his grades so that he can go on to college. Michael receives numerous visits from "big-time" college football coaches who are impressed by the films that SJ has put together for recruiting purposes.

The film offers a bit of real-life drama and controversy as both Leigh Ann and Sean are University of Mississippi (Ole Miss) alumni and encourage Michael to accept an offer to attend their alma mater. The NCAA investigates the situation and accuses the Tuohys of taking Michael into their home just so that he will play at Ole Miss. The NCAA is more concerned about other families doing the same thing, a possible recruiting violation, than they are in assuring that Michael has a home and a decent life. The Tuohys are eventually cleared of any wrongdoing and Michael does indeed decide to attend Ole Miss, where he will enjoy national acclaim and eventually get drafted by the Baltimore Ravens in 2009, get traded to the Tennessee Titans for the 2014 NFL season, and then finished his career with the Carolina Panthers in 2015–2016.

The Blind Side is a heartwarming film and very well made. The story behind the book and film is even more impressive considering the plight of this former homeless youth who proved, if given a chance, that he had much to offer society. But there are many other homeless youths like Michael. What if they do not find their Tuohy family? What's to become of them?

It is also important to point out that while critics and moviegoers alike thoroughly enjoyed The Blind Side, there was one major critic of the film, Michael Oher himself. Oher has stated that he did not feel like the film depicted his life in a realistic manner. Among other things, Oher was not a reserved loner type kid; instead, Michael claims he was quick with a smile and a roar of a laugh. Oher also claims that the film simplified the troubles of his homeless youth; but, this is understandable as a feature film has to condense material to fit a reasonable time length. In particular, Oher was disappointed that the racial tension was downplayed and that race had a much more profound impact on the lives of Oher and his family (Howe 2020). Oher has many other criticisms of the film's portrayal of his life with his adopted family; still, Michael remains friends with the cast of The Blind Side (Howe 2020).

SUMMARY

Children and play go hand-in-hand. Play should be encouraged, as it develops a child's imagination, intelligence, perceptual-motor development, and it is a healthy activity. Sport represents an evolutionary growth of play. Sport may be formalized or performed informally. Proponents of youth sport participation often point to the idea that sport builds character and contributes to ideals of sportsmanship. There is a good deal of debate over whether sports "builds character," particularly whether abiding by societal rules is a sign of good character. Sport participation is tied to the idea of personal identity. For many youths, being an athlete is a big part of who they are.

The origin and development of organized youth sports can be traced to the rise of industrialization and urbanization of the United States and Canada midway through the nineteenth century was the emergence of leisure time for many children, especially urban youth. Over the years, numerous sports were created and formal youth organizations formed to help indoctrinate youths into structured physical activities. Participating in formal sports is so well indoctrinated in the United States (as well as most parts of the world) that they become an integral part of culture. Formal youth sport participation is encouraged for many reasons, among them: to develop motor skills; develop physical fitness; develop healthy, strong identities; promote the values of society; develop social competencies; to have fun; and, to teach sportsmanship. Despite their many benefits, there are a number of criticisms of formal sports, including: an over-focus on winning; over-zealous coaches and parents; and an emphasis on specializing in one sport.

When sports no longer provide the most important thing to kids—having fun—they are very likely to abandon formal sports (by age 13) in favor of informal sports. Informal sports are those which are player-controlled, free from governing bodies and adult supervision, and allow the participant an opportunity to have fun in a self-expressing format. Informal sports include running/jogging, biking, dancing, ultimate Frisbee, weight-lifting, skate boarding, bicycle riding, jogging, and so on. They also include most of the extreme sports described in Chapter 3.

All too often, youths are not as physically active as they should be. As a result, physical education programs in the schools becomes critical for the overall health and mental well-being of youth. Ideally, PE and formal sport programs also incorporate the ideals of sportsmanship.

KEY TERMS

Athletic Stress Forces that cause bodily or mental strain.

Bodily Strain Physical impairment caused by excessive demands on the body.

Character Individual personality and behavioral traits, both good and bad, which define who a person is.

Character Development Gaining qualities that will make a person better able to deal with life's problems; many believe sports enhance character development.

Hot Housing The forced maturing of young children via over-programming.

Informal Sports Those which are player-controlled, free from governing bodies and adult supervision, and allow the participant an opportunity to have fun in a self-expressing format.

Little Leaguism A term used to describe youth sports that have become bureaucratic, standardized, efficiency-driven, rationalized, calculated, and predictable.

Mental Strain Distress caused by internal pressure that the youth places on self-performance.

Muscular Christianity A term used to describe the religious philosophy of teaching morals and values through sport.

Soccer Mom Someone who drives her children to soccer games and watches them compete.

Sportsmanship Conduct and attitudes considered as benefiting participants, especially in regards to a sense of fair play, courtesy toward teammates and opponents, game officials, and others involved in sporting contests, as well as grace in losing.

Traumatic Brain Injury (TBI) Head injuries (e.g., concussions) brought on by a severe blow to the head that lead to temporary or permanent brain damage.

DISCUSSION QUESTIONS

- What do you think of the Michael Oher story depicted in Popular Culture Box 6? That is, do you think the Tuohys helped Michael just because they wanted him to play at Ole Miss, or were their intentions good? Explain.
- What are some of the reasons why parents encourage their children to participate in sports? What do you think are positive reasons and what are negative reasons?
- How does participation in youth sports correspond to a child's mental and physical development? What are some steps that can be taken to make sure that a child's mental and physical development progress in an acceptable way?
- What are some of the key differences between formal and informal youth sports? Why is informal youth sport becoming more popular in the twenty-first century?
- Do you think that sports "builds character"? What does this phrase mean to you, and how can it be applied to youth sports in particular?
- Do you think that adults should stop their children from playing contact sports such as football and soccer due to the risk of brain concussions? Explain. Consider in your answer the fact that far more youth suffer traumatic brain injuries from bike riding and skateboarding than they do playing football.
- Do you think that Marv Marinovich went too far in his conditioning of his sons? Do you see any benefits of "hot housing" either in sports or some other sphere of life?
- Did you play any youth sports and, if so, do you think that contributed to your mental and physical development?

CHAPTER 7

High School and College Sports

"John Doe Scores Six Touchdowns in Final High School Football Game," reads the local newspaper article. Doe has the perfect combination of speed and power, two important tools for a running back. Doe has set state records in career touchdowns scored and rushing yardage. College recruiters are drooling over the hope that Doe might play for them. Community members from Doe's high school assume he will star in football at the college ranks. Unfortunately, Doe does not possess the perfect combination of study habits and academic grades. He has struggled every year to remain academically eligible for high school sports and, recently, Doe has learned that he has failed the SAT. His low high school grade point average does not qualify him for colleges offering football scholarships. Doe had spent far more time preparing himself for college as a football player than college as a student. What will he do now? Academic eligibility is just one of many concerns related to sports in the educational setting.

Interscholastic Athletics and Academics

Nearly all secondary schools offer interscholastic athletics. In the United States, and most other nations of the West, colleges and universities also routinely field sports teams. Sports and education would seem to go hand in hand. As discussed in Chapter 6, proponents of sports in schools often cite the long-held belief that sport teaches positive character traits and values (such as teamwork, dedication, loyalty and success due to hard work) that will transcend from the playing field onto the game of life. The schools themselves benefit from the increased commitment of alumni and local supporters. Others, however, argue that the priority placed on sport programs often distract the school (administrators, students and parents) from prioritizing educational goals (e.g., intellectual development through a rigorous curriculum). In addition, they claim that the costs involved in promoting and recruiting are not offset by ticket sales and contributions, and that teams are detrimental to the ultimate bottom line.

THE CONSEQUENCES OF INTERSCHOLASTIC SPORT PARTICIPATION

High school and college athletes may receive fame and accolades from peers, community members, and the traditional and social media. Males have long enjoyed the benefits of being an athlete in high school and college and more recently females have also begun to experience the attention. Data provided by the National Federation of High Schools

(NFHS) reveals that high school sports participation increased overall for the 29th consecutive year (2017–18 school year) (NFHS 2018). Led by an additional 15,009 participants in girls' sports programs, the total number of high school sport participants fell just shy of 8 million (7,980,886). The number of girls participating in high school sports reached an all-time high of 3,415,306 and boys' participation also set a new standard at 4,565,580 (NFHS 2018). (Note: We will provide a sport-by-sport breakdown later in the chapter.)

For the student-athletes, sport participation in high school has many potential positive consequences. Sport participation allows the introvert an opportunity to socialize and make friends with other students; this is especially important for students who are not usually the "life of the party." Having friends is important for many reasons and chief among them is realization that you have a trusted someone that you can talk to, confide in, and make plans with outside of school. The social environment is rife with social problems including students who are mean-spirited and bullies. Belonging to a team means that you have others who will have your back. Participation in high school sports affords participants with a chance to become a "hometown hero" following individual and team success. Hometown fans will cheer for you and success results in many potential accolades, including applause and public affirmation. High school sports often provide local communities with a rallying point of local pride. In addition, individuals who play sports feel an increased attachment to the school, school values, and community.

High school athletes enjoy positive attention because sports achievements generally receive more attention than academic ones. One reason for this is the idea that cheering for a sports team can unite members from the school and the greater community in a more tangible manner than academic accomplishments. With this in mind, interschool sports competitions provide a means of unifying the entire school. For example, individuals from diverse racial and social classes as well as kids from different subcultural groups are afforded a bonding opportunity through cheering for their high school sports teams and athletes. Teachers that support school sports are generally more respected by students than those who do not support sports. The school benefits indirectly by sports because of the social control apparatus that accompanies participation. Athletes must abide by a number of rules in order to remain eligible. These rules apply to both on the field behavior (team rules, league rules, and so forth) and off the field behavior (grades and personal behavior).

Kendellen and Camire (2017) examined the life skill development and transfer experiences of former high school athletes to see whether the skills learned in high school sports can be conducive to the development of various life skills. "The findings illustrate specific examples of life skill development in sport and subsequent life skill application in life by the same participant, thereby providing evidence for the occurrence of the process of transfer" (Kendellen and Camire 2017:395). The authors found empirical evidence consistent with the notion that such life skills such as autonomy (e.g., self-control), competence (coping with stress), and relatedness (e.g., social responsibility) developed in high school sport can be transferred and applied in other life domains.

Furthermore, research has shown that, in general, despite the time and energy spent on sports (e.g., training, practice, and game day) participation does not lead to poorer academic performance or lower academic aspirations (Nixon and Frey 1996; Gorman 2017). Researchers at Michigan State University found that students who participated in vigorous sports did 10 percent better in science, English, math and social studies compared with other students (Gorman 2017). Female athletes achieved the highest GPA of all high school students, significantly higher than female nonathletes (Gorman 2017). The NCAA (2020a) reports that that the likelihood of an NCAA athlete earning a college degree is higher than it is for nonathletes as 86 percent of Division, 71 percent of Division II, and 87 percent of Division III athletes earn degrees, while just over 58 percent of other students earn a four-degree in six years or less (Nadworny 2019).

There are, however, a number of potential problems associated with interscholastic and intercollegiate sport. Sport specialization has led many athletes to concentrate on just one sport, year-round, instead of enjoying participating in multiple sports. Proponents of sport specialization, however, argue that when athletes concentrate on one sport, they increase their chance of becoming dominant in that sport. Sports are often fields of elitism. The elite interscholastic and intercollegiate sports (football and basketball) generally dominate the athletic budgets of schools. Elite athletes often have such inflated egos that they begin to think they are better and more important than other students. Cheating in its multiple forms (e.g., violating rules of sportsmanship, taking performance-enhancing drugs) undermines the idealism of sport as an institution of character building. The excessive pressures to win often "cheat" participants from the fun of playing sports. Many athletes become disenchanted by the over-emphasis on rules and the pressures to win. They end up feeling like they are doing work rather than engaging in play. The authoritarian coach may also ruin the sport experience of participants. We will address these topics in the following pages.

High School Sports

Youth sport participation is mostly about having fun. When athletes reach high school the pretense of having fun is overtly replaced by an emphasis on winning. The best athletes receive the most playing time while others are relegated to the bench and supporting roles. The responsibilities of the high school athlete are far more intense than those of the nonathlete, as far as school-related activities are concerned. The high school athlete must manage educational, athletic, and social responsibilities that are very time consuming and too demanding for many young people. High school athletes not only have to study and do classroom assignments, but they must also attend athletic practices. Research has also shown that negative life stresses affect student athletes much more than non-student athletes (Petrie and Anderson 1996). Thus, high school athletes may face stress from off the field sources (e.g., homelessness and victimization of abuse), like their nonathlete peers, but also on the field stress—something nonathletes cannot encounter. Finding the proper balance between educational, athletic and social time requirements potentially presents challenges too difficult for young people. On the other hand, athletes that are successful at accomplishing this balance as teenagers should have an advantage in adulthood. The careers they will be entering, especially in the fast-paced twenty-first century, will probably involve multi-tasking, and the need to balance many competing responsibilities will come to the forefront.

Academic Requirements

While students participate in high school sports they are generally required to maintain a minimum academic requirement for athletic eligibility. Most students today would be surprised to learn that during the 1970s and early 1980s many high school jurisdictions did not have a minimal academic requirement for athletic eligibility. It was argued that academic requirements were unfair to disadvantaged youth. Some people even believed that sport participation was a right rather than privilege. Predictably, the lack of a minimal academic requirement led to many athletes concentrating on sports and ignoring academics. Today, it is common for all high schools to maintain minimal academic requirements for sports participation, such as 2.0, or a C average. However, such requirements may vary from state to state; from city to city; and, by school to school (e.g., some private schools may require a higher GPA).

While high schools do not maintain national requirements for athletic participation, universities and colleges do have minimum requirements for incoming high school students. At Division I (D1) schools, incoming high school students must have graduated from high school with a minimum of a 2.3 GPA in the 10 NCAA-approved core courses, with a combined seven in English, math, and science prior to the start of their senior year. There is a 2.2 GPA requirement in10 NCAA-approved core courses for Division II (D2) schools (Schlabach 2020). Students must also earn an SAT combined score or ACT sum score matching the core-course GPA on the NCAA sliding scale for Division 1 athletic qualification (Next College Student Athlete 2020). These tests were not administered in 2020 due to the SARS-CoV-2 global pandemic that hit the United States really hard and as a result the NCAA Eligibility Center waived the standardized test score for incoming freshman student-athletes in both D1 and D2 (Schlabach 2020).

There are no minimum academic standards for high school students entering Division III sports leagues, students must be in good academic standing and must be making progress toward graduation (as defined by individual schools) and taking a minimum of 12 semester or quarter hours while enrolled (regardless of individual school rules) once the athlete is competing at the Division III level (NCAA 2014a). Graduating high school students who want to play at National Association of Intercollegiate Athletics (NAIA) schools must graduate from high school and meet two out of three of the following requirements: (1) Achieve a minimum of 18 on the ACT or 860 on the SAT; (2) Achieve a minimum overall high school GPA of 2.0; and (3) Graduate in the top half of their high school class.

Athletic eligibility for student-athletes is a subject of great scrutiny. Administrative offices must constantly monitor the academic progress of high school athletes.

INTERSCHOLASTIC PARTICIPATION AND THE PROBABILITY OF COMPETING AT THE NEXT LEVEL

As previously stated, the NFHS (2018) reports that nearly 8 million students played high school sports during the 2017–18 school year. Football (11-player) remains far and away the most popular sport for high school boys, with more than one million participants but it's no longer the overall most popular participatory sport in high school, having been replaced by outdoor track and field (the number one sport for girls). (See Table 7.1.) The number of high school student-athletes playing 11-player football has been dropping slightly for the past decade and, in many cases, it has been replaced by 6-, 8-, and 9-player football (NFHS 2018). The estimated number of participants in 6-, 8-, and 9-player football (which small schools often adopt when they don't have enough students for 11-player teams) is going up but it still only accounts for about 30,000 players nationwide (Cook 2019). A number of high school students who have turned away from contact and/or violent sports (mostly out of fear of concussions) are playing more passive sports such as badminton, archery, fencing, bass fishing and Ultimate Frisbee (NFHS 2018). In 2017, Vermont became the first U.S. state to recognize Ultimate Frisbee as a high school varsity sport (*Associated Press* 2017a).

Table 7.1: Top Fourteen High School Sports by Total Number of Students Who Participated in Them, 2017–2018

Sport	Total	Boys	Girls
Outdoor Track and Field	1,088,689	600,097	488,592
Football (11-player)	1,039,243	1,036,842	2,401
Basketball	963,780	551,373	412,407
Soccer	864,844	456,362	390,482
Volleyball	507,559	*60,976	446,583
Cross Country	493,613	270,095	223,518
Baseball	488,859	487,097	*1,762
Fast-Pitch Softball	369,450	*1,589	367,861
Tennis	349,286	158,518	190,768
Swimming and Diving	314,529	138,935	175,594
Wrestling	266,589	245,564	*21,124
Lacrosse	210,217	113,313	96,904
Competitive spirit (cheerleading)	166,520	*3,851	162,669
Golf	154,845	144,024	*9,821

*(Source: NFHS 2018; *Statista 2018)*

The NCAA (2018) reports that the percentage of all high school athletes moving up to the NCAA to compete at the next level is 6 percent. The highest percentage is Men's Ice Hockey (11.7 percent) followed by Baseball (7.1 percent), Football (6.8 percent), Men's Soccer (5.6 percent), Women's Basketball (3.9 percent), and Men's Basketball (3.4 percent).

ATHLETIC ADMINISTRATION

With such large high school athletics participation numbers comes the need for administrative control and oversight. Many of today's administrators were trained in academic administration and not in athletic administration. As a result, most schools have added to their operating budget the costs of athletic administrators who oversee the sports program and such issues as academic eligibility and grievances (challenges to ineligibility). These athletic administration positions developed slowly and gradually. As secondary schools have grown in size (especially through the consolidation of school districts) and interscholastic programs expanded (particularly because of the addition of girls' programs), the need for sport administrators became increasingly evident. At many of the larger high schools, the athletic department has an athletic director (similar to the college ranks).

Athletic directors inevitably exert great influence in the forming of policies and practices at their respective schools and athletic conferences. Furthermore, a number of high school associations sponsor athletic directors' conferences and meetings that further strengthen their role and power. Athletic directors typically oversee standards of eligibility for interscholastic athletic competitions, contest regulations and preparation for out-of-town games; meet with tournament management; establish and define high school athletic policies; oversee athletic awards policies and banquets; administer the purchase, issuing and general care of equipment; direct athletic budgets; oversee safety essentials, programs and travel; manage the general layout and maintenance of athletic facilities; oversee intramural activities and the development of junior high school programs; and administer legal aspects of interscholastic activities.

One of the biggest demands on high school administrators is finding enough money to fund athletic and academic programs. Most high schools face financial challenges, and it becomes almost a trick to find a way to support athletic programs, especially in light of their importance to student athletes, their parents, the student body, and the community as a whole.

Clearly, there is a great deal of work involved in interscholastic sports that goes unnoticed by most fans and participants of high school sports. Another important aspect is dealing with the media: sending out press releases and notices of games, interacting with sports reporters from newspapers and television, and monitoring the stories that appear about the teams. In many U.S. cities high school sporting events are covered as aggressively as college and even national sporting events.

ATHLETIC TRAINING AND ECONOMICS

Among those providing overt benefits to sport participants are the athletic trainers. The National Athletic Trainers Association (NATA), the governing body of athletic training, describes as athletic training as encompassing "the prevention, examination, diagnosis, treatment and rehabilitation of emergent, acute or chronic injuries and medical conditions" (NATA 2019a). "Athletic trainers (ATs) are highly qualified, multi-skilled health care professional who render service or treatment, under the direction of or in collaboration with a physician, in accordance with their education, training and the state's statues, rules and regulations" (NATA 2019a). NATA provides a Code of Ethics stressing principles of ethical behavior that should be followed in the practice of athletic training.

The association sponsors certification through the NATA Board of Certification (NATABOC). "Historically the practice of athletic training was confined to the collegiate sports setting with an emphasis on caring for injuries in tackle football. It was not until the 1970s that this situation changed significantly, as the services of athletic trainers began to be recognized as extremely valuable in the high school sport setting" (Pfeiffer and Mangus 2002: 23). Despite the obvious need for, and the benefits of, athletic trainers, just 37 percent of public secondary schools and 28 percent of private secondary schools in the U.S. have a full-time athletic trainer on staff (NATA 2019b; Pike et at 2017). A number of schools have a part-time athletic trainer, doctor or emergency medical staff personnel. Nonetheless, millions of high school athletes compete without access to a certified athletic trainer to assure that their medical needs are being met.

When school boards face budget constraints, sports and the arts are usually the first victims of cuts. Understandably, academics must always be the first priority at all schools (and at every level of education); but it is always disappointing when extra-curricular activities are eliminated. (This economic reality helps to explain, in part, why there are so few full-time athletic trainers.) All across the United States and Canada school budgets are subject to cuts. When school budget cuts result in the elimination of the funding for sports teams, many sports booster groups spring into action in an attempt to save school sports.

College Sports

For many sports fans, college sports are more important and entertaining than professional sports. College football, for example, commands huge legions of followers, and the sheer number of teams guarantees a greater number of total games and spectators each weekend for college football than for professional football. The focus and attention given to collegiate sport in the United States is unparalleled compared to the rest of the world. Nearly every college and university in the United States has a sports program and fields multiple teams. Many of these teams play in organized leagues and just as many teams engage in intramural sports. Furthermore, many college sports (e.g., football and basketball) have a longer history than professional sports. As Richard Goldstein (1993) notes, "As far back as the 1820s, the meadows at Cambridge and New Haven were scenes of semi-organized mayhem for college men. On the first Monday of the school term at Harvard and Yale, the sophomores would battle the freshmen in games that ostensibly involved kicking a round canvas ball, but seemed mostly directed at kicking the opponent" (3).

All sports and games have rules. "Regulation of college sports began with debates over the still-being-formulated rules of the game themselves, before moving on to ask who should be allowed to play and under what conditions" (Shulman and Bowen 2001: 12). Once the rules of the game were established (allowing for modifications over the years), there grew a concern about the enforcement of the rules. This concern was fueled by the reality that, if left unsupervised, many people involved in sports (as with all other social institutions) would violate the rules and the spirit of the game in order to gain an unfair advantage during competition. Corruption and blatant cheating in sport forced the creation of supervising bodies.

Today, collegiate sports are governed by a number of large administrative bodies, such as the National Collegiate Athletic Association (NCAA); the National Association of Intercollegiate Athletics (NAIA); and the National Junior College Athletic Association (NJCAA). Membership in the NCAA is generally considered the most prestigious but the NAIA has great value as well. The NJCAA may serve as a means to an end (e.g., a sports career after high school) or as a stepping stone (to transfer to the NCAA or NAIA to continue one's sports career). NCAA athletics is divided into three tiers: Division I, which is "big-time" sports, and further divided for football into the Football Bowl Subdivision (FBS) and Football Championship Subdivision (FCS); Division II (in between "big-time" sports programs but those that will offer scholarships); and, Division III (athletic programs that choose not to offer athletic scholarships to their student-athletes).

Just as we provided the odds of high school students moving on to college to continue their sports career, the NCAA (2018) provides data on the percentage of all NCAA athletes to compete at the major professional level—and this figure is just 2 percent. The highest percentage of NCAA athletes moving on to the professional level is Baseball (9.1 percent), Men's Hockey (5.6 percent), Football (1.5 percent), Men's Soccer (1.4 percent), Men's Basketball (1.1 percent), and Women's Basketball (0.9 percent).

The National Collegiate Athletic Association (NCAA)

In college sports, the most dominant ruling body is the National Collegiate Athletic Association (NCAA). The purposes of the NCAA are clearly spelled out on page 1 of the 2019–20 NCAA Division I Manual. (The complete manual is nearly 450 pages long.) These purposes are:

a. To initiate, stimulate and improve intercollegiate athletics programs for student-athletes and to promote and develop educational leadership, physical fitness, athletics excellence and athletics participation as a recreational pursuit;

b. To uphold the principle of institutional control of, and responsibility for, all intercollegiate sports in conformity with the constitution and bylaws of this Association;

c. To encourage its members to adopt eligibility rules to comply with satisfactory standards of scholarship, sportsmanship and amateurism;

d. To formulate, copyright and publish rules of play governing intercollegiate athletics;

e. To preserve intercollegiate athletics records;

f. To supervise the conduct of, and to establish eligibility standards for, regional and national athletics events under the auspices of this Association;

g. To cooperate with other amateur athletics organizations in promoting and conducting national and international athletics events;

h. To legislate, through bylaws or by resolutions of a Convention, upon any subject of general concern to the members related to the administration of intercollegiate athletics; and

i. To study in general all phases of competitive intercollegiate athletics and establish standards whereby the college and universities of the United States can maintain their athletics programs on a high level [NCAA 2020b].

The NCAA is an administrative body designed to enforce the rules of college athletics. It is also an organization of all the colleges and universities that voluntarily belong to it. Thus, the NCAA could not exist without the mutual agreement of member institutions. "The NCAA has been described as the fox watching the henhouse of college sports, but the Association's consolidation of power cannot be attributed only to its own ambitions; schools had demonstrated repeatedly that they were unable to protect themselves from themselves and, at the same time, that they had no desire to disband their programs. In response, the NCAA has organized and managed the flow of big money" (Shulman and Bowen 2001: 16). Over the years, the NCAA has tweaked the rules and guidelines of intercollegiate sport in response to growing problem areas (e.g., steroid use, gambling, cheating, fans who want more action that leads to scoring, etc.).

As an administrative body that is supposed to represent the needs of member institutions, the NCAA is expected to fairly administer punishments and sanctions when member schools are perceived to have violated the rules. Unfortunately, the NCAA does not act with distributive justice. Consider the manner in which the NCAA handled Syracuse University's perceived athletics violations in its attempt to keep star basketball player Fabricio Paulino d Melo (Fab Melo) academically eligible in January 2012 when Syracuse was the number one ranked team in the country with a 20–0 record. Syracuse self-disclosed when it submitted a waiver to the NCAA explaining medical and personal difficulties for Melo, a 7-foot center from Brazil. Melo had been declared ineligible to play following the Fall 2011 semester; he rewrote a paper, the professor changed his grade, and Syracuse determined that no violations of the university's academic integrity policy had occurred. (As college professors themselves, the authors know that it is routine for many students to seek help with a paper at the tutoring center.) The NCAA investigated SU and found that somewhere between one and seven athletes benefited from academic impropriety over a span of seven years (Carlson 2016). In the grand scheme of college athletics such violations would typically be considered minor. However, the NCAA laid the hammer on SU and head Coach Jim Boeheim by suspending Boeheim for nine games, stripped (vacated) Boeheim and SU of 101 wins, and took scholarships away from the basketball program. (Note: Melo died of medical issues—described as "natural causes"—in February 2017 at the age of 26 in his home in Brazil.)

With the shocking extreme punishment of Syracuse athletics in mind, college sports observers and especially those at SU looked on with great interest as to what sort of punishment the NCAA would levy against the University of North Carolina when it was found that the institution had lost full control of academics and athletics, as more than 1,870 athletes were involved in faulty academic classes over a span of 18 years (Carlson 2016). Many observers predicted that UNC would receive the "death penalty" (the popular term for the NCAA's power to ban a school from competing in a sport for at least one year). Alas, this was not the case. In fact, UNC received no penalties! A shocking development, unless of course, you are among the people that view the NCAA as a corrupt organization. The NCAA ruled that because UNC "made available deficient Department of African and Afro-American Studies 'paper courses' to the general student body, including student-athletes" that the university did not violate NCAA rules (Norlander 2017). In September 2019, the University of Kansas confirmed it received a notice of allegations from the NCAA which included multiple Level 1 allegations against its men's basketball program (Carroll 2019). The verdict was not available at the time of this writing. Will Kansas receive a punishment similar to Syracuse University or the University of North Carolina? What do you think?

The NCAA has time after time inconsistently made decisions on matters of infractions and this is just one of the major criticisms of this administrative body. Another major criticism is the idea, which dates back for decades, that the NCAA acts as a cartel with the member universities as the network of connected businesses guided by an administrative body. Economists "generally view the NCAA as a cartel. They hold this view because the NCAA has historically devised rules to restrict output (the number of games played and televised) and to restrict competition for inputs (student-athletes)" (Fleisher, Goff and Tollison 1992: 5). The administrative offices of the NCAA do seem to enjoy flexing their muscles over member institutions but these affiliates also hold power. "The NCAA is a relatively ineffective cartel primarily because of the market structure in which it operates. The most destructive feature of this market structure, from the NCAA's standpoint, is the heterogeneity of member interests" (Koch and Leonard 1981: 253). Although it is questionable whether the NCAA would even want to act like a cartel (thereby viewing members' interest as a "destructive feature"), it is true that member colleges have a great deal of influence on the NCAA. For example, in 2014 the Division I "Power 5" conferences flexed their collective muscles in order to establish their own autonomy. Later in this chapter we will discuss the power moves being made by the athletes as they flex their muscles against the NCAA.

The role of the NCAA is to supervise the organization of college sports, the conduct of athletes, coaches and others involved with college sports, and the academic qualification to which athletes must adhere. However, because the NCAA would cease to exist if colleges and universities opted not to be a part of the organization, it must also bend to the desires of the membership, or at the very least, the powerful member schools.

National Association of Intercollegiate Athletics (NAIA)

The National Association of Intercollegiate Athletics, headquartered in Kansas City (Missouri), is the governing body of nearly 250 member colleges and universities with 77,000 student-athletes competing in 21 conferences which awards 27 championships (NAIA 2020). Organized in 1937, the NAIA has administered sports programs and championships while attempting to balance the overall college experience with an emphasis on academics. According to the NAIA (2020) the organization provides the tools and opportunities to support their institutional strategic priorities. "Return on Athletics (ROA) is the NAIA's proprietary approach to the management of collegiate athletics. Through data analytics, ROA provides institutional-level insight so members can maximize the impact athletics has on enrollment, student success, and financial viability" (NAIA 2020). NAIA provides member facts and figures which include: Average full-time enrollment, 1,400; private institutions, 82 percent; faith-based institutions, 65 percent; average number of sports, 16; and average number of student-athletes, 293 (NAIA 2020).

National Junior College Athletic Association (NJCAA)

There is also an association that oversees junior colleges in the United States, the National Junior College Athletic Association (NJCAA). NJCAA was founded in Fresno, California, in 1938 and oversees community colleges and institutions accredited by the appropriate state and/or regional accrediting agency. The mission of the NJCAA is to foster a national program of athletic participation in an environment that supports equitable opportunities with the educational objectives of member colleges (NJCCAA 2020). The NJCAA is divided into several divisions and regions. The NJCAA sponsors awards (e.g., All-American, Academic All-American, All-Regional and All-Tournament, Coach of the Year Awards, Service Awards, and the Loyalty Cup Award) and national championships. The NJCAA offers college athletes a chance to participate in structured conferences and tournaments which will provide increased exposure and publicity and potentially lead to an opportunity to play in the NCAA for their remaining years of eligibility. Not all junior colleges belong to the NJCAA. Junior colleges in California, for example, belong to the California Community College Athletic Association (CCCAA). There are 108 member schools in the CCCAA.

Academic Requirements, Recruitment, Scholarships and Maintaining Eligibility

High school athletes that hope to participate in collegiate sports must first graduate from high school and complete 16 core courses: four years of English; three years of math (Algebra 1 or higher); two years of natural/physical science (including one year of lab science if the high school offers it); one additional year of English, math, or natural/physical science; two years of social science; and four additional years of English, math, natural/ physical, social science, foreign language, comparative religion, or philosophy (NCAA 2020c). High school students must also earn at least a 2.3 GPA in the core courses and earn an SAT combined score or ACT sum score matching core-course GPA on the Division 1 sliding scale, which balance the student's test score and core-course GPA. If a student does not meet all the Division I academic requirements they may not compete in their first year at college; however, if the student qualifies as an academic redshirt, he or she may practice during their first term in college and receive an athletics scholarship for the entire year (NCAA 2020c).

Elite high school athletes are often recruited; that is, colleges seek them out, rather than the athlete seeking out a college. The recruitment of college athletes dates back to the period of 1895–1905 when there was widespread recruitment of schoolboy athletes (Bowen and Levin 2003). What has changed the most about recruiting over the past 100 years is the aggressive nature of recruiters today, some of whom do not even provide "lip service" to educational values (Bowen and Levin 2003). A related trend in sports such as ice hockey is the recruiting of athletes who have had extensive experience playing on club teams or even national teams, often honing their athletic skills after graduation from secondary school. "The result is a roster that contains a number of somewhat older, more experienced players" (Bowen and Levin 2003: 49). The recruitment of athletes has often led to some controversies and NCAA violations, such as providing top athletes' family members jobs and housing near the school that their sons and daughters attend. Recruiting violations took a new twist when celebrities got involved in a recruiting scandal in recent years. (This will be elaborated upon in Pop Box 7 below.)

Today, promising athletes will receive letters of invitation from college officials in the athletic department to visit their campus and may be invited or encouraged to attend sport camps on campus or those run by college coaches that are off campus. The recruitment process can be stressful to both the athlete and the sports programs (especially the coach). "Coaches are under enormous pressure to recruit the most outstanding high school athletes each year, since this has become the key determinant of competitive success in major college sports. The governing collegiate administrative bodies have many rules (e.g., the number of phone calls and unofficial and official visits to a recruit) regarding recruitment, and violations are punishable by such means as a reduction in the number of scholarships an athletic department many offer. The intensely competitive nature of the recruiting process is aggravated by the perception, real or imagined, that many coaches and institutions use negative or illegal recruiting tactics" (Duderstadt 2003: 192). Illegal recruiting tactics may include rival recruiters spreading misinformation, lies or innuendos to prized athletes in such ways as suggesting the other school is about to be placed on probation, they are going to raise admissions requirements, or that the head coach is about to quit or be fired.

The stress that a coach (and their staff) at a high profile school experiences due to recruiting (especially in basketball) is highlighted by the fact that one or two great players can make a program. The fact that such a high profile player may only stay at a school for one or two years before being lured away to the professional ranks adds to the pressure of recruiting from the coaches' perspective. The athlete being recruited also experiences stress. This young athlete must make the "right" decision. Among the athlete's concerns are playing time, the team's chances of winning, the amount of television exposure, the coaches' ability to "teach," the social life of the college, the academic environment, and the support system designed to help the serious academic-minded athlete. When the athlete decides what college to attend, he or she signs a "letter of intent." The letter of intent, which is treated as a legal contract, states that the athlete promises to attend a particular school for four years. If the athlete changes his or her mind and wants to transfer to a different Division I school, he or she may forfeit a year's eligibility and must sit out a year. An athlete who wishes to turn professional may do so but risks losing any remaining college eligibility.

Understandably, high school athletes, typically, hope to earn athletic scholarships to attend college. This is not an unusual situation, as many colleges offer academic financial support to numerous students who do not play sports. Athletic scholarships (some are full and some are partial) provide financial assistance, usually in the form of "room and board" (paying for admissions, textbooks and school supplies) as well as per diem (meal allowance). Sports programs are limited to a certain number of scholarships they may offer. As a result, this puts a great deal of pressure on young athletes and their families as they may have to weigh other options. If a graduating high school student-athlete does not receive a scholarship to a Division I school, he or she may either try out for the team as a walk-on (a nonscholarship athlete that tries out for a sport but pays all of their own expenses), or opt to play for a NCAA Division II or Division III school, an NAIA school, or a NJCAA school. College athletes may participate in athletics in non–Division I schools for a number of reasons, including: D-I schools did not show an interest in the athlete; the athlete received a better scholarship offer at a D-II, NAIA school, or Junior College; a non–D-I school was a better "fit" (e.g., closer to home) for the athlete; or, an opportunity for increased playing time. Approximately 40 percent of all NCAA athletes (and there are nearly one-half million in sum) compete in Division III athletics, the largest of the divisions. There are over 445 institutions that make up D-III, 80 percent private and 20 percent public. These athletes are not on scholarship and yet they still compete athletically in addition to their academic and personal commitments. As a result, many people consider D-III sports as "pure" sports because these athletes are perceived as playing for the sheer love of the sport.

Once student-athletes reach college they must remain academically eligible as determined by the "NCAA Eligibility Center" which calculates grade-point average (GPA) based on the grades you earn in NCAA-approved courses. Only the best grades from the required number of NCAA core courses are used and grades from additional core courses are used only if they improve the student's grade-point average (NCAA 2020c). Once a student-athlete is enrolled at an NCAA school they must meet the GPA requirement of the school they are attending and make continued progress toward graduation (40 percent of required coursework for a degree must be completed by the end of the second year, 60 percent by the end of the third year, and 80 percent by the end of their fourth year) in order to maintain their academic eligibility. Division II athletes must maintain a 1.8 GPA (essentially a "D" grade) after 24 semester or 36 quarter hours; 1.9 GPA after 48/72 hours; and, 2.0 after both 72/108 hours and 96/144 hours. The NCAA does not have a nationally adhered-to minimum GPA for Division III; instead, athletes must meet the institution's requirement.

The Student-Athlete, Activism and Economics

The life of student-athletes is generally quite regimented and time consuming, especially if they are involved with "big-time" athletics as the demands on their time increases accordingly to the amount of attention their sport garners. College athletes (in-season) will typically follow a six-day-a-week practice schedule that includes team workouts, film sessions, conditioning, and weightlifting. Thus, the student-athlete faces all the challenges experienced by non-athletes (e.g., social adjustment, career exploration, and school work) along with unique challenges that include scheduling classes that do not conflict with athletic commitments, visiting the athletic trainer for injury treatment, traveling for road games, learning an athletic play book, studying game films, and training. Different sports will emphasize certain aspects of training over others (e.g., football players will be encouraged to lift weights more than synchronized swimmers). The NCAA limits the amount of time an athlete may practice but most coaches know how to manipulate the rules by finding loopholes. Weight-lifting without coaches present is a good example of non-reported practice time. It used to be that athletes, such as football players "would disperse for the summer and return to campus in July or early August, just in time for fall camp." However, "during the past decade, though, programs have all but hemmed their players within the school's ZIP code because of intense offseason workout regimes" (McCollough 2020: B6).

Many student-athletes experience a time crunch because of travel. In some cases, college athletes will be on the road for days at a time. Often, when student-athletes return to campus they have to immediately go back to class and, in some instances, take scheduled exams. During the off-season, student athletes are still expected to work out and maintain their conditioning program. Some may participate in informal practice sessions with teammates. Student athletes, as representatives of their school and sports team, are often expected to donate their personal time for charity events and the promotion of their school and their sport. In addition to athletic and academic demands are the many personal responsibilities (grocery shopping, house-cleaning, dating, and family, for example) that every other college student has. Clearly, student-athletes are very busy.

Student-athletes have historically been under the thumbs of coaches, athletic directors and the colleges they play for but much of that has changed in the twenty-first century. A significant inspiration for today's sense of empowerment resides with former UCLA basketball player, Ed O'Bannon who, along with his brother (Charles), led UCLA to the 1995 national championship while winning the Wooden Award (1995) and being named the 1995 NCAA tournament "Most Outstanding Player." Most relevant to our primary point here is that O'Bannon also brought forth a lawsuit against the NCAA (*O'Bannon v. NCAA*) because he believed they were using his image and style of play as the basis for a star player on a video game. "In a landmark decision, U.S. District Judge Claudia Wilken ruled in favor of former UCLA basketball star Ed O'Bannon and 19 others in a lawsuit that challenged the NCAA's regulation of college athletics on antitrust grounds. She issued an injunction prohibiting the NCAA from enforcing its rules on money given to athletes when it comes to their names, images, and likenesses" (*Associated Press* 2014b). "Lawyers for O'Bannon and the others had sought to have millions of dollars put in trust funds for the athletes, but Wilken included a cap on payments" in her ruling (*Associated Press* 2014b). Wilken did, however, rule that "schools that used players' names on jerseys and likenesses in video games had to guarantee an athlete at least $5,000 a year in licensing revenue, paid into a trust fund that could be tapped once he used up his eligibility" (Wolff 2014). Shortly after the Wilken ruling, the NCAA filed an appeal. In September 2015, the Ninth Circuit Court of Appeals reversed the key aspects of the District Court. In March 2016, O'Bannon's lawyers appealed the case to the Supreme Court of the

United States. The Supreme Court refused to hear the case, keeping the Court of Appeals decision in place. To learn more about the O'Bannon case, read his first-hand account in *Court Justice: The Inside Story of My Battle Against the NCAA* (2018).

Seemingly, the judicial system had upheld the NCAA's interpretation of amateurism and its sense of control over student-athletes. However, the State of California took notice of the O'Bannon case and ruled in 2019 that California student-athletes had the legal right to hire agents and make money from endorsement deals with sneaker companies, soft drink makers, and other sponsors, just like the pros (Beam 2019). "The first-in-the-nation law, signed by Gov. Gavin Newsom (D) and set to take effect in 2023, could upend amateur sports in the U.S. and trigger a legal challenge" (Beam 2019: B2). Newsom used an explanation promoted by many others before, that "other college students with a talent, whether it be literature, music, or technological innovation, can monetize their skill and hard work" and so too should student-athletes (Beam 2019: B2).

Essentially, this law opens the door for college athletes in the state of California and gives them the opportunity to earn money. Other states worried that all the top athletes would attend school in California, prompting lawmakers to draft similar laws. By mid–2020, Colorado and Florida had also passed legislation allowing athletes to make money via their own endorsement deals. In other states, individual athletes hired lawyers to demand the right to make money off their own name, image, and likeness (Berkowitz 2020). Nebraska lawmakers followed the pay for play trend in July 2020. The NCAA is fighting this movement to empower athletes, as they could lose millions of dollars in revenue. In a California federal appeals court ruling, it was ruled that the NCAA's limits on "education-related" compensations [e.g., tuition, room and board] for athletes violates antitrust law. However, the court also found that the NCAA's limits on athlete pay not related to education are necessary for "preserving amateurism." "Jude Milan Smith concurred with the panel's decision even while writing that the NCAA is 'a cartel of buyers acting in concert to artificially depress the price' that college athletes could receive for their services on a free market" (Cunningham 2020).

In recent years, and motivated by the O'Bannon case, many student-athletes that play "big-time" (money-generating) sports have also demanded that they should receive a salary, or some sort of financial compensation (other than tuition and room and board) from the collective nearly one billion dollars generated annually from the student-athletes' labor. As *Associated Press* sports columnist Paul Newberry (2019a) explains, "The NCAA just doesn't get it. Under pressure from all sides—legislators, advocates, athletes, pretty much anyone who can spot an injustice when they see it—the group that governs college athletics [has] revealed a fierce determination to keep an iron grip on the two things it cares about the most. Money and power" (p. B2). The NCAA's effort to placate the athletes is to allow "side hustles"—such as the endorsement deals described above—rather than discuss greater financial compensation for those directly responsible for the lucrative sums of money generated by "big-time" sports. We have to remember too that the NCAA is made up of member institutions and they are the ones that profit directly from "big-time" athletics and, consequently, they too are fighting this demand by student-athletes. At Ohio State, for example, athletic director Gene Smith attempts to justify not paying athletes by saying, "One of our principles is not to move to a model where we turn athletes into employees. Whatever we come up with will not be something where we actually pay players. That's just not going to happen for us. We believe in the collegiate model, not the professional model" (Newberry 2019a). To be fair, colleges pay huge sums of money in facilities (e.g., training centers and new stadiums) and much of the money generated by "big-time" athletics is used to fund all the other athletic programs on a given campus—most of which do not generate enough revenue to self-sustain. This issue is very much a fluid one and it will remain as a divisive one for years to come.

The relationship between student-athletes and economics became abundantly clear in 2020 during the COVID-19 pandemic as college sports programs, especially football, attempted to reopen at the risk of the health of student-athletes. In mid–June, 30 UCLA football players issued a powerful letter condemning the university for failing to protect their health and safety. "They demanded an independent health official to ensure the COVID-19 protocols are followed, whistle-blower protection to report violations, and the right for players to decide whether to attend sports events without fear of retaliation or loss of scholarships" (Hussaini and Lipoff 2020: A11). This demand came within the context of student-athletes testing positive for COVID-19 during football camp at numerous colleges across the nation. "College students on athletic scholarships put their bodies and time on the line in exchange for tuition, room and board. The debate over pay for college athletes has always been about fair compensation for risk and efforts. COVID-19 has only added to those risks, as the group of UCLA football players recognized" (Hussaini and Lipoff 2020: A11). In August 2020, a group of Pac-12 football players banded together and threatened to boycott playing the 2020 season if a list of demands was not met. Many of these demands were already put forth by the UCLA athletes along with new demands: preserve all existing sports by eliminating excessive expenditures; end lavish facility expenditures; guarantee medical expense coverage; and, add medical insurance selected by players for sports-related medical conditions including COVID-19 illness to cover six years after college athletics eligibility ends (Axe 2020). Shortly after this, the Pac-12, along with the Big Ten, Mid–American, and Mountain West conferences announced that they would postpone their fall sports. However, lured by economic considerations, pressure from athletes, coaches, and parents of athletes, along with the adoption of emerging, more effective and rapid COVID-19 testing options, by late-September, the Big Ten, Pac-12, Mountain West, and Mid–American conferences changed their minds and decided to start their reduced-scheduled football seasons by the end of October or early November. This meant that all 10 FBS conferences decided to play football during the 2020 pandemic. (Note: The draft of this third edition was completed prior to the conclusion of the 2020 college football season; by the end of October, however, there were numerous outbreaks of COVID-19 involving college football games that led to postponements and cancellations.)

In addition to the backdrop of COVID-19 in 2020 was the national, and global, Black Lives Matter (BLM) social movement that also empowered student-athletes to challenge the authoritarian power of coaches and colleges. By mid–June 2020, students from multiple schools had taken a stand against racism. Consider these examples from Harris (2020):

- Oklahoma State running back and Heisman Trophy contender Chuba Hubbard tweeted that he would have nothing more to do with the Cowboys after seeing his head coach Mike Gundy wear an OAN (One America News Network) t-shirt. OAN is a far right cable news channel whose anchors have been critical of the Black Lives Matter social movement along with other progressive social movements promoting equality. Many other former and current Cowboy players came to Hubbard's immediate defense saying there was a culture of racism at the college. Gundy and Hubbard were part of the university's press conference wherein Gundy never actually apologized for anything but promised to bring about a change in the football culture.

- At the University of Texas, a group of athletes demanded a number of changes including, the renaming of several buildings, the donation of athletic funds to Black organizations, and the replacement of the school's fight song, "The Eyes of Texas."
- At Clemson University, a former football player accused a white assistant coach of using the n-word; current players came to the defense of the former players and led a peaceful on-campus protest against systemic racism. Counter protestors displaying Confederate flags organized a demonstration prior to the anti-racism protest, offending many players.
- The University of Iowa fired their strength and conditioning coach after several former players accused him of mistreating Black players.
- Many student-athletes across the nation participated in BLM protests.

Add to these stories the case of Colorado State University which shut down all football-related activities indefinitely following complaints from many football players of alleged racism and verbal abuse in the football program (Adelson 2020). Allegations included: the lack of pay for the African American coaches on the staff, concerns over nepotism following the hiring of new head football coach Steve Addazio in December 2019, racially insensitive comments that created a harmful culture, and accusations that the athletics department was not providing accurate information to local and state officials and ignoring COVID-19 guidelines (Adelson 2020).

Student-athletes have come to realize, especially in this current social climate, the power that comes from their activism and collective actions.

Sports Administration

Collegiate sports, like all other large business enterprises, are overseen by administrative bodies. As we have already learned, there are a number of large administrative bodies (i.e., NCAA and NAIA) that oversee the sporting operations of member schools; in turn, each college and university hires an administrative staff to oversee its own sports programs. On college and university campuses, mind you, there are an alarmingly large number of administrators (especially when compared to the more important position of full-time faculty). And yet, the bigger the sports presence on a college campus, the greater the need becomes for sports administration. Typically, this administrative staff is under the direction of the athletic director (AD). The athletic director has a staff of employees, often consisting of other administrators. The AD must administer protocol to assure that the actions of his or her staff, coaches, trainers and student-athletes properly conform to the expectations and demands of the college/university and the governing membership body as a whole. As administrators, athletic directors do not always have a sports background; instead, they usually possess general administrative skills that assist them in their goal of running a smooth and compliant department. It is common for athletic directors to belong to the National Association of Collegiate Directors of Athletics (NACDA), an association consisting of more than 15,700 individuals at more than 1,700 institutions throughout the United States, Canada and Mexico (National Association of Collegiate Directors of Athletics 2020).

Many institutions also have a Sports Information Director (SID), who in turn, may have a staff consisting of other administrators. A sports information director has functions similar to that of a public relations employee and provides statistics, team and player information about the college or university's sports team to news media. The SID, depending on the school, can have a very important role in assuring that the institution looks good to the general public as well as to the media. The SID office is usually responsible for the production of official publications, game notes and statistics and game programs. SID generally belong to the College Sports Information Directors of America (CoSIDA) association. CoSIDA was founded in 1957 and is a 3,100-plus member national organization comprised of the sports public relations, media relations and communications/information professionals throughout all levels of collegiate athletics in the United States and Canada (CoSida 2020).

The athletic department at nearly every college and university is an entity devoted entirely to varsity sports, and athletic directors enjoy freedoms that most other college and university department heads do not. Like most administrators, athletic directors are well compensated for their position and responsibilities. However, while top administrators are generally paid far more than faculty, athletic directors at "big-time" schools are generally paid far less than their high profile coaches. With this in mind, some college and university coaches actually have more power than athletic directors. Nonetheless, the AD has a number of important responsibilities that may include any or all of the following: properly assessing the athletic landscape at the college, especially in relation to scheduled opponents; knowing when to fire or not renew a contract of a member of the coaching staff; knowing how to pick the "right" coach for the job that needs to be filled; creating a schedule of opponents that best suits a particular sport; seeking funding and overseeing development of new facilities, including practice and playing facilities for all sports but especially the money-generating sports; keeping up with the growing craze of new uniform color and design schemes, while still balancing the expectations associated with tradition; finding a way to keep the student body involved; being aware of, and obtaining, any necessary certifications, especially for trainers; being able to entertain booster and alumni groups; and maintaining a proper support administrative staff. Some athletic directors keep a low profile and choose to lead by example, while others attempt to make themselves well-known via instituting relatively dramatic changes in the sports programs. On some occasions, the AD will succeed and on other occasions he or she will not. Depending on the power of the AD, they may be the point person to address the many issues being raised by student-athletes (as discussed previously).

Coaching

Coaches, as the old cliché goes, *coach*. They coach others in the rules of the game and methods of training, and ideally, help to develop the skills of athletes. One might assume, then, that coaches are highly trained people. But, this is not always the case. At the youth sports level, for example, the coach may simply be a parent of one of the kids playing. Generally speaking, as each level of sport competition increases, so too does the level of training that coaches go through.

High school coaches are usually employed in either a full-time or part-time position at the school they coach at. High school coaches have a number of job duties, including finding assistant coaches; holding tryouts for students, evaluating the tryouts' skills during practice, including perhaps time trials; holding practice for team members; overseeing the selection of team captains, even if that means leaving it completely up to the players themselves; developing talent; identifying the best positions for players; assuring that students attend scholastic classes; and, preparing athletes for upcoming competitions. Many schools will require a general bachelor's degree or a coaching degree and state certification when applicable.

It has become increasingly common for high school coaches to be required to pass a certification program or the very least take a number of courses on coaching. The NFHS advices that coaches check with their school administration or state association to confirm certification requirements. The NFHS offers a Coach Certification Program that is national in scope and is promoted as a way for a coach to better serve the student, the school, the community, and the profession of coaching (NFHS 2020).

The United States Sports Academy (USSA) offers certificate programs designed to help people become a part of the coaching profession. The USSA claims to be the largest sports university in the world specializing in sports management, sports medicine, and coaching (USSA 2014a). The Academy offers three levels of certification designed to help coaches: CEB 572 Coaching Certification Level I (includes topics on ethics, sports administration, coaching methodology, conditioning and nutrition, injury prevention, and immediate care and rehabilitation); Coaching Certification Level II (includes skills development, techniques, drills and playing strategies); and Coaching Level III (includes coverage in human movement and its relationship to sports activities) (USSA 2014b).

Collegiate coaches are employees of the institution and may, or may not, teach college courses (it would be more common for D-III coaches to teach classes than coaches at Power 5 conferences in the elite sports). At smaller colleges, such as D-III schools, the collegiate coach is likely to hold tryouts to fill positions. At schools that offer scholarships, most players are recruited to play. Major colleges may hold tryouts for walk-ons (student-athletes that practice but rarely, if ever, play in a game). Coaches of major sports will have a full coaching staff, while other coaches may have just one assistant. Coaches of major sports will also have a full staff helping to take care of the daily details of operating a sports program. Collegiate coaches almost always have played the sport that they coach, many were not star athletes but have the ability to coach. Collegiate colleges have usually either climbed the ranks starting in high school or served as an assistant coach at a college or university.

The primary role of a collegiate coach is to teach athletes. "Coaching is teaching in its most perfect and rewarding form. No matter what the sport, coaches are basically giving information, waiting for a response, and then giving feedback on that response" (Dorfman 2003: xi). Coaches are perceived by athletes as leaders, teachers, and mentors, and therefore they must think before speaking, be clear communicators, speak with clarity, be consistent yet flexible, and learn to establish a connection to all team members.

At "big-time" colleges and high schools, the coach is often the most recognized personality on campus and perhaps in the community. For example, in Syracuse, New York, a city lacking many visible celebrities, men's basketball coach Jim Boeheim is a first-tier celebrity. The media plays a major role in the development of the coach as a celebrity. In the case of Boeheim, it helps that he is a member of the Hall of Fame, the second winningest coach in Division I history, an assistant coach for the U.S. national team that has won gold medals and is very outspoken (sometimes to a fault). In his 2014 book, *Bleeding Orange: Fifty Years of Blind Referees, Screaming Fans, Beasts of the East, and Syracuse Basketball*, Boeheim does not hold back on his personal opinions about others in basketball and the media. The insights provided in *Bleeding Orange* impart an excellent look into the world of coaching and is a must-read for those who are curious about the life of a coach.

Coaches like Boeheim who lead winning teams are often celebrities at their schools and in their communities, and are often better known (and better compensated) than college presidents (and especially college professors!).

AUTHORITY, POWER, AND CONTROL

When dealing with athletes, the role of the coach, at any level, is to provide leadership, direction, order, structure and discipline. Coaches, then, are in a position of authority. A person of authority is in a position of power because he or she can influence the thoughts and behaviors of others. Some coaches attempt to gain complete control over the actions of athletes while others take a more democratic approach to coaching. Coaches who have the ability to handle authority well generally know how to manage people. When coaches attempt to assert their power position, they place their credibility on the line. "A leader who knows how to manage athletes can direct their mental and behavioral efforts toward a common goal—a goal established by the leader. This becomes the organizational/team credo" (Dorfman 2003: 4). The credo becomes the first expression of a coach's power position. It is important for coaches to establish their authority on day one. The coach will explain to his or her athletes what is expected from each of them as individuals and teammates. A coach can get the message across without being a raving maniac. Dorfman (2003) cites Bill Walton's (a basketball star at UCLA and in the NBA) reflection of Coach John Wooden's handling of a difficult or resistant player. According to Walton, Wooden would tell that player, "I admire and respect your position. We'll miss you here at UCLA. We've enjoyed your time. Thanks for coming" (Dorfman 2003: 5). In this manner, Wooden was polite to his defiant players but made it clear that it was still his way or the highway.

There is a distinction between power and authority. Coaches who crave absolute power are like dictators. Coaches who want to establish authority are really concerned with gaining control. "Coaches don't want power; at least, the ones who care about the players they coach aren't power-hungry. What coaches want is *control*—control over the many variables that affect their on-the-job performance" (Warren 1997: xvii). This idea is easy to grasp, as each of us would like to have some level of control—at least in our own lives. Of course, we all realize, sooner or later, that there are few variables in life that we can control. The manner in which we deal with adversity is what sets us apart from one another. This is especially true with coaches. Inevitably things will not go as planned. The players will look toward the coach to see how he or she is handling adversity and will generally feed off the coach's cues.

However, as we learned in the discussion on student-athletes, coaches today must be far more willing to take the perspective of players. They must also learn that the power trip many coaches (especially coaches of "big-time" sports) once enjoyed is far more likely to be challenged today. And, the universities are more likely to listen to athletes as they can promote their voices via social media and potentially garner support from the public.

Full time coaches, such as those found in the college and professional ranks, generally work long days (e.g., reviewing game films, preparing their athletes for competition, recruiting); especially during their respective seasons. All coaches have their own coaching styles and philosophies. The primary goal of all coaches, however, is to be successful. The ability to recruit gifted athletes and improve the skills of athletes will lead to coaching success. Ultimately, successful coaches have gained control of their team and individual athletes by getting them to accept the credo of hard work, dedication and sacrifice.

Elite college coaches are compensated quite handsomely for their time and dedication. Coaches at elite colleges and universities are often the highest paid employees on their campus. According to Forbes, the highest paid college coaches in 2019 were: Nick Saban (Alabama, football), $9.4 million; Dabo Swinney (Clemson, football), $9.3 million; Mike Krzyzewski (Duke, basketball), $9 million; John Calipari (Kentucky, basketball), $8.6 million; and Jim Harbaugh (Michigan, football), $7.7 million (Badenhausen 2019). Following LSU's 2019 football championship head coach Ed Orgeron had his salary increased to $8.7 million.

One might wonder whether coaches (or any elite athlete, celebrity, or CEO) are worth this level of compensation. At the elite schools, where the highest paid coaches reside, a number of sports programs (e.g., football and men's basketball) generate large sums of money and are focal points for community members and alumni. Thus, their rate of return on investment (ROI) is justifiable. However, if student-athletes continue to gain power and are compensated for their work—which is responsible for the large sums of money in college athletics—we may see that the ROI have to be adjusted accordingly.

Hazing

Among the more persistent problems associated with sports is hazing. "Hazing is an all-encompassing term that covers silly, potentially risky, or degrading tasks required for acceptance by a group of full-fledged members" (Nuwer 2004: xiv). Crow and Rosner (2004) incorporate the aspects of humiliation and shaming in their legal interpretation of hazing. They define hazing as "any activity expected of someone joining a group that humiliates, degrades, abuses, or endangers, regardless of the person's willingness to participate" (200). Susan Lipkins (2009) describes hazing as a process, based on tradition, that is used by groups to discipline members and to reinforce a hierarchy. Like Crow and Rosner, Lipkins incorporates the idea that hazing activities can be humiliating, demeaning, intimidating, and exhausting, all of which results in physical and/or emotional turmoil. Bawan, Pascual and Gabriel (2017) describe hazing as "the infliction of physical, social, psychological harm upon the person of an applicant to student organization or group as a prerequisite for admission. It is done as part of a ritual that people (such as college students) must go through before they are allowed to become members of the group" (p. 110–111). Hazing is fairly common in sports, fraternities and sororities, the military and street gangs. Incidents of hazing date back to 387 BCE with Plato's account of the savagery of young boys' hazing behavior. Hazing was common during the age of the rise of European universities (1400s). Nuwer (2004) states, "Martin Luther endured hazing at Erfurt as a student. Later, in 1539, at Wittenberg, he advocated hazing as a means of strengthening a boy to face and endure life's challenges" (p. xxv). At American universities hazing was a method first utilized by upperclassmen against freshmen to "keep them in line." According to Ronald Smith (1988), hazing in American sport can be traced back to Harvard University in the late 1700s.

> The sophomore-freshman hazing in sport became institutionalized in the early fall "rush." Annually, on the first Monday of the fall term in the late 1700s, Harvard sophomores would challenge individuals of the freshman class to wrestling matches. If the sophomore should by some chance be defeated by being thrown down, then the juniors would challenge. If the juniors lost, then the seniors would take on the freshmen. "It was a kind of initiatory process for newcomers," a member of the Harvard class of 1805 stated. The tradition of rushes or class battles, though not necessarily wrestling, was found on most nineteenth-century college campuses [Smith 1988: 19].

Since the early 1800s, and until recently, hazing has endured as a relatively acceptable form of freshmen indoctrination into the subcultural world of sports by upperclassmen. In this regard, defenders of hazing practices view hazing as a "rite of passage" which all recruits must endure before becoming accepted as a member of the team.

WHY DOES HAZING STILL OCCUR?

While there is no definitive answer to the question, "Why does hazing still occur?," many believe it has something to do with ideals of masculinity. Boys have a long history of attempting to prove their masculinity through the primal means of physically dominating and humiliating other, generally younger and weaker, boys. While this explanation seems applicable to males, what about females? Girls and women in sport have become increasingly common and popular for the past two generations and desire to be taken as "seriously" as boys and men in sport, so it is perhaps not surprising that females are taking on many of the same character traits of their male counterparts. Another plausible contributing explanation as to why hazing still exists is the reality that nearly all societies in the world are filled with acts of extreme violence including murder and war and acts of mild to moderate forms of violence (e.g., bar fights, fights between rival sports fans). To be shocked that hazing still occurs is to be surprised that violence of any kind exists.

In most cases hazing is a tool utilized by upperclassmen, or higher ranking personnel, as a means of conveying to freshmen, or newcomers, the privileged status of being a higher ranking individual. Groups such as fraternities, sport teams, the military, street gangs and other organizations tend to reward with power and status individuals who are perceived as making the group better. Hazers are looked upon as providing a group service by teaching newcomers precedence while toughening them up (Nuwer 1999). New recruits must show the experienced members of the group that they are "worthy" of admission. The tradition of hazing has long been upheld as an important ritual by groups and organizations that value extreme loyalty to the "team." The willingness among new recruits to endure a hazing ritual demonstrates the power and status of the group or team.

Hazing generally operates under the cloak of secrecy. Perpetrators and participants of hazing seldom admit to their involvement. The secret nature of hazing serves as a bonding experience among the participants. Those who perpetrate hazing have already experienced the victimization of hazing and easily justify victimizing newcomers. Newcomers who successfully survive their hazing experience look forward to the day when they become hazers. It becomes advantageous for all involved in hazing not to say anything to officials who may view such behavior negatively. Thus, a perpetual cycle of reinforcement guarantees the continuation of hazing. The adage "What was good enough for me is good enough for them" applies with hazing.

Proponents of hazing argue that such ritualistic behaviors stimulate team loyalty, bonding and solidarity—we're all in this together. The ever-growing legions of people (e.g., school administrators, faculty, concerned parents, and targets of hazing) who are against hazing argue there is no place for degrading or humiliating activities in team-building (Meagher 2005). Unfortunately, humiliating newcomers is a big part of hazing. In fraternities and male sports teams, newcomers are often humiliated in a sadomasochistic manner. Nuwer (1999) argues that sadomasochistic sexual assaults or threats of such assaults in fraternal hazing may be performed by older members to demonstrate their male dominance over newcomer males. (This is also the case in prison, where dominant males will rape weaker males. Such acts are not viewed as homosexual but rather as a sign of power and dominance.) Male dominance sometimes manifests itself in a sexual manner against women (e.g., gang rapes) (Nuwer 1999). Milder versions of male dominance over rookies are common in professional sports. In Major League Baseball, for example, rookies endure annual initiation rites. Rookies were generally made to dress like women (e.g., Bryce Harper was made to dress as a member of the U.S. Olympic women's gymnastics team; Mike Trout as Lady Gaga; Manny Machado in a ballet tutu; and Carlos Correa as Wonder Woman) (*Associated Press* 2016). In the era of cell phone cameras and social media many of these sexualized hazing incidents were observed by the general public and led to a negative reaction by many, including high school and college officials that believed the professional ranks of athletics were sending a negative message to athletes for tolerating any type of humiliating hazing behavior. In 2016, Major League Baseball created an anti-hazing and anti-bullying policy (A.B.1.) forbidding: bullying (verbal and physical); rookie hazings, pranks, and player rituals that can be viewed as derogatory, offensive, or insensitive to individuals (including fans); and, rookie initiation rituals (MLB 2016). The policy also states that the player's actual or perceived willingness to participate in said hazing does not excuse the activity. Beyond humiliation experienced by some, there are times when people are physically injured and sometimes killed during hazing activities.

Tolerance for hazing is at an all-time low among school and league officials. They believe hazing is an inappropriate behavior and have therefore created policies forbidding it. These officials are not alone in their quest to end such violence as hazing is illegal in nearly all U.S. states. "As of 2019, there were 44 states that have passed laws prohibiting hazing. Of those, only 10 states have laws that explicitly make hazing a felony when it results in death or serious injury" (Stewart, Tilghman, Fox, Bianchi, and Cain 2020). Hazing has become equated as a type of bullying. Englander (2013) argues that there are three characteristics of bullying: power imbalance (the bully wields greater power); repeated occurrence (it is not a single event); and intentionality (the acts were not accidental but committed on purpose). *Bullying* itself is viewed as an intentional act of aggression that is meant to harm a victim either physically or psychologically (Lipkins 2009). While many bullies operate alone and target individuals perceived as vulnerable, hazers target members from their own social group. Despite the active attempts of many school administrators, concerned parents and a number of coaches and athletes to end hazing, it continues to persist in high schools and colleges.

HIGH SCHOOL HAZING

The National Federation of High Schools (NFHS) defines hazing as any humiliating or dangerous activity expected of a student to belong to a group, regardless of his or her willingness to participate (Porter 2018). High school bullying practices often associated with high school hazing have the potential to bring bodily harm or even death. Among the hazing practices are tattooing, piercing, head-shaving, branding, sleep deprivation, physical punishment (paddling and "red bellying"), kidnapping, consuming unreasonable/unacceptable foods or beverages, being deprived of personal hygiene and/or inappropriate sexual behavior (Porter 2018). "It's a common misconception that newcomers to a group embrace its hazing rituals. Realistically, no one wants to be abused, humiliated or embarrassed" (Porter 2018). Youth athletes often prepare themselves for high school sports hazing as they have undoubtedly heard stories about such acts prior to trying out for the team. Some can handle it, or tolerate it, while others may be traumatized by it. For those who are distressed by a hazing victimization comes the increased risk of suffering from physical or psychological side effects that may lead to addiction. Some of the risks associated with teen hazing are: depression, anxiety, injury, and resulting peer pressure that may lead to other harmful effects such as drug abuse (Christopher 2020). High school hazing can occur in sports, band, performing arts, and programs such as the Reserved Officers' Training Corps (ROTC) (Christopher 2020).

The NFHS and the National Interscholastic Athletic Administrator's Association's (NIAAA) Leadership Training Institute (LTI) offer workshops and conferences designed to help athletic administrators find ways to prevent hazing in their schools. Because hazing is often ingrained into certain group cultures it becomes difficult to combat. And this is in spite of the realization that high schools typically have strict anti-hazing policies and those who take part are punished. Coaches who condone hazing will lose their jobs (Christopher 2020). As of 2019, there were 44 states that have passed laws prohibiting hazing; ten of those states have laws that explicitly make hazing a felony when it results in death or serious injury. "Many of these laws include language that defines hazing as a method of 'initiation' or 'pre-initiation,' but hazing activity extends far beyond initiation" (Stewart, Tilghman, Fox, Bianchi & Cain 2020).

Despite all legal, moral and ethical attempts to combat hazing, the practice remains very common at high school campuses across the United States; and, nearly half of those who have ever played high school sports were victimized by hazing. Consider some of these statistics as evidence of the prevalence of high school hazing: 1.5 million high school students are hazed each year; 91 percent of all high school students belong to at least one group, and nearly half of them (48 percent) report being subjected to hazing activities; 43 percent were subjected to humiliating activities and 30 percent performed potentially illegal acts as part of their initiation; both males and females report high levels of hazing; 24 percent of students involved in church groups are reportedly hazed; 70 percent of NCAA athletes report being hazed initially in high school; and, 25 percent were first hazed before the age of 13 (*Inside Hazing* 2014). Hazing is a type of ritualistic behavior that gives hazers a sense of power, entitlement, and occasionally sadistic pleasure (Nuwer 2004). "High school hazing of freshmen and rookies can be particularly vicious when directed toward nonconformists struggling to find an identity. In fact, hazing is part of a larger culture of violence and destruction" (Nuwer 2004: xvi). High school hazers may not view themselves as bullies, but in essence, that is what they are. High school administrators are increasingly coming to view hazers as bullies and want to stop hazing altogether in their schools.

General statistics provide a worthy overview of the prevalence of hazing, but specific stories detail some of the horrific acts that constitute hazing. We will share just a few short stories here, beginning with a 2019 incident at De La Salle Collegiate High School in Warren, Michigan, where football players were victimized with broomsticks in a sexual manner during alleged hazing incidents at the Catholic high school (Miller 2019). The football team, which has won three state championships in five years, was well aware of the hazing but failed to report it (Miller 2019).

Two boys were arrested and cited after a member of the Cottage Grove High School (OR) junior varsity football team was sexually assaulted in the boy's locker room as part of a hazing incident in September 2019 (Deffenbacher 2019). Cottage Grove PD Chief Scott Shepherd confirmed the account that described the victim being assaulted with a broomstick with as many as 10 people present. Cottage Grove HS is a part of the South Lane school district which has policies prohibiting sexual harassment and hazing. The policy defines sexual harassment as including, but not being limited to, physical touching of a sexual nature, sexual gestures and sexual activity or performance (Deffenbacher 2019). Recall earlier in our discussion on hazing when Nuwer (1999) stated that sadomasochistic sexual assaults were part of an attempt for older males to show their dominance over newcomer males. Sadistic, homoerotic types of hazing happen far too commonly in football across the nation. Deffenbacher (2019) reviews a number of other sexual assaults with broomsticks—known as "brooming"—including: Damascus High School (MD), four Maryland teens, all 15 year olds, were charged as adults with first-degree rape following the gang-style-attack of two younger players in the boys locker room; a former Seymour HS (CT) was charged with assaulting a teammate with a broomstick during a 2015 hazing incident; other criminal investigations for brooming have been reported at schools in Long Island (NY) (2004), New Mexico (2008), Vermont (2011 and 2012), South Carolina (2013), New Jersey (2014), and in Washington state (2015). Brooming occurs in other sports as well, including wrestling. Two Greater Latrobe Junior HS wrestling coaches were charged with child endangerment and failure to report January (2020) hazing incidents that were captured on surveillance cameras. Four 15-year-old boys were also charged with hazing and possessing an instrument of a crime (wooden broom handle) as they were seen on the surveillance video restraining their teammates and sodomizing them with what appeared to be a wooden broom handle (Signorini 2020).

The NFHS cites examples of coaches getting fired for turning a blind eye to hazing incidents: in California, some members of the varsity girls' soccer team forced four freshman girls to drink alcohol until the girls vomited or collapsed; in New Jersey, freshmen soccer players were physically abused and thrown in the mud as part of an annual hazing event (Jonas 2017).

College and University Hazing

The NCAA (2016) defines hazing as "any act committed against someone joining or becoming a member or maintaining membership in any organization that is humiliating, intimidating or demeaning, or endangers the health and safety of the person. Hazing includes active or passive participation in such acts and occurs regardless of the willingness to participate in the activities. Hazing creates an environment/climate in which dignity and respect are absent." The NCAA (2016) states that it is a myth that hazing creates bonding activities that brings teams closer together as, in reality, hazing is associated with lower team cohesion and can put personal, academic, and athletic goals out of reach. Many students have actually lost their lives during hazing incidents. Since 1970, at least one college student has died nationwide each year because of an initiation gone wrong (Mandelaro 2014; Nuwer 2018). "Other harms of hazing are more hidden as people respond to stress in individual ways. Some appear not to be bothered, while others cope by avoiding all contact with hazers. Others may develop symptoms of post-traumatic stress disorder, such as nightmares, depression and feelings of shame" (NCAA 2016).

The NCAA (2016) reports that 74 percent of student-athletes experience at least one form of hazing while in college, with the most frequently reported hazing behavior among student-athletics being participating in drinking games (47 percent of hazings). Twenty-three percent of student-athletes report having to drink large amounts of alcohol to the point of getting sick or passing out as part of a hazing activity (NCAA 2016). The NCAA (2016) cites data on the hazing experience of student-athletes and reports that 69 percent disagreed that hazing made them feel more like a part of the group; 78 percent disagreed that they felt a sense of accomplishment; and 82 percent disagreed that they felt stronger. A quarter of all student-athletes who had been hazed believed that their coaches knew about the hazing. Interestingly, only 27 percent of men and 29 percent of women reached out to family members if they had been hazed (NCAA 2016).

Most likely, you were aware that hazing occurs at many colleges—and this despite all efforts to end it—but maybe (unless you participated in a marching band) you were unaware that hazing takes place with marching bands, too.

One infamous case involves the Florida A&M University (FAMU) band and an incident that took place in 2011. The hazing of band members was similar to gang initiations witnessed by author Tim Delaney during his gang research, wherein a recruit had to run a gauntlet of existing members who threw punches and kicked the recruit as he tried to navigate the line. FAMU members had to endure a hazing known as "Crossing Bus C" in which they had to run from the front of the bus to the back through a gauntlet of band members. Drum major Robert Champion "crossed bus C" in 2011 and died as a result of the blows he endured (Hudak 2014). The state medical examiner testified that Champion was hit at least 8–10 times and could have been hit as many as 40–50 times on the band's bus. Champion had a massive hemorrhage in his soft tissue and lost over half of his blood supply (WESH.com 2014). During investigations it was found many members of the Marching 100 (FAMU's band) were not enrolled in school or should have been ineligible to perform because of poor grades (Hudak 2014). Champion's parents sued FAMU, alleging the university allowed a hazing tradition to fester in the band (Hudak 2014). (Note: In 2015, the family of Champion settled a lawsuit against the university by accepting a $1.1 million payment and an apology from the school.)

Although the hazing procedure is voluntary, prosecutors contend that Champion's band mates were guilty of manslaughter. Champion's death led to charges against 15 band members involved in the incident. Most of those accused were sentenced to combinations of community service and probation but Dante Martin, who was considered the "ringleader" (or "president" of Bus C, according to court records) of the hazing incident faced up to 15 years in prison. In early January 2015, Martin was sentenced to prison for 77 months despite the prosecutor's attempt for a harsher punishment. Judge Renee Roche chose a more lenient sentence because it had been demonstrated that Champion had been a "willing participant" in the ritual (CBS News 2015; Saunders 2018). Martin's attorneys filed an appeal, arguing that the state's hazing law was unconstitutional because it was overly broad and vague. In part, "Martin's attorneys contended that the hazing law was overbroad because it criminalized constitutionally protected speech and conduct" (Saunders 2018). The case reached the Florida Supreme Court wherein the ruling by the 5th District Court of Appeal was upheld and the defense arguments rejected (Saunders 2018).

Fans of college football have long recognized the collaboration of football and performances by the marching band, but the death of Robert Champion led to a renewed interest in investigating incidents of hazing in marching bands and developing prevention strategies to combat them (Silveira and Hudson 2015). Research indicates that nearly 30 percent of respondents indicated that they observed some form of hazing in their marching band, with the most common acts of hazing involving public verbal humiliation or degradation which generally went unreported (Silveira and Hudson 2015). Incidents of hazing in marching bands continue despite the FAMU incident. At Bowie State University (MD) the marching band—known as the Symphony of Soul (SOS)—was suspended and Band Director Adolph Wright voluntarily resigned because hazing incidents were brought to the attention of the university's administration. The university said that the marching band had a document, known as "The Constitution," that encouraged the hazing of new members. School officials said that there were several incidents of hitting and students being forced to do things against their will (Roby 2018). In October 2019, Ohio University announced that it had issued an administrative directive to its marching band—the Marching 110—to immediately stop all non-academic group activities following reports of hazing allegations. This directive came one day after the university issued a cease-and-desist order to three sororities governed by the Women's Panhellenic Association and one professional fraternity after it received reported allegations of hazing concerning the organizations (WKYC 2019).

Most universities and colleges include hazing guidelines in their student conduct policies and address incoming freshmen at orientation on the topic; schools with fraternities and sororities are especially likely to address hazing. Hazing involves ritualistic behaviors that often cause mental and physical harm to those who are forced to participate. A number of athletes are deterred from joining high school and college sports because of the threat of hazing. Those involved in hazing risk being suspended and held criminally responsible for such behaviors. Hazing shames and humiliates athletes at least as much as it builds team camaraderie as proponents claim. For the good of high school and college sports, hazing should not be tolerated any longer.

Connecting Sports and Popular Culture

Box 7: Operation Varsity Blues

In 2007, University of Texas–Austin's tennis coach Michael Center was named the U.S. Professional Tennis Association (USPTA) National College Coach of the Year. In 2019 he led his team, the Longhorns, to the NCAA finals, where they won the National Championship. A year later he was in prison. Center served a six-month federal prison sentence for taking a bribe in 2015 to certify a student applicant, the son of Silicon Valley venture capitalist Chris Schaepe, as a scholarship athlete even though the young man was not in fact a competitive tennis player. Center plead guilty to accepting $100,000 from Schaepe, $40,000 of which went to the UTA tennis program, and $60,000 of which went into his own pockets (Richer 2020).

The corrupt deal between Center and Schaepe was brokered by William "Rick" Singer, a con artist who bribed dozens of college coaches and administrators in order to have them recruit the children of his wealthy clients so that they would have an unfair advantage that would allow them to get into elite colleges. But unbeknownst to Center and Singer, the scam was being investigated by the U.S. Department of Justice, which revealed what came to be called Operation Varsity Blues (named after a popular 1999 movie) in 2019.

Singer, the mastermind of the scheme, is accused of taking over $25 million to broker the deals. The founder of a bogus charity called The Key Worldwide Foundation (which he said was set up to help "disadvantaged children") Singer had initially found a loophole in getting students from wealthy households into highly competitive elite colleges by exploiting the extra time that applicants with learning disabilities were given to complete their entrance exams. After pleading guilty in March of 2019 to charges of racketeering conspiracy, money laundering, and conspiracy to defraud the U.S. Government, Singer explained to the court what he called his "side door" technique: "There is a front door of getting in," he testified, "where a student just does it on their own. And then there's a back door, where people go to institutional advancement and make large donations, but they're not guaranteed in. And then I created a side door that guaranteed families to get in" (Spitznagel 2020). Singer knew that getting a diagnosis of a learning disability for an applicant would not be difficult, and would allow extra time during college-entrance exams. While contemptible, he had not yet broken the law. But by 2008, he began arranging for ringers to take the applicants' exams for them or paying proctors to "correct" tests, all the while taking large "contributions" to his bogus tax-exempt Foundation from the grateful parents. He found a further loophole in college sports, and started bribing coaches, recruiters and other college administrators to admit his clients' children as bona fide student-athletes.

Singer's methods were ingenious and well as contemptible. He had high school athletic records altered, and focused on non-competitive sports (which receive far less publicity), even going so far as to photo-shop applicants' heads onto genuine athletes' bodies to create fake athletic profiles. In the case of one of his clients, TV actress Lori Loughlin (of "Full House" fame), he came up with a clever way to get her two daughters accepted into the University of Southern California, by focusing on rowing crew. As Matthew Ormseth of the *Los Angeles Times* writes: "But one pastime was particularly suited to Singer's scheme. According to court documents, when it came to helping.... Loughlin, he turned to a sport with large rosters, little fan or media scrutiny, and wide latitude in recruiting female athletes—as well as one position that requires little physicality" (Ormseth 2019). Loughlin's daughters had never rowed competitively, nor apparently were they aware of their mother's skullduggery. Even more despicable was the way Singer knowingly took advantage of Title IX when he focused on crew as a target. "Schools with high-profile football programs use the sport as a Title IX counterweight, allotting women's rowing programs as many as 20 scholarships.... As a result some crew programs have rosters of 40 or 50 rowers—enough, perhaps, to stow away one or two in the recruiting process who didn't belong" (Ormseth 2019).

When the scandal was exposed to the light of day, Americans were shocked to learn that officials from such elite schools as Georgetown, Stanford, the University of Texas, Wake Forest, Yale, UC Berkeley, UCLA, UC San Diego, UC Santa Barbara, and the University of Southern California had been involved in such chicanery. Even more attention-getting was the fact that prominent celebrities like Loughlin had knowingly paid Singer huge sums of money to get their already-highly privileged children into these institutions. Another noteworthy actress involved was Felicity Huffman, one of the stars of the hit TV series "Desperate Housewives." Huffman admitted to paying Singer $15,000 to assist her daughter to cheat on the SAT and boost her test scores. Huffman served eleven days behind bars and paid a fine of $30,000. While initially denying the accusations against them, Loughlin and her husband, clothing designer J. Mossimo Giannulli, finally admitted to paying Singer $500,000 to get confirmed acceptances to the University of Southern California for both of their daughters. Loughlin was sentenced to 2 months in prison, and fined $150,000 fine, while Giannulli was sentenced to 5 months in prison with a $250,000 fine.

Ultimately more than 50 people have been charged in the federal Varsity Blues probe, with over 25 parents having plead guilty. What is particularly offensive about the scandal is the fact that it deprived genuine student-athletes of the possibility of being admitted to colleges based on their actual athletic abilities. Liz Greenberger, president of RowLA, a nonprofit organization which teaches rowing and other life skills to girls from low-income communities, was incensed when she learned that coaches from that sport had been involved in such corruption. One of the young girls she was hoping would be recruited to a collegiate rowing program asked her, "Does this mean I could be competing against those girls for a spot, and not get the spot because their parents have a lot of money?" Sadly, Greenberger told her, "Yes. That's exactly what it means" (Ormseth 2019).

It's interesting to note that the scandal was named in honor of the 1999 fan favorite movie *Varsity Blues,* about a small town college football team. James Van Der Beek stars as Jonathan "Mox" Moxon, a backup quarterback with a strict moral code. After becoming the new quarterback and team captain when his best friend Lance Harbor is injured in a game, Mox is shocked to learn of the unethical behind-the-scenes behavior of their legendary Coach Kilmer (played by Jon Voight), whose teams have won 22 district championships. Kilmer wants to win a 23rd by any means necessary and pressures his players to take performance-enhancing drugs, lies about their injuries, and endangers their health by having them play at risk of serious injury. When Mox stands up to Kilmer and opposes his win-at-any-cost mentality, Kilmer threatens to alter his high school transcripts so he won't be able to use the scholarship he has won to Brown University. In the end, Kilmer's ruthlessness is exposed, and Mox's teammates refuse to play for the coach. They then rally behind Mox who calls the plays to win the district championship. In *Varsity Blues* good sportsmanship triumphs, and the lead character gets into an elite college by his own academic talents, unlike the case with the Operation Varsity Blues bogus "student-athletes" and their enablers.

SUMMARY

Nearly all high schools and colleges offer a variety of sports. High school sport participation has been climbing for three decades especially as a result of the increased opportunities for girls. As with youth sports discussed in the previous chapter, sport participation is promoted for health and social skills purposes. Research has shown that life skills developed in sports have a carry-over effect in the development of various other life skills.

High school sports are less about having fun and more about skills development and winning. The best athletes receive the most playing time while others are relegated to the bench and supporting roles. A number of key aspects of high school sports were discussed, including the need to meet academic requirements in order to participate; projections of the likelihood that high school athletes will go on to compete at the next level; athletic administration; athletic training; and economics.

For many sports fans, college sports are more important and entertaining than professional sports. College football, for example, commands huge legions of followers, and the sheer number of teams guarantees a greater number of games and spectators each weekend for college football than for professional football. The focus and attention given to collegiate sport in the United States is unparalleled compared to the rest of the world. Nearly every college and university in the United States has a sports program and fields multiple teams. There are a number of governing bodies that oversee college sports including the NCAA, NAIA, and NJCAA. Of growing interest in the sociology of sport is the increasing role of activism among student-athletes as they attempt to gain power and economic control over their labor. In turn, sports administrations must now address the emerging changing collegiate sports landscape both socially and economically.

Coaches are central to the high school and college sports world. As each level of sport competition increases, so does the level of training that coaches go through. At one time, many coaches were also teachers, but this has changed dramatically at the collegiate level when sports became a commercial enterprise. Like athletic directors, coaches must learn to meet the changing needs and desires of student-athletes.

A persistent problem found in the world of high school and college sports is hazing. Despite concerted efforts among school officials and lawmakers, hazing remains relatively commonplace. The growing number of injuries, as well as negative media attention, has made this ritual no longer an acceptable practice.

KEY TERMS

Activism The purposive action designed to bring about political or social change.

Athletic Director A person who has full control over all aspects of college athletics, including the department's employees (staff, coaches, and student-athletes).

Athletic Scholarships Either full or partial, these provide financial assistance, usually in the form of room and board (paying for admissions, textbooks and school supplies) as well as per diem (meal allowance).

Athletic Trainers Professionals who specialize in proper health care for athletes and in prevention, evaluation, management and rehabilitation of injuries.

Authoritarian Coach An overbearing coach obsessed with winning who may ruin the sport experience of participants.

Authority A person in a position of power who influence the thoughts and behaviors of others.

Bullying An intentional act of aggression that is meant to harm a victim either physically or psychologically.

Cheating In school sports it can take multiple forms (e.g., violating rules of sportsmanship, taking performance-enhancing drugs), all of which undermine the idealism of sport as an institution of character building.

Coaches Individuals who guide athletes on the rules of the game, methods of training, and ideally, help to develop the athletes' skills.

Elite Athletes Those considered the best in their sport; they are often shown special favor by coaches and schools.

Elite Deference Refers to the special privileges that are afforded athletes.

Hazing An all-encompassing term that covers silly, potentially risky, or degrading tasks required for acceptance by a group of full-fledged members.

Illegal Recruiting Tactics These may include rival recruiters spreading misinformation, lies or innuendoes to prized athletes in such ways as suggesting the other school is about to be placed on probation, they are going to raise admissions requirements, or that the head coach is about to quit or be fired.

Letter of Intent Treated as a legal contract, this states that the athlete promises to attend a particular school for four years.

National Collegiate Athletic Association The NCAA supervises the organization of college sports, the conduct of athletes, coaches and others involved with college sports, and the academic qualification to which athletes must adhere. It attempts to act in the best interests of college athletics.

Practice Any meeting, activity or instruction involving sports-related information and having an athletics purpose, held for one or more student-athletes at the direction of, or supervised by, any member or members of an institution's coaching staff.

Recruitment Where colleges seek out an athlete, rather than the athlete seeking out a college.

Sport Specialization Concentrating on just one sport, year-around, instead of enjoying participating in multiple sports.

Walk-on A nonscholarship athlete who tries out for a sport.

DISCUSSION QUESTIONS

- Why has sport participation in high school continuously increased for the past three decades?
- What are some of the pluses and minuses of participating in interscholastic sporting events?
- Did you ever stop playing a formal sport because it "ceased to be fun" and, if so, what exactly were the reasons it stopped being enjoyable?
- Why do many American sports fans prefer college sports to pro sports?
- What is the NCAA and how did it come into existence? What are its chief functions today?
- Should student-athletes serve as activists and agents of social change?
- Should student-athletes be paid for their services? Give your reasons pro or con.
- Are you aware of any hazing incidents? Why is hazing a concern in youth sports, and what can be done to prevent it?

CHAPTER 8

Deviance in Sport

All sports are guided by numerous rules and regulations. Some of these rules seem rather silly and relatively meaningless. Golf, for example, has a few trivial rules that are strictly enforced. One such rule was cleverly articulated in a *Seinfeld* episode ("The Big Salad") where Kramer describes his golf outing to Jerry and Elaine. Kramer was playing with his friend, Steve Gendason, who on the fifteenth hole picked up his ball and cleaned it. Elaine wondered what the big deal was. Kramer responded, "Umph, sorry! But the rules clearly state that you cannot clean the ball unless it's on the green. The rules are very clear about that." Jerry concurred; the rules are very clear about that. Consequently, Kramer penalized Gendason a stroke. Gendason became extremely angry with Kramer and almost came to blows with him. Elaine still did not understand the seriousness of the rule. Kramer, once again explains to her, "A rule is a rule. And let's face it. Without rules there's chaos."

The *Seinfeld* episode illustrates the prevailing theme of deviance—if you break the rules you are subject to sanctions or punishments. As we have already learned from the earlier chapters, the social institution of sport is not immune from deviant or criminal behavior. Among the types of deviance in sport to be discussed in this chapter are on-the-field forms; off-the-field acts; performance-enhancing drug use among athletes; and illegal and pathological gambling.

Explaining Social Deviance

Sport promotes many of society's desirable character traits, including notions of fair play and sportsmanship; compliance to social expectations; hard work and dedication toward a desired goal; and, a commitment to excellence. Unfortunately, the sports world often falls short of such idealistic aspirations as many participants stray from social norms and expectations. When this happens, we enter the realm of social deviance.

Although most people tend to believe that they understand what the word "deviance" means, the sociological study of deviant behavior reveals that a number of circumstances influence how some behaviors come to be defined as deviant while others are defined as acceptable. Bear in mind, that behavior is not inherently deviant; it must be labeled as deviant in order to *be* deviant. Most definitions include the basic idea that deviance entails any behavior that violates cultural norms and that such violations may lead to punishment. For the purposes of this text, the authors define *deviance* as any act or behavior that is likely to be defined, by some members of society, or specific subcultural groups, as an unacceptable violation of a social norm and elicits negative reactions from others. By definition, people who commit such deeds are deviants. For example, it is widely understood among athletes that what happens in the locker room stays in locker room. In other words, do not air "dirty laundry" to the public. From this example, it becomes clear that deviant behavior is not necessarily criminal behavior. Conversely, all criminal behavior is a matter of social deviance.

There are a number of theoretical explanations of social deviance. Sociological theories are grounded by the belief that deviance is caused by environmental factors (e.g., family, community, and other social factors). They incorporate a diverse, multi-causal framework in their explanation of deviant behavior. In an attempt to support their theories about deviance and crime, sociologists utilize empirical data. Our discussion begins with functional and anomie/strain theory.

FUNCTIONALIST AND ANOMIE/STRAIN THEORY

Anomie theory, sometimes called strain theory, was articulated by Robert Merton, who borrowed Emile Durkheim's term *anomie*. Many of Durkheim's ideas were used in the formation of functionalist theory. Intrigued by Durkheim's focus on morality and his notion of anomie, Robert Merton examined the role of strain on individuals. Whereas Durkheim believed that anomie was the result of rapid social change, Merton believed that anomie, or strain, was a condition that existed permanently in certain societies, such as the United States. Merton introduced the concept of "dysfunction" to describe American society. Dysfunctions have a negative effect on society. Merton viewed the U.S. as a dysfunctional society because it places an over-emphasis on the cultural goal of economic success. Merton stated that American society provides many appropriate, legitimate, or institutionalized means for attaining the success goal for a majority of the people of society. However, Merton argued that not everyone is equally endowed with desire or opportunity to reach the success goal. Merton believed that when certain members of society become frustrated and feel a strain because they cannot attain the cultural desired goals legitimately, they turn to illegitimate means. Thus, Merton believed that deviance was a result of the social strain that anomie created.

Merton's anomie theory (first published as "Social Structure and Anomie" in 1938) is based on the premise that society encourages all persons to attain culturally desirable goals, but the opportunity to reach these goals are not equal for all members of society. Furthermore, when people have difficulty reaching their desired goals they will feel strain. Some people become so frustrated that they resort to illegitimate (deviant) means of getting ahead. Thus, an MLB player who has a goal of hitting 50 home runs in one season but does not quite have the strength to hit so many homeruns (the success goal) may instead choose a deviant adaptation and take performance-enhancing drugs.

SUBCULTURE/CULTURAL DEVIANCE THEORY

By the 1950s and early 1960s, sociologists were studying deviant behavior in the context of the new sociological term "subculture." A subculture refers to a group of people who possess distinctive cultural values, ethnicity, or some other trait that distinguishes it from other groups in the greater society. There are many subcultural groups within any society, including athletes.

Subcultures are formed when group members identify common goals, values, and traits that unite them. In this regard, the subculture becomes a reference group for individual members. One trait that may unite members of subculture is common activity, such as playing sports. As we learned in Chapter 4, athletes share a common lingo, or language, that has symbolic meaning to them. Reinforcing particular mannerisms and language are examples of reference points that unite subculture members. In many cases, the subculture's values and norms supersede that of the greater society. Consequently, members engage in behaviors that are acceptable within the subculture, but may be considered deviant by the greater society. For example, skateboarders—in need of paved areas to skate—might choose to skate in front of a government building (e.g., City Hall) because of its ramps, rails (stairway rails), and adjacent parking lots. To the skaters, this is a logical place to skate. Chances are, however, local ordinances will forbid skateboarding on government property, and thus, these skaters will be labeled as "deviants" by the greater society (especially the police and government workers). In short, subcultural theorists believe that deviants who violate certain rules adhere more closely to the norms of their subculture group than that of the larger society. In sports, individual athletes will feel the pressure to conform to team rules and expectations (e.g., hazing) and may do so in order to solidify their attachment to the group.

SOCIAL LEARNING AND DIFFERENTIAL THEORY

As the term "social learning theory" implies, individuals *learn* how to become deviant within a social context. An individual learns behavior through interaction with others, whether directly (being taught) or indirectly (through observation, imitation, and modeling). Through interaction with others, individuals learn of the norms, beliefs, attitudes and values treasured by the interactants. That is to say, people learn by observing the behavior of others. A young aspiring ball player will closely watch the behavior of other ballplayers, especially professional athletes. The young athlete will model his or her behavior to that of the observed by mimicking (e.g., chewing on sunflower seeds, wearing a ball cap backwards in the dugout, using a fist bump instead of a "high five" for a greeting). Most people model their behavior after influential others. Generally, this is acceptable. However, if the model (e.g., the anti-hero) engages in deviant acts, the observer is likely to see this behavior as acceptable and engage in the same type of activity.

Social learning takes place through a three-step process: acquisition, instigation, and maintenance of an observed behavior. *Acquisition* involves the initial introduction to a behavior; *instigation* occurs when the individual actually participates in a given behavior; and *maintenance* refers the persistent engagement of the acquired behavior. If we apply this perspective to performance-enhancing drug use, we would see a scenario such as: an individual observing a teammate taking a performance-enhancing drug, such as anabolic steroids, and learning about the perceived benefits of drug use; followed by the individual deciding to try anabolic steroids and learning how consumption is to occur (e.g., via a needle injection); and then, continued usage of anabolic steroids. (Note: We will discuss performance-enhancing drugs later in this chapter.)

Edwin Sutherland, a leading social learning theorist, emphasized the idea that it takes more than an occasional observation of deviant behavior on the part of the observer before it becomes an acquired behavior. Sutherland argued, in his differential association theory, that it takes continued association and reinforcement in order for a behavior to be indoctrinated. Thus, the more an individual associates with deviants (and criminals) the more likely he or she will learn and accept these behaviors, values, attitudes and beliefs (Sutherland and Cressey 1978). Based on this theoretical explanation of deviance, if athletes associate with deviant significant others rather than conforming significant others, they are more likely to become deviants. Further, if athletes are taught various methods of cheating by significant others, they are more likely to accept these behaviors.

Labeling Theory

At one time, labeling theory was the most prominent symbolic interactionist approach to the study and explanation of deviant behavior (the lack of consistent empirical verification has led to its decline in popularity). Labeling theory examines the effects of a "label" being placed on a person and his or her subsequent behavior. For example, what effect does the negative label of "choker" being assigned to an athlete have on the subsequent behavior of that person? That is, will the athlete continue to perform poorly ("choke") in pressure situations or will the athlete rise to the occasion and perform well in pressure situations in an attempt to prove that he is not a "choker?"

Labeling theorists believe that no one wants to acquire a label that they themselves consider to be an inaccurate assessment of their character (e.g., that he or she "chokes" at critical points of a game or competition). Everyone attempts to *negotiate* their *role-identity*. However, the allocation of labels is often determined by "outside" others, such as media personnel, fans, and coaches. As a result, we cannot control the labels that others bestow upon us. Labeling theory also states that when an individual continually receives negative feedback from significant others and then begins to accept the negative label, a self-fulfilling prophecy has been created. The self-fulfilling prophecy occurs when people take to heart the labels bestowed upon them, come to see themselves in regard to those labels, and then act correspondingly to those labels. In short, they come to see themselves as others have labeled them. Thus, labeling is an important factor in the creation of a deviant identity. For instance, athletes who are constantly referred to as "chokers" or "losers" might internalize such a label, lose self-confidence and thereby perform unsuccessfully.

Conflict Theory

While functionalists argue that there exists a consensus on values, norms and beliefs regarding such issues as morality and expectations of proper behavior, conflict theorists highlight the imbalance of power found in society, especially in light of economic and social inequalities, and therefore claim expectations of proper behavior are forced on all participants. Conflict theorists argue that those who control the means of production are in a social position to dictate to others what is "right" and "wrong" behavior. Class distinctions play an important role in complex societies. In sport, coaches, athletic directors, and owners possess power and make the rules that players must follow. These power elites are in a position of control and can impose their will and ideas of what constitutes deviance.

From a conflict perspective, the most important variable in determining behaviors that are proper and those that are deviant is the possession of power. If we consider ideals of proper dress attire, for example, athletes at all levels of competition are subject to rules dictating how they should dress, especially on game day (e.g., high school football players generally wear their team jersey on game day); when they travel (e.g., collegiate athletes are expected to dress a certain way as to "look good" coming off the team bus); during the game (e.g., jersey tucked in, consistent color in shoes and socks); and during post-game interviews.

In Chapter 11 we will discuss Colin Kaepernick and his kneeling during the national anthem while he was a member of the San Francisco 49ers. Many people do not know the story behind the military's involvement with the NFL and its forced patriotism thrust upon players and spectators. As recently as 2015, the Department of Defense was still paying the NFL millions of dollars for such things as military flyovers, flag unfurlings (those football field size American flags that are ritualistically unfolded and refolded), emotional color guard ceremonies, enlistment campaigns and, national anthem performances (Schmitz 2017). Initially, there wasn't a set policy about what NFL teams were supposed to do during these ceremonies; some teams remained in the locker room until after the rituals were finished. In 2009, the NFL "encouraged" players to stand during the anthem (Schmitz 2017). Over time, it became an expectation to stand during the anthem and any violation of that norm was viewed as an act of defiance—and in the case of Kaepernick and other players that protested police brutality against unarmed blacks vilified. During Trump's presidency the issue of not standing during the anthem became very political and a power move between the establishment (the power group) and those who would dare express their differing viewpoints during the anthem.

On the Field Deviance

The most likely culprits for on-the-field deviance are the athletes and coaches themselves. Normative forms of deviance are abundant and especially manifest themselves in the form of denial of wrongdoing or the failure to admit to deviant behavior. For example, soccer players may occasionally be guilty of a "hand ball"—the illegal touching of the ball—but they will not report such violations to the referee; nor would their competitors expect them to do so. Perhaps the most famous case of a hand ball occurred in the 1986 World Cup quarterfinal game between Argentina and England. In this game, Argentine star Diego Maradona credited God for his goal against England. (The goal is known as the "Hand of God" goal in soccer lore.) Maradona appeared to punch the ball into the goal but officials allowed it despite the complaints by the English team. In 2005, Maradona admitted that he struck the ball with his hand (Bechtel 2005).

ATHLETES AND DEVIANCE

In the spirit of respect for the game, baseball players are expected not to attempt to "steal" signs between the opposing pitcher and catcher. A batter might look behind his shoulder to see what signs a catcher flashes to the pitcher and runners on base (especially second base) may try to steal signs and relay them to his teammate who is at bat but acts of deviance such as these are mild. They are especially tame in comparison to one of the biggest scandals of sign stealing of all time when the Houston Astros stole the 2017 World Series from the Los Angeles Dodgers. Astros players, including pitcher Mike Fiers, admitted to stealing signs during home games throughout the 2017 season by using a camera positioned in center field. The camera was connected to a television monitor in the tunnel between the Astros' dugout and clubhouse and team employees or players would communicate expected pitches by banging a trash can to signal off-speed pitches (Brandt 2019). Former Boston Red Sox pitcher Carson Smith added to the sign stealing allegation when he posted on Twitter that he would send signs to certain batters. Smith said, following the 2019 season, that the "Astros went to extreme measures, undoubtedly still do, and it's paid off for them" (Brandt 2019: B3). It had become such "common knowledge" that the Astros cheated that Major League Baseball launched a full investigation and concluded that indeed the level of cheating by the Houston club was widespread. In early January 2020, MLB Commissioner Rob Manfred said Astros general manager Jeff Luhnow and manager A.J. Hinch were suspended for the 2020 season and that the Astros were fined $5 million (the maximum allowed by MLB) and would lose their first-round and second-round draft picks in 2020 and 2021. Shortly after the penalty was levied, Astros owner Jim Crane announced he had fired Luhnow and Hinch (Castillo 2020a). The investigation also found that bench coach Alex Cora received signals from the team's replay review room via text message. "Two months into the season, Cora and a group of Astros players developed a system to better communicate catchers' signs directly to a batter. A person would bang a trash can to indicate the forthcoming pitch type. One or two bangs usually meant an offspeed pitch. Silence signaled a fastball" (Castillo 2020a: D5).

MLB considers the matter of the Astros 2017 cheating scandal as closed. But tell that to the Los Angeles Dodgers franchise and their millions of fans who watched in disbelief that the powerful NL team had lost the Series (the Dodgers had one of the best records in the history of MLB and were close to breaking the all-time won-lost record). Columnist Bill Plaschke (2020) wrote, "This is now and forever fact that after a Major League Baseball investigation revealed Monday [January 13] that the Astros used technology to cheat during their championship season." The Dodgers were cheated. "The Dodgers won't get to claim the title. That damage has already been done. That parade has already been lost" (Plaschke 2020: A7). Plaschke added that MLB should have forced the Astros to hand over the championship trophy to the Dodgers, like they do in many other sports after it is determined that the "winning" team had cheated. But, that was not the case as MLB failed to show backbone. MLB officially labeled the Houston Astros as cheaters but said "no" to doing the right thing. Astros owner Jim Crane offered a weak sentiment apology that did not go over well with the Dodgers. The 2019 NL MVP, Cody Bellinger, did not hold back in his reaction following the verdict. "I thought Jim Crane's [apology] was weak. I thought Manfred's punishment was weak, giving them immunity. I mean these guys were cheating for three years. I think what people don't realize is Altuve stole an MVP from [Aaron] Judge in '17. Everyone knows they stole the right from us" (Castillo 2020b: D6). Aaron Judge of the NY Yankees—the team the Astros beat in the AL championship to reach the World Series—also expressed his anger and said that the Astros should be stripped of their 2017 World Series Championship. Judge said of Houston, "You cheated and you didn't earn it. That's how I feel. It wasn't earned. It wasn't earned the way of playing the game right and fighting to the end and knowing that we're competing, we're competitors. The biggest thing about competition is laying it all out on the line, and whoever is the better player, better person comes out on top" (Didtler 2020: B1).

In the aftermath of the Astros cheating scandal, there was talk by many pitchers in baseball that another type of on-the-field deviance would likely be dished out to Houston players; namely, that Astros batters could expect to be thrown at, and hit with fastballs on multiple occasions throughout the 2020 season. There was even an over/under number set for betters to bet on how many times batters would be thrown at. Many people were also referring the club as the Houston Asterisks to draw attention to the call by many in baseball (beyond the Dodgers organization) that if MLB was not going to take the title away from Houston that there should at least be an asterisk next to their name in the record book (Walker 2020). The COVID-19 pandemic resulted in a shortened 2020 season and as a result, retaliation on the part of pitchers of MLB clubs against the Astros was very limited. And, immediately following the conclusion of the 2020 MLB season, A.J. Hinch was hired as manager of the Detroit Tigers.

So, what can the Dodgers, Yankees and all the MLB teams and their fans do? They would have to move past the 2017 season. The Dodgers would make it to the World Series the following year (2018) and play the Boston Red Sox. And what are the odds that once again the Dodgers would be beat by a team that was found guilty of cheating by stealing signs? In an almost unbelievable bizarro world connotation, the Red Sox were also found guilty by MLB for cheating (in-game use of video to revise sign sequences provided to players) (Blum and Golen 2020). In this true-life story, or nightmare, depending on your perspective, Alex Cora, the former bench coach of the Astros in 2017, was now the Boston manager in 2018. Upon completion of the sign-cheating scandal by the Red Sox, MLB Commissioner Rob Manfred found that Boston did improperly use its video replay monitor to decode opponents' signs during the 2018 season and he implicated Alex Cora. Manfred did not discipline players but instead determined that the scheme was operated by the team's designated replay room operator (Verducci 2020). This decision did not set well, as clearly the replay operator must have been actually sharing this information with either coaches or players. For fans of MLB, the Dodgers, Yankees, and anyone else who does not like to see games won by cheaters, this ruling had a foul stench attached to it.

Using any sort of device to steal signs in baseball goes against the rules but, if the punishment does not fit the crime and the crime leads to a championship, how can we expect such on-the-field forms of deviance to end?

As a follow-up to Alex Cora, Boston fired him a day after (January 14, 2020) Manfred implicated him in the sport's sign-stealing scandal. However, in November 2020, Boston rehired Cora as their manager. Apparently, the adage of "cheaters never win" is not exactly true for people like Cora and Hinch.

In 2020, the Dodgers would win the World Series. The 2020 season was like no other due to the COVID-19 pandemic. The season was shortened to 60 games and the playoff rounds expanded to four. The final three playoff rounds were played on neutral sites with the World Series held at Globe Life Field, Arlington, Texas. Spectators were limited to a little more than 11,000. For MLB Commissioner Manfred, this was a good thing as the Dodgers fans that stayed in the stadium for the trophy presentation booed mercilessly at Manfred as he attempted to speak. (During his ruling on the Astros cheating scandal of 2017, Manfred attempted to downplay the importance of winning the World Series trophy by referring to it as a "piece of metal"—a comment that drew the ire of everyone connected to baseball, including players, management, and fans alike.) If this game was played at Dodger Stadium (the Dodgers were the "home" team when they won Game 6, the deciding game), there would have been five times as many people booing the commissioner. Maybe booing a league commissioner is itself deviant? Or, maybe a league commissioner referring to a championship trophy as merely a "piece of metal" is deviant. What do you think?

Cheating occurs in all sports. In baseball, beyond stealing signs, players have sought unfair advantages ever since the game was invented. Doctoring (e.g., "corking") their bats, tampering with balls (e.g., making cuts in the ball in order to grip it more easily), and taking performance-enhancing drugs are among a few examples. One cheater that got caught taking PED during the "steroid era" (generally considered to have run from the late 1980s to the late 2000s) is one-time AL MVP, Jason Giambi. He offered his take on the Astros scandal by saying, "Everybody is always looking for an advantage. It's no different than PED. There's always going to be things in this game when you're talking about people making a lot of money and wanting to win" (Miller 2020). Such an attitude does little to placate fans who pay their hard earned money to watch a game and cheer for their favorite team only to learn later that the other team was cheating. But, Giambi states that he sleeps well at night and is not worried about his cheating past as he reports that many fans are willing to give him a second chance (Miller 2020).

Other examples of on-the-field deviance, and one that can occur in nearly all sports, is point shaving. Point shaving involves a player(s) throwing" a game or performance (e.g., taking a "dive" in boxing; dropping a touchdown pass; deliberately missing free-throws in basketball) for money (usually from gamblers) or other goods and services. Athletes and coaches that engage in a pattern of harassment via such means as racial or sexist taunts are another example of on-the-field deviance.

There are athletes, just like non-athletes, who take drugs. Athletes who take performance-enhancing drugs will be discussed later in this chapter. Additionally, we will provide a few examples of athletes who have taken recreational drugs and were punished when it was later discovered. Conversely, it stands within reason that many athletes have taken drugs and were high while playing sports. One case in particular stands out and bears mention here, and that instance involves Dock Ellis, who threw a no-hitter on June 12, 1970, for the Pittsburgh Pirates while high on LSD. As reported by Larry Getlen (2014) in the *New York Post*, Scipio Spinks (Houston Astros) and Dock Ellis were young MLB pitchers who "had taken the era's free-love-and-free-drugs ethos to heart." Ellis reports that he pitched every game (138–119, career win-lost record) in the major leagues under the influence of drugs. As for the night he pitched a no-hitter while on acid, Ellis states, "I didn't know if I was facing Hank Aaron, Willie Mays or Mickey Mantle. I was just out there throwing a baseball and having a great time" (Getlen 2014).

Coaches and Deviance

As we learned with the Astros and Red Sox World Series scandals, coaches may be involved in deviant behaviors too. Coaches have also been known to lie about their resumes; belittle players in practice and sometimes in public; teach players how to get away with certain on-the-field acts; throw tirades (e.g., throw chairs, kick dirt at an umpire's feet); shove fans during post-game celebrations; use profanity in a public place; and, encourage athletes to take PED (especially in an individualistic sport).

NFL head coach Bill Belichick and the New England Patriots have been labeled as "cheaters" as a result of a number of on-the-field variations of deviance beginning with the Spygate incident of the 2007 season. The NFL's office found Belichick and the Patriots guilty of unauthorized video recording of opposing teams' coaches in order to pick up their play signals—a tactic that would provide the Patriots with an unfair advantage. "That little ethical lapse cost the Patriots a first-round draft pick and a quarter of a million dollars, not to mention a half-million-dollar withdrawal from Belichick's bank account" (Newberry 2019b: B2). According to the NFL's office, Belichick had been conducting unauthorized videotaping for the past decade, thus casting doubts on the legitimacy of their Super Bowl (as well as other) victories during that span. The controversy surrounding the cheating scandal led to the term "Spygate." In 2015, cheating allegations once again surrounded Coach Belichick, the New England Patriots and their long-time quarterback, Tom Brady, in the form of "Deflate-Gate." Deflate-Gate is a reference to the NFL's discovery that 11 of the 12 footballs used by the Patriots during their January 16, 2015, AFC Championship Game victory over the Indianapolis Colts were deflated up to 2 pounds below NFL standards. A deflated football is easier to grip and throw and easier for running backs to hold onto while opponents try to rip it from their possession. The NFL suspended Brady for the first four games of the 2015 season, fined the Patriots $1 million, and took away two draft picks as punishment for deflating footballs used in the 2015 AFC title game.

The New England Patriots have been involved in other highly controversial games as well: "The Snowplow Game" and the "Tuck Rule Game." The Snowplow Game refers to an incident that occurred at Schaefer Stadium, the old home of the Patriots, on December 12, 1982, when the Pats played the Miami Dolphins. The game was played under horrible weather conditions and with 4:45 remaining in the game and the scored tied at 0–0, the Patriots had the ball on the Miami 16-yard-line and were preparing to kick a go-ahead field goal. "Patriots Coach Ron Meyer sent stadium snowplow driver Mark Henderson in to clear a spot on the field. Henderson, who was working at the stadium as part of a work-release program at a prison, drove the John Deere machine to the line of scrimmage, which was considered acceptable, because officials were calling for a snowplow to locate the line of scrimmage—but he turned and also cleared the spot where Smith would be kicking. Smith converted the field goal and the Patriots won, 3–0" (Doyle 2015). Legendary Miami coach Don Shula called the incident the most "unfair act" ever in NFL history (Doyle 2015). Still holding a grudge against the Patriots, and following the Deflate-Gate incident, Shula referred to Coach Belichick as "Beli-cheat" (Doyle 2105). The Belichick-Brady era, one of the most successful coach-quarterback eras ever, began with the infamous "Tuck Rule Game" on another bad weather game night in New England on January 19, 2002. The opponent for that playoff game was the Oakland Raiders. With less than two minutes remaining in the game and with Oakland in the lead, cornerback Charles Woodson blitzed Brady and appeared to knock the ball out of the quarterback's hand. Raiders' linebacker Greg Biekert recovered the ball at the Oakland 47-yard-line, thus all but guaranteeing an Oakland victory. The game officials, however, ruled that Brady had not fumbled the ball but instead had "tucked" the ball in his possession while trying to throw a pass, leading to a ruling on the field that it was an incomplete pass (which would allow the Patriots to maintain possession of the ball) and was not a fumble (which would have given the Raiders the ball). The "Tuck Rule," which was created just three years earlier, was eliminated from the rulebook a decade later (Doyle 2015). In 2019, the Patriots gave us "Spygate 2.0." The Patriots admitted that one of their production teams filmed the Cincinnati Bengals sideline during their game against the Browns in Cleveland, supposedly for a Web series known as "Do Your Job." (The Patriots played Cincinnati in the regular season opener.) In June 2020, the NFL office handed down their punishments: $1.1 million in club fines; loss of a 2021 third round draft pick; and, the Patriots' TV crews not being allowed to shoot games during the 2020 season (Patriots Wire 2020).

The *American Psychological Association* (2014) conducted survey research on nearly 20,000 collegiate student athletes and found that the behaviors of coaches had an influential impact on the behaviors of athletes. For example, college athletes who have abusive coaches are more willing to cheat in order to win than players with more ethical coaches. Men's teams were much more willing to cheat than women's teams, according to the study, and men's football, basketball and baseball teams reported the highest willingness to cheat at large Division I universities where players are often under intense pressure to win (*APA* 2014). Athletes from both men's and women's basketball teams were much more likely to report that they had abusive coaches than any other sport. Measuring abuse comes in a variety of forms, including coaches who put down athletes in front of others, screaming insults, and shoving or kicking athletes. The *APA* (2014) reported that abusive behavior by college coaches has been a growing concern following several high-profile incidents of coaches being fired or sued by players for alleged abusive behavior. "The study did not determine whether abusive coaches actively encouraged or permitted cheating by their teams, but there was a correlation between abusive coaches and an increased willingness by players to cheat in order to win" (*APA* 2014).

REFEREES AND DEVIANCE

Referees and officials are only human. They sometimes make mistakes. Honest mistakes are forgivable. Dishonest mistakes and improper behavior are examples of deviance. Officials have been known to make mistakes on the number of downs in a football game leading, to a team having a fifth down. Sometimes they put extra time on the clock that gives one team another chance to win; perhaps, undeservingly so. Other times, officials misinterpret rules, giving one team an unfair advantage. And in one odd case (2007), veteran NBA referee Joey Crawford challenged San Antonio Spurs star player Tim Duncan to fight! The NBA suspended Crawford indefinitely. In 2008, umpire Brian Runge was suspended for one game for bumping into New York Mets manager Jerry Manuel before ejecting him from a game.

Crawford's and Runge's embarrassing behavior paled in comparison to the shameful behavior of Tim Donaghy, who so soiled the reputation of the NBA that its very integrity is in jeopardy. In 2007, the FBI began its investigation into the allegations that veteran NBA referee Donaghy influenced the outcome of professional basketball games on which he or associates of his had gambled on the outcome during (at least) the 2004–05 and 2005–06 seasons. The disgraced Donaghy resigned from the NBA and NBA Commissioner Stern attempted to ease the concern of fans and related parties by saying the actions of Donaghy were an isolated incident. During the 2007–08 NBA championships finals, Donaghy stated in court that NBA officials tampered with games to assure certain teams advanced through the playoffs. Kobe Bryant (Los Angeles Lakers) was asked about Donaghy's possible tampering with NBA games during the 2008 finals. According to *Sports Illustrated*, 2008, Bryant's answer was elusive and he apologized for his nonanswer by saying, "I'm sorry to be Belichicky"—a reference to Bill Belichick's vague responses to the media when he was asked about Spygate (28). Donaghy claimed that the NBA routinely encouraged referees to call bogus fouls to manipulate games (in order to extend playoff series as long as possible—because longer series equates to higher revenue) and ignore calls against star players (Goldman 2008). Long-time NBA fans have long heard about the reality of the "Jordan Rules"—meaning, fouls that would be called against other players would not be called against Michael Jordan—and the double standard that he enjoyed while playing in the NBA.

In light of the Donaghy case, NBA fans, in particular, and fans of all sports renewed their paranoia that "the game was fixed" mentality any time their favorite team appeared to fall victim of a perceived bad call from a referee or other game officials. (For more on the Donaghy scandal see Pop Box 8.)

Spectator Deviance

Much of spectator deviance is violent and occurs off the field (this topic will be discussed in further detail in Chapter 9). Some forms of spectator deviance are normalized. For example, many fans still try to sit in seats better than their own and then act surprised when they confronted by the proper seat-holders. Some spectators sneak alcohol and other forbidden products into sporting events. They may attempt to use cameras at events where they are forbidden. In the pre–BLM movement it was considered especially deviant when spectators did not stand during the playing of the national anthem, especially when males ignored the etiquette of removing their hats, and still others neglect to put their right hand over their heart. Most people still consider such breaches of behavior as deviant. However, with the increased frequency of players taking a knee during the anthem we have crossed into the realm of social boycott and politics. Some people wonder why the anthem is a part of sporting events at all; after all, we seldom stand to attention and sing the anthem at the start of other events such as the beginning of a movie at the theater or at places of business before one's work shift begins. The origins of singing the anthem before sporting events is debated but it became institutionalized at baseball games during World War II (Carlson 2011). (We will revisit this topic in Chapter 11.)

Other forms of spectator deviance are not normative and involve a direct confrontation between spectators and athletes. For example, in 1993 a crazed Steffi Graf fan stabbed her primary rival, Monica Seles, during a break in a tennis match in Germany. Houston Astros right fielder Bill Spiers was attacked on the field in the bottom of the sixth inning during a game at Milwaukee in 1999. Kansas City Royals first base coach Tom Gamboa was attacked during a 2002 game in Chicago by a father and son who ran onto the field. William Ligue, Jr., was sentenced to 30 months of probation for two counts of aggravated battery in the September 2002 attack on Gamboa. In April 2004, Ligue violated his parole when he was charged with breaking into a car in suburban Harvey and led police on a brief chase. If Ligue had been incarcerated for his unprovoked attack on Gamboa he would not have been free to commit his other crimes.

Spectators have increasingly been interfering with baseball players attempting to make plays near the edge of the stands. In many sports, spectators throw objects at players. It seems that many spectators interpret the price of admission as an opportunity to act in any manner they see fit. This is not true, of course. There are many possible explanations for the general lack of civility displayed by some spectators. Many are upset with players who act arrogant and are far-removed (especially financially) from the typical fan. Some spectators believe they need to "protect" their home turf and team's honor and direct their deviance toward opposing fans and players. In this regard, spectators are known to taunt, verbally or physically abuse and fight one another in the stands. Generally, it is only a handful of spectators at any given game that engage in violence, but on other occasions, such as with European soccer hooligans, entire groups or clubs of spectators may fight one another (see Chapter 9 for a further discussion of hooliganism). Ideally, spectators should realize that the rules of fair play and sportsmanship apply to them as well as the athletes themselves.

It is a matter of debate as to who the deviants are in this next scenario. The Arizona Diamondbacks (D–Backs) organization is always upset when the team hosts the Los Angeles Dodgers as there are generally far more Dodgers fans than D–Backs fans in the stands. (The NFL Arizona Cardinals have the same problem as a large percentage of the spectators of Cardinals home games consist of the road team's fans.) The Diamond-backs mandate that any Dodgers fans sitting behind home plate and visible to television cameras must cover up their Dodgers gear. This begs the question: Should spectators be allowed to wear sporting gear of their favorite team if they are cheering for the road team? What do you think?

Off the Field Deviance

Athletes, referees, coaches, and even marching bands may be involved with a wide variety of off-the-field/court deviant behaviors, including deviant sex scandals, criminal activities, recreational and performance-enhancing drug use, and illegal gambling.

As predicated by a long tradition, fans of the SUNY Oswego men's hockey team used to throw bagels onto the ice following the first goal against arch-rival SUNY Plattsburgh. The Administration now forbids this tradition.

DEVIANT SEX SCANDALS

Deviant sex scandals come in a variety of forms. Some are far more serious than others. Most likely, the first major sex scandal that one thinks of is the disturbing pedophile scandal at Penn State University involving then-football assistant coach Gerald Arthur "Jerry" Sandusky. Sandusky served as Joe Paterno's assistant from 1969 to 1999. He also ran a non-profit charity serving underprivileged and at-risk youth called "The Second Mile." Following a two-year grand jury investigation, Sandusky was arrested in 2011 and charged with 52 counts of sexual abuse of young boys over a 15-year period from 1994 to 2009. He is currently serving a 30- to 60-year sentence after being convicted of 45 counts of sexual abuse of 10 boys (Smallwood 2014). In 2019, a judge upheld the earlier decision.

Sandusky met boys via his charity organization. Many boys testified against Sandusky in his pedophilia case. Because he often brought the boys to the Penn State campus so that he could show them the football facilities, the football program was tied to the Sandusky case. It was revealed that a number of people involved in the football program were both well aware of what was going on and some even witnessed acts of pedophilia committed against the boys by Sandusky at the facilities. The NCAA investigated and was outraged by what they deemed as a total lack of institutional control and responsibility. "The arrests of two university officials—then vice-president for finance and business Gary Schultz and then-athletic director Tim Curley—raised flags of an internal cover-up; the two were charged with lying about whether then-graduate assistant Mike McQueary told them that he saw Sandusky raping a boy in a Penn State locker room shower and for not reporting the rape to the police" (Proffitt and Corrigan 2012). The scandal also prompted the firing of Hall of Fame head coach Joe Paterno and the ousting of then-university President Graham Spanier. In July 2012, the NCAA considered giving the football program the death penalty but instead announced significant penalties against Penn State and its football program, including a $60 million fine, a four-year postseason ban, the loss of 10 scholarships per year for the next four years, a limit of 64 total scholarships for players on the roster (the norm is 85), five years' probation, and a very symbolic gesture of vacating all its football victories (111 wins) from 1998 to 2011 (Thamel 2012). A year later in 2013, the NCAA reduced its sanctions against Penn State by gradually restoring scholarships. In 2014, the NCAA took away the remaining postseason ban and in 2015, the NCAA buckled yet again and restored Joe Paterno's victories. (Note: Paterno, 85, died in January 2012, two months after he was fired.)

Despite the NCAA's turn toward leniency against Penn State, this horrific deviant sex scandal will remain in the public's consciousness for years to come.

It would be nice, although naive, to think that sex scandals involving college sports programs and alleged cover-ups are limited to Penn State. In fact, we can stay in the Big Ten conference for another horrific example. This case involves incidents of sexual abuse against young athletes dating back to 1978 and extending to 1998 and yet it was only recently that it drew national media attention. In May 2020, Ohio State University announced that "it would pay $41 million to resolve some of the lawsuits stemming from several hundred sexual assault claims made against a doctor for the school's athletic department. The payouts to 162 people represent close to half the former athletes and other students who have filed lawsuits against the university because of assaults committed by Richard H. Strauss during his nearly 20 years [1978–1998] as a team doctor" (Witz 2020). The athletes, which included wrestlers, football players and others, were assaulted after being sent to Strauss for treatment of injuries or for physical examinations before their seasons began. The assaults ranged from groping and requiring the athletes to strip down unnecessarily (so that Strauss could ask them questions about their sexual behavior under the guise of medical treatment) to showering and taking saunas with them (Witz 2020; Edmondson 2018). Rocky Ratliff, who represents 38 of the former athletes who were not a part of the payout, called the $41 million settlement "pathetic," especially when it is compared to the nearly $30 million the school will pay the football coach Ryan Day over the next four years of his contract (Witz 2020). (Note: Strauss committed suicide in 2005.)

Ohio State reported in its own 182-page report, which detailed, sometimes in graphic terms, the abuse administered by Strauss (who was also a professor at the college) that more than 50 athletic department staff members and others had been aware of the doctor's misconduct but did not try to stop him (Witz 2020). Unnamed in the report was Jim Jordan (R), a U.S. Representative for Ohio's 4th congressional district since 2007 and a member of the House Oversight Committee. Several former wrestlers said that Jordan, an assistant coach from 1987 to 1996, was among those who turned a blind eye. Jordan has defiantly denied any knowledge of any kind of abuse (Edmondson 2018). Jordan disparaged some of the former wrestlers and stated, "I never saw, never heard of, never was told about any kind of abuse. If I did I would have dealt with it. A good coach puts the interests of his student-athletes first" (Edmondson 2018). Former OSU wrestler and Ultimate Fighting Championship star Mark Coleman said that Jordan would have to have dementia to have forgotten what happened (Edmondson 2018). Coleman was joined by other former wrestlers who claimed that Jordan was well aware of the abuse but turned a blind eye to it. One of the former wrestlers, Mike DiSabato, was very upset with Jordan's denials (Jordan claimed that the wrestlers had a political agenda and that they were part of a conspiracy, including, perhaps the "deep state") and said that "Jordan doesn't get to call me a liar to the entire world. He doesn't get to call the victims of systemic sexual abuse liars. He doesn't get to act like he wasn't in the sauna with us every day being subject to voyeurism" (Edmondson 2018). Another former player, and current wrestling referee (identified in court papers as "John Doe 42"), claims in a new lawsuit that he told Jordan and another coach two decades ago that Strauss masturbated in the shower in front of him but Jordan and then head OSU coach Russ Hellickson just shrugged off the shocking claim. John Doe 42 claims that Jordan and Hellickson responded, "Yeah, that's Strauss," according to the lawsuit filed (November 2019) in federal court in Columbus, Ohio (Dzhanova 2019).

The $41 million that OSU agreed to pay victims is a fraction of the $500 million that Michigan State (another Big Ten school) paid to settle a lawsuit by 332 victims of Larry Nassar, a team doctor who was convicted of sexually abusing hundreds of young girls and women. Nassar is the former Olympic doctor for USA Gymnastics. Nassar is also a former Michigan State faculty member and the former doctor for the university. He is currently serving a 40 to 175 year prison term for committing several sex crimes after hundreds of girls, mostly gymnasts, who accused him of sexually abusing them when they saw him for help with their injuries. In 2018, 150 women confronted him about the abuse during his trial (Garcia 2020).

Nassar, a doctor of osteopathic medicine, performed osteopathic manipulation wherein he would have to use his hands to move a patient's muscles and joints with techniques that include stretching, gentle pressure and resistance. However, according to criminal complaints Nassar's victims described how he would also put his fingers into their vaginas and anuses with his bare hands (Adams 2018). Nassar pleaded guilty to the charges and admitted that as a doctor, he was in a position of authority over his victims, and that he used that position to coerce them to submit to the penetration. All of the victims in the Michigan cases were under the age of 16 and three were younger than 13 (Adams 2018). During their investigations into Nassar, more than 37,000 videos and images of child pornography, including images of prepubescent children engaged in sex acts were found (Adams 2018).

Cheerleaders may also be involved in deviant sex scandals. In 2020, the University of Kentucky announced that it had fired all four of its cheerleading coaches after a three-month investigation found instances of "hazing activities, alcohol use and public nudity" by the school's cheerleading team at off-campus events (Bonesteel 2020). The college began the investigation after a tip from a cheerleader's family member alleging inappropriate conduct by squad members and inadequate oversight by coaches during off-campus trips. Among other things it was discovered that while on trips, some team members demanded that others on the team perform "basket tosses," in which people were thrown off a dock into a lake while topless or bottomless, and that it was done in full view of coaches; and that on other occasions cheerleaders ordered others to "perform lewd chants and wear outfits that did not include underwear" (Bonesteel 2020).

CRIMINAL ACTIVITIES

In a number of instances, those involved in athletics may become involved with criminal activities. By definition, a deviant behavior that violates a law constitutes a crime. People in the sports industry have been involved in deviant and criminal activities off-the-field for as long as there have been sports. However, in recent decades the number of athletes, sports agents, coaches and owners involved in criminal activity has seemingly skyrocketed. One merely has to listen to a *SportsCenter* broadcast, read a daily newspaper's sport section, or go online to find examples of crime in sports. The crimes range from misdemeanor offenses to felonies and include racketeering, fraud, extortion, murder, murder-for-hire, disorderly conduct, drug sale and distribution, spousal abuse, threatening people with weapons, running prostitution rings and so on. Some sport commentators argue that athletes committing crimes was as common in the past as it is presently, but that there were control mechanisms designed to protect the special privilege of athletes in the past that do not exist today. Thus, there only *appear* to be more crimes committed by athletes today than in the past.

It would be pointless to try to provide a complete list of deviant and criminal activities that involves athletes' off-the-field; however, we will provide a brief description of a few stories here. In 2017, an FBI investigation into cash payments being made to high school athletes as an enticement to play at specific schools led to the arrests of 10 people, including assistant coaches from Arizona, Southern California, Oklahoma State, and Auburn. "An Adidas marketing executive also was arrested, along with a tailor known for making suits for NBA stars in a case that alleges bribes were exchanged to influence high-level recruits' choice of schools, agents and financial advisers. The federal probe also implicated Louisville in paying a player to attend the school, leading Coach Rick Pitino and athletic director Tom Jurich to be placed on administrative leave. Louisville has since started the process of firing Pitino for cause" (*Associated Press* 2017a). Shortly thereafter, both Pitino and Jurich were officially fired.

In 2019, ten former NFL players were charged in a multi-million-dollar scheme to defraud the league's health care benefit program by submitting false claims for medical equipment; including devices used on horses, the Justice Department reported (Balsamo 2019). "The players were charged in two separate indictments filed in federal court in Kentucky, accusing them of conspiracy, wire fraud. Prosecutors allege they submitted nearly $4 million in phony claims, leading to payouts of about $3.4 million between June 2017 and December 2018" (Balsamo 2019).

The lucrative world of top-tier international soccer events such as the World Cup, WC qualifiers, CONCACAF Gold Cup (the U.S. plays in this qualifying region), and the Copa America (South America's regional championship) has regular led to corruption charges both in terms of which country can host the World Cup and what media companies can attain broadcast and marketing rights. In 2020, two former Fox television executives were facing federal charges for wire fraud and money laundering in connection with a long-running investigation into alleged bribery and corruption in international soccer (Baxter 2020a). The U.S. attorney in the Eastern District of New York alleged that Hernan Lopez (the then-head of Fox International Channels) and Carlos Martinez (chief executive of Fox Networks in Latin America) used bribes to gather confidential information during the bidding for broadcast rights to the 2018 and 2022 World Cup tournaments. FIFA later added an extension to Fox through the 2026 tournament (Baxter 2020a). "Prosecutors charged Lopez and Martinez with making bribes in annual payments of millions of dollars to South American soccer officials in exchange for the broadcasting rights to the world's biggest tournaments" (Baxter 2020a). ESPN had held the U.S. broadcasting rights since 1994 prior to Fox attaining them.

Doping and Performance-Enhancing Drugs in Sport

Many athletes take recreational drugs for the primary purpose of relaxation (recreation) and pain relief and while drugs such as marijuana can help individuals attain both of these desired goals, they do not help an athletes' performance. However, as the concept of "performance-enhancing" implies, other drugs can help an athlete increase their level of performance. In certain sporting venues, the term "doping" is used and is applied to the use of any banned athletic performance-enhancing drugs used by competitive athletes. While it is the athletes who take the drugs, a number of others may be involved in the administering of illegal drugs and in the cover-up of drug testing designed to keep sports clean.

When it comes to international sporting competition, the World Anti-Doping Agency oversees anti-doping policies and regulations within sport organizations and governments across the world (World Anti-Doping Agency 2020).

Blood-Doping

Blood doping refers to a specific type of performance-enhancing technique that involves attempts to increase an individual's oxygen-carrying red blood cells, which in turn improves an athlete's performance. The most common technique involves the injection of an athlete's own blood. This type of blood doping was rampant during the Olympics of the 1970s. Many athletes were suspected and ultimately shown to be guilty of this practice (Houlihan 1999). Although blood-doping was not officially considered cheating by the IOC before 1986, it was considered deviant and dishonorable within the athletic community (Voy 1991). The development of synthetic erythropoietin (EPO) modernized the blood-doping transfusion method as athletes could now take injections and blood transfusions of synthetic chemicals that carry oxygen and result in a boost in energy. Such a method is banned under the World Anti-Doping Agency's (WADA) "List of Prohibited Substances and Methods" (Bryner 2013). EPO is a hormone that is produced naturally by the kidney and promotes the formation of red blood cells by the bone marrow and even though it can be measured in the blood, athletes use EPO injections to enhance performance. EPO has a medical purpose and that is to help treat anemia. However, blood doping or EPO use comes with a risk as a blood count that is too high becomes too thick, and that makes it hard for the heart to push the blood around the body and may lead to a stroke or a blood clot (Bryner 2013). The sudden increase in the units of blood or red blood cells can cause dangerously high blood pressure, put the doper's heart at risk for failure, and increase the risk for other types of infections (Ramachandra et al. 2012). In some rare cases, total heart failure is possible.

Performance-Enhancing Drugs and Aura of Success

By design, competitive sports are all about winning. Generally, athletes rely on conditioning, practice and good diet in their attempt to outperform their opponents. All too often, athletes may use unusual and illicit means in an attempt to gain an edge over their competitors. An example of an unusual enhancement method is "cupping." Cupping drew the attention of the public because Michael Phelps used this performance-enhancing technique during the 2016 Summer Olympics in Rio de Janeiro. Cupping, and a similar treatment known as coining, have their roots in East Asian therapy. What is cupping? *Cupping* involves heated glass cups applied tightly to an area of the body creating suction as a way of stimulating blood flow to facilitate healing energy. The technique leaves a highly visible circular mark on the body following the technique. As a swimmer, it was easy to see all the suction marks on Phelps's body. Phelps is the most decorated Summer Olympian of all time with 28 total medals (23 gold, 3 silver, 2 bronze). Gymnast Larisa Latynina of the former Soviet Union is the next closest with 18 total medals (her 9 gold medals are tied for second highest) (Evans 2020; Bailey 2017).

It is illicit PED that garner the most attention in the sports world. Examples of performance-enhancing drugs (PED) include: Creatine, anabolic steroids, steroid precursors (e.g., androstenedione, "andro" and dehydroepiandrosterone, DHEA), amphetamines and other stimulants, and caffeine (Mayo Clinic 2020a). PED, such as anabolic steroids in particular, have an aura of success and therefore pose as a temptation to competitors.

Anabolic steroids are drugs that resemble androgenic hormones such as testosterone. "The effects of anabolic steroids mimic those of testosterone. Naturally synthesized hormones, such as testosterone, are types of lipids. They have a four-ring carbon skeleton and are synthesized in the adrenal cortex, ovaries or testes. Production of testosterone takes place in the male testes and the female ovaries; it is present in the male at significantly higher levels than in females, two of the main effects being androgenic and anabolic" (Lenehan 2003: 2). An excessive amount of testosterone provides an athlete with an advantage over the competition. When this testosterone is introduced to the body in an unnatural manner, it becomes a form of cheating. Testosterone's main effects are androgenic, which controls the secondary sexual characteristics in the male (e.g., deep voice and hair in the "growth areas") and anabolic, which controls the growth and development of many body tissues, the most obvious being muscles (Lenehan 2003). Any anabolic steroid that builds up muscle tissue will also cause secondary sexual changes, and therefore, as Lenehan (2003) suggests, steroids should really be referred to as anabolic-androgenic steroids. Despite this reality, most people use the term "anabolic steroid." Anabolic steroids are synthetic versions of naturally occurring hormones. Athletes consume steroids in hopes of gaining weight, strength, power, endurance and aggressiveness. The anabolic effects help to accelerate the growth of muscle, bone and red blood cells. When combined with a strenuous conditioning program, steroids do in fact aid the athlete in reaching the goal of added strength, quickness, and bulk muscle.

Here is a theoretical model of how steroids work: the steroid hormone enters the cell and binds to a receptor molecule; the bound hormone enters the nucleus and activates specific genes to produce proteins; and these proteins, in turn, bring about the cellular changes triggered by the hormone.

The introduction of anabolic steroids into the body can have numerous unintended consequences, such as upsetting one's nitrogen balance, which can lead to a state of "catabolism" (the negative nitrogen balance leads to muscle consumption). Protein is an essential element for building muscle tissue. Muscle growth will occur under two conditions: (1) With heavy training and weight-lifting, the testosterone binding capacity increases—aiding the athlete in reaching the goal of added strength, quickness, and bulk muscle and (2) the body must retain more nitrogen (from protein) than it loses through the ongoing process of nitrogen excretion. In short, taking anabolic steroids represents an unnatural approach to muscle gain. Furthermore, steroids actually accomplish what they advertise. The "typical" steroid user is a white male, 18 to 45 years old (but most likely is between 25 and 30) who may have a part-time, minimum wage job and a minor criminal record (Yesalis 1998). The obsession of young males with muscle gain and physical appearance has been referred to as "reverse anorexia"—when one believes he is not muscular (enough), when a rational person sees him as very muscular (Yesalis 1998).

It is against federal law to possess and distribute steroids in the United States unless it is under direct medical supervision and for rehabilitative purposes. And yet, there are many athletes who have fallen prey to the temptation of the aura of success that surrounds anabolic steroids. Again, this should not come as a surprise to anyone as from the time of the ancient Aztec warriors and Greek and Roman athletes, to the contemporary era, athletes have searched for a way to gain an edge over their competition. In the United States, athletes at nearly every level of sporting competition—from high school through the professional ranks—and those involved in weight-lifting, or anyone who wants to bulk up on their muscles, are likely candidates to take PED. Every sport, and especially MLB, has had PED scandals involving their athletes.

The United States is far from alone when it comes to taking PED. Russia, for example, has been under a doping cloud for years and especially since 2014. A 2016 WADA doping report revealed that systematic doping among Russian athletes represents a vast "institutional conspiracy" that covered more than 1,000 athletes in over 30 sports (competing in the summer, winter and Paralympics) and corrupted the drug-testing system at the 2012 and 2014 Olympics. WADA investigator Richard McLaren stated that the conspiracy involved the Russian Sports Ministry, national anti-doping agency, and a state-level cover-up (*Associated Press* 2016). The report provided evidence of manipulation of drug samples at the 2014 Sochi (Russia) Winter Games, held from 7 to 23 February.

The Sochi Games represents the first time Russia hosted the Olympics since the collapse of the Soviet Union. Suspicion arose immediately during the Games as Russian athletes won twice as many medals as in 2010. In December 2014, German television channel ARD reported on allegations of corruption and systematic doping throughout Russia. In November 2015, WADA declared Russia's anti-doping agency noncompliant and shut down the national drug-testing laboratory. Track and field's governing body, the IAAF, suspended the Russian track federation in a ban that remains in place today [still in place as of 2020] (*Associated Press* 2019a). In May 2016, *The New York Times* published damaging testimony by Grigory Rodchenkov, the former director of the anti-doping laboratory in Moscow, wherein he admitted that he switched out dirty samples for clean ones as part of a state doping program at the 2014 Winter Games and other major events. Follow-up investigations by the IOC led to the retesting of old samples from the 2008 and 2012 Olympics, eventually banning dozens of athletes from Russia and other countries (*Associated Press* 2019). Russia competed at the 2016 Games in Rio de Janeiro with a reduced squad after dozens of athletes failed vetting of their drug-test history by sports federations; the Paralympics kicked Russia out completely. Russia is not allowed to compete under its own flag (the Russians compete as independents) and Russia has been banned from competing as a nation in athletics since 2015 (*BBC* 2019). The Russian flag and national anthem ban will continue through the 2020 Olympics (which were postponed to 2021 because of the 2020 COVID pandemic) and 2022 World Cup (*BBC* 2019). The integrity of the entire international Russia sports athletics programs is under the shadow of steroid use and abuse shame.

As further evidence of the prevalence of steroid use in sports, U.S. federal authorities charged 27 people in a horse drugging scheme. "Horse racing, already in the midst of a crisis over the number of equine fatalities in the sport, was dealt another severe blow to its credibility" as a result of a PED scandal (Cherwa 2020: D3). "Federal prosecutors in New York put forth the indictments alleging 'widespread, corrupt schemes by racehorse trainers, veterinarians, [performance-enhancing drug] distributors, and others to manufacture, distribute and receive unadulterated and misbranded PED and to secretly administer those PED to racehorses" (Cherwa 2020: D3). What's next? Will we start to see drug testing at the Westminster Kennel Club Annual Dog Show? Well, maybe not dog shows, but dog sledding, yes. In 2017, it was revealed that the governing body of the world's most famous sled dog race (Alaska's grueling, 1,000-mile Iditarod) found that four dogs belonging to Dallas Seavey tested positive for a banned substance, the opioid pain-killer Tramadol. It was the first time since the race instituted drug testing in 1994 that a test came back positive (*Associated Press* 2017c).

The aura of success that surrounds anabolic steroid use has made stars out of athletes that might never have achieved such levels of performance without cheating, but eventually, nearly all big-name steroid users are punished one way or another.

Human Growth Hormone (HGH)

HGH is a synthetic human growth hormone that has generally been used as a therapy technique for nonathletes. Parents of short children have increasingly turned to HGH for their children in an attempt to stimulate growth. If parents believe HGH will assist growth development in children, it is just a matter of time before HGH is applied for other purposes. As Hoberman (2001) suggests, "Inevitably, some parents will want HGH to boost the athletic potential of their children" (115). HGH may also be used by adults who have a growth hormone deficiency not normally expected due to aging, and those who want to increase exercise capacity, bone density, muscle mass and decrease body fat (Mayo Clinic 2020b). HGH has become increasingly popular with athletes because it has the same aura of success as steroids but is much harder to detect via drug testing. "HGH is an endogenous peptide hormone involved in the regulation of a diverse of physiological processes including linear growth; protein, carbohydrate, and lipid metabolism (which includes effects on body composition such as anabolic and lipolytic actions); cardiovascular health; physical performance; and well being" (Evans-Brown and McVeigh 2009: 268).

One of our first introductions to HGH in the sports world occurred in June 2005, when Tim Montgomery, the world's fastest man, told a federal grand jury that he used HGH and a steroid-like "magic potion" provided by the alleged ringleader of the BALCO (Bay Area Laboratory Cooperative) steroids scandal. The *San Francisco Chronicle* reported that Montgomery admitted to a grand jury that Victor Conte gave him weekly doses of growth hormone and a steroid-like drug known as "the clear" (because it is undetectable in drug tests) over an eight-month span ending in the summer of 2001. Since this time, athletes have spent thousands of dollars to regularly inject this drug in the hopes of increasing athletic performance.

Athletes who take any type of PED must also find a way to cheat the drug testing system implemented by governing agencies. Minnesota Vikings player Onterrio Smith, who has a history of violating the NFL's substance-abuse policy, has a unique way to beat the system. He was briefly detained by police at the Minneapolis–St. Paul International Airport on April 21, 2005, after a search of his travel bag revealed suspicious vials of white powder. Smith explained to officers that it was dried urine used in conjunction with a device called "The Original Whizzinator." The dried urine is used for making a "clean" urine (*The Post-Standard* 2005). The Whizzinator is a device sold on a web site by a company called Puck Technologies in Signal Hill, California. It is worn like a jock strap with a prosthetic penis attached to it (Hamilton 2005). The device comes in different sizes and "skin" colors. It is believed that the Whizzinator is used extensively in baseball as well. Based on data collected analysis on the effectiveness of HGH testing, one does not need a Whizzinator. HGH tests in sports around the globe analyzed at labs accredited by the World Anti-Doping Agency in 2013 found zero positive test results; that's right, not a single positive test (*The Citizen* 2014b). In 2014, the NFL created a new HGH test for its players as part of its mandatory, random HGH blood test. Time will tell if they catch anyone. If the tests continue to fail in catching HGH users, expect the incidence of HGH use to increase.

Negative Aspects of Taking Performance-enhancing Drugs

There's a fundamental question to ask with regard to athletes who take performance-enhancing drugs and that is, "Why shouldn't athletes be allowed to take PED?" After all, humans are always striving to be the best they can possibly be. We saw the moon and went there. We are sending space probes into outer space and submarines to the deepest depths of the oceans, all because our species has a desire to explore and conquer challenges. We put up with digital music that modifies the true sound of instruments and voices and we enjoy movies and TV shows that are also artificially-enhanced (e.g., computer-generated imagery, or CGI) for our entertainment. We enjoy smartphones that can do things most people couldn't even have imagined a generation or two ago. In other words, we are always trying to improve upon our seemingly natural limitations, so why shouldn't we support willing athletes who want to take PED to improve their performance? Currently, regardless of athletes' willingness to take PED, sports' governing bodies have a strict list of approved and unapproved substances. As educators, we have to look at the big picture; however, when it comes to PED consumption there are indeed a number of variables to consider.

First, because governing sports bodies regulate the use of PED it gives the user an unfair advantage over the athletes who remain "clean." Thus, we are not getting a true measurement of competitive performance if one competitor is using PED and the other is not. This reality ties directly to the second issue concerning the consumption of PED, namely, that athletes who are on the "juice" are not having their natural (or "true") athletic ability measured. Third, because it is illegal to take banned PED, such as anabolic steroids, it is a form of cheating. Fourth, athletes who cheat are violating ethical codes of proper behavior. Fifth, athletes who take PED and become successful will have the ultimate effect of encouraging others to take PED, putting them at risk for many of the medical problems associated with various PED. Sixth, while it is one thing for other adults to take the assumed risk of taking PED, because athletes serve as role models to youth, they may also be indirectly encouraging under-aged athletes. Seventh, that there are athletes who are willing to cheat to get ahead is a reflection of a greater moral crisis in society, wherein people from all walks of life are willing to cheat and harm others so long as they succeed. And finally, and arguably the most important reason we should be concerned about athletes who take PED, is the potential for medical harm to the users.

Anabolic steroids such as testosterone, progesterone, estradiol, zeranol and other growth hormones do promote muscle growth and strength. However, prolonged use has been implicated in breast, prostate and testicular cancer, heart disease, sexual and reproductive disorders, immunodeficiencies and liver damage, as well as abnormal growth and premature sexual development in young girls. The Mayo Clinic (2014) provides an extensive list of the medical risks associated with PED use. For example, anabolic steroid use may have the following serious side effects: for men, prominent breasts, baldness, shrunken testicles, prostate gland enlargement, infertility, and impotence; for women, a deeper voice, enlarged clitoris, increased body hair, baldness, and infrequent or absent periods; both men and women risk severe acne, increased risk of tendinitis and tendon rupture, liver abnormalities and tumors, increased low-density of lipoprotein (LDL), cholesterol (the "bad" cholesterol), high blood pressure, heart and circulatory problems, aggressive behaviors ('roid rage or violence), psychiatric disorders such as depression, drug dependence, infections or diseases such as HIV or hepatitis if the user injects the drugs, and in teenagers, inhibited growth and development, and risk of future health problems (Mayo Clinic 2014). A number of risks are associated with HGH use: carpal tunnel syndrome; increased insulin resistance; Type 2 diabetes; swelling in the arms and legs (edema); joint and muscle pain; for men, enlargement of breast tissue (gynecomastia); and, increased risk of certain cancers (Mayo Clinic 2020b).

In addition to the fair play, moral, ethical, and health-related issues connected to PED use, another fundamental question remains—can steroids actually affect a player's ability to hit a homerun? There has been no evidence to suggest that steroid use increases the hand-eye coordination so critical in one's ability to hit a ball. However, logic would dictate that a steroid-enhanced athlete, because he or she is stronger, will be able to hit the ball farther because of increased strength and power. In sports like football and rugby, where brute strength is often critical, it is easy to see how steroids can affect play. In track, where victories are often measured in tenths or hundreds of seconds, any little advantage is enormous.

Proponents of PED use suggest that the sport governing bodies that drug test their athletes are actually violating the Fourth Amendment, which, among other things, protects persons against unreasonable searches and seizures. Sport governing bodies, however, have taken the perspective that, if athletes are unwilling to protect themselves and the integrity of the game, they will step in and make rules; violators of these rules will be treated as deviants and punished.

The authors believe that athletes will continue to take performance-enhancing drugs in the future (for as long as the "winning is everything" doctrine remains dominant) despite the negative message they send youngsters, the unethical nature of taking steroids, the possible negative consequences of poor health (including possible death), suspension and expulsion from the sport, and possible jail time. Furthermore, we believe that the next wave of performance-enhancing techniques is just beginning to emerge. What is this next wave? Genomics. Genomics involves the genetic manipulation of one's DNA (Deoxyribonucleic acid), the chemical compound that contains the instructions needed to develop and direct the activities of nearly all living organisms (National Human Genome Research Institute 2014). Each DNA strand consists of four chemical units, called nucleotide bases, which make up the genetic "alphabet." An organism's complete set of DNA is called a genome. "Virtually every single cell in the body contains a complete copy of the approximately 3 billion DNA base pairs, or letters, that make up the human genome" (National Human Genome Research Institute 2014). Genomics has great implications for medical science (and eventually, for athletic competition) as virtually every human ailment has some basis in our genes. The medical profession has been conducting research, especially via the Human Genome Project, in order to treat birth defects and a limited number of diseases. It may only be a matter time before medical scientists can manipulate our chemical make-up in order to fight disease and prolong life expectancy. If the medical profession can do all that, it seems reasonable to consider that this technology will find its way in the sports world. And if sports' governing bodies find it hard to test for HGH, testing for genomics-enhancement may be all but impossible.

Gambling

Nearly all of us have participated in some form of gambling, whether it involves purchasing a lottery ticket; playing church bingo; placing a bet at the track (or at an off-track location); casino gambling; playing cards for money; or making bets with friends, coworkers, or family members. Gambling among friends and co-workers is often called recreational gambling. A good example of recreational gambling involves a group of friends playing poker for minimum stakes or placing a small wager on a game.

The idea of recreational gambling, however, has taken on a far more serious tone as major casinos and governments, both local and state, are figuratively pushing gambling in our faces. Everywhere we turn, there seems to be an opportunity to gamble. This all began relatively simply enough with casinos in Nevada and then Atlantic City. The Indian Gaming Regulatory Act of 1988 triggered the spread of casinos on Indian reservations. Most state governments promote gambling via legalized lotteries; they justify their actions by claiming that lotteries help to generate increased revenues. (This seems to be a flawed sense of logic as people would have spent their gambling money on something more tangible such as consumer goods or services.) As of 2020, there were 501 American Indian gaming operations in the United States and they were owned by 246 of the nation's 573 federally-recognized tribes (500 Nations 2020). These gaming tribes operate in 29 of the 50 states (soon to be 31 states) with annual revenue from all Indian gaming exceeding $32 billion which represents 43 percent of all casino revenue in the United States (500 Nations 2020). The largest Indian casino (600,000 gaming square feet) is located in Thackerville, Oklahoma.

As of 2020, only two states had no legalized gambling whatsoever—that includes no lotteries, online-gambling, horse-racing, dog-racing, jai-alai or casinos—Utah and Hawaii. Just two decades before, only two states had legal gambling. At present, both Utah and Hawaii are considering legal forms of gambling as a means to generate state revenue. Many states have allowed the installation of a new generation of high-tech slot machines at race tracks and off-track betting (OTB) parlors creating "racinos"—slots at raceways. There is a growing trend of these racinos to include table games such as black-jack, poker and roulette.

GAMBLING IN SPORTS

At major casinos, especially those found in Nevada, gambling is not limited to card games, roulette wheels, slots, and dice; there are also sport books, where gamblers can legally place bets on a wide variety of sporting events. In 1992, via the "Professional and Amateur Sports Protection Act of 1992," (Pub. L. 102–559), Congress made almost all sports gambling illegal, believing that the substantial sums wagered on sporting events are potential threats to the integrity of the competition. Sport books in Nevada and Atlantic City were "grandfathered" (meaning they were exempted from the legislation) (Will 2000). My how things have changed in recent years. In 2018, by a 6–3 ruling, the U.S. Supreme Court eliminated Nevada's monopoly on legal sports betting by striking down the 1992 law that forbade states from not permitting it. In other words, the Supreme Court did not legalize sports gambling nationwide but, instead, made it possible for states to legalize sports gambling. As another example of how things have changed, in September 2020 basketball legend Michael Jordan (the majority owner of the NBA's Charlotte Hornets) took stake in ownership of DraftKings, a Boston-based sports betting site. The NBA allows even those directly involved in the league to have involvement with sports betting and fantasy sports businesses (subject to safeguards required under league rules to prevent actual or perceived conflicts of interests). A league owner directly involved with a gambling site would have been inconceivable just a few years earlier and deemed scandalous a decade earlier.

States across the union have opted for casino, lounge (sports books), and online sports gambling as the primary method of addressing legalized sports betting. As of this writing, nearly two dozen states have legalized sports betting (McGreevy 2020) and many others introduced sports betting bills. The state of California is trying to legalize sports gambling but influential Native American tribes that operate more than 60 casinos in the state have fought to maintain their monopoly (McGreevy 2020). In New York, legal bets can only be made in designated sports lounges—or sportsbooks—at Upstate New York's four full-service commercial casinos or at any of the seven full-service casinos operated by the state's Indian nations (Cazentre 2020). On the other hand, in Delaware, Vegas-style odds and betting options are offered, including single-game wagering and the soon-to-be launch of online sports betting (Legal Sports Betting 2020).

The primary reason for allowing legalized sports betting is the perceived regulation of gambling and the generation of tax revenue. This is understandable as a great deal of money is wagered on sports in the United States (as with many other nations around the world). It is estimated that the Super Bowl alone results in $6.8 billion in gambling (Cazentre 2020). Most of the money gambled on the Super Bowl, as with sports gambling in general, is wagered illegally. The exact figure is hard to ascertain as, after all, such wagering is done illegally (e.g., through bookies) which is a risky endeavor as the gambler must trust the bookie to pay off if they win and they have to worry about collection on debts if they lose and cannot afford to cover their bet. In 2014, NBA Commissioner Adam Silver said that illegal sports gambling in the U.S. was $400 billion per year in the U.S. alone (Weissmann 2014). Silver may have been ahead of this time or simply read the handwriting on the wall about the impending legalization of sports gambling, as evidenced by his op-ed piece in *The New York Times*, November 13, 2014, detailing why sports gambling should be allowed and concluding with this statement, "I believe that sports betting should be brought out of the underground and into the sunlight where it can be appropriately monitored and regulated" (Silver 2014). In his opinion piece, Silver describes how, despite legal restrictions, sports betting is widespread and is a thriving underground business that operates free from regulation or oversight. Silver points out that there is no solid data on the volume of illegal sports betting activity in the United States, but estimates put the figure at $400 billion wagered annually. Silver further cites domestic and global trends on sports betting that should lead to legalized sports gambling with strict regulatory requirements and technological safeguards. He also pushes the point that he wants to ensure the integrity of the game, but leans toward legalizing gambling on sports, especially within the NBA (Silver 2014).

This $400 billion figure may seem high as it would equate to about $1,700 wagered by every American adult every calendar year (Weissmann 2014). We know that every adult American does not wager that much money on sports per year but big-time gamblers wager far more than that amount and maybe the calculations work out but most likely they do not. Regardless of the actual dollar amount of illegal sports gambling, the FBI is concerned because organized crime groups often run the big illegal gambling operations. They use the money from illegal gambling to fund other criminal activities, like trafficking of humans, drugs, and weapons. These operations may also be involved in tax evasion and money laundering. The FBI echoes our concern too that gamblers may be at risk of extortion and violence, which bookmakers may use to collect debts (FBI 2020). As Best and Luckenbill (1994) explained decades ago, whenever a good or service is forbidden but the demand for it continues, an illicit market will emerge; and such is the case with sports gambling. Making sports gambling legal should, in theory, reduce the crime associated with it and increase tax revenue.

Public opinion polls indicate that the vast majority of Americans favor legalizing gambling on professional sports but significantly less are in favor of gambling on college sports. According to a 2019 poll by The *Associated Press*–NORC Center for Public Affairs Research, 60 percent of respondents want betting on professional sports to be legal in their state while just 42 percent want betting on college sports to be legal in their state. When distinguished by those who are very interested in sports, 69 percent think betting on professional sports should be legal and 52 percent say the same about college sports. Among those who are not very interested in sports, 50 percent favor betting on professional sports and 38 percent support wagers on college sports. Men are somewhat more likely than women to support gambling on professional sports, 65 percent to 56 percent. Forty-five percent of men and 40 percent of women think betting on college sports should be legal. Politically, 65 percent of Democrats and 59 percent of Republicans want legal gambling on pro sports while 47 percent of Democrats and 41 percent of Republicans think it should be legal to bet on college sports (*Associated Press* 2019b).

There's an adage in gambling, "If you can't afford to lose, you can't afford to gamble." This helps to explain why many people do not gamble and why big-time gamblers will wager far more than $1,700 per year. It also reminds us that sports gambling comes with the risk of unexpected key injuries of players; players taking a "dive" or involved in point shaving; managers who may gamble and therefore alter their lineups; referees that might be on the take; and, so forth. In other words, whether it's legal to gamble on sports or not, there are still elements of deviance that raise concerns about gambling in the first place. Because of such concerns, sports leagues generally have rules forbidding players and managers from gambling on sports. Consider the fact that Pete Rose, one of the best baseball players ever, is stilled banned for life from MLB because of his involvement with gambling. Rose has admitted that he gambled against the Cincinnati Reds' opponents when he was a manager but never bet against his own team either as player or manager. For years Rose had denied that he gambled on baseball as he knew to bet on a single game would have been enough to cause his expulsion from baseball. While vigorously denying that he gambled, in 1989 Rose voluntarily accepted a permanent place on baseball's ineligible list (Delaney 2007). In his 2004 autobiography, melodramatically entitled *My Prison Without Bars,* he finally admitted that he did indeed bet on Reds games, but stated he had never bet against the Reds (which would have made him liable for criminal prosecution).

Problems Associated with Sports Gambling

There are those who are concerned about gambling of any sort as they are worried that gambling will contribute to problem and pathological gambling. Problem gambling refers to people who have urges to gamble despite continuous negative consequences (e.g., emotional distress, financial problems) from wagering. Pathological gambling, or compulsive gambling, is far more severe and may lead the gambler to face several social (e.g., problems with relationships, breakup of the family, loss of employment) and economic costs (e.g., bankruptcy, inability to pay bills and take care of self and family members). Some pathological gamblers turn to Gamblers Anonymous for help with their addiction.

Another problem associated with gambling includes those who do not abide by the adage that if you cannot afford to lose, you should not gamble. There is a simple reason why multi-billion dollar casinos exist—the House always (eventually) wins. Winning big in any type of gambling is a risk; just consider the odds of winning the Powerball—if you play only one set of numbers, it is 1 in 292,201,338. Some people who go to casinos win small amounts of money (hundreds or thousands of dollars) while some people are losing millions and most people lost everything that they gambled. While living in Los Angeles, Tim Delaney constantly heard people say they were going to Las Vegas for the weekend but referred to "Sin City" as "Lost Wages."

Other concerns include the worry that the ease of gambling will result in an increased number of participants, both those adults who had never gambled and youths. Will this lead to a nation of gambling addicts? The federal government is concerned with e-gambling wherein gamblers engage in online gambling by setting up bank accounts in foreign banks and gambling with that money resulting in lost tax revenue. In an attempt to address this issue, in 2006, President George W. Bush signed into law a bill that makes it illegal for banks and credit-card companies to settle payments for online gambling sites. Something that is not discussed nearly enough is the realization that the gambling industry does not produce any tangible products for society. It merely provides a means for people to spend money gambling instead of buying consumer products.

One of the big selling points for legislators when it came time to consider legalizing sports gambling was the promise of tax revenues. "Tax revenue has fallen far short of projections in four of the six states where gambling on sporting events started last year, according to an Associated Press analysis" (*Associated Press* 2019c). Rhode Island expected to generate more than $1 million a month for its state budget through its 51 percent tax on sportsbook proceeds but only took in about $50,000 a month from late–November 2018 through February 2019 (*Associated Press* 2019c).

As we have learned in this chapter, the institution of sport is not immune to unethical, illegal, or deviant forms of behavior. Most people involved with sports recognize this and either live with it, or are trying to change it for the better. It is important to note, however, that for all the focus upon deviancy in sports in this chapter we remember that sportsmanship is not dead. We learned of the role of sportsmanship in youth sports in Chapter 6 and will revisit the topic in Chapter 16.

Connecting Sports and Popular Culture

Box 8: Tim Donaghy: A Foul Referee

Tim Donaghy, Tommy Martino, and James "Baba" Battista grew up together in a working-class Catholic neighborhood near Philadelphia, where they played basketball at Cardinal O'Hara High School before drifting apart. Their lives were brought together again 25 years later when they became involved in one of the largest betting scandals in the history of organized sports. Donaghy was for 13 years a professional referee for the NBA. He was also an inveterate gambler. In January of 2007 Battista, by this time a bookie who operated in the shadows of the law, arranged a meeting with Donaghy and their mutual friend Martino and made a proposition which the 3 came to call "the marriage." If Donaghy would provide inside information that Battista had picked, he'd be given $2,000 each time Battista's team won. Martino would be the go-between, to avoid the referee and the bookie ever being seen together in public. Donaghy, during the 2007 and 2008 seasons, would gather details from the team locker rooms, from players, and from other officials regarding the upcoming games and pass the information on to his two buddies. "Using burner phones, Donaghy would call Martino and inform him of his pick for the game he was officiating. Martino would then relay the pick to Battista.

Battista and Donaghy were never to speak directly. Battista would spend the day betting heavily on Donaghy's selection. In total, according to a person with knowledge of their operation, he hoped to get down about $1 million of his investors' money in each of Donaghy's games" (Eden 2020).

The friends' nefarious plan worked like a charm, until the FBI—doing an unrelated investigation—got wind on a wiretap of the Gambino mob organization that gamblers were making huge amounts of money thanks to a corrupt referee who seemed to be deliberately throwing games. FBI agents were able to trace this tip to Donaghy, who, when confronted by them, immediately agreed to rat out his collaborators for a lighter prison sentence. He also agreed to wear a wire, as the FBI was hoping to do an elaborate investigation of possible further corruption by game officials. However, an anonymous tip to a *New York Post* reporter nipped that in the bud, and Martino and Battista were arrested shortly thereafter. In August of 2007 Donaghy pled guilty and admitted to receiving $30,000 for passing information on to his bookie friends, but denied that he had thrown any games. Martino, in turn, admitted in April of 2008 to conspiracy to commit wire fraud and conspiracy to transmit gambling information. He received a year in jail, while Donaghy and Battista (who refused to cooperate with the FBI) were sentenced to 15 months in a federal prison.

While the Battista/Martino/Donaghy gambling connection can only be traced to 2007, court documents show that Donaghy had been betting on games since at least March of 2003, more than four years and four NBA seasons before he was caught (Eden 2020). Many have wondered about the quickness of the sentencing and the relatively small amounts of illegal money that Donaghy, Martino, and Battista admitted to procuring. As Scott Eden, in his 2019 ESPN re-examination of the scandal points out, "If it were shown that Donaghy had indeed fixed the games he reffed, it would reveal an uncomfortable truth, one that almost everyone—leagues, teams, fans, gamblers—would prefer to ignore: just how easy and profitable it is to fix an American sport" (Eden 2020). By looking at many of the games at which Donaghy had officiated, Eden felt that obvious fouls on teams he was betting for were not called, whereas dubious fouls were often called on the teams he was betting against. This seemed to constitute deliberate throwing of games. To paraphrase an earlier betting scandal, "Say it ain't so, Tim!"

In 2019 an entertaining movie, entitled *Inside Game*, gave a slightly fictionalized account of the 3 childhood friends' monumental fraud and its impact on their families and associates. Starring Scott Wolf (of TV's *Party of Five*) as Tommy Martino, Will Sasso (star of *Mad TV* as well as the character "Curly" in the 2012 reboot of *The Three Stooges*), and Eric Mabius (from TV's *Ugly Betty*) as Tim Donaghy, the film "efficiently checks off the requisite true crime drama tropes, but the smart money is on the strong performances of the cast, particularly Sasso's brow-mopping, pill-popping mastermind" (Rechtschaffen 2019). However, its lighthearted mood skirts the larger implications of the scandal.

Just how far did the referee cheating scandal really go? The Donaghy case continues to fester well after a decade after it was first discovered. In September of 2020 sports reporter Tim Livingston issued a 10-part podcast entitled "Whistleblower" which "takes on a major sports scandal that has mostly been swept under the rug with a mix of savvy PR and media incentives" (Da Costa 2020). Livingston spent over 5 years further investigating the case, interviewing former basketball players who suspected Donaghy at the time of deliberate bad calls; members of the mafia; other sports journalists with knowledge of behind-the-scenes shenanigans; FBI members who felt the NBA had too quickly shut down any internal investigation once their own had been outed by the press; as well as Donaghy himself. To Livingston, "it felt like no one had properly investigated the wider implications of referee culture in the NBA, the NBA's own complicity as an institution, and the FBI's perspective on Donaghy's activities" (Da Costa 2020). Ultimately, the Tim Donaghy scandal continues to leave a foul stench.

SUMMARY

All sports are guided by numerous rules and regulations. Generally speaking, rule-breaking behavior is considered deviant. Theoretical explanations that attempt to explain social deviance reveals that matters of deviance are not always clear and somewhat open to interpretation.

Four general categories of social deviance were discussed in this chapter: on-the-field deviance; off-the-field deviance; the use of performance-enhancing drugs; gambling. On-the-field forms of deviance involve athletes who violate the rules and social expectations of the game (e.g., sign stealing) during the course of their athletic performances; coaches (e.g., those that throw tirades, throw chairs, kick dirt at umpires, and cheat); referees (e.g., tampering with the outcome of the game); and spectators that interfere with the playing of the game. Examples of off-the-field forms of social deviance discussed in this chapter centered on deviant sex scandals and various criminal activities that occur away from the field/court.

Doping and performance-enhancing drugs in sport represent a serious form of social deviance. Athletes take PED because of the aura of success that surrounds the use of drugs that increase strength and endurance and thus, enhance athletic performance. The use of such techniques as blood-doping, ingesting PED, and HGH, and genomics, compromise the integrity of sports competition, fair play, ethics, and morality.

There are many forms of gambling in sports, both legal and illegal. Throughout the history of sport competition sports leagues have attempted to curtail the gambling habits of all those involved with sports but recent legalization that allows people to gambling on sports may potentially compromise such efforts. A number of problems (e.g., emotional distress and financial and personal problems) associated with gambling were discussed.

KEY TERMS

Anomie Theory Developed by Robert Merton, the premise that society encourages all persons to attain culturally desirable goals, but the opportunity to reach these goals is not equal for all members of society.

Blood-doping Attempts to increase an individual's oxygen-carrying red blood cells which, in turn, improves an athlete's performance.

Bookies People who determine gambling odds and receives and pays off bets.

Cupping The process of placing heated cups to an area of the body creating suction as a way of stimulating blood flow to facilitate healing energy.

Deviance Any act or behavior that is likely to be defined, by some members of society, or specific subcultural groups, as an unacceptable violation of a social norm and elicits negative reactions from others.

Deviants Those who violate social norms dictated by the group or greater society.

Differential Association Theory The view that it takes continued association and reinforcement in order for a behavior to be indoctrinated.

E-gambling Gambling on the Internet.

Genomics The use of genetic engineering to enhance athletic performance.

Labeling Theory The theory which examines the effects of a "label" being placed on a person and his or her subsequent behavior.

Performance-Enhancing Drugs Substances used to improve performance; this term often refers to anabolic steroid use in sports by professional and amateur athletes. Other substances include human growth hormone (HGH), stimulants, and diuretics.

Self-fulfilling Prophecy Occurs when people take to heart the labels bestowed upon them, come to see themselves in regard to those labels, and then act correspondingly to those labels.

Social Learning A theoretical perspective that puts forth the notion that individuals learn how to become deviant via a three-step process: acquisition, instigation, and maintenance.

Sport Books Legally placed bets on a wide variety of sporting events, allowed in some casinos.

Subculture A group of people who possess distinctive cultural values, ethnicity, or some other trait that distinguishes it from other groups in the greater society.

DISCUSSION QUESTIONS

- Why is it difficult to define the term "deviance"?
- Do you think it is okay for athletes, coaches, and others directly involved in sport should be allowed to social protest on-the-field? Why or why not?
- How does blood doping work? Do you think that infusing your own blood into your body prior to a sporting event is an act of social deviance?
- Many entertainers (e.g., musicians and actors) have their performances enhanced via artificial means (e.g., digital editing software and artificial/electronic music) and consumers and producers have accepted such productions; and yet, there is an outcry against athletes who use artificial means (e.g., performance-enhancing drugs) to reach peak performance. Why does such a double standard exist and why is this fair, or not fair?
- What are some of the ethical issues raised by using performance enhancing drugs?
- Is there a moral distinction between legal and illegal gambling on sport?
- Do you know anyone who has a pathological gambling problem? How did their behavior affect his or her life and their family's lives?
- Do you think it is okay to legally bet on pro sports? Do you think it is okay to legally bet on college sports?

CHAPTER 9

Violence in Sport

In his classic 1945 article "The Sporting Spirit," George Orwell proclaimed, "Serious sport has nothing to do with fair play. It is bound up with hatred, jealousy, boastfulness, disregard for all rules, and sadistic pleasure in witnessing violence. In other words, it is war minus the shooting." Orwell wrote this article for London's *Tribune* after attending a "friendly" football (soccer) match that took place in England between Chelsea FC and FC Dynamo Moscow. Due to the war, soccer had been put on hold since 1939 and fans and athletes alike were excited by the resumption of their favorite sport. The match was played before a crowd officially listed at 74,496 (but with witnesses, including Orwell, claiming there were well over 100,000 spectators) and Orwell was not impressed by what he witnessed on- and off-the-field (*Dangerous Minds* 2014). Instead, he criticized the idea that international sporting events foster such ideals as brotherhood and understanding among diverse people, claiming that sports promote nationalism and that spectators and players alike thrive more on the ideals of ultra-competitiveness and the win-at-any-costs mentality. He commented on how easily the players chose to ignore the rules and used means of violence in order to gain a competitive edge. The spectators too were, according to Orwell, willing to suspend the concept of civility in preference of a favorable outcome. Orwell's disdain toward sports in general, and soccer in particular, was reinforced a few years later in his classic novel, *Nineteen Eighty-four* (typically referenced as *1984*). In a classic quote from this novel, Orwell not only puts down football (and the general populace), he also makes reference to what sport sociologists have been saying for decades—that sports are the opiate of the masses. Orwell (1949) states, "Heavy physical work, the care of home and children, petty quarrels with neighbors, films, football, beer and above all, gambling filled the horizon of their minds. To keep them in control was not difficult" (154).

When it comes to violence in sport, little has changed since Orwell expressed his concerns. Then again, many of the most popular sports of any generation are characterized by acts of violence, intimidation and aggression; and, when we consider that sports are a microcosm of society, is anyone really surprised by this reality? That athletes often use the analogy of "going to war" with their opponents when preparing for a sporting event is further testament to Orwell's observations about the violent nature of sports. It would also seem to be true that acts of violence on the playing field are what draws so many fans to sports. It has been shown in hockey, for example, that increased violence exhibited by a hockey team leads to increased attendance at games (Jewell, Moti and Coates 2012).

What Is Violence?

Broken bones, torn ligaments, missing teeth, fist fights, blood, scars, concussions, and occasional deaths are just a few of the risks confronting athletes when they play sports. The fields and courts that athletes play on are often environments filled with hazards and violence. "Not even the risky and labor-intensive settings of mining, oil drilling, and construction sites can compare with the routine injuries of team sports such as football, ice hockey, soccer, and rugby" (Delaney 2002: 1560). Competitors in all spheres of social life attempt to gain an edge over the competition. As we learned in Chapter 8, there are times when some people will use deviant means (e.g., taking performance-enhancing drugs) to gain an edge. In this chapter, we shall discover that many people associated with sport utilize violence as well.

DEFINING INTIMIDATION, AGGRESSION AND VIOLENCE

Intimidation, aggression and violence are aspects of sports, just as they are a part of society in general. As with most of human history, we live in violent times. Governments, rebels, and terrorists have longed used violence (e.g., war) as a means of reaching a desired end and individuals and groups of people have widely used violence as a way to solve or create disputes. Violence in sport occurs at all levels: youth, high school, college, professional and amateur. Certain sports, such as basketball, football, rugby and hockey, are designed for assertive, physical contact between competitors. In 2017, of all the team sports, basketball caused the most total injuries treated in U.S. hospital emergency departments (with all age categories included—"younger than 5" through "65 and older") with 500,085, followed by football (341,150), and soccer (218,926) (III 2020). The sports activities that have the highest total number of injuries treated are personal exercise, with or without exercise equipment (526,000); in between basketball's and football's total injuries is bicycle riding (457,266); and in between football and soccer is playground equipment injuries (242,359) (III 2020). (Note: The data on sports injuries used from the Insurance Information Institute comes only from those treated in hospital emergency departments; thus, the actual total numbers of injuries by sport is higher than those cited.)

Other sporting activities we participate in that result in a large number of annual injuries are riding ATVs, mopeds, minibikes, etc. (214,761), trampolines (145,2017), skateboards (98,486) (III 2020). Many other sports and recreation activities can also cause harm, including auto racing, which contains an element of violence in the very fact that at any time during a race a crash may occur that leads to the destruction of an automobile and serious injury and potential death to drivers and in some instances, to spectators. In 2017, a number of other sporting activities caused a significant number of injuries: horseback riding (48,353); racquet sports (28,310); water skiing, tubing, and surfing (20,463); and tobogganing and sledding (13,954) (III 2020). Apparently, the whole idea behind encouraging kids to go outside and play is to get them injured and toughened up for the big, bad world!

Participants, spectators, and fans of violent team sports seem to enjoy the element of risk involved. For example, it has often been said that die-hard hockey fans love to watch the fights between players as much as they enjoy the actual hockey skills displayed by the players. Player fights are an example of violence in sport. Despite attempts by hockey leagues such as the NHL to place a focus (e.g., by imposing penalties against overly-violent plays) on the wonderful skills necessary to play hockey, the fans still like to see fights. Athletes that play in violent sports view such risks as "part of the game." Volumes of literature exist in an attempt to explain why violence is so prevalent in society and these explanations are applicable to sports as well. (Note: The same theories described in Chapter 8 to explain deviance in sport are applicable in explaining violence in sport as well.)

Some theorists, such as Sigmund Freud, take a biological perspective to explain violence, claiming that it is a part of human nature to be aggressive, or violent. In this regard, humans are violent because they have needed to be in order to survive as a species. Freud used the concept of an "id" to refer to the part of human personality that is governed by innate, aggressive desires; the "superego" to refer to society that tries to reign in the whims and basic desires of humans so that they can live in a civil society; and the "ego" which is the part of the personality that seeks a balance between the id and superego. In sports, especially the aggressive-by-design sports, those involved react in a primal way to competition and perceived threat. The superego would be the league's governing body and corresponding rules, and the ego would be the way in which sports attempts to maintain an "acceptable" level of aggression and violence. Sociologists would look at the influence of reference groups and the manner in which each of were raised; that is to say, were acts of aggression positively or negatively reinforced by agents of socialization. Pappas (2004) and associates state that in sport, reinforcement for acts of violence come from a variety of sources which can be grouped under three categories: (1) the immediate reference group of the athlete, especially coaches, teammates, and family; (2) the structure of the sport and the implementation of rules by governing bodies and referees; and (3) the attitude of the fans, media, courts of law, and society in general (293). If such focal concerns as toughness, courage and a willingness to be aggressive and violent are positively reinforced, they are more likely to occur and continue.

Intimidation and aggression are linked to violence. Intimidation is a common method of trying to gain an advantage over a competitor. *Intimidation* involves words, gestures and actions that sometimes may threaten violence or aggression in an attempt to pressure and put fear in the opponent. A tennis player may use loud grunting sounds while playing and flash intimidating grimaces toward an opponent. In a pre-fight promo, former heavy-weight champion Mike Tyson once threatened to eat an opponent's children and is quoted as saying, "I try to catch them right on the tip of his nose because I try to punch the bone into the brain." An athlete attempts to intimidate his or her opponents in an attempt to demonstrate power and dominance. Intimidation is often a vital tactic in battle and competition. However, intimidation is only successful if the intimidator is capable of backing up such words, gestures and actions or if the opponent is weaker and easily intimidated. Acts of intimidation can also backfire. Intimidation in sport is of lesser consequence than aggression and violence.

The authors define *aggression* in sport as verbal and physical behavior grounded in the intent to successfully accomplish a task even if it means to frighten, dominate, control, or harm, physically or psychologically, an opponent. Aggression is often linked with violence. Aggression is an important feature of performance success in many sports. Coaches teach and encourage aggressive behavior and teammates reinforce it; after all, it is better to be aggressive than passive in contact sports. In several sports (e.g., football, wrestling, hockey) aggressive behavior is *required*. And yet, even in contact sports where aggressive behavior is expected, there are boundaries of acceptability, and athletes who exceed these boundaries face penalties by game officials for exhibiting behaviors that can be labeled hostile or physically abusive. For example, in football, a defensive end that is rushing the quarterback is expected to be aggressive in his pursuit of the quarterback. However, he may not hit the quarterback above the shoulders or after the ball has been thrown. A passive approach to rushing the quarterback will generally not produce a positive outcome for the defensive team. Thus, the defensive end who is attempting to tackle the quarterback needs to be aggressive to be successful; he does not have to harm the opponent, he just has to tackle or hit him hard.

There are two forms of *sport aggression*: instrumental aggression and reactive aggression. Instrumental aggression refers to behavior that is non-emotional, task oriented and driven by the quest for achieving a goal without necessarily intending to cause physical harm to another (Delaney 2002). Thus, instrumental aggression may involve the physical form (e.g., direct contact and body blows) or the nonphysical form (e.g., athletes that try to "psyche" out the opponent; verbal taunts; "talking trash"; or jokes about one's sexuality and family members). While instrumental aggression is primary concerned with "getting the job done," the second type of aggression in sport, reactive, is spurred by the heat of the moment type scenarios. Thus, reactive aggression possesses an underlying emotional component in behavior with the primary goal of inflicting bodily injury or physical harm to an opponent (Delaney 2002). Because of the emotional aspect of reactive aggression, the term "expressive violence" is sometimes used interchangeably. An example of reactive aggression is baseball's "brush-back" pitch. A brush-back pitch involves the pitcher throwing the ball at or near the opposing batter in an attempt to send a message. Sometimes the pitcher will deliberately hit the batter in an attempt to intimidate the opponent and opposing team and such a stimulus will result in an aggressive response. In nearly any sport, an act that leads to a player getting injured will result in reactive aggression on the part of the injured player's teammates. Not surprisingly, reactive aggression often leads to violence.

Violence involves the use of physical force designed to injure, harm or abuse another person, or property. *Sport violence* can be defined as intentional aggressive physical behavior that causes harm to an opponent. While many sports are aggressive and violent by design there are instances (as we shall see later in this chapter) when certain acts of violence exceed the acceptability threshold level.

Contextually, violence in sport is evaluated differently from the general violence found in society. Simon (1985) argues that violence generally involves the use of force, but reminds us that every use of force is not violent. The tennis player, for example, uses force in serving, but few people would characterize a serve in tennis as an act of violence. It is possible, however, that a serve in tennis could be used in an aggressive, intimidating, and ultimately violent manner when the player serves *at* the opponent rather than at a place on a court where the opponent cannot return the serve.

Some sports, especially American football, have elements similar to the military and war. The language of football is filled with military references, for example, throwing a "bomb"; "blitzing" the quarterback; linemen working in the "trenches"; the quarterback as a "field general"; entering "enemy territory"; and so on. Rank is important in the military and in sports. The military designates personnel by titles (ranks) and expected corresponding duties. In the U.S. Army, for example, the private is subordinate to a sergeant, who reports to a platoon sergeant, and all of these people must submit to the authority of officers that range from lieutenants to generals. On the battlefield, a squad is composed of privates who are directly under the supervision of a squad leader, who is under the supervision of a platoon leader, usually a lieutenant. The chain of command goes all the way to the generals, and ultimately the commander-in-chief (the president).

In football, a team (squad) performing on the playing field (battlefield) is under the command of the quarterback (on offense) or the middle linebacker (usually) on defense. The offensive and defensive leaders receive their "orders" from their respective coordinators (assistant coaches), who are under the command of the head coach. The coach must report to a general manager, team owner, and ultimately, the league's commissioner. Furthermore, athletes and military personnel are subject to external and internal sanctions for committing deviant acts, and rewards for following orders and executing directives successfully. It should be noted, however, that among the glaring differences between sport and the military is the realization that literally killing the opponent is not an objective of sport. Also, in sport, many efforts are made to assure fair play and balance in available "weapons" (e.g., protective equipment, a ban on performance-enhancing drugs), whereas in the military, gaining an unfair advantage over the opponent is a goal consciously sought.

Many coaches, fans and even teammates expect athletes to perform at peak levels and to win by any costs, including inflicting injury onto an opponent. Players themselves often describe the game as a "battle" and have stated that they "are at war" with the other team. Immediately following the September 11, 2001, attacks on the World Trade Center and Pentagon and the subsequent start of the war on terrorism, many players consciously attempted to stop using war-analogous terms when describing their sporting exploits. However, by the mid–2000s, it became common once again for athletes to use the "going to battle" mantra.

Violent Sports

In order to achieve success, athletes in many sports have found value in being aggressive. In violent sports, it is often important for athletes to step up their level of aggressiveness to the point where certain forms of violent acts are encouraged and expected. While most athletes recognize that they are likely to get injured while playing sports, few are prepared for a post-career marred by chronic pain and brain dysfunction due to head injuries and concussions. In the following pages, we present a brief description of examples of violent sports.

Football

The most popular sport in American society is football, and by its very design and purpose, football is a violent sport. Football involves controlled collisions, sometimes at high speeds, highlighted by near hand-to-hand combat among linemen, hard hitting blocks that knock opponents down, and gang-style tackles are among the violent elements of football. Players are taught to be aggressive; they readily accept this expectation. Fans love the aggressiveness and violence of football and scream encouragement for their brave "gladiators" to destroy the opponent. The aura of football is *controlled* aggression and violence. Players of the past assumed certain risks, such as bone and muscle injuries, but football players are now concerned about long-term brain damage, generally as a result of one big blow or repetitive blows to the head. Football players understand that they must find a way to be aggressive and limit themselves to acceptable forms of violent acts, while trying to avoid serious injuries.

As we mentioned earlier in this chapter, there were more than 340,000 football injuries in 2017 that led to treatment in hospital emergency departments. When we breakdown this statistic into age groups we see that it is youth between "5 to 14" that have the greatest number of such injuries with more that 171,000; the age category of "14 to 24" represents the second highest number (136,296). There were 384 emergency room-treated football injuries in 2017 among those "65 and over" (III 2020).

Because of the violent nature of football a number of prominent people have said publicly that they would not let their sons play the game. Basketball superstar LeBron James, who once played high school football, said that he would not allow his sons to play football. James's former Miami Heat teammate Dwayne Wade has expressed relief that his boys have not yet shown an interest in playing football (Winderman 2014). President Barack Obama has said that he would have to think twice about letting his son play football if he had one. A number of NFL stars themselves have said that they would not let their sons play tackle football at an early age. Among these stars: Troy Aikman has a concern for head injuries; Adrian Peterson, simply said he wouldn't let his son Adrian Jr., play the sport; Drew Brees said in 2012 that the thought of his sons playing football scared him and, as we learned in Chapter 6, he promotes flag football (Football 'N' America); and, speaking hypothetically because he doesn't have any sons, Brett Favre said he would be very leery of them playing football (DeLessio 2014). The thing that scares all of these folks and millions of other parents across the United States is a fear over the violence of the sport in general and the possibility of a head injury in particular.

NFL Commissioner Roger Goodell has made player safety among his top priorities and has taken a hard stand against players who violate the NFL's rulebook that addresses unnecessary roughness. Rule 12, Section 2, Article 8 of the *Official NFL Playing Rules* (2014) states that "there shall be no unnecessary roughness" which includes, among other specific behavioral limitations, the rules that no player shall use any part of his helmet to spear an opponent and that no illegal launching into a defenseless opponent is allowed. A number of other rule changes throughout the past decade have been put into place to safeguard players as well, including banning head-to-head contacts; protecting "defenseless" players from taking shots above the shoulder; when a player loses his helmet, the play is immediately whistled dead; during field-goal and extra-point attempts, the defense cannot position any player on the line directly across from the snapper (who is considered to be in a defenseless position); a much stronger return-to-play guidelines for players who suffer concussions, with each team mandated to consult with an independent neurologist whenever there is a head injury; equipment changes designed to reduce concussions; banning the lowering of the helmet to initiate contact; and, spotters who watch for players that demonstrate concussion symptoms and removing them from the game (NFL.com 2010; Battista 2020). In 2016, Pop Warner banned kickoffs in its youngest divisions and simply placed the ball at the 35-yard line to start the next series of downs. Pop Warner also implemented a policy to limit contact (e.g., hitting, blocking and tackling) during practices.

Defensive players gang tackle a running back in a display of acceptable sport violence (courtesy Cardinal Sports Imaging).

Hockey

Hockey is an aggressive sport known for its rough play and tough athletes. It is not uncommon for a single professional hockey player to receive hundreds of stitches and incur numerous broken bones over the course of his career. The stereotype is that almost every player will have lost his teeth by the end of his career, either from getting hit with a puck or a stick or from fighting with other players. Sports commentators often remark after a hockey player has been injured and quickly returns to action, "What did you expect, he's a hockey player?!" The implication is that hockey players are so tough that they always play through pain and injury. The sport of hockey is conducive to fighting and overly aggressive play by its very design. For example, the slippery surface that hockey is played on may lead to inadvertent contact that opponents may take exception to. The enclosed rink with sideboards to slam into also encourages violent physical contact. Hockey players are "armed" with "clubs" (hockey sticks) and skate with blades; both are dangerous items used for violence under other conditions.

Hockey players, as with athletes in most sports (especially American football), are getting larger and faster and are in better shape than ever before. When these elements are added to a culture that encourages physical, aggressive play, acts of violence are almost certain to follow. In fact, a certain number of violent collisions are expected and demanded by coaches and teammates. Fans especially love to watch hockey fights. Certain players, known as "goons," are famous for their aggressive behavior. Hockey proponents warn that if fighting in hockey were eliminated (through regulations) the core hockey audience would stop being fans of the sport.

In a sport that requires even its weakest players to be aggressive, fighting is an integral part of the game. During hockey fights players may gouge at an opponent's eyes, rub their gloves across the face of an opponent, and engage in any other number of violent acts. Beyond these infractions, there are other times when excessive aggressive behaviors turn into fistfights. In the past, it was common for every club, at every level of the sport to employ "enforcers" or "goons" specifically to fight. Coaches send goons on the ice for a number of reasons, including when they want to "send a message" to their opponents, when the opponent has a big lead, or when a star player on their own team was hit too hard (the goon is there to defend the star teammates). Enforcers were generally well respected by teammates and adored by fans. It is now rare for clubs to have players whose primary purpose in the sport is to fight. With the elimination of enforcers from the NHL the number of fights per game has gone down, but they have not disappeared. Consider, during the 2018–19 season (1,271 games), there were 0.19 fights per game compared to the 2001–02 season when there were 0.65 fights per game (Hockey Fights 2020).

As for hockey injuries, there were 44,353 injuries that were treated in hospital emergency departments in 2017, with the age category of "14 to 24" having the highest number (18,333) and youth ages "5 to 14" with the second highest (13,862). There were 481 such injuries for the age group "65 and over" (III 2020).

SOCCER

Soccer is known more for its violence off the field than it is for player violence on the field. However, as Christopher Merrill (1993) explains, soccer was once a brutal sport characterized by players who often took cheap shots against opponents. Merrill writes:

> Soccer may be a brutally simple sport, but for much of its history it was simply brutal. From the beginning, it seems, humans have loved to kick things—balls, doors, skulls; in the records of every civilization there is evidence of kicking games like soccer. Chinese court games, Japanese *kemari,* Pueblo kickball, the ball games of the ancient Egyptians, the *calcio storico* still played in Italy, village football—"the mob game for ruffians" the English invented or imported from the Continent, codified into the modern game of soccer in 1863, then exported around the

world—in almost every culture humans have relaxed from the tedium of daily life by kicking something round over plains and fields, through streets and cities, in courts and stadiums [15].

Soccer is a deceivingly violent sport filled with acts of intimidation and aggression. The world's best soccer players, among them Lionel Messi, Cristiano Ronaldo, Sadio Mane, Luka Modric, Neymar and Virgil van Dijk, can intimidate opponents just as former and present basketball players as Kobe Bryant, Michael Jordan, LeBron James, and Steph Curry did. Acts of intimidation may include verbal taunts and heated exchanges between players. Aggression can take many forms including: putting close-contact pressure on an opponent; running at an opponent and shoulder charging them; slide tackling, which can involve clean or dirty variations; kicking an opponent; stepping on an opponent's cleats; mid-air collisions; bicycle kicks that are designed to strike an opponent as much as to strike the ball; and, in extreme cases biting an opponent (i.e., Luis "Cannibal" Suarez who bit an opponent during the 2014 World Cup).

Plays that go beyond the rules of the game are punishable by yellow or red cards, with each color designated to address the level of the infraction. The less serious of the two, yellow cards, are issued when there is unsporting behavior or dissent by word or action on the part of a participant (on-pitch players or off-pitch players, coaches, medical staff, etc.) that infringes the rules of the game. The red card is more serious and results in ejection from the game. Two yellow cards result in a red card and ejection. Red cards are generally issued when a player spits, becomes violent or overly aggressive, or uses offensive or threatening language. When an act is deemed more serious than a red card ejection, a player might be subject to suspension. In 2014, Ricardo Ferreira, a defender in a fourth-division soccer league in Switzerland, was suspended for 50 years after a post-match incident in which he kicked a ball in a referee's face and sprayed him with water (*Sports Illustrated* 2014). Now *that* is a serious penalty.

There were 218,926 soccer injuries treated in U.S. hospital emergency departments in 2017. As with American football, the largest number of soccer injuries occurred in the "5 to 14" age category (98,746); followed by 84,016 among those "14 to 24"; and 34,044 in the "25 to 64" age category (III 2020). There is a growing awareness that continuous blows to the head (e.g., via headers designed to "pass" the ball or an attempt to score a goal) may cause concussions and brain trauma in a soccer player's post-career.

Boxing

Boxing is a carryover sport from ancient times. Inherent physical risk, intimidation, and aggression are built-in features of this sport. Aggressiveness is not only encouraged in boxing, it is reinforced in its norms and expectations. To be passive in this sport is almost certainly going to lead to defeat and injury. Every boxer who puts on a pair of gloves and enters the ring risks substantial harm, including possible death, to both the opponent and himself or herself. The primary goal of contemporary boxing is pretty much the same as in the past—knock out the opponent. It is the repeated blows to the head that are of special concern in boxing as they may lead to post-career problems. Nearly half (8,063) of those injured to the point where they were treated in a hospital emergency department were in the "14 to 24" age category and 7,400 were in the "25 to 64" age category (III 2020).

Many people in contemporary society believe that boxing should be outlawed because of its primitive brutality. Despite the historic and continued corruption that surrounds boxing it is the threat presented by mixed martial arts (MMA) that is leading the way to the slow death of boxing. This is not to say that boxing does not have a place in the sports world; after all, there is the growing number of women boxers (the 2004 Academy Award Winner for Best Film, *Million Dollar Baby*, dealt with this phenomenon) in contemporary society which further leads to the chagrin of boxing detractors.

The violence that surrounds boxing is not limited to the ring and the two designated fighters. There are occasional brawls during the pre-fight weigh-ins (boxers must get their weight measured) that may include the boxers themselves or their team representatives (e.g., managers, trainers, bodyguards). Post-fight brawls may involve the boxers and their representatives and even fans; in some rare cases, a fan may enter the ring (e.g., the "Fan Man" who entered the ring during a fight via a flight suit powered by a motorized fan). However, the greatest level of violence still occurs inside the ropes. Some fighters are beaten to death, others sustain serious injuries, and some are knocked unconscious. A rather bizarre form of violence occurred during a heavy-weight fight between Evander Holyfield and Mike Tyson in 1997. Tyson took a bite out of Holyfield's ear during the match. Such an act of violence is deemed unacceptable even in a sport where participants are allowed to literally beat each other.

Mixed Martial Arts (MMA)

Mixed martial arts is an extreme combat sport in which contestants are allowed an amalgamation of fighting techniques including bare-handed boxing and a variety of martial arts such as kickboxing, judo and karate. MMA involves a combination of standing striking techniques such as boxing, karate, Thai-boxing, along with grappling techniques like judo, Greco-Roman wrestling and jiu-jitsu (Sanchez and Malcolm 2010). With roots dating back to the ancient Egyptian sport of pankration (see Chapter 3) MMA fighting has gained a considerable amount of popularity in recent years, mostly at the expense of boxing. Fans enjoy watching the violently brutal battles between competitors and cheer for landed punches and take downs. A few of the more common MMA leagues include Ultimate Fighting Contest (UFC), Pride Martial Arts and K-1 Martial Arts.

Competitors fight inside a cage or ring for a number of rounds until submission of one competitor, a knockout, or an official's decision. The goal of the sport is similar to boxing, to take down your opponent, with more options than simply hitting someone. By its very design, this sport is very violent and can lead to any number of short- and long-term injuries. Intimidation and aggressive behaviors are more of an aspect of this sport than even boxing. The most common categories of injuries in MMA and UFC are fractures—broken bones—as fighters wear little, if any, protective equipment. The bones endure quite a bit of stress in these types of fights and bones can break. Hand injuries (e.g., broken and jammed fingers, ligament tears) and knee injuries (knees are often twisted or forced into awkward positions during fighting maneuvers and grappling and tearing the anterior cruciate ligament is very common) are the next two most common types of injuries. Concussions are the fourth most common category of MMA and UFC fighting as fighters do not wear any protective head gear and are therefore susceptible to head injuries. If the fighter sustains a concussion it is critical, as with all other sports and non-sports, that they do not return to fighting until they are fully healed, since they are at risk of developing a degenerative brain disease known as CTE (to be described below) (Gleiber 2020).

Each of the sports discussed here—football, hockey, soccer, boxing and MMA—have at least one thing in common; namely, that the level of violence and the opportunities for blows to the head in these sports have led to a growing concern over chronic ailments, including post-concussion issues, suffered by athletes following their post-career lives.

There are so many other dangerous sports that routinely lead to injuries and death including sky diving, base jumping, cave diving, bull riding, gymnastics, cheerleading, and horseback riding. Horseback riding, for example, led to nearly 50,000 (48,796) injuries treated in hospital emergency departments in 2017 and represents one of the few sports tracked by III wherein more than half of the number of injuries comes from the "25 to 64" category. Horseback riding can be dangerous to horses too, especially when they are involved in racing. In May 2019, two horses crashed into one another during a race at Del Mar (CA) and both were killed instantly, an extremely rare result (Cherwa 2020). It seems as though it is a little known fact how many horses die each year at racetracks (most are injured and have to be euthanized); for example, 23 horses died at famed Santa Anita Park in California during a 14-week period, and 87 horses died in Pennsylvania race tracks in 2018 (*Penn Live* 2019).

Chronic Traumatic Encephalopathy (CTE)

Although all athletes understand that the possibility of getting injured on the playing field/court is a reality, most of them do not consider the long-term post-career health problems that confront them. Athletes who play collision and violent sports are especially susceptible to post-career health issues which may include Chronic Traumatic Encephalopathy (CTE). CTE is a progressive degenerative disease of the brain found in athletes (and nonathletes) with a history of repetitive brain trauma, including symptomatic concussions as well as asymptomatic subconcussive hits to the head (Boston University Alzheimer's Disease Center 2014). It has been known since the 1920s that repetitive brain trauma associated with boxing may produce a progressive neurological deterioration, originally termed "dementia pugilistica" and more recently described as CTE (McKee et al. 2009). The term "punch drunk" was often used by non-professionals to describe aging former boxers with CTE. Recent reports have also confirmed CTE in retired professional football players and other athletes who have a history of repetitive brain trauma. "This trauma triggers progressive degeneration of the brain tissue, including the build-up of an abnormal protein called tau. These changes in the brain can begin months, years, or even decades after the last brain trauma or end of active athletic involvement. The brain degeneration is associated with memory loss, confusion, impaired judgment, impulse control problems, aggression, depression, and eventually progressive dementia" (BUADC 2014). Finkbeiner, Max, Longman and Debert (2016) found that long-term psychiatric and psychological problems follow sport concussions in adults. The authors also state, however, that there is not nearly enough research in the area of CTE and its connection to psychiatric and psychological problems to draw significant conclusions.

While the main risk for CTE is thought to be repeated head injuries, experts are still learning about the risk factors (Mayo Clinic 2020). A concussion is believed to be the most common source of CTE. Concussions are a frequent occurrence in contact sports, with nearly 4 million sports-related concussions occurring annually in the United States and perhaps up to half of these go unreported. Athletes who incur several concussions during the course of their career have a 17 percent likelihood of developing CTE (McKee et al. 2009). CTE is most common in sports with high rates of concussions: rugby, ice hockey, football, lacrosse, wrestling and boxing. According to Complete Concussion Management (CCM) (2018), for adult athletes (18 years and older), rugby has the highest incidence of concussion rate both in match play (3 per 1,000 participants) and practice (0.37 per 1,000). Men's tackle football was second with 2.5 concussions per 1,000 for match play (third for concussions experienced during practice, 0.30/1,000). Interestingly, Women's ice hockey came in third for match play concussion rates at 2.27 per 1,000 and second for practice concussions with 0.31 per 1,000. What makes this interesting is that Women's hockey is non-contact, but has a higher rate of concussion compared to men's hockey—which is full body contact (CCM 2018). Ranked third through eleventh in concussion rates are: Lacrosse; soccer; wrestling; basketball; softball and field hockey (tie); baseball; cheerleading; and, volleyball (CCM 2018).

There are no clear symptoms of CTE and some of the possible signs and symptoms of CTE can be associated with other conditions. Nonetheless, a few proven CTE symptoms include: difficulty thinking (cognitive impairment); impulsive behavior; depression or apathy; short-term memory loss; difficulty planning and carrying out tasks (executive function); emotional instability; substance misuse; and suicidal thoughts or behavior (Mayo Clinic 2020c). It is important to note that CTE can only be diagnosed after death (CDC 2019b). Because of this, many athletes have put into their wills that they want to donate their brains for CTE research.

In 2016, Brandi Chastain, a famous member of Team USA Women's Soccer—and perhaps best known for scoring the winning shootout goal in the 1999 World Cup final against China and for the jersey-shedding celebration that followed—agreed to donate her brain to the Concussion Legacy Foundation and researchers at Boston University, pioneers in the study of concussions and CTE (Branch 2016). Chastain was motivated to do this because, as of 2016, no female athletes had been diagnosed with CTE. The sample size for examination of brains for CTE was just 307 in 2016, only 7 of which were women's (no athletes). They were found to have CTE and they had a history of head trauma (Branch 2016). Three years later and researchers at Boston University report that only two women have ever, anywhere, been diagnosed with CTE (McAlpine 2019). In contrast, 99 percent of the former NFL players (110 of 11) studied were found to have CTE (Moran 2017). Such data would suggest that there is likely a relationship between exposure to football and the risk of developing the disease (Moran 2017). However, the BU researchers also believe that other factors (e.g., substance abuse, other head traumas, or a genetic component) beyond concussions may be involved in athletes being diagnosed with CTE (Moran 2017). Female athletes don't want to be left behind in the CTE research and as a result 20 former soccer players (including Chastain and Michelle Akers) have agreed to create the first all-female study cohort dedicated to understanding CTE. The final step of the research process will involve the athletes donating their brains after death to have them studied for CTE (McAlpine 2019).

As of 2020, there are still many questions that surround CTE. Researchers seem to agree that experiencing concussions or other brain injuries, especially over a period of many years, is a leading cause of CTE. The CDC (2019b) reports that CTE has been diagnosed in people with and without a history of head or brain injuries and that most people with a history of head or brain injuries do not develop CTE. Nonetheless, the public perception is that concussions may result in CTE in later life and many contact sports, especially football, seem to be affected by an increasing number of parents who do not want their children playing tackle football. Football's reaction is a proactive one as they are doing whatever they can to improve the safety of football, especially when it comes to head injuries. However, current efforts at minimizing the chances of suffering a head trauma in football, hockey, soccer and other high-incident rates of concussions are not satisfying to many.

Research has shown that former NFL players face a great number of post-career health issues including Alzheimer's, amyotrophic lateral sclerosis (ALS), severe depression and chronic traumatic encephalopathy (King 2010); significant decreases in regional cerebral blood flow across the entire brain, abnormally high instances of dementia, cognitive impairment and depression and a higher risk for permanent brain damage (Amen et al. 2011); and premature death (generally by middle age), mood disorder (mainly depression), memory loss, paranoia, poor cognitive insight or judgment, outbursts of anger or aggression, irritability, apathy, reduced concentration, agitation, hyperreligiosity, and tragic death (e.g., suicide, police chase, self-inflicted wounds) (McKee et al. 2009). More recent research has found a link between a longer NFL career and a higher risk of cognitive, mental health problems. When compared with former kickers, punters, and quarterbacks (positions that are protected the most by NFL rules), men who played any other position (e.g., running back, linebacker, and defensive linemen) had a higher risk of poor cognition, depression, and anxiety. Concussion symptoms persisted even 20 years after the athletes last played football (Roberts et al 2019). Many former NFL players have donated their brains for CTE research. In 2013, the NFL reached a tentative settlement of nearly $1 billion over concussion-related brain injuries among its 18,000 retired players and families that demanded compensation. By 2018, more than $500 million in claims were approved. Attorneys for the retired players adjusted their estimates on the total payout of expected claims, saying that the settlement would likely reach $1.4 billion (CBS News 2018).

Hockey players are certainly subject to head injuries. And like their football playing counterparts, hockey players who suffer from concussions are displaying the same symptoms suffered by football players. Data on reported concussions indicate ranges from 4.6 to 7.7 per 100 NHL players per season (Tahirali 2015). Hockey players who sustained concussions during a recent season will experience acute microstructural changes in their brains, according to a series of studies published in the *Journal of Neurosurgery*, and they are likely to suffer chronic injuries later in life from head trauma (Klein 2014). In 2009, Reggie Fleming became the first ice hockey player known to be tested for CTE. While Fleming died at the age of 73, test results revealed that he had suffered from dementia and CTE for thirty years as a result of playing hockey without a helmet throughout his career. Hockey players wear helmets today but the threat of CTE is just as real today as when Fleming played, as a number of players, including long-time enforcer Bob Probert and Derek Boogaard (his brain was tested at Boston University) and the suicides of Rick Typien and Wade Belak were all tied to CTE symptoms.

There is a growing concern over the relationship between playing soccer and suffering a head injury, with players suffering the same CTE symptoms as football and hockey players. Soccer is unique in comparison to other sports in that it is the only sport in which participants purposely use their head to hit the ball. Soccer players may hit the ball with their head on average 6–12 times a game and may practice heading the ball hundreds of times outside of match play (Neurological Wellness Institute 2016). "Some researchers have suggested that using your head to hit the ball in soccer is associated with abnormal brain structure, abnormal brain activity, and abnormal brain function such as cognitive impairments" (NWI 2016). During the 2018 World Cup, Morocco midfielder Noureddine Amrabat sustained a concussion when he collided with Iranian midfielder Vahid Amiri during his team's opening round match. Because of the concussion, Amrabat has no memory of playing in his first World Cup ever. Amrabat said of the match, "Five, six hours, gone. Totally gone. When you think about it, it is a little bit scary" (Baxter 2018: D2). The team doctor sprayed water on Amrabat and slapped him on the face, seemingly to wake him from his stupor. FIFA would later absolve itself from any responsibility in the team decision to field him again so quickly. He was sent to the hospital following the match and it was determined he had suffered a concussion. Five days later, he was back in the lineup for Morocco's match versus Portugal (Baxter 2018).

Before football started receiving so much attention for concussions, boxing was the sport most commonly associated with head injuries and post-career health problems. There is little wonder why boxing is linked to concussions as the sport involves blows to the body and especially the head. "Boxing's controlling bodies and the government have made some attempts to put into place a number of regulations, such as the Muhammad Ali Boxing Reform Act, that seek to minimize the dangers" (Kennard 2019). The Muhammad Ali Boxing Reform Act (H.R. 1832—Muhammad Ali Reform Act), commonly referred to as the Ali Act is a federal law that was introduced in 1999 and enacted on May 26, 2000, by the 106th Congress (Congress.gov 2000). We have read the Ali Act itself and it does not address violence, concussions, or CTE; instead it addresses coercive provisions placed in a boxer's contract (e.g., it prohibits a boxing service from requiring a boxer to grant any future promotional rights as a requirement of competing in a professional boxing match that is a mandatory bout under the rules of the sanctioning organization) (Congress.gov 2000). There is no doubt about it, boxing can cause great harm to the participating athletes. According to the American Association of Neurological Surgeons, 90 percent of boxers sustain a brain injury (Kennard 2019). Boxing is believed to account for fewer deaths than some other sports but the numbers of boxers suffering brain damage are believed to be much higher than recorded (Kennard 2019). CTE and disease duration is the longest in boxers, with many former boxers living for decades past their boxing days with smoldering and yet symptomatic conditions (McKee et al. 2009). Boxers with CTE are likely to suffer from forgetfulness, confusion, falls, alcohol abuse, depression, anxiety and characteristics of a "punch drunk" (McKee et al. 2009). One of the world's best known athletes was former boxer Muhammad Ali. Ali had long suffered from Parkinson's disease, a degenerative brain condition that many doctors say can be brought about by punches to the head. Ali's own neurologist told the Associated Press that he didn't think Ali's condition was the result of head blows, and yet the symptoms were consistent (Dahlberg 2012). "The list of boxers who suffered from brain damage is a long one, and goes back a long ways. [Joe] Louis had dementia symptoms late in life, while Sugar Ray Robinson developed Alzheimer's disease in his later years. Jerry Quarry, a heavyweight contender who fought Ali twice, died at age 53 from dementia pugilistica, while his brother Mike, a light heavyweight, died from the same thing at age of 55" (Dahlberg 2012). With the intent of boxing to deliver blows to the body, including the head, there is no wonder boxing is associated with CTE and other health problems.

MMA fighting represents a far greater risk of CTE and other post-career health concerns for its athletes than does boxing. MMA is sometimes categorized as a "combat sport" (other combat sports include boxing, kickboxing, Muay Thai, wrestling, and other traditional forms of martial arts) because the athletes use striking, grappling, or weapon-related techniques under specific rules of engagement to stimulate parts of real hand-to-hand combat (Curran-Sills and Abedin 2018). Engaging in MMA exposes athletes to inherent risks including subdural hematoma, fractures, tears, muscle and ligament sprains along with electroencephalographic abnormalities as a result of neck holding maneuvers (White 2007) and a number of facial injuries, including lacerations, along with a number of overall injuries (Bledsoe et al. 2006). "The current literature has examined associations between injuries and potential risk factors such as age, sex, weight, match outcome and bout length. A meta-analysis of these studies has revealed that contests in the heavyweight class, title fights, bouts that last longer, bouts that are decided by knockout (KO), technical knockout (TKO) or decision, and the loser of a bout resulted in higher rates of injuries" (Curran-Sills and Abedin 2018). Furthermore, about one-third of professional MMA matches end in knockout or technical knockout and these knockouts are generally the result of a severe blow or blows to the head, indicating a higher incidence of brain trauma than football, boxing, kickboxing or other martial arts (Blackwell 2014). Lockwood and associates (2017) acknowledge that MMA is an emerging combat sport that is gaining popularity worldwide and reiterate that repetitive head injuries incurred while fighting will likely lead to neurological consequences. The researchers also state that more research needs to be conducted on combat sports such as MMA.

The future of many popular sports such as football may be in the balance because of concussion-related injuries.

Sport Violence and the Law

Sport participants realize there is always a chance of injury when playing sports. This concept is based on the English common law notion of *volenti non fit injuria*, or voluntary assumption of risk. Assumption of risk assumes that both management and labor understand the medical hazards inherent within sport (as with many other employment occupations). Injury, or harm, may occur as a result of actions that are within the realm of acceptable assumption of risk, or outside the realm of acceptability. In his 1859 publication *On Liberty*, British philosopher John Stuart Mill distinguished between *self-regarding* acts and *other-regarding* acts. Self-regarding acts refer to behaviors that may cause harm only to the individual performing them; and therefore, fall within the realm of acceptable violence. Other-regarding acts, however, are those which may cause harm to others; and therefore, fall outside the dominion of acceptable forms of violence. Mill (1859) argued that individuals should have the right to engage in risky behaviors (without interference) if they want because it is no one else's business what one does with one's own life. On the other hand, individual behaviors that cause harm to others are not acceptable and are subject to interference (e.g., government legislation or oversight by some regulatory agency). Robert Simon (1985) refers to Mill's concept as "The Harm Principle." In brief, The Harm Principle states that the only justification for interference with personal behavior is to prevent harm to others (Simon 1985).

Athletes often risk personal harm. For example, a wide receiver who runs a pattern across the middle of the field and stretches himself to reach for a ball while surrounded by defenders realizes that he is vulnerable and will be hit hard. The wide receiver understands that his actions run a risk for harm (a self-regarding act) but runs such a pattern anyway. However, the wide receiver does not agree to be hit early, late, or illegally (other-regarding acts) by defenders. Although athletes have historically understood the risks involved in playing sports, an increasing number take exception to other-regarding acts. For example, in the past, it was uncommon for batters to charge the mound after a pitcher sent a "warning" pitch near the batter. Today, it has become commonplace for batters to charge the mound. These batters, as with many other athletes, are less tolerant of others whose behaviors may cause them harm. As Delaney (2002) explains, "While the concern with violence in sport is nothing new, what is new is the degree of legal intolerance to forms of player violence and player resistance to blind acceptance of risk of bodily harm. Legal forms of resistance by professional athletes are evidenced by the many cases in sports law and the growth of civil and criminal litigation" (1561).

The 2020 global pandemic presented the sports world with an example of a gray area in the notion of *volenti non fit injuria*. During summer college football camps many football players were asked to sign a COVID-19 liability waiver. While each college created their own version of the waiver, the student-athletes were essentially being asked to risk their health, and possible lives, to play football (without pay), and to promise not to sue if they got the virus (and possibly died from it or spread it to others). Initially, some colleges threatened their football players that if they refused to sign the waiver they would be prohibited from participating in team activities, denied admittance to athletic facilities, and might be cut from their teams—putting their athletic scholarships and academic futures in jeopardy (West 2020). In late-August, the NCAA ruled that Fall athletes would not have to sign a COVID waiver; their scholarships would not be taken from any athlete that did not feel safe to play sports; and, preserved the athletic eligibility of athletes if Fall sports were canceled. As it turned out, nearly all Fall sports were canceled except for football at many major conferences.

Over the years, efforts have been made to differentiate between acceptable forms of sport violence (sanctioned violence) and those which are not (unsanctioned). A most useful typology of on-the-field violence among athletes originated with Michael D. Smith (1983, 1996). His typology involves four categories: brutal body contact, borderline violence, quasi-criminal violence, and criminal violence.

1. *Brutal Body Contact.* This category of sports violence includes physical acts that conform to the official rules of the game and are accepted as part of the action and, therefore, are legal under the law. Examples include delivering extreme punches to an opponent in boxing, hard tackles in football, certain variations of elbowing an opponent in basketball, checking in hockey, and stick whacks in lacrosse. As Smith (1996) explains, "It is taken for granted that when one participates in these activities one automatically accepts the inevitability of contact, also the probability of minor bodily injury, and the possibility of serious injury. In legal terms players are said to 'consent' to receive such blows (*volenti non fit injuria*—to one who consents to injury no injury is done)" (162–163). With "brutal body contact" athletes are suspending the usual moral standards of acceptability found in civil society. A pedestrian on a sidewalk does not consent to a blind-sided tackle from another pedestrian. A football player does give such consent. Thus, athletes on the playing field are working with a type of sports morality or ethics that is acceptable during game time, but a different type of ethical and moral behavior when they

interact in the everyday world. In essence, morality and ethics are modified in the sports. But, as we will see, such modifications do have their limits.

2. *Borderline Violence.* This category of sports violence involves behaviors that violate the official rules of the sport and the law of the land but are widely accepted by all concerned as conforming to the norm of sport ethics when used as part of competitive strategy (Smith 1983; Delaney 2002). Examples include the "brush back" pitch in baseball, fist fights in hockey, late hits in football, high tackles in soccer, bumping cars in auto racing and talking smack in basketball. During the course of the game, such acts may be subject to sanctions (penalties). In auto racing, there is a difference of opinion as to how "aggressive" a driver can be in an attempt to pass another car. Some drivers believe that if you make contact causing the other driver to spin out, that is unacceptable; conversely, there are some drivers who believe any tactic (other than purposely putting a driver at risk of serious harm) used to pass an opponent is acceptable. When "questionable" contact is made, there are often flare-ups between drivers and their teams at the immediate conclusion of a race. As Smith (1996) explains, "Borderline violence is essentially the province of referees, umpires, and other immediate game officials, higher league officials and law enforcement authorities seldom becoming involved. Sanctions never exceed suspension from the game being played, and perhaps a fine" (165). These behaviors are often "expected," encouraged and positively reinforced within the sports world. "Borderline violence is tolerated and justified on a number of grounds, most of which boil down to some version of the 'part of the game' argument" (Smith 1996: 165).

3. *Quasi-Criminal Violence.* Involves assaultive physical acts that violate the formal rules of a given sport, the law of the land, and the informal norms of player conduct (Smith 1996). Examples of quasi-criminal violence include swinging a bat at a player in baseball, kicking a player in the head in rugby or soccer, and sucker punches in any sport. Quasi-criminal violent acts usually result, or could have resulted, in serious injury, which brings it to the attention of top league officials (Smith 1996). Athletes usually condemn this form of violence and fines or suspensions are often imposed. Quasi-criminal behaviors may generate outrage from the public but they are generally viewed as a sport problem to be handled internally and not involving courts of law (Nixon and Frey 1996). Smith (1996), however, states that some episodes of quasi-criminal violence in professional sports have resulted in litigation. An example would be a basketball player "cold-cocking" (punching) an opponent in the head rendering them unconscious.

4. *Criminal Violence.* This category consists of behaviors that are obviously outside the boundaries of official rules of the sport, the law of the land and players' informal norms, and are handled by the law. It should be made clear that if something is illegal outside of sport, it is also illegal *in* sport and this notion dates back to the case *R v. Bradshaw (1878) 14 Cox C.C.83* which states, "No rules or practices of any game can make lawful that which is unlawful by the laws of the land." Consequently, athletes that commit criminal violence on-the-field are subject to arrest and criminal prosecution. Deliberate or premeditated attempts to injure or seriously disable another athlete are examples of criminal violence.

Athletes and Off-the-Field Violence

Most athletes display the positive character traits promoted by proponents of sport. That is, they are disciplined, hard-working, engage in good sportsmanship, and maintain a positive work ethic. However, as we learned in Chapter 8, some athletes and other members of the sporting world engage in deviant behaviors. In this chapter, we have learned about the sometimes violent nature of sports. Athletes are taught to be aggressive and to use a proper amount of violence when their sport dictates such behaviors. As former NFL player Tim Green points out, NFL players have to tap into their dark sides in order to play effectively: "The difference between an NFL player and the average guy on the street is not that the player is more likely to break someone's nose. The NFL player has simply learned how to tap into the dark side of the human psyche. We all have it, that dark side. Most football players can turn that on and off like a blender. You need to be bad on the playing field, vicious and mean, that's part of the game. That is the game" (Green 1996: 65). However, once athletes leave the playing arena, they are expected to disengage from their dark side and "turn it down." Most athletes are successful at this disengagement; others, however, have a harder time and may find themselves in off-the-field forms of violence, including domestic violence.

An example of an athlete involved in off-the-field violence that would also involve pre-diagnosed CTE is Aaron Hernandez, who had Stage 3 (out of 4) of the disease, which can cause violent mood swings, depression, and other cognitive disorders. The former New England Patriots player was convicted of first-degree murder and sentenced to life in prison without parole on April 15, 2015, for a deadly late-night shooting. Hernandez, 25, was considered a top tight end in the NFL after a stellar college career at the University of Florida (where trouble surrounded his life as a Gator). His NFL career began in 2010 and he was a standout immediately. In 2012 he signed a five-year, $40 million contract extension with the Patriots. In February 2013, Hernandez's friend Alexander Bradley was shot in the face after partying with Hernandez at a Miami strip club; Bradley later filed a lawsuit alleging Hernandez was the shooter. On June 17, 2013, the body of Odin Lloyd was found near Hernandez's mansion in North Attleborough, Massachusetts. The police traced evidence back to Hernandez—Odin was dating the sister of Hernandez's fiancée. On June 26, 2013, Hernandez was charged with first-degree murder and five firearms violations. The Patriots announced his release less than two hours after his arrest. Following his murder conviction in April 2015, Hernandez was indicted on a witness intimidation charge relating to the 2013 shooting of Bradley. On February 14, 2017, Hernandez was acquitted of the 2012 double homicide of Daniel de Abreu and Safiro who were shot to death in their car during a drive-by shooting in Boston's South End neighborhood. On April 19, 2017, Hernandez was found hanging by a bedsheet in his prison cell. On September 21, 2017, it was revealed that Hernandez had been suffering from CTE at the time of his death. His CTE was caused by repeated head trauma (Bertram 2020). Hernandez's life began with him as a victim of child abuse wherein allegedly his father regularly beat him, his brother and mother. He undoubtedly could have suffered serious head trauma then. The rest of his short life was spent playing football. Bearing in mind our review of CTE and the realization that the medical profession does not have all the answers on this disease, it is hard to say whether or not playing for the NFL is what caused his CTE. In September 2017, the lawyers of Hernandez opted to sue the NFL with such a claim. They argued in U.S. District Court that the league and the Patriots failed to protect their players' safety. In February 2019, a federal judge dismissed the $20 million lawsuit.

College and professional athletes are all quite young, relatively speaking, and they are in top physical shape, like to enjoy themselves, and often like to party in nightclubs. It seems the more public athletes are, the more likely trouble is going to find them, or they will find trouble. We hear of athletes involved in a number of different acts of violence off-the-field, generally they entail fights, but once in a while, gun fire is involved. It is realistically understandable that athletes may get in trouble from time-to-time, as a number of people in their age category do.

Perhaps the single category of crime that draws the attention of the public the most is domestic violence. Pappas et al. (2011) found a correlation between athletes who participate in violent sports with sexual aggression. Their research indicates that 60 percent of athletes at a major university had used verbal coercion to obtain sexual favors, and 15 percent had used physical force to obtain said favors. They also found a higher rate of physical battering cases and sexual assaults than non-violent sport athletes. But we have to wonder, does playing violent sports contribute to off-the-field violence or were such athletes drawn to playing violent sports because they already used violence as a coping mechanism (before playing violent sports)? Grange and Kerr (2011) suggest that players experience a protective frame when they are within the boundaries of their sport. Within these boundaries, players can count on their teammates and coaches to help them play within the rules of the acceptable levels of violence so that they are free to enjoy the physicality of the sport. When the athlete is removed from this protective frame, they become vulnerable to exceeding the limits of acceptable levels of violent behaviors.

Grange and Kerr (2011) propose a theory that articulates four kinds of motivation for aggression: play (e.g., sports which allow for approved aggression); power (e.g., exhibiting dominance over others); anger (e.g., engaging in violent behavior in response to something another person has done to upset the athlete); and thrill (e.g., engaging in dangerous activities simply to see what results will follow). Athletes that have trouble with violent behaviors off-the-field are likely having trouble controlling the final three types of motivation for aggressive behavior. There is also research that suggests when athletes who play violent sports drink alcohol off-the-field they are more likely to engage in violent acts (Jewell et al. 2012; Pappas et al. 2004; Grange et al. 2011). The idea behind such research rests with the idea that since alcohol tends to reduce inhibitions, the athlete's primal need to act aggressively has lost its filter. Alcohol use has also been linked to spectator violence.

A number of highly publicized incidents have occurred in the past years. One of the most talked about was that involving Ray Rice (Baltimore Ravens) who was recorded punching his then-fiancée (and now wife), Janay Palmer, in an elevator of the Revel Hotel and Casino in Atlantic City in February 2014, knocking her out cold. The video shows the couple arguing with one another and Rice lunging at Palmer as he tries to intimidate her. Palmer angrily responds with a backslap across Rice's face as they make their way to the opening elevator doors. Palmer keeps her head down and Rice lunges a few more times in an attempt to intimidate her. When Palmer attempts to stand up to him, Rice delivers a devastating blow, knocking her out. He drags her limp body out of the elevator and we see an approaching parking lot guard (Perez 2014). The incident led the NFL to revamp its personal conduct policy. In September 2014, the Ravens released Rice, suspending him indefinitely but he was later reinstated. No other team signed him, ending his career.

Following the Ray Rice case, Major League Baseball and the National Basketball Association put into place policies addressing domestic, sexual, and child abuse. All offer therapy, counseling and allow leagues to independently investigate incidents (Skrbina 2018). The NHL, however, still does not have a set policy on domestic violence. It does mandate domestic violence, sexual assault, and sexual harassment training for all of its players. The program was developed by the NHL and NHL Players' Association, which involves all 30 teams going through hour-long educational sessions with outside professionals (NHL.com 2016). Defenseman Slava Voynov was suspended indefinitely in October 2014 from the NHL following a no contest plea involving incidents of domestic violence with his wife. The Los Angeles Kings then suspend the player in 2015. Voynov returned to his native Russia, played hockey there, and has now applied for reinstatement with the NHL (following his conviction being dismissed by a judge in Los Angeles). In turn, the NHL suspended Voynov for the 2019–20 season but made him eligible as of July 1, 2020. The NHL still reviews each case on an individual basis rather than initiating a league-wide and uniform policy on domestic violence issues (*USA Today* 2019).

Athletes that commit domestic violence are not, of course, restricted to North American sports, as such incidents are common across the globe (we do not have the space to document many such cases). One example is Columbia where intimate-partner violence against women rose by 33 percent during the past two World Cups in general and it also happened with the players and their partners (Salazar 2018). A case cited in Columbia involved soccer star Pablo Armero and his altercation with his wife Maria Bazan. Police arrested Armero for battery and took him into custody following an incident. Two summers later Armero was playing for the Columbian national soccer team for a series of World Cup qualifying matches. To many, his inclusion on the national team was a tacit acceptance of domestic abuse (Salazar 2018). In 2010, a horrific case of domestic abuse occurred in Brazil. Bruno Fernandes de Souza, a Brazilian goalkeeper, was convicted to 22 years in prison for murdering his girlfriend and feeding her remains to his dogs. "After the courts had failed to rule on his appeal for several years, Bruno was briefly released. A second-division Brazilian team signed him within a month, and he played in five games to chants of, "We are all Bruno" (Salazar 2018).

NBA Commissioner Adam Silver echoed the opinion of sport sociologists, mental health professionals, domestic violence victims' advocacy groups and others when he acknowledged that domestic violence is a societal issue and needs to be addressed as such (Mahoney 2014). As a microcosm of society, we are not surprised that there are some athletes involved in domestic violence as this violent and unethical behavior exists throughout society. Sports leagues are not the only organizations that need to address the serious nature of domestic violence, as any civil society that tolerates or turns a blind eye to domestic violence should be ashamed of itself.

Spectator Violence

The focus of this chapter has been on the athletes, the violence they face on-the-field, the violence that some engage in off-the-field, and issues of violence and the law. But, we would be remiss not to mention another critical element of sport violence, spectator violence. Among the variations of spectator violence are verbal assaults, disrupting play, throwing objects (at opposing fans, athletes, coaches and referees), physical assaults (e.g., fighting, stabbings), and vandalism.

Verbal assaults refer to the use of obscenities, vulgarities, and threatening words directed by sports spectators at the targets of their scorn (e.g., other spectators, players, coaches, and game officials) (Wann, et al. 2001). As nearly anyone who has attended a sporting event in the United States (and nearly anywhere else in the world) can attest, numerous spectators use curse words, often with complete disregard for those seated nearby. It is very common at football and hockey games for fans to shout threatening words.

Disrupting play generally takes place in the form of a spectator(s) running onto the field or court. These deviants want to become "a part of the game" and usually mean no harm. They may want to shake hands with a player or kiss a player or even attempt to steal the ball. In fact, there is a subgroup of spectators, both male and female, who get attention by running onto the playing field nude. Most of these interferences are in good fun, and accepted as such. Yet ever since a fan ran onto the court and stabbed tennis player Monica Seles in 1993, there is an increasing level of fear that some fan disrupting play may actually cause physical harm and commit acts of violence aimed at players, coaches, or referees.

Spectators do not have to enter the field of play to cause possible physical harm to sport participants; they can simply throw objects. Any object can become a possible missile of harm, including batteries, coins, plastic beer bottles empty or full of some sort of liquid (e.g., beer or urine), electronic devices, belts and other clothing items, food items, snowballs, and so on. The throwing of objects may also be directed toward opposing fans. Particularly vocal visiting football fans can expect to have objects thrown at them by the home fans at most professional football games.

Physical assaults may occur either in the stands, restrooms, concourses, or outside a stadium. The most common type of physical assault involves fighting among spectators. People who fight at sporting events typically have been drinking alcohol. Generally, the fans that fight each other are cheering for opposite teams. There are other occasions when a fight may ensue for reasons that are unrelated to the sporting event (e.g., a chance meeting of rival gang members, alcohol-induced confrontations). Fights outside the stadium may, once again, be related to the sports event just attended or some other non-sports-related reason. Beyond fighting, stabbings and gunfire would be considered examples of physical assault. There have been incidents of spectators shooting other fans outside a stadium and of stabbings both inside and outside a sporting arena. For example, in September 2003, a Los Angeles Dodgers fan was shot and killed in a Dodger Stadium parking lot during a dispute following a game between the Dodgers and Giants. The murderer was a Giants fan and the victim a Dodgers fan. In 2011, a far more discussed incident occurred outside Dodger Stadium between Giants and Dodgers fans. Giants fan Bryan Stow was beaten unconscious by two men after opening day. Stow suffered a head injury and will have disabling brain damage that necessitates he have the assistance of caretakers for the rest of his life. After the attack, Stow sued the two men who attacked him (they were found guilty of the charges and ordered to pay part of the settlement), the Los Angeles Dodgers organization (who were found guilty of negligence and ordered to pay part of the settlement) and then-owner Frank McCourt (who was cleared of legal wrongdoing charges and financial responsibility). The Dodgers and McCourt argued that they should bear no responsibility for the attack and pointed out that Stow's blood-alcohol level was .18 percent—more than twice the legal limit for driving (he was on his way to his car to drive)—and witnesses gave accounts of Stow yelling at

Dodgers fans in the parking lot prior to the attack. Stow was awarded an $18 million dollar settlement (Fowler 2014).

The very threat of violence in the stands or parking lots may affect the scheduling of sporting events. Venues may be moved to neutral sites, night games may be moved up to day games, and in some rare instances, spectators may actually be banned from the game.

As with fighting, vandalism—the willful or malicious destruction or defacing of public or private property—may occur in the stands (e.g., ripping apart seats in the stands or toilets and sinks in the bathroom) or outside the arena (e.g., damaging vehicles, breaking neighboring store windows). Sports-related vandalism is usually caused by disgruntled fans, although a disturbing trend of victorious fans destroying property after winning a big game or championship developed in the 1990s.

SPECTATOR VIOLENCE IN THE UNITED STATES

As stated above, spectator violence takes many different forms. It would be impossible to quantify the number of verbal assaults, physical assaults, incidents of objects being throw, and so on. Therefore, here we will just mention a few of the more extreme cases of spectator violence in the U.S.

One severe example of spectator violence is the disturbing occurrence of sports celebrations (following championships) that turn violent and destructive. A victory celebration in Detroit after the Pistons won the 1990 NBA championship degenerated into a riot that left 7 dead. Three people died in rioting in Chicago following the Bulls' 1993 NBA championship. In 2002, sport celebrations turned ugly at College Park, Maryland, and Minneapolis. University of Maryland fans celebrated the school's first national championship in basketball by destroying property. Riot police were called in to restore order. University of Minnesota fans were celebrating their school's national championship in men's ice hockey (O'Toole 2002). Beyond the physical mayhem, a number of acts of vandalism occurred. In the College Park incident, six police cars were damaged and fire-fighters fought at least 16 separate fires. In Minnesota, street lights were damaged, furniture was torched, and rocks and bottles were thrown at police. While Maryland fans were causing havoc near their campus, fans of the losing team—Indiana—also took to rioting. Upset by their team's loss, fans torched couches, toppled street signs and threw objects at police. In Boston, fans rioted following their 2004, 2007 and 2013 World Series titles. Numerous arrests were made. In 2018, Eagles fans rioted following Philadelphia's victory in the Super Bowl; a great amount of property was damaged and dozens of arrests made. In sum, nearly 20 lives have been lost in the last forty years following victory celebrations of championships (Smith 2018).

Fans are allowed to cheer for their team and root against the opposing team. They are not allowed onto the field or court. Conversely, athletes should not run into the stands to confront fans. An infamous example of player-in-the-stands violence occurred on November 19, 2004, in an NBA game between the Pistons and Pacers when players went into the stands and fought fans and then the fans came onto the court and fought players. Another example of fans fighting players on the court occurred during a February 24, 1947, NBA game between the Syracuse Nationals and the Moline Blackhawks. The hometown Nationals fans became increasingly upset with the officiating and the perceived "bad calls" by the officials that went against Syracuse. After a particularly hard foul against a Syracuse player, home-grown John "Chick" Meehan, by Blackhawks player

William "Pop" Gates, a Hall of Famer and one of the first African Americans to play in the NBA, hundreds of Syracuse fans stormed the court to get at Gates. One fan pulled a knife and tried unsuccessfully to get at Gates. Fistfights broke out across the court (Kirst 2004). The NBA and *The Post-Standard* of Syracuse referred to the incident as a "race riot." The NBA responded by returning to an all-white sport the following year (Kirst 2004). The similarity between the two incidents (Syracuse and Detroit) is the fact that officials lost control of the game and players and fans reacted by responding inappropriately.

Spectators enter the playing fields and courts for reasons other than attempting violence. Even so, they risk disrupting play. "Rushing" the field or court after the game concludes has been relatively common in collegiate sports but has come under increasing disfavor. As a rule, spectators simply want to bask in the glory of their team's victory, especially if it was an unexpected victory or a monumental one. Although players and officials are seldom injured, the risk factor is very high. With most sports, when fans storm the court or field, they have no real direction; that is, there is no central place to converge. Football is different. When fans storm the field at the conclusion of a football game most of them head directly toward the goalposts. Their purpose is to knock down the goalposts and parade around the stadium with them. The goalposts are similar to a hunter's trophy—proof of victory. Tearing down goalposts has a long tradition in football. It is considered good clean fun. Most spectators and fans of the victorious team look upon fans tearing down the goalposts with joy and happiness. Tearing down goalposts reached its peak in 2002 with 17 reported cases. However, tearing down goalposts can have dire and even deadly consequences. For example, on homecoming weekend at the University of Minnesota–Morris, October 22, 2005, the goalpost became a symbol of tragedy. Spectators stormed the field to knock down the goalposts. As is the typical fashion, fans stand on the crossbar and jump up and down until the parts of the goalposts snap off. These "parts" are made of strong metal. At Morris, as the dislodged goalpost tumbled down, it hit a student and caused his immediate death due to severe head trauma. In 2003, a spectator at Toledo became a quadriplegic after being hit by a goalpost being carried out of the stadium. At Ball State, in 2001, a fan became paralyzed as he was hit by a falling goalpost. Thirteen people were injured, including two who were airlifted to hospitals following Oklahoma State's victory over archrival Oklahoma in 2012. The postgame celebration crowd on the football field was so thick it took officials 45 minutes to clear them away. Spectators were injured and the goalposts were destroyed by Ole Miss fans following their 2014 upset victory over Alabama. The university complained about the costs to replace to goalposts and immediately fans set up a special online site (this was pre–GoFundMe era) to raise money to cover the costs.

As a result of these and other tragic events, college administrators are trying to find ways to stop the tradition of storming the field and tearing down goalposts. Collapsible goalposts are used at some stadiums. The posts are made of aluminum. If the goalposts are already down it more or less defeats the purpose of storming the field. Some schools have goalposts on hydraulics so that they can collapse the goalposts quickly. Other schools grease the goalposts so that spectators cannot climb them.

INTERNATIONAL SPECTATOR VIOLENCE

The United States is hardly alone when it comes to spectator violence as it occurs in many other countries as well. Once again, it would be impossible and beyond the scope of this text to try and cover all the major incidents. So, we offer a sampling below.

One of the most extreme forms of violence found in society is terrorism (war would be the most extreme example of violence). Attending sporting events in the 2000s—especially after 9/11/2001—has been characterized by perceived threats of terrorism. Because of the threat of terrorism, spectators today are routinely subject to security checks outside every major sporting event. While we all hope that the reality of a terrorist attack at an American sporting event is unlikely to occur, there have been cases of terror attacks at sporting events in the past. The most infamous attack occurred during the 1972 Olympics, when 11 Israeli athletes were brutally murdered by Palestinian terrorists while the world watched in horror (see Chapter 13 for a further description).

As an example of the sign of the times, a riot broke out between rival soccer fans from Serbia and Albania and spilled onto the field involving rival players fighting each other and fighting with the fans following an incident involving a drone. Officials were already concerned with Serbia and Albania playing each other in an October 2014 European qualifying match, but tensions escalated in the 42nd minute when a drone carrying an Albanian nationalist banner (depicting Albania, Kosovo and parts of other countries considered to be culturally Albanian) flew over the soccer stadium in Belgrade, Serbia. Serbian player Aleksandar Mitrovic ripped the flag down as it flew over his head, upsetting the Albanian players who jumped him and starting a melee on the field. The violence quickly spread among the Serbian and Albanian spectators. The soccer match had to be suspended because of the brawl. For the unacquainted, Serbia and Albania have been at odds with one another for decades as Serbia refuses to recognize Kosovo's autonomy even while the international world does. Several members of the Albanian national team were born in Kosovo, so they have a special connection to the idea of an Albanian nationalist flag. Serbians are equally passionate against their unification (McCauley 2014). This incident has been dubbed the "Drone Brawl" and it is likely to be the first of many incidents involving drones at sporting events and non-sporting events alike.

Quick thinking on the part of French authorities may have averted a massacre during a soccer match held at the Stade de France in November 2015. Suicide bombers' explosive belts packed with shrapnel were designed to kill and main the crowds of fans. The explosives were designed to detonate at the same time as the terrorists' associates' bombs went off in the center of Paris killing 128 people. However, "a combination of solid security at the huge arena, quick thinking in a crisis, modern stadium infrastructure and apparent mistakes in the attackers' planning appears to have averted a massacre" (*Associated Press* 2015).

The passion of many soccer fans around the world often leads to packs of supporters who travel to towns and cities their favorite teams play. In many cases, encounters with rival packs of fans lead to brawls. Some fan bases are notoriously well-known by law enforcement. Perhaps the most infamous of all violent packs of fans are soccer hooligans. Hooliganism itself refers to violent and malicious behavior. When applied to sport, soccer hooliganism occurs when fans of soccer teams go on violent sprees of destruction that may involve verbal and physical violence, vandalism, physical altercations (often involving the use of weapons), rioting, burning objects, and causing general chaos. Soccer hooligans display behavior similar to street gangs. Their violence may occur before, during, or after soccer matches. Although many nations are home to hooligans, England's soccer hooligans are the most notorious. The English hooligans are so well-known that hooliganism has been referred to as the "English Disease." Other nations dread the arrival of England's teams because of the infamous acts of hooliganism that often accompanies them (Snyder 2001).

There are two general categories of soccer hooliganism: spontaneous and deliberate. "Spontaneous hooliganism" is unplanned and a relatively low-level form of disorder caused by fans at, or around, soccer matches. Spontaneous hooliganism occurs at the arena between rival fans who are seated (or standing) next to each other or during chance meetings (e.g., at city centers, bars, or train stations). "Deliberate hooliganism" refers to planned, organized violence caused by gangs of hooligans who have attached themselves to Futbol clubs and fight "firms" from other clubs at soccer matches or in areas far removed from the pitch.

As mentioned above, soccer hooligans have similarities with street gangs, including core members who interact at a high frequency rate, possession of a group name, identity by specific types of clothing and color, claims of a specific territory, and participation in violent and criminal behavior. As with gang members, soccer hooligans justify their behavior, usually by insisting that they are simply protecting their neighborhoods or teams from outside rivals. In this regard, soccer hooligans, like street gangs, find it their duty to fight rival groups. As a result, there are a large number of incidents (too many to list here) of hooligan violence. Internationally, authorities like to think that they have a handle on tracking soccer hooligan activity as advancements in tracking technology and the omnipresent and watchful (or intrusive) cameras in nearly all public areas help law enforcement keep an eye on their whereabouts at all time. And yet, in 2020, English police reported that violence between groups of rival futbol hooligans has been the worst they had seen for years (*Daily Mail* 2020).

The seriousness of soccer hooliganism cannot be overstated. Firms (gangs) of soccer hooligans not only target other firms willing to fight, but they also victimize innocent soccer fans who simply wish to cheer their team on to victory, free from violence. This helps to explain why *Sports Illustrated* (2006) demonized an English toy company for creating a line of soccer-fan action figures called "Little Hooliganz" in its weekly "Sign of the Apocalypse" feature.

SITUATIONAL FACTORS THAT LEAD TO SPECTATOR VIOLENCE

Spectators that participate in violence range from the soccer hooligan who uses sport as an excuse to fight to a normally mild-mannered fan who finds him- or herself caught up in some sort of collective behavior. Consequently, there are a number of situational factors that lead to spectator violence:

1. *Hypermasculinity.* Hypermasculinity refers to a belief among young males that honor and respect are the result of one's ability to physically dominate another. Hypermasculinity is especially important to lower socio-economic class males. This idea is similar to Miller's (1958) explanation of gang behavior and his use of focal concerns (trouble, toughness, smartness, excitement, fate and autonomy). These focal concerns become the basic feature of lower-class values and a way of life (Delaney 2006). Hypermasculine males tend to be attracted to sports that encourage physical play. When males who value trouble, toughness and other masculine traits come into contact with one another, the possible for violence exists.

2. *A Strong Sense of Identity.* Many spectators have such a strong connection to the sports team that their very identity is shaped by the team. Soccer hooligans, for example, view the soccer team as an extension of the community in which they are based and consequently an important source of identification and pride (Semyonov and Farbstein 1989). A strong sense of identification to the team coupled with hypermasculinity become two powerful situational factors that lead to soccer hooliganism. The soccer hooligan views the arena as a "battlefield" wherein turf must be protected. The soccer hooligan also views fans of an opposing team as the "enemy." Not only do the majority of soccer hooligans come from the lower social classes, but most spectators who act violently tend to be young males (16–25 years old) from lower socio-economic group. It should also be noted that spectator violence is more likely to occur in team sports than it is with individual sports because it is easier for fans to identify with a group, which represents community, than with an individual.

3. *Alcohol Consumption.* Most spectators that engage in sports violence have consumed excessive amounts of alcohol. This is especially true with fan disturbances at college and professional sporting events (especially during football games).

4. *Frustration.* Fans realize that despite their passion and dedication, they have no direct effect on the outcome of the game. Thus, their role as spectator has a built-in component of stress and frustration. Some people react violently when frustrated; the hypermasculine male is the most likely candidate. Logic would seem to dictate that fans of the losing team would be the most frustrated and therefore most likely to engage in violent behavior. However, as we have already shown, many sports riots occur when fans celebrate a championship.

5. *A Dense Crowd.* A packed stadium creates a certain anxiety among spectators. It is also a source of frustration because spectators feel as though their personal space has been violated. Standing room crowds, which are extremely rare in the United States but common in other parts of the world, also contribute to violence because people on their feet are more active than those who sit throughout the game.

6. *A Large Crowd.* A large crowd increases the probability of violent spectators. A large crowd also creates a sense of anonymity by individuals (Mann 1979). Members of large crowds feel a sense of power because they realize they greatly outnumber the security forces. A large crowd may also lead to a "mob mentality."

7. *Mob Mentality.* Individuals tend to lose their inhibitions and sense of "right" versus "wrong" when they become a part of a large crowd. They take on a group, or mob, mentality. As Gustave Le Bon (1952) explained in his "contagion theory," a "collective mind" forms within a large group and individuals abandon rational reasoning and become submerged into the groups' acts and mood (Vogler and Schwartz 1993). Individuals experience a heightened sense of suggestibility when they are a part of a "mob." At many sporting events, alcohol fuels a mob mentality. A good example of the mob mentality in sports is the storming of the football field by spectators in an attempt to tear down the goalposts. As some fans jump on the crossbars, others join in. They revel at being a part of a group and simply follow the cues of others. Destroying property is a behavior that most of these people would never engage in if not for the "mob mentality."

8. *Important Games.* As a general rule, the more important the game, the more

passionate fans become. Important events include playoff games, championship games and games against long-time rivals. If these rival teams are also from neighboring schools or cities, the importance of the game increases.

9. *In-Game Player Violence.* Spectators respond to stimuli on the field. If an athlete(s) on the field reacts in an aggressive manner such behavior is likely to stimulate the fans of the athlete(s). For example, Smith (1974) found that nearly 75 percent of the incidents of hockey spectator violence in the stands were preceded by player aggression on the ice.

These are among the typical situational factors that influence the likelihood of spectator violence. Spectator violence in sport is an all too familiar occurrence. Civil societies frown upon spectator sports violence and attempt to control it via the civilizing process.

Connecting Sports and Popular Culture

Box 9: "'Hit Somebody"

Perhaps nothing epitomizes violence in sports more than a hockey fight. In particular, the so-called "enforcer" or "goon" in hockey is always controversial. These are the players whose role—whether they admit it or not—is to aggressively taunt, retaliate, and often brutalize members of the opposite team. They are usually intimidating and frightening figures on and off the ice. Yet three of the most beloved figures in sports film history fall into this category: the Hanson Brothers, who appear in the 1977 film *Slap Shot,* directed by George Roy Hill, and starring Paul Newman as Reggie Dunlop, the over-the-hill player-coach of the fictional Charlestown Chiefs.

Dunlop realizes that the Chiefs are going nowhere. Their cheapskate owner (who Dunlop doesn't even know the identity of) refuses to do anything to get better players, and most of the team members are, to put it mildly, eccentric. But none of them are as bizarre as the three Hanson brothers, who are acquired for next to nothing and who seem wildly out of place in the locker room: they are innocent-looking, childlike men with long hair, coke-bottle eyeglasses, and a predilection for playing with toy racing cars. Dunlop is appalled by them, but when most of his other players are hurt he's forced to send them in. "Okay, guys," he says without any enthusiasm, "Let's see what you got."

Much to his astonishment, the Hansons on ice are maniacs. In a few short minutes they wreak havoc on their opponents, much to the delight of the home crowd. Dunlop and the other Chiefs watch in disbelief as the Hansons trip up, double check, and punch out the players on the other team. Dunlop, realizing that this display of brutality has revitalized the dispirited Chiefs and their fans, skates onto the ice to argue with the refs who have, quite rightly, ordered the Hansons out of the game. He senses that things are about to change for the Chiefs.

When it becomes clear to him that the Chiefs' owner has no interest in maintaining the team, meaning that they are going to fold and this will be their final season, Dunlop decides to unleash the Hansons. He encourages them and the other members of the Chiefs to fight dirty all the time. Amazingly, attendance increases and the Hansons become superstars.

In an iconic scene from a later game, the Hansons get into a pre-game brawl during the warm-up, when no officials are yet on the ice. As the National Anthem plays the three of them are shown with broken glasses, multiple cuts, and blood dripping from their faces. An irate referee skates up to one of them and sternly says that he runs a clean game and will be keeping a sharp eye out for any mayhem, to which he receives the immortal line: "I'm listening to the f*ckin' song." Chastised, the ref can only turn around and do the same.

When it comes to their final game, though, Dunlop wants a clean win. However, the Chiefs' main opponents, the feared (and equally fictitious) Syracuse Bulldogs, decide to fight fire with fire and fill their team with enforcers. When Dunlop realizes this, he gives the word to his teammates that they will go out in a blaze of glory. The Hansons are unplugged and the ice soon looks like a battle scene. But another Chiefs player, sickened and angered by the horrors he sees, decides to end the mayhem. He strips naked, except for his jockstrap, which shocks and silences the maddened crowd. It also offends the Bulldogs' goons, who feel that *that's* going too far. When one of the Bulldogs demands that a referee stop this at once he is refused, and angrily sucker-punches the official. This causes the game to be forfeited to the Chiefs, who end the season—and their last ever game—as champions.

Watching *Slap Shot* is a guilty pleasure for many hockey fans. The Hanson brothers are so over the top that it's impossible not to root for them. In the humorous words of writer Bill Danielson, "To invoke the name of the Hanson brothers is to invoke the purest spirit of joyful, violent mayhem; the exuberance of youthful, adrenaline-fueled energy. These brothers were introduced to the world in the film *Slap Shot* (perhaps the finest movie ever made) and remain indelibly burned into the memory of anyone who has ever seen them" (Danielson 2020). In fact, the three actors who played the roles (all of whom were professional hockey players themselves) still make appearances throughout the U.S. and Canada as the Hansons, although their constant traveling to charity events and memorabilia shows was curtailed in 2020 due to the ongoing Coronavirus crisis (Stubbs 2020). They even made it to the cover of *Sports Illustrated* in July of 2007—not bad for fictitious athletes. Still, as mentioned previously in the section of hockey violence, clubs today are eliminating enforcers or goons—fictitious players like the Hansons may be lovable, but their real-life versions most certainly are not.

While the Hansons may be heroes (or anti-heroes, depending on how one looks at it), there is another fictional goon who deserves mention—Buddy from Big Beaver, the subject of Warren Zevon's 2002 "Hit Somebody (The Hockey Song)." Zevon (1947–2003) was an unconventional singer-songwriter, best known for such strange hit songs as "Werewolves of London," "I'll Sleep When I'm Dead," and "Roland the Headless Thompson Gunner." But he had a sentimental streak as well, and wrote such plaintive love songs as "Searching for a Heart," "Reconsider Me," and "Poor Poor Pitiful Me." In "The Hockey Song" he manages to combine violence and sentiment. He co-wrote the song with the popular sports writer and columnist Mitch Albom, who notes on his blog, "This song came about when my friend Warren Zevon and I were talking one day. He said, 'You know, I'd like to do a sports song that nobody has done before.' And I said, 'Hockey.' And he said, 'What?' And I said 'I can't think of a single hockey song.' And he said, 'Great! You should write me one!'" (Albom 2015).

They sat down and co-wrote a plaintive song about Buddy, a Canadian farm boy who loves to play hockey but, unfortunately, isn't any good at it. All he wants to do is score goals like his hero Rocket Richard, but he's too inept and gawky to do so. However, like the Hansons, he has a talent for beating people up, and quickly makes it into the big time as an enforcer. "There's always room on our team for a goon," he's told over and over.

And so, as he makes his name as a brawler, Buddy keeps hearing the refrain "Hit Somebody!" (which is gleefully yelled throughout the song by Zevon's real-life pal David Letterman). But Buddy's only desire is to score a goal.

Finally, he gets the opportunity when a puck unexpectedly rolls near him right before he's going to fight it out with a goon from Finland on the other team. Buddy commits and, after twenty years of wanting to do so, takes a shot. Right after he does so he's cold cocked by the Finn and falls to the ice. As Albom relates, "Buddy spends his entire lengthy professional career as hockey's greatest goon (with a penalty box throne) … He only wishes to score just one goal. Then on his final night he finally gets his chance and narrowly succeeds, but gets hit in the head by a Finnish player in the process. Buddy doesn't care though since he sees the flashing red goal light before he loses consciousness and, it is implied dies on the ice" (Albom 2015).

A song about a hockey goon who goes to heaven—even the Hanson brothers might shed a tear for that.

SUMMARY

Broken bones, torn ligaments, missing teeth, fist fights, blood, scars, concussions, and occasional deaths are just a few of the risks confronting athletes when they play sports. Some sports, such as football, rugby and hockey, are designed for assertive, physical contact between competitors. Violence is often seen as "part of the game." Intimidation (the use of words, gestures and actions that sometimes may threaten violence or aggression in an attempt to pressure and put fear in the opponent) and aggression (verbal and physical behavior grounded in the intent to successfully accomplish a task even if it means to frighten, dominate, control, or harm, physically or psychologically, an opponent) are two other aspects that are a part of sports.

A review of the role of violence in five sports—football, hockey, soccer, boxing and MMA—was provided. In each of these sports, aggressive play is an expectation and the very design of the sport dictates that violent acts will occur on a regular basis. Another thing these sports have in common is the opportunity for blows to the head leading to concussion.

While all athletes understand that the possibility of getting injured on the playing field/court is a reality, most of them do not consider the long-term post-career health problems that confront them. There is a growing concern over Chronic Traumatic Encephalopathy (CTE), a progressive degenerative disease of the brain and its possible connection to various aggressive sporting activities. Brain degeneration is associated with memory loss, confusion, impaired judgment, impulse control problems, aggression, depression, and eventually progressive dementia. Long-term psychiatric and psychological problems follow sport concussions in adults. Millions of athletes endure concussions while playing sports each year. The medical field is studying the donated brains of dead athletes who have suffered multiple concussions and showed signs of CTE in order to learn more about this disease.

A review of sport violence and the law was another feature of this chapter. A typology of sport violence was provided: brutal body contact, borderline violence, quasi-criminal violence, and criminal violence.

Violence may follow some athletes off the field. They may get into fights (e.g., at nightclubs), and sometimes gunfire may be involved. However, the type of violence we hear the most about is domestic violence. A number of highly publicized incidents have occurred in the past years. One of the most talked about was Ray Rice. A video recording of Rice beating up his wife in a hotel elevator led to public outrage and action on the part of the NFL to articulate a policy on athletes and off-the-field behavior of violence. Other major sports leagues would also create policies on how to help prevent domestic violence in the first place and ascertaining a designated punishment for violations of the policy. While strongly condemning domestic violence, the NHL still handles incidents on a case-by-case basis.

The aggressiveness of the athletes is often matched by fans and spectators. Spectator violence has long been a feature of sports events. Among the variations of spectator violence are verbal assaults, disrupting play, throwing objects (at opposing fans, athletes, coaches and referees), physical assaults (e.g., fighting, stabbings), and vandalism. A more severe example of spectator violence is the disturbing occurrence of sports celebrations (following championships) that turn violent and destructive. Threats of terrorism and efforts to combat it are a permanent fixture of sporting venues domestically and internationally. Soccer hooligans represent a fixture at many soccer matches overseas.

There are a number of situational factors that lead to spectator violence, including, a strong sense of identity attached to the team; alcohol consumption; frustration; a large crowd; mob mentality; and in-game player violence.

KEY TERMS

Aggression in Sport Verbal and physical behavior grounded in the intent to successfully accomplish a task even if it means to dominate, control, or harm, physically or psychologically, an opponent.

Chronic Traumatic Encephalopathy (CTE) A progressive degenerative disease of the brain found in athletes (and nonathletes) with a history of repetitive brain trauma, including symptomatic concussions as well as asymptomatic subconcussive hits to the head.

Combat sports Sports that involve striking, grappling, or weapon-related techniques under specific rules of engagement to stimulate parts of real hand-to-hand combat.

Disrupting Play Generally takes place in the form of a spectator(s) running onto the field or court.

Harm Principle Philosopher John Stuart Mill's view that the only justification for interference with personal behavior is to prevent harm to others.

Hypermasculinity The belief that ideal manhood lies in the exercise of force to dominate others.

Instrumental Aggression Behavior that is non-emotional and task oriented and driven by the quest for achieving some nonaggressive goal.

Intimidation Behavior that involves words, gestures and actions that sometimes may threaten violence or aggression in an attempt to pressure and put fear in the opponent.

Mixed Martial Arts An extreme combat sport in which contestants are allowed an amalgamation of fighting techniques including bare-handed boxing and a variety of martial arts such as kickboxing, judo and karate.

Mob Mentality Collective thinking and action that develops when a group reacts nearly simultaneously to a stimulus.

Other-regarding Acts Behaviors which may cause harm to others and, therefore, fall outside the dominion of acceptable forms of violence.

Reactive Aggression Where one's primary goal is inflicting bodily injury or physical harm to an opponent.

Self-regarding Acts Behaviors that may cause harm only to the individual performing them and, therefore, fall within the realm of acceptable violence.

Sport Violence Intentional aggressive physical behavior that causes harm, occurs outside the rules of the game, is unrelated to ideals of sportsmanship, or which destroys the property of another sportsperson.

Terrorism The unlawful use of—or threatened use of—force or violence against individuals or property to coerce or intimidate governments or societies, often to achieve political, religious, or ideological objectives.

Vandalism The willful or malicious destruction or defacing of public or private property.

Verbal Assaults The use of obscenities, vulgarities, and threatening words directed by sports spectators at the targets of their scorn.

Violence Entails great physical force used intentionally by one person(s) to cause another person(s) harm or aggressive behavior which destroys the property of another.

Volenti non fit injuria The assumption of risk of injury in sport that athletes and management acknowledge may occur during the course of their sporting activity.

DISCUSSION QUESTIONS

- What are the differences between "intimidation," "aggression" and "violence" in sports? Give examples based upon your own knowledge or experience.
- What are examples of actions that would be deemed violent outside of the realm of sport that are deemed acceptable within the realm of sports?
- How might nonphysical forms of instrumental aggression be used by athletes to gain a competitive edge? Do you think this is acceptable behavior?
- Do you think football is in danger in light of the concern of concussions and CTE?
- Do you think that professional athletes are becoming more or less aggressive in their actions? Give some specific examples of athletes you are familiar with.
- Of the sports discussed in this chapter that may lead to post-career concussions, which sport in particular do you think is most likely to lead to athletes with post-career brain-related problems? Which other sports run a risk for post-career concussions? Explain your answer.
- Have you ever experienced spectator violence at a game? What might be the causes for this deviant behavior?
- Do you think it is a good thing that hockey clubs have been eliminating enforcers or "goons"?
- How should sports leagues frame their domestic violence code of conduct? What type of punishments would you designate for the varying degrees of domestic violence?

CHAPTER 10

Gender and Sport

A character on the long-lasting and popular TV series *The Simpsons*, Lisa Simpson is known for taking a stand on a variety of issues, including feminist concerns. In the "Bart Star" episode (November 9, 1997), Lisa appears at a youth football tryout prepared for one of her trademark confrontations by asking head coach Ned Flanders, "What position have you got for me?" She continues, "That's right, a girl wants to play football. How about that?" Lisa is left speechless when Flanders replies, "Well, that's super-duper, Lisa. We've already got four girls on the team." As it turns out, Lisa is decades too late in her quest to become a trailblazer for women's rights in sport participation. Had she made such a proclamation in the early 1970s, she might have been the first girl to play organized youth sport.

Unlike Lisa Simpson, Kathrine Switzer, then a Syracuse University student, was a true trailblazer in the women's rights movement as it pertains to sports. Switzer entered the 1967 Boston Marathon even though women were barred from long-distance running. She registered for the race as K.V. Switzer to avoid possible gender identification by race officials. At about the four-mile mark, Boston Marathon official Jock Semple charged after her in an attempt to tear off her bib. Semple yelled, "Get the hell out of my race, and give me those numbers!" (Siu 2014). Switzer ran with a male companion, Thomas Miller of Syracuse, who threw a block that tossed aside Semple. Switzer, with her friend Miller, kept running even as press trucks followed her, finishing the race at 4 hours and 20 minutes (Siu 2014). Switzer dispelled a long-held myth that women could not run 26-mile races, thus helping to pave the way for future female marathoners specifically, and women sport participants in general. The Boston Marathon, the world's largest such race, officially accepted female runners in 1972, a very important year in women's sports. Switzer continues to run marathons today and in 2011 she was inducted into the National Women's Hall of Fame for empowering women through running (Siu 2014). The number of women participating in the Boston marathon now is almost equal between men and women. In 2018, 45 percent of the 30,000+ entrants were women (Runner's World 2020).

As we shall see in this chapter, women's role in the sports world has grown a great deal during the past 50 years. However, it is also true that women have yet to receive equality and there are a number of different reasons for this.

Patriarchy's Influence on Female Sports Participation

Historically, women have been denied equal access to sport participation. Much of this had to do with the patriarchal (male dominated) design of most nations around the world throughout history. A patriarchy refers to a social system in which males serve as the primary authority figures. This generally extends to the father as the head of the household who has control over property and finances, men holding the top power positions in business and major corporations, and men holding the top political positions; in short, they control the decision-making positions in society. Because men hold the power positions in a patriarchal system, women were held to subordinate roles. Conflict theorists and feminists alike would remind us that those who hold positions of power will use any means necessary in order to maintain their advantageous position. In sport, this meant keeping females on the sidelines while males participated in, and benefited from, sport participation.

The patriarchal system is based upon a sexual distinction between males and females and the corresponding gender role expectations established by those in power (males). Sociologists point out that the terms "sex" and "gender" are a matter of social construction; that is to say, they are human creations and not defined by laws of nature. The term "sex" refers to one's biological classification (male or female). As we are aware, males and females differ biologically in regards to their internal and external reproductive organs and genitalia, types and levels of hormones and chromosomal structure (females have an XX and males an XY design). (Note: There are people who do not fit neatly into either category and may be referred to as *intersex* persons—those born with both male and female physiological characteristics.) As social scientists, sociologists are more interested in gender classifications than they are with sexual classification schemes. "Gender" refers to socially determined expectations placed on individuals because of their sexual category. Males and females are taught societal ideals of gender roles through the agents of socialization. Traditionally, males have been expected to act masculine, while females were expected to act feminine. Society dictates what it means to be masculine or feminine. Gender role expectations associated with femininity have encouraged girls and women to be passive, gentle, delicate, and submissive (Eitzen 2015). "These cultural expectations clashed with those traits often associated with sport, assertiveness, competitiveness, physical endurance, ruggedness, and dominance" (Eitzen 2015:239). Among other things, these traditional expectations based on one's sex denied women equal access to opportunities, not only to sports participation but also to college and to various occupations (Eitzen 2015).

Because sport has traditionally been viewed as a masculine endeavor, females born into a patriarchal system were discouraged from playing sports. However, as Morgan, Meier and Schneider (2001) explain, there is no sport that requires the possession of male genitalia in order to perform. Thus, if females are physiologically capable, why haven't they participated in sport in significant numbers before the 1970s? The answer must lie with culture, and in this case, a patriarchal culture. Needing some sort of justification to keep females out of sport, patriarchies created a number of myths associated with female sport participation.

Myths Associated with Female Participation in Sports

Myths associated with female sport participation reflect both medical ignorance and negative stereotypes of women. As Patricia Vertinsky (1994) points out, during the late nineteenth century, "medical practitioners, many of whom were men, utilized pseudo-scientific theories about the effects of the reproductive life cycle upon women's physical capabilities in order to rationalize the life choices of middle-class women and define limits for their activities" (39). Other researchers agree with Vertinsky's analysis. For example, Stanley (1996) argued that in the 1870s, the medical profession described the uterus as "a perilous possession" and the most dominant organ in the female body (29). Dr. Edward Clark of the Harvard Medical School wrote an immensely popular book, *Sex in Education: Or a Fair Chance for the Girls* (1873), where he claimed that educating girls after the onset of puberty was a fundamental mistake because nature "had reserved that time for the process of ovulation and the development and perfection of the reproductive system. Education interfered with this critical process because the body never did two things well at the same time" (Stanley 1996: 30). Education was considered unimportant for women because it might spoil women for family duties, thus "rendering them manly, indelicate, and unsexed" (Sack and Staurowsky 1998: 52).

Combining primitive medical knowledge with negative stereotypes of women would lead to the creation of myths. Among the myths we found were: A woman's uterus will fall out if she plays sports; if a woman is pushed too much physically, she will lose her emotional stability; muscles are masculine, therefore, female athletes who work out are un-feminine; and, the notion that women are too weak physically to play sport. If these sound like far-fetched ideas, which the authors would agree that they are, consider that present-day Saudi Arabia does not allow women to drive because, in part, many clerics believe that if women drive an automobile it will cause harm to their reproductive organs (*CBS This Morning* 2014). Finally, in 2018, Saudi King Salman bin Abdulaziz decreed that both men and women would be issued driving licenses starting in June 2018.

One of the oldest myths of women and sports centers on the idea that women are not strong enough to play sports. Research will confirm that the average male is physically bigger, faster and stronger than the average female. Consider, for example, data from the Centers for Disease Control and Prevention (CDC) (2017) which reveal that the average height and weight for adult men (ages 20 years and over) is 69.0 inches (height) and 197.8 pounds (weight); and for adult women, 63.6 inches and 170.5 pounds. The average waist circumference for men (40.3 inches) and for women (38.7) also reveals how overweight/obese Americans have become and further illustrates the need to mandate that children participate in sports and exercise and that adults stay active their entire lives. Using the Body Mass Index (BMI) calculator, males have a 29.2 BMI (a score of 30 or more equals obese) and females have a 29.3 average BMI (National Heart, Lung, and Blood Institute 2020).

This data does not mean that all men are stronger than all women, nor does it mean that an athlete must be large in order to succeed in sport. In many cases, women have more flexibility than men, which can be a big asset in many sports. The notion that women cannot compete in endurance sports such as running marathons has long been discounted. Furthermore, the one-time large gap in the performance of the top male long distance runner compared to the performance of the top female runner has been steadily decreasing for years. As described in this chapter's introductory story, Kathrine Switzer proved that women could run marathons even if her time of 4:20 is rather pedestrian today. In the 2018 Boston Marathon, the finish time for the top female runner, Worknesh Degefa of Ethiopia, was 2:23:30, a time just a little more than 15 minutes slower than the top male finisher, Lawrence Cherono of Kenya at 2:07:57 (*CBS News* 2019). Interestingly, the top women's time was better in 2014 when Rita Jeptoo finished the marathon in 2:18:37 (*Runners World* 2014). While the elite female runners are narrowing the gap compared to the elite male runners in long distance running, there are still far more elite male competitors for the top spot than there are women. When it comes to the designation of the fastest person in the world—the 100 meters race is used as the determinant—Usain Bolt (Jamaica) has the world record at 9.58 seconds and the fastest woman is Shelly-Ann Fraser-Pryce, also of Jamaica, 10.71 seconds (Church 2019).

There are other physiologically-based myths regarding female participation in sport. "Some critics believe that sport participation defeminizes women (meaning that it makes some women less attractive, either physically or mentally, in some men's eyes), or that women (or sometimes their not-yet-conceived children) might suffer some physiological damage" (Morgan, et al. 2001: 208). Any assertion that women are harmed as a result of strenuous physical exertion while men are not is inaccurate. Further, if men are allowed to engage in "risky" behavior, then women should be allowed the same bodily and mental risks (Morgan, et al. 2001). The concept of a "macho female athlete" is a derogatory term used by those who argue female athletes become too masculine through sport participation (Sabo 1996). Another myth related to the physiology of women is tied to the supposed delicacy of the female body. This myth is centered on the idea that women are easily injured; in particular, the breasts and reproductive organs are especially vulnerable. Female fragility is a big concern in patriarchal societies that view women primarily as care-givers to children.

Myths designed to keep women from playing sports are not limited to the physicality of the female body. They also extend to the psychological realm as well. "The 'myth of psychic damage' contends that women do not have the necessary psychological assets for athletic competition and, in contrast to men, women do not reap psychological benefit from sport. These notions are partly rooted in psychological theory…⌧. Within the framework of psychoanalytic theory, for example, nonconformity to traditional roles and stereotypes was considered pathological. Hence, women's interest and involvement in business, engineering, athletics, or other 'masculine' activities were clinically suspect" (Sabo 1996: 334–335). Women can, however, benefit from sport participation. Just as males supposedly learn how to become better leaders and team players, females who play sports often grow up to become leaders.

Patriarchal myths in sports designed to discourage female participation have nearly disappeared. There are still some lingering effects of these myths but most people in Western societies accept the idea that women should be allowed to play sports and realize that females do not face physiological or psychological damage for doing so.

DOING GENDER

Many feminists such as Barbara Risman (1956–) believe that an individual is labeled at birth as a member of a sex category, either male or female, and from that point on is held to acting accordingly. The individual generally succumbs to society's expectations, often through the use of, or the threat of, sanctions and therefore "does gender." Individuals who deviate from these expectations often have difficulty having typical interactions with other members of society (Delaney 2014). Feminists believe that such expectations reflect a patriarchal society that devalues what is defined as female or feminine, and claims that biological differences between males and females exist justify male dominance (Risman 1998). Thus, gender is not something that one has or something one is; instead, it something that one *does* (Delaney 2014).

The "doing gender" perspective was later extended by West and Fenstermaker (1995) to "doing difference," with the assumption that what we actually create through interaction is inequality. Risman (1998) believes that just as some people use race to guide interactional encounters despite its lack of biologically-based differences, people also use gender to determine where one stands in daily interactions. Risman argues that there is a great difference in how people are treated simply because of their gender categorization. "Gender polarization is the assumption that not only are women and men different, but that this difference is super-imposed on so many aspects of the social world that a cultural connection is thereby forged between sex and virtually every other aspect of human experience, including modes of dress and social roles and even ways of expressing emotion and experiencing sexual desire" (Risman 1998:2).

Pfister and Bandy (2015) posit that a socially constructed and gendered body is the medium for interactions and performances that are crucial to the (unconscious) construction and embodiment of gender. Categorization of gender carry over to "bodily practices" expected of men and women based on such social constructions. "Gendering processes occur all the time, everywhere, and in every interaction, including the field of sports, because individuals must present themselves as males and females" (Pfister and Bandy 2015: 223). Once again, then, gender is not something we are or have but something we *do*. And, as it generally is, socialization becomes the key to doing gender. As youth age, most have been bombarded with social expectations based on their gender and these expectations may, or may not, be reinforced at home and school, and by peers. If a junior high school girl expresses a desire to go out for the wrestling team, the manner in which she is encouraged or discouraged will help shape how she chooses to do gender.

The Early History of Women's Participation in Sports

As our discussion on the patriarchal nature of most societies and the negative myths associated with women's participation in sport implies, it is not surprising to realize that, until recent years, women have played a minor role in the history of sport. This is not to suggest that women did not participate at all in ancient sports but their role was very limited, even to the point of being barred from the ancient Olympics. Richard C. Bell (2008) points out that Homer (c. 800 BCE) wrote of Princess Nausicaa [a character in Homer's *Odyssey*] playing ball with her handmaidens next to a riverbank on the Greek island of Scheria, "When she and her handmaids were satisfied with their delightful food, each set aside the veil she wore: the young girls now played ball" and that Odysseus was awakened by the shouts of the girls engaged in their sport.

Through the Middle Ages and into the mid–1800s, most societies limited female sport participation to non-competitive, informal recreational activities. As recently as the 1800s, there was a dominant belief that each human had a fixed amount of energy (Bell 2008) and women were expected to exert their energy with child rearing and home making and to be supportive of men who participated in sports.

Pre–Civil War

Discrimination against women participating in sports can be traced back to the ancient Olympics when women were forbidden from participating. Anshel (1994) states that women could be sentenced to death for simply watching men compete. However, as we pointed out in Chapter 3, women of ancient Greece established their own games in honor of Hera, the wife of Zeus. Spartan women were actually encouraged to keep healthy (through physical activity) in order to be good "breeders" (Leonard 1988). During America's colonial period, wealthy women participated in a number of leisure activities, including horseback riding and foot racing. They were also spectators to men's sports. Women played cricket during the 1700s.

Prior to the Civil War, women as well as men participated in sports and leisure activities that were popular in their respective countries and social classes. Upper class women's sport participation was limited but generally included horseback riding and dancing. Middle- and lower-class women led lives that were more physical by necessity. Their recreational activities included dancing, horseback riding, skating, foot racing, and early versions of bowling and baseball (Howell 1982; Figler and Whitaker 1995). Bell (2008) states that sports for women prior to 1870 existed in the form of play activities that were recreational rather than competitive and, being informal and without rules, emphasized physical activity over competition. Men, on the other hand, were allowed much greater latitude in their physical pursuits. As a rule, men participated in more physical and aggressive sports than women and their everyday life events often presented physical challenges.

The Victorian Era

During the Victorian Era (mid- to late nineteenth century), upper-class women were treated as frail beings ruled by their hormones. It is important to note that hard physical labor was performed by lower-class and slave women on a daily basis prior to, and during, this era; a fact that seemed to escape the "educated" doctors of the wealthy class. Wealthy women were exposed to calisthenics in schools and private clubs, but most of the Victorian women participated in passive sports such as croquet, bowling, tennis, golf and archery. However, participation in these sports were for social purposes rather than competitive ones (Leonard 1988). Well into the 1870s, aristocratic women considered it vulgar to strengthen the body. But this would slowly change with the advent of women's colleges.

By the 1870s a number of women's colleges had opened their doors. Calisthenics became increasingly popular. The Wellesley College catalog of 1876, for example, "proclaimed that good health was absolutely essential to good scholarship" (Stanley 1996: 49). A number of colleges created remedial programs to prepare young women who could not successfully perform calisthenics. "Many students who previously had been excused from gymnasium work (mostly because of spinal curvatures or weak arches) received corrective therapy" (Stanley 1996: 49). Women's colleges of the late 1800s were helping to reverse the popular cultural belief that sport participation was harmful to women. Many physical educators believed that sports would stimulate an interest in all forms of physical exercise for women. Gymnastics classes would determine those women (and men) that were capable of more strenuous forms of exercise that sports required. While progress was being made on some fronts, women's sports were mostly restricted to intramurals (teams from the same college) even though men were beginning to play extramural sports (between different colleges). By the end of the century, however, things were beginning to change. The first recorded women's intercollegiate sporting event took place

on January 1, 1896; it was a basketball game between Stanford University and UC Berkeley. In front of crowd of 700 women, Stanford won 2–1 (Bell 2008; *Time Toast* 2014). A tennis match between Bryn Mawr and Vassar had been scheduled prior to this basketball game but it was cancelled because the Vassar faculty forbade intercollegiate sporting events for women (Bell 2008).

The patriarchal society imposed ideals of proper dress for men and women. Full-length dresses and unrevealing clothes were the standard for women. Such clothing was not conducive to sporting activities. However, in the late 1800s a sports breakthrough for women occurred. As Leonard (1988) explains, "Although the pale and fragile woman remained a cultural ideal until the 1930s, the rosy-cheeked girl on her bicycle was providing evidence that exercise made a woman healthier for housework and childbearing. Amelia Bloomer's bloomers allowed women to move, but modesty in appearance was still an important consideration in sports participation" (265). Middle-class women took to the bicycling rage of the 1890s as a means of testing the limits of female physical expression. Women dared to wear more comfortable and shorter dresses so that they could more easily ride a bicycle. Elizabeth Cady Stanton argued that bike riding "was the means, she said, by which health would be restored to an ever increasing number of nervous, overwrought women" (Vertinsky 1994: 79). Physicians may have embraced the idea of women riding bicycles for the mild exercise benefits it produces, but many during the Victorian era feared that the freedom the "wheel" brought to women would lure them away from the home (and housework) to remote spots alone with men where they might succumb to seduction (Rader 2004). Many members of society who embraced patriarchal notions also worried that women might ride bicycles to stimulate sexual organs (apparently through the vibration). Oddly, this same "logic" (genital stimulation as a result of vibrations) was not applied to horseback riding (as it is today). Feminists often view women cyclists as a symbol of emancipation from Victorian inhibitions, but the most enduring legacy of cycling appears to be tied to women who enjoyed riding because of the freer forms of clothing (Rader 2004).

The sport of tennis evolved during this era thanks in part to the less restrictive clothes worn by both men and women. Stanley (1996) states, "Gentlemen began to abandon their formal attire in search of the freedom of movement required by the new game. Some women could be found playing the faster-paced game and wearing less restrictive clothing. Women playing tennis strictly for its own sake were apparently novel. In fact, in 1893 when socialite Ava Willing Astor played a vigorous tennis match (wearing bloomers) it created quite a stir. So arresting was the sight that *Vogue* devoted special coverage to the spectacle" (76). Lawn tennis became increasingly popular with the women and men of the elite classes. Tournaments were designed so that only those of the "assured social position" were permitted to participate (Stanley 1996). By the turn of the twentieth century, "Sports had become a necessary activity for anyone wishing to gain entry to polite and refined society" (Stanley 1996: 77). Thus, anyone who was "someone" played sports. The masses, for the most part, were relegated to pursuits that assured basic survival.

The Early 1900s

It should come as no surprise that women were still being discriminated against in the early 1900s as they would not be granted the right to vote until 1920. During the

beginning of the twentieth century, more women became involved in various athletic activities. A group of wealthy sportswomen founded the Chicago Women's Athletic Club in 1903. Soon after that, other lavish women's athletic clubs opened in New York and other major cities around the country (Cahn 2003). Women's participation rates in sports received a positive boost in the early 1900s when they were allowed to participate in the 1912 Olympic Games in Stockholm, Sweden. (It should be noted that Olympic founder Pierre de Coubertin and the American Olympic Committee were against women participating.) Their participation in these Olympic Games was limited to swimming and diving. However, it was becoming evident that the cultural mores and gender expectations regarding women's sport participation were beginning to change in the early 1900s. For example, in 1923, a Women's Division of the National Amateur Athletic Federation was formed to stress "sports opportunities for all girls, protection from exploitation, enjoyment of sports, female leadership [and] medical examinations" (Simon 1991: 123). The idea of this sports "creed" was to encourage girls and women to play sports while at the same time reassuring these female athletes that they were not unfeminine just because they played sports.

Another milestone in women's sports during the early 1900s occurred in England when Gertrude Ederle swam the English Channel. "When Gertrude Ederle swam the English Channel in 1926, two hours faster than any of the men who had preceded her, people began to think that women might not be so weak" (Heywood 1998: 213). The athletic achievements of Babe Didriksen were likewise widely reported during the 1920s, but Heywood and Dworkin point out (2003) that "Babe was muscular and androgynous in the 1920s, but became increasingly 'feminine'—in the sense of growing her hair and wearing dresses—in the '30s and '40s in response to constant media criticism of her 'masculinity,' criticism that was a mask for fears about her sexuality" (p. xviii).

During the 1930s and 1940s several women's sports organizations were in place. They generally adopted position statements supporting educational-based sports programs for all girls and women. Track and field became popular sports for girls and women during the 1930s, '40s, and '50s. Beginning in 1924, the AAU (Amateur Athletic Union) sponsored annual national track and field events for women. The 1924 Olympics scheduled track and field events for women. Stanley (1996) recounted many stories by sports writers who covered the women's track and field events in a less than flattering manner (e.g., women could not handle the undue stress that competition placed upon their nerves); thus revealing that old cultural norms were prevalent among males in the sports world. Interestingly, the Great Depression drove most white women away from track and field (Rader 2004). The economic turmoil caused by the Great Depression led to most sports and recreation programs for women being canceled or scaled down due to budget cuts. Black women filled the void. Nearly all segregated southern black high schools offered varsity competition in basketball and track and field to their students (Rader 2004). In 1943, with the help of a group of Midwestern businessmen and the financial support of William Wrigley, Jr. (the owner of the Chicago Cubs), the All-American Girls Softball League was founded to help fill the void of the cancellation of Major League Baseball during World War II (AAGPBL 2014). (Note: Midway through the 1943 season the league's name changed and then it changed again at the end of the season to the All-American Girls Professional Ball League.) Although they faced a great deal of discrimination and were subject to jeers by many, the AAGPBL showed that women could play baseball and if given an equal chance could develop the skills necessary to master the

sport. (See "Connecting Sports and Popular Culture" Box 10 at the end of the chapter for a closer look at the AAGPBL and the movie *A League of Their Own*.)

The Cold War between the United States and the Soviet Union that began in the late 1940s helped to stimulate renewed attention to women track athletes. The U.S. men had competed relatively evenly with the Soviet men, but the Soviet women easily beat the U.S. women in the 1952 Olympics. Attracting white women to a sport that was now dominated by black women was viewed both as essential in the quest to compete with the Soviets and difficult due to the massive recruitment efforts that would be necessary to attract larger numbers of women to the sport. Campaigns actively touted that women could be track athletes and feminine at the same time.

Enthusiasts for women's track enjoyed some mild successes at the 1960 Rome Olympics when Wilma Rudolph won praise for both her track performances (a triple gold medal winner) and her femininity (Rader 2004). The astute reader may notice that this approach to female sports—that the athlete be both accomplished on the field while also being feminine—has continued to the present era.

POST WORLD WAR II

During the 1960s, many American women (e.g., Wilma Rudolph, Wyomia Tyus in track, Donna de Varona in swimming, and Peggy Fleming in figure skating) achieved Olympic fame and commercial success. Tennis stars Billie Jean King and Margaret Court were gaining much public acclaim, as well as relative wealth, for their sports achievements. However, these women were the exception to the rule, as there were few opportunities for women at all levels of sports (high school, college and professional). The women's movement of the 1960s that fought so hard for the equality of women in many spheres of social life all but ignored the sports world. But the women's movement did advocate a sexual revolution and launched an all-out attack on the traditional mores and norms that placed restraints on physical freedom and the enjoyment of bodily pleasures (Rader 2004). In the 1970s, the women's movement would find a "playing field"—sports— to test gender equality judicially. "With women's rapid postwar movement into the labor force and revived feminist movement, what had been an easily ignorable undercurrent of female athleticism from the 1930s through the 1960s suddenly swelled into a torrent of female sport participation—and demands for equity" (Messner 2001: 274). In short, women were becoming organized and were fighting the system via the system.

A large number of collegian women's sports organizations that existed prior to the 1970s became unified in 1971 under the direction of the Association for Intercollegiate Athletics for Women (AIAW). "The AIAW hoped to bring about more intense and higher level competition while avoiding the abuses threatening men's college athletics. The AIAW placed strong restrictions on recruiting and took other steps to avoid cheating on transcripts and recruiting, exploitation of students and too much emphasis on commercialism. The AIAW's hope [was] for a separate but equal and purer existence than the governing body of male college athletics" (Beezley and Hobbs 1989: 339). Among other things, the AIAW attempted to provide women with an opportunity to strive for excellence in sport; create new programs for women; and create local, state, regional, and national competitions. It emphasized educational achievement as well as academic and worked to secure the rights of female athletes who leave school to still be qualified for an Olympic bid (Morrison 1993). The AIAW stressed the importance of being a student first and athlete second. They instilled a set of rules and regulations to assure that female athletes maintained their grades for eligibility. The AIAW also fought for the rights of female athletes. With the passage of Title IX in 1972, it promoted the idea that women's intercollegiate sports were to be viewed as the same as men's intercollegiate sports. In this regard, the AIAW represents one of the early major social institutions fighting for gender equity in sport and education. After spearheading a new ideal of women athletics that encouraged millions of young women to participate in sports, the AIAW dissolved in 1982. The direction and supervision of women's athletics then came under the jurisdiction of the NCAA. "The AIAW left a heritage and a legacy of women leaders who examined, created, controlled, and supported a critical decade of intercollegiate athletics. That decade was a period of great accomplishment for women and for women's athletics" (Morrison 1993: 65).

The number of women in sports grew slowly throughout the 1970s. Women met a general resistance from the masses who still thought that sports were for boys and men; from male athletes who wanted to dominate a domain they considered their own; and the NCAA, which fought the inevitable growth of women's participation in sport. Women won this battle, of course, as they participate in sports at greater rates today than ever before in history.

The most momentous single event to affect women's participation in sport occurred with the passage of Title IX of the Educational Amendments Act of 1972. (This topic will be discussed in detail later in this chapter.) Women did not experience immediate benefits from Title IX; they would come later. There would be other factors that contributed to the growth of female participation in sports beyond Title IX.

Factors That Led to Increased Women's Participation in Sports

Female sport participants today owe a great deal to the general women's rights movement of the 1960s and the women's right to play sports movement that began in earnest in the 1970s. Every social movement needs trailblazers. We already discussed the role that Kathrine Switzer had in opening the Boston Marathon to women, but long distance running only seldom reaches the consciousness of most people, let alone sports enthusiasts. In the 1970s, baseball was still "America's sport" and yet the highly popular Little League Baseball was limited to boys. It was important then, for a trailblazer to emerge in baseball, and this pioneer would be Maria Pepe of Hoboken, New Jersey. In the summer of 1972, Pepe, then 12 years old, shattered the gender barrier in Little League Baseball. Pepe, who had a deep passion and desire to play baseball coupled with a mean fastball, tried out for the local Little League Baseball team. She made the team and played in three games. The governing body of Little League ruled her ineligible—because girls were not allowed to play—and threatened to strip the Hoboken Young Democrats team's status as a member of the Little League Association because it had allowed a girl on the team. After her coach informed Pepe of the news, with a heavy heart she turned in her uniform. Her plight made national attention. The National Organization for Women (NOW) worked with Pepe's family in an attempt to get her reinstated. Two years later, the New Jersey Superior Court ruled that girls must be allowed to play Little League Baseball. For Pepe, it was too late, as she no longer made the age requirement. In 1984, Victoria Roche, a 12 year old from Brussels, Belgium, became the first girl to play in the Little League World Series. While there have not been many girls to reach the LLWS (just 19 as of 2019), approximately 5 million girls have played Little League Baseball and Softball.

Billie Jean King was a major trailblazer in the fight for gender equity in sport. King was a brilliant tennis player who fought to end sexism in sport; especially the gender inequalities in pay (until the 1970s, women generally received about 10 percent of the amount of prize money available to men). King was able to convince other leading female tennis players to start their own women's circuit and formed the Women's Tennis Association. The feminist movement joined forces with King and helped to secure financial backing from the Philip Morris Tobacco Company, which promoted its Virginia Slims brand of cigarettes by sponsoring the WTA Tour (Rader 2004). A television contract further increased the prize money for women.

Beyond serving as an advocate for gender equity in salary (something that has not occurred yet), King was a feminist and an ostentatious tennis player who drew a great deal of attention on and off court during the changing cultural era of the 1970s. King made quite a stir when she told reporters that she did not want to have children and instead wanted to pursue her tennis professional career full time. Her attitude challenged the dying patriarchal order of American society. A far more flamboyant Bobby Riggs (a former triple-crown winner at Wimbledon in 1939) represented the voice of the "old school" patriarchal regime. In 1973, Riggs, who was 55 years old, challenged King, who was 29 years old and at the peak of her career, to a tennis match. Riggs (a famous braggart known as "the Mouth that Roared") was confident that because he was a man, not even a player as great as King could beat him. King refused to play Riggs, citing that she had nothing to gain by it.

Margaret Court, another leading women's tennis player, however, agreed to play Riggs on Mother's Day 1973. Riggs won in straight sets. King then changed her mind and decided to play Riggs in a tennis match to be broadcast on live television from the Houston Astrodome in September 1973. Millions of viewers, including both of these authors, remember viewing this spectacle when it first aired. Riggs entered the arena in typical chauvinist flair accompanied by scantily dressed women and teased and taunted King before the match. It was King, however, who had the last laugh, as she easily defeated the outmatched Riggs. This "Battle of the Sexes" (as it was billed) was mostly show, but it generated huge interest and debate among Americans, Canadians, and sports enthusiasts around the globe. A great number of women began to believe that girls and women should have the same rights as males to play sports. They were also ready to challenge any male who stood in their way.

Jay (2004) explains that the "Battle of the Sexes" showed that tennis could attract a mass audience. Furthermore, it "brought tennis out of the country club and into the mainstream. Combined with a new crop of dominant American players, the much-publicized match helped to make tennis one of the most watched sports of the 1970s and early 1980s" (171). Many stars emerged during this era, including Chris Evert and Martina Navratilova on the women's circuit and Arthur Ashe, Jimmy Connors, and Bjorn Borg on the men's circuit.

Throughout the 1970s a number of new opportunities presented themselves as many girls and women's sports programs were created in high schools and colleges. The desire of many girls to play sports coupled with an increasingly powerful feminist movement was responsible for a great deal of the growth in women's participation in sports. The numbers of girls participating in high school sports, funding, visibility, acceptance and popularity increased dramatically in the 1980s (35 percent of high school athletes were female) compared to the 1970s (7 percent) (Leonard 1988). The average number of sports programs offered per college for women grew from 5.61 in 1978 to 7.31 in 1988 (*Chronicle of Higher Education* 1988). The 1984 Los Angeles Olympics witnessed twice as many female athletes—about 2500—than any other previous Games (Leonard 1988). However, this number still represented just 23 percent of the total Olympic athletes in 1984 (Figler and Whitaker 1995).

Women's participation in sports would continue to grow throughout the 1990s; by this time there was a general consensus in Western societies that females should have equal opportunity to pursue sporting activities. The growth in sport participation was fueled by a health and fitness movement that encouraged women to work out. The development of physical strength and sports competence was now encouraged, rather than discouraged, for women. Many people believe that the greatest sports moment in U.S. women's sports history was the 1999 World Cup victory. The U.S. team played before sold-out stadiums every match and was viewed by millions across the globe on television. More than 90,000 fans packed the Rose Bowl to witness the championship match. The World Cup victory made celebrities of many team members, including Mia Hamm and Brandi Chastain, and turned the athletes into heroes for a countless number of young girls.

The emergence of Venus and Serena Williams in the mid–1990s represents another marker of social change (Jay 2004). Fans, sportswriters and critics commented on their every move. The Williams sisters served as a "commentary on race relations and gender norms, and the symbolism of being powerful black women in a nearly all white game" (Jay 2004: 238). Today, the sisters are world renowned tennis superstars who possess a combination of speed, strength, and charisma, along with a fashion sense designed to be marketed. As L. Jon Wertheim notes in his book *Venus Envy*: "In the year 2000, Venus wouldn't just surpass her little sister; she would establish herself as the dominant player in women's tennis. In addition to claiming the U.S. Open and Wimbledon titles, she would run off a thirty-five-match winning streak and win gold medals in both singles and doubles at the 2000 Summer Olympics. To top off what had already been a pretty good year, she signed a $40 million endorsement deal with Reebok that made her the richest female athlete in history" (Wertheim 2002: 3). By 2020, the Williams sisters, and in particular Serena, were still among the elite women's tennis players in the world.

Women have come a long way since their humble sport participation beginnings. Girls playing youth sports are now routine; millions of girls are playing high school sports just as there are millions of women playing collegiate sports; and, there are many professional women's sports leagues. Females today, like their male counterparts, take for granted that there will be plenty of opportunities to play sports and that they will meet little, if any at all, resistance in their desire to play sports.

Obstacles to Continued Growth in Women's Sports

While girls and women do not face the same level of resistance in their quest to play sports as females did 50 years ago, there are a number of potential obstacles that may interfere with the continued growth of women's sports participation. For example, there is a lack of women in power positions; economic concerns, including budget cuts; and a lingering holdover from days gone by, aesthetic idealism.

LACK OF WOMEN IN POWER POSITIONS

As the conflict perspective articulates, those in power will attempt to keep it—it is in their best interest to do so—while those without power will attempt to change the status quo. It should come as no surprise that there are many men and a few women who are still resistant to the trend of an increasing number of women in sports (including athletes, coaches and administrators, as well as people in peripheral positions in the sports world). It has been 50 years since the passage of Title IX (to be discussed later in this chapter), the legislation that helped to change the gender landscape of sports forever, and while there are large numbers of females playing high school and college sports, the power positions are still mostly held by men. A primary reason for this is that Title IX does not apply to the hiring of coaches and administrators. Instead, colleges must show that male and female athletes are provided equitably qualified coaches and that men's and women's teams are provided equitable administrative support.

In 1972, the year Title IX became law, over 90 percent of women's teams and programs were coached by women (Van Keuren 1992; Brennan 2013). The influx of money and the creation of many more coaching opportunities following Title IX led to a corresponding increased interest among male coaches to seek coaching positions in women's sports. In 2019, about 40 percent of women's college teams were coached by women; in contrast, only about 3 percent of men's college teams were coached by women (Hutchins, Curry, and Flaherty 2019). When it comes to sports administration, 89 percent of Division I athletic directors are men (Hutchins, Curry, and Flaherty 2019). When women are not given equal opportunities to serve as leaders—coaches and athletic directors—female athletes have less of an opportunity to look up to a female role model in their preferred domain of athletics. In turn, this is not conducive to the further growth of women in sports' power positions.

BUDGET CUTS

School sports programs always seem to face budgetary cuts and this is true at all levels of education. In a 2018 Public Schools Review report, it was emphasized that budgets have become so constrained that several school districts have drastically slashed or entirely cut their athletics program (Chen 2018). Throughout the lifetimes of the authors, dating back to their own respective school days, school districts have always seemed to complain that there is not enough money to fund athletics (and the arts). Trying to pass school budgets that involve any sort of increase comes under great scrutiny by property owners who feel the brunt of proposed annual budget increases. When this occurs, tough decisions have to be made. "For some schools, the cuts may come in the athletics departments, with a number of districts threatening to significantly decrease the athletic programs available to students or to do away with sports altogether. While this is not a choice most schools want to make, what other options do they have when money simply isn't there?" (Chen 2018). Consider for example, in the state of Pennsylvania, Governor Tom Corbett (R) announced a cut of more than $1 billion to public education—$550 million in cuts to public schools, and $625 million cut from the budgets of state universities (Chen

2018). Sports programs are deemed the "easier" option of where to make the cuts; after all, there have to be teachers, staff, and maintenance of the school facilities. Pennsylvania is hardly alone and many states face economic shortfalls. As it pertains to our primary topic of concern there, budget cuts can certainly represent an obstacle to continued growth in both girls' and boys' sports programs.

Colleges and universities face budgetary concerns as well, especially at the Junior College, D-II, and D-III levels as few sports programs actually generate the revenue to operate. Even at the D-I level, it is generally football and men's basketball that generate revenue. Furthermore, nearly all other sports, especially women's sports, are dependent upon this revenue to fund their own programs. (And thus another issue complicating the desires of college athletes wanting to be paid a salary, see Chapter 7.) At "big-time" colleges it has long been known that football and men's basketball programs are the two sports that are the most likely to generate large sums of money (they also spend a lot of money on themselves, such as significantly higher coaches' salaries, travel, and equipment) and thus it is important—even in a world where trying to reach gender equity is a huge concern—that they survive and thrive. However, the COVID-19 pandemic sidelined many revenue generating sports in 2020 and that caused a ripple effect of colleges dropping athletic programs due to financial shortfalls. Consider for example, that Stanford dropped 11 sports (men's and women's) amid financial difficulties caused by the coronavirus pandemic. Florida State announced a cut in 20 percent of its athletics department budget for the same reason. Other schools to drop sports programs include: Florida International (dissolved men's indoor track and field); Akron (eliminated three sports— men's cross country, men's gold, and women's tennis); Bowling Green (shutdown baseball); Furman (cut baseball and men's lacrosse); East Carolina (eliminated four sports, men's and women's swimming and diving and men's and women's tennis); and, Appalachian State (cut men's soccer, men's tennis and men's indoor track and field) (Beard 2020).

The elimination of programs represents a clear obstacle to continued growth in women's sports (and men's sports, for that matter).

AESTHETIC IDEALISM

We referenced Eitzen (2015) earlier in this chapter as he pointed out the cultural expectations of what it means to be masculine or feminine and how such expectations often clashed with the primary aggressive traits of sports. This led to a tradition of steering girls toward socially acceptable athletic pursuits. So-called acceptable sports, according to Eitzen (2015), had to possess "three characteristics: (1) they were aesthetically pleasing (e.g., ice skating, diving, and gymnastics); (2) they did not involve bodily contact with opponents (e.g., bowling, archery, badminton, volleyball, tennis, gold, swimming, and running); and (3) the action was controlled to protect athletes from overexertion (e.g., running short races, basketball where the offense and defense did not cross half-court)" (p. 239). Things seem to have changed quite a bit; after all, women have proven that they can compete in all sorts of sports, including the combat sports of boxing and MMA.

And yet, the myth that sport masculinizes females persists in many cultural circles. The long-held, traditional conservative perspective found in most societies, including the United States, that women who play sports will be viewed as or become "manly" scared away many females from playing sports (Knoppers and McDonald 2010). As Eitzen and Sage (2013) explain, "For years, women of physical competence were stigmatized as 'masculine' by claims that women who engaged in physical activities were not 'feminine.' This was like a doomsday weapon to discourse female interest and involvement in sport" (p. 321). It is not true that women participating in sport become biologically more like a male; so such a notion of sports masculinizing women reflects a culture's view on femininity. The notion of a masculinized female athlete is further stigmatized by a myth that simply playing a sport designated as masculine would make girls and women androgynous or gay.

While many in society are completely accepting of women participating in physically assertive sports there are others, including many of the athletes themselves, who are consciously aware of the perceived stigma of being labeled masculine. For example, in softball, the helmets worn by the athletes usually have a circular opening (a hole) cut in the back of the helmet so that girls' and women's ponytails can be viewed and not forced-tucked inside. This is done because cultural norms generally associate long hair with femininity and short hair with masculinity (although certainly not everyone accepts such genderized notions).

As a result of the concern for aesthetic idealism, females who play sports have traditional tried to be viewed as both athletic and attractive (feminine). They want to be taken seriously as athletes, and yet because of increased public exposure and an increasing number of marketing opportunities, female athletes also attempted to be femininely attractive. The advantage to being sexually attractive is directly connected to the long-held marketing notion put forth by advertisers that "sex sells." Thus, if women want to achieve financial riches, they have to promote themselves outside of sport in a sexual manner. And, if the adage that "sex sells" is correct, these women will have to possess aesthetic idealism—looking attractive and feminine. The aesthetic idealism notion that has predominated marketing leads to female athletes being known more for their bodies and sex appeal rather than their athletic skills. "By portraying sports women either as sex objects or as 'pretty girls,' the message sent to society is that sports women are not strong, powerful and highly skilled individuals" (Rawjee et al. 2011).

However, by the 2020s it had become quite clear that the antiquated adage of "sex sells" was quickly becoming a thing of the past as many social institutions were no longer adhering to it. The International Olympic Committee, which does not govern such things as the uniforms that athletes wear but does run the Olympic Broadcasting Services, made clear that the mantra of broadcasting the 2020 Tokyo Olympics (held in July 2021) would focus on "Sport appeal, not sex appeal," meaning that there would be no close-up camera shots on parts of the body (e.g., women's bottoms during beach volleyball, gymnastics, swimming and track). The athletes themselves were also taking a stand. For example, the Norwegian women's beach handball team refused to play in bikini bottoms during their bronze-medal match at the European Beach Handball Championship in July 2021. (Note: The Norwegian women were fined for not wearing the "proper" uniform but the traditional media and social media backlash was very much in favor of the athletes.) Days later, Germany's women's gymnasts wore full-body unitards during the 2020 Tokyo Olympics as a protest against the "sexualization" of the sport—a dramatic deviation from the sport's standard uniform of bikini-cut leotards. A focus on aesthetic idealism and "sex sells" had not completely disappeared but its tolerance was quickly dissipating.

CHEERLEADING: AESTHETIC IDEALISM OR SPORT?

When you think of cheerleading and cheerleaders do you think of girls and young women conforming to an aesthetically pleasing mode of appearance? Or, do you think of highly trained, competitive athletes? Either scenario may be correct. The first cheer-leaders were males at Princeton University who formed an all-male pep club. A graduate of Princeton, Thomas Peebles, took the Princeton cheers to the University of Minnesota, where football and fight songs were becoming very popular. In 1923, women were first allowed to be cheerleaders at University of Minnesota football games (Varsity.com 2014). By the 1960s, cheerleading could be found in nearly every grade school, high school, and college across the United States. Cheerleaders were viewed as promoters of their schools and communities and instilling "school spirit" (Varsity.com 2014).

Many folks outside of cheerleading do not view this activity as a sporting venture; in fact, they see it as a type of aesthetically pleasing activity wherein females conform to patriarchal notions of femininity. Female cheerleaders generally wear short skirts and often tight tops with the name of the school, or some other school insignia, embedded into the clothing. Cheerleaders encourage their teams during sports games via chant-ing clever, but simple, verses of support while jumping and clapping in rhythm with one another. It is unlikely that their support and attempts to get the crowd involved have any actual impact on the outcome of the game. And yet, there they are, sun, rain, or snow, cheering the team on. This type of cheerleading is seldom viewed as a sport and may, at best, be viewed as a sporting activity.

There is, however, a second type of cheerleading that is very much like a sport, com-petitive cheerleading. "Competitive cheerleading is when cheer squads compete against each other at a competition. At typical cheerleading competition, teams perform a 2 and half minute routine with music that includes stunts, jumps, tumbling" (Varsity.com 2018). Competitive cheerleading involves a great deal of strenuous practice time, and the use of athletic skills. It does not involve girls and young women standing on the sidelines and cheering for (generally) male athletes. The sport is taken so seriously that these female and male cheerleaders have club teams (like hockey) not affiliated with their schools. Competitive cheerleading still involves a degree of aesthetic idealism but it also meets the criteria of our definition of sport (see Chapter 1).

An additional aspect of competitive cheerleading is its relevance to Title IX discus-sions, as a designation of competitive cheerleading as a sport would allow the numbers of cheerleaders on scholarship to count toward participation compliance (proportion-ality). "In recent years, state legislatures, state departments of education and state ath-letic/activity associations have enacted statues and regulations decreeing competitive cheerleading to be an 'officially recognized' sport and imposing obligations on schools with regard to competitive programs" (Green 2019). The passage of such laws and rules has been done primarily for the purpose of ensuring that the same safety standards are in place for competitive cheer as is the case for all other interscholastic sports (Green 2019).

Sexism

Sexism is another obstacle confronting women in their attempt to reach equity in sport. *Sexism* is defined as behavior, conditions, or attitudes that foster stereotypical social roles based on sex and lead to discrimination against members of one sex due to preferential treatment aimed to assist members of the other sex. Sexism leads to inequal-ity. Historically, women have been victims of sexism far more often than men, but both men and women may be victimized by sexism. There are three primary forms of sexism, interpersonal, ideological, and institutional. *Interpersonal sexism*, or individual sexism, is the discriminatory, prejudicial, and stereotypical form of sexism that directly occurs between people wherein a person of one sex treats a person of the opposite sex in a pre-conceived notion of what constitutes gender-appropriateness based on gender roles. For example, when a boy yells at a girl that she is too weak to play football and suggests that she try out for cheerleading instead. *Ideological sexism* is the belief that one sex is inferior to another and stresses gender-appropriateness based on gender roles. Ideological sexism in sport has long prevailed and is exemplified by men who consider women too weak to play sports. An example of ideological sexism is provided by the remarks of Formula One head Bernie Ecclestone, who told reporters before the 2005 U.S. Grand Prix that "women should be all dressed in white like all the other domestic appliances" (Cannella 2005). The 74-year-old Englishman's comments were directed toward race car driver Danica Patrick. A year earlier Ecclestone told a female writer that not only were women like appliances, but also "they shouldn't be allowed out. You don't take the washing machine out of the house, do you?" (Cannella 2005). *Institutional sexism*, on the other hand, refers to sys-tematic practices and patterns within social institutions that lead to inequality between men and women. The lack of women in power positions in sport could be seen as a form of institutional sexism. Equal opportunity in sport for women and men will occur only when discrimination and sexism is removed from that social institution and society in general.

A surfer stretches before heading out to tackle waves at the North Shore in Oahu, Hawaii.

Sexual Harassment and #MeToo

Sexual harassment is a byproduct of sexist attitudes. Sexual harassment is a violation of U.S. law. *Sexual harassment* is defined as the making of unwanted and offensive sexual advances, sexually offensive remarks or acts, unsolicited verbal comments, gestures, or physical contact of a sexual nature, especially by a superior or a person in a supervisory position. As a once all-male domain, the world of sport is often an environment wherein sexual harassment may be found. In some instances, sexual harassment occurs between coaches and athletes. The coach has an advantageous position of power over the athlete. At times, the coach may use his or her position to force an athlete to have sex in return for favors such as increased playing time, or a starting position (at the expense of another athlete). Sexual relationships between coaches and athletes are generally discouraged and in many cases may be explicitly forbidden in athletic handbooks. Sexual harassment may also occur when a woman plays sports on a men's team.

The seriousness of the nature of sexual harassment led to the "#MeToo" social movement. The "#MeToo" movement focuses on the experiences of sexual violence survivors; it has earned a large response because sexual harassment and sexual assault impact people every day (Maryville University 2020). "The hope is that, if people are more aware of sexual harassment and how casually it is sometimes treated, then tolerance for it will decrease and support for victims will rise" (Maryville University 2020). It was actor Alyssa Milano's online call to activism (after the Harvey Weinstein sexual harassment revelations became a part of public discourse) wherein she asked the public to call out men who sexually harassed and assaulted women that spirited the movement. Milano, and others, called on all women who are victims of sexual harassment to share their stories on public platforms and use the hashtag #MeToo (Khomami 2017). While the social movement of "#MeToo" is relatively new, the ideas behind it have been a part of the consciousness of sociologists for centuries. The role of patriarchy, the low number of women in power positions, sexual myths regarding women, sexism, sexual harassment, and so forth, have long been the study and concern of sociology.

Equitable Pay

The most recognizable U.S. women's sports team is the national soccer team. The women have earned a great deal of respect throughout the international community. As described in Chapter 4, the U.S. Women's team has won half of the eight World Cups and was a runner-up in another. We also noted that the Men's World Cup draws a global audience roughly 3.5 times the size of the women's WC. Nonetheless, the U.S. women's team has been fighting for years for equitable pay. In March 2019, the American players filed a federal discrimination lawsuit in U.S. District Court in Los Angeles under the Equal Pay Act and Title VII of the Civil Rights Act against the U.S. Soccer Federation over unequal treatment and pay. The players alleged that they are victims of institutional gender discrimination that includes unequal pay. The lawsuit seeks class-action status. Despite public sentiment supporting the women and clearly a greater level of success on the pitch compared with the U.S. Men's team, the players faced a tough challenge in that the two U.S. national teams have separate collective bargaining agreements, and their pay is structured differently. Nonetheless, following their dominant 2019 WC title, the women held hope. The scene of the U.S. players dancing on the pitch and joining the throngs of spectators chanted loudly, "Equal pay! Equal pay!" was inspirational (*Associated Press* 2019d).

Using a very unusual and reactionary-throw-back justification as to why the U.S. Women should not win their equity pay case, lawyers for U.S. Soccer argued that "indisputable science" proved that women players were inferior to men and that playing for the men's team required a "higher level of skill" and "more responsibility" than playing for the women's team (Baxter 2020: D6). (Note: This reinforces what we wrote earlier about myths and patriarchy's role in sports, even though readers may have likely found it hard to believe that such beliefs could still be held in the 2020s.) Federation board members expressed outrage over the wording used in the legal fillings and U.S. Soccer president Carlos Cordeiro resigned because of it. In May 2020, a federal judge threw out the unequal pay claim but left intact the Civil Rights Act claims (Peterson and Blum 2020b). At the time of this writing, the players indicated that they planned to ask the 9th U.S. Circuit Court of Appeals to overturn the District Court's decision, meaning that this case may not be finalized until 2021 or later.

Another high-profile professional women's sport is tennis. Research indicates that more than 70 percent of men in the world's top 200 have earned more than their female counterparts in 2018 with prize money only equal at the majors (Levitt 2014). The U.S. Open is one such major that awards men and women equal prize money and this equity in pay is the result of Billie Jean King who threatened to boycott the U.S. Open in 1973 if men and women did not receive equal pay for their U.S. Open wins (Connley 2019).

In professional basketball, WNBA players realize that they cannot expect to earn the same enormous salaries as their NBA-male counterparts as the WNBA generates roughly $25 million annually from its TV deal with ESPN whereas the NBA's TV revenue from ESPN and TNT is 100 times that (Abrams 2019). However, men share in half of the revenue the league generates while women in the WNBA only earn 20–25 percent of the league's revenue. However, during the 2020 season—which was interrupted by the COVID pandemic—the players and league reached a tentative eight-year labor deal that would result in a 50–50 split of revenue and opportunities for the league's elite payers to earn far more money than they are currently (*Associated Press* 2020a).

LGBTQ+ AND SPORTS

Stephen Maddison (2000) explains that the rhetoric and ideology of the women's movements of the 1960s and 1970s assisted the gay liberation movement that followed. The attention that these second wave feminists brought to gay and lesbian issues led to a specialized subfield of sociology concerned with lesbian, gay, bisexual, and transgender (LGBT) persons. Since the early stages of the LGBT movement "Q" for "queer" and "+" for other categories of sexual identification have been added leading to today's ubiquitous acronym of LGBTQ+.

Many LGBT persons face prejudice and discrimination in society. Although it is a crime to discriminate against any person, U.S. law has designated a special crime status of "hate crime" (also known as a bias crime) whenever the victim identifies as LGBTQ+ and the offense committed was done because of the victim's sexual identity. LGBTQ+ persons often run the risk of being targeted by intolerant people in society in general and in sports in particular. As we have described in this chapter (as well as others), sports have historically been the exclusive domain for males who express the contemporary socially-accepted masculine characteristics. Just as female athletes have been expected to conform to socially-approved gender roles so too have LGBTQ+ athletes. Some try to keep their sexual lives private but others are more open.

Let's revisit the issues of sexuality that have confronted women in past centuries. In the 1800s, women were considered too frail to play sports. After women proved they could play sports, there were concerns that female athletes would become too masculine or engage in lesbianism. During the mid–1900s leaders of women's sports became aware of criticisms that female athletes were labeled as lesbians and "failed heterosexuals" (Cahn 1994). This was based on assumed associations between mannishness and lesbians and between masculinity and sport. Based on these assumptions, critics of women's sport now claimed that women athletes were "mannish lesbians who were unattractive to men" (Griffin 1998: 35). During the 1970s, the feminist movement had become quite strong. Lesbians no longer felt the need to hide their sexual preference. "The emerging gay and lesbian rights movement changed coming out from a personal declaration to a political statement and sparked the proliferation of a more visible and proud lesbian and gay subculture" (Griffin 1998: 41).

During the Reagan era (1980s) the U.S. became more conservative and lesbian athletes especially felt more compelled to keep their sexuality secret. In 1981, Billie Jean King held a press conference to reveal that a former lesbian lover was suing her for palimony. Most women on the professional tour knew King was a lesbian but kept it a secret, fearing loss of sponsorships. This reality affirms the perspective of that era that female athletes were accepted by society as long as they were heterosexual and that it was financially ruinous for lesbian professional athletes to publicly identify themselves (Griffin 1998). Martina Navratilova, another dominant female tennis player, was "outed" in an article in the *New York Post*. The public was not too surprised by this. The Women's Tennis Association, fearing loss of sponsorships, warned other players they would not tolerate another player coming out (Zwerman 1995). A general acceptance of lesbian athletes in sports like tennis and golf existed throughout the 1990s. This period of liberalism has been replaced by a focus on aesthetic beauty and athleticism in the 2000s. A new generation of professional tennis players and golfers has embraced femininity and has reaped the financial awards for doing so.

It has long been taboo for male athletes to "come out" as well due to the threat of loss potential corporate sponsorships, the desire of sports clubs to retain their masculine image, and the likelihood that teammates will not accept them as peers. Although there is a growing acceptance of gay men in most Western societies, male athletes work in an environment that is still dominated by machismo.

In an attempt to help LGBTQ+ athletes the NCAA has instituted inclusion initiatives that read in part: "As a core value, the NCAA believes in and is committed to diversity, inclusion and gender equity among its student-athletes, coaches, and administrators. We seek to establish and maintain an inclusive culture that fosters equitable participation for student-athletes and career opportunities for coaches and administrators from diverse backgrounds" (NCAA 2020d). The NCAA and other collegiate leagues, along with member schools, have a number of organizational resources designed to support LGBTQ+ athletes, coaches, and others involved in collegiate sports. When it comes to a transgender student athlete being allowed to participate in any sports activity the athlete's use of hormone therapy, if any, must be consistent with NCAA existing policies on banned medications (Mosier 2020).

There is some confusion among school officials and international governing bodies as how to define sexes for transgender athletes and whether or not to allow them to compete competitively in athletics as their new sexual identity. Jamey Harrison, the deputy director of the governing body of high school sports in Texas, for example, does not believe that anyone has it exactly right because if they did, everyone else would just do that. To Harrison's point, "established guidelines at the youth level that address things like hormonal treatment and sex reassignment surgery are nonexistent" (Andrews 2017). The issue first emerged in Texas in 2012, according to Harrison. Texas had rules that required female athletes to compete on girls' teams and males on boys' teams, but no rule that addressed how to decide someone's sex. Transgender students—those who identify as a different gender than their biological sex—did not fit into an existing category (Andrews 2017). Students that were transitioning were of a particular concern with regard to sport participation. "With no national governing body laying down rules, individual states have navigated the issue independently, weighing the shifting beliefs of schools, parents and athletes" (Andrews 2017). In 2019, two transgender high school sprinters in Connecticut who were transitioning to female sparked huge debates (mostly among adults) as to the fairness of their being allowed to compete as female on the girls' teams where they dominated the competition (*Associated Press* 2019e). Expressing a familiar argument in a complex debate for transgender athletes as they break barriers across sports around the world from high school to the pros, critics say that males that transition to female and compete as females have an unfair advantage (*Associated Press* 2019e). As of 2019, Connecticut is one of 17 states that allow transgender high school athletes to compete without restrictions; seven states have restrictions that make it difficult for transgender athletes to compete while in school (e.g., they must compete under the gender on their birth certificate or are allowed to participate only after going through sex-reassignment procedures or hormone therapies) (*Associated Press* 2019e).

Chris Mosier, a source previously cited above, is the first known transgender man to represent the United States in international competition (in 2015) in the gender they identify with and is a catalyst for change for the International Olympic Committee policy on transgender athletes. The policy, in part, states, "To require surgical anatomical changes as a pre-condition to participation is not necessary to preserve fair competition and may be inconsistent with developing legislation and notions of human rights" (Scott 2016). Other aspects of the IOC policy include: Trans male athletes face no restrictions but trans females must have testosterone levels below a certain point for at least a year before competing, and they must remain below that level throughout the eligibility period in order to compete (Scott 2016). Concern over testosterone or other androgens, commonly used to assist transition from female to male is what led to USA Powerlifting banning transgender athletes (Robert 2019). Posted as its "Transgender Participation Policy" (2019): "USA Powerlifting is not for every athlete and for every medical condition or situation. Simply, not all powerlifters are eligible to compete in USA Powerlifting" (Robert 2019).

The concern over levels of testosterone has been around for decades, as taking performance-enhancing drugs raises the level of the hormone. With the recent development of trans athletes competing in sports the concern was modified over worries that trans women may have a higher level of testosterone than females typically possess. As acknowledged in the IOC policy described above, athletes that transitioned from male to female may possess higher levels of testosterone and thus have an unfair advantage similar to taking PED. Consider the ground-breaking case of South African Caster Semenya, a track star who first gained attention for destroying the competition at the 2009 World Championships. Raised as a girl and having parents that insisted she was a girl, Caster was always a tomboy, quite muscular, and had a deep voice. Competitors at the 2009 World Championships openly questioned her sexuality. Caster was given a medical exam immediately following the competition where it was revealed that Semenya had three times the normal level of testosterone in her body. The International Association of Athletics Federations (IAFF), the governing body for track and field competition, subjected Semenya to "gender verification" to determine her eligibility to compete as a woman. For ten years, Semenya would undergo testing, investigations, rule changes, court decisions, and appeals, all the while mostly being allowed to compete. She won Olympic gold in 2012 and 2016. In May 2019, the Court of Arbitration for Sport turned down her appeal and upheld a new rule that to compete in women's races, runners must have "normal range" levels of testosterone—in other words, lower that Semenya's (Wood 2019).

There is an element of aesthetic idealism involved with Semenya and her legal ordeals that is disguised around "the purported goal of gender verification" as a means to prevent males from posing as females in sporting competition (Wood 2019: A11). Semenya has an unusually masculine body type compared to other women and it may be the case that she "has a disorder of sex development that causes naturally high testosterone levels, at least compared with other women" (Wood 2019: A11).

Issues related to LGBTQ+ athletic competition are relatively new and governing bodies attempting to deliver equitable solutions are fluid.

Title IX

As we mentioned earlier in this chapter, the most significant single event to occur for women in sport was the passage of Title IX of the Education Amendments of 1972 (20 U.S.C., Sect. 1681–1688). Congress enacted Title IX on June 23, 1972. Title IX legislation was the first comprehensive federal statue created to prohibit sex discrimination in education programs that receive federal financial assistance. This includes public elementary, secondary and post-secondary schools and public and private universities. Since nearly every educational institution is a recipient of some type of federal funding, nearly all educational institutions are required to comply with Title IX. Title IX is enforced by the Office for Civil Rights (OCR) of the U.S. Department of Education. This legislation requires educational institutions to maintain policies, practices and programs that do not discriminate against anyone based on sex. Under this law, males and females are to receive equal funding and treatment in all areas of education including athletics. The OCR has the authority to develop policy on the regulations it enforces.

Before Title IX, athletic budgets were overwhelmingly slanted toward male sports. Title IX was designed to eliminate such widespread examples of discrimination in educational settings. The implementation of Title IX meant that men would have to share the better facilities (gymnasium, weight rooms, swimming pool, etc.), the better practice times (women were usually given late night or early morning practice times), and most importantly, financial resources. "The impact of Title IX has been clear and dramatic. In

1972 only one girl in twenty-seven played a sport sponsored by her high school, and colleges spent a total of $100,000 on athletic scholarships for women. By 1996, one girl in three played a sport sponsored by her high school, and colleges spent a total of $180 million on athletic scholarships for women. The participation of women in college sports increased fourfold between 1970 and 1999, from 31,000 to 110,000" (Porto 2003: 13–14). Through the first decade of the 2000s, women's participation rates in college sports continued to increase. According to the NCAA (2011), there were 191,131 women competing in Division I, D-II and D-III overall in the 2010–11 year. This figure represents a fivefold increase since 1972 (Brown 2009). In the 2017–18 academic year, nearly half a million students (494,992) competed on nearly 20,000 (19,745) teams (Schwarb 2018). Of these totals, 216,378 student-athletes were female and 278,614 were male; whereas 54 percent (10,662) of the NCAA teams were female, compared with 46 percent (9,083) that were male (Schwarb 2018). The percentage of men's teams compared to women's teams is closest to a gender balance at D-1 with 53 percent of all teams are men's and 47 percent women's; and at D-II and D-III, they are both at 58 percent men's teams compared with 42 percent women's teams (Schwarb 2018).

TITLE IX AND COMPLIANCE

Any school in violation of Title IX can be penalized for non-compliance; such penalties usually result in the loss of federal funds. Although most schools are not in compliance with Title IX, no institution has lost money for violating Title IX. Many schools have, however, paid substantial damages and attorney fees because of lawsuits brought to court. There are three basic aspects of Title IX that apply to athletics: participation and accommodation (offering sports programs), athletic financial assistance (scholarships), and "other" athletic program areas.

1. *Participation and Accommodation.* To comply with Title IX institutions must show one of three things: proportionate (to the enrollment of the institution) athletic opportunities for male and female athletes; or demonstrate a history and continuing practice of expanding opportunities for the under-represented sex; or the provision of sports of interest to the under-representative sex. Title IX does not require institutions to offer identical sports programs but, instead, an equal opportunity to play. Thus, if a woman wanted to play football at Stanford, the university would not have to create another football team to accommodate the athlete's desire, but they would have to allow her to try out for the existing football team.
2. *Athletic Financial Assistance.* The total amount of athletic aid (scholarships) must be proportionate between female and male athletes. This is calculated by simple mathematics. If 53 percent of the participants are men and 47 percent are women, then 53 percent of the scholarship dollars must be awarded to men and 47 percent to women. Title IX does not impose scholarship limits by sport—the NCAA determines this.
3. *Other Athletic Program Areas.* Title IX mandates equal treatment in a number of other athletic program areas (benefits), including coaching, game and practice times, medical and training facilities, publicity, travel per diem, equipment and supplies (especially in regard to equal quality of equipment), locker rooms,

recruitment of student athletes, tutoring opportunities, laundry service, and practice and competitive facilities.

Title IX does not require that men's programs be cut to accommodate women's programs. It is each school's choice whether to cut men's programs in an effort to comply with Title IX or to add women's programs. Due to the decreasing amount of money available to an increasing number of schools, cutting men's sports programs is often viewed as the best fiscal decision. It is also important to note that the law protects men as well as women; consequently, men may charge an institution with violating Title IX.

Reactions to Title IX

The implications of Title IX were clear to all those involved in sports. Many males felt threatened by the passage of Title IX. As Francis (2001) explains, "Despite the phase-in, Title IX was met with resistance from coaches of men's teams, from university athletics directors, and from the National Collegiate Athletic Association.... The NCAA lobbied Congress to exempt athletics from Title IX, and, when this effort failed, brought suit challenging the regulations issues by the Department of Health, Education, and Welfare (HEW) to implement Title IX" (252). The NCAA merely postponed the inevitable enforcement of Title IX. University athletic directors worried that equal funding for women's sports teams would financially cripple the men's programs, especially the revenue producing football and basketball programs, but started the phase-in of women's sports by the end of the decade. By the late 1970s, the typical pattern was for a university to offer roughly equal numbers of men's and women's teams in nonrevenue sports.

In 1982, the AIAW was swallowed by the NCAA. The NCAA started offering national championship games in women's sports—a symbolic victory of equality. National championship games had previously been reserved for men's sports. Since 1988 and the clarification on the program-specific interpretation of Title IX, numerous lawsuits have been brought against university athletics programs, by both male and female athletes. Most of these lawsuits were initiated by athletes who sought to block their schools from dropping specific sport programs. "Female members of varsity teams objected to cutbacks that eliminated the teams in equal numbers for both sexes. Male members protested cutbacks that were imposed unilaterally on men's teams. In several cases, women members of club teams sought to compel their university to upgrade their teams to varsity status, a step that the university was unwilling to take for financial reasons" (Francis 2001: 253).

During the Bill Clinton presidential administration, Title IX took on a new momentum as the Office of Civil Rights laid down a new set of compliance guidelines (Rader 2004). Among the new rules was a stricter interpretation of proportionality—that the total number of varsity male and female athletes be in proportion to the general student body. Since women outnumber men in college (overall), women would now be required to receive a greater number of total scholarships than men. Colleges with football programs were in real potential trouble, as the football team was once allowed to offer 85 scholarships. This number would have to be reduced, but even then, other men's programs were in jeopardy if football continued. When football is taken out of the equation, women receive more athletic scholarships than men. Critics argued that women may not have the same interest level in participating in sport and therefore questioned the legitimacy of proportionality as the criteria for athletic funding. Defenders of proportionality argue that if given a chance, women may wish to participate in sports as much as men presently do.

During the 1980s and 1990s at least 170 men's college wrestling programs were eliminated (Rader 2004). A large number of men's swimming and diving, tennis and gymnastics teams have also been eliminated during this period. Roughly 400 men's college sports teams were dropped in the first 30 years since Title IX was passed (Brady 2002b). Men's programs continue to be eliminated in the 2000s. In 2011, the University of Delaware announced that it was demoting its men's track and cross-country teams to club status; and Delaware was just one of dozens of universities that had recently eliminated "low-profile" men's teams like wrestling, gymnastics and swimming in an effort, the universities say, to comply with Title IX (Thomas 2011). Delaware also announced that it was adding a women's golf team for the Fall 2011 season.

WHY IS TITLE IX APPLIED ONLY TO SPORTS PROGRAMS?

Proponents of Title IX argue that the legislation is still necessary and not unfair to men. They will point to data such as we provided here to indicate the low participation rates of women in collegiate sports prior to the implementation of Title IX on sports. Indeed, the number of women's teams has outnumbered men's teams since 1996–97 and, as we cited earlier, the number of women's teams in the 2017–18 academic year was 10,662 compared with 9,083 men's teams (Schwarb 2018). There are two primary reasons for this: (1) many women's programs have been added and (2) many men's teams have been eliminated because of Title IX.

Armin Brott (2018) states, more than 400 college teams have been eliminated since the implementation of Title IX, mostly men's programs. Consider, for example, that there are only 17 men's gymnastics programs in the country (2020) and if these go away, our Olympic efforts in men's gymnastics will be devastated (Olson 2020). In light of the COVID pandemic, numerous sports programs were dropped from colleges and universities (see earlier discussion on budget cuts). Decisions on which sports to drop usually depend on whether they are revenue generators or non-revenue sports and are they men's programs or women's programs. Pandemic-related cuts have affected men's and women's programs, with more men's than women's teams being cut.

Brott also points out something that few other commentators have managed to bring to the forefront and that is, "Why is Title IX applied only to sports programs?" Brott is correct when he points out that nowhere in the original language of Title IX of the Education Amendments of 1972 does it specifically state that sports programs are the programs and activities to be held up to compliance. What about all the other education programs and activities where females outnumber males? Activities such as the student newspaper or yearbook, student council, music and performing arts, and academic clubs, all statistically have far more females participating in such programs than males. Where is the accountability in these activities he ponders? This is an interesting question that is likely to get shot down by those who defend Title IX and its application to sports and attempts to reach equity.

College women play the Native American sport of lacrosse (courtesy Cardinal Sports Imaging).

Connecting Sports and Popular Culture

Box 10: Three Cheers for Cheerleading

As mentioned previously in the section on "Cheerleading: Aesthetic Idealism or Sport?" there is a double-sided view on this particular endeavor: is it merely an aesthetically-pleasing diversion, or a serious sport involving highly trained, competitive athletes? Popular culture has played a large role in how cheerleading is perceived, going back to the earliest days of sports in America. For, as Mary Ellen Hanson details in her book *Go! Fight! Win!: Cheerleading in American Culture*, it is a pure American phenomenon both in its inception and in its development. She writes: "Cheerleading, an American invention with roots in the institutions of sport and education, has become a staple in American culture. The cheerleader is a nationally recognized symbol invested with positive as well as negative cultural values" (Hanson, 1995: 1).

Over the years, cheerleading, which initially had been an amateur gathering of collegiate male sports fans (including future U.S. Presidents Franklin Roosevelt and George W. Bush, who cheered for their respective Harvard and Yale teams during their years in college), has become a highly structured activity primarily, but not only, involving female participants. Some people view it as wholesome extracurricular activity, while others consider it to be an exploitative form of entertainment. Hanson (1995) explains, "The cheerleader is an icon, an instantly recognized symbol of youthful prestige, wholesome attractiveness, peer leadership, and popularity. Equally recognized is the cheerleader as symbol of mindless enthusiasm, shallow boosterism, objectified sexuality, and promiscuous availability" (p.2). All of these characteristics can easily be seen in popular culture, with two particular stereotypes predominating: cheerleaders as "eye candy" and cheerleaders as "airheads."

In the early 1970s a series of lowbrow and small budget films were released in grindhouse and drive-in movie theaters, with titles like *The Swinging Cheerleaders, Revenge of the Cheerleaders,* and *Cheerleaders' Wild Weekend.* They made a huge profit, and later became staples on the then-new cable television channels HBO, Showtime, and Cinemax, always being shown late at night. As the titles suggest, the films had ridiculous plots involving dumb jocks and promiscuous cheerleaders, with copious nudity thrown in to keep the viewer's attention. In addition, NFL football teams in the 1970s deviated from the previous wholesome image of cheerleaders on the sideline and instead promoted cheerleaders wearing skimpy outfits and yelling sexually suggestive chants. The Dallas Cowgirls were especially prominent and even "inspired" a 1978 X-rated movie called *Debbie Does Dallas.* Hanson writes of the Cowgirls that "their hot pants, midriff revealing tops, and go-go boots outfit came to symbolize the essence of professional cheerleading: glamour, sex appeal, celebrity, and merchandising success" (Hanson, 1995). With such depictions in popular culture, it's not surprising that the image of cheerleading became rather tainted.

In regard to cheerleaders as airheads, recall *Saturday Night Live*'s popular recurring skit in the 1990s called "The Spartan Cheerleaders" about two clueless students at East Lake High School named Arianna (played by Cheri Oteri) and Craig (played by Will Ferrell). After being spurned by the real cheerleading squad, the Spartan Spirits, the two somehow purloined some uniforms. Not being welcome at football games, they began cheering for less popular sports. Arianna and Craig—whose enthusiasm is only rivaled by their awkwardness and cluelessness—arrive at increasingly less appropriate settings to lead their cheers, including a math competition, a bowling game, a ping-pong match, and a chess tournament. Their unbridled goofiness made the Spartan Cheerleaders two of the most famous "SNL" characters, and, while Oteri and Ferrell stopped performing as the Spartans in 1999, their "routines" live on today on countless YouTube sites and webpages, where one can relive their encounters with exasperated students played by such celebrities as Teri Hatcher, Paula Abdul, Jim Carrey, and Jennifer Love Hewitt (as Arianna's nemesis Alexis). In fact, the Spartan Cheerleaders have inspired many high school and college students to emulate them in performing at unlikely sporting events. And why not? Who says that chess tournaments don't deserve cheerleaders? Remember Craig and Arianna's spirited chant: "Well you want a victory/Well that makes you a wisher/Cause one thing that is for sure/You ain't no Bobby Fischer!"

By the 2000s cheerleading started to get more serious representation in popular media. The 2000 film *Bring It On!*, while initially dismissed as fluff by the critics, has since become a cult classic. Starring Kirsten Dunst, Eliza Dushku, and Gabrielle Union as rivals for the national championship, it is in some ways a satire of the cheerleading films of the 1970s. Instead of brainless bimbos, the characters in the film—while engaged in humorous adventures—are sympathetic and genuinely likeable. Written by Jessica Bendinger, the film is a sophisticated and savvy take on competitiveness, and much more feminist-oriented than previous movies on this topic.

As ESPN writer Katie Barnes says of *Bring It On*, "Some see it as just a teen comedy, but it's so much more than that. Widely released on Aug. 25, 2000, the film captures societal and racial tensions that reach far beyond the walls of high school. It is, in many ways, a piece of art that resonates as much today as it did then, especially for me" (Barnes 2020). Like many others, she admits to having watched the movie dozens of times, and still finds the characters' fight for equality and recognition to be inspiring. "What makes *Bring It On* so good isn't the one-liners or the catchy cheers, it's that 20 years later, it's more relevant than ever. The entire film is an exploration of appropriation and the way whiteness works in our culture. It tackles race, gender and sexuality in stunning ways. Somehow within 98 minutes, queer politics gets addressed too. It's a breakneck cultural mirror" (Barnes 2020).While admitting that some of the humor has not aged well, she calls it a "messy film" but adds: "Still, it is a film that I love both for its messiness and for what it strives to be, underneath misguided and dated locker room quips. It is both an artifact and a crystal ball" (Barnes 2020).

As a sign of the film's popularity, one can note the sheer number of sequels it produced, including *Bring It On Again* (2004), *Bring It On: All or Nothing* (2006), *Bring It On: In It to Win It* (2007), *Bring It On: Fight to the Finish* (2009), and *Bring It On: World-wide Cheersmack* (2017), with yet another sequel tentatively scheduled for 2022 in the works. It was even adapted into a Broadway musical version in 2012, with music and lyrics co-written by none other than Lin-Manuel Miranda of *Hamilton* fame. Still, it is the original 2000 movie that remains a fan favorite. Noted film critic Roger Ebert gave a lukewarm review when *Bring It On* originally came out, but nine years later re-evaluated it, calling it "The *Citizen Kane* of cheerleader movies." He added that, unlike so many other films in this particular genre, *Bring It On* "involved genuinely talented cheerleaders" (Ebert 2009).

And speaking of genuinely talented cheerleaders, in early 2020 Netflix broadcast a six-part docuseries entitled *Cheer* which became a surprise hit with fans and critics, generating a great deal of discussion about cheerleading as a legitimate athletic contest. Called "TV's first breakout hit of 2020" by *Rolling Stone* writer Lara Zarum, the series looks at an elite collegiate cheerleading squad, the Navarro Bulldogs from Coriscana, Texas, and their preparation, under the direction of their coach Monica Aldama, for the National Cheerleading Championship in Daytona, Florida. Zarum says, "The Navarro routine is among the most incredible feats of athleticism you'll see. Whiteley and his crew make the stunts look absolutely spellbinding, capturing the tumbling, spinning, and balancing from a wide variety of angles that emphasize the sport's gravity-defying dynamism. When the camera gets right in the middle of the action, the viewer feels like the one who's about to leap into the arms of a team member, or catch one. In some shots, girls vault up from below as if they're weightless, swooping up and into formation on top of their teammates; in others, the routines are slowed down, making the athletes' backbreaking work look as fluid and natural as a flock of birds taking flight" (Zarum 2020). As a mark of just how much of a hit *Cheer* became, it was the subject of a *Saturday Night Live* parody—the ultimate sign of pop culture success!

Back in the 1970s, Miller Brewing Company put out a series of advertisements for its reduced calorie beer, Miller Lite. Often appearing during commercial breaks in televised sporting events (and not coincidentally featuring such sports greats as Joe Frazier, Boog Powell, and Bubba Smith), the ads involved heated debates over just what made Miller Lite so great, with one side yelling "Less Filling!" and the other side yelling "Great Taste!" At the end, both groups would agree that these were not in fact mutually exclusive. Perhaps something similar can be said about the great debate over whether cheerleading is a form of aesthetic entertainment or a genuine competitive sport. As they used to say on *Monday Night Football*: "You make the call."

SUMMARY

Traditionally, women have been denied equal access to sport participation. Much of this had to do with the patriarchal (male dominated) design of most nations around the world throughout history. A patriarchy refers to a social system in which males serve as the primary authority figures. Because sport has traditionally been viewed as a masculine endeavor, females born into a patriarchal system were discouraged from playing sports. Needing some sort of justification to keep females out of sport, patriarchies created a number of myths associated with female sport participation. Many feminists believe that an individual is labeled at birth as a member of a sex category, either male or female, and from that point on is held to acting accordingly; and thus, one *does* gender.

As our discussion on the patriarchal nature of most societies and the negative myths associated with women's participation in sport implies, it is not surprising to realize that, until recent years, women have played a minor role in the history of sport. Changes in cultural attitudes toward women have led to dramatic increases in the number of girls and women playing sports today. Women have come a long way since their humble sport participation beginnings. Girls playing youth sports are now routine; millions of girls are playing high school sports just as there are millions of women playing collegiate sports; and, there are many professional women's sports leagues. Females today, like their male counterparts, take for granted that there will be plenty of opportunities to play sports and that they will meet little, if any at all, resistance in their desire to play sports.

There are still a number of obstacles interfering with the continued growth of women's sports participation, including a lack of women in power positions (e.g., coaching, sports administration), budgetary cutbacks, and a lingering holdover from past days that women should conform to expectations of aesthetic idealism that emphasize femininity and beauty—with the implication that being an athlete is not enough for female athletes. The discussion on aesthetic idealism is connected with cheerleading. There are two types of cheering, the traditional version where cheerleaders stand on the sidelines and cheer for others, and competitive cheerleading which is a sport.

The topic of sexism—behavior, conditions, or attitudes that foster stereotypical social roles based on sex and lead to discrimination against members of one sex due to preferential treatment aimed to assist members of the other sex—was discussed. Sexism leads to inequality. There are three primary forms of sexism: interpersonal, ideological, and institutional. Byproducts of sexism include sexual harassment and unequal pay, with women often receiving less than their male counterparts. Issues related to LGBTQ+ athletic competition are new and governing bodies attempting to deliver equitable solutions are fluid.

The single most momentous event to affect women's participation in sport occurred with the passage of Title IX of the Educational Amendments Act of 1972. In the fifty years since this landmark legislation was passed the number of girls and women playing sports has increased dramatically.

KEY TERMS

Cheerleading There are two types of cheerleading; one entails encouraging their teams during school games via chanting and jumping; the other is competitive cheerleading, a strenuous athletic competitive sport.

Doing Gender The idea that when people conform to cultural expectations based on a sexual category that they are *doing* gender.

Gender This refers to socially determined expectations placed on individuals based of their sexual category. In traditional cultures, males are expected to act masculine, while females are expected to act feminine.

Ideological Sexism The belief that one sex is inferior to another; it stresses gender-appropriateness based on gender roles.

Institutional Sexism Systematic practices and patterns within social institutions that lead to inequality between men and women.

Interpersonal sexism (or individual sexism) The discriminatory, prejudicial, and stereotypical form of sexism that directly occurs between people wherein a person of one sex treats a person of the opposite sex in a preconceived notion of what constitutes gender-appropriateness based on gender roles.

Patriarchy A social system in which males serve as the primary authority figures.

Proportionality In Title IX, the total number of varsity male and female athletes must be equal to the general student body.

Sex This refers to one's biological classification. Males and females differ biologically in regards to their internal and external reproductive organs and genitalia, types and levels of hormones and chromosomal structure (females have an XX and males an XY design).

Sexism Behavior, conditions, or attitudes that foster stereotypical social roles based on sex and lead to discrimination against members of one sex due to preferential treatment aimed to assist members of the other sex.

Sexual Harassment The making of unwanted and offensive sexual advances, sexually offensive remarks or acts, unsolicited verbal comments, gestures, or physical contact of a sexual nature, especially by a superior or a person in a supervisory position.

DISCUSSION QUESTIONS

- What does "doing gender" mean? How do you "*do* gender?"
- What is the difference between "sex" and "gender"? Why might this be significant in the discussion of women in sports?
- What is "gender stratification" and how does it relate to a patriarchal political system?
- What are some of the myths associated with female participation in sports? How did these myths arise, and how might one argue against them?
- What are some of the reasons the issue of female equity in sports became a major issue in the 1970s? How did Title IX try to address these issues, and what are the pros and cons that have arisen in trying to implement this policy in the past 50 years?
- Should the athletes on the U.S. Women's soccer team receive the same pay as their male counterparts?

- What is "aesthetic idealism" and why is it an issue in female sports?
- Do you think that cheerleading is a legitimate sport? Why or why not?
- What sort of obstacles do LGBTQ+ athletes face in sports?
- Why do you suppose that Title IX is applied only to sports programs and not to other scholastic programs such as the student newspaper or yearbook, student council, music and performing arts, and academic clubs?

CHAPTER 11

Race and Ethnicity in Sport

"The times, they are a-changing."

The lyric above is from a song title written by folksinger Bob Dylan and was released as the title track of his 1964 album of the same name. The song became an anthem for the civil rights and anti-war movements of the 1960s and propelled Dylan as a singer of protest songs and a politically charged artist (Kooper 2020). The lyric is quite apropos in 2020 sans an anti-war sentiment. Instead, it is relevant because of the socio-political civil rights social movements that gained great influence during that pandemic year.

Sparked by the death of George Floyd on May 25, 2020, the Black Lives Matter social movement took hold throughout the United States and in many other parts of the world as well. Calls for social justice and police reform spilled over to affect all social institutions, and nearly all spheres of life were influenced one way or another. The NFL said it would allow players to protest during the anthem; NASCAR banned the Confederate flag at its venues; Confederate statues and monuments and those of other racists were being toppled; the NFL's Washington franchise finally agreed to change its racist nickname; the country band "Lady Antebellum" finally dropped the pre–Civil War time period reference of "antebellum" and the Dixie Chicks dropped "Dixie" from their name; food brands such as Aunt Jemima, Uncle Ben's, Cream of Wheat, and Mrs. Butterworth, which perpetuated painful stereotypes, were shelved forever; and, the 32-season strong *Cops* television show was cancelled.

Racism in the United States

The United States has a long history of racism dating back to when the Europeans first started settling in the land that is now known as the United States of America and established an economic system centered on slavery. The first African slaves were brought to the North American colony of Jamestown in 1619, to aid in the production of such lucrative crops as tobacco and cotton. Throughout the seventeenth and eighteenth centuries people were kidnapped from the continent of Africa and forced into slavery in the American colonies. In 1776, the colonists declared their independence from England, the dominant imperialist in the colonies at that time, and followed their independence with the U.S. Constitution which guaranteed rights for white men, not for women, and not for slaves. The Constitution did not ban slavery and so it went on until the bloody Civil War (1861–65) between the Union (the Northern states) and the Confederates (the Southern states). Following their defeat in the war, the Southern states enacted racist Jim Crow laws that essentially denied freed slaves, and all African Americans, the rights given to white Americans. There has been continued racial tension and strife, prejudice, and discrimination, ever since.

Among the many social problems that continue to confront African Americans today is police brutality. As described in Chapter 4, Colin Kaepernick famously protested the several then-recent shootings of unarmed Black men during the summer of 2016. As a non-violent protester, Kaepernick remained seated on the bench. When asked by a reporter why he did not stand during the anthem, Kaepernick explained, "I am not going to stand up to show pride in a flag for a country that oppresses black people and people of color. To me, this is bigger than football, and it would be selfish on my part to look the other way. There are bodies in the street and people getting paid leave and getting away with murder" (Boren 2020). Colin's protests continued into the next game but he went from sitting on the bench to kneeling on the sideline. Soon after, he was joined by a few other teammates and then, members of other NFL teams. While he received limited support for his actions, he was condemned by President Trump, chastised by the NFL (e.g., NFL Commissioner Roger Goodell told the *Associated Press*, "I don't necessarily agree with what he's doing"), and much of mainstream America.

At the time of his protest, Kaepernick was a young and celebrated quarterback for the San Francisco 49ers and had the top-selling jersey among NFL players. The 49ers had a miserable 2016 season, finishing 2–14, and he started just 11 games. As of the fall of 2020, Kaepernick had not played in a NFL game since January 1, 2017, the last game of the 2016 season. No NFL team signed Kaepernick and many football observers believe it was because of collusion among the league's owners as a result of his protests.

Kaepernick appeared to be headed to football oblivion but then the George Floyd murder occurred. This was the incident that finally sparked the fires of discontent and stimulated the Black Lives Matter (BLM) movement to 40 days and 40 nights of protests (in some cities, such as Portland, Oregon, the daily protests lasted much longer) across the country and in many other parts of the world. Most of the protests were peaceful but many others were reminiscent of the 1960s riots that occurred in many U.S. cities. According to their website, "#BLM was founded in 2013 in response to the acquittal of Trayvon Martin's murderer. Black Lives Matter Foundation, Inc. is a global organization in the US, UK, and Canada, whose mission is to eradicate white supremacy and build local power to intervene in violence inflicted on Black communities by the state and vigilantes." #BLM was especially concerned about the manner in which so many African Americans were being mistreated by the police. Numerous video recordings were played by the news media and repeated in the social media. A cross-section of people were outraged. Demands to defund police departments (e.g., shift some of the budgetary money allocated for policing toward hiring professionals that should be handling noncriminal manners typically given to the police to handle) and ban a number of violent tactics (e.g., chokeholds and using a knee to the back of the head to pin a suspect to the ground) used by the police to contain suspects. The BLM protests that began in May (2020) were inspiring to many, including large numbers of people that were not African Americans. "In small, mostly white towns across the country, hundreds of people gathered to chant 'Black lives matter' and 'no justice, no peace' in the middle of the day. It felt like a moment not seen for generations" (Cineas 2020). The times were a-changing as these protests had a different feel to them because they were shifting public opinion in a number of social arenas (that will be described below).

Interestingly, Kaepernick's social revival, which did not include another stint with the NFL (at least as of 2020), reached a new height in 2020 when he was on his way to becoming a "media mogul." In July 2020 Kaepernick signed a deal with Disney that would begin with an ESPN docuseries about his life. This agreement followed a deal between Kaepernick and Netflix to create a new series starring the former NFL star (Desta 2020).

Given yet another chance to actually lead the country in a meaningful manner, President Trump was far more callous on issues of concern among #BLM. For example, on July 14, 2020, Trump gave a "rambling, campaign-style" talk in the Rose Garden at the White House. Following this appearance, Trump granted a one-on-one interview with Catherine Herridge, a CBS News reporter who asked Mr. Trump: "Why are African-Americans still dying at the hands of law enforcement in this country?" Upset by this question on race relations in the United States, Mr. Trump replied in a highly defensive manner, "So are white people. So are white people. What a terrible question to ask. So are white people. More white people, by the way. More white people" (Qiu 2020). This is a misleading response as Black Americans are killed at a far higher *rate* at the hands of law enforcement than are white Americans. Since 2015, *The Washington Post* has logged 2,499 white Americans killed by police for a rate of 13 per million, compared with 1,301 Black Americans for a rate of 31 per one million (Qiu 2020). In New York City in 2018, 73 percent of police shooting victims were Black, though Black residents comprise only 24 percent of the city's population (MacDonald 2020). A more sympathetic response would help ease Mr. Trump's perceived racist comment.

In addition to drawing attention to their discontent with law enforcement, the BLM movement took on the issue of the very odd honoring of the Confederacy throughout the South and shockingly in so many other parts of the country. It has long been baffling to most Americans why the Confederates have statues and monuments paying homage to their legacy of waging war against the United States, committing treason and perpetuating slavery. For the past few years leading up to the 2020 protests, over 110 Confederate monuments had been removed from public spaces but #BLM took matters in their own hands and knocked down at least another hundred more.

Allies of the #BLM targeted monuments of Christopher Columbus as well. Columbus, who mistakenly landed in North America while seeking a quicker trade route between Europe and India, China and the West Indies, is viewed as a racist because of his treatment (e.g., enslavement and genocide) of the indigenous people—who he named Indians, because he thought he was in India—and his actions that led to the genocide of native people (the Arawak/Taino people). In October 1492, Columbus landed in what is now the Bahamas, probably Watling Island (History.com 2020), claiming the land for Spain, even though people already resided there. Later that month, he sighted Cuba, which he thought was mainland China, and in December the expedition of three ships— the Santa Maria, the Pinta, and the Nina—landed on Hispaniola, which Columbus thought might be Japan. "The explorer returned to Spain with gold, spices, and 'Indian' captives in March 1493 and was received with the highest honors by the Spanish court" (History.com 2020). He was the first European to explore the Americas since Leif Erickson and the Vikings did so more than 500 years earlier. While imperialist Spain considered Columbus a hero, the same cannot be said about the indigenous people. Columbus and his men were responsible for introducing Old World diseases such as smallpox, measles, and influenza to the Taino population that weren't immune to the germs. In 1492, there were an estimated 250,000 indigenous people in Hispaniola (what is now known as the Dominican Republic), but by 1517 only 14,000 remained, according to the Oklahoma Medical Research Foundation (Lee 2020). "Some historians believe that the impact of European and African settlers in the New World possibly killed as much as 90% of the native populations and was deadlier than the Black Death was in medieval Europe" (Lee 2020). The Taino Museum (2020) states that in addition to being exposed to diseases, the Taino population was forced to work in the mines and fields for the Spanish and that by 1531 only 600 remained. "By 1531 the number was down to 600. Today there are no easily discerned traces of the Arawak/Taino at all except for some of the archaeological remains that have been found. Not only on Hispaniola, but across the Windward Passage in Cuba, complete genocide was practiced on these natives" (Taino Museum 2020). The "handwriting on the wall" for the attacks on Columbus' statues had been in place for years as many cities and states (i.e., Minnesota, Alaska, Vermont, and Oregon) had already replaced Columbus Day with Indigenous People's Day (Lee 2020). While it's true that if not Columbus, it was inevitable that someone else from the European imperialist nations would discover the Western World, it also likely that years from now people will look back at this era and wonder why there was a national holiday for Columbus in the first place.

While Columbus statues and monuments were being knocked down, or removed for safe keeping, so too were statues of other representatives of genocide being targeted by 2020 protestors. On the west coast of the United States, statues of Roman Catholic Saint Junipero Serra—known as "Father Genocide" by his detractors—were also targeted. "Serra was the founder of nine of 21 missions in California during the 18th century. As he spread Roman Catholicism throughout much of California, then a Spanish territory, many Native American tribes were decimated through the introduction of foreign diseases and the destruction of villages and native plants and animals. Native Americans also were forced to construct the missions and were subjected to harsh corporal punishment" (Campa 2020). The city council of Ventura City, California, voted to remove two Serra statues; another statue of Serra was forcibly toppled in San Francisco's Golden Gate Park a month earlier on June 19 (Campa 2020).

On June 27, 2020, Princeton University removed former President Woodrow Wilson's name from its Public and International Affairs School in the wake of nationwide protests against racism and police brutality. "The trustees concluded that Woodrow Wilson's racist thinking and policies make him an inappropriate namesake for a school or college whose scholars, students, and alumni must stand firmly against racism in all its forms," said Christopher L. Eisgruber, Princeton's president (Muller 2020). Wilson, who was U.S. president from 1913 to 1921 (as well as president of Princeton from 1902 to 1910), publicly advocated for and implemented racist policies, including resegregating federal government workers after they had been integrated for decades (Muller 2020). It should also be pointed out that as U.S. President, Wilson oversaw the passage of a great deal of progressive legislative policies (e.g., the Federal Reserve Act, Federal Trade Commission Act, the Clayton Anti-Trust Act, and pro-immigration rights) but such accomplishments are generally overshadowed by his acceptance and support of Jim Crow policies.

Returning to the disdain directed toward the Confederacy by the BLM movement and its supporters is a particular perceived source of racism and hatred, the Confederate flag. The Confederates used three different flags but the one we most identify as the enemy of the United States is the battle flag, or the "Stars and Bars." This battle flag has a red background (which is supposed to represent valor), with a blue X containing

13 stars—for the 11 seceded states plus Kentucky and Missouri. For a number of years, Southern states incorporated this battle flag in their state flags. It was not until 2020, and as a result of the BLM movement, that the last state, Mississippi, finally agreed to rid its state flag of an image of the "Stars and Bars." While most Americans view the flag as traitorous, African Americans generally view it as racist, and for good reason. William T. Thompson, a Confederate and founder of the newspaper that would become the *Savannah Morning News*, is the designer of the flag. He said of the flag, "As a people we are fighting to maintain the Heaven-ordained supremacy of the white man over the inferior or colored race" (LaCapria 2019). Ordaining the white race over the "inferior" race is a textbook example of racism. It is certainly understandable why so many Americans are offended by this flag. Today, the Confederate flag is often flown by the Ku Klux Klan and other white supremacists, which only heightens its perceived connection to racism, oppression, and slavery.

In the same July 14, 2020, interview with Mr. Trump described previously, Herridge asked, "You understand why the [Confederate] flag is a painful symbol for many people because it's a reminder of slavery?" Trump, who has always denied being a racist, said, "People love it. I know people who like the Confederate flag and they're not thinking about slavery." That Trump references people he knows who do not view the Confederate flag as a symbol of slavery instead of mentioning whether or not he has friends that *do* view it as racist certainly does not endear him with those who find it as a symbol of racism.

Racism in the United States is often very overt, or systemic, as demonstrated above, but it is also often quite subtle and ingrained in many aspects of American culture. Consider, for example, the stereotypical images of African Americans used on many popular food brands. During the month of June 2020, and "amid a national reckoning on racism," it was announced that the images associated with Aunt Jemima, Uncle Ben's, Cream of Wheat and Mrs. Butterworth would be discontinued because they "perpetuated painful stereotypes that negatively African Americans and women were perceived for generations" (Jones 2020). Conagra Brands, the maker of Mrs. Butterworth's, with its syrup bottles shaped like a matronly woman were "intended to evoke the images of a loving grandmother" but to some people, "she conveys a disturbing stereotype of a servile Black woman who is content to spend her life waiting on whites"; in other words, a clear appropriate of the "mammy" motif (Jones 2020). A "mammy" is a reference to a black woman who nursed white children or was a servant to a white family. It is viewed as an offensive term of belittlement based on a narrow view of the role of black women. According to history professor Gregory Smithers (Virginia Commonwealth University), the Aunt Jemima syrup bottle carries the same "mammy" concern as Mrs. Butterworth's as it creates a naturalized image of subservient black women existing to serve white people (Jones 2020). The images used for Uncle Ben's and Cream of Wheat have similar stereotypical concerns only as black males designed to serve. The initial image used for Cream of Wheat featured a fictional character dubbed "Rastus," a racist term for Black men depicted as simple-minded and irresponsible that arouse during the minstrel era. A toned-down version of this image was used years later (Jones 2020). David Lazarus (2020) believes that these "indisputably racist brands, and their bewildering longevity, speak to the power of marketing in reinforcing offensive stereotypes" (p. A8). Lazarus adds, "Simply put, if corporate America hadn't given its full backing to creating and promoting these images as sales tools, making them both culturally legitimate and highly profitable, it's debatable whether the country's racial divisions would have run so deep for so long" (p. A8). With all the other sources of racism in the United States it may seem like a stretch to suggest that these food brands should bear such a burden of responsibility but Jerome Williams, a business professor at Rutgers University, states, "There's very strong support for that premise. Corporate America perpetuated this situation" (Lazarus 2020: A8). Judy Davis, a marketing professor at Eastern Michigan University adds, "Advertising and marketing play an important role in selling whiteness. They have played a role in perpetuating an image that whites are superior" (Lazarus 2020: A8).

The world of popular culture is filled with all sorts of racist and prejudicial connotations directed toward every category of people. A few examples include two from music and one from television. From music, we have two country groups that have modified their racist names. The first is Lady Antebellum. The band claims that they chose their name after the pre–Civil War style "antebellum" homes of the South and yet somehow never took into account the slavery connotations behind the word when they originally named their band in 2006. They now report that they are "embarrassed" by this gaffe (Watts 2020). Many people wondered how they got away with using this name for so many years without public condemnation as the word "antebellum" refers to a period of time prior to a war, especially the Civil War, and slavery is among the first images that come to mind when hearing the word. The band now simply refers to itself as "Lady A" even though a black blues singer from Seattle, Anita White, already uses the name, thus creating yet another controversy surrounding the band's name. Upon learning of Lady Antebellum's decision, White said, "I was furious when I first found out that Lady Antebellum had appropriated the name. I was furious because I felt like yet another white person's privilege was going to be allowed to take something from another black person. Besides our lives, now you're gonna take our name, and that triggered me" (Lewis 2020). White and the band formerly known as Lady Antebellum worked things out via a Zoom meeting and they both decided to use Lady A (Lewis 2020). Like Lady Antebellum which changed its name due to the BLM social movement, another country musical act, The Dixie Chicks changed their name to The Chicks. The word "Dixie" is affectionate slang used to describe the Civil War–era South—a time when slavery was an acceptable and common practice (Miller 2020). The BLM social movement had an impact on the 32-season strong *Cops* television show and the six-part podcast *Running from Cops.* In light of events involving the police and African Americans, public scrutiny increased over shows like *Cops* for its "depictions of poor communities, its filmmaking tactics, and its messaging" (Jackson 2020). *Cops* always made the police look like the "good guys" and perpetrators as the "bad guys." This was not the first time, however, that *Cops* has been cancelled and it might not be the last time (Jackson 2020). The show was cancelled by FOX in 2013 because of its "intentional focus on Black, Latino, and low income neighborhoods and its highly selective portrayal of race" (Jackson 2020).

If you didn't already know (and how would that be possible?), issues related to race and ethnicity have a long and complicated history in the United States. A closer look at key concepts therefore is important and follows below.

SOCIAL CONSTRUCTION OF RACE AND ETHNICITY

Sociologists point out that the concepts of "race" and "ethnicity" are a product of social constructionism and that such categories of people exist merely because society has chosen to label people in racial or ethnic terms. With that in mind, we can define *race* as a category of people who share some socially recognized physical characteristic, such as skin color or hereditary traits that distinguishes them from other categories of people. The most common biological feature used to determine races of people is skin color—despite the reality that this is a very imprecise way of determining races. Thus a racial group is biologically determined through cultural constructs and interpretations. An *ethnic group* refers to a category of people who are recognized as distinct based on such social or cultural factors as nationality, religion, language, geographic residence, a common set of values, and so on.

In the United States, the federal government determines the categories of races and ethnicities and collects data on people based on their categories. Official classification of race and ethnicity is revealed in its Census form. In 2020, these categories included: Question #8, Is Person 1 of Hispanic, Latino, or Spanish origin? Response options include: No; Yes, Mexican, Mexican American, Chicano; Yes, Puerto Rican; Yes, Cuban; and, Yes, another Hispanic, Latino, or Spanish origin, with directions to fill it the boxes for Salvadoran, Dominican, Colombian, etc. Question #9 asks: What is Person 1's race? (This has to make one wonder why there is a Question #8?). Option responses include: White, with directions to fill in origin (e.g., German, Irish, English, Italian, etc.); Black or African Am, with directions to fill in an origin; American Indian or Alaska Native, with directions to print the name of the principal tribe; and then a number of other options that are mostly Asian: Chinese, Filipino, Asian India, Vietnamese, Korean, Japanese, Native Hawaiian, Samoan, Chamorro, Other Asian, or other Pacific Islander. There is also an option for "Some other race" with instructions to print race or origin.

The concepts of race and ethnicity are social constructs because, technically, we are all of the same race, or species, *Homo sapiens* (Latin words meaning "thinking person"), that first emerged in Africa approximately 250,000 years ago (Macionis 2010). Before people started migrating in large numbers from their homelands in the late 1500s, there was no concept of race. By the late 1500s, however, Europeans began to use the term race to describe diverse people. Around 1800, European scientists came up with three broad categories for humanity: Caucasian (for people from Europe and Western Asia) to designate people of light skin and fine hair; Negroid (derived from the Latin meaning "black") to refer to people with dark skin and coarse, curly hair typical of people living in sub–Saharan Africa; and Mongoloid (referring to the Mongolian region of Asia) to refer to people with yellow or brown skin and distinctive folds on the eyelids (Macionis 2010). Since the early 1800s, a number of academic disciplines utilize classification systems for race. In biology, race refers to a population of humans based on certain hereditary characteristics that differentiate them from other human groups (Marger 2006). Physical anthropologists distinguish racial groups either by phenotype—visible anatomical features such as skin color, hair texture, and body and facial shape—or by genotype—genetic specifications inherited from one's parents (Marger 2006).

The racial classification schemes described above all use cultural interpretations of physical characteristics in order to create categories of race. From a genetic standpoint, however, biologists would "tell us that people in various racial categories differ in only about 6 percent of their genes, which is less than the genetic variation that we find within each racial category. What this means is that from a scientific standpoint, physical variation is real, but racial categories simply do not describe that reality very well" (Macionis 2010: 57). If we used genetics to determine racial categories, cultural ideals might have to be changed in the face of certain realities. Consider, for example, Jews and Palestinians, who have been locked in a bitter struggle for more than a century, would have to face the reality that they share a common ancestry dating back 4,000 years to Abraham, the biblical patriarch of both Jewish and Arab nations (Kraft 2000). According to genetic research, the percentage of variation in the Y chromosome between Jews and Palestinians differ by only 1 percent, compared to a difference of 5 percent between Jews and Europeans (Kraft 2000).

It should be noted that there are some well-recognized and meaningful genetic differences between groups of people, "for instance between Ashkenazi and Sephardi Jews in terms of their risk to Tay-Sachs disease" (*Nature* 2009: 787). Nearly all people of northern European descent can enjoy milk and milk products, but about 75 percent of African American, Jewish, Native American, and Mexican American adults cannot digest much milk; nor can about 90 percent of Asian Americans (Delaney 2012). Lactose intolerance can be managed by taking a chemical called lactase which is available in pill form and in some dairy-based products such as specially formulated milk (vos Savant 2005). As another example, young blacks are twenty times as likely as whites to suffer from heart failure (1 in every 100 blacks under the age of fifty) (Delaney 2012). Interestingly, there is a specific treatment for heart disease that is most effective for blacks: BiDil. BiDil represents the first medication approved by the Food and Drug Administration for a specific racial group (Jewell 2005).

Still, it is important to emphasize that the social creation of racial and ethnic categories of people was not motivated simply by a desire to classify people based on physical traits and for medical reasons; instead, it has much to do with one category of people finding a way to feel superior over others and thus justifying their superordinate role over others. Feelings and/or delusions of superiority may lead to racism, prejudice, and discrimination of the subordinates all in attempt to maintain an advantageous social position.

RACISM, PREJUDICE, AND DISCRIMINATION

Racism involves any attitude, belief, behavior or social arrangement that has the intent, or the ultimate effect, of favoring members of one racial category of people over another. Racism involves denying equal access to goods, services and opportunities to people because of their racial category. In football, it has been common to relegate white athletes to the "thinking" positions (e.g., quarterback and middle linebacker) while designating black athletes to "reaction" positions (e.g., defensive back and defensive tackles). The idea that the quarterback position in football is a "thinking" position while playing defensive back is a "reaction" position serves as an example of a traditional, race-based belief that has contributed to stereotyping and discrimination in sport. Such beliefs are based on social construction (cultural determinations) rather than biological realities. As with gender and sexism (see Chapter 10) there are a number of ways to look at racism including such distinctions as: interpersonal, ideological, and institutional. *Interpersonal racism*, or individual racism, is the discriminatory, prejudicial, and stereotypical form of racism that occurs directly wherein a person of one race treats a person of a different race in a preconceived notion. *Ideological racism* refers to the belief that one sex is inferior to another and stresses racial-appropriateness based cultural notions (e.g., that members of one race are better suited for corporate jobs and members of another race are better suited for agricultural employment). During the era of slavery, members of the white race believed that Africans were inferior and used this ideology to justify slavery. *Institutional racism* refers to the systematic practices and patterns within social institutions (e.g., "redlining" in banking and real estate) that lead to inequality between members of different races.

Racism leads to prejudice and discrimination. Although the terms "prejudice" and "discrimination" are related, there are distinct differences. *Prejudice* can be defined as negative beliefs and overgeneralizations concerning a group of people involving a judgment against an individual based on a rigid and fixed mental image applied to all individuals of that group. "Ethnic and racial prejudices are characterized by several features, including categorical or generalized thoughts, negative assumptions about an individual based on group membership, and inflexible thinking" (Delaney 2012: 257). Because football started during an era in American history wherein blacks were still subjected to Jim Crow racist beliefs, they were not considered smart enough to handle the quarterback position and it was also believed that white teammates would not follow a black leader on the gridiron. Throughout much of the development of football over the years this prejudicial attitude persisted. (There was also a carry-over effect to other sports that blacks were not capable of leadership roles on ball teams.)

A common type of prejudice is the stereotype. *Stereotypes* are oversimplified and exaggerated beliefs about a category of people. The belief that whites make better leaders than blacks or that all black people make good athletes are examples of stereotypes. Some white athletes may make for good leaders on- and off-the-field but that does not mean all whites are naturally prepared to handle the rigors of leadership; and, not all blacks are great athletes.

Discrimination refers to behavior that treats people unequally on the basis of an ascribed status, such as race or gender. Discrimination can be viewed as applied prejudice (LeMay 2005). That is, while prejudice involves negative beliefs about a person without having knowledge of that person, discrimination refers to actual behavior that leads to unequal treatment. If we revisit the QB position in football, if a coach believes that an athlete is not smart enough to be a QB because he is black, the coach is guilty of prejudicial thinking. However, if the coach gives the athlete a chance to try out for the QB position he is not guilty of discrimination. On the other hand, if a coach has a policy wherein black athletes are not allowed to try out for quarterback, he is guilty of discrimination.

The Role of Genetics

Genetics itself refers to the field of science that examines how traits are passed down from one generation to the next (Robinson and Spock 2020). Genetics is the study of heredity and the variation of inherited characteristics. It is the genes of our parents that determine the physical makeup of a child but these genes do not dictate behavior as we have free will and are capable of learning via the socialization process, trial and error, reinforcement, and modeling (see Chapter 5). Drawing conclusions about a person's ability to accomplish some sort of task based on a socially constructed racial/ethnic category, then, is fraught with a lack of rationality and may lead to racist conclusions about people. For example, the idea that blacks are innately superior athletes and that whites are innately more intelligent reflect racial ideologies that lead to prejudice and discrimination in the sports world.

Based on all the scientific information that we have now, the origin of modern humans can be traced back to Africa within the past 200,000 years and evolved from their most likely common ancestor, Homo erectus. Such a notion often leads some to wonder, "If that is true, why aren't all people black, or dark skin, like Africans?" The simplest answer resides primarily with the presence of an amino acid derivative known as melanin, a natural skin pigment that provides human skin, hair, and eyes their color. It is melanin that protects the upper levels of the skin from being damaged by the sun's ultraviolet rays; it also decreases the body's ability to produce Vitamin D in response to sun exposure (Harris 2004). In general, the closer to the equator that one's ancestors come from the darker their skin color; and the farther from the equator, the lighter the skin color. There are, however, significant individual differences in skin color; moreover, a genetic variation known as albinism, in which the person has very little melanin, can and does occur in all racial categories (Delaney 2012). Natural selection favored lighter skinned people who live far from the equator because it is easier for UV rays to penetrate and produce essential vitamin D. In turn, darker skinned people that live close to the equator have the natural ability to block out deadly UV rays more easily (Smithsonian Natural Museum of Natural History 2020). From a biological standpoint then, differences in skin color help people to survive based on their geological residence. However, skin color has nothing to do with intelligence or innate athletic ability.

Beliefs of racial superiority based on genetics can have deadly results. The European colonies that were established in the New World and became the United States justified slavery on the ideological belief that black people were not equal to whites which helped to "justify" the ownership of one race by another race. Hitler's idea of the superior Aryan nation led to a justification of an "inferior" Jewish "race" that needed to be exterminated. In 1971, Martin Kane wrote an article, "An Assessment of Black Is Best," for *Sports Illustrated* and suggested that blacks dominate sports because American slave owners weeded out the weak blacks on plantations and made sure that strong black men and black women mated (thinking this would lead to stronger and better working slaves). Jimmy "the Greek" Snyder, a former sports analyst for CBS, suggested in 1988 that blacks made good ball carriers in football because they were bred to have big, strong thighs when they lived as slaves. Kane and Snyder conveniently ignored the millions of blacks with skinny thighs and were ignorant of the historical fact that the control of white slave masters over the sexual behavior of black slaves was never extensive enough to shape the genetic traits of even a small portion of the U.S. African American population.

Biological notions of racial predispositions are troublesome at the very least and deadly in more extreme cases. There are many flaws to the theory of genetic predisposition to sports. Primarily, there is no "pure" gene pool that guarantees an individual is genetically programmed to be an athlete, or a teacher or biologist for that matter. Further, the idea that blacks are naturally more gifted athletes is discounted by the fact that most blacks—like most whites—are not athletes and do not participate in sports. Focusing on physical attributes while ignoring work habits and intellectual characteristics is also problematic. It takes training, practice, dedication and positive reinforcement, among other social traits, for an individual to become a great athlete. Still, there are those who believe in the outdated concept of "born athletes."

In Chapter 10 we described how naïve the medical profession was in regard to women's frailty in during the Victorian era. As recently as the mid–1950s the medical profession considered the 4-minute mile a physical impossibility. Doctors feared that the athlete's heart or lungs might explode due to the stress of such a feat. In 1954, Roger Ban-nister accomplished the impossible when he ran a 3:59.4 mile. Bannister attributed his triumph to medical training, careful observation and logical deduction (Entine 2000). (Note: The current world record for the 4-minute mile is 3:43:13.) Bannister was a medi-cal student who trained himself to become a world-class runner. He had finished fourth in the 1,500 meters at the 1952 Olympics. Bannister later became a medical doctor. Ban-nister never claimed to be the best runner of his era. He attributed his accomplishments to hard work and training. Why is it then that some people cling to ideas of natural born athletes? Is there an "athletic gene" that gives some individuals an edge over others based on biology? Since blacks are dominating most major commercial sports in North Amer-ica, do they possess this athletic gene? Are people from Southern California, Hawaii, and the Pacific Islands better surfers than people from Kansas, Minnesota, and Winnipeg because they have a surfing gene, or is it because they have easy access to the ocean? Are Canadians better hockey players than residents of Chad because they possess a "hockey gene" or simply because of the many opportunities for Canadians to skate on frozen riv-ers and lakes? Sociologists quickly discount any such notion that genetics alone creates better athletes because of the possession of specific "sport genes." It is not genetics that dictates whether or not someone will be good at a particular sport, rather it involves such variables as opportunities to play certain sports, others that may serve as role models that inspire participation, family and peer reinforcement, and so on. Recall from Chapter 6 the exploits of Marv Marinovich, who attempted to "breed" genetically perfect athletes based on his perceived superior genes and of the women whom he believed also pos-sessed superior genes.

Sport sociologists do not discount that some individual athletes have physical advantages over others. Clearly someone with big hands will find it easier to grip and palm a basketball. Being tall also helps in basketball. Lance Armstrong's heart is 20 per-cent larger than the normal person's heart, giving him a great advantage in endurance sports such as bicycling. Armstrong does not have this advantage because he is a white person—he is a biological fluke. Andy Roddick has unusually flexible ribs and spine, enabling him to arch his back and rotate his arm much more efficiently than the average professional tennis player, which helps to explain why he can hit a 155 mph serve. Once again, all white people do not share this "advantage." Achieving athletic success involves many elements, but genes are not at the top of list.

Working hard, practice, and sometimes luck (e.g., remaining injury free) are ele-ments that help athletes win in sporting contests. Athletes are not born, they are made. Skin color is not a precursor to athletic superiority or intelligence.

RACE AND INTELLIGENCE

The role of intelligence in sports has been mentioned a couple of times already in this chapter; consequently, the attempted link between race and intelligence is worth a quick review here. As longtime imperialists, it is not a surprise that nineteenth-century Europeans first introduced the categorization of "races" of people. Viewing conquered people as inferior helped to justify the establishment of an overlord presence throughout a significant part of the world. Darwin's 1871 publication of *The Descent of Man and Selec-tion in Relation to Sex* reflected the prevailing view that non–Europeans lacked the same level of intelligence as Anglo-Saxon upper-class males (*Nature* 2009). In the 1950s, there was a eugenic concern in Britain that the "genetically inferior workers were out-breeding their superiors" (*Nature* 2009). The issue of race and intelligence became prominent in the United States during the late 1960s, in part in response to the civil rights movement. Edgar G. Epps, professor of sociology and chairman of the Division of Social Sciences at Tuskegee Institute, the famous Black foundation in Alabama, also mirrored the 1950s and 1960s era common belief of differences in race and intelligence by saying, "The fact that Negro students on the average, score below White students on most measures of academic achievement is well documented" (Wober 1971: 17).

With a concern over the relationship between race and intelligence came a desire to scientifically prove whether one race was more intelligent than others. French officials developed an IQ test as a way to measure intelligence but did so because they were trying to supplement teachers' assessments of their pupils. "In the hands of later psychometricians, the tests became increasingly reified and seemingly made more scientific by the development of the term 'g' to encapsulate 'crystallized' or 'general intelligence'" (*Nature* 2009: 787). The "g" term refers to general intelligence. Arthur Jensen's research (*Bias in Mental Testing*, 1980; *The g Factor*, 1998) on a "sociology of intelligence" is the benchmark which others who study race and intelligence often cite. "The sociology of intelligence refers most broadly to the ways in which a population and its members are affected (individually and collectively) by the dispersion in *g* in that population. It also refers to the ways in which a society responds to that dispersion in *g*, including beliefs and taboos concerning it, the evolution of institutions accommodating it, and social policies attempting to alter it" (Gottfredson 1998: 293). According to Park (2008), *g*, or general intelligence, is a biological inherited entity and this entity has a heritability of .80 (80 percent). "This means that 80 percent of the variation in intelligence within a population is explained by genetic differences. Only 20 percent is the result of environment—that is, having been brought up under different cultural conditions" (Park 1998: 406). The implication being that differences in intelligence are largely the result of genetic differences and consequently, any social program designed to raise the general IQ of people is essentially futile (Park 1998).

Critics of Jensen's proposition of *g* center on the accusation that IQ tests are culturally biased against American blacks. Claims of cultural bias have stymied discussion of intelligence in most social circles in contemporary society because anything that could be used to impugn the validity of tests for one group could be used to undermine their credibility for all groups (Gottfredson 1998). Differences in IQ measurements, then, were blamed on social class privilege and therefore deemed to be of no functional importance. Gottfredson (1998) argues that what critics of IQ tests are most concerned about is that, if a genetic basis for IQ differences is real it would undermine support for egalitarian social programs because these differences were "natural" and not social. Another criticism of Jensen specifically and IQ tests in general rests with the realization that there is no agreement about what intelligence actually is; that is, what criteria exactly should be measured in order to determine how intelligent someone is.

The general IQ test is an attempt to measure intelligence in rank order across an entire population in linear mode but such a scheme ignores other forms of intelligence, including social, emotional, craftsman, and the intuition of the scientist (*Nature* 2009). No one questions that intelligence is important in practical affairs. And, as Burhan and associates (2014) put forth, it's fairly reasonable to assume that intellectually competent individuals learn faster and are better at acquiring information, knowledge, and skills related to their occupations. But therein lies the important issue: we all need to possess intelligence in our particular occupations; that is to say, college professors need certain types of intelligence, plumbers another type, ambassadors another, and so on. This logical premise can be extended to sports as well. The quarterback does not need the intelligence of an academic to teach college courses and conduct empirical research, nor does he need to be able to fix a leaky faucet; he does, however, need to be football smart (e.g., possess the ability to read defenses, make audibles at the line of scrimmage, calculate the exact point to throw the ball downfield as the wide receiver runs a pattern, and so on). Is the ability to comprehend the examples of "football smart" provided here a matter of intelligence and the failure to understand the examples itself an example of a lack of intelligence? No, it is a matter of having knowledge in a particular area, in this case, football. Thus, the limitations of an IQ test. A common adage used to illustrate measurements of intelligence is akin to this: If we compare the IQ of a fish and a monkey and their ability to climb a tree, the fish will always look unintelligent and the monkey intelligent.

And yet, the NFL attempts to measure the intelligence of its draft picks via the Wonderlic Cognitive Ability Test (WCA). It is one thing to measure athletic skills (e.g., 40-yard dash speed, jumping ability, and physical strength) as they are not culturally-biased but it is another issue altogether to subject all draftees with the Wonderlic test. The Wonderlic test has been used by companies, universities, and the military since 1936 and is designed to measure one's intelligence with a variety of logical, numerical, and literacy-focused questions. The Wonderlic test is a 50-question, 12-minute, IQ-type test "that begins with a series of mind-numbingly easy queries and gets progressively more difficult" (Fisher 2014). Samples of Wonderlic questions are available online but here are two examples: "Paper clips sell for 21 cents per box. What will four boxes cost?" "A box of staples has a length of 6 cm, a width of 7 cm, and a volume of 378 cm cubed. What is the height of the box?" (Note: Each of the authors took a sample Wonderlic test and, thankfully, scored extremely high!) Former Bengals punter Pat McInally, an Ivy Leaguer, scored the NFL's only perfect 50 score (Fisher 2014). Other test result examples include: Tom Brady, 33; Peyton Manning, 28; Brett Favre, 22; and Keyshawn Johnson, 11 (Straight Forward Sports 2020). The Wonderlic is not an accurate predictor of NFL success as the low scores of Brady, Manning, Favre, and Johnson would indicate.

Racism in Sport

As we have documented already in this chapter, racism is an issue in most spheres of life. This includes the manner in which minorities feel they are being treated by the socio-political system in general and law enforcement in particular; having to confront racist imagery in the form of statues and monuments that glorify those responsible for racist behaviors; and, stereotypical brands of food that put African Americans in a subservient role and television shows that portray minorities from low income neighborhoods as the "bad guys" and law enforcement as the "good guys." So prevalent had issues of racism become that in 2020 millions of people from cities ranging from small to very large across the nation were willing to protest even though there was a global pandemic occurring at the same time of the marches. With the prevalence of racism in the Unites States, it is no surprise that racism exists in sports. Racism is not a new phenomenon in sports and it's not limited to the color of the skin of an NFL starting quarterback.

Racism in Sports in the Past

The roots of racism and discrimination in sports may be as old as sports themselves. Social class discrimination was common during the American colonial era and England's amateur rule was adopted "in order to block, or at least to limit, lower-class participation in modern sports; but social class has not been as high a barrier here as it was in Europe. In the United States, prejudices about race and gender have done more than class biases to hinder full development of modern sports" (Guttmann 1988: 119).

Following the end of the American Civil War in 1865, slavery was officially abolished by the 13th Amendment. Many social institutions, businesses and industry had to reexamine their inclusionary role in accepting blacks into mainstream society. Most of these institutions failed miserably. Sport, as a social institution, generally reflects the prevalent sentiment of any era. For example, in horse racing, it had been common practice that blacks were jockeys for their masters' horses in colonial and antebellum times (Guttmann 1988). Immediately following the Civil War most jockeys were still black. A black jockey, Oliver Lewis, rode the winning horse (Aristides) in the first Kentucky Derby in 1875. Further, all but one of the fifteen jockeys in the first Kentucky Derby was black. Isaac Murphy, a black jockey, won the derby in 1884, 1889 and 1891, and was considered one of the best jockeys of his era. However, spectators and fans of horse racing attributed a first-place finish to the speed of the horse rather than any skill on the part of the jockey, thus making it easier for white Americans to accept black jockeys (Guttmann 1988). This form of racism would end when white jockeys began to dominate the sport, as jockeys were now viewed as skillful athletes. The black jockey, in fact, became a symbol of racism.

According to Shropshire (1996), the lawn jockey is a symbol of racism. Lawn jockeys are small statues, approximately three feet high, of black jockeys featured with oversized lips and flared nostrils, usually dressed in bright red coats and holding a ring or lantern. Lawn jockeys have been around for hundreds of years. There are many possible explanations regarding the origin of the lawn jockey. One version has George Washington's eight-year-old slave "Jocko" as the inspiration of the original lawn jockey. "According to the anecdote, the slave froze while holding the reins of George Washington's horse after the crossing of the Delaware River in 1776" (Shropshire 1996: 20). Another explanation dates to the start of the eighteenth century when lawn jockeys were cast of solid iron or zinc, weighed 300 or more pounds, and were used as hitching posts, most frequently in front of tobacco shops (Hamilton 2018). The U.S. Patent Office issued patent no. 5,875 to Robert Wood of Philadelphia in 1872 for a "hitching post in the form, shape, and costume of a 'Jockey'" (Hamilton 2018). In this regard, it was made to appear that a slave was frozen as he held the horse of his master while the master and friends drank inside a tavern (Shropshire 1996). The racist connotations of the lawn jockey have led to their near complete disappearance, although some people have painted the figure white—assumingly to conceal the racist image.

Baseball became one of the first American sports to take a strong exclusionary position on the role of blacks. In 1867, the National Association of Base-Ball Players (NABBP) ruled that blacks would not be allowed to play in their league. As the first established baseball league, their policy forbidding members from a specific race from participating in sport would set the tone as an accepted practice for future American sports leagues. The NABBP's discriminatory policy "reflected the racism and segregation that were becoming facts of life in the North after the Civil War" (Bowman and

Zoss 1989: 136). The NABBP would disband years later, but it set the standard for future baseball leagues.

In 1876, baseball's National League was established. The National League became the premier league in all of baseball. (In 1901, the American League became baseball's second major league, establishing the structure that continues today.) As early as 1879, the National League and other lower-level leagues agreed to respect each other's player contracts and avoid raiding the rosters of other teams. However, this pact did not forbid the lower leagues from signing black players. During the 1880s, it is estimated that at least 55 blacks participated in organized baseball (Bowman and Zoss 1989). Just like blacks who first broke the color barrier in Major League Baseball decades later, these black players were subjected to a great deal of prejudice and discrimination. Spectators heckled any black player. White pitchers often intentionally threw at the heads of black players, white players tried to spike black players while sliding into base, and verbal taunts by white players against black players were common (Bowman and Zoss 1989). In 1887, organized baseball established the "National Agreement" which, in effect, eliminated blacks from the elite leagues. Thus, baseball was guilty of institutional racism, as the Jim Crow mentality had crept into "America's pastime."

Negro baseball would arise in response to baseball's color line and the establishment of separation ("separate but equal") in society. "As in the rest of American life, a period of experimentation with interracial activities, initiated after the Civil War, had been replaced by a period of increasingly rigid racial segregation. It was apparent to prospective black ballplayers that if they wanted to play baseball they would have to form all-black teams that played in all-black leagues" (White 1996: 128). The Negro leagues were not one solitary league in which all black baseball players played; rather, it is a collective term used to describe the various teams and leagues that existed from the early 1900s until the 1950s. Eventually, exhibitions between Negro League teams and Major League Baseball teams were played. These exhibitions drew huge crowds from both white and black America. "Triumphs over big-leaguers were savored, recalled, elaborated upon. If black players could not play in the major leagues, they could show that they belonged there" (Peterson 1984: 5). (Note: In 2020, Major League Baseball announced that the Negro Leagues' statistics and records would be considered part of the history of MLB.)

Although the Negro Leagues were never as popular as Major League Baseball, they provided many players an opportunity to play ball in a racist society. Jackie Robinson's integration into Major League Baseball would lead to the demise of the Negro Leagues, but it would also signal an end to segregation in baseball.

Perhaps the most well-known racist of the twentieth century is Adolf Hitler, who proclaimed his German people (the Aryan race) as the superior people of the world. Hitler had hoped to use the 1936 Berlin Olympics as a showcase for the superiority of fascism. James Cleveland "Jesse" Owens, a black American, would shatter Hitler's delusionary vision. Owens faced prejudice daily. As a track and field star at Ohio State, Owens and his black friends were forced to live in off-campus housing (away from white athletes) and were not allowed in university restaurants. Despite being a victim of racism, Owens flourished on the track. During one meet in 1935, Owens broke three world records—in the 220-yard dash, the 220-yard low hurdles, and the long jump—he also tied the world record in the 100-yard dash (Entine 2000). His selection to the American Olympic team was an obvious choice. But would he be accepted by Americans? After all, he was a victim of racism on his home campus. Because of nationalistic pride, however, most Americans adored Owens.

Owens was treated as hero by the vast majority of Americans. The myth of Hitler refusing to shake Owens's hand further added to his hero status (Guttmann 1988). (Note: Different reports indicate that Hitler snubbed Owens; other reports indicate that he did not shake any athlete's hands; and, still other reports claim Hitler only shook the hands of German and some Finnish athletes.) The sudden emergence of a black sports hero presented a dilemma for the churchgoing black community of his era. Black church leaders had "long made a point of downplaying athletic success, instead stressing schooling as a way to accelerate assimilation into white society and shake the image of black inferiority. That strategy had not opened many doors. Now sports offered a more promising path to acceptance" (Entine 2000: 173–174). Many black social leaders began to view sport as one of the best means of blacks becoming accepted, or assimilated, into mainstream society.

Like Owens, the boxing great Joe Louis provided a blow to racist ideology. In 1935, Louis beat Italian Primo "Italian Ox" Carnera in New York City. "That sixth-round knockout was particularly sweet for the black community with Mussolini's troops poised to conquer Ethiopia, an independent nation and another source of pride for many American blacks…. The white press conferred status on the young heavyweight for the fight was portrayed as a battle between Italian fascism and American democracy" (Entine 2000: 188). Although hailed by Americans as an American hero, Louis was also a victim of racism in the United States. "Despite his great talent, Louis at first had found it almost impossible to break through the race wall that had been reinforced in the years since Jack Johnson had been driven out of the sport" (Entine 2000: 189).

Basketball was another sport in which blacks were segregated from whites. Basketball slowly grew in popularity in the United States during the first three decades of the twentieth century. "By the 1930s, basketball had replaced track and baseball as the second most popular sport on college campuses, but professional basketball struggled for places to play…. Black youth often played basketball at community centers because few black high schools and relatively few colleges could afford gymnasiums, and black youth who attended integrated schools were often not allowed to participate in school activities" (Caponi-Tabery 2002: 41). For the most part, blacks and whites played basketball separately. When integration in education became a reality in the 1950s, not everyone eagerly accepted it. For example, on January 2, 1957, Iona College was scheduled to play Mississippi in a men's college basketball game at the All-American City Invitational in Owensboro, Kentucky. When Mississippi Governor J.P. Coleman learned that Iona had a black player on the team, he refused to allow Mississippi to play against them. The game is listed in the Iona record book as a 2–0 victory, the official score for a forfeit. There is no sign of the game in the Ole Miss record book (Fitzgerald 2001). Stanley Hill, Iona's black player, was shocked when he heard the governor state, "We're not going to play any blacks—against any blacks or with any blacks" (Fitzgerald 2001: B11). Hill was pleased when all the Mississippi players went to his hotel room to apologize (Fitzgerald 2001).

Whites and blacks played the game of basketball differently. White players' approach was to dribble, fake and move past the man guarding you for a lay-up or, if your path was impeded, for a "set shot." Blacks, however, incorporated jumping with their moves (Caponi-Tabery 2002). Thus, blacks introduced the jump shot to mainstream basketball. At one time, the racist term "Negro basketball" was applied to this style of basketball; it has since been replaced by such phrases as "street ball" and "hotdogging" (Caponi-Tabery

2002). The "slam dunk" was also introduced into basketball by black players. It was considered such an unnatural part of the game that in 1967 the NCAA instituted the "Alcindor Rule" banning the slam dunk. Kareem Abdul-Jabbar (then Lew Alcindor), a center for UCLA, was so dominant that the NCAA forbade the use of the slam dunk because it gave players like Jabbar an unfair advantage and was considered hotdogging (Caponi-Tabery 2002).

Major Racial Breakthroughs in American Sports

Historically, whites have dominated every aspect of sports in the United States, Canada, and Europe and this includes as sports participants, coaches, medical personnel, front office executives and owners. However, in some cases, even some white ethnic groups faced racism.

In Ireland, the political and socio-economic status of the Irish Catholic was similar to that of blacks in the United States. The Irish experienced poverty, degradation, and oppression at the hands of the English. The hatred that the Irish had toward the English would carry over as part of their "cultural baggage" in the New World. In the United States, the Irish were still discriminated against—because of the Anglo-Saxon cultural dominance. In many cities, prominent signs announced "No Irish Need Apply" on many business windows and doors. The Irish were certainly not Anglo—they were Gaelic or Celtic—and they felt insulted when referred to as Anglo. The largest number of Irish came to the United States during the 1840s because of the Irish potato famine.

Some of the Irish success in assimilation can be attributed to sports, especially boxing. "More has been written on Irish success in the American prize ring than about any other ethnic group in sport" (Wilcox 1994: 57). Boxing has long found appeal among the oppressed minorities. Boxing represents a rapid escape from poverty, prejudice and discrimination. Historically, the racial or ethnic group that dominates boxing is an oppressed group in that society. The Irish dominated boxing throughout the second half of the nineteenth century. Among the more prominent Irish-American boxers prior to the Civil War were Sam O'Rourke, Cornelius Horrigan, John C. "Benecia Boy" Heenan, James "Yankee" Sullivan, and John Morrissey. Sullivan demonstrated the "Irish way"— embrace American culture quickly and assimilation will follow all the more promptly. The "Irish way" was embraced by other European immigrant groups who had the racial advantage of being white in a white-dominated society. In the post–Civil War era, other Irish boxers also dominated. Among the more prominent fighters were Paddy Ryan, Jake Kilrain, John L. Sullivan, and "Gentleman Jim" Corbett. "World Champion from 1882 to 1892, Sullivan has been credited with anywhere between 75 and 200 victories in the ring. 'John L.' became the first modern sporting superstar" (Wilcox 1994: 58). The Irish would also participate in other sports like rowing but boxing remained as their key sport. Following the lead of the Irish, the next wave of European immigrants were the Italians. They too found it advantageous to embrace sports as a means of getting ahead and becoming assimilated in American culture. At the turn of the twentieth century Italians participated in bicycle riding and Greco-Roman wrestling and bocce ball. Italians also turned to boxing, baseball, and soccer.

We have shown that some blacks played professional baseball but it is Jackie Robinson who received credit for breaking the "color barrier." In 1947, Robinson signed with the Brooklyn Dodgers. So significant is this event that MLB officially retired Robinson's jersey number "42" from all MLB teams. Robinson was signed by Branch Rickey, base-ball executive of the Dodgers. As Rickey had foreshadowed, Robinson's integration into MLB was difficult. Robinson was the victim of numerous racist taunts by both players and fans. Robinson was a great player and quickly won over his Dodgers teammates who, for the most part, eagerly defended him from others. Pee Wee Reese, the Dodgers team captain, once put his arm around Robinson in an early game during the 1947 season to demonstrate to all that Robinson was accepted as player and teammate. Robinson was only human and he admits in his *Autobiography* that there times when the abuse tested his patience. The Philadelphia Phillies, led by manager Ben Chapman, were by far the most insulting and venomous. Robinson states that Chapman's and the Phillies' con-stant abuse was so awful that he almost went over the Phillies dugout to grab "one of those white sons of bitches and smash his teeth in with my despised black fist" (Robinson 1995: 60). But then Robinson remembered all that Rickey had warned him about and he regained his composure. The entire Dodgers team and organization were often the recip-ients of abuse because of Robinson's participation in baseball. Robinson, of course, went on to have a great career and receives credit for paving the way for other African Ameri-cans to play baseball. Just months after the Dodgers signed Robinson, the Cleveland Indi-ans owner Bill Veeck signed Lawrence Eugene Doby to play in the American League. He too went on to have a great career and became the first black player to hit a home run in a World Series game.

Charlie Sifford is known as "the Jackie Robinson" of golf as he became the first Afri-can American to break the Caucasian-only clause on the PGA tour when the Association finally issued him an "approved player" card in 1960 (Kupper 2015). When asked about the comparison to Jackie Robinson, Sifford replied, "If I was the Jackie Robinson of golf, I sure didn't do a very good job of it. Jackie was followed by a hundred great black ball-players. I was followed by no one" (Kupper 2015: B7). While Sifford is correct that the list is short, most people can think of Tiger Woods as an exception. Earl Lloyd is known as the first African American to break the color barrier in the NBA in 1950. Much of his NBA career was spent with the Syracuse Nationals where he became the first black player to win an NBA title in 1955 (Kirst 2015). Countless African Americans followed Lloyd to success in the NBA. Known as the "Jackie Robinson of hockey," Willie O'Ree, a descendant of escaped slaves, broke pro hockey's color barrier in 1958 as the first black player to skate in a NHL game (Pond 2020). (For a popular culture connection, see the award-winning film-festival favorite, "Wille.") O'Ree was playing his second season in the Quebec Senior Hockey League with the Quebec Aces when the Boston Bruins called him up for two games in 1958. O'Ree never disclosed to the Bruins that he had lost 95 per-cent of the vision in his right eye two years earlier after getting hit with an errant puck. As with the other African American trailblazers in sports, O'Ree endured racial slurs, threats, and fights (Bell 2017).

The Hispanic/Latino experience in American sports is quite different from that of whites and blacks. African Americans had long been the largest minority group in the United States, and as a result far more attention has been placed on the black experience in sports. However, Hispanics have for some time now been the largest category of people after white Americans. Latino players did not begin to enter the professional leagues in Amer-ican sports in any significant numbers until the 1950s. Unlike blacks, many Latino players faced discrimination because of language barriers. The inability of Latino and Hispanics to speak English infuriated many Americans. Many Latinos, such as Roberto Clemente, were unprepared for America's obsession with racial categorization. Puerto Rico, Clemente's home country, does not use racial categories when dealing with others. Clemente stated, "I don't believe in color; I believe in people" (Lomax 2004: 77). Latinos considered the Jim Crow practices of American society irrational. The resulting segregatory practices naturally upset Latinos. Because of hotel segregation, especially during barnstorming exhibitions in the southern states, there were times when the white players received police escorts through town so that their chartered buses could make it to the airport and ball fields on time. Blacks and Latinos had to take separate buses and fend through traffic on their own—sometimes missing flights to the next city (Lomax 2004). A number of professional teams that played Latino ballplayers hired assistants to help them deal with American culture. Still, black and Latino players did not feel that they should have to adapt to racist policies; rather, racist policies should be changed. One of the most significant early Hispanic athletes to play American sports was Roberto Clemente. Clemente was an awesome player who excelled both defensively as an outfielder and offensively with a career batting average of .317. He was the eleventh player to reach the career 3,000 hit club. Clemente played in an era before cable television and during a "dead" period in baseball (low scoring, which translates to lower interest on the part of fans). Those who saw Clemente play will remember his uncanny ability to flag down fly balls in the outfield and his ability to stretch a single into a double with his speed and reckless abandon on the base paths.

Nancy Lopez is another early Latino athlete to achieve greatness in her sport, golf. Lopez is a member of the Ladies Professional Golf Association (LPGA) tour. She first started playing golf at age 8 and by age 12 she won the New Mexico Women's Invitational (Chavira 1977). Lopez joined the LPGA in 1978. "Lopez won nine tournaments, including an unprecedented five in a row, was named Rookie of the Year, Rolex Player of the Year (also won in 1979, 1985, and 1988), Vare Trophy Winner (also won in 1979 and 1985), Golfer of the Year, and Female Athlete of the Year (Jamieson 1998: 343).

Jim Thorpe represents the most significant Native American to break into American sports. Thorpe was born circa May 28, 1888, near current-day Prague, Oklahoma. Thorpe's parents were both of mixed-race ancestry; his father had an Irish father and a Sac and Fox Indian mother and his mother had a French father and a Potawatomi mother. He was raised as a Sac and Fox with his native name, Wa-Tho-Huk, meaning "Bright Path," but was christened Jacobus Franciscus Thorpe (Biography.com 2014). Thorpe played multiple sports, including baseball, basketball, football, hockey, track and field and boxing. He was an All-American in football at the Carlisle Indian School. Perhaps his greatest sporting achievement occurred at the 1912 Olympic Games in Stockholm, Sweden, where he won the pentathlon and decathlon. Sweden's King Gustaf V declared Thorpe to be the greatest athlete in the world. Upon his return to the United States, he was honored with a ticker-tape parade in New York City as part of a hero's welcome home. However, a newspaper article revealed that Thorpe had been paid to play minor league baseball in 1909 and 1910. As a result, he was stripped of his amateur eligibility and forced to return his gold medals and his historic performance was erased from the Olympic record books (Biography.com 2014). Today, he would not have been classified as an amateur. But, even by the standards of the day, Thorpe was cheated of his Olympic glory because the 1912 rulebook stated that protests had to be made within 30 days from the closing ceremonies of the Games and the newspaper articles did not appear until six months later (United States Olympic Committee 2014). In 1982, long after his death, Thorpe's medals were restored and his name put back in the record books.

Beyond his Olympic glory, Thorpe was named by the Associated Press in 1950 as the greatest athlete of the first half of the twentieth century and the following year he was portrayed by Burt Lancaster in the film *Jim Thorpe: All-American*. Thorpe was also elected a charter member of the Pro Football Hall of Fame in 1963 (Biography.com 2014).

These stories represent a few select major racial breakthroughs in American sports.

Racism in Sports in the Present

In 1954, the Supreme Court (*Brown v. Board of Education of Topeka*) invalidated the *Plessy v. Ferguson* 1896 court decision that had created the "separate but equal" American policy. The significance of the *Brown* case cannot be overstated, for among blacks, as well as other minorities, it provided the spark of hope that had begun to build in the 1940s. The 1954 decision, among many things, guaranteed blacks the opportunity to attend public schools, including colleges. Coupled with the G.I Bill of Rights, it enabled large numbers of blacks to attend college in the 1950s. These same opportunities would open the doors for college athletic participation among blacks.

The transition from segregation to integration of some college sports teams between the late 1960s and the mid–1970s may best be illustrated by the University of Alabama. In 1968, Alabama had no blacks on athletic scholarships. By 1975, its basketball team had an all black starting lineup (Nixon 1984). In 1966, the University of Texas at El Paso (UTEP), known then as Texas Western, with five black starters, shocked heavily favored (and all-white) Kentucky in the NCAA men's college basketball final, winning 72–65 (Menez 2006). (In 2006, the film *Glory Road* was released and although the filmmakers took some dramatic license, the film is based on this historic meeting between Texas Western and Kentucky.) College coaches across the United States began to seek talented black athletes, assuming this was their ticket to success. As Lapchick (1991) states, UTEP's triumph over Kentucky is often hailed as a sign of a breakthrough against racism, but none of the five starters on the basketball team graduated from the university. According to Lapchick, if UTEP had a true commitment to ending racism, they would have worked with these athletes to ensure their graduation from college. Low graduation rates remain a concern of many college sport observers.

Even the casual observer has noticed that blacks dominate many American sports today (especially team sports with high earning potential). However, black domination in sport was then, and remains today, mostly limited to the role of participant (the workers) in the major commercialized sports. There are still few minority owners, general managers, managers, head coaches, and trainers. The primary reason minority members are underrepresented in power positions in sports is because of racism. "The most visible nonplaying personnel in sports are those who reside in the front office. These parties include chief executive officers, team presidents, general managers, and the head coach, who straddles the line between the field or court and the administrative offices. The front office also includes such professionals as team doctors, lawyers, and accountants" (Shropshire 1996: 76). Little has changed in the years since Shropshire's observation. Consider for example, the NFL. "When the NFL was first made to formally address the embarrassing lack of diversity in its coaching and front-office ranks back in the early aughts, a scant three of the league's 32 teams were helmed by minority head coaches. Seventeen years since the introduction of the Rooney Rule, which requires all clubs to interview at least one minority candidate for its openings at head coach and general manager, the grand total entering the 2020 season has inched upward to four" (Graham 2020). Since the Rooney Rule was initiated, the NFL, in its attempt to increase minority hiring, requires at least one minority candidate for any of the top coordinator vacancies and one external minority candidate for the senior football operations or general manager positions as well (Booker 2020a). When it comes to position coaches, nearly 70 percent (69.6 percent) of RB/WR/DB coaches are minorities but just 25.4 percent of OL/TEA/DL/LB, 12 percent of special teams, and 11.1 percent of QB coaches are of minority status and this is in a League where 70 percent of the players are minorities (Dahlberg 2020).

The NBA, on the other hand, is doing a much better job with minority hiring. Richard Lapchick (who along with James H. Frey were a part of the early formation of the North American Society for the Sociology of Sport), the Director of the Institute for Diversity and Ethics of Sport at the University of Central Florida, describes the NBA as a continuing "leader in racial and gender hiring practices. The NBA again earned an A+ on the issue of racial hiring, a B for gender hiring practices, and an overall grade of an A in the 2019 report card" (Lapchick 2019). In June 2020, the Arizona Coyotes hired Xavier Gutierrez as their team president and CEO, making him the first Latino at either position in NHL history.

Racism is a big problem in soccer throughout the world and is especially prevalent in Europe and South America. Christos Kassimeris (2008) argues that nationalism is the prime culprit for this reality. Leading up to World War II, a number of nations, especially Nazi Germany and fascist Italy, attempted to create perfect teams based on home-grown talent. Hitler in particular tried to prove the validity of his "Aryan race as the superior race" philosophy by winning international sporting events, including soccer matches. As it turned out, the Germans were (and still are) very good at soccer and they won without minorities on their teams. Many other nations followed this formula. And, as Kassimeris points out, for most of soccer's early history, the sport at the semi-professional and professional level was segregated, and very few racial and ethnic minorities were allowed to play at the club level. When clubs played at the international level, the soccer match takes on a far greater meaning than simply one team playing another; it takes on the meaning of one nation battling another nation for ideological superiority.

Following World War II, when the talent level of some minority players was too high to ignore, a number of clubs and national teams began to sign them. This upset many ultra-nationalistic fans of club teams. England, the primary European nation to stand up to Germany during the World Wars, became known for its notorious soccer hooligans who went to soccer matches in foreign cities as much to fight the locals as to cheer for their club or national team (see Chapter 9 for a discussion on hooligans). As the popularity of soccer continued to increase throughout Asia and Africa, a large number of fans of soccer clubs and national teams took on the battle-like mentality of the English. Fights against rival fans in the stadium and outside the stadium became routine. Players of races, ethnicities, and nationalities different from the competition were subject to racial taunts and chants. For many fans, nationalism takes precedence when cheering for their favorite teams. Fans of Poland recall Germany's invasion of their land at the start of World War II, while fans of England and France have an equal disdain toward the Germans. And so it goes on, as nationalistic fans from around the world with long memories take past injustices with them to the soccer stadium.

It has remained common in soccer for players and spectators to taunt black players with the racial chants involving the term "monkey." Consider this one of many examples:

In a very odd move, Italian soccer was condemned for using monkey paintings in their anti-racism campaign. Alexander Smith (2019) writes, "With players being racially abused by fans, newspapers printing insensitive headlines, and pundits using bigoted language, Italian soccer officials acknowledged this week that something needed to be done about endemic racism in their sport." The anti-racism campaign in the nation's elite league, Serie A, commissioned artist Simone Fugazzotto who created a series of paintings of different colored monkeys, and thought it would be a clever way to neutralize the monkey chants that Senegalese defender Kalidou Koulibaly is routinely subjected to by spectators. His idea was to refer to everyone as monkeys. Anti-discrimination groups such as "Kick It Out" called the artwork "completely inappropriate" (Smith 2019). Kick It Out and Football Against Racism in Europe (FARE) are two attempts to combat racism in soccer. Another form of discriminatory chanting involves homophobic "puto" chants, often associated with fans of the Mexican national soccer team. The term "puto" has been used to disparage homosexuality. The Mexican national team has pleaded with its fans to no longer use chants that include this word (Zeigler 2016).

Individual athletes often say or do things that are racist. For example, Philadelphia Eagles wide receiver DeSean Jackson shared an anti–Semitic post (that quoted a tirade against Jews by none other than Adolf Hitler) on social media over the July 4 (2020) weekend that was immediately condemned by the NFL. When called out on this, Jackson said, "My post was definitely not intended for anybody of any race to feel any type of way, especially the Jewish community. I post things on my site all the time, and just probably never should have posted anything Hitler did, because Hitler was a bad person, and I know that" (Maaddi 2020). Former Eagles president Joe Banner criticized Jackson on Twitter writing: "If a white player said anything about (African Americans) as outrageous as what DeSean Jackson said about Jews tonight there would at least be a serious conversation about cutting him and a need for a team meeting to discuss [it]" (Maaddi 2020).

In light of the Black Lives Matters movement, a number of players and leagues have fought to combat racism in sport in contemporary society. Consider these examples:

- In June 2020, Kansas State football players announced that they will boycott all team activities until administrators create a policy that would allow a student to be expelled for "openly racist, threatening or disrespectful actions" (*Associated Press* 2020b).
- Oklahoma State's coach Mike Gundy had his salary cut by $1 million and his contract shortened by a year as part of an internal review prompted by sharp criticism from his star running back for wearing a T-shirt that promoted a far-right news channel, One America News Network (OANN). Among other things, OANN is critical of the BLM movement and promotes falsehoods and conspiracy theories (*Associated Press* 2020c)
- A long time tradition at the University of Florida is under review in light of BLM social movement. The "Gator Bait" chant ("If you ain't a Gator, you're Gator bait") wherein Gator fans taunt opposing players and fans has links to slavery and an era when, according to historical accounts, alligator hunters used black children as human bait (Wharton 2020)
- In early June, FIFA announced that it would not sanction players demanding justice for George Floyd during matches which would usually go against FIFA policy prohibiting "any political, religious, or personal slogans, statements or

images" on equipment. Players from around the world, including Germany, England, and New Zealand, displayed various messages of support including: "Justice for George Floyd" and "We Won't Tolerate" (Douglas 2020)

- NFL Commissioner Roger Goodell announced that the League was wrong when they did not listen to Colin Kaepernick and other players who silently and peacefully protested during the playing of the national anthem at the start of games in the past but vowed that the NFL would allow such protests in the future (Litke 2020).
- Prior to the George Floyd killing, the state flag of Mississippi still included an image of the Confederate flag. Following Floyd's death, Mississippi State star running back Kylin Hill said that would not play another down of football if the state of Mississippi didn't change its flag. The Southeastern Conference and the NCAA immediately put pressure on the state of Mississippi as well. And sure enough, the state shortly afterwards agreed to finally change its state's flag (Russo 2020).
- NASCAR's Ganassi Racing fired driver Kyle Larson after he used a racial slur (the "n-word") during a live-streamed virtual race in April 2020 (Fryer 2020). Ganassi left the door open to reinstate Larson in the future and did so six months later [Booker 2020b].

Perhaps one of the biggest surprises in trying to right the wrongs of the past in light of the BLM social movement, and something worth special attention, was NASCAR's decision to ban the Confederate flag at all its venue. The Stars and Bars has long been associated with this sport of southern roots and a fan base that primarily consists of southerners. "For more than 70 years, the Confederate flag was a familiar sight at NASCAR races. Through the civil rights era right on through the season opener at Daytona in February [2020], the flag dotted the infield campsites and was waved in grandstands by fans young and old" (Gelston 2020). However, after having its woke movement, NASCAR said it would no longer be allowed. As the decision was made during the COVID-19 pandemic, spectators were not allowed at the racing venues, so it was not immediately known how NASCAR fans would react to such a bold move. NASCAR states that it will continue "to make diversity and inclusion a priority as it tries to expand the sport's reach beyond its largely white audience" (Booker 2020b).

We turn our attention now turn to one of the most blatant forms of racism in American sports, the use of Indian imagery.

The Use of Native American Nicknames, Logos, and Mascots

Sports teams routinely use nicknames, logos and mascots as a means of conveying a team identity. These nicknames, logos, and mascots possess symbolic meaning, usually meant to intimidate opponents because of their fierceness. For example, the NFL's Chicago franchise has "Bears" as a nickname and clearly, a bear is an intimidating figure. Wild bear do not roam the streets of Chicago so how is it that the nickname "Bears" was chosen? The Bears franchise originated from Decatur, Illinois, and when George Halas bought the team in 1922 he wanted a different nickname than the "Staley's" (founded in 1920 and named after the A.E. Staley Company, a starch manufacturer). Thus, the

"Staley's" had a natural connection to the team as it was the last name of the owner (much like the Cleveland Browns being named after former co-founder/owner and first head coach Paul Brown). Halas decided to use a more ferocious version of Chicago's Cubs (MLB) who were already beloved in the city. Many sports franchises have nicknames with symbolic meaning including: Major League Baseball's Colorado "Rockies" (located in the Rocky Mountains); the Minnesota Twins (for the Minnesota "twin" cities of Minneapolis and St. Paul); Milwaukee "Brewers" (Milwaukee is known for its beer breweries); and the NBA's Philadelphia "76ers" (as in the spirit of 1776). Other times the relationship is not so obvious and often the result of franchise relocation; for example, the Utah "Jazz" made sense when the franchise was still in New Orleans, the Los Angeles "Lakers" when they were still in the "Land of 10,000 Lakes" (Minnesota), and the Los Angeles Dodgers when Brooklyn fans actually had to dodge the cable trolleys in order to enter Ebbets Field. (The Dodgers were originally known as the "Trolley Dodgers.")

A number of sports teams use Native American imagery for their nicknames, logos, and mascots. Those who support such team nicknames as the "Braves" or "Indians" believe that they are honoring Native Americans. They believe that ritualistic behaviors like the "tomahawk chop" and the "war cry" are merely ways of cheering for the team. The manner in which fans defend their right to hold on to and embrace their cherished symbols of the team reflects a type of totemism. Totemism, as described by Emile Durkheim, is a primitive form of "a religious system in which certain things, particularly animals and plants, come to be regarded as *sacred* emblems (totems) of the clan. With totemism, an image or representation is placed on a totem pole. The images at the highest points of the totem were the most sacred. In addition to the physical aspects of totemism is the moral character. There are occasions when the members of the tribe come together at the totem and share a number of emotions, sentiments, and rituals" (Delaney 2004: 100). Ordinary items are transformed into sacred totems through special rituals and ceremonies (e.g., the wafer and wine at a Catholic mass which is ritualistically transformed into the body and blood of Christ). Team logos and mascots take on this totem quality for devout fans. It seems odd that people in the twenty-first century embrace totems, or symbols, with the same level of enthusiasm as primitive, pagan worshippers. However, sports often bring out the primitive inner being of people—including a passionate devotion to a belief or symbol. This type of devotion leads to at least two forms of defense: (1) That the nicknames are now a part of tradition and should be kept (Toglia and Harris 2014); and (2) That attempts to ban Indian imagery violates First Amendment speech and represents "political correctness" (Grose 2011). As is often the case, when someone invokes a claim of "political correctness" to avoid change it's because the issue at hand is a matter of social incorrectness.

Those who defend the use of Indian imagery in sports need to remember that no honor is given if none is received. That is to say, when people state that they are honoring indigenous people by naming sports teams in honor of "Indians" it is not an honor if the indigenous people do not see it as an honor. The Seneca Nation, for example, wants an end to the practice of more than 50 high schools across New York State using Indian imagery for their sports teams. Seneca Nation spokesperson Joe Stahlman states that the "Seneca Nation views the use of Native American names, references, and imagery for the logos and mascots of schools and their sports teams as blatantly offensive to the Seneca Nation and has no place in a multicultural society that values diversity" (Legare 2020).

In light of the fact that Native Americans were victims of *genocide*—the intentional attempt to exterminate a race of people by a more dominant population—a number of Native American groups, scholars, and sports fans consider the practice of using Indian imagery as a form of racism. Though there exist some other types of human mascots, Native American mascots are in a different category. Human mascots such as Hilltoppers, Oilers, Patriots, and 49ers are generally emblematic of the geographic area where their teams reside. Other human mascots (e.g., Crusaders, Friars, Knights, and Saints) have religious significance. Native American nicknames may be generic (e.g., Indians and Redmen), tribal (e.g., Florida State Seminoles, Utah Utes, Central Michigan Chippewas and Eastern Michigan Hurons), or they may focus on an attribute (e.g., Braves, Warriors and Savages). In most cases, Indian nicknames do not represent a specific regional tribe, but rather, that the team has the fearsome characteristic of "Indian savages." The idea of Indians as "savages" corresponds to the threat that Indians posed to the early settlers. Furthermore, in many cases, it served as justification for taking their land.

In addition, this attribution of Native Americans as mascots is similar to those teams that use nicknames such as Tigers or Bears. For example, there are no wild lions running loose in Detroit; instead the usage of the nickname and mascot "Lions" by Detroit's NFL franchise is to imply that the team embodies the power of a wild and ferocious animal. Native Americans, however, are human beings, not wild animals. Using imagery of Native people as though they are fearsome, savage beasts is as racist as it is derogatory towards an entire category of people. And this leads to another related issue, the cultural appropriation of Native people, or as Jennifer Dyar states, with their "Indianness." Dyar ponders the white obsession with Indianness and why it is they are the ones who can dictate the narrative of what it means to be an indigenous person. "Whether through vicarious participation in Indianness at a distance or through direct appropriation of Indian power and value, whites have attempted to distill Indianness until it is composed of nothing more nor nothing less than they desire. For centuries, Indians themselves have been excluded from the process of defining Indianness, powerless to curtail or alter white conceptions" (Dyar 2003).

THE TIMES ARE (FINALLY) CHANGING

In response to growing social pressure, Indian imagery in sports has been eliminated from a growing number of high schools, colleges and universities. One of the early universities to drop the Indian imagery was Syracuse University. SU dropped its "Indian" logo and mascot—The Saltine Warrior—in 1978, despite being one of the first institutions to employ Indian imagery. The Saltine Warrior, a precursor to FSU's Chief Osceola (which was created the same year SU dropped the Saltine Warrior), dressed in complete headdress and Indian clothing, performing "Indian" dances on the sidelines during football games. "Throughout the late nineteenth and twentieth centuries, Syracuse's Indian mascot was rooted in notions of 'noble savagery,' the 'vanishing Indian,' and eventually the Indian as wild creature" (Fisher 2001: 25). By the 1970s, there were protests from local Native American groups to end Syracuse University's usage of Indian portrayals. Additionally, university officials decided to eliminate the Indian imagery because "reason, truth, and fairness had prevailed over emotion, fiction, and prejudice" (Fisher 2001: 38). St. Johns University changed its name from "Redmen" to "Red Storm" in response to cultural sensitivity. These are just two examples of schools that have voluntarily disassociated themselves from Indian imagery. Other schools and professional sports franchises have been reluctant to change.

The Florida State University Seminoles, Mississippi College, and the Utah Utes are three universities that use Indian imagery to refer to specific tribes rather than a generic nickname. FSU utilizes an extensive amount of racist Indian imagery in sports including fans who wear face paint and do a tomahawk chop chant. The school also allows the use of a mascot dressed as an "Indian" who rides a horse, like Syracuse did decades ago. However, because the Seminoles refer to a specific tribe indigenous to the Tallahassee, Florida, region (home of the university) and seemingly have the support of the Florida Seminole nation, FSU has mostly escaped the negativity directed toward other colleges and professional sports teams that use Indian imagery. Some members of the much larger Oklahoma Seminole tribe, however, are not supportive of the Indian imagery even though the Seminole National General Council voted not to oppose the use of Indian imagery at FSU. Further, the same people who believe Indian imagery is offensive no matter what the circumstances also find FSU's imagery as insensitive to a particular culture. Supporters of the Florida State University's usage of the nickname "Seminoles" believe that they are honoring a regional, specific group of brave warriors who refused to compromise and be forced to move westward. The student mascot is a male dressed as "Chief Osceola," who wears moccasins, a tasseled leather "Indian" outfit, face paint and a large bandanna, hoisting a large feathered lance. One of FSU's most visible traditions (created in 1978) involves the home-football game performance of "Chief Osceola," atop a horse named Renegade, charging onto the football field with a burning spear and then dramatically thrusting it into the logo centered on the playing field. The FSU fans cheer in a wild frenzy. With input from the Mississippi Band of Choctaw Indians, the Mississippi College Choctaws have kept their team name while doing away with their mascot Chief Choc in 2005 (Apel 2015). The Ute Indian Tribe encourages the University of Utah to use the Ute name for the University's sports programs "with its full support" reads a memorandum of understanding between the two parties (The University of Utah 2020).

Without question, the most offensive nickname in North American professional sports is "Redskins." Many schools across the nation have banned the nickname; this includes the state of California which banned the use of "Redskins" at all schools in the state. The biggest culprit of the "redskin" nickname is the NFL's Washington franchise. Originating in Boston as the Braves in 1932, but changing its nickname to the Redskins in 1933, the franchise moved to Washington in 1937 and kept the offensive nickname. For decades, the authors of this text, nearly all others in academia, enlightened people in general, and Indian tribes, have argued that that the nickname was offensive based on the fact that dictionary descriptions for "redskins" are the same as they are for "n*igger"—that it's an "offensive term," or "offensive slang." People should be as uncomfortable saying the word "r*dskin" as they are saying the word "n*gger." In other words, the term "redskin" should be viewed as "the 'R' word" just as most people use the expression "the 'N' word" to refer to the offensive slang word for African Americans. Furthermore, it is more than ironic that the Redskins franchise is located in the U.S. national capital city. Washington, D.C., has long been the symbol of broken promises and treaties over the years to Native Americans. Dan Snyder, the owner of the Washington franchise since 1999, however, declared that he would never change the name. Then came the BLM movement of 2020; followed by the announcement that Washington would indeed, finally, drop the Redskins name and imagery. Adding to the controversy is the realization that many people are now upset with things named "Washington" because, like nearly all wealthy landowners in Virginia, George Washington owned slaves. Furthermore, the "D.C." in Washington, D.C., stands for "District of Columbia" with the territory of Columbia named after Christopher Columbus. Racial connotations abound with this NFL franchise, city, and nickname.

Did Snyder finally see the light and grow a social conscience and make the change because it was the correct thing to do? Not exactly. Instead, it was economic pressure from such major sponsors as FedEx, Nike, Pepsi, and Bank of America that led to the change. For an idea what kind of pressure was put on Snyder consider that FedEx had threatened to strip its name from the team's home stadium in Landover, Maryland, to the tune of $45 million and Nike stopped selling team apparel on its website. Undoubtedly, these major corporations saw that the "times were a changing" and their pressure on Snyder reflected this influence. Snyder did not admit that the nickname was racist and instead attempted to turn attention toward coming up with a new name and imagery. However, the July 2020 transition would not be as smooth as Snyder had hoped as 15 female former employees said that they were sexually harassed during their time with the team. The women did not accuse Snyder directly but rather the culture within the organization that he created. A month later (August 2020), new sexual harassment accusations were pointed directly at Snyder, raising the number to 40 women accusing him of sexual harassment either directly or indirectly (Florio 2020). Snyder pledged to make organizational changes in light of the impact of these two related social movements—BLM and #MeToo (the movement, with variations in names, designed to fight sexual harassment and sexual abuse). In the short term, Snyder decided to rename his franchise (for the 2020 season) the Washington Football Team. (Note: The outcome of these allegations was not available at the time of our writing this book.)

The authors have been promoting the need for name changes for other franchises as well (i.e., Cleveland Indians, the Atlanta Braves, and the Kansas City Chiefs) and there is good reason to think such changes will finally occur. The Cleveland Indians (MLB) have come under attack primarily because of their logo—a caricature of an "Indian" head smiling with huge glaring buckteeth and a single red feather, named "Chief Wahoo." Adopting demeaning and cartoonish images for the purposes of cheering for a sports team is tactless, offensive and is highly objectionable to Native Americans and many American Indian organizations have asked repeatedly for the Chief Wahoo logo to be replaced. Finally, and effective at the start of the 2019 season, Cleveland took the divisive Chief Wahoo logo off their jerseys and caps and stadium signs. Commenting on the move, MLB Commissioner Rob Manfred said, "Major League Baseball is committed to building a culture of diversity and inclusion throughout the game. [The logo] is no longer appropriate for on-field use" (Withers 2018). Many people had argued that the logo was not appropriate long ago, but anti-racist advocates are happy with the results if not the justification.

Slightly less objectionable to Native American groups is the generic nickname "Indians." Nonetheless, it is long past the time for Cleveland to drop this nickname. The Cleveland Indians organization claims that the nickname was chosen by Cleveland fans in a newspaper poll as an honor to Louis Francis Sockalexis, the first Native American to play Major League Baseball. The "Indian" identity has been absorbed into the collective consciousness of Cleveland Indians fans, and fans of baseball in general, forming a shared tradition and common rallying point (Staurowsky 1998). However, Staurowsky conducted an extensive content analysis of Cleveland newspapers from

September 1914 through March 1915, the period of time when the fan voting supposedly took place, and concluded that the eventual selection of the "Indians" name by newspaper readers was improbable and difficult to prove. Further, Staurowsky claims that the assertion that a fan recommended "Indians" to honor Sockalexis, although not impossible, has no evidentiary foundation in the articles chronicling fan or writer preferences. This revelation that the Cleveland story lacks credibility has been reported before in the mainstream press by the *Cleveland Plain Dealer* (Aran and Sangiacomo 1993) and by other sources. As an update, and as the authors had predicted, Cleveland did drop the "Indians" nickname and in July 2021 announced that the new nickname would be "Guardians."

The controversy facing the Atlanta Braves centers on such fan practices as the use of the "tomahawk chop," the "warwhoop," wearing "Indian" face paint, etc. The primary disdain directed toward the Atlanta Braves franchise by Native American groups is the generic use of the term "Braves" and the stereotypical usage of Indian imagery and the mockery of Native American history, culture and religion. When Native Americans wear face paint it is for events of cultural significance, such as wearing white while in mourning, green for endurance, blue for confidence and so forth. We would not accept a fan (let alone an entire franchise) showing up at a sporting event in blackface because of its racist undertones, so why do we accept non–Native Americans wearing face paint to look like an "Indian" or "Brave?"

The Kansas City Chiefs have some of the same issues as the Cleveland Indians and Atlanta Braves with regard to the use of stereotypical usage of Indian imagery. In August 2020, the KC franchise addressed some of these concerns as the Chiefs banned fans from wearing "Indian" headdresses and facepaint and were considering banning the "Arrowhead chop" (similar to the Braves fans' use of the "tomahawk chop").

Dana Williams (2007) describes how the use of Native imagery for sports teams exemplifies a racist practice that selectively targets Native Americans by displaying decapitated heads (as essentially that's what Naïve logos are) of previously replaced, abused, conscripted, and eliminated peoples has clear ideological and propagandistic purposes. "The symmetry with the genocidal practice of scalp-hunting should not be lost" (Williams 2007).

Native Americans are people. They are not mascots. Eliminating offensive Indian imagery is not a matter of "political correctness" but rather, a matter of *correctness*.

Connecting Sports and Popular Culture

Box 11: *Race* and **Race**

There have been many movies that deal with the topic of race and sports, many of which have been based on true stories. For people of a certain age, the first film that often comes to mind is a classic from over 50 years ago, *Brian's Song* (1971). It is often listed as one of the best sports films ever made. As Ray Didinger and Glen Macnow point out in their *Ultimate Book of Sports Movies*, "When we surveyed people for their all-time favorite sports movies, *Brian's Song* was on most short lists" (Didinger and Macnow 2009: 80). Indeed, the film is often mentioned as a personal favorite of people who are not otherwise noted for their love of tear-jerking movies. They add: "Larry Csonka, the Hall of Fame fullback, admits he choked up watching *Brian's Song*. It's hard to imagine Csonka

310 The Sociology of Sports

with that battle-scarred face and outta my way scowl getting all misty over a movie, but he swears it really did happen" (Didinger and Macnow 2009: 80).

Just what is it about this movie that can make grown men cry (especially grown men not usually identified with such behavior)? *Brian's Song* (which was originally made for television rather than for theatrical release) is based on a true story, and one which directly relates to race and sports. It details the friendship between Chicago Bears running backs Gale Sayers (played by Billy Dee Williams) and Brian Piccolo (played by James Caan). Williams and Caan would soon become famous for their roles in, respectively, *Star Wars* and *The Godfather,* but when *Brian's Song* was first aired they were unknown actors, which perhaps added to the power of the movie's reception since they both seemed to embody the roles they were playing. For in 1971 many viewers would have known of the real Sayers and Piccolo and their poignant friendship. Heated rivals who were competing for the same spot on the roster, Sayers and Piccolo initially had little reason to interact with each other off the playing field. More significantly, Sayers was African American and Piccolo was white, during an historic period when the Civil Rights Movement was still in its early stages and members of different racial and ethnic communities seldom if ever communicated with each other, let alone became friends. In addition, the two men came from different social and economic backgrounds.

As the film shows, once they begin to know each other, Sayers and Piccolo find that they have much in common. They are both pranksters who love to laugh when off the field (and frequently play good-natured practical jokes on each other), but are also hardworking and dedicated players when on the field. After becoming roommates when traveling to games their respect for each other deepens. Further shattering the racial boundaries of the time, their two wives also become the best of friends.

Sayers initially is chosen as the starting fullback instead of Piccolo, but Piccolo doesn't seem to resent this. He's happy for his friend's success and realizes that this is all for the good of the team overall. In fact, when Sayers in injured in a game against the San Francisco 49ers, tearing the ligaments in his right knee, Piccolo takes it upon himself to aid in his recovery, going so far as to bring a weight machine over to Sayers' home and helping him in his rehabilitation efforts. He does so even though, in Sayers' absence, Piccolo is given the starting fullback position, leading the Bears to a 17–16 win over the L.A. Rams and being given the game ball afterwards. While it would seem to be detrimental to his chances to remain in that position should Sayers return, he puts such thoughts aside as he aids his friend and helps him get back onto the field.

While Sayers does recuperate, he is quickly hampered by a second injury, this time to his left knee. Around the same time, Piccolo, at the young age of 26, also begins to decline. He is losing weight unexpectedly and is no longer able to run as fast as before. After going to the hospital for a checkup he receives a dire diagnosis—he has terminal cancer. The last part of *Brian's Song* deals with the ways in which Sayers reciprocates for the support previously shown to him. It is now his turn to help a stricken friend, and he remains by Piccolo's side throughout the agonies of his final days. The film ends with a powerful flashback of the two men in their prime, racing each other in a park, and a voiceover asks that Piccolo be remembered not for how he died but rather for how he lived. (Sayers died in 2020 at the age of 77.)

In understanding the initial impact of *Brian's Song* (which was based on Sayers' 1971 autobiography *I Am Third*) it should be noted that the Made-for-TV film appeared just a year after Piccolo's untimely death at the age of 26. Many football fans were still shaken by this, and the movie was an emotional experience for them. But another important point is that in 1971 racial unrest was still a very real issue across the country (as it sadly still is in contemporary America), with rioting, violent protests and the rise of Black Nationalism all constant themes on daily television news broadcasts.

Brian's Song, by showing that African Americans and whites could, at least potentially, work together, and by emphasizing the ways in which true friendship can override racial antagonisms and misunderstandings, was not only a popular motion picture, it inspired many other sports films dealing with race.

A more recent sports film dealing with an actual person is 2005's *Coach Carter,* starring Samuel L. Jackson. It is based on the true story of Ken Carter, a winning basketball coach at Richmond High School in Richmond, California, who made a pact with his team, the Oilers, that they all regularly attend their classes and maintain at least a C+ average. He has clear expectations for his players, knowing that regardless of their athletic achievements most will not do well in life without getting a proper education. Even though the team has a shot at the State Championship after going undefeated in the regular season, Carter is livid when he finds out several players have reneged on their agreement to study, and enforces a lockdown, making them all hit the books. In his glowing review of the film, Roger Ebert writes: "Ken Carter's most dramatic decision, which got news coverage in 1999, was to lock the gymnasium, forfeit games and endanger the team's title chances after some of his players refused to live up to the terms of the contract. The community of course was outraged that a coach would put grades above winning games; for them, the future for the student athletes lies in the NBA, not education" (Ebert 2005).The film has become a fan favorite, and Ken Carter—both the real man and his movie version—continues to inspire by demonstrating the true virtues of being a coach.

Another sports movie about a real-life athletic hero, which came out in 2016, has the clever title *Race.* This takes on multiple meanings, since it is all about Jesse Owen's incredible victories at the 1936 Olympic Games (described in detail earlier in this chapter), in which he won four gold medals, much to the chagrin of the Olympics' racist host, Adolf Hitler. Owens (portrayed in the film by Stephan James) became a hero to millions of sports fans of all races, but the film deals with the complexities of his dramatic triumphs. As Karly Cox points out, "Owens was dedicated to sport, which is shown in *Race* to elevate him above everyday concerns. However, his dedication also required an additional level of self-sacrifice due to the challenges of segregation and the pressures of being a role model" (Cox 2016). While his incredible performances showed the world that Hitler's "Aryan superiority" beliefs were both bogus and evil, Owens, upon his return to America, continued to face discrimination in his home country. The movie gives us much to reflect upon in regard to racial inequality at home and abroad. Cox concludes that "ultimately, *Race* does what all great sports films do: celebrates victory on the track. But in the coda, it punches you in the gut: heading to a dinner held in his honor back home, Jesse isn't allowed in through the front door, and has to go through the back. Director Stephen Hopkins isn't scared to draw parallels between the horrors of Nazism and the supposedly civilized US—and this is perhaps *Race'*s greatest strength" (Cox 2016).

The fight for social justice continues, and sports movies provide us with a provocative way to better understand such issues, especially those films that focus on real-life civil rights heroes and their struggles for equality.

SUMMARY

The Black Lives Matter social movement had a significant impact on society in general and in the sports world in particular at the start of the 2020s. The racism experienced by so many Americans for so long was being challenged in a loud and visible manner. Statues and monuments constructed to honor those who promoted hate, racism, and slavery were toppled and the names of once-revered public figures that were placed on prominent buildings were removed, all in the name of fighting racism. Athletes, sports teams, and sports leagues were taking a real stand against racism. NASCAR even banned the Confederate flag at all of its racing venues.

Sociologists point out that the concepts of race and ethnicity are a product of social constructionism and that such categories of people exist merely because society has chosen to label people in racial or ethnic terms. Other key terms including racism, prejudice, and discrimination were discussed. The role of genetics was explored. Racists that promote an ideological belief that one race is superior to others often attempt to use genetics to support their prejudicial and discriminatory arguments. Flaws to the theory of genetic predisposition apply to sports, especially the outdated notion of "born athletes." Certain unique physical characteristics however can enhance one's chances of performing well in sports.

Racism in sport is explored in some detail and begins with a look at past examples including the exclusion of Black athletes from professional and collegiate sports. A number of major racial breakthroughs would occur as key figures (i.e., John L. Sullivan; Jackie Robinson; Lawrence Dolby; Earl Lloyd; Roberto Clemente; Nancy Lopez; and, Jim Thorpe) finally broke racial barriers. Racism still exists in the present and reveals itself in a number of ways, including limited minority members in key top decision-making positions (e.g., General Manager and Owners of sports franchises); soccer players that are racial taunted around the world; athletes that take abuse from fans; and, coaches with outdated and reactionary ways of thinking.

One of the most blatant forms of racism in American sports involves the use of Indian imagery in team nicknames, logos, and mascots. As a sign of progress, a number of sports teams at all levels are finally getting rid of their racist nicknames including the worse violator of all, the NFL's Washington franchise. Native Americans are people. They are not mascots. Eliminating offensive Indian imagery is not a matter of "political correctness" but rather, a matter of *correctness*.

The issue of race provides yet another example of sport serving as a microcosm of society.

KEY TERMS

Black Lives Matter A global social movement designed to end discrimination and racism against African Americans.

Discrimination Behavior that treats people unequally on the basis of an ascribed status, such as race or gender.

Ethnic Group A category of people who are recognized as distinct based on such social or cultural factors as nationality, religion, language, geographic residence, a common set of values, and so on.

Genocide The intentional attempt to exterminate a race of people by a more dominant population.

Indian imagery A type of racist cultural appropriation based on stereotypical caricature of indigenous people that leads to ignorant distorted views.

Institutional racism The systematic practices and patterns within social institutions that lead to inequality between members of different races.

Prejudice Negative beliefs and overgeneralizations concerning a group of people which involves a judgment against someone based on a rigid and fixed mental image of some group of people that is applied to all individuals of that group.

Race A category of people who share some socially recognized physical characteristic (such as skin color or hereditary traits such as facial features) that distinguishes them from other groups of people and are recognized by themselves and others as a distinct group.

Racism Any attitude, belief, behavior, or social arrangement that has the intent, or the ultimate effect, of favoring one group over another.

Stereotypes Oversimplified and exaggerated beliefs about a category of people.

Totemism As described by Emile Durkheim, a primitive form of a religious system in which certain things, particularly animals and plants, come to be regarded as *sacred* emblems.

DISCUSSION QUESTIONS

- What is the Black Lives matter social movement and what is its impact on sports?
- Identify the three different types of racism and provide an example of each.
- What is the difference between discrimination and prejudice? Can you think of some examples where this might pertain to the sports world?
- What is the role of genetics, if any, in the development of individuals as athletes?
- Why are there so few minority owners, managers and coaches in sporting teams today? What do you think could be done to try to change this?
- What do you think about the controversy over using Indian imagery for athletic team names and mascots?
- What are some examples of racism in sports today?

CHAPTER 12

Economics and Sport

We learned in previous chapters that people play sports for many reasons. Young people are mostly driven by the desire to have fun and as we age and continue to play sports we do so for intrinsic reasons such as staying in shape, forming bonds with others, the sheer joy of being involved with athletics, or as an excuse to get out of the house. The sports world is also about extrinsic rewards such as fame, adulation, and economic fulfillment. Professional sports, "big-time" college sport programs, and other sporting activities not quite at the elite level have a strong connection with the social institution of economics.

As we shall see in this chapter, economic considerations center on such things as sports as an extension of consumerism; sports entertainment; sports marketing and corporate sponsorship; player endorsements; sports stadium deals; economic benefits for owners; and increased salaries for athletes. Ask yourself, then, what are all of these economic considerations dependent upon? The simple answer, "sports!" If sports aren't played, revenue is not generated, and if revenue is not generated, how can anything else connected to economics pan out? This explains why, at the professional level, owner lockouts and players strikes are bad business for everyone. Except for rare and isolated cases, you do not hear of colleges locking out student-athletes or players going on strike for a better contract deal (although this could be a real possibility in the future). All this means that the money will keep on rolling in so long as people do not mess things up. That is, unless something really bizarre occurs, say a global pandemic, or an apocalypse.

On the plus side, we have not been confronted by an apocalypse, yet (read the authors' *Beyond Sustainability* book if you want to learn about the possibility of an apocalypse via a mass extinction). However, we were hit with a global pandemic in the year 2020. We have mentioned the SARS-CoV-2, or COVID-19, pandemic by name a few times in this updated edition of *The Sociology of Sports* and for good reason as the entire world was shaken by this nouveau disease. So many common mannerisms such as hugging loved ones, shaking hands with associates, and high-fiving each other at a ballgame are perhaps altered forever. Why, MLB players were told they could no longer spit (e.g., tobacco or seeds) while playing baseball for goodness sakes! (This last mannerism is, perhaps, best to be banned regardless of the situation.) The relevant concern for us is the lack of sports and, in particular, the lost revenue because of the cancellation of sports.

The sports world was interrupted by COVID-19 in mid–March, just prior to college basketball's huge money maker (over $1 billion) "March Madness"; as the NBA and NHL regular seasons were nearing an end, and with their respective playoffs looming, and prior to the start of the MLB season. Internationally, soccer leagues were shut down for months before restarting sans spectators in the stands and the 2020 Olympics were postponed until 2021. NASCAR resumed after a short hiatus but without spectators. Golf did the same thing. In July 2020, MLB started a 60-game season, although Toronto was not allowed to play home games in Canada due to the Canadian government's fear of Americans entering their country. The NBA decided to conclude its season with the playoffs in a protective "bubble" format at the ESPN Wide World of Sports Complex at the Walt Disney World Resort in Orlando, Florida; the WNBA continued its season under the "bubble" format in Bradenton, Florida; and the NHL played a few games and moved quickly to their playoff season with all playoff teams playing in Canada due to its ability to better handle the COVID-19 pandemic. Meanwhile, most high schools and college sports leagues across the country closed down fall sports. Primarily because of economic considerations (it is estimated that college football is a $7 billion industry), college football started its 2020 season (with some conferences starting later than others) and faced one hurdle after another (including those described in Chapter 7); eventually, all the FBS conferences would start. (Note: At the time of this writing, the college football season was still in progress and it was unclear whether the season would be completed.) While some sports were wrapping up their respective seasons in a bubble format, the NFL season began. Without a bubble format there were many instances of COVID-19 cases resulting in the rescheduling of games. (Note: At the time of this writing, the NFL season was still in progress.) The NHL became the first of the 2019–20 major team sports to complete its season (September 28, 2020) following 9 weeks in the Canadian bubble format (with zero positive COVID-19 cases); the WNBA successfully completed their season on October 6 (with zero positive COVID-19 cases); the NBA crowned its champion on October 11 following a three-month bubble for the Finals teams (with zero positive COVID-19 cases); and, MLB completed its season on October 27 (the last three playoff rounds were played in a bubble format and resulted in one positive COVID-19 case detected during the final World Series game).

As football attempted to complete its 2020 season, other Fall sports were put in limbo. College basketball, another sport with huge economic impact, was delayed a few weeks but efforts were made to play an entire season. (Note: The season had not begun by the time we finished writing this third edition.)

While the pandemic caused upheaval in the sports world throughout much of 2020 (and likely 2021), it did bring us something unprecedented as all four of the major North American sports (football, baseball, basketball, and hockey) and a number of other major sports (e.g., tennis, soccer, golf, and NASCAR) were played at the same time. Major League Baseball expanded the number of teams allowed to play in the playoffs (because of the short 60-game season) resulting in yet another unprecedented event—8 playoff games played on one day (September 30, 2020). Sports fans went from starving for any sort of sporting activities throughout the Spring and most of the Summer to an overload of sports by the end of Summer, beginning of Autumn. Los Angeles sports fans in particular were recipients of great sports fortune as the Lakers and Dodgers won championships just 16 days apart.

When people rang in the New Year on December 31, 2019, they had no idea what 2020 had in store for them. Many college sports program never resumed, a death by economic considerations brought on by a global pandemic. The people who bring us sports tried desperately to give us sport consumers what we wanted and what many of us *needed*.

Some deemed that no price seemed too high if it meant getting back to "normal"—like having sports and taking them for granted like we always had before. Maybe, at least for a few years, sports fans will no longer take sports for granted.

Economics, Social Stratification, and Socio-economic Status

The term "economy" refers to the social system that coordinates a society's production, distribution, and consumption of goods and services. With such responsibilities as overseeing production and distribution of goods (e.g., necessities and luxury items) and services (e.g., police, fire and health care), the economy clearly represents a major social institution. *Economics* refers to the social science that studies economic activity in order to better understand the processes involved in the economy.

Economies contain different sectors. Generally we think of three basic sectors: primary, secondary and tertiary. The primary sector consists of the direct extraction of natural resources from the environment, such as drilling for oil and gas, mining, fishing, ranching and farming. The secondary sector involves transforming raw materials into physical products (goods) and may include refining petroleum into gasoline, turning metals into automobiles, and mass-producing a wide variety of consumer products. The secondary sector is the central feature of industrial societies. The tertiary sector, or service sector, consists of producing and processing information and providing services and includes such activities as research, engineering, finance, technological support,

Corporate commercial advertisements adorn the outfield of Dodger Stadium.

teaching, entertainment and sports (Delaney 2012). Geologist Matt Rosenberg (2020) believes there are 5 sectors of the economy: primary, secondary and tertiary (as described above); quaternary, related to the tertiary sector but with a focus on intellectual activities often associated with technological innovation, or "knowledge economy"; and quinary, which includes the highest levels of decision-making in a society or economy (e.g., top executives or officials, science, universities, nonprofits, health care, culture, and the media) and some economists may also include domestic activities performed at home. John Spacey (banking and telecom industry) argues that there are 8 sectors to the economy: primary; secondary; tertiary; quaternary; quinary; public (e.g., public education); private (privately owned businesses or organizations such as a family-owned restaurant); and, voluntary (e.g., housework, caring for children and the elderly).

As a multi-billion dollar industry, the economic study of sport is well warranted. Consider that, in 2018, the North American sports market had a value of about $71.06 billion; the figure is expected to rise to $83.1 billion by 2023 (Gough 2019b). According to Sport England (2020), sport and physical activity contributes £39 billion to the UK economy. The economic clout of sports can be felt at the professional levels as well as with "big-time" college sports. At some top NCAA football programs, football can generate $150 million and as much as 75 percent of college sports revenue annually (Birnbaum 2020). Industry analysts believe that a lost football season would wipe out $7 billion in total revenue and the implication would reach far beyond the economic realm—since the start of the COVID-19 pandemic and through late July schools had cut, dropped, or suspended 61 Division I teams and 176 programs across all NCAA levels (Birnbaum 2020). These statistics reinforce why we mentioned in the chapter's introductory story the desperation behind many colleges and their desire to have a 2020 football season.

The economics of the sports world includes a multitude of employees directly related to the games played (e.g., athletes, coaches, administrators), the owners that pay all the bills, and those indirectly associated to the games played (e.g., vendors, parking lot attendants, and bars and restaurants near the stadium). As we shall learn later in this chapter both the owners and athletes stand to earn huge sums of money. Considering that many of the highest paid athletes in contemporary sports come from humble beginnings it is sports that provided them with an opportunity for upward mobility, an opportunity they might not likely have found in some other profession. It's not surprising then, to realize that many of the highest paid athletes came from lower socio-economic backgrounds, which are disproportionately composed of minority members. Consider for example, that African Americans (20.8 percent) are more than twice as likely to be living in poverty than are whites (10.1 percent) and poverty rates for Hispanics (17.6 percent) are much closer to Blacks than whites (Poverty USA 2020). The sociological study of economics and sports uses this reality to contend that when the most commercialized sports are dominated (as players) by individuals from racial and ethnic minorities there is a perceived, or real, ideology that sports offer the best, or only, chance to get ahead (upward mobility). This is, of course, an indictment on the socio-economic system of a given society.

Those most attracted to sports as a means of upward mobility are from the lower socio-economic classes. Socio-economic classes are a component of the stratification system that exists in all groups, organizations and societies. Geologists may concern themselves with such things as the layers of the Earth's sub-surface, but sociologists are concerned about the "layers" found in the social world. *Social stratification* is a ranking system of members of a social system into levels having different or unequal evaluations; it reveals patterns of social inequality. Most societies have three major dimensions of stratification: social prestige, political (power), and economic.

While many people are concerned with power and prestige, it is money that they really want; and, if economic success brings power and prestige, then it's all the better. As a result, the economic dimension of stratification systems is what holds most people's attention and focus. The economic dimension involves two key variables: income and wealth. Income refers to the amount of money that a person, or family, receives over a period of time; generally a calendar year (e.g., reported income on a tax return). In 2019, the top three highest paid athletes in the world were tennis star Roger Federer ($106.3 million; $6.3 million in salary/winnings, $100 million in endorsements); soccer star Cristiano Ronaldo ($105 million; $60 million from salary/winnings and $45 million in endorsements); and, soccer star Lionel Messi ($104 million; $72 million from salary/winnings and $32 million from endorsements) (Badenhausen 2020). The top 100 highest-paid athletes earned a combined $3.6 billion in 2020 (Badenhausen 2020). One of things most of these top highest-paid athletes have in common is there lower socio-economic backgrounds. The second element of economics is wealth. Wealth refers to the total value of everything that a person or family owns, minus any debts owed. It is similar in meaning to the term net worth. The wealthiest athletes in the world are basketball Hall of Famer, shoe magnate, and NBA owner Michael Jordan ($1.9 billion); Formula One auto racer Michael Schumacher ($800 million); golfer Tiger Woods ($740 million); and former basketball player and current businessman Magic Johnson ($600 million) (*The Richest* 2020).

Economic success is often equated with social prestige, as people with name recognition and appeal generally garner more attention and respect in western societies than the poor. Sociologists use the term *socio-economic status* (SES) to measure social prestige. SES is a composite term that includes a person's income, wealth, occupational prestige, and educational attainment. People have the greatest chance of improving their SES if they reside in a society (i.e., the United States) with an open stratification system. An open stratification system allows people to climb, or fall from, the socio-economic ladder. In the "class system" of the United States both ascribed and achieved statuses have significant effects on people's income, wealth, and social position. An *ascribed status* refers to any trait assigned to an individual at birth, such as one's race/ethnicity, sex, and nationality. In many societies, including the U.S., certain ascribed statuses may present greater opportunity for social mobility; conversely, other ascribed statuses may present more challenges due to such social realities as prejudice and discrimination. For example, those born in wealthy families generally enjoy a higher status than those born in poorer families. In addition, wealthy persons will have opportunities presented to them that the poor will not (e.g., access to better schools, private tutoring, and job "connections"). However, achieved status also plays a role in the class system. An *achieved status* is any trait assigned to a person through individual effort and merit, hard work, determination, and making successful personal and economic decisions. Gaining the status of "college graduate" or earning a prestigious employment title (e.g., Full Professor, CEO, or partner in a law firm) are examples of achieved statuses. Young athletes that climb the ranks and reach the top tier of the sport profession have gained upward mobility and a higher SES because of an achieved status.

Sports as an Extension of Consumerism

Social mobility is possible in the class system primarily because of the opportunity to amass capital; conversely, the lack of capital leaves someone in the lower socio-economic classes. Capital accumulation is a fundamental driving force of capitalistic economies (Glyn 2006). To be successful, capitalistic economies must mass-produce consumer items (goods) designed for consumption and it must have a population large enough and with enough personal financial assets to purchase them. This economic theory of an increasing consumption of goods and services as economically desired is known as *consumerism*. When businesses develop products that consumers desire or demand, such as sports, great profits can be realized.

The origin of consumerism is a matter of some historic debate as traces of consumer interest and behavior extend throughout much of human history. Consumerism became significant in the late-eighteenth-century Western Europe (Stearns 2001). That consumerism coincides with the rise of industrialization is not a coincidence. Newly-formed factories were able to mass produce items that were once rarely available to the masses. The corresponding introduction of shop-keeping provided the conduit between the factory assembly-line and the eager to purchase consumers. The steady rise of a middle class with enough disposable income to guarantee a large consumer purchasing base only further fueled production. As the cycle continued to increase consumerism takes hold. As sociologist Jean Baudrillard (2006) noted, consumption is an active mode of relationship between people, objects, the community, and the mode of systematic activity upon which a cultural-economic system is based.

Consumerism had become so common by the end of the nineteenth century that Thorstein Veblen wrote of *conspicuous leisure* and *conspicuous consumption*. According to Veblen (1899), conspicuous leisure refers to nonproductive use of time, and conspicuous consumption refers to purchasing items not necessary for basic survival. Throughout most of history, humans had to work hard and steadily to secure the basic essentials of survival (e.g., food, water and shelter). Agricultural life, much like farming today, entailed working throughout the day with little or no time for recreation and leisure. It was the rise of industrialization and the shift in labor from agriculture to industry that led to a set number of working hours per week and free hours for leisure. Veblen's idea of a leisure class with disposable free time is still very relevant today as billions of people around the world find time to attend sporting events or watch them on television or online. Veblen's notion of conspicuous consumption is also very relevant today. While there are at least one billion people today working hard to secure enough items for daily survival, there are billions of people who live beyond the subsistence level. Many people today not only have enough disposable income to purchase items far removed from basic subsistence, they purchase items in an attempt to flaunt their success. Nixon and Frey (1996) were among the classic sport sociologists to recognize this trend a generation ago by describing conspicuous consumption as "a public display of material goods, lifestyles, and behavior in a way that ostentatiously conveys privileged status to others for the purpose of gaining their approval or envy" (211). In the time since Nixon and Frey wrote about the public display of a privileged status, the social networking era has arisen. People on social network sites like Facebook. Instagram, or Twitter are well aware of their friends' leisure exploits via countless posts of travel, fun, and attending sporting events.

It's interesting that sports today are such a significant aspect of consumerism as sports themselves are an enigma. On the one hand, they *are* games. Games are usually associated with play and play with frivolous, nonserious activity. Organized sporting activities—sports—are far different from children's games. Sports are so pervasive in society that they comprise a multi-billion dollar industry. Much of the business of sport involves providing a "product" that is marketable. As a result, much of sport is designed for entertainment appeal—"Give the fans something to cheer about!" It is important to provide an entertaining product because people have so many options as how to spend their leisure time and money. This adage helps to explain why fans will pack a stadium to watch a winning, entertaining team, but will stay away from games involving losing or boring teams (an "inferior" product). The sports industry must compete with all the other consumer entertainment-driven businesses. And there are many options available, sports or otherwise.

In an attempt to reach an ever-expanding market, the sports industry has paid increasing attention to its entertainment appeal and methods of marketing its product to consumers. Successful sport franchises must realize that they do not exist in isolation from the vagaries of demand and the consumption ethic (Bodet 2009). Indeed, to be successful today, sports organizations must offer new, creative, and fulfilling experiences in greater quantities or risk dissolution. Thus, in addition to presenting a successful product on the playing field, sports organizations should be prepared to offer consumers all sorts of options, including exciting apparel options for purchase (e.g., a variety of team jerseys to purchase), food and beverages beyond the typical, and free promotional items. Moital, Bain, and Thomas (2019) agree with Bodet's general assessment that sports franchises and facilities must recognize the consumption needs of consumers if they wish to satisfy them. The bottom line is, if spectators, fans, and corporate sponsors stop consuming sports as consumption products, the riches enjoyed by many in sports (e.g., professional athletes, franchise owners, and college administrators) will disappear (Funk, Mahony, Nakazawa, and Hirakawa 2001).

Sports Entertainment

Both of the authors teach college students. We meet new students every semester. Nearly all students indicate that their primary reason for attending college is to "find a good job." Most students expect to receive a high salary right after graduation. (These expectations are usually crushed by reality!) For the most part, however, students looking for a productive career realize that they will be working for most of the rest of their lives. Inevitably, sociology professors (as professors in most disciplines) will hear such questions as, "What type of jobs can I find with a sociology degree?" and "How much money will I earn?" Although students may be disillusioned with the answers, they never expected to hear of an option that involved a profession where they could earn so much money that they could retire after 5 or 10 years. High paying jobs like that don't even exist. Or do they? Yes, in fact they do. Usually these positions are found in the field of entertainment (e.g., movie and television stars, popular singers, and elite athletes).

Sports are a part of the entertainment business. Elite members of the sports industry will earn huge sums of money. The average annual salary for players in any of the four major American sports leagues is more than most people will earn in a lifetime.

According to data compiled by Statista the average annual player salary (in millions, USD) in the sports industry in 2019–20, by league was: NBA, 8.32; Indian Premier League (IPL), cricket, 5.3; MLB, 4.03; English Premier League (EPL), 3.97; La Liga, Spanish soccer league, 2.55; NHL, 2.69; Serie A, Italian soccer league, 2.23; Bundesliga, German soccer, 1.98; and MLS, 0.41 (Gough 2020b).

While most people will have to work most of their lives, most professional athletes believe that they *should* be paid enough money during their brief sports career so that they do not have to work after retirement—usually sometime in their late 20s or early 30s. Who enters any profession thinking that they can work for 5 to 10 years, earn millions of dollars, and live in comfort without needing to work again for the rest of their lives? Obviously, there are many of us who would love to be in that position. Such is the design of economics in sport in contemporary society. The sports industry is a field where even marginal professional athletes can expect to earn millions of dollars annually. Today's athletes are lucky to be a part of such an odd profession. In contrast, as recently as 1981 many Major League Baseball players took jobs during the baseball strike because their salaries were far more in line with the median salary of all U.S. workers.

Athletes are the most important aspect of the sports world and the sports world is a part of the entertainment sector of business. For the vast majority of the world's population sports serve as a primary form of entertainment. Some people like to attend sporting events and spend money and others like to watch sports via some version of media (e.g., radio, television, streaming, books and magazines). Media and marketing executives are well aware of our love for sports and are willing to try almost anything to encourage the masses to consume sports-related products. In turn, sports fans are indeed willing to consume the products produced for our consumption. These products include purchasing tickets for ballgames, purchasing the clothing attire of our favorite athletes and teams and purchasing the products advertised by marketers and endorsed by athletes. The names of corporate sponsors are prominently displayed in the sports world. We see advertisements at stadiums; dozens of sponsors' labels cluttered over nearly every inch of a race car and the drivers' jumpsuits plastered in advertisements; and, advertising is so extreme in soccer that the players' jerseys display a corporate sponsor's name instead of the name of the franchise, making the name of the corporate sponsor more important than the team name. With the popularity of certain sports, like soccer, the corporate sponsor receives exposure from a large audience which justifies the huge amount of money they spend for the rights to promote their name and products. As we shall learn in Chapter 15, the television media enjoys the same benefits of a large audience but with the added bonus of multiple advertisers that are all willing to spend huge sums of money related to the audience of the sporting event. Advertisers for the World Cup have exposure to billions of people, the Super Bowl over 100 million viewers, and the Final Four in Men's College Basketball, the World Series, and so on, all generate huge audiences.

There is so much money attached to the sports world—over $71 billion in North America alone—that there is little wonder that athletes are making millions of dollars. Very few of us workers are involved in professions wherein we are directly responsible for a multiple-billion dollar industry and that is why we work for most of our lives at relatively low wages and top tier athletes work for far fewer years and yet make much more money than we do.

Symbiosis: The Sports World and Corporate Sponsorship

When two unique institutions work together in an intimate association or close union with one another, such as the sports world and corporate sponsorship, we have a symbiotic relationship. (Note: The sports world has many symbiotic partners.) The corporate sponsor invests money into a sports entity (e.g., individual player, sports franchise, or college), helps to promote the sports entity, and de facto, represents the sports entity. In turn, the sports entity has its own image shaped by the corporate sponsorships it accepts as a working partner. If the corporation's brand does not align with the team's identity there is little benefit to them if the fans do not consume their product (e.g., it becomes known that the corporation is involved in illegal or immoral behavior) (Peluso, Rizzo, and Pino 2019). Conversely, if the sports entity itself becomes involved in questionable acts (e.g., the owner refuses to drop its racist nickname), the corporation may drop its sponsorship.

It is common for sports entities to have multiple corporate sponsors but generally there is one primary benefactor, the one whose corporate image is most prominently displayed in the stadium and during press interviews. Even the lowest professional and college levels of sports have corporate sponsors. In small markets, the sponsor may be localized in its sales and services (e.g., a local grocery store or restaurant) and that is fine as such smaller businesses cannot afford larger sponsorship fees nor can they handle a massive clientele. This is why, the larger the sporting venue the larger the corporate sponsor tends to be.

Understandably, corporate sponsors expect to receive a "return on investment" (ROI). An ROI measures the efficiency of an investment and is determined by the profit made from the original investment in comparison to the value of the investment at a future date. Thus, if you invested $5,000 and the investment is worth $7,500 after two years, your annual ROI would be 25 percent. The ROI measures the efficiency of a company, or investor. Professional and college coaches, for example, can be evaluated from an ROI perspective by examining their salary in relation to wins, especially quality wins over quality opponents and their share of team expenses. When/if the time comes that college athletes get paid to play the ROI formula is likely to be used to calculate dollar value. In 2020, Under Armour (UA) informed UCLA that it wanted to terminate the record-setting $280 million deal the apparel giant signed with the school in 2016, citing UCLA's inability to provided unspecified marketing benefits as required by the contract between the two parties (Bolch 2020). Any loss of revenue would be doubly devastating to a UCLA athletic department already facing a massive budget deficit even before the COVID-19 pandemic led to cancellation of revenue-generating sport seasons. From UA's perspective, it didn't receive the expected ROI given UCLA's recent struggles in its marquee sports of football and basketball (Bolch 2020). In this scenario, UA has argued that symbiosis was not achieved.

Corporate sponsorships are a form of marketing and advertising. There is a key difference between advertising and corporate sponsorship, however. Conventional advertising is designed to send a specific message to a targeted audience whereas sponsorship is about increasing brand awareness and enhancing the brand image (Smolianov and Aiyeku 2009). With the varying degree and numbers of sports entities in existence the sports world is a haven for corporate sponsors and when one sponsor leaves, surely another is ready to take its place.

Phil Schaaf's (2005) analysis of the potential benefits for sponsors who wish to identify their product with an athlete or sports program are as true today as when he first described them years ago:

- Reaching an event's audience at the event and through the available media.
- Building brand identity with on-site visibility and naming rights.
- Potential customers sample the product or service.
- Employee rewards and incentive programs may be created involving the property.
- Creating programs within the event.
- Leveraging special mailing or customer lists.
- Selling the product at the event via concession access privileges [167–169].

Corporate leaders also recognize that their sponsorship of a particular athlete may establish, maintain, and enhance their identity.

Player Endorsements

Athletes have been endorsing products for companies dating back at least to 1905 when star baseball player Honus Wagner signed a contract with Bud Hillerich who in 1894 had begun producing a trademarked baseball bat containing the engraved name, Louisville Slugger. Wagner befriended Hillerich while he played ball for the Louisville Colonels. Wagner's contract allowed Hillerich to commercially sell baseball bats with Wagner's signature on them in stores. Wagner's name or likeness appeared in advertisements for chewing gum, gunpowder, soft drinks, Gillette razor blades, cigars, and other products (The Pop History Dig 2020). Today, it is common for businesses to pay athletes to promote all sorts of products based on the commonly held belief that consumers are likely to purchase products endorsed by athletes. Marketing and academic research tends to support this belief. Chen and associates (2019) found that individuals are more likely to buy a particular pair of basketball shoes if they were celebrity endorsed. The sports celebrity influence on purchasing has a greater influence on younger consumers than older ones and they are more susceptible to interpersonal influence and fear of negative evaluation. Lin and Chen (2012) found that "the greater the susceptibility to interpersonal influence, the greater the tendency to buy on impulse. Likewise, the greater the fear of negative evaluation, the greater the impulse buying tendency" (p. 353).

Collectively, corporations spend billions of dollars on player endorsements. Many elite athletes may earn more income from their endorsement contracts than from their salaries to play sports. All elite athletes are not created equal. It helps to be an elite athlete in the "right" sports. The popular sports (e.g., football, baseball, soccer, and basketball) provide great visibility for its elite athletes and as a result, endorsement contracts are more likely be extended to them. The obvious reason for this is that marketers need spokespersons that have popular appeal and name and face recognition. Consider that from 2012 to 2019, 16 athletes each made more than $100 million solely from endorsements (Csiszar 2020). Overall, the list of the top 30 pro athlete endorsement deals is dominated by basketball and tennis players with a total of 15 spots (Csiszar 2020). Listed below are the top ten endorsement earners from 2012 to 2019:

- Roger Federer (tennis), $489 million; notable endorsements: Barilla, Mercedes-Benz, Rolex, Wilson Sporting Goods

- Tiger Woods (golf), $403 million; Hero MotoCorp, Monster Energy, Nike, Rolex, Upper Deck
- LeBron James (basketball), $393 million; Beats Electronics, Coca-Cola, KIA Motors, Nike
- Phil Mickelson (golf), $346 million; Amgen, Callaway Golf, Intrepid Financial Partners, KPMG, Rolex
- Cristiano Ronaldo (soccer), $256 million; Altice, DAZN, Electronic Arts, Herbalife, MTG, Nike
- Kevin Durant (basketball), $213 million; Alaska Air Group, Google, Nike
- Lionel Messi (soccer), $202 million; Adidas, Gatorade, Huawei, MasterCard, PepsiCo
- Rafael Nadal (tennis), $189 million; Babolat, KIA Motors, Nike, Telefonica, Tommy Hilfiger
- Rory McIlroy (golf), $175 million; Nike, Omega, TaylorMade, United Health Group, Upper Deck
- Novak Djokovic (tennis), $167 million; Asics, Head, Lacoste, NetJets, Seiko Watch Corp [Csiszar 2020].

Clearly, it pays to be an elite athlete as the benefits extend far beyond the playing field and onto marketing endorsements.

The Globalization of Commercial Sport

Sports are consumed throughout the world. In Chapter 1 we discussed the global popularity of soccer (played in more than 200 countries), cricket, basketball, field hockey, tennis, volleyball, table tennis, baseball, American football, rugby and golf. Sports events such as the World Cup and the Olympics draw the attention of nearly half the world's population. Americans are surely not the only ones involved in sport consumerism.

The global consumerism of sport introduces us to the concept of globalization—a term that has been a part of discourse for well over a century. Modernization and the development of nation states transformed the concept of community to encompass the greater society, and eventually the world community. As noted sociologist Emile Durkheim (1912/1965) pointed out, "There is no people and no state which is not a part of another society, more or less unlimited, which embraces all the peoples and all the States with which the first comes in contact either directly or indirectly; there is no national life which is not dominated by a collective life of an international nature. In proportion as we advance in history, these international groups acquire a greater importance and extent" (p. 474).

Globalization generically refers to the worldwide movement toward economic, financial, trade and communications integration by incorporating the perspectives of diverse cultures from around the world. It involves the transfer of capital, goods and services across national borders. With these ideas in mind, *globalization* may be defined as a socioeconomic system in which the constraints of geography on social and economic arrangements recede and people become increasingly aware that they live in an interconnected world (Delaney 2012). The increasing interconnectedness of the nations of the world has led to an evolutionary transformation of heterogeneous cultures into a homogeneous culture that transcends all topographical boundaries placed on maps.

Globalization is fueled by the wealth and influence of multinational corporations (MNC). MNC are not a new phenomenon, as commerce among nations dates back at least to the time of the Phoenicians, whose trading ships sailed from what is now Lebanon to foreign lands more than 3,000 years ago. From that point on, trading routes via shipping have crisscrossed the globe. Today, most people across the world have long been aware of the United States because its capitalistic system has created some of the most powerful MNC business operations in the global market. Numerous American products such as Pepsi and Coca-Cola and fast-food restaurants such as Pizza Hut and McDonalds, for example, are found worldwide and are enjoyed by billions of culturally diverse people. Companies such as Nike "demonstrated how in the post–1970s world of new transnational corporations, money was free to move anywhere it could find quick profit" (LaFeber 1999: 151). The Nike swoosh symbol is recognized internationally. Just as people around the world are familiar with many American corporations and their products, so too are Americans aware of such international MNC as Altice, KIA Motors, Mercedes-Benz, Omega, Rolex, and Telefonica (all of which were companies identified as sources of endorsements for the top ten athletes in endorsement deals described previously).

Certainly sports represent an aspect of awareness of an interconnected world as many world-wide sporting events (i.e., the Olympics and the World Cup) connect people's collective consciousness of each other's presence, or representations. People around the world are increasingly aware of our brand of football and are fans of the NBA and MLB. The NHL is a worldwide respected brand in sports as well. Conversely, Americans have become increasingly interested in European and Mexican soccer, especially the Premier League, La Liga, Serie A, and Mex. Anyone with an ESPN app can look up the scores in these leagues very easily. It is also quite common for sports fans to not only watch international sporting events but also to consume clothing attire.

The Role of the Owners

Professional sports teams may be owned by individuals (i.e., Jerry Jones, Dallas Cowboys; and Jeffrey Lurie, Philadelphia Eagles); a family (e.g., the Glazer brothers, Avram, Bryan, Joel, and Edward, sons of late billionaire Malcolm Glazer owns Manchester United; and the Steinbrenner family—through Yankee Global Enterprises, LLC—owns the New York Yankees); a group, such as club members, aka, socios (Real Madrid and FC Barcelona) or an ownership group (Guggenheim Baseball owns the Los Angeles Dodgers); and, publicly owned by shareholders (the Green Bay Packers). With many professional sports franchises valued at more than $1 billion, it stands to reason that owners of professional sport teams are very wealthy people. While the exact net worth of owners is somewhat variable based on the source of information (we are citing The Richest. com), it is generally understood that the wealthiest American sports franchise owner is Steve Ballmer ($40.8 billion), Los Angeles Clippers (NBA). He is followed, in order, by David Tepper ($11.6 billion), Carolina Panthers (NFL); Mickey Arison ($11.4 billion), Miami Heat (NBA); Philip Anschutz ($11.2 billion), Los Angeles Galaxy (MLS) and the Los Angeles Kings (NHL), and part owner of the Los Angeles Lakers (NBA), Los Angeles Sparks (WNBA), and Swedish football club Hammarby IF; Stephen Ross ($10.3 billion), Miami Dolphins (NFL); Stanley Kroenke (7.8 billion), Los Angeles Rams (NFL), Colorado Rapids (MLS), the Colorado Mammoth (NLL), and part owner of the Arsenal

FC (Premier League); Daniel Gilbert ($7.4 billion), Cleveland Cavaliers (NBA); Robert Pera ($6.9 billion), Memphis Grizzlies (NBA); Marian Ilitch ($6.5 billion), Detroit Tigers (MLB) and Detroit Red Wings (NHL); and, the tenth richest is Charles Dolan ($5.5 billion), New York Knicks (NBA), New York Rangers (NHL), and New York Liberty (WNBA) (Binns 2019).

Sport Cartels and Sport Monopolies

Owners work within the confines of sports leagues and the league commissioner they put into power. Professional sport leagues have often been characterized as sport cartels by economists. "A cartel is a collective of firms who, by agreement, act as a single supplier to a market" (Downward and Dawson 2000: 31). From a sociological perspective, cartels are bureaucratic, large-scale social organizations. Many sports leagues take on the primary characteristics of cartels. The authors define a sports cartel is an economic body formed by a small number of independent teams within the same league that make decisions on matters of common interest (e.g., rules, revenue-sharing, expansion, scheduling, and promotion) and exchange money as resources. Buying and selling players and establishing minimum league salaries are examples of collective financial decision making made by league officials. "In a cartel mutual behavior is by agreement only and these agreements need to be enforced. If they are not, or better opportunities for members of the cartel appear elsewhere, then they can break down. Paramount to the success of a cartel thus is the ability to reconcile potential conflicts of interest within the group" (Downward and Dawson 2000: 36). Sports leagues that act as a cartel provide economic advantages for all the owners in the cartel.

Cartel business activity is essentially illegal in the United States—as established by the Sherman Antitrust Law. Enacted in 1890, and named after Senator John Sherman of Ohio, it authorized federal action against any combination of trusts which engaged in a conspiracy to restrain trade or stifle competition. Companies, for example, that engaged in business across many states were thought to be in violation of the Sherman antitrust legislation. Sports leagues often extend business across many states. They also control player salaries, another feature of a cartel. The Sherman Act, however, was vaguely worded and has been difficult to enforce.

Over the years, the courts have allowed a variety of exceptions to the cartel behavior of many American corporations and businesses, especially in sports (Daymont 1981). Among the more significant court decisions was the 1922 Supreme Court decision that essentially ruled Major League Baseball free from antitrust legislation (Metzenbaum 1996). Supreme Court Justice Oliver Wendell Holmes "reasoned that the antitrust laws did not apply because baseball could not be considered interstate commerce" (Metzenbaum 1996: 275).

In 1922, Oliver Wendell Holmes, speaking for the majority, delivered the Supreme Court's opinion adjudicating Baltimore's case. The court considered the facts and then ignored them. Baseball, concluded the learned jurists, was not interstate commerce. Although baseball teams traveled from state to state, baseball games were merely "exhibitions" of talent and they were always played within the boundaries of a single state. This bizarre interpretation of the law was reaffirmed fifty years later in *Flood v. Kuhn*. In that decision, written by Harry A. Blackmun, the justices admitted that the predecessors had made a mistake, but they refused to correct the "established aberration" [Guttmann 2004: 137].

The 1922 Supreme Court decision afforded Major League Baseball an exemption from antitrust legislation and the burden of fair competition dictated by the open, democratic market. The other major sport leagues never enjoyed the immunity given to MLB, but they too received a variety of protections by the courts and Congress that enabled owners to monopolize their industry and operate their sport leagues as cartels (Sage 1996). "This has enabled owners to engage in collusion, price and wage fixing, and various restraints of trade (e.g., leaguewide negotiation of TV contracts), thus maximizing their profits. It has also protected each franchise within a league from competition because the number of franchises is controlled by the team owners; no franchise is allowed to locate in a given territory without approval of the owners" (Sage 1996: 265). Essentially, the ruling said that organized baseball was primarily a sport and not a business, and therefore not subject to antitrust laws and interstate commerce regulations.

The NFL, like MLB, also enjoys a special exemption from the government. "Section 501(c)(6) of the Internal Revenue Code lists 'professional football leagues' as worthy of tax-exempt status, a lingering result of legislative maneuverings that facilitated the NFL-AFL merger in 1966" (McCann 2014). A 501(c)(6) designation is usually applicable to a charity but "a trade association that helps its members cooperate and achieve a common purpose, like a chamber of commerce that promotes local businesses or a guild that advocates for plumbers or accountants" is also valid (McCann 2014: 28). Working as a trade association to help its members succeed falls under the cartel umbrella. In 2014, U.S. Senator Cory Booker (D-NJ) became the latest member in Congress to propose amending 501(c)(6) so that the NFL and nine other professional sports leagues, including the NHL, USTA and the PGA Tour, no longer qualify (McCann 2014).

In response to occasional threats from members of Congress seeking to revoke the NFL's tax-exempt status, the league announced in April 2015 that it would voluntarily give it up to eliminate the distraction it caused. Robert McNair, chairman of the NFL's finance committee and owner of the Houston Texans read from the league's official statement, "The owners have decided to eliminate the distraction associated with misunderstanding of the league office's status" (Hiltzik 2015). Among the consequences of this move is that the NFL will become even more secretive than ever as they will no longer have to publicly report its financial dealings (e.g., the salary of the Commissioner). "This annual disclosure is virtually the only glimmer the public gets at the workings of this huge business enterprise, since 31 teams are private businesses and don't make public disclosures of their own. The exception is the Green Bay Packers, which is owned by 350,000 public shareholders and releases financial data annually" (Hiltzik 2015). While details of such financial dealings as the commissioner's salary might not be released by the NFL, such information is attainable. For example, in April 2020, an internal league memo obtained by NPR revealed that Commissioner Roger Goodell decided to slash his April salary to $0 and that executive pay reductions and furloughs of employees due to COVID-19 would take effect. It was also revealed that Goodell was slated to make up to $40 million in 2020 (Mai 2020). There was no word about how long Goodell would work for free.

Generally speaking, individual colleges and universities (as well as high school sport teams) are not viewed as cartels. However, the NCAA is. Economists generally view the NCAA as a cartel for a number of reasons, including that it:

1. Sets input prices that can be paid for student-athletes
2. Regulates the usage of those student-athletes in terms of duration and intensity

3. Regulates output in terms of the number and length of athletic contests
4. Occasionally pools and distributes the profits of the cartel earned from activities such as the television football package
5. Disseminates information concerning transactions, market conditions, and business accounting techniques
6. Polices the behavior of cartel members and levies penalties for infractions [Koch and Leonard 1981: 253].

During the 2020 Senate Judiciary Committee hearings on student-athletes' attempts to gain the right to earn money on their own name, image, and likeness (NIL), Senator Cory Booker (D-NJ) slammed the NCAA as a cartel (Wells 2020). Senator Lindsey Graham (R-SC), who presided over the hearing, said if college programs use NIL as a recruiting tool it will "unleash holy hell on young college athletes" and added that he doesn't want to get into a situation where schools "have a bidding war for recruits" (Wells 2020). The different perspectives taken by these two senators reflect the Democrat position of siding with the workers (student-athletes) and the Republican position of siding with big business (the NCAA and its conferences) but also, the concern of many (regardless of their politics) that the Power Five conferences are likely to benefit disproportionately as they are in an advantageous position (e.g., more media exposure) to recruit top athletes they may potentially benefit from their NIL.

Despite the many similarities to illegal cartels, the NCAA and professional sports leagues are usually immune to antitrust policy in the United States. They are essentially business cartels that seem to enjoy an economic monopoly. A monopoly is when one company controls a commodity or service in a particular market, or has such control over a commodity or service that it is capable of manipulating prices. Professional sports league act as unregulated monopolies wherein each league regulates itself almost exclusively without government interference. League officials can determine rules, schedules, promotions, expansion, media contracts, sanctions, and reward systems.

Of particular economic importance to sport league monopolies is their ability to negotiate their own television contracts. Economic growth in sport is due primarily to television revenue. And although it is true that some teams hold such high status that they can negotiate partial broadcast rights and keep their own revenue (e.g., Notre Dame home football games; University of Texas Longhorns Network; and the New York Yankee Network), revenue sharing dominates most American sport leagues.

Sports leagues resemble cartels but do not monopolize an entire business. Thus, sport leagues are more like cartels than monopolies. As Downward and Dawson (2000) explain, "The co-operation between teams required in cartels can echo monopoly behavior. However, it also implies less rigidity and conformity of behavior than implied in a monopoly *per se*, in which power must, by definition, reside with the league. In a cartel mutual behavior is by agreement only and these agreements need to be enforced. If they are not, or better opportunities for members of the cartel appear elsewhere, then they can break down. Paramount to the success of a cartel, thus, is the ability to reconcile potential conflicts of interest within the group. While aspects of a cartel's activities can resemble a monopoly … the concept of a cartel is a better conceptual description of a sporting league" (36). One of the critical elements of a cartel is to monopolize the market. The sport league attempts to limit the number of franchises and the placement of franchises in order to maximize the profits of all the teams in the league, as well as the league itself.

As a cartel, sports owners represent an oligarchy. An *oligarchy* occurs when power is in the hands of a few. And when power is in the hands of the few, the masses (fans) are generally at a major disadvantage. Owners often flaunt their power in the face of loyal fans. They charge outrageous prices for game tickets, parking, merchandise, and food concessions. Season ticket holders in particular carry the brunt of the economic burden. For example, NFL season ticket holders are required to purchase the meaningless preseason (exhibition) games. Adding insult to injury, the preseason tickets are stamped as "Game 1" and "Game 2"—as if they are real games. The season home opener game is stamped as "Game 3." Season ticket holders are not given a choice on whether they want to purchase the preseason games—they are automatically included in the season ticket package—and they cost the same dollar amount as real games even though the general public can usually get them at half-price (because preseason games generally do not sell out). (Delaney is a former long-time season ticket holder of an NFL franchise.)

However, being forced to pay for preseason tickets, overpriced tickets, and so forth pales in comparison to the worst atrocity committed by owners; namely, franchise relocation (discussed in Chapter 4). If an owner decides to relocate a franchise fans have little recourse, legal or otherwise. No matter how loyal fans are to a team, franchise permanence is not guaranteed. The franchise remaining in the local community is critical to fans. Making profits is critical for owners and it is often their top concern; fans are left to support the team unconditionally or risk losing their team.

Sports Stadiums

Communities have to decide just how badly they want to keep or attract a professional sports franchise, and whether the taxpayers will incur the costs of building a stadium or pay renovation on existing stadiums. An owner of an existing sport franchise may threaten to relocate the franchise if a new stadium is not built, or renovations not made. A potential new franchise owner may hold competing communities at bay by waiting for the best stadium proposal from local community leaders. Support for seeking and securing a professional sport franchise at public expense usually comes from coalitions of urban elites: local politicians; businesses, especially restaurants and hotels; developers; construction firms; local mass media; and, of course, the pro-sport industry. Proponents argue that sports facilities eventually pay for themselves and usually require little beyond initial public backing for the bonds that finance them. Backers note the economic impact for nearby restaurants and other related businesses. Consequently, the public (taxpayers) often foot the bill for new stadiums and stadium renovations. Local governments offer public subsidies in order to keep existing sports franchises or to attract potential new franchises. The scarcity of professional sports teams and the tremendous fan interest in having a major sports franchise in their city fuels the desire for municipalities to offer deals attractive enough to entice a sports owner to relocate.

Nearly all stadiums are built with public subsidies, especially through revenue bonds. During the 1960s and 1970s a number of cities financed new stadiums for professional sports teams. The "cookie cutter" stadiums—the circular, fully enclosed, two-sport ballparks—made infamous in St. Louis, Atlanta, Cincinnati, Pittsburgh, and Philadelphia served their purpose and gave municipalities their money's worth, but were aesthetically unappealing. "The functional facilities opened to glowing reviews between 1966 and 1971. They were hailed as modernistic, space-age edifices with no poles obstructing views, symmetrical dimensions in the playing field and cutting-edge features such as huge scoreboards with computerized animation" (Dodd 2005: 1C). These stadiums ranged in cost from Atlanta-Fulton County Stadium at $18 million (first game on April 12, 1966) to Philadelphia's Veterans Stadium at $52 million (first game played on April 10, 1971) (Dodd 2005). By the end of 2005, the cookie cutter stadiums had all been demolished and replaced with newer stadiums—at great cost to taxpayers.

In addition to the "cookie cutter" stadiums that have been replaced by newer, flashier stadiums, the Houston Astrodome, formerly a symbol of progress and a source of pride for Houstonians—and once proclaimed as the "Eighth Wonder of the World"—was replaced as the home of Astros in 1999. The Astrodome opened in time for the 1965 Astros home opener at a cost of $35 million. A little more than three decades later, this "modern wonder" was deemed outdated by MLB. Today, the Astros play at Minute Maid Park, a stadium funded by a combination of private and public financing (taxpayers funded 68 percent of the $250 million price tag). The retractable roof certainly makes the stadium more aesthetically pleasing to fans and players alike although it does not compare to stadiums that incorporate scenes of nature in the background (i.e., Dodger Stadium with views of palm trees and the San Gabriel Mountains behind the outfield; Folsom Field, Colorado; LaVell Edwards Stadium, Utah; and, AT&T Park, San Francisco). Globally, many stadiums incorporate natural beauty within their sightlines including: Newlands Cricket Ground, South Africa; Monte-Carlo Country Club, Monaco; Arnos Vale Ground, Saint Vincent; HPCA Stadium, India; and Roy Emerson Arena, Switzerland, to mention just a few.

While new stadiums, understandably, come with a higher price tag, many of them are increasingly becoming more environmentally-friendly. And this is certainly a good thing as, "major sports arenas, ballparks, and stadiums consume massive amounts of nonrenewable energy and have historically placed significant burdens on their cities' public utilities" (Kellison, Trendafilova, and McCullough 2015: 63). Sports facilities consume large amounts of water and electricity and are responsible for waste output, carbon dioxide emissions and raw materials usage (Kellison et al 2015). But, many stadiums have attempted to answer the call to "go green." The need for filtrated clean air has become especially important in light of the COVID-19 pandemic. "The billions of dollars spent on state-of-the-art sports facilities over the last quarter-century have made high-efficiency air filtration systems more common, thanks in part to the pursuit of green and healthy building certifications. Upgrades will likely increase in the post-coronavirus era too" (Campbell 2020: B2). Filtration systems are measured based on the Minimum Efficiency Reporting Value (MERV) scale and the minimum standard for Leadership in Energy and Environmental Design (LEED) certification which are designed to protect people inside stadiums as much as possible from airborne microbes. Stadium construction must also meet environmental impact standards as well. In 2016, Golden 1 Credit Union Center, home of the Sacramento Kings, became the first LEED Platinum certified arena in the world. In 2020, the Los Angeles Clippers' plans for a privately financed billion-dollar arena complex in Inglewood received unanimous approval for the city council. Billionaire Steve Ballmer wanted to make sure that his basketball (plus other venues) arena met both environmental guidelines and that his facility would be "the single greatest place in the world for basketball [and] a basketball palace with no peer" (Greif 2020).

Among the stadiums that are becoming increasingly sustainable is the solar-powered pavilion at Chase Field (Arizona Diamondbacks) which generates clean energy for the grid as well as the stadium itself, contains LED concourse lights, low-flow sinks, EV charging stations, and concession stands that save the grease (from their churro dogs and other food items) in order to recycle it into a biodegradable diesel fuel (Hunt 2019). Other Energy-smart stadiums include: Lusail Stadium, Qatar, an 80,000-seat capacity stadium that will use solar panels to reduce temperature to 27 degrees Celsius even when its 40+ outside; Antalya Stadium, Turkey, the country's first solar-powered stadium, will generate power via solar panels and divert it back to the grid on non-game days; Tokyo Olympic Stadium, Japan, scheduled site of the 2020 Games (because of the COVID-19 pandemic the Games were postponed for a year); Mercedes-Benz Stadium, Atlanta, where over 4,000 solar panels were installed at the stadium and surrounding areas (primarily above car parks); Stadio della Roma, Italy, expected to be completed by 2023, which will be built based on LEED standards; and T-Mobile Arena, Las Vegas, which uses high-efficiency LED lighting throughout to reduce energy usage were among the criteria used to help this desert stadium attain LEED gold certification (Unwin 2019; Delaney and Madigan 2021). It is common now for stadiums to have separate trash and recycling bins; tailgaters are often provided recycling bags to encourage the recycling versus simply throwing everything in the trash bin. The Green Sports Alliance, an environmentally-focused trade organization, works with teams, leagues, conferences, venues, corporate partners, governmental agencies, athletes, and fans to promote a healthy sports environment by covering five areas: pre-event planning and communication; waste management at the event; carbon-management at the event; water management at the event; and, post-event measurement, reporting, and goal setting (Green Sports Alliance 2020).

Sports stadiums that are becoming increasing aesthetically-pleasing and environmentally-friendly are a wonderful thing, especially if financed by private funds. However, when owners hold communities hostage and threaten to relocate their franchise if they do not get better publicly-financed stadium deals, they become a source of divisiveness.

ECONOMIC BENEFITS FOR OWNERS

In major team sports it is common for most franchises to be valued over $1 billion. All NFL franchises are worth over $1 billion and the leader of the pack is the Dallas Cowboys and this despite the fact that in the past 20 years they have reached the playoffs just 7 times. According to Forbes (2020), the Cowboys were valued at $5.5 billion in 2019; followed by the New England Patriots ($4.4 billion); New York Giants ($3.9 billion); Los Angeles Rams ($3.8 billion); and rounding out the top five, San Francisco 49ers ($3.5 billion). Even the least valued NFL franchise, the Buffalo Bills ($1.9 billion), is worth close to $2 billion dollars, and is followed by the Detroit Lions ($1.95 billion); Cincinnati Bengals ($2 billion); Tennessee Titans ($2.15 billion); and the Cleveland Browns ($2.175 billion) rounding out the bottom five least valued franchises (Forbes 2020a).

At $5.0 billion, the New York Yankees were the highest valued MLB team in 2019 and this dollar value is twice what it was just 5 years earlier (Forbes 2020b). The next four highest valued MLB franchises are the same as five years ago: the Los Angeles Dodgers ($3.4 billion); Boston Red Sox ($3.3 billion); Chicago Cubs ($3.2 billion); and the San Francisco Giants ($3.1 billion) (Forbes 2020b). In 2014, only the top five highest valued MLB franchises were worth more than one billion dollars while in 2019, only one franchise, the Miami Marlins, was worth less than $1 billion ($980 million) (Forbes 2020b).

All 30 NBA franchises were valued at over $1 billion in 2019 with the top five as: New York Knicks ($4.6 billion); Los Angeles Lakers ($4.4 billion); Golden State Warriors ($4.3 billion); Chicago Bulls ($3.2 billion); and the Boston Celtics ($3.1 billion) (Forbes 2020c). The NHL does not enjoy the vast richness of the other three major North American team sports and had just five franchises valued at one billion dollars or above in 2019: New York Rangers ($1.65 billion); Toronto Maple Leafs ($1.5 billion); Montreal Canadiens ($1.34 billion); Chicago Blackhawks ($1.085 billion); and, Boston Bruins ($1 billion) (Forbes 2020d). Eleven NHL franchises are valued at less than one-half billion dollars with the Arizona Coyotes the lowest valued at $300 million (Forbes 2020d). When considering the value of sports franchises much of it has to do with the facilities (e.g., home stadiums) as franchises such at the Dallas Cowboys, New York Yankees, Los Angeles Dodgers, New York Knicks and Rangers, play at venues worth over one billion dollars themselves.

When looking at the highest valued franchises in the world it is not surprising that so many come from the United States and the four major team sports leagues. According to Forbes (2020e), the richest sports teams in the world in 2019 were: Dallas Cowboys; New York Yankees; Real Madrid; FC Barcelona; New York Knicks; Manchester United; New England Patriots and Los Angeles Lakers tied for seventh; Golden State Warriors; and the New York Giants (Forbes 2020e). The only other non–North American teams to crack the top 25 are Bayern Munich at 17th place and Manchester City at twenty-fifth (Forbes 2020e).

As demonstrated above, the value of top tier sports franchises is astronomical but how do we measure the economic value to the owners? The ROI would be a great indicator. Let's look at a few examples. In 1994, Jeffrey Lurie, the owner of the Philadelphia Eagles (NFL), had to take out a loan to purchase the franchise for $185 million. Today, he owns over 90 percent of the franchise and it is valued at $3.1 billion. That is a pretty good ROI. Philip Anschutz purchased the LA Galaxy for $28 million in 1998 and, to date, he's made around $300 million in returns (Binns 2019). Marian Ilitich (the second richest self-made woman in the United States) and her late husband purchased the Detroit Red Wings in 1982 for a mere $9 million and have received 7,677 percent ROI (Binns 2019).

How do we explain the value of sports franchises? The answer to this question is both difficult and simple. On the one hand, it seems odd that an industry worth multi-billions of dollars is based on games that we all played as children. On the other hand, it is quite simple, as we all love to be entertained. When you combine the two seemingly diverse ends of the spectrum to these answers we can see the overlap as we once enjoyed playing sports when we were young and now we enjoy watching top-tier performances in our adulthood. Add to this the realization that as long as we have free time and money to spend on non-essential needs, we will continue to spend money on entertainment and sports are among the most popular forms of entertainment. Sports franchise owners that were savvy enough to spend huge sums of money in the past, and had their intelligence questioned about such investments, have been laughing all the way to the bank ever since.

The owners enjoy a number of economic benefits along the way too. They receive financial assistance for new stadiums and renovations to old stadiums (e.g., adding "luxury" or "corporate" suites); they enjoy revenue from a number of sources, including parking, gate receipts, concessions, television and other media contracts; and, receive a number of tax breaks and incentives via a number of "tricks" not afforded to most of us such as "showing a loss" (e.g., deducting player contracts they inherited when initially purchasing a sports franchise as well as deducting these same contracts in the future as players age because they have "depreciated") so that business expenses can off-set huge profits. When owners sell a franchise they also receive a huge tax break because the money earned from the sale is treated as capital gains—and therefore taxed at a lower rate than other sources of income such as salaries and wages. The Internal Revenue Service, for example, allows the owner to claim 60 percent of that cost for the franchise and 40 percent for player contracts. Further, owners may pay themselves exorbitant salaries which are counted as operating expenses (Zimbalist 2000). Thus, even when sports owners say they "lost" money and can show it on paper as a loss, they have most likely already made a huge profit. It should also be noted that businesses that purchase sports-related commodities (e.g., game tickets, food and skyboxes) can write these costs off as business expenses. As this mere sampling of financial perks afforded owners helps to illustrate, there is very little wonder why owners hold onto their franchise even when they claim to be losing money.

Periodically, sports owners like to flex their economic muscles and demonstrate their power. This can be accomplished in such ways as "cutting" players who can no longer perform, suspending players for misbehavior, refusing to renegotiate contracts of players having a "break-out" season of peak performance, and so on. These displays of power are conducted on the micro level and generally affect one player at a time. Occasionally, team owners exert their power at a larger, macro level. They may engage in collusion (e.g., an informal agreement among owners to a "ceiling" salary, or "black-balling" a specific player) or in extreme cases, "lockouts." Collusion is a secret undertaking by two or more people engaged in for the purpose of fraud. In the mid–1980s, the owners of MLB were found guilty by arbitrators who ruled that they were colluding to suppress the pay of free agents. A lockout occurs when negotiations between players and owners have deteriorated to the point where owners simply close down operations and keep players from playing. Generally, lockouts follow failed negotiations where owners are claiming a loss and players are perceived to be demanding too much from them.

The Role of the Players

The players play the most important role in sports. Sports would literally not exist without players. Coaches are important, league officials that organize schedules, team officials that organize travel and hotel arrangements, and so forth are all important but they pale in comparison to the role of players. Think back to when you were a child playing sports and you realize that the only thing needed besides other kids was the basic equipment, such as bats and balls if you are playing baseball, and a field big enough to play in. Certainly, as the level of competition increases there is a corresponding need for involvement from others but when it comes down to the most basic needs of sports, players are the unquestionable key. In this regard, organized sports are no different than any other business; the workers are the most essential. We are reminded of this time and time again.

Like other businesses, however, the owners and managers of the means of production seem to forget about and/or choose to ignore this most fundamental reality. Through most of the early history of professional sports players were not even allowed to sell their services to the highest bidder, a fundamental right of all workers. This restriction on the players' ability to sell their services to the highest bidder was known as the reserve clause. Today's professional ballplayers would be appalled by the restrictions of past reserve clauses. Contemporary athletes can thank Curt Flood, a baseball player for the St. Louis Cardinals for the change in this system as he became the first MLB player to challenge the reserve clause in the early 1970s. Because of Flood, players have more rights and freedoms today than at any other time in sports history.

So, what is the "player reserve clause?" The player "reserve clause" system utilized by professional sports through the early history of sports is a prime example of a past injustice where the economic benefit was primarily to owners. The reserve clause eliminated interclub competition for players' services, as once a player signed a contract with a professional sports team, he or she became the "property" of the team. The team holding the player's contract had the sole right to unilaterally negotiate with players. The reserve clause, in essence, meant that players had no control over the team for which they played during their entire playing careers. This "forced loyalty" explains, in part, why players in the past stayed with just one team.

Throughout most of its history, professional baseball enjoyed a formal exemption from the Sherman Antitrust Act. Football, hockey and basketball generally benefited from lax enforcement of antitrust laws as well. Sports owners have typically argued that the reserve and draft systems promote competitive balance and are therefore necessary. The players, naturally, have a different perspective; they view the reserve clause as indentured servitude. The reserve system did, after all, make a drafted athlete the *property* of a team for his whole career. The signed (to a contract) athlete's skills and abilities were "reserved" for the original owner. The reserve clause guaranteed that a player could not join a rival team without the owner's permission. The marketplace for an athlete can be described in economic terms as a "monopsony." *Monopsony* refers to a market situation in which there is only one buyer. In sports, a monopsony refers to a situation where a seller (the player) is limited to only one buyer (the owner who the athlete is currently under contract or who has drafted them). The buyer controls the market because the seller is not allowed to sell his skills elsewhere in a free and open market.

A variation of the reserve clause, the option system, was used in football and basketball. Under the option system, a player was free to seek employment with another team one year after his contract had expired if the original owner did not re-sign him (at 90 percent of the previous year's salary) (Vogler and Schwartz 1993). During much of the 1960s and 1970s, the NFL implemented the "Rozelle Rule"—named after then–NFL commissioner Pete Rozelle. The Rozelle Rule was a highly restrictive and secretive system designed to impede a player's attempt to sell his services to the highest bidder after playing out his option year of his contract. Any team that signed such a player was obligated to pay compensation (draft choices, money, or both) to the original team. No team was informed (prior to signing a player after his option year) as to what the compensation would be. Because of the Rozelle Rule, only four players who had played out their options were signed by other clubs between 1963 and 1976. The owners of professional sports had quasi-literally "owned" the athletic talents of their players.

Most athletes took offense to this. They believed that their skills should be marketed in the same manner as people in other industries with the right to "sell" themselves to the team that made them the best offer. The majority of athletes realized that they were powerless in their struggle with ownership over the reserve clause and other restrictive practices that made them the property of sports owners. Eventually, a "sacrificial lamb" decided to challenge the reserve clause. This pioneer in the fight for economic rights for athletes was Curt Flood.

Curt Flood

Curt Flood was an outstanding centerfielder for the St. Louis Cardinals. He was a three-time All Star and seven-time winner of the Gold Glove for his defensive skills. Flood hit higher than .300 six times during his 15-year MLB career that began in 1956 and had a lifetime batting average of .293. Following the completion of the 1969 season, the Cardinals attempted to trade Flood (along with Tim McCarver, Byron Browne and Joe Hoerner) to the Philadelphia Phillies (for Dick Allen, Cookie Rojas, and Jerry Johnson). Flood refused to go. Among other things, Flood viewed Philadelphia as a racist city and the Phillies as a team with little hope of reaching the playoffs, plus he wanted to stay in St. Louis. He also felt insulted by the idea that he was being treated as a piece of property because of the reserve clause. The late 1960s were rebellious years with anti-war protests, civil rights movements, and a general questioning of "The Establishment." Maintaining policies just because "that's the way we have always done it" no longer seemed valid to an increasingly large percentage of the American population.

Flood received the backing of the Players Association and former U.S. Supreme Court Justice Arthur Goldberg (who argued on Flood's behalf) and decided to forgo a relatively lucrative $100,000 contract to challenge the legality of the reserve clause. On January 16, 1970, Flood filed suit against MLB and its reserve clause in a case known as *Flood v. Kuhn* (407 U.S. 258) Kuhn was the MLB commissioner at the time. Flood sat out the entire 1970 season while he battled MLB. The Cardinals were forced to pay compensation (two minor leaguers) to the Phillies. Flood's *The Way It Is*, an autobiography which detailed his moral and legal objections to baseball's reserve clause, was published in 1970. In 1971, Flood joined the Washington Senators but his time away from baseball and his increasing age led him to quit the Senators after playing just 13 games. In June 1972, the Supreme Court ruled against Flood and upheld baseball's exemption from antitrust statutes. Justice Harry Blackmun's "majority opinion quoted from 'Casey at the Bat' and cited the fiction of Ring Lardner. Blackmun ... recited the names of Ty Cobb, Babe Ruth, and eighty-six other legendary players. Confronted with economic injustice and legal absurdity, the justices wallowed in nostalgia" (Guttmann 2004: 137).

However, Flood's legal challenge of the reserve clause helped pave the way for Andy Messersmith and Dave McNally's 1975 successful challenge. In that year, baseball arbitrator Peter Seitz ruled that since Messersmith and McNally played for one season without a contract, they were "free agents" and allowed to place their athletic skills up for the highest bidder. After the Seitz decision, MLB commissioner Kuhn feared that baseball would be overrun by greedy ballplayers to the point that the game would not be able to survive (Wilson 1994).

Flood died of throat cancer in 1997 at the age of 59. In honor of Flood's attempt to empower players' rights against the oligarchic power of owners, the "Curt Flood Act of 1998" was passed. This legislation makes it clear that major-league baseball players are covered under antitrust laws.

Player Benefits and Increased Salaries

Curt Flood's challenge of baseball's reserve clause helped to change the face of sports forever. However, this change was relatively slow. Kuhn's proclamation that baseball was going to be driven to bankruptcy by greedy players did not come to fruition. As Wilson

(1994) explains, "Arbitration was undoubtedly a victory for the players, but Kuhn's picture is overdrawn. Between 1973 and 1989, fewer than one thousand cases were filed for arbitration out of a group of eight thousand eligible players; and of those cases, only 8 percent were actually arbitrated" (p. 112). However, the power of player unions would continue to increase after the Flood court case.

Sports unions are quite different from traditional unions. Consider for example, a teacher's union wherein a single employer (school or school system) dictates salary ranges for teachers or professors based on their rank and experience. Sports unions deal with many employers (all of the individual teams) and do not negotiate a set wage (beyond a minimum salary) for players based on years of service; instead, sports unions establish collective bargaining parameters. There is far greater turnover in sports union membership than in traditional unions as players, on average, come and go in just a few short years. Unlike other workers, sports union members do not have to worry about franchise owners shipping their industry overseas for cheaper labor. Like traditional unions, however, sports unions fight for better compensation, benefits and working conditions (e.g., better locker rooms, training facilities, travel provisions, and so on). The unions negotiate higher minimum salaries and better health and pension plans.

By the 1990s, it had become commonplace for players to come and go from one team to the next and athletes were beginning to reap the benefits (financial and otherwise) associated with being able to sell themselves in the open market. The greatest impact on today's huge player salaries (and owners' profits) is the result of the media, primarily television, and the nearly unthinkable sums of money they pay respective leagues for broadcast rights. Earlier in the chapter we shared data on the average annual player salary in select sports leagues for the 2019–20 season. Some of the individual player's salaries of today likely shock those who played professional sports 40+ years ago. Consider for example: Kansas City Chiefs (NFL) Super Bowl MVP quarterback Patrick Mahomes agreed to a 10-year contract extension in 2020 worth $503 million; Mike Trout of the Los Angeles Angels (MLB), 12-years for $426.5 million; Mookie Betts of the Los Angeles Dodgers (MLB), 12-years for $365 million; Christian Yelich of the Milwaukee Brewers, 7 years at $188.5 million; Stephen Curry of the Golden State Warriors (NBA), $40.2 million for the 2019–20 season; Cristiano Ronaldo of Juventus (Serie A), $105 million in salary and bonuses for the 2020 season; and Lionel Messi of FC Barcelona (La Liga), $104 million in salary and bonuses. (Note: Messi reported that all Barcelona players would take a 70 percent salary cut as a result of the shutdown caused by the COVID-19 pandemic. As the season did resume, it is not clear, as of this writing, just how much players' salaries were actually reduced.) The salaries of many professional athletes were in flux in 2020 as a result of the COVID-19 pandemic, as most leagues reduced player salaries pending the number of games played. Minor League Baseball players were in dire straits in 2020 as their entire season was scrapped. MLB instructed all 30 teams to pay their minor leaguers $400 per week through May 31, and all teams eventually committed to extending those payments through at least June 30 (Glazer 2020). Most MLB teams agreed to pay those stipends through September 7, the scheduled completion of minor league baseball (Torres 2020). When MLB started its season on July 23, 2020, clubs were allowed to expand their player pool to 60 which included top prospects so that they could be around the club's coaches and partake in intra-squad scrimmages and the like. In some cases, the minor leaguers got the opportunity to play with the big-league club (Anderson 2020).

The Role of Sports Agents

Curt Flood's challenge of the reserve clause and subsequent successful legal battles by athletes against ownership coupled with the rise of power of player unions have greatly benefited professional athletes economically. However, many of today's elite athletes earn high salaries and other benefits because they have entrusted their financial careers to sports agents. Some of these agents have become nearly as famous as their clients, due to their high-powered negotiating skills. Drew Rosenhaus, for instance, is one of the best known American Football sports agents and was reputedly the inspiration for the character "Bob Sugar" in the popular 1996 film *Jerry Maguire*. Rosenhaus, nicknamed the "Shark," and his agency Rosenhaus Sports Recreation (RSR), which he cofounded with his brother Jason, represents nearly 100 active NFL players. The 98 clients of RSR had contracts with a combined value of $1.2 billion. RSR had earned $34.6 million as of September 21, 2019 (Forbes 2020f). While many people who follow sports closely have likely heard of Drew Rosenhaus, he only ranks as #18 on the list of top earners in agent commissions. Scott Boras leads the list of top American sports agents, earning an astounding $118.8 million in commissions with his renowned Boras Corporation, the world's top baseball representation agency (Forbes 2020f). Atop the Forbes list of the world's most powerful sports agents for 2019 is soccer's Jonathan Barnett who negotiated more than $1.28 billion in active contracts but whose commissions exceeded $128 million (Forbes 2020f).

The primary role of agents, as implied above, is to represent the interest of athletes, especially in contract negotiations. Agents also handle sponsorships, public relations, and financial planning (Angst 2019). "Professional athletes often are signing their first professional contracts in their late teens or early 20s and rarely have the experience or education to fully understand the legal complexities involved. In the case of high-profile athletes, those contracts are for hundreds of thousands or millions of dollars, and athletes need guidance handling those finances" (Angst 2019). Sports agents, then, need to be proficient in writing and understanding contracts, negotiating, possess an expert knowledge of their clients' sports, collecting and analyzing data and statistics, promotions, networking, and salesmanship (Angst 2019). While not completely necessary, sports agents should possess a law degree or have a strong legal understanding of contracts. Some sports leagues or players associations will require agents to be certified in order to represent players (Angst 2019). It is also critical for sports agents to understand the market and comparable worth of their athletes in relation to other athletes. Knowing the general managers of teams across the league(s) is also helpful when it comes time to negotiate. Having a love of sports, good people skills, sales skills, and persistence are good qualities for sports agents (Angst 2019). Anyone thinking about becoming a sports agent should realize that there are only so many top-tier athletes and that most of them are earning relatively smaller salaries and, thus, the total value of commissions are not always high. Sports agents will work long hours, making themselves available 24/7 for countless athletes, travel a great deal, and must constantly keep up with market trends, all the while dreaming up new perks for their athletes to negotiate in their contracts.

The perks that sports agents manage to negotiate for their clients, as we shall see below, are quite lucrative and creative:

- Former Los Angeles Dodgers pitcher Kenta Maeda is contractually guaranteed uniform #18, which he took off the back of catcher Mitch Garver when he was traded to the Minnesota Twins in February 2020. The eight-year contract Maeda originally signed with the Dodgers in 2016 also required the team to pay for four round-trip business-class tickets between Japan and the U.S. annually, an interpreter, as well as travel, visa, and housing expenses for a personal assistant (Baxter 2020c).

- The New York Yankees gave pitcher Masahiro Tanka a $35,000 moving allowance, a $100,000 housing allowance, an interpreter at a salary of $85,000, and four first-class round-trip airline tickets between Japan and New York (Baxter 2020c).
- When Bryce Harper signed with the Philadelphia Phillies before the 2019 season, in addition to his $330 million contract that was filled with bonus incentives, it also guaranteed him a hotel suite on the road and the right to purchase a luxury suite for home games. Near years earlier, when Harper left junior college to sign his first contract with the Washington Nations, the team agreed to pay for eight semesters of college, a common perk for many baseball players (Baxter 2020c).
- Players such as Giancarlo Stanton and Evan Longoria who leave states with no state tax (i.e., Florida, Texas, and Washington) to play in states with a state income tax will have in their contracts that the team must pay those taxes (Baxter 2020c).
- Pitcher Charlie Kerfeld's second big league contract guaranteed him 37 boxes of orange Jell-O to match the #37 on his orange Houston Astros jersey [Baxter 2020c].

The expression "It's good to be the king" is all too relevant when you are a top-tier athlete and have a leading sports agent working on your behalf.

Connecting Sports and Popular Culture

Box 12: Moneyball

When it comes to economics and professional sports, one of the central issues relates to payroll. Just how much money does a particular sports franchise have to play with when it comes to issuing contracts? This is a very real concern for owners and managers from smaller market teams who have to compete with other teams who can buy their best players from them once they become available as free agents.

Such a dilemma faced Billy Beane, the general manager of the Oakland Athletics, in 2001. The A's had gone all the way to the World Series that year, losing to their archrivals the Yankees but still amazing fans with their stock of talent. But the three star players, Johnny Damon, Jason Giambri, and Jason Isringhausen, had all become free agents after the fantastic winning season, and there was no way the A's, the lowest salaried Major League team, could keep them from going elsewhere.

Realizing that he had to somehow replace these big name players in order to remain competitive, but also realizing that his payroll was extremely limited in comparison to other teams like the Yankees, Red Sox and Dodgers who are also looking for the same talent, Beane was at his wits' end. The journalist Michael Lewis detailed how Beane (himself a former professional baseball player) resolved the problem in his entertaining best-selling 2003 book *Moneyball: The Art of Winning an Unfair Game*, which itself became the basis for a 2011 film, also called *Moneyball*. Directed by Bennett Miller, written by Aaron Sorkin and Steve Zaillian, and starring Brad Pitt as Beane, the movie went on to be nominated for six Academy Awards (including Best Picture, Best Actor for Pitt, and Best Supporting Actor for Jonah Hill).

In the film version of *Moneyball* (which like most adaptations takes various liberties with the original source), Billy Beane becomes exasperated by the A's seasoned scouting team, who keep arguing for players who are far too costly for the A's to even consider. Just when he's at his wit's end, Beane meets Peter Brand (Jonah Hill), an awkward-looking economist who recently graduated from Yale University with rather unorthodox views on how to draft players. At first Beane can't comprehend the number-crunching theories of Brand (a fictionalized version of several real people from Lewis' book) but he finally catches on to the basic cost-benefit analysis the young economist is advocating. Brand is an advocate of the so-called "sabermetrics" approach (which was developed by the real-life Bill James), which looks for objective rather than subjective measures which often go against conventional wisdom. "For all its complex terminology, *Moneyball*'s sabermetrics is fairly simple. The theory posits that while individual star players can bring a match home, a combination of talents, with each player playing their own part, is more valuable. And by investing in such undervalued resources and divesting from overvalued ones, small teams can even odds in favor of bigger teams" (Rago 2020).

For instance, Brand argues, instead of following the scouts' advice to somehow go after name players, it would make much more sense to draft players who are "under the radar," either because they have been deemed by other teams to be past their prime or because they are too young and unimpressive to even be considered. Brand convinces Beane that players should be selected by their on-base percentages (OBP). The focus should be solely upon the specific needs the team has, and how the players to be chosen can fit those needs.

An impressed Beane hires Brand as the Athletics' assistant general manager, even though he has no previous experience and has never even played baseball, unlike the scouts like Grady Fuson (played by Ken Medlock) and the A's manager Art Howe (played by Philip Seymour Hoffman), who scoff at the confusing statistics rattled off by the nerdy-looking economist in their midst. Much to their astonishment, Beane overrules them and firmly supports Brand.

At first the new method advocated by the A's proves unsuccessful and leads to much ridicule from fans and sportswriters, as well as from the team's own staff. But Beane is able to convince the owner that things will soon change and he is vindicated when the Athletics win 19 straight games.

One can see how Beane's competitive spirit is rejuvenated by this unorthodox approach to choosing players, although even he expresses doubt over some of Brand's choices, such as the seemingly over the hill outfielder David Justice (played by Stephen Bishop) or the injured Scott Hatteberg (played by Chris Pratt), a catcher who had been let go by the Red Sox after damaging a nerve in his elbow. But when Howe ignores the new strategy and chooses to play his own more traditional lineup, he is overruled by Beane, who insists that Hatteberg be put in as first baseman, a position he'd never played before.

Much of the heart of *Moneyball* consists of the growing friendship between the driven Beane (who, because of the unbearable tension he feels before every match, refuses to watch the game in process) and the unprepossessing but headstrong Brand, who is convinced that his method is the best one for modern teams to use, regardless of how much traditional-minded baseball lovers might despise it as being too cold or mathematical. Both, in their own ways, truly love the game of baseball. For them, while money is a prime aspect, it's not the only or even the most important part of the game.

The climax of the film deals with a game against the Kansas City Royals. If the A's can win, they will set an American League record for most consecutive wins. Beane's daughter convinces him to break his superstition and go to watch the game. But, as if to prove he'd been right all along to avoid doing so, Beane watches in horror as the A's drop an 11–0 lead. The Royals even the score at 11–11 as the game nears its end. However, proving that sabermetrics can save the day, Hatteberg, much to Howe's surprise, scores the game winning home run.

As with most movies based on real-life people, *Moneyball* takes creative liberties with the truth. "In the film, Beane fires Fuson after the latter questions Beane's radical approach to scouting. In actuality, Fuson had made an amicable exit from the team after gaining a reputed position with the Texas Rangers. Howe, too, was depicted as hostile to Beane's progressive ideas and set in his ways. Howe, in an interview with SiriusXM's Mad Dog Radio, expressed his displeasure about his portrayal, saying, '…it is very disappointing to know that you spent seven years in an organization and gave your heart and soul to it and helped them go to the postseason your last three years there and win over 100 games your last two seasons and this is the way evidently your boss [Beane] feels about you'" (Rego 2020). Still, Brad Pitt's winning performance, and the film's fascinating look at the inner workings of baseball, helped to make *Moneyball* a perennial favorite for lovers of sports films.

Although the A's were defeated in the 2002 post-season and didn't make a return appearance in the 2002 World Series, Billy Beane did achieve a sense of vindication when the owner of the Boston Red Sox (a team that had been desperate for a World Series victory since 1918) offered him a lucrative contract for $12.5 million to become general manager. But Beane turned down the offer, even though it would have made him the highest-paid general manager in history at that time. From a purely economic perspective this made no sense. But from the perspective of someone who loves and is loyal to his team it makes perfect sense. Beane has continued to be a front office executive with the Oakland A's right to the present day. As the film points out at its end, the Red Sox did incorporate sabermetrics into their strategy, and two years later went on to win the 2004 World Series. *Moneyball* makes it quite clear that (to quote a famous line from another baseball film, *A League of Their Own*) while there may be no crying in baseball, there certainly will be a lot of number-crunching for as long as the game continues to be played.

Summary

Economics refers to the social science that studies economic activity in order to better understand the processes involved in the economy. In this chapter, we examined the role of economics in the sports industry. The economics of the sports world includes a multitude of employees directly related to the games played (e.g., athletes, coaches, administrators), the owners that pay all the bills, and those indirectly associated to the games played (e.g., vendors, parking lot attendants, and bars and restaurants near the stadium). Sports can provide upward mobility (directly or indirectly) for many athletes and as such, improve their socio-economic status. As a multi-billion-dollar industry, the economic study of sport is well warranted.

Social mobility is especially possible in the social class economic system because of the opportunity to amass capital; conversely, the lack of capital leaves someone in the lower socio-economic classes. Capital accumulation is a fundamental driving force of capitalistic economies. To be successful, capitalistic economies must mass-produce consumer items (goods) designed for consumption and it must have a population large enough and with enough personal financial assets to purchase them. This economic theory of an increasing consumption of goods and services as economically desired is known as consumerism. When businesses develop products that consumers desire or demand, such as sports, great profits can be realized.

Sports have great entertainment value as billions of people are willing to consume products produced by this industry. Corporate sponsorships and player endorsements help to fuel the sports industry's enormous economic engine. Sports enjoy an international cross-over in appeal leading to the globalization of commercial sport.

The owners of professional sports can amass great wealth if they own top-tier franchises in favored sports leagues. The owners have many advantages that allow them to profit from sports; they work within a monopolistic system with little legal interference, and make decisions similarly to an oligarchy. Many owners enjoy a huge return on investment as the value of their franchises continue to rise.

Players today have more rights and freedoms than at any other time in sports history, due to such pioneers in the fight for economic rights as Curt Flood. Thanks in large part to sports agents, players are in great position to earn large sums of money. The sampling of salaries and perks negotiated in their contracts and provided in this chapter are a testament to this reality.

KEY TERMS

Achieved Status A social or economic standing achieved through high levels of education and/or successful personal and economic decisions.

Ascribed Status Social or economic standing inherited by those born in wealthy families, higher than those born in poorer families.

Collusion A secret undertaking by two or more people engaged in for the purpose of fraud.

Consumerism The economic theory of an increasing consumption of goods and services as economically desired.

Economic Dimension A stratification system involving two key variables: income and wealth.

Economics The social science that studies economic activity in order to better understand the processes involved in the economy.

Economy The social system that coordinates a society's production, distribution, and consumption of goods and services.

Globalization A social process in which the constraints of geography on social and cultural arrangements recede and in which people become increasingly aware that they are receding.

Lockout Occurs when negotiations between players and owners have deteriorated to the point where owners simply close down operations and keep players from playing.

Monopoly Occurs when one company controls a commodity or service in a particular market, or has such control over a commodity or service that it is capable of manipulating prices.

Monopsony Refers to a market situation in which there is only one buyer.

Oligarchy A power structure in which control is in the hands of a few.

Option System An arrangement in which a player is free to seek employment with another team one year after his contract has expired if the original owner did not re-sign him.

Social Stratification A ranking system of members of a social system into levels having different or unequal evaluations; it reveals patterns of social inequality.

Socio-economic Status A composite term that includes a person's income, wealth, occupational prestige, and educational attainment.

Sports Cartel An economic body formed by a small number of teams within the same league that make decisions on matters of common interest (e.g., rules, revenue-sharing, expansion, scheduling, and promotion) and exchange money as resources.

Wealth The total value of everything that a person or family owns, minus any debts owed.

DISCUSSION QUESTIONS

- In which economic sector would you place sports? Explain.
- In what ways are sports a part of the entertainment business?
- Would you buy a product primarily because it was endorsed by an athlete? Is it important to you that the athlete actually uses the product he or she endorses?
- Is it okay for marketers to use the sex appeal of athletes to promote their product? Why or why not?
- What is "collusion" and why have Major League Baseball owners been accused of engaging in it?
- Explain the symbiotic relationship between the sports world and corporate sponsorship.
- Do you think professional athletes are paid more than they are worth? Why or why not? Do you think entertainers in general are overpaid? Why or why not?
- Do you think there will ever be a ceiling on the amount of money athletes are paid and that team owners earn?

CHAPTER 13

Politics and Sport

In January 2020, Tim Delaney attended an international conference in Santiago, Chile with the intention to study first-hand the social protests being waged by students, the economically poor, and anarchists that had been going on for months. The protestors wanted social change and the ouster of President Sebastian Pinera who they perceived as an egotistical tyrant who refused to step down from office despite his ineptness as a leader. Delaney and his travel companions (whom had family residing in Santiago) witnessed many areas of Santiago besieged with clashes between protestors and the police; fire-bombings; and, anti-government graffiti on government, public, and private property buildings, statues, and trees. Many areas looked like war zones.

On January 28, we attended a futbol match between host Colo-Colo and Palestino-Campeonato AFP Planvital. Police were on horses, foot, and motor vehicles outside the stadium and scores of police were highly visible inside the stadium. We sat in a general admission area. The fencing around the perimeter of the pitch had razor sharp wiring atop a tall fence. Sports fans in general and spectators at futbol matches were using the matches as opportunities to hurl anti–Pinera chants such as: "Pinera is a Mother F*cker. Assassin Just Like Pinochet." Another crowd favorite involved spectators enthusiastically jumping up and down chanting, "He who doesn't jump is a cop." A "cop" signifies something more than simply a police officer; they are viewed as oppressors and representatives of the government. The term "cop" then, is similar to when Americans call police officers a "pig." There were political chants throughout the televised match and many protestors inside the stadium tried to make sure that their protest banners were visible. As for the match itself, Colo-Colo won 3–0 and the fans exited Estadio Monumental Stadium (capacity of 47,347) in a happy and festive mood.

Little did we know, at the time, that this futbol match would turn into a flashpoint of even greater political protests. Exiting the parking lots and trying to get onto narrow city streets in this residential neighborhood was similar to many large sports events in the U.S. On the same street we were attempting to enter, a police vehicle sped at an excessive speed running over an exiting fan. Immediately, a number of fans tried to come to the rescue of the injured fan but an armored police vehicle used a water cannon to stop them. The fan died shortly afterwards. A detective later admitted that the vehicle was driving too fast. However, the police driver was minimally punished. This incident sparked an "All Fans Protest" movement. Futbol fans of all Primera Division teams (D1) and Primera B de Chile (D2) teams (16 teams in each league) united in protest against the incident. Chilean fans assured me that uniting all soccer fans toward a common goal is nearly impossible, but an exception was made because of the Colo-Colo incident. Fans blocked entrances to soccer stadiums across Chile in an attempt to keep people from attending games; security cameras were destroyed. The owners of futbol teams wanted the games to continue as they wanted to keep making money. These protests would continue for some time and the protestors used such chants as: "Streets with blood, fields without futbol"—meaning, there should not be soccer matches while blood is being spilt on the streets. Pitch invasions occurred throughout the matches that were played. There was at least one futbol fan shot to death by the police. By the time Delaney left Chile there still was no official response about the incident from the government.

Upon returning to the U.S. in early February there were visible signs of international travelers who were well aware of the spreading global novel corona virus. Within a few months, the pandemic was causing havoc in the U.S. and American cities were facing protests, violent clashes between protestors and the police and buildings on fire. The social protests, as in Chile, would spill over into the sports world.

These are the types of issues that will be discussed in this chapter.

The Role of Politics and Governments

Politics and governments have intruded into the domain of sports throughout the ages. The terms politics and government are not used synonymously, but in juxtaposition with one another. Politics refers to the methods, activities, or tactics of government,

Political protests at a soccer match between Colo-Colo and Palestino-Campeonato AFP Plan-vital in Santiago, Chile (courtesy Carlos Benavides).

or governing, of a society, and the administration and control of its internal and external affairs; it is the guiding influence of government policy. The political system operates on behalf of the government. The government is the political unit that exercises authority via laws and customs.

Governments in general, and politicians specifically, demonstrate significant interest and support of sports and for a variety of reasons. For example, the prevailing sport creed often includes values such as respect for authority, commitment to success, hard work and dedication, and perseverance and these sentiments are also the same cherished "ideals" of acceptable behavior for citizens deemed by governments around the world. As demonstrated throughout this text, the social institution of sport is intertwined with all the other social institutions of society (e.g., education, family, military, economics, religion, and the media) and by showing support (financial or otherwise) for sports politicians potentially gain favorable access to the people found within these realms. This helps to explain why many politicians like to participate in such traditions as throwing out the "first pitch" of a baseball game and making a visible appearance at sporting events, whether it is a local community sporting event or a nationally televised championship game. The overall popularity of sports is an automatic draw to politicians who hope to identify with the people. There is a certain risk, however, when politicians put themselves at the mercy of fans that do not care for their politics. As a memorable example, Mr. Trump appeared at Nationals Park in Washington for Game 5 of the 2019 World Series. When he was introduced during the game he was met with boos and jeers of a "high-decibel, visceral loathing usually reserved for visiting teams" and chants of "Lock Him Up!" similar to the manner that Trump's supporters shouted "Lock Her Up" in reference to Hillary Clinton who ran against him in the 2016 presidential campaign (Ali 2019; Allyn 2019). During the game, spectators also unfurled a "VETERANS FOR IMPEACHMENT" banner behind home plate (Allyn 2019). It is important for politicians to realize that when they appear at any sort of a "stronghold" of the opposition party that they are not likely to gain political favor.

Political Power and Authority

A number of sociologists, economists, and political scientists have attempted to explain the concepts of "power" and "authority," their role, and how they operate in society. Power and authority are exercised in nearly all social relationships, including small groups and large organizations and societies. George Homans, a social exchange theorist, focuses on micro-level relationships and views power and authority as similar concepts. According to Homans (1961) a person who has *influence* over other members of a group has authority. Possessing influence occurs when an individual has the ability to provide valuable rewards. Likewise, power is defined as the ability to provide rewards. Homans believes that those with power and authority are small in number but that is not really true as every organization has a hierarchical system wherein the people at higher levels are in the position to provide rewards (or punishments/sanctions) to those at lower levels. Subordinates will accept the authority and power of leaders as long as they feel they are being treated equally (distributive justice). Subordinates will become upset when they are not treated fairly and will challenge the power and authority of the superordinates.

Max Weber viewed power as the ability to exercise one's will over others, despite their resistance. In this regard, a thug who commits a mugging against an innocent passerby has exercised physical power over another in order to take what he desires. From a political perspective, legislators have the power to pass laws even if we disagree with them. Weber defined authority as power attached to a social position. In the United States, we elect people to political office and these politicians then have the legal authority to make decisions that affect us. In sports, game officials and referees have the authority to enforce the rules of the game and are allowed to implement punishments within a predetermined manner (via the rulebook). Ruling bodies, such as the NCAA, NAIA, and professional sports league offices, have the authority to levy sanctions against member institutions and participating athletes, coaches, and other team personnel.

Conflict theorists emphasize the role of power as a force that reveals social inequality throughout society. They claim that the dominant power group forces its values upon the rest of society, the subordinate groups. Karl Marx, whose works led to the formation of conflict theory, argued that power is attained strictly through economic means. He felt that those who control the means of production (the bourgeoisie) have power over the workers (the proletariat). In this regard, the owners of professional sport franchises hold a position of power over the players. The sports world is a multi-billion-dollar industry. Therefore, from an economic standpoint, sport represents power. Our discussion of sport owners (see Chapter 12) highlighted the fact that, for the most part, only wealthy individuals, groups and corporations can afford to own sport franchises.

The Role of Government in Sport

Governments around the world use sports as a tool for promoting the interests of politicians. The following represents a glimpse at the primary role of the government in sport in the United States.

1. *Rules and Safety.* Perhaps the most important role of the government is to assure the safety of its citizens. This includes providing safe sporting environments where safety rules are enacted, monitored, and enforced. "Without rules on civility and the resolution of conflicts, public life deteriorates into a jungle of passions" (Wiebe 2003: 35). Rules regarding safety in sport include categorizing sports that are legal (e.g., football, basketball, baseball) or illegal (e.g., street luge, BASE jumping); setting age requirements for participation (usually expressed in terms of minimum age requirements); requiring safety personnel at ball games (e.g., trained rescue workers and ambulances at football games); restricting locations to those suitable for certain sports (e.g., BASE jumping may be allowed in "designated" areas); and, making laws that designed to stop discrimination (e.g., Title IX, which ensured that women had the right to play sports in federally-funded schools).

   There are other ways in which governments attempt to safeguard the public order, including protecting sports fans in public places via the placement of safety signs, caution cones, and barriers to control traffic flow, and mandating a large number of law enforcement officers and private security personnel. In addition, governments have to be concerned with the potential for fan violence, which can arise due to longstanding team rivalries, inebriation, provocation, and racial tensions. This is a particular problem in countries where sport hooligans or thugs are prevalent. Special care must be taken to monitor the potential for violent outbreaks, and police and medical personnel have to be available to contain the after-effects if violence does occur.

2. *Physical Fitness.* For thousands of years, warriors have prepared for the battlefield by training on the athletic fields. The original Olympics involved sports that accentuated the skills of soldiers. Medieval lords used such sports as jousting to train knights. The often-cited quote "The Battle of Waterloo [1815] was won on the playing fields of Eton" revealed the English belief that sports helped to prepare the English soldiers for battle. Baron Pierre de Coubertin, a French nobleman, pushed for the reintroduction of the Olympics after the pitiful performance of French soldiers in the 1870–71 Franco-Prussian War. Coubertin believed that France's military prowess could be re-established by means of a national fitness and sports program.

By the end of the nineteenth century, the Muscular Christianity movement had taken hold in the United States as an ideal of honorable sporting prowess. Muscular Christianity helped to generate the development of sports and fitness programs in the United States—primarily for boys—in the early twentieth century. The government's support of the playground movement was another sign of its role in encouraging health and fitness. During the 1950s, general fitness programs were the norm at schools.

Unfortunately, the U.S. government has done an inadequate job of maintaining health and fitness programs, especially in the schools. Obesity rates for children, as well as adults, in the United States remain high. The CDC (2019c) reports that 18.5 percent, or 13.7 million, of children and teens aged 2 to 19 were obese in 2018. The prevalence of obesity increases as children age, reaching 20.6 percent among 12 to 19 year olds. Childhood obesity is most common among Hispanics (25.8 percent), followed by non–Hispanic blacks (22.0 percent), non–Hispanic whites (14.1 percent), and non–Hispanic Asians (11.0 percent) (CDC 2019c). The rate of obesity for American adults in 2018 is more than twice as high as children, 42.4 percent (CDC 2019d). Adult obesity is highest among non–Hispanic blacks (49.6 percent) followed by Hispanics (44.8 percent), non–Hispanic whites (42.2 percent), and non–Hispanic Asians (17.4 percent) (CDC 2019d). Obesity is associated with many poor health conditions including heart disease, stroke, type 2 diabetes, and certain types of cancer (CDC 2019d). Many schools have been forced to cut physical education and sports programs due to financial reasons. It is not a mere coincidence that as physical education programs have been increasingly disappearing or de-emphasized, the youth of today are increasingly overweight and out of shape. The U.S. government must reinvest in America's fitness programs. Daily physical education (for all able-bodied children) must become mandatory. After all, good healthy habits established in childhood are more likely to be maintained in adulthood. And with the increasing costs of health care, it is in everyone's (the government, as well as individuals) best interest to maintain good physical health. (Note: We will revisit this issue in Chapter 16.)

3. *Promoting Prestige.* Sports provide opportunities for heroic performances, which in turn are prestigious. Athletes and teams that overcome huge odds to win a gold medal or world championship; a fallen athlete who finishes a race despite a great deal of pain; and host communities who make visitors feel welcomed are among the few ways of attaining honor, respect and prestige. Governments like to take advantage of opportunities that make them "look good," especially in front of the global community. It is this very quest for prestige that provides governments

with the incentive to fund sports programs and training centers. At the local level, community businesses and local governments support various sports teams (e.g., a Pop Warner football team, or high school sport teams) as a way of gaining a favorable presence in the community. Such an impression within the community is, of course, a sign of prestige.

The discussion on franchise relocation (see Chapter 4) revealed how prestigious owning a professional sports franchise is for local governments. A city is not a "major league" city until it owns a major sport franchise. A city that loses a sports franchise suffers a major loss of prestige. The reasoning goes, if a city cannot hold onto and support a major sports franchise, how are they going to conduct more mundane forms of business? Contrastly, a city that "wins" (or "steals") a sports franchise experiences an increased level of prestige. This reality helps to explain why local governments are so willing to give "sweetheart" deals to sports franchises. Such governments believe that the costs of owning a sports franchise are more than offset by the rewards of prestige.

Nations of the world find it important to win at international sporting events, as it gives them "bragging" rights in at least one social sphere. The governments of "power nations" want to beat other sporting elite nations because they believe it helps to justify their political ideology. The politicians in power can bask in the reflected glory of being identified with a winning team, especially one that has excelled on an international level.

Successfully hosting an international sporting event may also provide prestige. Consider China's hosting of the 2008 Summer Olympics. As the Chinese nation took political hit after political hit because of human rights issues, it became increasingly important for that society to "look good" within the international political world.

4. *National Identity.* Many nations possess an international identity because of their sporting prowess. For them, it becomes especially important to win the sports that they are "supposed" to win. Brazil, for example, took an international sporting beating as a result of its failure to win the 2014 World Cup it hosted and especially because of its humiliating 7–1, semi-final loss to Germany. On the other hand, when a nation beats a reigning power, the victory is all the sweeter. Furthermore, when a nation performs well when it was not expected to, they have positively contributed to their identity.

5. *Politicians Who Use Sports for Identity.* Sports reflect the culture of a society and provide a nation with a sense of prestige and national identity. As a result, politicians like to attach themselves to athletes; especially those who win championships. Politicians with varying rank from local community council members to the president of the country have taken advantage of the popularity of sports in an attempt to shape a positive identity with the citizens. A nation's top political leader shows respect for sports because of its cultural importance. In the United States, this tradition dates at least to President Theodore Roosevelt. Presidents routinely invite NCAA champions and professional sport champions to the White House for official photo-taking publicity shots and general "clowning" around. Nearly all presidents of the twentieth and twenty-first centuries have had a true love for sports; enhancing their identity via sport was "natural." President William Howard Taft, for example, had a brother who owned a professional

baseball franchise and regularly attended professional baseball games. Taft started the annual custom of president's attending the opening day game. President John F. Kennedy's advisors used his love for touch football to "evoke images of youth and vigor" (Wilson 1994: 271). President Gerald Ford, although perceived by the media as a bit of a klutz, played football at the University of Michigan. Ronald Reagan was a football announcer, aside from being an actor, before becoming president, and his most famous acting role was as Notre Dame football great George "the Gipper" Gipp in the 1940 film *Knute Rockne, All American*. President Bill Clinton possessed a great love for his home state University of Arkansas basketball team. George W. Bush, a sports cheerleader at Yale, was the former owner of the Texas Rangers (MLB) and remains an avid fan of baseball. Barack Obama had a true passion for sports and was often shown playing basketball during his eight years as president; he even had the White House tennis court adapted so he could play both tennis and basketball on the outdoor court. It was also well-known that he was also a huge fan of the Chicago White Sox (MLB). Every year, Obama would fill out a bracket on ESPN for the Men's NCAA Basketball Tournament. In addition, Presidents Jimmy Carter, Clinton, Bush, and Obama all have their identities attached to being avid runners, and all have been identified with public advocacy of physical fitness—ironically enough, during a time when more and more Americans are becoming obese and out of shape. While certainly not a runner, the obese Donald Trump routinely played golf; in fact, he spent twice as long on the links as Obama—the man he often criticized for golfing too much—and even golfed regularly during the COVID-19 pandemic (MSN 2020).

At state and local levels, politicians from all ranks of government turn to sporting contests as a way of increasing a positive identity within the community. If a high school team from a small city or town wins a state championship it is understood among the townspeople that the mayor should be at the victory celebration. And generally speaking, politicians seldom skip out on publicity opportunities that place them in an environment where people are already celebrating and experiencing joy and happiness.

6. *Integration via Sport.* The U.S. government uses sports as a way to integrate different groups. Sport possesses integrative properties because it represents one of culture's broadest common denominators and politicians love to appeal to a cross-section of voters (Lapchick 2003). Recent immigrants to the U.S. can immediately feel a part of society through sports (as participants, fans, and spectators). Rich and poor, white and black, young and old, conservative and radical can all join together and become one collective when they cheer for the same team. Supporting local high school and college sports is an effective method of becoming a part of the community. Politicians are aware of the integrative power of sports. For example, "It is because sport is such a potent integrative symbol that congressmen combine romanticism and rationalism in their attitude toward it. They shift easily from seeing sport as the quintessence of private, voluntaristic behavior to seeing it as vital to the national purpose, a trust as sacred as the Constitution itself or a national monument" (Wilson 1994: 273–273).

At a national level, the integrative properties of sport provide diverse members of a society an opportunity to form a national identity. Thus, recent immigrants to the United States will find assimilation easier when they cheer for American teams involved in international competition. Every nation of the world attempts to integrate its citizens in order to maintain stability. Sport is the common vehicle world-wide that is used to help citizens form a national identity.

Politics and American Sports

Despite the fact that many of the major American sports have foreign roots, the United States has succeeded in constructing its own sporting culture. With industrialization and the conclusion of the Civil War, the United States witnessed a rapid expansion of sports during the late 1800s and early 1900s. Commercial backing, the creation of governing bodies, and improvement in media technology (e.g., telegraph service, newspapers) coupled with an increasing number of Americans who enjoyed leisure time helped to create an American sporting culture that was unique from its colonial founders. The American sport culture was quite distinctive with its considerable emphasis on the team sports of baseball, American football, basketball and hockey (the "Big Four"). Bairner (2001) claims that "the emphasis on team sports as opposed to individual activities is itself a peculiarly American characteristic" (p. 95). This claim is not entirely accurate, as team sports such as hockey are a fabric of national identity in Canada and soccer is the very essence of such nations as Brazil, Argentina, England, Spain, Italy, and Germany. What distinguishes American sporting culture from the rest of the world is a love for a wide variety of sports. Most people around the world are passionate about one sport. Although it is true that most American fans have a favorite sport, many are passionate for the sports played in each season. That is, any given fan will pay close attention to football during the fall, basketball and hockey during the winter and baseball in the spring and summer. Numerous other sports, including auto racing, tennis, golf, and lacrosse will also grab the attention of Americans during the season of their primary sports team preference.

Baseball played an important role in the development of the United States throughout the late nineteenth and twentieth centuries. Baseball was referred to as the "National Pastime." Playing baseball was encouraged by the U.S. government because the sport highlighted cultural ideals of fair play, individualism within the team framework, team spirit, respect for authority, and competitiveness. The integrative function of baseball was also viewed as a positive attribute of the sport. "One of the most dramatic developments in modern America was the migration of huge numbers of people from the rural communities to the rapidly growing cities. The game of baseball moved with them, not only physically but in some metaphysical sense as well. Indeed, for many young men, the game provided them with a sense of belonging otherwise absent from their new life experience" (Bairner 2001: 98). The integration function was also deemed important as a means of "Americanizing" immigrants. Any boy, despite his national origins, that played baseball was in effect creating an identity as an American. This sporting identity was, however, as imperfect as American society itself. For example, racism and sexism were found in both domains.

The Cold War sparked increased governmental involvement and political importance of Americans participating in international sporting events. The Soviet bloc nations were using sports as a way to promote their political ideology. The United States felt compelled to answer in kind. As Bairner (2001) states, "During the Cold War, sport clearly had a part to play in the promotion of American values. International events, such as the Olympic Games, acquired a new significance" (p. 112). The United States was working at a disadvantage. First, the U.S. was still using true amateur athletes in international sports competitions, whereas the Soviet bloc nations were using athletes trained by the government since early childhood. They were hardly ideal amateurs. Second, the Soviet bloc nations spent more money on their athletic training facilities than the U.S. Further, the primary sports in the U.S. were football and baseball, neither of which were Olympic sports. (Note: Baseball was added as an official Olympic sport at the 1992 Barcelona Games, dropped after the 2008 Beijing Games, and did return to the 2020 Tokyo Games held in 2021 due to COVID-19.) Americans have always been more interested in their national sports than in international sports. The typical NFL and MLB fan would rather have their favorite team win the league championship than have the American national team win an international sports tournament.

U.S. government involvement in sport reached a new high in the 1970s. Legislation such as Title IX (see Chapter 10) had a dramatic impact on American sports. During the 1970s, the government also set its political attention toward the international sport scene by establishing the United States Olympic Committee (USOC). President Gerald Ford appointed a Commission on Olympic Sports in 1975 in an attempt to organize the governorship of U.S. amateur athletics. As a result of the presidential commission, the Amateur Sports Act of 1978 was passed. This act established the USOC as the chosen organization of the U.S. government to oversee, promote and support amateur athletic activities involving the United States in athletic competitions with foreign nations. Although the intentions of the Amateur Sports Act of 1978 were good, the legislation did not solve the problem of how amateur sports should be funded. The USOC had historically prided itself as the only national Olympics association that did not receive any government support—even though the government had given minimal support in the past. A decade later, the Olympic Coin Act of 1988 was passed and enabled the USOC to sell silver and gold commemorative coins printed by the U.S. Treasury.

The idea of international sporting events as a quasi-political field had played witness to a variety of political boycotts throughout the years in such competitions as the Olympics. President Jimmy Carter decided to have the U.S. boycott the 1980 Moscow Olympic Games because of the Soviet invasion of Afghanistan, thus demonstrating the United States federal government's willingness to politicize international sporting events. (The irony of this condemnation has not escaped political observers as the U.S. would invade Afghanistan in late 2001.) A boycott is a form of collective action intended to pressure the target group to change its position or behavior. Soviet bloc nations returned in kind and boycotted the 1984 Los Angeles Olympic Games, still the most profitable (for the host country) of all the Games. In ancient times wars ended so that the Olympics could be played. The modern Olympics on the other hand have been used as much as a political tool as an athletic event. (We discuss the modern Olympics in further detail later in the chapter.)

As described by *The Washington Post* writer Adam Goldman, the U.S. government, via the CIA, sometimes incorporates elements of the sports world with its "influence operations" in foreign countries. Influence operations involve covert action programs conducted by the CIA in an attempt to win the hearts and minds of the local people or turn them against a particular ideology. Before the U.S. invaded Haiti in 1994, for example, the CIA distributed soccer balls to Haitian people. An official said, "It made them feel good about Americans. We were trying to prepare the way for the military" (Goldman 2014). Interestingly, the CIA, in addition to the deployment of drones, satellites, spies, informants, and tracking devices, also considered waging war with toys. Beginning in about 2005, the CIA began secretly developing an Osama bin Laden action figure with the face painted with a heat-dissolving material designed to peel off and reveal a red-faced bin Laden who looked like a demon with piercing green eyes and black facial markings (Goldman 2014). The goal of the short-lived project was to spook children and their parents, causing them to turn against the actual bin Laden and his ideology— through an influence operation. The CIA said that the "Devil Eyes" project never reached fruition although prototypes were made. The CIA turned to Donald Levine, the former Hasbro executive who was instrumental in the creation of the G.I. Joe toys, to design the "Devil Eyes" bin Laden action figure.

Athletes and Politics

Earlier in this chapter we discussed politicians who use sport for a sense of identity and opportunities to improve their own political standing with voters. In this section, we will discuss athletes who turned to politics for a new identity and sense of power and describe some examples of athletes who use their celebrity status to protest social injustice.

Former athletes have a number of potential advantages over non-athletes when running for political office. Their name recognition provided by the sports world is chief among them. The numerous political positions available and voter apathy are two other significant factors contributing to their success. In many nations around the world there would be fewer opportunities for an athlete to become a politician; however, the United States has more elections than any other democracy. Voters not only fill positions that are typically appointive in other countries, such as judges, but they also select officials for many more layers of government, from the town or county to the federal level. Voters even select nominees for the ballot through primaries, instead of relying on party organizations to designate candidates" (Fowler 1996: 430). In short, thousands of candidates compete for elected office each year. The large number of election opportunities clearly paves the way for nearly anyone to get elected to some level of political office including one of the authors. Ideally, candidates who will serve the needs of their constituents the best will be elected to office. Obviously, this is not always the case. In many instances unqualified persons who seek only to improve their own personal standings or serve as a figurative puppet for a political party may be elected. Much of the blame resides with voters who choose candidates for reasons that have little or nothing to do with political qualifications. Voter apathy among the majority of citizens contributes to the problems of democracy as well. When thousands of election opportunities are combined with the voter apathy, unqualified candidates being elected to political office is often the result. Furthermore, even when a president is elected on an overwhelming mandate (as Barack Obama was in 2008) they can effectively lose their ability to govern within two years if public opinion turns against them (as it did in 2010) because every two years all of the seats in the House of Representatives and about a third of the seats in the Senate are up for grabs via elections again. For Obama, this pattern repeated itself as he easily won reelection (2012) but became a lame duck two years later. Midterm elections are a good way to try to keep the president in check but they may also result in very little significant policy being enacted (Mounk 2014).

When it comes to former athletes who run for office they may, or may not, be qualified. Each athlete would have to be evaluated on a one-by-one basis. To be fair, it should be pointed out that being qualified for a political office is not necessarily a characteristic of eligibility to run for office. For example, "By law, almost anyone can seek a seat in Congress; for the Constitution sets only three criteria for members: age, citizenship, and residence in the state" (Fowler 1996: 430). Athletes are certainly capable of meeting these three requirements. Further, most athletes possess the most basic characteristic of other candidates (especially those already in office) and that is, they have greater wealth than most people do. Athletes turned candidate will likely enjoy the benefit of name recognition with voters. It is often said by sports commentators that popular coaches, especially following a national championship, could run for office.

FORMER U.S. ATHLETES WHO TURNED TO POLITICS

As described earlier in this chapter, a number of U.S. presidents were involved in sports, or were sportsmen, before their political careers began. Abraham Lincoln was an equestrian, swimmer, wrestler, runner, and jumper; Theodore Roosevelt pursued baseball, lacrosse, polo, horseback riding, tennis, football, boxing, and rowing; Woodrow Wilson played and coached football; Franklin D. Roosevelt swam, rode horseback, and sailed; Harry Truman was an avid walker and umpired baseball games; Dwight D. Eisenhower played baseball and football in his youth and played football at West Point (once making a tackle against legendary Jim Thorpe), and in later life enjoyed golfing and fishing; John F. Kennedy swam, sailed, golfed, played tennis, and played touch football; Lyndon B. Johnson was a swimmer, equestrian, hunter, and fisherman; Richard M. Nixon played football at Whittier College; Gerald Ford played football at Michigan (earning the most valuable player award on the 1934 Michigan team and participating in two All-Star games) and later coached at Yale while pursuing his law studies (he also turned down professional offers from the Green Bay Packers and Detroit Lions); Jimmy Carter played basketball in high school; and Ronald Reagan played football at Eureka College (Leonard 1992). George H.W. Bush was the captain of his baseball team; Barack Obama was an avid basketball player, as well as a devotee of golf; and Donald Trump played baseball in high school and continues to golf regularly. As these examples demonstrate, political leaders at the highest level participated in sports before they turned to politics. In the following pages, a number of other athletes who have successfully run for political office will be discussed. This is not, of course, an exhaustive list but instead provides ample evidence of the fact that the world of athletics and politics often intersect.

Among the more popular, or well-known, former U.S. athletes who have gone onto political careers are Joe Biden, Jack Kemp, Bill Bradley, Steve Largent, and Jesse "The Body" Ventura. While certainly less accomplished on the athletic field than these other athletes, Biden climbed much higher in the political realm as he was elected President of the United States in 2020 in addition to serving as Vice President for two terms (under Obama). Biden played baseball in high school and is a member of the Little League's Hall of Excellence. Jack Kemp was a star quarterback for 13 years with the AFL Buffalo Bills and San Diego Chargers. He led the Bills to back-to-back AFL championships in 1964 and 1965. Kemp co-founded the AFL Players Association and was elected president for five terms. His sports exploits and name recognition helped his initial election bid. Kemp, a Republican, served in the House of Representatives (representing the Buffalo area and western New York) from 1971 to 1989. He failed in a 1988 bid to earn the Republican Party presidential nomination but served as secretary of Housing and Urban Development for four years in George H.W. Bush's administration. Kemp was selected as Bob Dole's 1996 presidential running mate against Bill Clinton (and Al Gore). Clinton and Gore won in a landslide victory. (Ed Rutkowski, a teammate of Kemp's with the Bills, was also elected Erie County executive.)

Bill Bradley, a Rhodes Scholar after starring for Princeton's basketball team, where he was a three-time All-American (averaging 30.2 points per game throughout his three-year varsity career), played in the NBA for 10 years and won two NBA Championships with the New York Knicks (1970 and 1973). Bradley's excellence in professional basketball was honored by the Knicks when they retired his number 24 jersey. Bradley also served as captain of the 1964 gold-medal winning U.S. Olympic basketball team. Bradley turned his popularity in basketball into immediate success in the political arena. After retiring from basketball in 1977, Bradley ran for the U.S. Senate in New Jersey in 1978. He won and would serve 17 years in the Senate. Bradley ran unsuccessfully for the 2000 Democratic presidential nomination, losing out to Al Gore.

Steve Largent, never the fastest or the most gifted wide receiver, worked hard throughout his 14-year NFL career with the Seattle Seahawks and earned his induction into the Hall of Fame. The Oklahoma native was elected to the U.S. House of Representatives as a Republican in 1994. He was re-elected three times, always receiving more than 60 percent of the vote. He identified himself with the Religious Right and led a revolt against House Speaker Newt Gingrich, whom he blamed for congressional loss in 1998. Largent relinquished his House seat to run for state governor in 2002. He lost his bid in a close election, being defeated by state senator Brad Henry by less than 7,000 votes. He served as the CEO of a cellular phone lobbying organization until May 2014.

Although professional wrestling in the United States is not considered to be a sport, we have decided to include Jesse "The Body" Ventura on the lists of athletes who have turned to politics. Ventura is a former Navy SEAL, professional wrestler, actor, mayor (Brooklyn Park, Minnesota) and talk show host. A controversial man outside and inside the political arena, Ventura can credit his successful election as governor of Minnesota to his flamboyant personality. Ventura changed his wrestling nickname of "The Body"—a reference to his persona as bully with great physical prowess—to "The Mind"—to reflect a qualification deemed more desirable in the political world—during his foray into politics. Ventura, a member of the Reform party, served as governor from January 1999 to January 2003 but did not seek a second term. Ventura remains active politically but does not currently hold a political office.

There are other notable American athletes who have gone onto politics. Provided here is a sampling of some of the more notable examples. Bob Mathias, a decathlon Olympian the 1948 Summer Games, served four terms as U.S. House Representative from 1967 to 1975. Ben Nighthorse Campbell (son of a Portuguese immigrant mother and Northern Cheyenne Indian father) is a former Republican senator from Colorado (he did not seek re-election in 2004). Elected to the U.S. Senate in 1992, Campbell was the first Native American to serve in the Senate in more than 60 years. He also served in the U.S. House of Representatives from 1987 to 1992. Campbell is a former three-time U.S. National judo champion (1961–63) and represented the United States at the 1964 Olympic Games in Tokyo. While serving in the Senate, Campbell was a member of the Senate's Committee on Indian Affairs. He remains as an outspoken critic of the use of Indian nicknames, mascots and logos in sports. Jim Bunning, MLB Hall of Fame pitcher, who had 1,000 strikeouts and 100 wins in both leagues, returned to his home state of Kentucky and was elected as a city councilman and then state senator. In 1986, Bunning was elected to the U.S. House of Representatives and served in the House from 1987 to 1999. He was elected to the U.S. Senate from Kentucky in 1998 and served two terms as the Republican junior U.S. Senator. In 2009 he announced that he would not run for reelection in 2010. (He was succeeded by current U.S. Senator and presidential hopeful Rand Paul.) Jim Ryun (R–Kansas), a three-time Olympic track star and former mile and 1,500-meter world-record holder, is a congressman. J.C. Watts, a two-time Orange Bowl MVP with the University of Oklahoma, played football in the Canadian League. Upon the completion of his CFL career, Watts was elected to the U.S. House of Representatives in 1994. Watts served four terms in Congress before leaving politics in 2003. Watts was one of the highest profile African Americans in the Republican Party. Former professional bodybuilder Arnold Schwarzenegger, who at age 23 became the youngest Mr. Olympia (holding the title for six straight years), was elected governor of California in 2003 in a special recall election to replace then-governor Gray Davis. Schwarzenegger was then elected to a full term in November 2006 where he served until January 2011. Heath Shuler, a prolific quarterback at the University of Tennessee and former Washington Redskins quarterback, was elected to the U.S. House of Representatives in 2006 and would serve three consecutive terms before deciding not to run for a fourth term. In 2014, Mark Gilbert, who played seven games for the Chicago White Sox, became the first former MLB ballplayer to be named a U.S. ambassador (to New Zealand and Samoa) (Townsend 2014). Joe Runyan a former NFL offensive tackle served two terms in the U.S. House of Representatives but quit politics in disgust after expressing frustration with this fellow Republicans over the government shutdown before the 2014 elections (Griffin 2016). Tom Osborne, the former legendary football coach of the Nebraska Cornhuskers was elected to Congress in 2000 as a Republican and served three terms. Curiously (because he was known to break the rules as a player throughout his 14-season playing career that ended in 2009), Runyan was named the NFL's rules czar in 2016 (Griffin 2016). In 2020, Tommy Tuberville (R), the former football coach of the University of Auburn, won his bid to become an Alabama U.S. Senator.

As these examples indicate, a number of former U.S. athletes have gone on to life of politics following their athletic careers.

INTERNATIONAL FORMER ATHLETES WHO TURNED TO POLITICS

The United States is not the only country with political leaders who were previously sports stars. Throughout the world former athletes have entered the realm of politics. Just as in the United States, some of these athletes have risen to the ranks of president. One example is Russia's long-time president Vladimir Putin, a one-time KGB agent, who is a martial arts expert and who still enjoys putting on displays.

Among some of the many other international star athletes that have gone on to political careers is Sebastian Coe, a British middle distance runner who dominated the 800 and 1500 meter races during the early 1980s, is the only man to win the Olympic gold medal in the 1500 twice (Moscow in 1980 and Los Angeles in 1984). He is one of the most decorated athletes in British history. Coe, a Conservative, was elected to the Parliament from 1992 to 1997, but lost his re-election bid. In 2000, Coe was elected to the House of Lords. He led London's successful bid to host the 2012 Summer Olympic Games and now serves as president of the organizing committee for those Games. Coe had to convince members of the International Olympic Committee that London's transport system could be overhauled and that there was public support for the Games.

A number of former Canadian NHL players have enjoyed success in the political arena after their playing careers were over. Howie Meeker's sporting and political professions overlapped, as he won the federal by election in the Ontario riding of Waterloo South in 1951 while he was still playing hockey for the Toronto Maple Leafs. The Conservative member of Parliament did not seek re-election in 1953. After retiring from hockey, Meeker became a Canadian hockey broadcasting icon who entertained viewers for 30 years with his trademark folksy phrases. Frank Mahovlich, who played professional hockey for 22 years (NHL and WHA), never ran for political office, but he was appointed to the Senate in 1998. He belongs to the Fisheries and Oceans and National Finance Senate committees. Ken Dryden, a former goaltender for the Montreal Canadians, successfully ran for office in the Parliament. He was named to the cabinet as minister of social development. There are rumors that Dryden ultimately plans on running for prime minister. It is reasonable to assume that if Wayne Gretzky stepped into Canada's political arena that he could successfully run for nearly any political office, including prime minister.

Manny Pacquiao, a former eight division boxing champion, was elected to the Philippines' House of Representatives in 2010; he was reelected in 2013. Imran Khan, Pakistan's most successful cricket captain (he led his national team to 1992 Cricket World Cup Championship), started his own political party, Pakistan Tehreek-e-Insaf (PTI; "Movement for Justice") in 1996 and after a rough start he emerged as one of the most powerful politicians in Pakistan. He became a member of the National Assembly from November 2002 through October 2007 and was elected again in 2013 when his party gained 35 seats in the National Assembly. Vitali Klitschko, a former heavyweight boxing champion, was elected president of Ukraine and took office in June 2014.

At least 15 former cricketers turned to politics following their careers. One example is Imran Khan, a Pakistani politician who founded the Pakistan Tehreek-e-Insaf (PTI) party immediately after his retirement as one of the most successful cricketers ever and was elected Prime Minister. Indian star Mohammad Azharuddin won the Lok Sabha elections from Moradabad. Sri Lankan star cricketer was an active politician during his play days (Bhalerao 2014).

Many international soccer stars have turned to politics. For example, Brazil's Romario de Souza Faria, known simply as Romario, is an elected politician in Brazil. Arguably, the most successful international athlete turned politician is George Weah, a former professional soccer player who was one of the greatest strikers of all time and played for some of the best teams in Europe. After retirement, Weah served as Senator from Montserrado County (elected in 2014) and then went on to become president of Liberia in 2018. Weah had a tough challenge, as president as Liberia was rebuilding following war (Themner and Sjostedt 2019).

Like our list of former American athletes who found a life in politics, this look at international athletes who became politicians is also a mere sampling. The point of the discussion was to demonstrate how these individuals used their fame in sport to gain a platform and name recognition in politics following their sporting careers.

Athletes Who Protest

Athletes, especially elite and/or outspoken ones, are regularly interviewed by the media on topics beyond sports, including political issues. As described above, some athletes and coaches have such strong political feelings about social issues that they run for political office following the conclusion of their athletic careers. Other athletes express their political views, in the form of social protest, while they are still actively playing sports and, as a result, put their careers at risk. While it is more of a generalization than the rule, it is more typical for conservative white athletes and coaches to run for political office and left-leaning (those who want social change) athletes and coaches to become involved in social protest movements. Minority athletes protest in an attempt to end social injustice in its varying forms. As we have learned throughout this text, and especially in Chapter 3, blacks and other minorities were mostly excluded from "big-time" sports and it wasn't until the 1960s that blacks began to play collegiate, professional and international amateur sports in significant numbers. Coincidentally, the 1960s was a decade filled with social activism (e.g., civil rights movements and women's rights movements), protest (e.g., anti–Vietnam War), civil disobedience (e.g., many American cities were scenes of bloody and deadly rioting) and counter-culture movements (e.g., hippies and recreational drug users). As products of their environment, many black athletes of this era involved themselves with social activism as well. For example, black players refused to play in the AFL All-Star Game in New Orleans in 1965 to protest the blatant racism and discrimination of that city (Wright 2012).

In 1964, Cassius Clay (age 22) won the world heavyweight boxing title from Sonny Liston in a stunning upset. Younger fans loved Clay's bravado and older fans spoke of his potential for greatness. Shortly after winning the crown, however, Clay joined the Nation of Islam and changed his name to Muhammad Ali. (In 1975 he would convert to Sunni Islam.) Most Americans did not understand why Ali would do this and he began to lose favor with mainstream Americans. In 1967, Ali, still the reigning world heavyweight boxing champion, refused to be drafted into the U.S. Army. It should be noted, however, that Ali initially considered honoring the draft, thinking he would be given special consideration and worrying that he might lose out on economic benefits via commercial promotions if he refused the draft. However, the Nation of Islam would not go along with this and Ali would eventually become an outspoken critic of the war (Wright 2012). His public outspokenness against the war coupled with his Muslim beliefs made him one of the most polarizing sports figures in the U.S. As Harry Edwards described at the time, "There was so much consternation concerning the war and Ali that the fighter became symbolic of almost every rift in society" (Wright 2012).

On June 4, 1967, Ali met with members of the Negro Industrial Economic Union (later renamed the Black Economic Union) and several hundred other concerned individuals in Cleveland for a summit on socio-political matters. The NIEU was formed by Jim Brown, himself a highly visible social activist who had retired from the Cleveland Browns at the end of the 1965 season as the all-time leading rusher in NFL history (many people still consider him the greatest football player ever). At the meeting with Ali and Brown were a number of other high profile athletes, including Bill Russell, Lew Alcindor (who would later change his name to Kareem Abdul-Jabbar), Bobby Mitchell, Sid Williams, Jim Shorter, Walter Beach, John Wooten and Curtis McClinton (Wright 2012). All of these athletes were united in making a concerted effort to support Ali and to take a stand against those who supported racist overtones. Ali had claimed conscientious objector status but later in 1967 he was found guilty of trying to avoid the draft and sentenced to prison for 5 years. He remained free as he fought the sentence but he was barred from fighting (his boxing license was revoked). Due to a loophole in Georgia (they did not have a boxing commission), Ali fought Jerry Quarry in 1970 (he won with a KO, 3rd round). In 1971, the Supreme Court ruled in Ali's favor.

Perhaps the most famous international political protest waged by American athletes occurred in the 1968 Mexico City Olympics when Tommie Smith and John Carlos gave their black-power salutes (a one-armed raised fist) with heads bowed down during the playing of the national anthem.

Following the turbulent 1960s there were a number of instances wherein athletes have made political statements and protests but nothing quite compared to the protests of Ali, Brown, and Smith and Carlos. There have been times when black leaders would call upon black athletes to use their sports celebrity status and media forum to promote political causes designed to put a spotlight on racial discrimination in the United States or in other parts of the world but, generally, most were reluctant to do so; after all, they were doing well financially and could help socio-political causes in their own way. In 1990, Michael Jordan faced a great deal of pressure to get politically involved in the North Carolina senatorial race. Black writers and leaders asked Jordan to support Harvey Gantt, former mayor of Charlotte, in his tight race against five-term Republican Senator Jesse Helms. Helms, a long-time opponent of civil rights who, among other things, led a filibuster against the creation of Martin Luther King, Jr. Day, had released a scare-tactic political ad called "White Hands" in a distressed plea designed to get the white vote. Black leaders had turned to Jordan, who went to college at the University of North Carolina, to "endorse Gantt in his quest to become the South's first black man elected to the Senate since Reconstruction" (*Republicans Buy Shoes* 2014). Jordan, however, had other things on his mind. He was on the verge of winning his first NBA title and was in the early stages of amassing his nearly $2 billion fortune (see Chapter 12) by selling shoes. As such, Jordan attempted to avoid anything controversial and when asked why he would not support Gantt, Jordan infamously quipped, "Republicans buy shoes, too" (Badenhausen 2011). For the unacquainted, in 1983, Nike had just $1 million in total sales but their fortunes would change when they signed Jordan to a shoe endorsement deal in 1984 (Helin 2013). By 1989, Nike was making a fortune off of Jordan's shoes and in 1989 they started a campaign featuring Jordan and Spike Lee, with the slogan, "It's gotta be the shoes."

For many, it was clear that to Jordan selling shoes was far more important than political activism. He was criticized by many black writers for "not being black enough" and for profiting by the white corporate structure. In a 1992 interview with *Playboy*, Jordan addressed his critics by saying, "I realize that I'm black, but I like to be viewed as a person, and that's everybody's wish. That's what Martin Luther King fought for. In some ways I can't understand it because here we are striving for equality and yet people are going to say I'm not black enough?" And while Jordan has, for the most part, avoided controversy, he has his detractors because of his lack of political involvement. Jordan also indicated that he was a good role model because of his success. When asked about not supporting Gantt in 1990, Jordan gave a reasonable response: "I chose not to because I didn't know of his achievements, I didn't know if there were some negative things against him. Before I put myself on the line, at least I want to know who this guy was. And I didn't, but I knew

Jesse Helms and I wasn't in favor of him. So, I sent Gantt some money as a contribution. But that was never publicized" (*Playboy* 1992). Jordan was also aware that Jesse Jackson and other activists criticized him. His response was, "I never bow to that pressure because I always keep my opinions to myself. I avoid those types of endorsements from a political standpoint. That's just me. That's my prerogative to do. If you don't like it, lump it" (*Playboy* 1992). It certainly is Jordan's prerogative to avoid making political statements and often athletes do just that in order to keep their off-the-court/field beliefs private.

Most athletes are concerned that making their political views public might overshadow their athletic careers or alienate a large segment of their fans and so they avoid political activism during their playing careers. However, there are times when people must act and such was the case in late 2014 and carrying over into 2015, as athletes at all levels of competition (high school, college and professional) made political statements about a social issue that had gripped American society; namely, a number of high profile cases involving police officers killing black citizens suspected of committing crimes. Four cases in particular caught the public's attention and would later influence the behaviors of athletes. On August 9, 2014, Michael Brown, a young black man, was shot dead in Ferguson, Missouri, by police officer Darren Wilson as he tried to arrest him. On November 24, 2014, it was announced that the grand jury did not find enough evidence to indict Wilson. Rioting ensued (Somashekhar and Kelly 2014). A number of people believe that Brown had his hands up in the air to indicate that he posed no threat, and protestors and rioters used this "hands up, don't shoot" gesture and phrase throughout their protests. In Staten Island, New York, police attempted to arrest Eric Garner for allegedly selling illegal cigarettes, a crime he had committed numerous times prior (he had been arrested 30 times since 1980, with many of the arrests for selling loose cigarettes) (*Conservative Tribune* 2014). Garner refused to be handcuffed and police officer Daniel Pantaleo is seen (via a recording of the incident) putting a chokehold on the 350-pound Garner. It is against police policy to use a chokehold in New York City. In the recording Garner can be heard repeatedly saying, "I can't breathe." The asthmatic Garner suffered a heart attack and died on his way to the hospital (Bloom and Imam 2014). A series of protests (some violent, most peaceful) across the nation included protestors holding signs that read, "I Can't Breathe." (Note: The only person arrested for this incident was the bystander who recorded it.) In Cleveland, police officers shot and killed twelve-year-old Tamir Rice on November 22, 2014; authorities say the officers mistook the child's air gun for a real firearm (the police had responded to a 911 call about a black male—"probably a juvenile"—pointing a pistol—"probably fake"—at people in a park) (Ly and Hanna 2014). On December 12, 2014, the shooting was ruled a homicide. (As of this writing, there wasn't a conclusion to the case.) In August 2014, John Crawford was shot and killed while he was holding an air rifle as he walked through a Wal-Mart in Ohio. Police were responding to a call when they shot him shortly after encountering him (Balko 2014).

What do these four cases have in common? Among other things, the victims were black and the police officers were white; but, equally relevant to this publication is the decision of many active athletes to publicly protest the incidents. On November 30, 2014, five St. Louis Rams players raised their hands (to go with the protesters chant and gesture of "hands up, don't shoot") in solidarity with protesters upset at Michael Brown's death as they exited the tunnel to the playing field. One of the players, Jared Cook, told reporters, "We wanted to do something.… This is our community" (Fantz 2014). Another one of the Rams protesters, Tavon Austin, referring to Brown's killing and the ensuing violence, said, "What happened was a tragedy, period. There are things out there bigger than football and we notice that" (Fantz 2014). Rams Coach Jeff Fisher told reporters that the players would not be disciplined and that they were just exercising their right to free speech. The St. Louis Police Officers Association was "profoundly disappointed" with the football players (Fantz 2014). Following up on their promise to help the residents of Ferguson, the five Rams players attended the Urban League of St. Louis Christmas Party on December 19 and contributed $10,000 to purchase gloves, hats, socks, underwear, and other items to be distributed at the event (Fallstrom 2014).

The death of Eric Garner and his last words of "I can't breathe" became synonymous with social protests during the middle of the last decade and it was certainly hoped that the corresponding protests would put an end to such police brutality perpetrated against blacks. However, as we discussed in the previous chapter, the death of George Floyd on May 25, 2020, and his same fatal last words of "I can't breathe" showed that this was not the case. Floyd's death sparked a renewed sense of social protest by the BLM movement. However, this time, it was a little different as many mainstream white Americans finally said enough is enough and joined in the protests. The 2020 sports season, or what there was of it, would be greatly impacted by the Floyd tragedy. That the protests generally occurred during, or prior to, the playing of national anthem, would only add to the amount of attention garnered.

Protesting During the National Anthem

Many people, athletes included, have protested at various times in their lives and this includes during the playing of the national anthem at sporting events. For younger people, the athletes most closely associated with protesting during the national anthem is Colin Kaepernick formerly of the NFL's San Francisco 49ers and then some of his teammates and other professional football players (see Chapters 4, 8 and 11). We know why athletes (or anyone else for that matter) would protest during the playing of the national anthem as it will draw attention to the social act and spark conversation about the underlying issue. It is also understandable that there would be a backlash against such action. Let's take a closer look at this polarizing issue.

The title of the U.S. national anthem is the "Star-Spangled Banner" and it was written by Francis Scott Key, a lawyer-poet born to massive slaveholding wealth in Maryland which made him one of the richest men in America. Key certainly enjoyed his wealth and that led him to support slavery and described it as a national "peculiar institution" (Stiehm 2018). He was a slave owner himself and an anti-abolitionist who at times fought in court both for and against slaves seeking their freedom. He would prosecute abolitionists who founded the anti-slavery movement in the 1830s. He was also a founding member of an organization that sought to return captured slaves to their homelands (Charles River Editors 2017). He served as an advisor to President Andrew Jackson, another anti-abolitionist, slave owner, and racist whose actions were tantamount to the genocide of Southeastern Native American people, leading to the infamous "Trail of Tears" (Dan 2019). (Note: These are among the reasons why people want his image removed from the $20 bill and replaced by ex-slave and abolitionist leader Harriet Tubman.) By any measure of ethics and morality and certainly by today's standards, Key was not the right person to pen the national anthem.

The story of Key and the writing of the "Star-Spangled Banner" began when British forces landed in Maryland on August 19, 1814, and moved toward Washington, D.C. Key was alarmed at the ease by which the British invaders defeated an "outclassed and poorly led American force" (Vogel 2020). The British would burn every vestige of American power in the capital, including the White House, the State, War and Navy headquarters, the Capitol and with it the Supreme Court and the Library of Congress. The light of the fires could be seen as far away as Baltimore to the north and Fredericksburg to the south. Soon after dawn on September 13, the British would next bombard Baltimore, firing 200-pound explosive shells from ships two-and-a-half miles away. But, Key saw the American flag still flying over Fort McHenry at twilight and found hope and inspiration to write a poem about his observations. The British were beaten during this battle and then soundly defeated at Plattsburg, New York, in the "Battle of Lake Champlain" thus ending the invasion of the British imperialist forces. During the Civil War years later, the Union would find Key's lyrics meaningful when the American flag survived attack from Confederate forces. But it was still not until 1931 that the "Star Spangled Banner" would become the national anthem (Vogel 2020).

Despite such violent images in the lyrics of the national anthem, they serve as an inspiration to many. So, why then, do so many people despise the lyrics? To be clear, it is not the often-cited and sung first stanza of the anthem that enrages critics, it is the third stanza which includes: "No refuge could save the hireling and slave; from the terror of flight or the gloom of the grave." It is here where Key's racist and pro-slavery ideology comes to the forefront. Anyone who is not a racist would have to ask, why even include such lyrics? Today, proponents of the national anthem ignore this stanza in their nationalistic defense of the anthem.

Nationalists have the attitude of—"America, love it or leave it"—as they blindly support the status quo and believe that everything in the country is perfect and that no changes are needed. They do not see racism, sexism, elitism, and they do not acknowledge "Black Lives Matter." Instead, they counter with "All Lives Matter." Patriots on the other hand believe in the adage of—"America, stay and make it better." Those who support patriotism love their country but recognize that there are many problems and argue, or protest, that things need to be changed. Patriots acknowledge that all lives matter but point out that some people (i.e., African Americans and Hispanics) face discrimination and hardship simply because of their race or ethnicity. They even acknowledge that not all white people have an easy life but point out that such circumstances are not because of their race, as is the case with many Blacks and Hispanics.

The national anthem is played at sporting events prior to the start of the game. This is a nationalistic ideal embraced by most people. They dutifully standup, remove their hats (if they are males), and place their right hand over the heart. Some sing along, but most do not. Few, if any, think about the words of the anthem and their meaning. They enjoy the pomp and circumstance of military involvement and military jets that flyover outdoor stadiums, especially at NFL games. They do not think about how their tax dollars are paying for the military's expense to have a presence at ballgames. Most probably think that the NFL and other leagues cover the costs, but that is not the case. As a result of all this, military involvement at sporting events becomes synonymous with the playing of the anthem and from this perspective any dishonor shown during the anthem is a direct affront on the brave men and women who fight to "keep our nation free." However, this is a misguided belief as athletes and others that protest during the playing of the national anthem are not directing their protest at the military, they are directing it at a country and its supporters who have turned their backs on freedom and equality for all—the patriotic way of viewing the country.

Perhaps we should rethink the playing of the national anthem at sporting events. It is a puzzle why it is played at sporting events but not in other arenas of life such as the workplace, movie theaters, restaurants, on romantic picnics for two, concerts, and so on. So why then, is it performed at sporting events and when did this tradition begin? The answers to these questions are a little unclear. As Peter Jensen Brown describes in his ESPN blog, the idea that it began at the 1918 World Series (Ferris 2014) is not true. Newspaper articles indicate that the earliest known example of the "Star-Spangled Banner" being played at a baseball game was on May 15, 1862 (Brown 2016). Brown states that it is possible the anthem could have been sung before or during any number of games throughout the 1800s except that records did not survive, or have not been found. There are many articles indicating that it was a part of sporting events throughout the late 1800s. It was also played before picnics, fairs and other holiday events that might feature orators, races, or a band concert (Brown 2016). The Brooklyn Bridegroom (one year before they were first called the Trolley Dodgers) had a band that marched on the field playing the song (Brown 2016). It became more commonplace to include the anthem during the Spanish-American War. Later wars, such as World Wars I and II, likely contributed to the tradition becoming intractably ensconced in the American sporting tradition (Brown 2016). During the World War II era, most stadiums were now equipped with sound systems, meaning live bands were not necessary to play the "Star-Spangled Banner." With the official designation of the "Star-Spangled Banner" as the national anthem in 1931 it became increasingly popular to play the song at baseball games (where it was moved from the 7th-inning stretch to the start of game) and the newly formed National Football League. During the war, the anthem was played during every game. At the conclusion of World War II, NFL Commissioner Elmer Layden called for the league's teams to play the song at every game, stating, "The National Anthem should be as much a part of every game as the kick-off. We must not drop it simply because the war is over. We should never forget what it stands for" (Waxman 2017). The roots of playing the national anthem at sporting events had been transformed into a sort of national identity and any disrespect shown during this tradition was labeled unpatriotic.

However, as previously explained, a large number of Americans believe the time has come to finally face up to its long racist history, of which the author of the "Star-Spangled Banner" and the song itself were now identified. When Kaepernick protested during the anthem in 2016 he was mostly left on an isolated island and treated like a leper that needed to be quarantined. U.S. Women's soccer star, and outspoken critic of inequality, Megan Rapinoe, who protested during the anthem in the 2019 World Cup, seemed destined to reside on this same leper island as Kaepernick. However, in 2020, the majority of Americans welcomed Kaepernick back as a sort of martyr for the cause of equality. The BLM social movement of 2020 led athletes in every major sport to protest during the anthem when sports attempted to resume during the COVID-19 pandemic. European soccer leagues opened first and players in most countries protested in favor of BLM in one form or another. The respective leagues did not punish them. MLB, WNBA, NBA, and MLS players all protested at the start of the season during the playing of the anthem. Players in all sports took a knee during the anthem; referees joined in the silent protest in the NBA; the NBA allowed the athletes to use a simple form of protest on their jerseys in place of their own names; WNBA players left the court during the anthem on opening day; most athletes wore "Black Lives Matter" t-shirts; the NFL gave the green light to players who wanted to protest once the season started; and so on. The tide had completely reversed; at least, among the athletes and countless supporters. Still, there were those who were upset over these actions and vowed not to watch sporting events where players were allowed to protest during the anthem.

The solution to the problem of athletes protesting during the anthem is simple. Either end racism and inequality in all of its forms, or stop playing the national anthem at sporting events. Those who prefer the status quo, warts and all, wish that all the athletes who protest during the national anthem be kicked off the team. But, then came the murder of George Floyd, the BLM social movement, and a growing throng of supporters for equal rights and an end to racism. The status quo was obviously no longer acceptable.

International Sports

Many nations around the world attempt to promote their socio-political ideology on the playing field. As Tomlinson and Young (2006) explain, "The political exploitation of the global sports spectacle and the cultural and economic ramifications of its staging have been critical indices of the intensifying globalization of both media and sport" (1). Ideally, the sports environment provides a civil, universally accepted way for rival and friendly nations to compete. To assure the smooth functioning of international sports competition, each nation must abide by international rules that apply both on the field and off the field. The creation of international rules was, according to Tomlinson and Young (2006), greatly established by the foundation and growth of the International Olympic Committee (IOC) and the Federation International de Football Association (FIFA). Participating nations must realize that international rules may differ from those of their home nation. International basketball rules, for example, include a different three-point line than the one used in either the NBA or NCAA. Off the field issues usually come under the realm of foreign policy. As Nafziger (1995) states, "Foreign sports policy must comply with international law, including that governing nation groups such as the Commonwealth of Nations.... The Olympic Charter best evidences international custom pertaining to sports competition, Olympic or not. The Rules of the Charter are administered by a 'supreme authority,' the International Olympic Committee (IOC). The IOC is a corporate body having juridical status and perpetual succession.... Although the IOC is a nongovernmental organization that cannot in itself compel state obedience, its rules best evidence current international practice and therefore have legal significance" (241). Thus, it is important for competing nations to understand international rules of the game and the legal authority of governing bodies. Developing coherent sports policy is an important and necessary function of government. Developing a suitable international sport policy assures that all participants, including the individual athletes as well as the governments of competing nations, fully understand the rules on and off the field.

Once an international sport policy is established, governments are ready for international sport participation, and there are a variety of political uses of international sport competitions.

POLITICAL USES OF INTERNATIONAL SPORTS COMPETITION

Ever since the reintroduction of the modern Olympic Games, the importance of international sport competition has increased tremendously. Nafziger and Strenk (1978) argue that there are six political uses of international sports competition: international cooperation, national ideology and propaganda, official prestige, diplomatic nonrecognition (and recognition), protest, and conflict. Of these categories of political uses of international sport competition, "only diplomatic nonrecognition and conflict are improper official uses of sports competition according to international law, although variations on the other uses may constitute unfriendly acts. Within this margin of discretion, it is necessary for governments to clarify their objectives" (Nafziger 1995: 239).

1. *International Cooperation.* Ideally, sports foster cooperation and fair play between competitors. Nations that participate in international sporting competitions have, more or less, agreed to abide by international law. International sporting events provide a playing field where all participants play by the same rules that are, ideally, enforced fairly.

2. *National Ideology (identity) and Propaganda.* Most nations attempt to use sports as a propaganda tool. Governments hope to showcase their athletes' triumphs as examples of national ideological superiority. Before the Soviet Union and East Germany attempted to demonstrate their perceived political ideological superiority via sport, Adolf Hitler had attempted to do the same thing during the 1936 Berlin Olympics (see Chapter 11). Prior to the start of the 2018 Men's World Cup held in Russia, a Russian legislator drafted a bill imposing a fine of 10,000 rubles ($160 USD) against anyone who criticizes the national team. Vitaly Milonov told the *Associated Press* (2018), "This is not just about football. This is about our national identify." As it turned out, Team Russia exceeded expectations and reached the quarter-finals, losing to Croatia on penalty kicks, 3–4. The world's nations, including the United States, continue to use international sporting events as an opportunity to showcase their athletic prowess as a sign of political ideological superiority. Tracking medal counts are important for nations that seek to showcase their political ideology as superior to others. The staggered stage set (gold medal winners are elevated above silver medal winners who are elevated over bronze medal winners) used to award medals to champions also reflects a power status. There are critics of this Olympic tradition of elevating gold winners over the others because they view such ceremony as elitist. These critics would prefer a technique used in the Special Olympics where all participants are treated equally. The idea of applying such an egalitarian format to international sporting events such as the Olympics and World Cup is not at all popular with the masses, who believe winners should acknowledged for all their hard work.

3. *Official Prestige.* Concepts related to official prestige include a national identity and self-image. International sporting events provide a golden opportunity for nations of the world to earn prestige and a positive self-image. Victories gained on the playing field provide an affirmative national identity. Emerging nations are afforded an opportunity to create an image for themselves via international sporting events. Nations often use the sports world as a means of developing a national identity because it is easier to develop talents of athletes than it is to locate

other precious commodities (e.g., oil, gold, diamonds, etc.). Nigeria and Kenya, for example, have found it easier to develop prestige via their reputation as nations with great distance runners than by developing a strong international banking economy or space program. Each nation must learn to adapt to the level of natural resources and level of technology it possesses. In addition, by encouraging the talents of local athletes, nations can give a sense of hope to individuals who might otherwise despair of or even rebel against the government. And the identification certain countries, such as Brazil and Argentina, have with World Cup victories bolsters the esteem of their citizens.

4. *Diplomatic Recognition and Nonrecognition.* When a nation is allowed to compete in international sporting events, it becomes symbolic of political recognition. This often occurs during various Olympic Games. For example, Bosnia and Herzegovina (a former republic of Yugoslavia) was allowed to use its own national flag and anthem in the 1992 Barcelona Olympics. Bosnia and Herzegovina were among several small nations that emerged from the break-up of Yugoslavia, a heterogeneous country that was created after World War I by the victorious Western Allies. (Before Yugoslavia was ravaged by war during the 1990s, Sarajevo had played host to the 1984 Winter Olympic Games.) When a new nation sends its athletes to an international sporting event, it represents an innocent way to institute official contact. Thus, sports help to serve as a transitional step in the official diplomatic recognition of new governments. However, recognition can be denied a nation when other countries refuse to compete against it in sport. The former East Germany gained its official recognition via international sporting contests, thus separating itself from West Germany. The former South African government that employed a social system of apartheid (separation of races) felt the brunt of international nonrecognition in the sporting world, as most nations refused to compete with them on the playing fields. This former elite sporting nation suffered tremendously because of this nonrecognition. The racist South African government eventually collapsed.

5. *Protests.* The international sporting environment provides a major venue for protesting perceived social injustices. Social protests can occur at two levels: the individual or small group and the national or multi-national level. At any time, any number of athletes may attempt to stage a political protest during an international sporting event. If this individualistic act of protest is deemed unacceptable by the nation represented by the protestor(s), the athlete(s) risks great condemnation both nationally and internationally. On the other hand, the protesting athlete may actually gain sympathy through his or her public display of discontent. Perhaps the most famous protest conducted by American athletes during an international sporting event was exhibited by Tommie Smith and John Carlos, who gave black-power salutes during the medal ceremonies for the 200-meter race (Smith finished first and Carlos third) in the 1968 Mexico City Olympics. Smith and Carlos each raised one black-gloved hand during the playing of the national anthem. They were subsequently banned for life from all Olympic competition and ordered to leave Mexico. Of note, Harry Edwards, the sociologist who coined the term "sport sociology" (see Chapter 1), who was friends with the two athletes, had been the one who suggested the protest gesture to them. The protest perpetrated by Smith and Carlos was designed to send a global message about their feelings that the

American society was racist. The majority of Americans were outraged by this public display meant to dishonor the United States. On the other hand, a number of people view the political gesture made by Smith and Carlos as a heroic stand against injustice. In January 2020, the IOC warned Olympic athletes that protests such as kneeling and hand gestures (e.g., the raised fist) during medals ceremonies and competition was still banned and would not be tolerated at the 2020 Tokyo Games. The IOC wants no visible signs of political demonstrations. The outspoken Megan Rapinoe, a star athlete on the U.S. Women's Soccer team—that was expected to win a gold medal—responded by saying "We will not be silenced" (Associated Press 2020d: B5). As we know, this concern was moot as the 2020 Games were postponed and scheduled to be held in 2021.

Individuals and groups may lead protests. However, protests at the national level also may occur. Protests at the national level generally involve a nation, or a number of nations, who engage in a boycott. The boycott is a type of sanction (punishment) directed toward the governmental policies of another nation(s). South Africa fell victim to an international sports boycott because of its repressive government. South Africa instituted its system of apartheid in 1948. The movement toward isolating (punishing) South Africa from the international sporting world began in 1964 when it was banned from the Tokyo Olympics. In 1970, the International Olympic Committee issued a permanent ban against South Africa, forbidding it from future Olympic competition until it ended its system of separation.

6. *Conflict.* The sports world mirrors the greater society, one that is filled with conflict and war. As explained in Chapter 9, conflict and violence are a part of sports (see, for example, the "Drone Brawl"); the international sporting arena is no different. Sport competition itself may lead to conflict and violence; for example, when athletes tangle in the "heat of the moment." This type of conflict and violence is generally short-lived and isolated. Conflict that started on the playing field sometimes spills over outside the sports arena. For example, in one rare case, a war broke out because of the events that took place on the playing field of an international sporting contest. In 1969, a best-of-three World Cup qualifier game between El Salvador and Honduras sparked an incident known as "The Soccer War." The intense rivalry between these two nations peaked when El Salvador won the best-of-three match, causing hostility. The borders between the two nations were closed. Six thousand people died and millions of dollars in damage occurred during the short war that followed. Clearly, these two rival nations had political conflicts (e.g., a long-standing dispute over the exact location of a border and the huge numbers of Salvadorans who had migrated into Honduras) prior to this short-lived war (four days), but the spectator violence that took place during the qualifying matches was enough to upset both nations to the point of war.

Conflict and violence directed at international sport participants may come from the outside and impose themselves upon the sports world. For example, in 1972, the Black September Movement (BSM) used the 1972 Munich Games to stage a violent conflict aimed at Israeli athletes. The BSM wanted to promote the recognition of Palestine and demonstrate its disdain toward Israel. The Palestinian terrorists broke into the Olympic Village and took Israeli athletes and coaches hostage. All hostages were eventually killed. The 2005 movie *Munich* recounts the tragic moments of this massacre and the subsequent hunting down of the terrorists by Israeli military personnel.

The Modern Olympics: The Ultimate International Sports Stage

The Modern Olympic Games, although often claiming a sense of idealism, have fallen far short of such lofty principles. When Baron Pierre de Coubertin, a French nobleman, attempted to establish the Modern Games, his intention was not solely to encourage the valued principles of sportsmanship and fair competitive games. Rather, it was the sad performance of French soldiers in the 1870–71 Franco-Prussian War that prompted de Coubertin's belief that France's military prowess could be re-established by means of a national fitness and sports program. Born in Paris on January 1, 1863, de Coubertin was just a child when France suffered its humiliating defeat at the hands of the Prussians at Sedan in 1870 (Guttmann 1992).

De Coubertin believed that a national physical education program was the best means of "restoring the vigor of French youth and grandeur of France" (Senn 1999: 2). He came to this conclusion because "he had been taken with the character-building claims of the game-playing curriculum of the upper-class-male British public schools. He proposed that sport be extended to all in what he called a 'democracy of youth'" (Kidd 1995: 233). De Coubertin faced far more obstacles getting his Olympic dream started than he did in establishing physical education programs for French youth. De Coubertin was confronted by political intrigues, antagonisms, and conflicts. Convincing athletes from different nations, such as Germany and France, to compete together under unified rules was another major challenge confronting De Coubertin. From the very first modern Olympic Games, held in Athens in 1896, de Coubertin realized that the Olympics would always be consumed by political interference. In 1908 he concluded, "The Games have become an affair of state" (Senn 1999: 2). Senn (1999) states that early Games "had become a focal point of state policies and national ambitions. Ultimately, participation in the Games became a public affirmation of international recognition, and the possibility that some governments might even object to Games' practices arose, as the Russians did to the flying of the Finnish flag at the London Games of 1908. The Olympic Games has seemed at times something like a disabled boat adrift in stormy international waters" (p. 2). Competing nations in the early Modern Games argued over what sports should be played, an argument that continues today. "The American sport czar James E. Sullivan, for example, argued that track and field constituted the most important sports and that most of those other types of competition should be excluded. Coubertin vigorously rejected this thought, insisting the Games should consist of many different types of competition" (Senn 1999: 3).

Sullivan wanted track and field as the centerpiece of the Olympics because the United States dominated in those sports. American journalists documented every early success of American athletes, proclaiming such international victories as evidence of the superiority of the United States' social system (Riess 1995). The 1904 St. Louis Games were completely dominated by American athletes; however, it should be pointed out that 432 of the 554 competitors were from the USA. The U.S. won seventy of 74 track and field medals, twenty-nine of 30 in rowing, and all the medals in boxing, cycling, wrestling, and women's archery (Riess 1995). Nationalism was in full display by the 1908 Olympics. "Four years later at the 1908 London games, where national teams were employed, chauvinism became a dominant factor. By mistake, the host nation failed to display the American flag at the opening ceremonies. In response, several Americans carried their own U.S. flags in the opening parade and were the only athletes who did not dip their flags in respect when marching before King Edward VII. This gesture was seen as an affront to Great Britain, and British judges seemed to retaliate by cheating American athletes" (Riess 1995: 28). Martin Sheridan, the American standard-bearer of the U.S. flag, responded to King Edward and Great Britain's perceived slight by stating the American flag dips to no earthly king.

The ceremonial opening parade of athletes remains a hallmark of the Olympics. Athletes march together by nation carrying their flags. This is a proud moment for the athletes and the nations they represent. It often brings chills to participants and viewers alike. There are a few detractors of this form of nationalism, but such critics should try explaining themselves to the athletes who relish this opportunity to represent their nation. For example, tell the Palestinian swimmers of the 2008 Olympics that athletes with national uniforms and flags marching during the opening ceremonies is not a good idea. There is no Olympic-sized pool in the territories the Palestinian athletes represent. Their training consisted of swimming in a 17-meter pool (Halpern 2008). Furthermore, there was no budget to help support the Palestinian athletes. In short, there was little hope for these athletes to win medals in the 2008 Olympics—wearing their national uniforms and hoisting their flag during the opening ceremonies was their "gold medal." Would you take that opportunity away from them?

The great public exposure afforded by the Olympics all but guarantees political involvement (Hill 1992). The modern Olympic Games have been plagued by political involvement and national self-interest. U.S. President Theodore Roosevelt and the city of St. Louis are credited with injecting politics into the modern games for the first time in 1904. Chicago was originally selected by the International Olympic Committee to host the games. St. Louis was already planning to host its Louisiana Purchase Exhibition World's Fair the same year and organizers managed to get the IOC to change its decision through pressure from Roosevelt (*Los Angeles Times* 1992). Politics have continued to play a negative role in the Olympics.

POLITICAL PROBLEMS WITH THE MODERN OLYMPICS

International sporting events are vulnerable to any number of political problems. Corruption, political boycotts, drug scandals and economic issues are among the primary politically-charged problems of the modern Olympic Games.

1. *Corruption.* The true level of corruption involved in the Olympics may never be known. Corruption may involve crooked judges who are paid to give high scores to specific athletes and low scores to his or her leading competitors and any number of other forms of illegal and unethical behavior. Among the more commonly known forms of Olympic corruption involves providing illegal payments and bribes to members of the International Olympic Committee from delegates of potential host cities who try to influence members of the IOC to vote favorably for their city. Former IOC President Juan Antonio Samaranch admitted that it would

be difficult for any city to secure the Games without some sort of "donation." It is also expected that "gifts" ("hidden" as souvenir-related expenses) will be provided to Committee members if a city hopes to secure a nomination to host the Games. Allegations of corruption are common when representatives of bidding cities are willing to lavish "expected" gifts to unscrupulous IOC members.

    Olympic-related corruption is not limited to the IOC, as host cities or nations may also be involved in corruption. A Swiss member of the IOC said that roughly a third of the $55 billion spent on the 2014 Sochi (Russia) Winter Olympics had disappeared due to corruption (Ernst 2014). Boris Nemtsov, former deputy prime minister of Russia, said that bribes and kickbacks were common at Sochi and that he was trying to interest the IOC on that matter for quite a while but to no avail. "Until now, there's been no clear acknowledgement of the issue, even though the facts are widely available. The attitude is that 'all is well' and if there's any corruption it's a problem for the host country and not the IOC" (Ernst 2014).

2. *Boycotts.* A number of private groups have boycotted the Olympic Games. For example, European political leftists and socialist workers organizations protested the Olympics during the 1920s and 1930s. The NAACP, Jewish organizations, and half of the American public (according to a 1935 Gallop poll) protested American involvement in the 1936 Berlin Games (Wilson 1994). However, when private groups and organizations attempt to disrupt the playing of the Games, they are unsuccessful. Significant and influential boycotts of Olympic Games are those perpetrated by a coalition of nations. For example, Israel was excluded from the 1948 Games because of an Arab-led threat of boycott. However, for the most part, before World War II, there was little interest among the nations of the world to boycott the Games. This would change in the 1950s. Olympic boycotts occurred in 1956 over the Soviet invasion of Hungary and the British invasion of Egypt. A number of nations also boycotted the 1976 Montreal Games because New Zealand was allowed to participate. (New Zealand was stigmatized at that time because of its refusal to boycott South African sports.) Guttmann (1992) claims that the "era of the boycott" began in the 1970s. A number of nations sympathetic with the plight of Palestine boycotted the 1972 Games. Twenty nations from Africa agreed to boycott the 1976 Montreal Games if New Zealand was allowed to participate. The African nations were upset with New Zealand because it allowed one of its rugby teams to play in South Africa, which was a violation of the international boycott imposed on all South African sports. China not only threatened to boycott the 1976 Games if Taiwan was allowed to participate in Montreal, the Chinese government threatened to renege on a trade agreement crucial to the Canadian economy. Taiwan enjoyed IOC recognition and host Olympic nations must welcome athletes from any country in good standing. The IOC was eager to have mainland China participate in the Olympics and as a result allowed them to participate. Nationalist China (Taiwan) was asked to participate under either a Taiwan or IOC flag. It refused and boycotted the 1976 Games.

    The 1980s witnessed the biggest and most significant political boycotts of the Olympics. A U.S.-led boycott of the 1980 Moscow Games was prompted by the 1979 Soviet invasion of Afghanistan. This boycott, in turn, resulted in a Soviet Union led 15 nation boycott of the 1984 Los Angeles Games. President Jimmy

Carter initially had a hard time convincing foreign nations—let alone the United States Olympic Committee—to agree with his decision to boycott the Moscow Games. The U.S. had alienated the African nations by not joining them in their 1976 boycott and many European nations had questioned Carter's reasoning and justification for his political boycott of Moscow (Wilson 1994).

The Carter Administration's demand for a boycott by the USOC of the Moscow Games was based on what appeared to be unclear policy concerns. The Administration variously argued principles of diplomatic protection of its nationals, deterrence and retribution. The President first justified the boycott on the grounds of a presumed danger to American athletes and spectators, which was the rationale parroted by the Soviet Union to justify its boycott of the 1984 Games. After having advanced this rationale for the compelled boycott, the White House later changed its mind by asserting that the real reason for the boycott was to deter future aggression and to send the Soviets 'a signal of world outrage.' [Nafziger 1995: 239].

In the end, the largest Olympic boycott ever—61 nations in all—responded to Carter's request that athletes stay home to protest the Soviet invasion of Afghanistan. Ironically, decades later, the U.S. would invade Afghanistan although for entirely different reasons.

Despite the Soviet led boycott of the 1984 Summer Games, Los Angeles earned a record $222 million-plus profit. (Peter Ueberroth, the organizer of the event, became famous for his managerial skills, and was shortly thereafter appointed the commissioner of Major League Baseball, serving from 1984 to 1989.) Of note, Nationalist China competed as Taiwan and the People's Republic of China competed as China. The 1988 Seoul Games enjoyed a near "normal" participation rate among the nations of the world. South Africa was still banned from the Games but only six invited countries (North Korea, Cuba, Ethiopia, Nicaragua, Albania, and the Seychelles) refused to participate (Figler and Whitaker 1995). The "Era of the Boycott" appears to have concluded. The 1992 Barcelona Games represents the first Olympiad since 1972 that no country boycotted. A record 169 nations took part in the opening 1992 parade. Participation rates continue to soar into the Third Millennium. Many human rights groups called for a boycott—either by athletes or by world leaders attending the opening ceremonies—of the 2008 games in Beijing, in protest for China's occupation of Tibet and alleged human rights violations perpetrated on its inhabitants. In 2014, a number of individuals and political groups attempted to organize a boycott, or at the very least, draw attention to socio-political issues of concern. For example, the Circassians (an ethnic group from the North Caucasus, an area in southwest Russia) demanded that the Games be moved unless Russia made a formal apology for the nineteenth-century Circassian genocide (Putin refuses to acknowledge their historical presence or any of their grievances) (Smith and Balkiz 2014). LGBT groups wanted the Sochi Games boycotted because of Russia's anti–LGBT stance and their "gay propaganda" laws (Leslie and Tilley 2014). Thus, while it may be true that the era of mass boycotts ended in 1992, it is highly unlikely that there will never be individual athletes, political groups, or nations that will ignore the opportunity to make an international political statement at the global level considering the international platform the Olympics provide.

It is worth noting that when the Games are boycotted by nations, regardless of the reason, it is the athletes that suffer the most. We have all heard how Olympic athletes work their entire lives to compete in the Olympics. It becomes a time-consuming pursuit to the point of near exclusion of a "normal" life. To have the Games boycotted (or in the case of the 2020 Summer Games, postponed) is devastating to athletes. According to Michael Phelps, the owner of the most Olympic gold medals and total medals ever, the vast majority of Olympic athletes suffer mental problems and symptoms similar to PTSD. No stranger to mental health issues himself, as he has freely discussed in many forums, Phelps serves as the narrator and executive producer of *The Weight of Gold*, an HBO documentary that premiered in August 2020. Phelps interviewed several high-profile athletes and they echo his desire that the U.S. Olympic and Paralympic Committee, and their respective federations, invest in and encourage mental health counseling. Phelps is particularly upset that no one seems to care enough to help these athletes and believes Olympic athletes are treated just as "products" (Bumbaca 2020).

3. *Drug Use and Drug Testing.* Another problem facing the Olympics is one that exists at all levels of sports, drugs and the subsequent drug testing policy. Just as illegal drug use and drug testing is a major focus of governing bodies in American sports, so to is it a concern in the Olympics. Decades ago, sports fans marveled at the accomplishments of East German athletes; today, of course, we know the results are tainted because of illegal drug use. Athletes taking performance enhancing drugs such as anabolic steroids predates the East Germans. Hoberman (2005) explains that the doping of athletes "was evident long before the anabolic steroid epidemic began during the 1960s. As early as 1939, before doping was being recognized as a societal problem, a Danish exercise physiologist was reporting that the use of stimulants by athletes was fueling 'the record-breaking craze and the desire to satisfy an exacting public'" (p. 216). Descriptions of illegal drug use in the Olympics having reached "epidemic proportions" dates back decades (Coe 1996; Hoberman 2005) and continue today (see Chapter 8 for a discussion on Russian doping in the 2012 and 2014 Olympics). The culture that accepts athletes taking drugs must be changed if effective drug enforcement is to prevail. This culture includes the athletes, trainers, coaches, governments and fans of sport. They must all agree that taking performance enhancing drugs not only risks the health of the athletes but ultimately compromises their performance.

4. *Economic Issues.* Host countries compete with each other intensely in order to have the Olympic Games held in one of their prominent cities. Partly this is done for prestige purposes, due to the great attention the country will receive from the mass media during the events. But the primary motivating factor seems to be the perceived economic benefits that will accrue from tourists, commercialization, and other revenue-enhancing areas connected with the events. Yet, with the noted exception of the 1984 Los Angeles Games, which were a great financial success, it is debatable just how positive the economic impact has been on the host cities. Most cities have claimed to have ended up losing money, although it is often said that the long-term benefits of adding new stadiums and other facilities more than makes up for any initial financial loss. Still, as Helen Jefferson Lenskyj (2000) points out, this too is debatable:

Evidence from three decades of Olympic industry disasters has demonstrated what is arguably the most serious and sinister implication for citizens living in Olympic cities and states: the threat of disenfranchisement. The generally negative social, economic, and environmental impacts of hallmark events, as well as the documented concerns and experiences of anti–Olympic and Olympic watchdog groups on four continents, provide irrefutable evidence that Olympic bids and preparations exacerbate the problems of already disadvantaged populations. While some of the promised economic boosts may eventuate, there is little evidence that the people "at the bottom of the food chain" will reap any benefits. A beautified, gentrified city with state-of-the-art professional sports facilities has no value to men, women, and children whose basic human needs are not being met [192–193].

To illustrate this concern over economic losses all the more, Brazil reports great economic loss following their hosting of the 2016 Summer Games. Brazil says that it spent $13 billion in public and private money to organize the Olympics—although some estimates suggest the figure is closer to $20 billion—and today, many of the arenas are left empty and ROI was not realized. It took a government bailout to hold the Paralympics and corruption scandals plagued the Games (*Associated Press* 2017d). On the other hand, because of the Olympics Rio has a new subway line extension, high-speed bus service, and "a renovated port filled with food stands, musicians and safe street life in a city rife with crime" (*Associated Press* 2017d).

Idealistically, the Olympics are a symbol of cooperation among diverse nations. In reality, the Olympics are ripe with political problems and issues. Promoting one's ideology through international sport dominance remains as a characteristic of the elite nations of the world. Hosting an Olympics is usually associated with prestige but often brings with it debt, controversy and protests. If only the Olympics were about the games (sports) that people play and not the politics of the Games.

Connecting Sports and Popular Culture

Box 13: *Olympia*: A Faustian Bargain

In Renaissance Germany, legend tells of a learned doctor named Faust who wanted unlimited knowledge and pleasure. The devil, knowing of his desires, made Faust a bargain—if the doctor signed over his soul to him, Faust in turn would be granted 24 years of hedonistic gratification, wealth, wisdom, and immense power over others. Faust reveled in his experiences, but when the 24 years were up realized to his horror that he would now spend an eternity in hell. In the words of Jesus, "for what shall it profit a man, if he shall gain the whole world, and lose his own soul?" (Mark 8: 34–38).

The story of Faust comes to mind when considering the career of Leni Riefenstahl (1902–2003). A beautiful actress, talented photographer, daring athlete, and pioneer female film director, she was the mastermind behind one of the greatest sports films ever made, 1938's two-part documentary *Olympia*. While filming the 1936 Olympic Games in Berlin, Riefenstahl came up with many innovative techniques for capturing athletes in motion, including tracking shots, extreme close-ups, digging trenches in which to place cameras and cameramen, and even filming underwater. Her opening shots of the Olympic torch being passed from hand to hand have influenced all subsequent Olympics, and her style remains highly influential to the present day. "Riefenstahl has often been called the greatest woman documentary filmmaker—although she would have bridled at the 'woman.' No feminist, she wanted nothing less than her due as a great artist" (Rollyson 2007).

And yet, this triumphant work is also one of the most controversial films ever made. For Riefenstahl, in order to film the proceedings, was given carte blanche by the official host of the Olympics, the German Chancellor Adolf Hitler. He allotted her the then-astronomical budget of $7 million, complete control over what to film, and gave her years to edit it to her satisfaction. Very few directors have ever had such power.

Olympia was not Riefenstahl's first film sponsored so lavishly by Hitler. In 1935 she premiered her infamous *Triumph of the Will*. Documenting the annual Nazi Party rally at Nuremberg in 1934, it captures for posterity the charisma of the new German Chancellor. In iconic imagery we see Hitler's plane coming down from the clouds, as the film depicts him like a God descending from above to rescue "his people." While watching the adoring crowds cheer their supposed savior, we cannot help but also think of the millions soon to perish under his mad regime. Riefenstahl's movie, made at the very beginning of Hitler's career as German Fuehrer, did much to legitimize his rule in the eyes of its original viewers.

It is no wonder, then, that a year later Hitler would give his acolyte complete control to capture the Olympic Games, which had been scheduled to be held in Germany long before he came to power. He would use this event for propaganda purposes, and he had found the perfect person to aid him in this endeavor. "All of Riefenstahl's work celebrated power and elevated strength and the body beautiful over all other values. This 'fascist aesthetic' permeated Riefenstahl's work as an actress in her popular 1920s films and, most famously, in her documentary, *Olympia*, about the 1936 Olympic games, hosted by Hitler in Berlin" (Rollyson 2007).

Riefenstahl had opportunities that very few directors ever get: a budget to meet her needs, a compliant crew, an event of historical importance to focus upon, and most of all total command over how to capture it. In *Olympia* she created a masterpiece, but at what cost? "Regardless of Riefenstahl's aesthetics, *Olympia* cannot be separated from its Nazi connections—or the ways it was used to glorify German athleticism and justify the subjugation of others" (Blakemore 2016).

Can one watch *Olympia* without being aware of the horrors to come, or even the horrors of the time—Jewish athletes denied the right to participate, racist bigotry expressed by the crowd, Nazi insignias and salutes prominent throughout, and Hitler and his henchmen ever present in the stands, like Roman emperors of old, cheering on the German athletes and scowling at all the rest?

Olympia is a complex film. For instance, as discussed earlier in this text, America's black athlete Jesse Owens set records during the 1936 Olympics and Riefensthal's cameras capture these for posterity. As Nicholas Barber points out, "in Riefenstahl's defence, her representation of Owens is entirely positive. Repeatedly described by the commentator as 'the fastest man in the world,' Owens is shown not just winning four gold medals, but beaming at the camera afterwards. No other athlete in the film makes anywhere near as much of an impression. Nor is Owens the only black competitor to feature in *Olympia*. Knowing what we do about Nazi Germany, the film's obsession with race is troubling: the commentator notes that the line-up in the 800-metre final has 'two black runners against the strongest of the white race.' But this fixation has its subversive aspect. The 'black runners'—John Woodruff and Phil Edwards—finish the 800-metres in first and third place. It's hard to see how this sequence could have served the Nazi cause" (Barber 2016).

Nonetheless, Riefenstahl's constant emphasis on physical beauty, particularly that of the German male and female athletes, resonates uncomfortably with the known "Aryan Superiority" ethos already being espoused by the German leader and his followers.

"Whenever you start to be hypnotised by *Olympia*, though, you are jolted back to reality by a shot of Hitler, up in the stands, clapping and cheering when the Germans are doing well, drumming his fingers on his uniformed knee when they aren't" (Barber 2016). *Olympia* is a tainted film, simultaneously capturing the best and the worst aspects of the modern Olympics.

After the war Riefenstahl denied knowing Hitler's real motives, and claimed that she was only an artist, without any political aspirations or ideological views. Historians, sociologists and ethicists continue to debate how plausible her denials really are. "But her most prominent defense, which she repeated for the rest of her life, was that she was simply an artist whose profound focus left her no room to consider politics or world affairs. Historical records prove otherwise. Riefenstahl claimed to her death, for instance, that *Triumph of the Will* was an act of reportage, yet ample contemporary documentation makes clear that she was an active participant in planning the 1934 Nuremberg rally—and that the rally was planned primarily for the purpose of producing the film" (Zax 2020). She likewise played an active role in determining how the various Olympic athletic events were to be staged for her cameras and made sure that her cameras had a special focus on her beloved Fuehrer. While never a member of the Party, her writings make it clear that she was a Nazi sympathizer and a genuine admirer of the person she once called "the greatest man who ever lived," Adolf Hitler (Rollyson 2007).

Riefenstahl lived to be over one hundred, but only directed two more movies after *Olympia*, once during the Nazi regime, and once at the very end of her life. No one doubted her talent, nor her directorial skills, but for the rest of her long life after the war she was unable to secure funding from any studios, and had countless thwarted film projects she was not able to complete due to her controversial reputation. Boycotted, denounced, and reviled by many, she died knowing that her legacy would forever be tainted by the bargain she made as an artist with history's most evil leader.

Like Doctor Faust, Leni Riefenstahl learned an age-old lesson: when you dance with the devil, you get burnt.

SUMMARY

Politics and governments have intruded into the domain of sports throughout the ages. The primary role of government in sport in the United States comes in the form of rules and safety; promoting physical fitness; promoting prestige; the provision of a national identity; and, politicians who use sports for a positive identity and to attach themselves to popular athletes. At state and local levels, politicians from all ranks of government turn to sporting contests as a way of increasing a positive identity within the community. On the national and international levels, they often try to connect athletic victories with their own governmental policies.

A number of athletes will enter politics following the conclusion of their athletic careers. This explains why so many politicians played sports when they were youths, in high school, college, and in some cases, professionally. It is common for politicians to have photo-ops with athletes and it is always quite apparent those who played sports and those who did not based on the ease, or lack thereof, of the interactions between them. Internationally, it is also quite common for former athletes to go into politics.

While some sportspersons go on to politics after their playing careers, a number of athletes become active politically via social protest. Protests at sporting events have been common for eons in the United States, especially since the 1960s. It has become increasingly common for athletes to protest social injustice during the playing of the national anthem, which can potentially lead to some very heated differences of opinions on the appropriateness of such social acts. In this, the "Black Lives Matter" era, all sorts of subjects including the "Star-Spangled Banner" and its lyricist are being examined by current day standards.

International sports competition, especially since the reintroduction of the modern Olympic Games, are often very political as well. Political uses of international sports competition include: international cooperation; national ideology and propaganda; official prestige; diplomatic nonrecognition (and recognition); protest; and conflict. The modern Olympic Games provide the ultimate international sports stage wherein sporting competitions are held against the top athletes of the world. While the sporting competitions always live up to their hype, the Olympics themselves have a number of political problems including: corruption; boycotts; drug use and drug testing; and, economic issues.

KEY TERMS

Apartheid Government-sanctioned separation of races.

Authority According to George Homans, a person who has *influence* over other members of a group. Authority is considered to be a type of legitimate power.

Boycott A form of collective action, in athletics involving withdrawal from participation, intended to pressure the target group to change its position or behavior.

Government The political unit that exercises authority via laws and customs.

Political Sports Identity Politicians who attempt to raise their level of prestige by attaching themselves to successful and popular athletes.

Politics The methods, activities, or tactics of government, or governing, of a society, and the administration and control of its internal and external affairs; it is the guiding influence of government policy.

Power According to Max Weber, the ability to exercise one's will over others, despite their resistance.

DISCUSSION QUESTIONS

- Have you ever attended a sporting event where protestors and the police physically confronted each other? How would you react if you were leaving a stadium in a foreign country following a soccer match and political protests led to violence?
- All nations must be interested in the physical well-being of their citizens. Should sports participation, particularly in the schools, be subsidized by government money? Why or why not?

- How do sports provide opportunities for promoting prestige among nations? Should citizens identify with their nations' sport teams during such international events as the Olympics or World Cup?
- Why might an athlete be a viable candidate for political office? What abilities, demonstrated on the playing field, might be applicable to holding a political position? What are some criticisms that could be given for supporting athletes who run for office?
- Are the ideals of the Olympics too lofty? Or do they still basically serve the goals of their initiators, who hoped to alleviate world tension and foster a sense of international cooperation?
- Should the national anthem be played at sporting events? Should athletes that protest during the anthem be praised or condemned? Explain.

CHAPTER 14

Religion and Sport

The game is on the line as the home team lines up for a last second, game-winning field goal attempt. The tension in the air is heightened when the visiting team calls a timeout in an attempt to "freeze" (add pressure to) the kicker. Tens of thousands of spectators in the stadium and millions of fans watching on television hope for the best. Many of these fans, assuming that a higher power exists, offer up silent prayers to God for divine intervention. "Please, God, let the kicker make this field goal," pray the fans. Meanwhile, many of the opposing team's fans are praying to God that the kicker will miss the field goal. Whose prayers will God answer? Why do people think God cares whether the field goal is good and one team wins, or whether the field goal is missed and the other team wins? Why do people believe there is a God to pray to, for that matter? These are among the questions that prevail in an examination of sport and religion.

In this chapter, the role of religion (including prayer) in sport is examined. We will examine the social institution of religion, the relationship between sport and religion, the similarities and differences between sport and religion, and the secularization of sport (including a look at sport superstitions).

The Institution of Religion

Throughout humanity our species has struggled to survive among the bigger, much stronger, and faster species that inhabit the earth. Humans learned to rely on cunning ingenuity and eventually developed a superior intellect. This intellect allowed for the creation of tools that help the human species rise to the top of the food chain. Along with an evolving intellect came a thirst for answers to life's dilemmas that seemed overwhelmingly complicated to the average person. Lacking scientific knowledge, early humans developed crude, elementary forms of explanation. Humanity simply personified the forces of nature, thus creating a universe of spirits that were held accountable as explanations for natural phenomena (Prebish 1993). Along with totemism (discussed in Chapter 11) Animism was among the earliest forms of religion. "Animism maintains that everything has two aspects, a physical manifestation and a spirit or soul. This duality enabled early humanity to explain the difference between life and death, as well as the images present in dreams. The presence in these spirits or *anima* suggested both a life after death and the existence of realms other than the human" (Prebish 1993: 5). Over time, most religions shifted their belief systems from multiple gods to the concept of one true God.

How do people learn about religion? Much in the same manner that they learn about sport; that is, through the agents of socialization. Sport and religious participation are generally taught in early life through exposure to the ideals of each institution from significant others. Through participation individuals cultivate an increasingly more sophisticated level of understanding and knowledge of religion, as they do sport. Most people who are introduced to sport or religion early in life and had such ideals reinforced throughout childhood are likely to maintain their participation throughout their lifetimes. Prebish suggests, however, that people constantly seek more knowledge about sports than they do about religion.

Defining Religion

Religion developed as a source of explanation for life's uncertainties. Religious explanations are not based on empirical science, but rather, a belief system. Science and religion are often at odds because of this fundamental difference. Whereas people of science rely on empirical data collection and analysis, religious adherents rely on faith and spiritual beliefs. A belief is a conviction of certainty about specific matters even without evidence of its truth. Every religion is structured on a system of beliefs. Religious beliefs are centered on an unquestioned conviction of ideals to which members of a particular religion adhere. Fans of Notre Dame University believe that "God made Notre Dame number one," but they have no empirical "proof" of this. Nonetheless, religious adherents form a sense of community based on their beliefs and spirituality. In his *The Elementary Forms of Religious Life*, Durkheim (1965/1912) put forth the notion that religion is eminently social and serves as source of solidarity and identification for individuals within a society while reinforcing the morals and social norms held collectively within a society. While his basic ideas about religion still hold true today, Durkheim worked with a functionalist assumption that there is a consensus on norms and values in society. The authors define *religion* as a system of beliefs and ritualistic behaviors which unite a group of like-minded people together into a social group who adhere to ideals of spirituality.

Sociological Perspectives on Religion

The sociological perspective on religion represents a subfield of sociology with a distinguished pedigree as "virtually all of the leading lights of early sociological devoted considerable attention to the sociology of religion in one way or another" (Christiano, Swatos, and Kivisto 2016:4). Questions related to religion—what religion is, how it works, how it came into being, and why it persists or recedes—were among the most pressing issues that early sociologists (i.e., August Comte, Karl Marx, Emile Durkheim, Max Weber, Georg Simmel) confronted (Christiano et al 2016)). The diversity of religious beliefs and disbeliefs is what makes religion sociologically interesting and worth studying.

Sociologists study religion from a variety of perspectives, so let's take a quick look at three sociological perspectives on religion here—functionalism, conflict and symbolic interactionism. Functionalists believe that religion remains a strong social institution in society because it serves many functions. (An understanding of the functions of religion will help the reader to better understand the similarities and differences between sport and religion to be discussed later in this chapter.) A function is an activity, purpose, service, or behavior that contributes to the maintenance of group, organization, or society. Functions of religion commonly cited among sociologists include the following:

1. *Religion Provides Order and Meaning to Life.* Religion helps to provide structure and order in the daily lives of adherents. It helps to explain and justify the role of individuals in the social world in order to move onto the next life. Religion offers simple and reassuring explanations about the meaning of life.

2. *Psychological Support.* A chief function of religion is providing for the psychic needs of its followers, especially by providing emotional and spiritual support in times of crisis. With the death of a loved one, many people find comfort within the religious community because of the psychological support offered. Psychological support is also provided in happy times as well (e.g., marriages, confirmations, baptisms, and so on).

3. *Self Esteem and Identity.* Another function of religion that helps individuals is the affirmation of social status. Through religious membership, adherents enjoy a sense of belonging to a community of like-minded people, which in turn upholds the positive aspects of religious identity. A positive identity is acquired primarily through social interaction with others. This positive sense of identity, in turn, increases self-esteem.

4. *Social Solidarity and Integration.* As religion continues to alter the identities of individuals, a community of like-minded people forms. The integrative property of religion remains as one of the primary functions of religion; after all, the word "religion" comes from the Latin word "religare," meaning "to bind together." Religion shapes the group into a common way of thinking and adhering to common beliefs and values, where shared perspectives shape a "we" feeling (e.g., "we Baptists," "we Catholics," "we Hindus").

5. *Ceremonies of Status.* Ritualistic behavior among group members reaffirms the social solidarity between them. Ceremonies of status are a form of ritualistic behavior that represents the passing from one level to the next. Baptisms, bar mitzvahs, confirmations, and other religious ceremonies characterize major steps in development for the younger members of the religious community. Such rituals indoctrinate the next generation into the mindset of the religious group; they also reinforce the collective sentiments held by those with full status.

6. *Social Control.* All religions have a set of rules that adherents are expected to abide by. Religious tenets (e.g., the Ten Commandments, the Golden Rule, the Koranic rules) are designed to keep believers in line with the norms, values, and beliefs of group. Most followers practice the beliefs taught to them by religious leaders in their daily lives. In some societies, the social control power of religion is as important as (or the same thing as) the government. In Western societies, such as the United States, there is generally a separation of church and state principle that allows civil law to supersede religious law in civil matters.

7. *Provision of Holidays.* While adherents are supposed to live a certain lifestyle at all times, there are days of the week, month, or season that are reserved as special days, worth elevating to high status. The provision of special holidays is a jolt of religious reality that interrupts the daily, often mundane, life with a clear reminder that there is a greater purpose for living. The world of sports has many parallels to the "functions approach" as sports provide meaning to many people's lives; psychological attachment does develop; one's identity is attached to a favorite team; cheering with fans of the same team is uplifting; ritualistic behaviors abound in sport via routines and superstitions (to be discussed in greater detail

later); sport participants know they must behave in a certain manner or risk disqualification; and sports fans love "game day" and the playoffs are all the more exciting because of it.

As we learned in Chapter 2, functionalism is based on the idea that there is a general consensus in values and norms in society and that all people willingly integrate the prevailing sentiments into their lives. Conflict theorists, however, believe that the prevailing norms and values of society's institutions, including religion, are forced upon the members of society that do not adhere to a given religious belief system. When adherents from two different religions cannot get along, conflict may occur. If conflict escalates to violence or war, those in power will use force to bring people under control. People intolerant of others' religious beliefs tend to develop a "we" or "us" versus "they" or "them" scenario. The "us" vs. "them" mentality is a cornerstone ideal of sports competition for both participants and fans.

If you recall from Chapter 2, symbolic interactionism focuses on how people interact with one another through the use of symbols. Religion is filled with symbolic behavior; in fact, it is nearly dependent upon the use of symbols and rituals. The use of symbols is just as obvious in the sports world. Plays are designed in diagram form with certain shapes (e.g., "X" and "O") having symbolic meaning for offensive and defensive players and arrows are then added to the diagram to illustrate the direction specific athletes are supposed to go. Athletes on the playing field flash signs back and forth to each other more often than gang members on the streets. The use of tracking baseball games in a program requires a symbolic language all to itself. In short, religion and sport are both filled with symbolic forms of communications via signs, gesturing and language. Elements of totemism come into play from the symbolic interactionist approach as well as athletes are driven to "win a (championship) ring" or "win a trophy" not because the ring or trophy itself has great meaning, but rather because it is symbolic of something cherished.

The Relationship Between Religion and Sport

Emile Durkheim argues that the relationship between sport and religion is sociological, rather than psychological or biological. From a Durkheimian perspective, the relationship between religion and sport represents the meeting of the sacred and the profane. Durkheim (1912) described sacred items as those objects that we show reverence toward (e.g., a blessed rosary); they are set aside from the everyday items. In contrast, profane items are the ordinary, everyday objects (e.g., computers, cell phones, DVDs). Durkheim viewed religion as a social phenomenon, rather than a psychological one, because of its ritualistic behavior and use of symbols. As Birrell (1981) explains, "The conceptual definition of *ritual*, and the related concept *symbolic system*, on which this discussion of sport is based, are most familiar from Durkheim's *The Elementary Forms of Religious Life* where he presented his thesis concerning religion as a social rather than psychological experience" (p. 356).

Charles Prebish (1993) believes that the ritualistic behavior and use of symbolic language found in sport today qualifies it as religion. Furthermore, because followers of sport treat it as sacred, sport *is* religion. Harry Edwards (1973) claimed that if a universal popular religion exists in the United States, it is found within the institution of sport. This religious experience in sport is not confined to the actual participants (the players) but also extends to the fans. And, if sports fans believe, and players view, a sport as a type of religion, then it, in fact, becomes a religion. Bain-Selbo and Sapp (2016) argue that the human drives and needs that compel some people to be a part of a particular religion are the same drives and needs that compel some to be a part of sports world in some way. "That is, we believe the activities and beliefs associated with religion per se are similar, if not identical, to the activities and beliefs of athletes and fans of sport. We are saying that sport can be religious for some in the same way that participating in the activities of a mosque, temple, or church can be religious. Sport can function like a religion in that it meets the same needs and desires satisfied or promised by formal religions" (Bain-Selbo and Sapp 2016).

Not all sport sociologists argue that sport is a religion in the same manner that Methodism, Presbyterianism, or Catholicism is a religion; rather they claim that it is a secular or civil religion. Novak (1993) explains, "Sports are religious in the sense that they are organized institutions, disciplines, and liturgies; and also in the sense that they teach religious qualities of heart and soul. In particular, they recreate symbols of cosmic struggle, in which human survival and moral courage are not assured. To this extent, they are not mere games, diversions, pastimes. Their power to exhilarate or depress is far greater than that. To say: 'It was only a game' is the psyche's best defense against the cosmic symbolic meaning of sports events" (153). To put it simply, sport can give *meaning* to a person's life, and for many it is the primary way they give importance to their own existence.

The relationship between religion and sport is also extended to the fact that both of these social institutions have great meaning to the vast majority of people around the world. Let's take a closer look at the number of adherents that both of these institutions have in order to quantify the popularity of sports and religion. Research conducted by the Pew Research Center (2019) reveals that 65 percent of American adults describe themselves as Christians, down 12 percentage points over the past decade, while the percentage of religiously unaffiliated (atheist, agnostic, or "nothing in particular") Americans continued to rise, reaching 26 percent, up from 17 percent in 2009. That leaves 9 percent of Americans for some other religion (i.e., Jewish, Muslim, Hindu). The younger the age cohort, the greater the percentage of unaffiliated: "Silent Generation" (born 1928–45), 10 percent; "Baby Boomers" (1946–64), 17 percent; "Generation X" (1965–80), 25 percent; and "Millennials" (1981–96), 40 percent (Pew Research Center 2019). Data compiled by Statista reveals that 65 percent of Americans are sports fans, with 27 percent as "avid" fans; while 35 percent are not at all fans of sport (Gough 2020c). In 2012, six in 10 Americans reported being sports fans; which was a dramatic increase from 50 years earlier, when just 30 percent of Americans considered themselves sports fans (Beneke and Remillard 2014). As this data indicates, the number of Americans claiming to be religious continues to decrease while the number of sports fans continues to increase.

Similarities Between Sport and Religion

Harry Edwards (1973) argued that the universal "popular" religion of the United States is sports. To be considered a religion, sport must possess a number of characteristics common to religion. Edwards refers to thirteen essential features that sport shares with religion. Having researched the numerous similarities between sport and religion, as cited by Edwards and other sport sociologists, the authors have established a list of twenty-one similarities between these two powerful social institutions.

1. *Belief Systems.* Edwards (1973) argues that both sport and religion have a body of formally stated beliefs that are accepted on faith by a great number of adherents. Belief systems are centered on a creed that followers abide by in varying degrees. Fans are told to have "faith" in their team, especially in times of turmoil, much in the same manner that religious people are told to have faith in times where they doubt their religion or "God's plan." The philosopher William James (1897) coined the phrase "the will to believe" to express the view that sometimes believing that an event will occur can actually help make it happen. This can be applied to both athletes and fans, who feel that their strong dedication to winning might actually tip the scale and make victory occur.

2. *True Believers.* Neither sport nor religion can survive without followers, or true believers. Both social institutions rely on converting new members into their belief systems. This is accomplished through the socialization process (see Chapter 5). "True believers" are those who so strongly support the religious or sport ideals that they defend such social institutions passionately. They are unyielding in their support.

3. *Providing Testimony.* Religion and sport both have their pundits who promote their respective social institutions. Sports fans everywhere love to proclaim, "We're number one!" Religious adherents also believe that their religion is "number one" as well.

4. *Patriarchal Dominance.* Both institutions have been, historically, dominated by men. The passage of such legislation as Title IX and a greater acceptance of women in sport have lessened the male dominance once found in sport. Many of the world's major religions have failed to embraced gender equity. In the Catholic Church, for example, women are not allowed to join the ranks of priesthood. Muslim women are often treated as a distant second-class citizen to the male Muslim. Hindu and Islamic nations seldom have women athletes or women's teams because women are not allowed to expose any parts of their bodies in public. Such a practice is clearly not conducive to gender equity. Both sport and religion have "ruling patriarchs"—males who carry the most influence within their respective institutions. The ruling patriarchs are often treated, and act, as saints or gods.

5. *The Worship of Saints and Gods and Superstars.* As described above, the institutions of sport and religion have their saints and gods who personify the respective ideals of their institutions. Sports fans often idolize and "worship" athletes as if they are gods, much in the same manner religious adherents blindly revere and adore a variety of religious leaders. The various sports halls of fame are especially symbolic of the level of worship bestowed upon athletes by sports fans. Further, sport fans demonstrate their commitment to their earthly gods (superstars) by regularly reading the sports pages for more information about their heroes and by collecting various sports memorabilia (e.g., autographed baseballs and other items and a wide variety of sport-related souvenirs) which are symbols of their faith in their gods. Religious adherents often have various religious items (e.g., crucifixes, holy books in their homes) that they also pay homage. Both institutions also have their "martyrs." With sport, Notre Dame football great George "the Gipper" Gipp, Yankee baseball legend Lou Gehrig, and Pat Tillman (see Chapter 4) might be considered in this category.

6. *High Councils.* Religion and sport are both consumed with rules and expectations

of proper behavior. Rules are designed to maintain consistency within a group or society. Often, these rules contain moral and ethical undertones. As a result of rules and the need to enforce the rules, both social institutions have ruling councils that create, maintain, and interpret their respective rules. The Catholic Church, for example, requires that its priests remain celibate in order to preserve their purity and closeness with God. The hierarchy established in the Church will enforce such rules. In sport, such councils include the NCAA, USOC, and the various ruling professional sport league offices.

7. *Scribes.* Another commonality between sport and religion is the reliance on scribes to maintain the history of their social institutions and promote public awareness regarding the ongoing, daily events of the tradition. Scribes are clearly more visible in sports than in religion as traditional and social media coverage of sports and sporting events is a 24/7 proposition.

8. *Seekers of the Kingdom.* Both sports and religion have hard-core, diehard followers who believe so strongly in the tenets they have been taught that they take the teachings literally and are willing to do anything to reach the "promised land." For the religious person, the "kingdom" may be Heaven or a higher reincarnated life form. In sport, the "kingdom" is the sporting event itself, especially when the game is played in a revered stadium or arena—and this scenario is true for both the athlete and the fan.

9. *Psychological Support.* As mentioned earlier in this chapter, one of the primary functions of religion is to provide psychological support to its adherents, especially in time of emotional crisis (as well as during happy occasions). Athletes and coaches are capable of providing psychological support to one another as well. Coaches (especially at the nonprofessional level) often console athletes after an individual failure or team loss. Teammates, also, generally support one another in time of crisis. In addition, coaches and teammates are there to celebrate victories with one another as well.

10. *Pilgrimages to a Shrine.* Diehard religious adherents and sports fans must have a destination, a promised land, to guide their paths through life. Depending on one's religion, hearing Mass at the Vatican, or saying prayers at Mecca, represent ideal destinations. In sport, the various halls of fame may be viewed as shrines honoring heroic figures accompanied by tales of greatness. Attending major sporting events and beloved stadiums are also viewed as shrines. The 1989 film *Field of Dreams*, with its mantra "If you build it, he will come," ably captures this mystical aspect.

11. *Buildings for Events.* Believers and followers of sport and religion generally have a place, sacred ground, where they meet to worship as a group. It is true that religious believers and sport followers can both practice their religion at home, but most will commune with others. Thus, both religion and sport provide physical locations which may qualify as "shrines" for people to worship collectively. All societies provide buildings (e.g., churches, synagogues, and mosques) for followers to worship and pay homage to their saints and gods. The parallel between sport and religion is obvious in this regard, as most towns and cities in the nation have a ball field, high school stadium, and perhaps a university or major league stadium.

12. *Use of Symbols.* People communicate symbolically. Symbols are objects, ideas, and actions that possess meaning for those who adhere to such beliefs. Both religion and sport employ the use of symbols that possess a shared meaning for

participants. Religion has such symbols as the Cross, the Star of David, the Rosary, and the Mezuzah, and sport has such symbols as championship trophies and rings, medallions, and ribbons. The Olympic torch as a symbol of pure, undying sportsmanship is another such example.

13. *Written Dramas.* In an effort to keep the attention of their followers, both religion and sport have created dramas to captivate adherents. Religion relies on prayer books as a means to keep followers interested in their teachings as well as provide guidelines for "proper" behavior. The sports world has playbooks and training manuals for athletes and media guides and programs for sport fans.

14. *Scheduled Events.* The primary reason for scheduled events is to keep followers in a routine of ritual. Religious people are expected to attend services on a regular basis; consequently, religious leaders designate specific days and times for adherence to such services. The sports world heavily promotes its schedule and has the assistance of the media. Cipriani (2012) refers to these scheduled celebrated days as "feast days."

15. *Special Days.* The routine can become boring, even to the strictest adherent to sports or religion. As a result, both the sport and religion create a number of "special" days to stimulate and excite followers. Religion promotes these special days (e.g., Easter, Passover, Christmas, and Hanukkah) as a time to re-commit to religious ideals and tenets. The sports world usually promotes special days at the conclusion of each season. Thus, the World Series (which follows the end of the regular and playoff season in MLB); the Super Bowl (which crowns the NFL champion); "March Madness" (the NCAA men's basketball championship single-game elimination series); and the World Cup and Olympics are viewed as pinnacle days in sports.

16. *Collective Emotions.* Religious followers who share the same belief and come together in the form of a religious community often share collective emotions through ritualistic behaviors. The collective emotions shared by sports fans are especially obvious as they outwardly display their emotions: happiness and elation following a victory and sadness and despair following a loss. Both religion and sport allow men, in particular, the rare opportunity to cry in public and generally express their deepest emotions in an unabashed way.

17. *Ritualistic Behavior.* "Both sport and religion employ intricate rituals which attempt to place events in traditional and orderly view" (Slusher 1993: 173). Religious services include a large number of ritualistic behaviors. Catholics, for example, make the sign of the cross after placing their index finger in a bowl of holy water upon entering the church. They kneel, sit, stand, and repeat. They shake hands with one another and receive communion. In religion, ceremonies and rituals are practiced to give order to man's existence (Slusher 1993). The sports world is also filled with ritualistic behavior; although such behavior is often tied to superstitions. Chandler (1992) argues that many rituals in sports are designed simply to assert superiority, these rituals of superiority are global, and that these rituals of dominance simply underscore the sporting competitor's objective: to win." Ritualistic behaviors are used to galvanize a community of adherents around a set of values (Hoffman 1992). (We will discuss the role of ritualistic, superstitious, and magical behavior in sports later in this chapter.)

18. *Competitive Nature.* Both sports and religion are in competition with challenges

within their respective social institutions from competing elements. Each religion seeks to convert as many followers as possible in an attempt to outnumber its "enemies." Religions, by their very design, are unique and different, and each one believes it is "right" and therefore, by default, the others are "wrong." Consequently, each religion is in competition with the others. The sports world is a "battlefield" of competition. Once again, by design, sports have as its primary goal for one athlete or team to demonstrate its superiority over competitors.

19. *The "Us" vs. "Them" Scenario.* This scenario was described earlier in the chapter. Sports fans cheer for their favorite sports team (or athlete in non-team sports) creating an "in-group" which automatically makes those who cheer for rival teams members of an "out-group." In many societies where there is a dominant religion it is not unusual for adherents to view followers of different religions as members of an out-group.

20. *Prayer.* Religious leaders and adherents, athletes, and sports fans utilize prayer as a means of attaining a favorable outcome. Although prayer in the religious world is generally thought of as within the sacred realm and prayer in the sports world as profane, there remains a common thread between the two. In all cases, those who rely on prayer are hoping for "divine" intervention. They have lost "faith" in human ability and have searched for unearthly assistance. The role of prayer in sport will be discussed later in this chapter.

21. *Sense of Identity.* Sport, as religion, helps to provide individuals with a sense of identity and self-esteem by creating a sense of belonging and providing meaning to life. Both sport and religion provide opportunities to reaffirm social solidarity through the creation of a bond among members, thus forming a sense of community. Bonding leads to feelings of identity, loyalty, commitment, and self-esteem.

Social identity theory helps to explain the "us" vs. "them" scenario as people's self-concepts are often based on their membership in social groups (e.g., sports teams, religions, nationalities, occupations, sexual orientation, racial and ethnic groups, and gender) (Tajfel 1978; Tajfel and Turner 1979). Although it is common for sports teams to have participants from different religions, research conducted by Alamri (2015) has found that many Muslim students' participation in sporting activities within the public high school environment presents many challenges, most notably when it comes to prayer. In their study of how Arabic Muslim female athletes are treated Maesam and associates (2010) found that they were placed in a framework of their identity based on religion. As someone who tried to unite all Americans, former president Barack Obama gave a speech in 2016 promoting the idea of accepting Muslim sports heroes to which then-Republican presidential candidate Donald Trump tweeted, "What sport is he talking about, and who?" This led to then-Oklahoma City Thunder center Enes Kanter to tweet in response, "I think we have amazing athletes. Like Muhammad Ali, Kareem Abdul-Jabbar, and Hakeem Olajuwon. Legends" (Trister 2015). The Muslim experience is just one example of what people from one religion endure when in a country of a different dominant religion. People who do not identify with any religion risk being placed in an out-group by all religious adherents.

As shown here, there are clearly many similarities between sport and religion. In fact, it is difficult to argue with those who claim sport *is* religion; or at the very least, a

A religious mural on the side of the Library Building at the University of Notre Dame that overlooks the football field is affectionately nicknamed "Touchdown Jesus" because Jesus appears to be signaling "touchdown."

quasi-religion. There are, however, a number of significant differences between sport and religion as well.

Differences Between Sport and Religion

The differences between sport and religion are highlighted by the fact that sport is centered on the profane, everyday, tangible world, whereas religion is centered on the sacred, spiritual world. The major distinctions between sport and religion are listed below.

1. *Sports Are Real and Religion Is Spiritual.* Although sports fans express "faith" in their team, this is not the same thing as religious faith. Religious adherents pay homage to a "sacred" world (the afterlife) that is not visible and that is promoted by people who cannot show empirical proof of their spiritual claims. Sports, on the other hand, are real, tangible, and visible. Sports fans and athletes need no other verification of the validity of sport than simply to observe the phenomena before their very eyes. Sports fans must have "faith" that their team or favorite athlete will prevail, but no such faith is necessary to verify its existence. Religious adherents are told to have faith in an entity unseen and unverifiable. Religious beliefs are based on a leap of faith. Sports fans keep tangible records and hope for victories in *this* world rather than the world to come.

2. *Sports Are a Part of the Here and Now.* Related to the first difference between sport and religion, sports are not only "real," they are a part of the here and now. The world of sport provides us with concrete time and space situations bound by the laws of nature. Time and space constraints also mean that sport is a human event that rests *within* humans (Slusher 1993). The religious realm transcends time and space; it speaks of an afterlife, a world *outside* of human confines.

3. *Sports Are Materialistically Driven.* Because sports are a part of the profane world, and economic success is a powerful force (especially in Western culture), sports are materialistically driven. Athletes want big salaries. Sports owners want big profits. Sport sponsors want their athletes to win and promote their products. The media wants to sell commercial time in an attempt to make broadcasting profits. At every level, economics and materialism are a critical aspect of sport (see Chapter 12). Religion, because it is a part of the spiritual world, is for the most part nonmaterialistic. The primary goal of religion rests with providing adherents eternal salvation in the afterlife (or the next life). It should be pointed out, however, that because religion is a part of the everyday world, it relies on economics and materialistic goods for its survival. Most religions collect (and expect) money from its parishioners in order to "pay the bills." Some churches actually seek to make profits. The Catholic Church, for example, is said to own more real estate than any other entity in the world. And many prominent religious figures, especially those that lead "megachurches" are noted for their extravagant lifestyle and opulent display of wealth. Still, the ideals for religious leaders and religions in general continue to be austerity, simplicity and concern with spiritual rather than material well-being.

4. *Rationalism.* Although both sports and religion have rules, sport is organized rationally and not supernaturally. The sports world is based on secular, civil rules that are equally applied to all. Religion is based on spiritual rules and faith and admits its dependence on the nonrational (Slusher 1993). Religious athletes sometimes find conflict between their religious beliefs and commitments and the civil rules of sports. Attempts to embrace religious diversity combined with the American fundamental principle of the "separation of church and state" will assure that conflicts between these two institutions will steadily increase for as long as people cling to religious ideals in a civil and secular environment such as sports.

5. *Ritualistic Behavior Is Used Differently.* Religion and sports both utilize rituals; however, in sports, rituals are instrumental and goal-oriented; whereas, in religion, rituals are expressive and process-oriented. For sport fans, the ritualistic behavior of consuming a hot dog and peanuts at a baseball game is far different from the ritualistic behaviors associated with going to religious services for a religious person.

6. *Buildings for Events.* Although both religion and sport provide buildings for events, these structures take on different meanings. As Novak (1993) explains, a ballpark is not really a temple, but it is not a "fun house" either. Sports spectators are allowed, and expected, to yell and scream while they support their favorite player(s) and teams. Stadiums and arenas are viewed as secular meeting places where participants can relax and release a number of their inhibitions. Conversely, most religious services are conducted inside buildings where

adherents are expected to abide by moral protocols (e.g., acting dignified and respectful, or being "moved" by spirituality on cue). Of course, there are moments during sports events where solemnity is also expected, such as during the singing of the national anthem and "moments of silence" to honor the passing of socially significant persons.

7. *Attempts to Provide Answers to the Meaning of Life.* A major difference between sport and religion rests with religion's desire to explain the meaning of life, and an afterlife, while sport does not attempt such a grandiose ideal. Because religion is consumed with the spiritual realm, attempting to explain the meaning of life is among its primary goals. Sport, because it is immersed in the secular, everyday world, makes no proclamations regarding the meaning of life.

8. *Clear-Cut Winners.* Although religion attempts to explain the meaning of life, it does so without scientific, empirical proof. Any answer to life's dilemmas provided by religion is suspect at best. Further, different religious perspectives may yield contrasting answers. Sport, however, provides clear-cut winners. Someone wins the game or race and the others do not. No religion has been able to correctly claim they are "right" or they are the "winner." While the spiritual realm remains unknown, the sports world is non-ambivalent.

9. *Choosing a Religion or Sports Team (or Athlete) to Follow.* Most people who are religiously affiliated support the religion that they were raised in by their parents and family and they were likely indoctrinated (e.g., baptized) into that religion when they were too young to choose their own religion to follow. Chances are, most people will not take the time to explore all the world's religions, let alone the major ones, before choosing which religion works best for them. People are free to change their religious affiliation later in life, but most will not. Choosing a favorite athlete or sports team to follow is mostly different. While it is true that many die-hard sports fans will dress their babies, toddlers and young children in the sportswear of their favorite team, growing children are far more likely to choose their own athletes or teams to cheer for than they are to change their religion.

10. *Public Display of Religious Imagery.* Blame "political correctness" (or simply correctness) or a real attempt to avoid being exclusionary, but governments (e.g., public schools and government offices) at all levels, local, state and federal, consciously attempt to avoid making public displays of religious imagery. This is why a town square might have a "holiday tree" instead of a Christmas tree, even though we all know that no other religious holiday incorporates a pine tree in its holiday celebration. The sports world works differently. If a city's sports team wins a championship it may be common for government employees and local merchants to wear the home team's sports imagery. In some cases, a parade through city streets adorned with banners and flags of the sports team imagery is common; and this, despite the fact that it may offend fans of other sports teams that live in the city or non-sports fans who do not want to be subjected to such public displays of imagery.

Despite the differences between sport and religion, the two social institutions remain connected by the numerous similarities. While some would state that religion is far more important than sports, others would be of the opposite opinion.

The Role of Prayer in Sport

It is fairly common for people to appeal to a higher authority in times of stress and hope. In the sports world, both sport fans and athletes have been known to pray for favorable outcomes. The role of prayer in sports, especially in school sports, is one of the more controversial topics in the discussion of the relationship between sport and religion.

Turning to Prayer

Why do people turn to prayer? In the religious realm, prayer fosters the contemplative attitudes of listening and receptivity; it brings adherents closer to God. In the strictest sense, religious prayer is the preparation for contemplation and discussion with God. According to Keating (1994), prayer is supposed to reduce the obstacles caused by the hyperactivity of individuals' minds and lives so that adherents can concentrate on their "discussion" with God (or some other spiritual entity). Religious people who believe in a "Higher Power" assume that God can do anything; after all, God is "all powerful." To move into the realm of prayer is to be open to infinite possibilities (Keating 1995). Belief in religious prayer is equated to a belief in a God, or "Holy Spirit," that is capable of anything. If God is capable of anything, then certainly influencing the outcome of a game is within the control of God. Prayer would seem, to some, as a "logical" path of communication between individuals and God when requesting a favorable outcome. *Prayer* can be defined as a solemn request for help or an expression of thanks addressed to a higher power or an object of worship.

Although prayer, in the strictest sense, is a part of the religious realm, it has crossed over into the sports world as well. Athletes may pray for safety and protection during competition, for a good individual or team performance, and especially for a victory. Sport participants (e.g., athletes, coaches, trainers and team owners) may engage in the team pregame prayer in an attempt to help unify the players into one collectivity. We see athletes point upward, as if Heaven or God is located in the sky above us, following a favorable sports outcome (e.g., hitting a homerun, throwing a touchdown pass, or striking out a batter); current and former athletes such as Tim Tebow making genuflections on the playing field as a sort of prayer or homage to God; Phil Jackson incorporating tenets of Zen Buddhism in his coaching and administrative guidance; and Muslim athletes who choose to maintain their Ramadan fast even though they still participate in sports in a weakened physical state (Beneke and Remillard 2014).

For the most part, sports leagues ignore the behavior of athletes praying on the playing field/court, so long as the rest of their antics conform to the rules. But, sometimes acceptable forms of religious expression cross over the lines of acceptable behavior, making it difficult for game officials to know exactly how to interpret the emotional displays of athletes. For example, Kansas City Chiefs safety Husain Abdullah was penalized for unsportsmanlike conduct when he slid to the grass and dropped to his knees in prayer after he returned a Tom Brady interception for a touchdown in a September 29, 2014, Monday Night NFL game between the host Chiefs and the visiting New England Patriots. The officials cited Rule 12, Section 3, Article 1 (d), "Players are prohibited from engaging in any celebrations or demonstrations while on the ground" (ESPN.com 2014a). Officials immediately threw their yellow penalty flags onto the ground. The officials then explained their ruling to Chiefs head coach Andy Reid. Abdullah, who is a devout

Muslim (who took a year off from football to make a pilgrimage to Mecca and who also fasts during Ramadan), admitted after the game that his celebration was pre-orchestrated because he knew before he reached the end zone he would drop to his knees in thankful prayer. After the game, Reid said, "When you go to Mecca [referring to the end zone], you should have the privilege to slide anywhere you want to slide" (Petchesky 2014).

This should have been the end of the story except that a number of people took to social media questioning whether there was a double standard in penalizing Abdullah for saying a prayer on the field when Christian players are allowed to do so. The Council on American-Islamic Relations, a civil liberties and advocacy organization, issued a statement the day after the game asking the NFL to look into the penalty (ESPN.com 2014a). Abdullah told the *Associated Press* (2014a) that he assumed he was penalized for the slide and not the prayer. Nonetheless, the NFL, in its concern to avoid looking like it supports a double standard on athletes and prayer, said that Abdullah should not have been penalized for unsportsmanlike conduct (*Associated Press* 2014a).

It's not just the athletes who turn to prayer for a favorable outcome; many sports fans do so as well. They may make proclamations such as, "I promise to be a better person, just let my team win," as they bargain with God or some spiritual entity for divine intervention. People who turn to prayer for a favorable sporting outcome, however, choose to ignore this basic question—Why would God answer such mundane prayers? Nonetheless, 20 percent of Americans believe that God influences the outcome of sporting events (Beneke and Remillard 2014).

The comedian Lewis Black puts all this into a nice perspective: "There is nothing more obnoxious to an avid sports fan—okay, to me—than an athlete telling the audience after a big victory that God was the reason for it. As Jeff Stillson puts it so well in his act: 'I like football games, but I hate the interviews after the games, because the winning players always give credit to God while the losers blame themselves. Just once I'd like to hear a player say, "Yeah, we were in the game ... until Jesus made me fumble. He hates our team. Jesus hates us."' It implies that the losers on the other team just didn't love God enough to have enough faith in the Supreme Being" (Black 2008:36).

Prayer in School

The United States, in theory, has a separation of church and state policy. However, religion intrudes in state affairs in a variety of ways, including the 1954 addition of the phrase "Under God" to the pledge of allegiance to the flag; the addition of "In God We Trust" on U.S. currency in 1956; the requirement to place one's right hand on the Bible in a court of law; and, prayer in public schools. The role of prayer in school is an especially hot topic. "For the greater part of this century, controversy has raged over the separation of church and state in the United States. Perhaps no issue has so fueled this controversy as religion in the public schools. Today, fifty years after *Everson v. Board of Education*, which brought Thomas Jefferson's famous phrase, 'a wall of separation between church and state' into modern Establishment Clause jurisprudence, the debate rages on. Despite the passage of more than thirty years since the *School District of Abington Township v. Schempp* and *Engel v. Vitale* decisions, which held that school-sponsored bible reading and prayer, respectively, are unconstitutional, public school religious exercises still breed controversy" (Ravitch 1999: 3).

Many school districts simply ignore constitutional mandates forbidding bible reading and prayer in public schools. The growing power of conservative religious groups ("the Christian Right") in the United States has led to organized campaigns to influence school policy in favor of religious inclusion in public schools despite the rights of people who hold differing religious views or those who refrain from organized religion altogether. "United States history is replete with examples of religious exercise in public schools facilitating discrimination and intolerance against religious minorities and dissenters. In some cases, the discrimination has been an unintended byproduct of the exercises. At other times, it has been a significant purpose behind them. Regardless, a disturbing trend of discrimination results when public schools engage in religious exercises" (Ravitch 1999: 4).

Interestingly, the first organized attempt to keep religion out of schools came from conservative Protestant groups who wanted to keep Catholicism out of the newly formed public schools in the mid–1800s (Greenawalt 2005). In 1844 two riots, known as the Philadelphia Bible Riots of 1844, resulted as a reaction against Catholic immigration and participation in the public schools. The riots "were fueled by a fear of increasing religious and cultural pluralism as well as by anti-immigration zeal (Ravitch 1999: 4). More than twenty people were killed during the riots (Delfattore 2004). Until the mid–1800s, with few exceptions, religious pluralism was restricted to the different Protestant sects that existed at the time. Religious zealots, of any denomination, are not known for their tolerance for other people, they do not believe in what they preach: brotherhood to all. As Ravitch (1999) explains, "During the mid-nineteenth century, Catholic children were sometimes whipped and beaten in public schools for refusing to engage in school-sanctioned religious exercises; a priest in Maine was tarred, feathered, and ridden on a rail as the result of a dispute over bible reading in the public schools; and other incidents occurred throughout the country" (6). In 1878, the Supreme Court decided in the *Reynolds v. United States* case that George Reynolds, a resident of the Utah Territory and an active member of the Church of Jesus Christ of Latter-Day Saints (Mormon), could not practice his religious belief of polygamy (Smith 1987). Examples of religious intolerance in the United States continued throughout the twentieth century and persist today.

Much of the current debate over prayer in public schools involves gray-area situations about where the lines should be drawn in respect to religious activity (Delfattore 2004). Schools try to appease student-led, volunteer prayer groups, while staying within legal guidelines. As one form of compromise, many states and school districts have instituted moments of silence to replace oral prayer to begin the school day (Greenawalt 2005). The Anti-Defamation League (2020) summarizes the role of prayer in public schools: "Organized prayer in the public school setting, whether in the classroom or at a school-sponsored event, is unconstitutional. The only type of prayer that is constitutionally permissible is private, voluntary student prayer that does not interfere with the school's educational mission." The fact that students can pray silently to themselves is evidence that God, or some other spiritual entity, is in the schools; and because religious adherents believe that God is everywhere, they do not have to fret over constitutional mandates. Despite the clarity of the "separation of church and state," by all indications, the debate over prayer and religious expression in school will continue for some time. However, the focus of our attention here rests with the role of prayer in sport. Specifically, we are most interested in the demonstration of religious expression, including prayer, in sports in school and on the playing field. In 2000, the Supreme Court passed a ruling

(6–3) that forbids invocations at school activities, including pre-football game kickoffs, even when students organize them.

In 2006, the authors conducted a survey on college students from a public state university and a private Catholic college regarding sports and prayers. In 2020, we asked students a number of similar questions but the structure of the questionnaire was different and did not allow for an easy comparison and, therefore, just the 2020 data appears in the Tables 14.1–14.5. In our 2020 survey, there were 84 respondents from a public state university (54 females and 32 males) and 72 respondents from the private college (42 females and 30 males). Of the public state university respondents, 44 percent said that they considered themselves a religious person while 56 percent said that they were not; while 65 percent of the private Catholic college considered themselves a religious person and 35 percent did not.

Survey respondents were asked, "Should prayer be allowed in sports in public schools?" Fifty-eight percent of public state university respondents said "yes" while just 42 percent said "no." When controlled by gender, 63 percent of males and 55 percent of females said "yes." Eighty-five percent of private Catholic college respondents said "yes" that prayer should be allowed in public schools with 91 percent of males and 81 percent of females saying "yes" (see Table 14.1).

Table 14.1. Should Prayer Be Allowed in Sports in Public Schools? (in percent)

	Public State University			Private Catholic College		
	Combined	Males	Females	Combined	Males	Females
Yes	58	63	55	85	90	81
No	42	37	45	15	10	19

Although the survey question was not an open-ended instrument, a number of respondents wrote that they were in favor of prayer in sports in public schools only if it was voluntary and not forced onto the team or spectators. What we did not ask is, "What prayers should be said?" Should it be "Prayers from all religions?" Should it be "Prayers from just the dominant religion?" In an attempt to be inclusive, should it be "Prayers from all the religions of team members?" These are issues to be addressed in the future.

Respondents were asked, "Should prayer be allowed in sports in private schools?" This is an issue that seldom comes to the forefront of public concern for the simple fact that these schools are private and not publicly supported. (If a private school is publicly supported, it is a concern.) As suspected, an overwhelming percentage of respondents indicated that they were in favor of prayer in private school sports. Eighty-four percent of respondents from the public state university and 97 percent of respondents from the private Catholic college were in favor of prayer in sports in private schools. There was an equal percentage (97 percent) of males and females from the private college in favor and 91 percent compared 81 percent of females at the public university in favor of prayers in sports in private schools (see Table 14.2).

Table 14.2. Should Prayer Be Allowed in Sports in Private Schools? (in percent)

	Public State University			Private Catholic College		
	Combined	Males	Females	Combined	Males	Females
Yes	84	91	81	97	97	97
No	16	9	19	3	3	3

Over the past couple of decades an increasing number of athletes have incorporated religious gestures (e.g., making the sign of the cross or pointing toward the sky) on the playing field or court. Respondents were asked if they think it is okay for athletes to make religious gestures (e.g., the sign of the cross) after some athletic achievement on the playing field/court (see Table 14.3). The results of this question were a little surprising as 43 percent of public university students strongly agreed that some sort of religious gesture was okay following an athletic achievement while just 28 percent of private college students strongly agreed. However, 66 percent of private college students agreed while 50 percent of public college students agreed. Results for the private school respondents were identical for males and females.

Table 14.3. After Some Athletic Achievement on the Playing Field/Court, It Is Okay for Athletes to Make a Religious Gesture (in percent)

	Public State University			Private Catholic College		
	Combined	Males	Females	Combined	Males	Females
Strongly Agree	43	50	37	28	28	28
Agree	50	40	56	66	66	66
Disagree	1	0	3	3	3	3
Strongly Disagree	6	10	4	3	3	3

The bond shared among many religious athletes extends beyond the bond among teammates. One example involves professional and collegiate football players from opposing teams kneeling together in prayer on the field after the conclusion of the game. While other teammates go to their respective locker rooms a number of opposing players join together for a public display of prayer. With this idea in mind, respondents were asked whether it was okay for athletes from opposing teams to join together in prayer on the playing field (see Table 14.4).

Table 14.4. It Is Okay for Athletes from Opposing Teams to Join in Prayer on the Playing Field? (in percent)

	Public State University			Private Catholic College		
	Combined	Males	Females	Combined	Males	Females
Strongly Agree	24	24	24	33	37	31
Agree	60	63	56	58	57	60
Disagree	16	12	19	4	0	7
Strongly Disagree	0	0	0	4	7	2

The vast majority of public (84 percent) and private college students (91 percent) agreed that it is okay for athletes from opposing teams to join in prayer on the playing field with 24 percent of public college students strongly agreeing and 33 percent of private college students strongly agreeing. It should be noted that some respondents wrote that they were in favor of athletes praying together when a player has been injured.

Anyone who has attended a sporting event or watched a sporting event with a group of friends or family has likely witnessed fans praying for a favorable outcome. Why is this the case? Why do people think praying has a correlation to winning? Fans may pray for a favorable outcome because they know they have no direct influence over the play of the game. Rather than rely on the skills of their favorite athletes to successfully prevail, fans turn to prayer. Do sports fans really think prayers help? Delaney (2001) conducted research on the Southern California Browns Backers (SCBBA) (an NFL booster group) during the 1990s. He asked members whether praying can influence the outcome of a Browns game. Only 19 percent agreed and 4 percent strongly agreed. During interviews conducted with members of the SCBBA, one respondent told Delaney (2001), "If all it took was prayers, the Browns would have won at least three Super Bowls by now" (p. 93). Millions of Browns fans are still praying for a Super Bowl victory, or a Super Bowl appearance for that matter. Not only have their prayers not been answered, Cleveland temporarily lost their franchise shortly after this research was conducted. There are millions of other fans who have also never had their prayers answered when praying for a favorable outcome in a sporting event. And yet, many cling to their faith in prayer. And what happens if an equal number of people from the two playing teams playing each other are praying for a favorable outcome? Why do some fans have their prayers answered and others do not?

Athletes may also turn to prayer in hopes of a favorable outcome. This is quite disconcerting for most fans. After all, fans want to see confidence in their favorite players, not moments of doubt or signs of a reliance on variables outside of individual talent. Uncertainty and doubt are primary reasons athletes turn to prayer in sports. "Because sport competitions involve a high degree of uncertainty, it is not surprising that many athletes use religious prayer to make them feel as if they have some control over what happens to them on the playing field" (Czech, et al. 2004: 9). Thus, fans that rely on prayer do so because of the frustration and stress they experience due to the fact they have no direct influence on the game, while athletes turn to prayer because of their insecurities and doubts. Czech and associates (2004) believe that "many times, Christian athletes utilize their belief system as a performance enhancement technique. More specifically, prayer has been used as a coping mechanism for stress, to help with team cohesion, and to promote a morally sound life" (p. 4). In this matter, athletes who turn to prayer may do so because it adds to their self-confidence. This newly charged self-confidence, athletes believe, helps to motivate them to perform better. In their 2020 study, Delaney and Madigan asked respondents whether or not praying can influence the outcome of the game (see Table 14.5).

Slightly more than half (53 percent) of private college students responded that they agree (13 percent strongly agree) that praying can influence the outcome of the game while less than a quarter (24 percent) agreed or strongly agreed that praying can influence the outcome of the game. Thirty-eight percent of public state university students strongly disagreed that praying can influence the outcome of the game.

Table 14.5. Praying Can Influence the Outcome of the Game (in percent)

	Public State University			Private Catholic College		
	Combined	Males	Females	Combined	Males	Females
Strongly Agree	5	12	0	13	20	7
Agree	19	0	30	40	37	43
Disagree	52	50	52	31	30	31
Strongly Disagree	24	38	17	17	13	19

This brief analysis on the role of prayer in sports indicates that a substantial number of college students—both public state university and private Catholic College—believe that prayer in a variety of contexts is acceptable. The most significant difference between public and private school students is the ability of prayer to influence the outcome of the game; not surprisingly, Catholic school students were more likely to believe in the power of prayer than were public state university students. Fans and athletes alike have not relied solely on prayer for a positive intervention in their sporting endeavors. Many have turned to magic and superstition. Such behaviors reside in the secular world of sport.

Secularization and Sport

The social institutions of sport and religion are filled with ritualistic behavior. People turn to ritualistic behaviors for a variety of reasons. Malinowski (1927) suggests that ritual, or magical behavior, is associated with high risk activities. Risk is expressed in terms of physical danger to the participants or when the possibility of failure in an important endeavor is possible (Womack 1992). Fortes (1936) argued that uncertainty plays a role in ritualistic behavior and that ritual is associated with behavior designed toward the safety of the group (rather than with individuals). Douglas (1966) believes that ritual is used to deal with elements of psychic danger, as well as with physical danger and threat of deprivation (Womack 1992). Turner (1967) states that rituals are a way of demonstrating conformity to expected behavior while Geertz (1965) claims that rituals are an effective form of social control (Womack 1992). Czech and associates (2004) state, "Throughout history, people have used rituals based on religion, magic and/or superstition to cope with uncertainties in their lives" (p. 9).

Rituals in Sport

Ritualistic behavior possesses a number of qualities. According to Womack (1992), there are five key components of ritual:

1. *Repetitive.* It occurs again and again in a given context, or certain elements tend to be repeated throughout the behavioral sequence.
2. *Stylized.* It is formal, rather than spontaneous.
3. *Sequential.* There is an orderly procession from beginning to end. Transposition of elements within a ritual is thought to diminish its efficacy.
4. *Non-ordinary.* It is distinct from ordinary mundane activities and is not essential to technical performance.
5. *Potent.* It is believed to be either innately powerful, or powerful in controlling supernatural beings or forces [192].

Ritualistic behaviors are very common in sport, as many athletes, coaches, and fans engage in any number of rituals before, during or after the game. Fans of sport may wear specific clothing while viewing or attending a game, and in some cases, not wash the clothing for as long as the winning streak continues; eat certain foods; listen to specific music; take specific routes to the game or a friend's house to watch the game; and, engage in pre-game tailgating and postgame festivities (e.g., meeting at certain "watering hole"). Highly identified fans may go through more ritualistic behaviors than athletes. They believe that their actions, somehow, contribute to the outcome of the game. Athletes may engage in a variety of rituals, including preparatory rites (pre-activity rituals that may include the shower routine and the refusal to shave on game day); day-of-game rituals (a specific meal or time of day to eat, putting clothes on in a specific order, or wearing "lucky" clothes under the uniform); pregame rituals (especially in terms of "warming up" for the athletic event, a field goal kicker who refuses to leave the field until he makes a practice field goal attempt); activity-specific rituals (behavior that psyches an athlete to play); and in-game rituals (e.g., a baseball pitcher that jumps over the foul line on his way to the pitching mound, eating seeds, and the routine of LeBron James to throw powder in the air).

Ritualistic behaviors help to relieve anxiety and stress and help athletes concentrate and face the competition with confidence. As Gmelch (1994) explains, "Rituals usually grow out of exceptionally good performances. When a player does well he seldom attributes his success to skill alone. Although his skill remains constant, he may go hitless in one game and in the next get three or four hits. Many players attribute the inconsistencies in their performances to an object, item of food, or form of behavior outside their play. Through ritual, players seek to gain control over their performance" (p. 355). Womack (1992) concludes that ritual is important in sport for the following reasons:

1. Ritual helps the player focus his attention on the task at hand. It can be used by the player to prevent anxiety or shut out excessive environmental stimuli—such as the chanting of fans—from interrupting his concentration.
2. Ritual can signal intent to the other team. Specifically, ritual can be used to "threaten" the other team.
3. Ritual provides a means of coping with a high-risk, high stress situation.
4. Ritual helps establish a rank order among team members and promotes intra-group communication.
5. Ritual helps in dealing with ambiguity in interpersonal relationships, with other team members, and with people on the periphery of the team, such as management and the public.
6. Ritual is a "harmless" means of self-expression. It can be used to reinforce a sense of individual worth under pressure for group conformity, without endangering the unity of the group.
7. Ritual directs individual motivations and needs toward achieving group goals [200].

Rituals in sports are a way to regulate one's mental state, provide calmness and self-confidence, and provide a positive distraction from the task ahead. Still, regardless of the rituals employed, ultimately it is talent, skill, and ability that generally prevail. However, the element of luck inherent in any sporting event allows both fans and athletes to attribute outcomes to their specific ritualistic behaviors.

Magic

A number of ritualistic behaviors are grounded in the world of magic. Magic, like religion, assumes that supernatural powers exist; however, whereas religion is oriented to the otherworldly, magic is oriented toward the instant, sensible goals. Religion concerns itself with eternal salvation while magic is focused on the needs of the here and now. Religion preaches that adherents should behave in specific ways that are consistent with their teachings in order attain eternal salvation. People who turn to magic hope to manipulate events in such a way as to gain an advantage over their competitors. The world of religion deals with sacred items such as emblems and symbols of faith (e.g., a Christian cross, Star of David, Crescent Moon, or Dharmachakra). *Magic* is defined as the appeal to supernatural powers for outcome assistance.

In contrast, the world of magic relies on profane items as symbols of magical power (e.g., a lucky penny, rabbit's foot, pendant, Valknut, sigil, and the circled dot). According to *Magicians Magazine* (2017) there are ten types of magic: mentalism (e.g., telepathy, hypnosis, clairvoyance, and psychokinesis); arcane (manipulation of dark forces and powers); sleight of hand (fast hand movement to create the illusion of magic); roving magic (popular with children shows and other social functions); utility and prop (a set or stage that has utilities and props already set up for the show); elemental (involves the complete control and use of the four main forces of the earth; fire, water, earth, and air); levitation (involves the use of some other unseen force, like a magnetic force, to actually levitate objects, including people); traditional magic (theatrical tricks); card tricks (sleight of hand, such as side slips, palming, false cuts, false shuffles); and escapology (an "escape artist" that risks their life in attempt to escape a dangerous situation).

Sports fans are likely to have thought of a number of variations of magic that athletes use from the list above, including hypnosis and sleight of hand. Gmelch (1994), an anthropologist and former professional baseball player, believes that while relying on magic would certainly seem to be illogical, it does in fact serve valuable functions. Gmelch classifies magic into three categories:

1. *Rituals.* Rituals emerge from exceptionally good performances. That is, the behaviors that preceded an outstanding performance are repeated because they are deemed to possess magical power.
2. *Taboos.* Taboos refer to behaviors that are avoided because they are deemed bad luck. "Taboos usually grow out of exceptionally poor performances, which players often attribute to a particular behavior or food. Certain uniform numbers may become taboo" (Gmelch 1994: 355). Gmelch admits to his own "pancake taboo"— he refused to eat pancakes during the baseball season because he once ate pancakes before a game in which he struck out four times. Athletes today may refuse to stop on the foul lines on the baseball field as they run out to the field or back to the dugout.
3. *Fetishes or Charms.* Material objects such as coins, old bats, or horsehide covers from old baseballs are credited with possessing special powers. "Ordinary objects acquire power by being connected to exceptionally hot batting or pitching streaks, especially ones in which players get all the breaks. The object is often a new possession or something a player finds and holds responsible for his new good fortune" [Gmelch 1994: 355].

SUPERSTITIONS

Irrational beliefs in the power of magic are tied to superstitions as well. *Superstitions* can be defined as beliefs or practices resulting from ignorance, fear of the unknown, or a belief in magic or chance. Superstitions can be found in all cultures. They can also be found in sports. Superstitions are fragmentary remains of past rituals, systems of thoughts, and belief systems that have lost their original meaning to those who believe in them in the present. Put another way, "Superstitions are the living relics of ways of thought much older than our own, and of beliefs once strongly held but now abandoned and forgotten. Absurd as some of them now seem in the light of knowledge, all were serious in their beginnings" (Hole 1969:7). Deol and Singh (2017) believe that superstitious beliefs are an outcome of ignorance and lack of rational thinking, and emphasize that this is the case because, after all, they are merely beliefs. "Beliefs become notions, then it becomes opinions, and they begin to prevail in society as well as the sports world" (Deol and Singh 2017: XX). Superstitious persons find causal relations between certain behaviors and outcomes where they do not really exist. Deol and Singh (2017) consider athletes, especially top athletes, as among the most superstitious people. "Some top class athletes believe that their superstitions enhance their performance and alter the outcome of competition, but in fact, practice and confidence is the key to success in athletes" (Deol and Singh 2017). In more extreme cases of superstitious beliefs, sport participants and fans alike come to see a breach in certain superstitious behaviors as a "jinx." (Note: The concept of a "jinx" is discussed in "Connecting Sports and Popular Culture" Box 14.)

The belief in superstitions reflects the idea that elements other than personal ability affect behavioral outcome. Athletes that rely on superstition do so in an attempt to gain some sense of control over an event. Gaining any type of "edge" in athletic performance is the goal of all athletes. In their research on NCAA track and field athletes, Todd and Brown (2003) found a positive relationship between athletic identity and superstitious behavior, suggesting that student athletes high in athletic identity use more superstition in sport competitions.

Superstitious behaviors are different from preperformance routines. Preperformance routines, such as relaxation techniques and focusing and coping strategies, are learned behavioral and cognitive strategies which are deliberately used by athletes to assist physical performance (Bleak and Frederick 1998). Engaging in superstitious ritual, much like preperformance routines, provides the athlete with a feeling of control or sense of calm prior to athletic participation. Ritualistic superstitious behaviors are usually personalized by individual athletes; that is, many athletes have their own quirky behaviors separate from general taboos found in their sport.

B.F. Skinner (1948) found that the acquisition of superstition as a conditioning process is the result of unrelated events that have been linked together. Thus, if an athlete wears blue socks (instead of the normal white socks that he or she typically wears) and breaks a personal losing streak, the athlete will attribute (link) the newfound favorable outcome to an unrelated procedure (wearing blue socks) if he or she is superstitious. If subsequent connections are made between the new ritual (e.g., wearing blue socks) and a favorable outcome the behavior becomes routinized as a superstition. When superstitious behaviors become a part of the regular pregame ritual the superstitious athlete will continue such behavior even when positive reinforcement (a favorable outcome) fails to occur. *Sport superstitions* can be defined as ritualized routines that are separate from athletic training and that are performed by athletes because they believe such behaviors are powerful enough to control external factors (e.g., supersede the talents and game preparation of opponents).

Generally speaking, superstitious behaviors in sports fall under the belief in magic or chance, rather than ignorance or fear of the unknown. As with other forms of ritualistic behaviors, athletes engage in superstitious behavior as a way to reduce their level of anxiety before and during the game. There is a fair amount of research that indicates ritualistic behaviors can assist athletic performance. Schippers and Van Lange (2006) found that the state of psychological tension was mediated when athletes had an external locus of control (superstitious ritualistic behavior) and that this was especially true when uncertainty (of outcome or performance) is high rather than low, and when the importance of the game is high rather than low. Blackwell (2015) believes that the "real value in superstition or ritual is the boost of confidence and sense of control that they provide a sports person." Domotor, Barquin and Szabo (2016) found that athletes are more likely to engage in superstitious behavior as the importance of the sporting event increases, when athletes' level of uncertainty in their own skills is in question, and as the level of difficulty in the challenge increases. Wright and Erdal (2009) state that professional athletes were more superstitious during difficult tasks than easy tasks; thus, the bigger the game, the more superstitious someone would be. Wann and Goeke (2018) provide a review of past research on superstition and stress reduction and found that athletes who activate good-luck superstitions can improve sport performance (e.g., golf putting) and that superstitions are most beneficial when the competition is greatest or the game is close (superstition is not needed when the team is enjoying a huge margin in score differential). Wann and Goeke examined the superstitious behaviors of sports fans and found that such behaviors are most often prominent because fans realize they have little control over the outcome of their favorite teams' games so they resort to superstitions in an attempt to reduce their own stress while also trying to positively influence the outcome of the game.

There are many superstitious behaviors among hockey players. For example, because of the importance of protective clothing and padding, players spend a great deal of time putting on equipment in a very precise, routinized manner. During on-ice warm-ups, hockey players employ a number of superstitious ritualistic behaviors. Team rituals may involve players skating towards the net in a particular order and with each player's movement a deliberate pattern. Usually the players skate by their goalie and give him a tap and offer words of encouragement. Every team has a player that *has* to be the last one off the ice or a player who has to be the last one to shoot a puck in the goal (Keating and Hogg 1995). In contrast to Deol and Singh (2017), Todd and Brown (2003) found that research conducted on Division I and Division III hockey players reveals that the frequency of superstitious behaviors engaged in by the two levels of athletes is quite similar. Thus, the level of competition does not determine the use or frequency of superstitious behavior.

One of the more unique stories tying sports and superstitions together involves baseball teams that stay at the Vinoy Renaissance St. Petersburg Resort & Golf Club, "the lodging chosen by most big league teams" when they go to Tampa Bay to play the Rays (Garcia-Roberts 2014). Players have rushed downstairs to the lobby in the middle of the night scared of something in their rooms; they have claimed to have witnessed images of people in their rooms; there are rooms with faucets that turn on and off by themselves; flickering lights; and a woman in a painting that suddenly appears to be trying to claw outside of the canvas are among the scary things athletes from a variety of teams have claimed to encountered at the Vinoy. Gus Garcia-Roberts, a writer for *American Way* magazine, investigated the hotel himself but did not experience any unusual happenings. The desk clerk told Garcia-Roberts that he "mostly blames baseball players' superstitions for spreading the hotel's haunted reputation." Certainly, the images these athletes claimed to have seen fall under the definition of superstition's parameters (Garcia-Roberts 2014).

Although logic dictates that superstitious behaviors have no direct bearing on the outcome of the game, if athletes believe in superstitions it may provide them with a psychological edge. This edge may lead to victory. In this manner, superstitious behavior is more likely to lead to a favorable sporting outcome than prayer.

Connecting Sports and Popular Culture

Box 14: "Don't Jinx Me": The *SI* and *Madden NFL* Cover Curse

Two best friends are anxiously watching the end of the game. Their favorite team is about to pull the biggest upset in history when one friend says to the other, "Can you believe we are actually going to win this game?" Disturbed by this comment, the other friend says, "Don't say that, you just jinxed us." The second friend is expressing a concern that many of us can relate to; namely, when you call attention to something before its action is concluded, bad luck will follow. Superstitious people believe in things like a jinx primarily because they believe that unrelated events are somehow related. Just as we discussed in this chapter about athletes and fans who engage in certain superstitious behavior like wearing a "lucky" shirt or having the same "lucky" breakfast every game day because it will, somehow, bring good luck, people also believe in bad luck. A jinx is an example of bad luck.

A jinx may be a verbal or visual expression that violates the code of superstitious people that says one is not supposed to talk about the conclusion of a game until the game has in fact concluded. To speak of victory before it occurs is a form of premature celebration and for superstitious people it is akin to the "kiss of death." Thus, if your favorite team is about to kick a winning field goal at the end of the game, you and everyone around you are supposed to keep calm and remain silent and let the course of action take place. Sure, you may be thinking to yourself, "If he makes this field goal we win and I will celebrate this for a long time"; but, for superstitious persons, you are never to speak the same expression out loud.

It is odd that sports fans, and athletes alike, believe that if someone in the stands or at home says aloud, "we are going to win this game" before the outcome is truly no longer in doubt, that such an utterance will cause a misfortune to those (e.g., the field goal kicker) who did not even hear the vocal breach of etiquette. But believing in a jinx is not unique to sports fans. Anyone who believes in magic or superstitions is likely to fall for the fallacy of a belief in a jinx. College students, for example, may believe in jinxes. If one friend says to another, "Why are you studying so hard? You know this material, you are going to ace the exam," the other student may say, "Don't jinx me! I haven't taken the test yet." Some people believe that whenever two people say the same thing at the same time that is a jinx. Thus, if Paul and Wendy both say at the same time, "I love pepperoni pizza" that is supposed to be bad luck. However, if either Paul or Wendy immediately replies "jinx" following the simultaneously spoken phrase, the other one alone has bad luck. Furthermore, the person who says "jinx," following the simultaneously spoken phrase may add an addendum by saying something like, "Jinx, you owe me a soda," and the other person is obligated to buy the soda.

Some people believe so strongly in jinxes that they actually believe it is possible to jinx someone while they are engaged in a behavior. For example, if your team is on defense when the opposing team is trying to kick the game-winning field goal, superstitious people will attempt to "jinx" the kicker via some made-up jinx ritual like waving both hands in the direction of the kicker or by making any number of physical and/or verbal gestures. If the kicker misses the field goal the person(s) who attempted to jinx the player will actually take credit for the outcome—"The kicker missed the field goal because I jinxed him."

The idea of a jinx is very relevant to the sports world as so many people are superstitious and believe in such irrational things as jinxes. Sports, the actual games played, are often devoid of rationality because of their strong emotional component. The authors consider themselves rational folks and yet when it comes to sports and cheering for a favorite team or player, they too realize that emotion often supersedes rationality. There are long-standing jinxes that most sports fans have heard of, the *SI* (*Sports Illustrated*) cover jinx and the *Madden NFL* cover jinx.

The *SI* cover jinx refers to a long-running theory, or what some people describe as an "urban legend," that proposes that any player who makes the cover will suffer a decline in their performance, often immediately but sometimes in the longer term (LeBron 2014). Aware of their image, *Sports Illustrated* put on its January 21, 2002, cover the caption "The Cover that No One Would Pose for, Is the SI Jinx for Real?" Instead of an athlete, the cover featured a black cat. The *SI* jinx concept can be traced back to August 16, 1954, when Milwaukee Braves third baseman Eddie Mathews became the first person to make the cover (*Atlanta Journal Constitution.com* 2014). Right after his cover shot reached the newsstands, the Braves' 9-game winning streak ended and Mathews suffered a broken hand which cost him to lose seven games of playing time (*Atlanta Journal Constitution.com* 2014). There are multiple examples from every decade that seemingly substantiate the concept of the SI jinx as players and teams suffered misfortune following their appearance on the magazine's cover. Conversely, there are far more examples of when a "jinx" did not follow an appearance on the *SI* cover. Statistical regression would seem to explain the notion of the so-called "jinx." Players and teams make the cover of *SI* because they are performing at a very high level and statistically-speaking, it is only a matter of time before they revert back to the norm of athletic performance. Thus, there may be a correlation between landing a SI cover and then a drop in performance but it is far-fetched to suggest that there is a cause-and-effect relationship.

The same situation applies to the *Madden* cover jinx. (FYI: John Madden is a former NFL coach—he won a Super Bowl as head coach of the Oakland Raiders—and is also a sportscaster.) The *Madden* cover jinx refers to the cover photo of an NFL player on the *Madden NFL* video game developed by Electronic Arts Tiburon for EA Sports. There are various versions of the *Madden* game, with the first one released June 1, 1988; it was called *John Madden Football 1988*. The name of the game has changed often but always includes "Madden" and a year. A new game comes out every year but oddly the game is always a year off, in other words, *Madden NFL 21* was released prior to the scheduled start of the 2020 NFL season and not prior to the 2021 season. The cover photo is chosen on the performance of an active NFL player from the season prior; thus, the cover photo of *Madden NFL 21* is chosen because of the statistics of an NFL player from the 2019 season.

Nearly every NFL player chosen for the *Madden* video game has suffered a playing misfortune. As Petite and Marshall (2020) describe, "More than 25 years into the iconic franchise's history, there's almost no escaping the *Madden* Curse. Since Garrison Hearst broke his ankle in 1998, shortly after starring on the cover of *Madden NFL 99*, most players who starred on the game's cover have suffered an injury the following season. Of the 22 players who have been selected to grace the cover of *Madden* games through this season [2020], 16 have had troubling or abruptly shortened seasons following their cover debut—including several who suffered season-ending injuries shortly after their game hit shelves."

If you're a fan of football and believe in jinxes, you better hope your favorite player doesn't end up on the cover of *Madden NFL*. Baltimore Ravens quarterback Lamar Jackson is on the cover of *Madden NFL 21*, is he now cursed to suffer from the *Madden* cover "jinx?" By now, the answer has been revealed.

SUMMARY

The institution of religion arose from the need to explain and understand life's mysteries. Religion provides a meaning or interpretation of life, reinforces the morals and norms held by the collectivity, and provides many functions. Sport sociologists point out that many of the human drives and needs that compel some people to be a part of a particular religion are the same drives and needs that compel some to be a part of the sports world in some way. Religion and sports have nearly equal adherents in the United States, with 74 percent of Americans describing themselves as religious and 65 percent of Americans considering themselves as sports fans. Fifty years ago, the gap between religious and sports adherents was much higher.

Twenty-one similarities between sport and religion were described in this chapter, contributing to the assertion that it is difficult to argue with those who claim sport *is* religion; or at the very least, a quasi-religion. There are, however, a number of significant differences between sport and religion as well. Ten specific differences between sports and religion were described. Despite the differences between sport and religion, the two social institutions remain connected by the numerous similarities. While some would state that religion is far more important than sports, others would be of the opposite opinion.

The role of prayer in life, and in sport specifically, is a fascinating topic. Many firmly believe in the power of prayer to provide solace, hope, and a positive outcome with some sort of challenge or need. Such a notion does not hold up to empirical research as there is no proven connection between prayer and a desired outcome and that is especially true in sports. After all, for every prayer for one outcome, there is another prayer for the opposite outcome. Thus, it is impossible for prayer alone to cause the outcome of a sporting contest.

In addition to prayer, a number of people turn to more secular sources that will provide a positive outcome, rituals, magic and superstitions. Rituals in sports are a way to regulate one's mental state, provide calmness and self-confidence, and provide a positive distraction from the task ahead. Still, regardless of the rituals employed, ultimately it is talent, skill, and ability that generally prevail. Magic, like religion, assumes that supernatural powers exist. Sport superstitions are ritualized routines that are separate from athletic training and that are performed by athletes because they believe such behaviors are powerful enough to control external factors (e.g., the talents of opponents).

KEY TERMS

Belief A conviction of certainty about specific matters even without evidence of its truth.

Function An activity, purpose, service, or behavior that contributes to the maintenance of a group, organization, or society.

Magic The appeal to supernatural powers for outcome assistance.

Prayer A solemn request for help or expression of thanks addressed to a higher power or an object of worship.

Preperformance Routines Learned behavioral and cognitive strategies which are deliberately used by athletes in order to assist physical performance.

Religion A system of beliefs and ritualistic behaviors which unite a group of like-minded people together into a social group who adhere to ideals of spirituality.

Religious Beliefs Ideals to which members of a particular religion adhere.

Sacred Items Objects and behaviors that are deemed part of the spiritual realm and are set apart from the ordinary; they are worshipped.

Sport superstitions Ritualized routines that are separate from athletic training and that are performed by athletes because they believe such behaviors are powerful enough to control external factors (e.g., supersede the talents and game preparation of opponents).

Superstitions Beliefs or practices resulting from ignorance or fear of the unknown, or a belief in magic or chance.

DISCUSSION QUESTIONS

- Why do fans pray at sporting events? Do you think they seriously believe that God will be influenced by their prayers and that God really cares who wins?
- What are some of the similarities between sports and religion?
- How are sports and religion different from one another?
- One definition of "religion" is that it is an institution that binds people together. Do you think it is possible for anyone to believe that sport is a religion in the same manner?
- Do you think that prayer should be allowed in sports in public school? If yes, should the prayers of all religions be said at sporting events of just a select religion?
- What are some athletic superstitions that you are familiar with? Do you have any yourself?
- Do you think that religious celebrations in sports, such as praying after a touchdown, should be banned? Why or why not?

CHAPTER 15

The Media and Sport

There is an old philosophical question, "If a tree falls in the woods and no one is there to hear it, does it make a sound?" With the growing influence of the mass media over sport, we might amend this question to, "If they hold a sports event and the media is not there, is it really a sports event?" Today, nearly all sporting events are covered by some aspect of the media. Whether it is mainstream media (e.g., television, radio, newspaper) or social media coverage (e.g., Twitter, Facebook, Instagram, streaming services), the media are there to report sports—and sports at all levels including youth, high school, college and professional. The role of the media in sports has not always been as inclusive as it is today, but the mass media and mass interest in sport grew together and now enjoy a symbiotic relationship. The results of this convergence between the media and sports will be discussed throughout this chapter.

ESPN, a 24-hour sports network, is the leading representative of emphasizing entertainment over sport. This is most clearly exemplified by the fact that the "E" (for "entertainment") comes before the "S" (for "sports") in ESPN (the "P" and "N" stand for "programming" and "network" respectively). Some viewers would find it hard to imagine ESPN without the "E" aspect of its coverage. Other viewers would prefer that the "E" was eliminated and the coverage restricted to the "S"—sports coverage without all the frills and sidebars and seemingly nonstop studio conversations with media, sports experts and/or celebrities. Instead of endless attempts of describing the game from the "E"ntertainment perspective, most die-hard sports fans would prefer a focus on "S"port highlights. However, all indicators point to a continuing emphasis on the entertainment value of sports rather than sporting value of sports as we move through the twenty-first century. Dhonde and Patil (2012:1) concur that "the world of sports has transcended from purely athletic competition into entertainment and celebrity" but point out that this switch in focus has led to a larger sports audience.

The Institution of the Media

The media, or more specifically, the press, has enjoyed much power throughout the past few centuries. The creators of the U.S. Constitution were so passionate about the rights of the press that the First Amendment guarantees the freedom of speech and freedom of the press. Dating back to the era of the penny press (one-page newspapers sold for a penny so that the masses could afford to read the news), the media have attempted to inform the masses of important news events. As the freedom of the press is guaranteed by the Constitution it is the sworn duty of the president of the United States to protect the media from any attacks. A failure to do this would be considered an impeachable offense. But what happens if the president is the one who attacks the press and it not held accountable for such actions? The answer is simple; we have an attack on democracy itself. Any sort of attempt to silence the press, especially journalists, is a sure sign of corruption.

The U.S. Constitution defends the press because of its importance as a major institution of society. The press is an aspect of the mass media. Providing news, information, and entertainment are the trademarks of the contemporary mass media. The term "media" has been used since the 1920s. According to Real (1996), "The term *media* refers to all communication relays and technologies" (9). The word "mass" refers to the large size of the media's audience (Ryan and Wentworth 1999). Put together, the mass media become the medium by which large numbers of people are informed about important happenings in society.

The mass media has grown from its humble printing press beginnings to its current omnipresent existence due to the incorporation of the ever-expanding level of technology. Prior to the twenty-first century, the media were divided into two major categories: the print media, which include newspapers, magazines, and books; and the electronic media, which include television, radio, motion pictures, sound recordings, and the Internet. Currently, we divide the media into two other categories: traditional media (e.g., print media such as newspapers, magazines, and books; terrestrial radio; television; and, motion pictures, sound recordings, and billboards) and social media (e.g., internet-based and computer-mediated technologies that facilitate the exchange of news, information, ideas, entertainment) and other forms of expression via virtual and web-based communities and networks (e.g., Twitter, Facebook, Instagram, YouTube). When it comes specifically to news, traditional media reigns supreme, primarily because news is researched by journalists and reporters—the keys to democracy. A primary sign of the deterioration of democracy and human rights in the U.S. and around the world are the attacks on the traditional news media when they report factual news but have it referred to as "fake news" or "alternative facts" because such factual information runs counter to an ideology or belief system (Delaney 2021). Declaring the media as the "enemy of the state" is a sign of tyranny and cannot be tolerated, especially if a nation refers to itself as a democracy. Mainstream news must also commit to maintaining high levels of integrity.

While traditional, mainstream media is more controlled and subject to rigorous review, social media operates much like a "wild west" where seemingly anything goes with little control over content. Many people have forgotten that any news or information attained via social media outlets is highly suspect until it can be verified as factual by an independent fact-checking website (i.e., Snopes.com) or by peer-reviewed academic sources. Social media platforms such as Twitter and Facebook are filled disreputable sources of information, including from high-ranking government officials.

Those of us worried about the institution of the media are most concerned by the world of social media, a place where people can lie, spread false and unfounded conspiracies, organize rallies of hate, and incite violence with little, or very delayed, response to close down such provokers of true false news. Furthermore, there are numerous fake accounts found on social media platforms, some of which may present themselves as a real account (i.e., a variation on SportsCenter) and there is the ever-growing concern of the "get it out first" mentality wherein a news platform wants to be the first to get a new story out even while the story is still developing and may change.

While social media has serious problems when it comes to providing factual news, and it has, essentially, destroyed the print media (e.g., newspapers are dying across the country and much of the world, and *Sports Illustrated* is now a monthly publication instead of a weekly), newspapers have adapted by offering a digital media aspect in an attempt to maintain subscribers. Social media allows us to watch and share videos and photos, read and write blogs, post on social networking sites and have online conversations (Newman et al 2017). Athletes, coaches, and league offices often taken advantage of social media platforms because they can control the message being sent to the public rather than potentially having their message framed for them; or, worse yet, not having a platform to send their message. The audience for news information on sports is huge and social media helps to fill the void that traditional media cannot. It is safe to say that social media platforms will remain popular, at least until the next step in the evolutionary process of the media's continuing transformation.

Two youths use technology to play the NBA 2k video game and to update their ESPN fantasy football team (courtesy Todd Delaney).

The Relationship Between the Media and Sports

The relationship between the media and sports has grown extensively over the past couple of centuries. Let's take a quick look at the socio-historical development of this symbiotic relationship. Throughout the nineteenth century, sports became increasingly important in American society. The print media were there since the beginning. As Rader (1984) states, "Even early in the nineteenth century, print media—whether in the form of weeklies, newspapers, fiction, biography, or autobiography—enhanced public interest in sports" (18). The print media quickly took notice of the rise of a leisure class and the growing popularity of sports on college campuses. "To increase circulation, newspapers frequently became promoters of sports. As early as 1873, James Gordon Bennett, Jr., the eccentric owner of the New York *Herald*, began awarding cups and medals to intercollegiate track and field champions" (Rader 1984: 19).

The sports page was taking shape in many newspapers in the 1880s and 1890s. By the 1920s, the sports page was a fixture in all major daily newspapers. Readers of the sports pages in the early twentieth century enjoyed sports columns for the same reasons people enjoy them today; that is, the sports pages provide information consisting of clear-cut winners and losers and provide continuity and orderliness to a segment of life. The sports pages became so popular by the early twentieth century that writers began to specialize in sports. Throughout most of the twentieth century as the popularity of sports and newspapers grew, a number of people were employed as sports journalists and sports journalists. The development of such new media technology as radio, motion pictures and television was also applied to the world of sports in an attempt to reach the largest possible audience.

LINKING THE MASS MEDIA TO SPORTS

As previously stated, newspapers began to cover sports in the late 1800s. William Randolph Hearst, publisher of the *New York Journal*, is often credited as the first person to develop the "sports section" of a newspaper (McChesney 1989). By 1900, the sports section represented about 15 percent of all general news covered in leading newspapers (Eitzen and Sage 1989). Throughout the early half of the twentieth century newspapers contributed to the popularity of sports. Along with sponsoring sporting events, newspapers provided sports information to growing leisure class that featured millions of sports fans who thirsted for information about their favorite athletes and sports teams. The print media became the conduit between the masses and their desire for sports information. Sports information and sensational story-telling on the part of sports journalists helped to establish athletes as stars worthy of adulation.

Rader (1984) claims that newspaper sportswriting in the pre-television era fell into three large, sometimes overlapping categories: the tall tale, verse, and the true story. The tall tale, the oldest form of storytelling, is the result of oral accounts of great feats. The verse refers to poetic-style writing of sportswriters. Grantland Rice's depiction of Notre Dame's famous "Four Horsemen" and their 1924 victory over powerful Army is the classic example of the verse style of sportswriting: "Outlined against a blue-grey October sky, the Four Horsemen rode again. In dramatic lore they are known as Famine, Pestilence, Destruction, and Death. These are only aliases. Their real names are Stuhldreher, Miller, Crowley, and Layden" (Rader 1984: 21). The true story approach to sportswriting revealed the frailties and failures of athletes.

Newspaper stories were enhanced by accompanying photographs. This proved to be especially significant. "The emergence of sports sections, and the growing use of photography helped to establish the beginnings of an individualization of sport in which star individuals began to inhabit the public imagination" (Whannel 2002: 31). The introduction of cigarette cards that featured photos of athletes aided the creation of star status among the elite ball players. Cigarette cards, which are believed to have originated in France around the 1840s, were cardboard stiffeners used as promotion (Whannel 2002). (Cigarettes were sold loosely or in paper packs that required a stiffener in the late 1800s and early 1900s.) These cards usually featured "glamour shots of women (as most smokers were men), but a series of sport cards were introduced in the United States toward the end of the nineteenth century. Tobacco companies assumed that male smokers cared the most about three things: sport, women, and the military (Whannel 2002).

Other forms of print media include magazines and books. Before the sport section appeared in newspapers, a number of magazines and books were written, and continued to be written, about athletes and sports. Magazines on horse racing, hunting, and fishing were popular since the 1830s. During the twentieth century every sport developed its own specialized magazines, and many popular magazines such as *Sports Illustrated*, *Sport*, *Inside Sport*, and *The Sporting News* enjoy a huge circulation. Books have existed for centuries. The mass readership of books coincided with mandatory education laws (which transformed a nearly completely illiterate mass into a literate one) and industrialization (which allowed for the production of dime novels around the time of the U.S. Civil War). There were a variety of books written on the topic of sport dating back to the late nineteenth century. During the twentieth century it became popular to have books written on sports teams and individual athletes from a wide range of sports. Athletes, with the assistance of ghost writers, often write books about their sporting exploits. At times, these books include the "tell all" variety where the athletes expose the "secret" world of sport. Baseball player Jim Bouton's *Ball Four* (1970) remains a classic must-read. "Tell all" books remain in vogue today, as evidenced by Jose Canseco's *Juiced* (2005), an exposé about the alleged rampant abuse of steroids in professional baseball; as it turned out, many of Canseco's allegations turned out to be true.

Beginning in the early twentieth century, motion pictures brought to life many sporting stories and events that fans had only heard about. Cinema newsreel was very popular in England and the United States by the 1920s and 1930s. "By 1919, 50 percent of the British population went to the cinema once or twice a week. During the 1920s and 1930s there was a substantial increase in investment in cinemas, with around one thousand being built between 1924–1931. The introduction of sound at the end of the twenties provided a boost to industry and encouraged investment in new cinemas.… By 1940 the average weekly audience was 21 million" (Whannel 2002: 32–33). In the United States, an estimated eighty-five million Americans saw one movie per week (Eitzen and Sage 1989). While movies such as *Knute Rockne, All American* (1940), *The Pride of the Yankees* (about Lou Gehrig, 1942) and *Somebody Up There Likes Me* (about Rocky Graziano, 1956) were popular films, oddly, sports movies were a rarity until the 1970s. Today, a number of sports movies have enjoyed great success. (Sports movies were previously discussed in "Connecting Sports and Popular Culture" Box 1 as an example of the pervasiveness of sports in society.)

A major breakthrough in sports coverage occurred with the introduction of the radio. Sport stories retold in motion pictures and books are dated by the time they reach their audience. Magazine sport stories are relatively recent and newspaper coverage is at least a day removed from the sports event. But radio provided immediate coverage—and to a large audience. "If cinema brought action and movement, radio provided immediacy and it brought sport into the domestic sphere for the first time. In both Britain and the USA early radio broadcast experiments were underway by the start of the 1920s. The percentage of households with radio rose rapidly in the inter-war period, from 10 percent in 1924 to 71 percent in 1938. In the USA, too, radio rose to prominence and sport broadcasts played a significant role in its popularity. By 1929 one-third of American households had radio" (Whannel 2002: 33).

Fans across the U.S. listened to the radio for the play-by-play accounts of sporting events, especially baseball, boxing, horse racing, and football. Unlike the newspaper, which informed sport enthusiasts about sporting events *after* they occurred, radio provided sounds and descriptions of sporting events *while* they occurred. In spite of the overwhelming presence of television in sports, radio broadcasts remain popular today. In certain markets local games of interest may not be televised but are offered on the radio. Many fans listen to sporting events on the radio while they are at work or riding in their cars. Some fans become so attached to the voice and personality of their favorite radio announcers that they listen to the radio while watching televised broadcasts (with the television volume muted).

The next major break-through of media technology to the sports world was television. Television fundamentally changed sport. It not only provides immediacy, as radio, but it also provides all the action and movement of motion pictures. "Like the radio, this medium allows live reporting, but because it transmits not only sound but also live images, the feeling of 'being there' is even stronger for television spectators than for radio listeners. So, with television, major sporting contests are no longer available just to spectators witnessing the event in person, but also to many millions more who can view the spectacle in their own homes, thanks to their television sets. The added value stemming from this medium is evident: close-ups, replays, slow motion, the different angles from different cameras, and cameras that follow the action. It can be more exciting to be spectator in front of the television screen than to be a spectator in the stadium, far away from the playing field or arena floor" (Beck and Bosshart 2003: 10).

According to Duncan and Brummett (1987) there are four dimensions of televised sports in the contemporary era: narrative, intimacy, commodification, and rigid time segmentation.

1. *Narrative.* Televised sports programs are presented in a predictable fashion using predictable plots and familiar characters. Then again, as Hilliard (1996) explains, "The athletic contest itself provides a basis for narrative." In other words, a sporting event is a story that unfolds before the viewer and the job of the commentator is to simply describe the events.
2. *Intimacy.* Televised sports programs provide viewers an opportunity to become closer to the sport participants. Intimacy "refers both to the visual closeness of the television viewer to the subject matter and to the development of an emotional attachment between actor and viewer. The development of audience identification with characters is a principal means by which viewers' attention to the narrative is maintained" (Hilliard 1996: 116).
3. *Commodification.* In an attempt to keep viewers tuned to televised commercials, television executives look for advertisers whose products fit the needs and interests

of the viewing audience. Today, a great number of televised commercials are elaborate and entertaining and more than keep the interests of viewers. In the case of the Super Bowl, millions of viewers tune in to the game *primarily* to watch the commercials! Furthermore, there is as much discussion in the media the Monday after the Super Bowl about the commercials as there is about the game itself.

4. *Rigid Time Segmentation.* It has often been said that soccer will never be a marketable success in the United States because it does not possess built-in stoppages of play that allow for the airing of commercials. In an attempt to remedy this, many televised soccer matches superimpose commercial brand logos on-screen. Most other sports events are organized into short, rigid blocks of time that allow for commercials during timeouts or stoppages of play. An obvious example of this is the "television timeout" after the first dead ball every four minutes (16:00, 12:00, 8:00, and 4:00 minute mark in each half) in college basketball. The "TV timeout" allows for a regular presentation of commercials. (More recently, the "TV timeout" has been described as a "media timeout." But let's be honest, do radio stations or newspapers have the power to stop the game for a commercial break?) It also stops the flow of the game and allows coaches to save timeouts for more critical times. And it provides TV commentators time to discuss the plays and compare them with past performances and other arcane bits of information.

Television is critical for the economic success that all those in sports enjoy. The revenue generated by television all but guarantees that major North American sport franchises operate at a profit. And despite the long, drawn out pregame hype that coincides with such sporting events as the Super Bowl, without television, these games would hardly be *events.* The very fact that the media, especially television, are responsible for creating events ties to the question in the introduction of this chapter: Without the media, is it really a sporting *event*?

Today, with the advent of cable and satellite television and streaming Internet broadcasts, nearly any game is accessible to sports fans. Television is responsible for creating billions of sports consumers around the world. The interactive design of streaming video broadcasts allows viewers to watch the game and comment about it in a shared forum with others. This enhances the experience for people who do not find joy in watching the game without outside interference and disruption. (Technological advancements in the mass media, including the social media, since the development of cable television will be discussed later in this chapter.)

FUNCTIONS OF THE SPORTS MEDIA

As with the media in general, the sports media serve a number of functions, including the following:

1. *Information.* The sports media provide scores, statistics, highlights, and general information on a variety of sporting events, athletes, and teams. Information on sports may also come in the form of interviews and live coverage.

2. *Interpretations.* Coverage of sporting events and the provision of information are accompanied by media interpretation, and possible biases. ESPN's Mel Kiper, Jr., makes a living providing his "NFL Draft Analysis"; which, of course, is based on his interpretation of potential draftees. Sport media "experts" offer opinions

on teams they think will make the playoffs (e.g., what teams are "on the bubble" and which ones will be selected as "at large" bids for the NCAA tournament?) or whether or not a particular athlete will break a record, or who will win a boxing match, auto race, and so on.

3. *Entertainment.* The sports media are all about entertainment. As mentioned earlier, the "E" comes before the "S" in ESPN, signifying the importance placed on entertainment. The wide variety of sporting events available all but guarantees that the sports media will find any number of sporting events worthy of coverage and description.

4. *Excitement.* People love sports because they find them exciting. The game or event itself is enough to draw fans' interest to sports. Stimulating arousal and excitement in fans helps the media serve an affective function.

5. *Escape and Diversion.* Sports provide people with an opportunity to "lose themselves" for a period of time while they immerse themselves in a sporting event. Ideally, sports allow people to temporarily escape from frustrations and life problems. Unfortunately, the highly identified fan may actually incur greater affective costs if the sporting event does not turn out favorably. Thus, if a person watches sport for an "escape" from problems and then his or her favorite athlete or team loses, it is like adding salt to an open wound.

6. *Economics.* The mass media have completely changed the design and financial makeup of the sports world. The economic aspect of the media in sport will be discussed later in this chapter both in terms of their positive and negative role.

7. *Integration.* Sports provide people with a chance to bond with fellow fans. This is true for the spectators in the stands who cheer for the same team as well as friends bonding together at home or at a bar while watching sports. Friends who watch historic sporting events together are linked together forever and think of each other whenever the game or key play is replayed. At the macro level, members of a nation can unite together while cheering for their national teams during international sporting events.

8. *National Identity.* International media sports coverage places a bright spotlight on the host city and nation. This is especially true for World Cup games, the Olympics and the Super Bowl. The fact that the whole world is watching is a source of pride and national identity [Beck and Bosshart 2003].

The link between the mass media and sport is firmly entrenched. In fact, they enjoy a symbiotic relationship where each social institution attempts to create the most marketable product possible. The sports media, especially television (and in particular specialty networks like ESPN that are dependent on sports for their 24-hour entertainment broadcasts) need sports in order to provide an endless supply of entertainment programming. As a result, these networks pay huge sums of money for the broadcast rights of various sports events. At the same time, the sports industry needs the mass media in order to keep functioning as an elite social institution, and one that handsomely rewards those involved with great finances. The mass media and sport institutions cooperate with one another but they are not dependent on each other. The media can survive without sports because people will always find something to watch on television, listen to on the radio, or read in the print media. Furthermore, sports have existed throughout recorded history, and there are enough athletes to play sports and fans who will follow sports whether the media covers them or not. The ancient Greeks managed to stage the Olympics and other Panhellenic games long before the existence of the mass media; surely modern sports can survive without the media. Still, never before in the history of humanity has sport received such a mass popularity, due primarily to the symbiotic relationship between sports and the media.

During the COVID-19 pandemic we were all reminded of the degree to which the sports media is dependent upon live sporting events. Starting in mid–March of 2020, sports channels suddenly and very unexpectedly found themselves without any live sporting events to broadcast or discuss. Networks like ESPN "still had news and archival content, but watching it without live events is bizarre" (Barton 2020: E1). For months, ESPN and other sports programming networks (i.e., CBS, Fox, NBC, and Turner) relied on airing games from the past and jumped on any bit of sports news they could find. ESPN turned to Korean baseball to fill the void of missing MLB games, as Korea handled the pandemic crisis better than the United States and decided to have baseball sans fans in the stands. In addition, the sports industry realized that without games, there were no broadcasts of games, which meant a loss of great revenue streams. Both the sports world and the mass media were reminded very clearly just how much they depended on their symbiotic relationship.

Pandemics aside, the merger between these two social institutions has created a number of both positive and negative outcomes.

The Media's Positive Impact on Sport

Although sports survived for millennia without media coverage, the structure of contemporary sport has benefited tremendously because of its relationship with the media. Perhaps the most significant aspect of the media's role in sport centers on economics.

Economics

A great deal of the economic success that commercialized sports enjoy is the result of the media and its commitment to sports entertainment programming. The sports media, especially television, pays humongous sums of money for the broadcasting rights of various commercial sports. Consider, for example, that through the 2022 season, the NFL was paid more than $5 billion a year from selling its broadcasting rights (Young 2019). In Chapter 12, we explained how this money helps players and owners to earn great incomes. With the scheduled completion of the next collective bargaining agreement in 2022 it is expected that the payout will be much higher. As of the end of the 2019 season, the three major NFL TV networks (CBS, Fox, and NBC) were at the tail-end of their nine year deals to air NFL's Sunday's games, earning $1 billion a year from CBS, $1.1 billion from Fox, and $950 million from NBC (Young 2019). ESPN has a separate contract that gives it the exclusive rights to air NFL's Monday night games that expires at the end of the 2021 season; the value of that deal is more than $1 billion per year. The NFL also gets $1.5 billion from AT&T's DirecTV to distribute its Sunday Ticket package (Young 2019). While the NFL, understandably, benefits the most from its economic relationship with the media, the other major sports leagues do quite well for themselves. The National Basketball Association makes roughly $2.6 billion annually off of its broadcasting rights from ESPN and Turner Sports; Major League Baseball gets about $1.5 billion under its current contract deals with ESPN, Turner, and Fox; and the PGA Tour was paid roughly $700 million per season split between CBS, NBC, and The Golf Channel (Young 2019). At the time of this writing it was too soon to tell what sort of compensation would be worked out between the major sports entities and the media due to the loss of games during the pandemic. However, as early as April 2020, it was projected that TV ad spending in the U.S. would decline by an estimated 22.3 percent—20.3 percent, or $10 billion to $12 billion during the first half of 2020 alone (James 2020).

Sport leagues and conferences as a whole benefit from the economic infusion by the media. Additionally, television and other media outlets are capable of making stars out of high profile sports journalists, reporters and announcers/broadcasters.

Social Events and Spectacles

The media have the power to transform a ball game into a social event or spectacle. When the media become involved in a sporting event a number of elements arise. "First, the media will hype the game in order to draw more attention and awareness to the event. Increased awareness leads to a greater number of viewers, which equals more advertising revenue and results in more profits. Second, by the very fact that the media have chosen to broadcast a particular game reveals the importance of it. Third, many people attend the game not only to support their team, but in hopes of being 'seen' on television. In other words, the game has now become a social event" (Delaney and Wilcox, 2002: 206). People will do almost anything to be on television. ESPN's Game Day (college football pregame show) crew attends sporting events and broadcasts hours before the start of that game, drawing huge crowds. In nearly all cases, those who show up want to be seen on television as much as they want to attend a media-staged pep rally hours before the start of the game. During a game, fans cheer wildly when the camera is turned in their direction. The game and the crowd combined are social events and spectacles when television coverage is involved.

During the early years of television, the coverage of sport was limited primarily to the "Big Four" professional sport leagues (NFL, MLB, NBA, and NHL), "big-time" college sports, and to a lesser degree, the more marketable individual sports (professional tennis, auto racing, and golf). Coverage of the Olympics is another big-time sporting spectacle. With the advent of cable and satellite television and the introduction of ESPN came the realization among television sports executives that sports coverage would have to extend to a variety of sports in order to fill in "blank" (times when few or no major sporting events occur) airing spots. During its infancy (and before it attained the rights to major sporting events) ESPN broadcast a wide variety of sports—including world championship Frisbee, badminton, table-tennis, and calf wrestling—from around the globe. Among the more popular nontraditional American sports covered by ESPN during its early history was Australian Rules Football. ESPN created cult followings during the late 1980s and early 1990s with its Aussie football coverage.

The exposure to a wide variety of sports is viewed as a positive function of the media because millions of people, especially youth (see Chapter 6), may be disenchanted with commercialized sport and yet still enjoy sports, leisure and recreation in general. Exposing the public to viable alternatives to commercialized sports may help stimulate youth, and adults, into participating in healthy sporting endeavors.

It also noteworthy to mention that sporting events can be special events beyond the game itself in a number of ways including: high schools and colleges often schedule class reunions and Homecoming or Alumni weekends based on a sporting event, especially a football game in the fall; people have proposed marriage at a ballgame, sometimes with stadium officials' cooperation so that the proposal is shown on the stadium's big screen (with the nerve-wracking possibility that the person asked might say no!); a number of people have used sporting events or venues as a place to hold wedding ceremonies; soldiers who make a surprise home visit and meet their unsuspecting family members, who are being honored under some sort of guise to maintain the surprise, at a sporting event; and so on.

Public Forum

The success of sports broadcasting is dependent upon two critical issues, the actual broadcasting of the sporting event and access to the athletes for insightful and exclusive comments. The mass media creates a public forum where athletes can discuss aspects of the game. For their part, sport leagues, including the NCAA, have rules that make it mandatory that athletes make themselves available to the media for post-game interviews. This intrusion into the athlete's inner world extends to the locker rooms where athletes shower and dress. "Potentially, all parties involved with sports benefit from this relationship. The media are given a product to sell; the sports fans are given 'inside' information about the events of the game; and the athletes are given an opportunity to present and review events from their perspective" (Delaney and Wilcox 2002: 207).

With the advent of social media platforms—web-based technology and applications that enable the flow of communication, photos, videos, and so forth—athletes, coaches, and others from the sports world can now create their own public forums and control the flow of information. Among the more popular current social media platforms are Twitter, Instagram, Facebook, Google+, and YouTube. This freedom adds to the challenge of traditional media in their attempt to create a narrative of a sporting event or sports story. There are a number of social networks for sports fans as well, including: SportsFanLive, Phanoto, FanCake, and Bantr.

Media Ethics

As with all social institutions (and people), the media is expected to adhere to ethical practices. *Ethics* generally refers to moral principles that govern a person's behavior or conduct while performing an activity (e.g., reporting on news stories). Morality involves a distinction between "right" and "wrong," a clarification that should seem straight-forward until we factor in the role of values and bias. Proper ethical behavior, then, involves some gray areas. When we discuss ethics in relation to the media there are many gray areas including: should the story be told; is the story being told fair; does the story violate privacy laws and considerations; and so on. Journalists and broadcasters in particular have an obligation to maintain ethical standards.

The topic of media ethics can fall under both "media's positive impact on sport" and "media's negative impact on sport." In the first two editions of this text we placed the discussion of media ethics in the "negative impact" discussion but that was unfair to the vast majority of media personnel who attempt to adhere to ethical reporting. The media serves a positive function when it maintains principles of ethical reporting and broadcasting. According to the Ethical Journalism Network (2020), there are five key principles of ethical journalism: truth and accuracy (e.g., getting the facts correct, providing all relevant facts, and seeking corroborative information); independence (maintaining an independent voice, a voice free from the interests of certain political, corporate, or cultural influences); fairness and impartiality (impartial reporting builds trust and confidence); humanity (journalists should do no harm, being aware of the impact of the words and images being conveyed to the audience); and accountability (if an error in reporting was made, it must be acknowledged).

A failure to uphold ethical standards can place the media in the category of a negative impact on sport. If a reporter finds something that will paint an athlete or sports organization in a negative light they should give the subject of the story a chance to tell their side of story. If an athlete, especially a young one who is inexperienced dealing with the media, says something dumb that they immediately regret the reporter should give the athlete a chance to revise their story and/or to immediately apologize.

ENTERTAINMENT

One of the primary functions of the sports media is to provide entertainment. Sports are commercialized, but most fans realize that commercials are a price worth paying when sports coverage is the return. Providing information, entertainment, and a temporary escape from the everyday life activity is perhaps the most enjoyable feature of the sports media. Despite any warranted criticisms of ESPN, sports fans are glad it exists. Originally funded by the Getty Oil Company through the use of 625 television cable systems and a satellite for transmission, ESPN initially reached just 20 percent of the nation's television viewers. Today, ESPN (along with its sister networks that include ESPN2, ESPN News, ESPN U, ESPN 360, ESPN Deportes, and so on) is available to most everyone in North America. ESPN inspired other networks to increase the quality of their sports broadcasting (i.e., Fox created Fox Sports 1, NFL Network, MLB Network, and the NASCAR Network). The growth of cable and satellite television has assisted the sports industry in their attempt to entertain us, the sport viewers. Many sports fans start their days with ESPN's SportsCenter so that they are up to date with all the latest sports news and entertainment.

When the sports industry resumed major sporting events during the COVID-19 pandemic sans fans in the stands, the sports media was there to try and enhance the entertainment experience by infusing computer-generated-imagery (CGI) during its broadcasts. Virtual spectators at MLB games were shown doing "the wave" and, to make it look more realistic, with a number of fans not standing at the right time. Many sporting events incorporated cardboard cutouts of fans to make it look like people were attending the game. Efforts such as these were done in the name of providing entertainment to enhance the viewing audience.

The Media's Negative Impact on Sport

Undoubtedly, the media have quite an influence on sports. The distinction between the media's positive role and negative role in sport is often a matter of perspective. For example, the Chicago Cubs used to play only day games at Wrigley Field. Major League Baseball and the Chicago Cubs organization realized that greater broadcast revenue could be generated with televised night games. In order to do this, lights were added to the ballpark. This modernization of one of professional baseball's oldest stadiums was not initially popular with most Cubs fans, who preferred the tradition of day games. Ultimately, the fans' voices were secondary and lights were added in an attempt to attract increased revenue via night time broadcasts of Cubs games (there are more people available to watch games at night than during the day when people work and children go to school). Was television's influence that led to lights being installed at Wrigley Field positive or negative? The answer lies with one's perspective. On the one hand, a long-standing tradition was destroyed; on the other hand more people had access to Cubs games both live and on-television.

Some examples of the media's negative role in sport are detailed in the following pages, bearing in mind that there is room for disagreement on these outcome evaluations.

ECONOMICS

As stated earlier in this chapter (and in Chapter 12), the media—primarily television—have positively impacted the economic fortune of athletes and team owners. The large sums of money provided by television to the sports industry led to, among other things, dramatically higher salaries for athletes in all commercial sports and greater profits for franchise owners. Although the yearly salaries of most athletes in commercial sports are usually higher than the lifetime income of average Americans, contemporary athletes continue to demand more money and greater "perks." Still, the owners will claim that they have a difficult time covering the operating expenses (e.g., player and personnel salaries and travel and maintenance costs) of a ball club. In order to cover their expenses, sports owners and event promoters have continued to raise ticket and concession prices. It has become increasingly difficult for families to afford the price of attending a ballgame, auto race, international sporting event, and so on. The Fan Cost Index (FCI) is used to measure how much it costs a family of four to attend a major sporting event in the U.S. The FCI factors: four tickets (calculated with average ticket prices for that venue); four small soft drinks; two small beers; two game programs; parking; and two adult-size caps (the least expensive).

In 2019, the FCI for MLB was $234.38 USD, with the Chicago Cubs the costliest venue at $370.12 per game and the Arizona Diamondbacks the cheapest FCI at $142.42 (Gough 2020d). The average ticket price for MLB is $33.00, but with the most home games per season at 81, MLB franchises make their profits via volume. As one might expect, and in contrast with MLB, the NFL has the highest average ticket price ($102.00) per game (8 regular season home games) and highest FCI ($540.52) (Gough 2020e; Shaikin 2019). The costliest venue in the NFL (based on FCI) in 2019 was the Los Angeles Chargers ($830.56) and the least expensive FCI venue in the NFL in 2019 was the Cincinnati Bengals ($403.20) (Gough 2020e). As for the other major American sports leagues, the NHL has an average ticket price of $76.00 and a FCI of $425.00; the NBA has an average ticket price of $74.0 and FCI at $421.00; and Major League Soccer (MLS), an average ticket price of $34.00 and FCI at $250.00 (Shaikin 2019). To put these numbers in perspective, consider that the median income for a family of four in Los Angeles County was $78,672.00 (in 2019); after accounting for the costs of housing, child care, health care, food, transportation, and taxes, that family would be left with $3,413.00 in discretionary income for the year, $284.00 per month (Shaikin 2019). If this family of four attends a ballgame of the five major team sports, their discretionary income disappears in one big chunk.

INFLUENCE OVER SCHEDULING AND RULE CHANGES

Television has great influence over the sports industry when it comes to scheduling games and with start times. The actual date of a game may be moved to accommodate television. This is especially true for high profile games and events and especially the playoffs (and tournaments). "The start time of games are nearly always scheduled in an attempt to maximize viewership. This is most evident during playoffs, where networks worry about broadcasting a night game during the week. If the game starts too late in the Eastern time zone, viewers may turn off the game before the end because it is so late. But, if the game starts too early in the Pacific time zone, potential viewers are still at work, or driving home from work" (Delaney and Wilcox 2002: 209). Scheduling start times to accommodate television broadcasts is often upsetting to coaches and players as well as viewers and spectators.

Television has also played a role in a variety of rule changes in sports. The television timeout in televised sports events (especially in basketball and football) is especially frustrating to spectators and viewers, and sometimes to the athletes and coaches as well (e.g., when the television timeout stops a team's momentum). The television timeout is designed to provide structured stoppages in play in order to broadcast commercials—which is the source of revenue for television. A number of rule changes in sports have been influenced by television in an effort to provide more action. Television executives realize that American viewers want to watch sporting events with action that leads to scoring. Over the past few decades a number of rules changes have been enacted to increase offense (action). Three examples from baseball include lowering the pitcher's mound, which takes away a certain amount of the "edge" that the pitcher has (the higher the hill, the greater the edge the pitcher has), moving the outfield fences closer to home plate, and decreasing the foul ball territory (and replacing it with high-priced luxury seats). The enactment of the 3-point shot rule dramatically changed the game of basketball. Teams that find success from "behind the line" can reduce a deficiency or build a big lead quickly. The 3-point shot was first introduced in college basketball in the 1980–81 season. It was introduced in the NBA on a trial basis a season earlier. The American Basketball Association already had the 3-point shot, which spearheaded the NBA's interest in this exciting rules change.

CONTROLLED PRODUCTION

The media provide information to listeners and viewers. This information is filtered through a restricted presentation of descriptions of events. The presentation of televised sports involves a highly structured and controlled production. Because of the complexity involved with producing a sports event, it is important to control as many variables as possible. The production staff generally includes a "hierarchical division of labor, typically between the producer, the director, commentators, camera operatives, vision and sound mixers, and technicians. Each individual has clearly defined responsibilities, which they are expected to fulfill despite any deficiencies in equipment [and] Each is employed in a particular role according to skills and previous experience, although flexibility is also a desired quality. The pressures involved are not just of time but also of uncertainty, in that producers have to react to unpredictable occurrences both within the event and external to it" (Brookes 2002: 22). Thus, the game itself may be unscripted, but the production of the sporting event is as organized as possible. Ideally, the production of the televised sporting event meets the expectations of the viewers.

In most cases, the viewers are relatively happy with the production of televised sporting events. Viewers want and expect accurate information and descriptions of events. There are times when television (and radio) announcers flat-out miss calls (e.g., use the wrong name of an athlete, fail to see a penalty that was clear to viewers), announcers think and act as if *they* are as important as the sporting event, television breaks away to commercials too quickly (action is missed) or return from commercials too late (action is missed). Any die-hard fan can attest to the numerous mistakes of media personnel during the production of any given game. This is because many viewers are actually more knowledgeable about sports (or a particular sport or game) than those announcing it. The media provides much of what fans expect and desire. However, they do so in a very controlled context. This is especially true in sports highlights shows (e.g., ESPN's *SportsCenter*). The mass sports media discuss the topics that *they* want to discuss. The notion of a controlled context holds true for social media platforms too as they control the narrative and the highlights that will be accessible to viewers.

The controlled aspect of production allows media outlets an opportunity to shape people's perception of events. As the leader in sports entertainment broadcasting, ESPN has great influence sport consumers. Its attempt to dominate the sports market includes the controlled production of an award show known as *The ESPYs* (Excellence in Sports Performance Yearly Awards). *The ESPYs* is an awards show created and produced by ESPN wherein media stars (mostly movie and television entertainers) present various awards to athletes. Fans are allowed to vote for specific plays (chosen by ESPN) in each category and the winners are announced at the annual ESPYs show. This light-hearted production is a clear example of the marriage between the mass media and athletics.

LOSS OF HEROES

Heroes have most likely existed throughout history. One becomes aware of heroic deeds through two primary means: first-hand observation of heroic deeds and through some form of communication. Before written languages were created, stories of heroes were passed down from one generation to the next (and undoubtedly they were embellished every step of the way). With written language, tales of heroic deeds were expressed in poems and short stories. Over time, technology improved and expanded upon these early versions of communication, leading to the creation of a mass media that included newspapers and eventually, radio, motion pictures, television, satellite, and the Internet. All of these media outlets have helped to establish hero status for certain individuals. However, as quick as the media often is to bestow hero status to some athletes, the media is just as quick to reveal stories of an athlete who has fallen short of heroic behavior, thus knocking him or her off the hero pedestal.

Throughout most of the history between sports and the media, journalists and others involved in the media kept the private lives of athletes out of their commentary, which in turn kept the hero myth alive for many athletes who did not lead ideal lives. For example, most people did not know that during Mickey Mantle's entire baseball career he had a drinking problem. This was not revealed until years after his career ended and Mantle admitted that he could have been an even greater player if he had taken better care of his body. Today, the private lives of many athletes have become overly public. As a result, fans know too much about their sports heroes (and athletes in general). Furthermore, in this era of social media, many athletes themselves expose their own "dirty laundry" via Twitter or Facebook posts. If a public outcry ensues due to the content of the post/tweet, the athlete will delete the comment from their account, issue an apology and move on. The problem remains after the post is deleted, however, as fans remember the athlete's damaging or crude comments and begin to feel less admiration, which is a contributing factor in the demise of a once heroic figure. (See Chapter 4 for a more in-depth discussion on heroes.)

In short, the media are capable of placing someone on a hero pedestal and equally capable of knocking someone off it. To their credit, however, the media generally provide an athlete an opportunity (public forum) to tell his or her side of the story or a chance to publicly apologize, and therefore provide the avenue for "fallen" athletes to regain their positive image. The fact remains, though, that the media are partly responsible for the decreasing number of sports heroes found in contemporary society.

The Media's Portrayal of Gender

The topic of gender and sport was discussed in Chapter 10; among other things we pointed out how women do not receive equal pay in comparison with their male counterparts. With regard to media portrayal, women in sports were mostly downplayed, or ignored completely. Very successful teams (i.e., the women's soccer team) could not be ignored but the media coverage was small compared to men's teams. The media's portrayal of women in sport also involved the "sex sells" concept; although this type of production still exists to some degree, it is disappearing.

One final point worth making has to do with the amount of media coverage given to women's sports compared to men's sports. It is clear to anyone who follows sports that far more attention is given to men's sports than women's sports. But is this difference a matter of a preference toward men's sports, or a media bias? For the time being, at least, it seems that more men *and* women prefer to watch men's sporting events. And while the total coverage of women's sports is less than compared to men, the amount of coverage has certainly increased in the past generation.

Sport Journalism and Broadcasting

As described at the beginning of this chapter, freedom of the press in the United States is guaranteed by the Constitution and this is because the media serves a critical function in any democracy. To go against the press is to go against democracy. The importance of investigative journalism cannot be overstated as journalists are the ones who are paid to investigate corruption and other newsworthy stories. "Often, investigative newspersons write such good stories that the unethical, immoral, and illegal activities of corrupt persons are revealed and consequences follow" (Delaney 2021: 48–49). These consequences may include attempts to distract or discredit the report with false claims of "fake news," attacks on journalists, journalists being incarcerated, and the deterioration of democracy itself (Delaney 2021).

Sports Journalism

On the surface, it may seem that the work of sports journalists pales in comparison to the reporting of journalists around the world attempting to shine the light on the darkness of humanity and the deterioration of democracy, human rights, and rational thought and in many cases, that would be correct. However, as we have explained, billions of people around the world love sports and they want information and news stories. Furthermore, as a microcosm of society, the evils (e.g., racism, sexism, elitism, corruption) of the world spill over into the sports world and therefore become worthy of serious journalism. In this regard, sports journalists and broadcasters are relatively influential people in shaping public opinion on a variety of sports-related topics.

Journalists provide information to an audience. Sports journalists, of course, focus on elements related to the institution of sport. As the popularity of sports grew from the beginning of the twentieth through nearly the entire century, a number of people were employed as sports journalists. It was common for sports coverage to account for nearly 20 to 25 percent of the content of major newspapers in most cities. As a result, sports journalists have experienced a certain level of prestige within the newspaper business, as sports coverage represents the largest specialization within most newspapers. The sports department of a typical daily newspaper often consisted of a separate editor, desk editor, sub-editors, and reporters. We talk in the past tense because the last couple of decades of the twentieth century and especially now, the twenty-first century, played witness to a diminishing role for sports journalists in traditional newspapers. A number of top columnists and reporters embraced the trend for instantaneous broadcast of information the moment it happens to the public via the electronic forms of media. These journalists may still have a job writing columns in newspapers but they also have Twitter accounts and their own blogs, or they work for sports networks like ESPN to give "expert" opinion on sporting matters. No longer do top journalists have to wait until the next morning to get their story out nor do they have to worry about being edited (at least not to the say degree as in the past).

There are many similarities between news and sports journalists. For example, just as news journalists, sports journalists generally have a degree in journalism. As news journalists, sports journalists provide information; specifically, on sporting events and stories of relevance to either athletes, sports teams, or the institution of sport in general. As with other news reporters, sports journalists are trained to be and expected to be objective and neutral in their reporting. Sports journalists, like news journalists, generally write stories of relative importance; however, with major news events such as the "Black Lives Matter" and "#MeToo" social movements spilling over into the sports world, there are a number of sports journalists writing stories of great social importance. Sports journalists who write serious, newsworthy stories are utilizing the "hard" news approach to journalism. The hard news style is more factual and objective in content. It reflects the serious nature of sports journalism. In hard news articles, journalists often seek out "experts" in the field to provide quotes for their articles. This helps to bring legitimacy to their reports. It also makes it "hard" news. In contrast, there are journalists, both in sports and out of sports, who prefer to cover "soft" news. Soft news journalists discuss gossip and scandals. Scandals of any kind are often covered by journalists. Sports scandals follow this pattern. The soft news approach also involves journalistic coverage of local sporting events, such as high school ball games. These sport journalists are dealing with the profane, everyday world of sports where the coverage is expected to be "light" and noncontroversial. These sport journalists generally enjoy a regular audience, but such an audience is localized. The sport journalist who covers the everyday sporting events serves an important function for smaller newspapers that rely on hometown coverage of sporting events, perhaps including a slant in storytelling that favors the home team.

Sports Broadcasting

Sports broadcasting is a specialized version of broadcasting wherein persons with great sports knowledge, and generally a degree in broadcasting, describe sporting events to an audience that may number in the tens of millions. A sports broadcaster is someone who provides coverage of a sporting event using a variety of different media outlets, including radio, television, and social media. Some sports broadcasters concentrate on one particular sport, doing commentary, while others will lend their broadcasting skills to a variety of sports. The best-known and most recognized occupation within the sports broadcasting field is that of game announcer or commentator. Generally, a sports announcer and commentator will work as pairs during the broadcast consisting of the play-by-play announcer and the color commentator. The play-by-play announcer describes the play and explains to the viewers what is happening while the game or event is in action; the color commentator chimes in when there is a break in the action sharing personal knowledge and game experiences (Career Explorer 2020). This is why the color commentator is generally a former athlete (who is in a position to offer expert analysis) and the announcer has a degree in broadcasting (who is in a position to maintain a professional broadcast).

The mass audience of sports fans and consumers affords opportunities for a number of sport broadcasters to become stars in their own right. In this regard, sports broadcasters may attain celebrity status by virtue of their occupation. ESPN sports anchors (as well as those on other major sports networks) in particular reach the homes of millions of viewers. The celebrity status enjoyed by the top sports journalists and broadcasters is often both exciting and filled with "perks."

Sports broadcasters often serve as icons for fans. The "voice" of a particular team is heard repeatedly by fans. Many fans listen to that same "voice" for years, even decades. Among the "old-school" broadcasters who enjoyed iconic status were Red Barber, Mel Allen, Curt Gowdy, Francis Dayle, "Chick" Hearn, and Vin Scully. Present-day broadcasters that enjoy great fame include Dick Vitale, Al Michaels, Mike Tirico, and Joe Buck. Former NFL coach turned sports broadcaster John Madden enjoys such an iconic status that his name is used to sell the official annual NFL video game that is a hit with youth today.

Sports broadcasters and journalists are such a big part of sport that they are eligible for various sports halls of fame. For many fans, broadcasters and journalists bring to life sporting events they have not seen and recreate images of games and events they have seen. There is no doubt that the media will continue to have a strong role in sports.

Technology and Social Media

As described throughout this chapter, the primary role of the media is to provide information. Sports fans love, crave and enjoy sports information, especially about their favorite athletes and teams, and they also want the latest statistics and up-to-date scores of a variety of sporting events. It seems as though as the level of technology increases so too does our desire for sports information. Thus, when fans once had to rely on newspapers and radio and later basic television coverage, they made do with what they had. Then came cable television and satellite TV, and sports information outlets grew and so too did our desire to consume it. The introduction of electronic technology, or social media, fueled our thirst for instantaneous information. Live streaming put sports information and video in the palm of our hands. Is it any wonder we are becoming a nation of sports junkies with an ever-increasing desire for instantaneous gratification?

TECHNOLOGY

Technology exerts a great deal of influence in nearly all spheres of life. Technological advancements in the mass media and communications have had a tremendous influence in the sports world. Sports fans who want inside information about athletes do not have to turn to sports highlight shows—which should focus on highlights instead of insipid stories of athletes—as many athletes have their own personal Web sites or blogs and readily share personal thoughts via social media platforms such as Twitter. Personal social media outlets provide athletes with a forum where they can control the production and presentation of their lives. Sports fans may also set up social network sites or blogs on their favorite (or most despised) athletes and teams. Blogs are similar to personal journals or diaries but they are posted online for others to read. All major sport teams have official Web sites where fans can visit and learn about the team, specific athletes, the organization, upcoming events, news stories, and so on.

The primary concern of sports fans is receiving information on games and sporting events. To this end, technology of the early twenty-first century has revolutionized sports coverage much as television had decades ago. Sports fans not only enjoy the opportunity to view numerous sporting events every day of week thanks to cable television and satellite coverage, but they also now have live sports streaming. If there is a game broadcast anywhere in the world, a satellite can beam the broadcast in an instant around the globe. One merely needs to possess the proper technology to receive such broadcasts. Satellite television is popular in many parts of the world, including Europe. Not only has the quantity of sporting events available to consumers increased, thanks to digital technology the quality of the broadcasts has also improved tremendously.

Cable and satellite TV coverage of sport represents the mere beginning of the technological advancements that have led to the proliferation of sports programming and consumer availability. Advances in computer technology have led to dramatic memory increases and high-speed data transfer rates. This technology combined with satellite technology makes it inevitable that unlimited sports broadcast programming will be available online. Right now, fans can visit official Web sites of major sports leagues and gain access to a wide variety of sports information, statistics, and play by play of accounts of games in progress. Most sites have audio links as well. Generally speaking, official Web sites are relatively sophisticated. At MLB.com, for example, a baseball diamond is presented graphically. It shows the location of any base runners and "locates" the defensive players on field. Statistics are provided for the batter's history against the pitcher, as well as the pitcher's history against the batter, and so on. In short, there is no shortage of sports information available online. International travelers are especially happy with the information available online because they can find sports information and ball game results wherever they are.

Undoubtedly, technology in this area will continue to advance at a rapid pace. The broadcast media will continue to find new ways to entertain sports viewers. There will be more cameras used in sports broadcasts than viewers can possibly imagine. There are already cameras nearly everywhere, including helmet cam, goalie cam, cameras in the floors at NBA games, overhead cameras at football games, cameras inside race cars, and so on.

Technology will be infused in sport in a variety of ways. For example, the authors predict that inevitably, tiny transmitters will be incorporated inside hockey pucks and digital lines will be installed over the goal line in an attempt to reach undisputable evidence of whether a goal was scored. The NFL could also utilize this technology by installing a transmitter inside a football and digital devices used at yard makers in order to determine such things as first downs and whether or not the ball crosses the end zone. At this pace, technology will continue to play a significant role in presenting and shaping sporting events.

The key development in sports media development is interactive, computer-based applications that allow sports fans to share ideas and information with digital and print elements. Advancements in graphics will work side-by-side with continued improvements in electronic devices (e.g., cell phones, tablets, I-pads, and so forth) that are increasingly improving because of technological advancements, making it easier for video chats and streaming videos. These developments will lead to employment opportunities in such areas as graphic artist, digital photographer, instructional designer, production assistant, and desktop publisher (Learn.org 2020).

Social Media

As we described in the beginning of the chapter, social media has increased its presence in the sports world tremendously. This development mirrors the overall trend of most people in the twenty-first century spending a great deal of time communicating with one another virtually. We turn to the electronic world for a great deal of news, entertainment, and sports content. Social media, then, refers to cyber-communication and the countless array of "internet based tools and platforms that increase and enhance the sharing of information. This new form of media makes the transfer of text, photos, audio, video and information in general increasingly fluid among internet users" (*Social Media Defined* 2014). People use social media for business and pleasure via such platforms as Twitter, Instagram, Facebook, YouTube, LinkedIn, and so on, all with the inevitable conclusion of forming virtual worlds of reality.

Sports are a part of all forms of social media. We can text each other sports information, we can stream ball games online on computers or smartphones, we can post sports-related photos on Facebook, and tweet sports-related messages on Twitter, and we use our cellphones to show our electronic game tickets to gain entry to sports venues. Athletes and sports teams themselves also use social media in an attempt to control select messages to the public. Sometimes people act too hasty and post things they wished they hadn't and even when they delete it the content still exists in the cyberworld. Often, people will take screen shots of posts or repost tweets which helps to keep the content available even after it is deleted by the person who made the original post. Social media outlets like Facebook and Twitter help to identify sports trends. This identification process is accomplished when a site suddenly sees a huge spike in common-themed posts or tweets. Thus, when something huge occurs in the sports world and people immediately use social media to talk about it and then others follow suit, we have a "trending" phenomenon.

We conclude this chapter with one more story of the increasing relevance of social media and sports and that is, when one attends a sporting event, especially a televised event, one must always be ready to be caught by the camera and put on air and risk being turned into a meme. And the circumstances may not be of our choosing. Some readers may recall the 1993 *Seinfeld* episode ("The Lip Reader") in which George Costanza was caught on air eating an ice cream sundae and making a mess of himself. The on-air announcers mocked George and said things like, "hey buddy, they have a new invention, it's called a napkin." The camera stayed on George for a full eight seconds, which is quite a while and plenty of time for people viewing the tennis match to see George. So ashamed was George's girlfriend that she broke up with him! Something like this could not happen in real life, could it? Well, of course it can. One much-discussed incident from years ago involved a man shown sleeping at an April 13, 2014, baseball game between the host New York Yankees and the visiting Boston Red Sox. An ESPN camera found the sleeping Yankees fan and the announcers mocked him unmercifully. The scene was similar to the *Seinfeld* episode in that the reaction of those viewing the unsuspecting man caught on camera involved laughingly mocking the spectator. In the case of Andrew Robert Rector, the Yankees fan who admitted in court documents that he "napped" during the game, he filed a $10 million lawsuit against ESPN New York, Major League Baseball Advanced Media and the Yankees for defamation and intentional infliction of emotional distress, contending he was mocked on air which resulted in "substantial injury" to his "character and reputation" and "mental anguish, loss of future income and loss of earning capacity" (ESPN.com 2014h). The defamation lawsuit was dismissed shortly afterwards (Salinger 2015). The lesson should be clear to all of us: be careful what you say and do at all times (and always have a napkin handy!) or risk being turned into a meme that may live on forever in the cyberworld.

Connecting Sports and Popular Culture

Box 15: Athletes and Social Media Presence

As of the first quarter 2020, there were over 2.6 billion monthly active users on Facebook, making it the biggest social network worldwide. There were almost 3 billion people using at least one of the company's core products (Facebook, WhatsApp, Instagram, or Messenger) each month (Clement 2020a). There are over one billion people that use Instagram every month; half of these people use Instagram Stories every day; and 63 percent of users log in at least once per day (Newberry 2019). Another popular social media platform is Twitter. As of the first quarter of 2019, Twitter averaged 330 million active users (Clement 2019). The primary thing all these social media sites have in common is the ability of users to reach a potentially large audience by amassing followers. Sites such as Facebook, Instagram, and Twitter allow users to post messages and upload photos or short videos.

Understandably, the world's top athletes enjoy their presence on social media as they can initiate the narrative of any story of their choosing. Athletes can connect with their fans easily by sending brief messages at an instant and like all other social media users; they can upload photos and short videos in an attempt to enhance their stories. Unlike most of the billions of social media users, however, top athletes have up to hundreds of millions of followers. It's not just the social aspects of social media that attracts athletes to platforms such as Facebook, Instagram and Twitter; it is the business aspects afforded to them as well. "Most professional sportspeople have advertising and sponsorship contracts and social media provides them with an outlet to promote their preferred brands even further" (Clement 2020c). Thus, social media platforms represent big business to athletes. Consider that, "in June 2019, the average media value of an Instagram post by Cristiano Ronaldo was 861,304 U.S. dollars. In second place was Neymar, whose posts were worth half a million dollars" (Clement 2020c). The attractive visual nature of the Instagram platform is particularly beneficial for channeling brands and for marketers to promote their products (Clement 2020c).

When it comes to followers, the athletes with the largest numbers come from the world's most popular sport. The top two athletes on Facebook, as of June 2020, were Cristiano Ronaldo (122.28 million) and Leo Messi (90.16 million) (Clement 2020b). Ronaldo and Messi were also the two most-followed athletes on Instagram as well, with Ronaldo with over 197 million followers and Messi with over 140 million followers (Clement 2020c). When the three major social media platforms (Facebook, Instagram and Twitter) are combined 63 of the top 100-most-followed athletes in 2019 were soccer players; 21 of the 30 fastest-growing athletes on social media were also soccer players. The leading American on the list of most popular athletes is LeBron James. "Led by James, current and retired NBA players were tied with cricket as the second-most represented sport behind soccer, claiming 11 of the top 100 most-followed athletes" (Weber 2020). The top ten athletes in total followers of the three major social media platforms in 2019 are: Ronaldo (399.6 million followers); Neymar (236 million); Lionel Messi (230.1 million); LeBron James (121.8 million); Virat Kohli (117 million); David Beckham (112 million); Ronaldinho (103.8 million); James Rodriguez (95.3 million); Gareth Bale (89.2 million); and Andres Iniesta (83.8 million) (Weber 2020).

The numbers of followers top athletes enjoy on social media platforms is staggering and, clearly, they represent a presence that traditional media cannot match.

SUMMARY

The institution of the media plays a vital role in democracy and in the United States, the freedom of the press is guaranteed by the Constitution. Providing news, information, and entertainment are the trademarks of the contemporary mass media. Currently, we divide the media into two other categories: traditional media (e.g., print media such as newspapers, magazines, and books; terrestrial radio; television; and, motion pictures, sound recordings, and billboards) and social media (e.g., Internet-based and computer-mediated technologies that facilitate the exchange of news, information, ideas, entertainment, and other forms of expression via virtual and web-based communities and networks such as Twitter, Facebook, Instagram, and YouTube). Both forms of media play a role in sport.

The link between the mass media and sport is firmly entrenched. They enjoy a symbiotic relationship where each social institution attempts to create the most marketable product possible. Presently, sports and the mass media are loyal partners. The merger between these two social institutions has created a number of both positive and negative outcomes.

Sports journalism and broadcasting both play vital roles in the presentation of sports to an audience eager to consume it. Sports journalists, like news journalists, generally write stories of relative importance; however, with major news events such as the "Black Lives Matter" and "#MeToo" social movements spilling over into the sports world, there are a number of sports journalists writing stories of great social importance. Sports broadcasting is a specialized version of broadcasting wherein persons of great sports knowledge, and generally having a degree in broadcasting, describe sporting events to an audience that may number in the tens of millions.

Athletes utilize social media in attempt to control the narrative of events, to connect with their fans instantly, and for business purposes as well. In 2019, seven athletes had more than 100 million followers on the three major social media platforms with Ronaldo (399.6 million) leading the way.

KEY TERMS

Cigarette Cards Believed to have originated in France around the 1840s, these were cardboard stiffeners used as promotion.

Freedom of the Press A right guaranteed by the U.S. Constitution to those in the American media.

Mass Media The medium by which large numbers of people are informed about important happenings in society.

Narrative The matter in which a news story is told, sometimes by the participants themselves and other times by those in the media.

Print Media Part of the traditional media which includes newspapers, magazines, and books.

Social Media Internet–based and computer-mediated technologies that facilitate the exchange of news, information, ideas, entertainment, and other forms of expression via virtual and web-based communities and networks (i.e., Facebook, Instagram, and Twitter).

Social Media Platforms Web-based technology and applications that enable the flow of communications informally with others.

Sports Journalists Those who provide sports information to an audience via reporting.

Streaming A technological advancement in sport broadcasting that allows sports fans to watch sporting events via social media platforms.

Traditional Media Aspects of the media that include the print media, terrestrial radio, and television.

Trending A process that occurs when a social media site suddenly sees a huge spike in common-themed posts or tweets.

DISCUSSION QUESTIONS

- Why does ESPN place the letter "E" (for "entertainment") prior to the letter "S" (for "sports") in its network name? Do you think this is significant?
- Explain the importance of the "freedom of the press" in a democratic society.
- Why is the connection between sports and the mass media called a "symbiotic" one? What are some of the positive and some of the negative aspects of this interconnection, in your view?
- Identify five positive impacts of the media on sports. Describe five negative impacts of the media on sports.
- How can sports journalists and broadcasters potentially affect the way fans view sports?
- Why are athletes so popular on social media sites? Describe how athletes benefit from the use of social media platforms.

Chapter 16

Sportsmanship and
Why We Love Sports

Writing a textbook on the sociology of sport is a bit like being a patriot; that is to say, while we have acknowledged the fact that the institution of sport is far from perfect and have pointed out its major flaws, the authors do, in fact, love sports. To be a patriot, in the political sense (see Chapter 13 for a distinction between the concepts of "patriot" and "nationalist"), is to love one's country enough to point out its flaws and yet still show a desire to want to correct things to make it better all the while stilling loving it. To think that any nation, like any social institution, is without flaws is to be naive, ignorant, or delusionally arrogant. In the same manner, it would be impossible to speak of the institution of sport and not point out its blemishes or to think it is a perfect social institution (as a nationalist would do when reflecting upon their nation). Still, we fully understand why billions of people around the globe love sports as its redeeming qualities far exceed its negative ones. The fact that sports are interconnected with every major social institution found in society combined with the realization that sports exist around the world and throughout history is a testament to its staying power. Furthermore, sports give meaning and excitement to the lives of billions of people so how can anyone deny its role in society?

Nearly all fans enjoy sports because at its simplest, sports involve physical activity and games. If you think of your favorite sport, you can likely recall playing it with your friends during your youth, a time when things likely seemed simpler than adulthood. For example, organized football is so complicated and regulated but the game of football itself is fun. There's something about running on the field, playing catch, and trying to score a touchdown that seems to have a bit of poetry in motion to it. Watching big-time college or professional football is not the same thing but while we watch such games we can still recall what it is like to just play the game. Think of your own favorite sport and recall why you love it so much. Does it bring a smile to your face?

In this final chapter, we will take a look at some of the other reasons why we love sports and conclude by emphasizing the importance of sportsmanship.

Fantasy Sports

Fans who love sports enjoy watching the competition that games and sporting events provide. They love to follow their favorite athletes and teams. However, for a large number of people, real sports do not provide the same level of excitement as it does for

428

fans of sports; instead, they prefer make-believe sporting events also known as "fantasy sports." In this era of virtual and cyber reality it should not be surprising to realize that many people enjoy, or even prefer, fantasy sports over real sports. Fantasy sports are mock sports but treated as quasi-real by those who participate in them. Enjoyed by men and women, young and old, fantasy sports participants have formed a wide variety of fantasy sports leagues. According to the Fantasy Sports & Gaming Association (FSGA) (2020), there are more than 60 million fantasy sports players in the United States and Canada. Of these participants, 80 percent play fantasy football.

With fantasy sports, participants are afforded an opportunity to act as an "owner" or general manager of a fantasy sports franchise and "draft" players via a mock draft for their teams. The make-believe fantasy sports teams compete against other fantasy teams via real-life statistics of the players. Thus, if someone is involved in a fantasy NFL sports league, they "draft" real-life players from all the NFL team rosters forming their own make-shift team. Other players in the league do the same thing. The statistics generated by players on a week-to-week basis are entered into a program that allows for a point system (based on the achievements of the real-life players' performances) in order to determine weekly and seasonal winners and losers. When drafting players and while the league is in session, it is helpful to have an understanding of statistics, the rules of the game, up-to-date knowledge of real-life player injuries, and how players match-up against certain teams. A lack of knowledge of players' statistics will likely be a determent to success in the fantasy world. That there are "losers" in a fantasy world is of itself sociologically and philosophically intriguing; after all, the idea of escaping to a fantasy world has historically been equated to a utopian world where all of one's whims and desires are met. Such is not the case with fantasy sports. How sad it is that one can be a loser in one's own fantasy? Nonetheless, millions of fantasy sports participants enjoy the remote social interactions they have with others.

Fantasy sports have been around for several generations and have evolved from their humble 1960 beginnings "when then Harvard sociologist William Gamson started the 'Baseball Seminar' where he and his colleagues would form rosters that earned points based on players' final statistics, such as their batting average, runs batted in, earned run average, and wins" (Delaney 2012: 95). Each participant paid an entry fee and a winner was declared at the conclusion of the fantasy league. Today, with the help of cyber-technology, fantasy sports leagues are far more advanced and extremely popular. In addition, nearly every kind of sport is available as a fantasy sport league. Many leagues allow people to play game-by-game or week-to-week rather than an entire season. In addition, the overall popularity of fantasy sports also has an impact in the real world presentation of sporting events, as the traditional media (i.e., ESPN) often provide data specifically for fantasy aficionados. They give statistical analysis of players for fantasy sports leagues and have programming designed to help participants to choose what players to play on a given day.

Fantasy sports are increasing in popularity as they provide entertainment for tens of millions of participants and, consequently, it's a reason why people love sports.

Video Gaming

Video gaming represents an aspect of the sports and recreation world that is enjoyed by billions of people globally. With its roots dating back to the arcade game phenomenon of the 1960s and the introduction of the first personal computers and home gaming consoles in the 1970s, video gaming has long been a staple activity both domestically and globally. The once upon time stereotypical profile of a gamer as a male teen slacker has been transformed to that of an older, nearly equal male and female gender demographic. Data provided by Statista reveals the age breakdown of video game players in the United States in 2020: Under 18 years, 21 percent; 18 to 34 years, 38 percent; 34 to 54, 26 percent; 55 to 64 years, 9 percent; and those 65 and older, 6 percent (Gough 2020g). Those in the 45 to 54 age category spend the least amount of time video gaming. Americans aged 15 to 19 spend 49 minutes on gaming or leisurely computer use during an average weekday, and more than 90 minutes doing so during weekends or holidays. Some 11.6 percent of gamers in the U.S. admitted to playing video games for more than 20 hours a week, while another 11.4 percent claim to spend between 12 and 20 hours a week gaming. In 2019, 46 percent of American gamers were female (Gough 2020g).

It is estimated that there were roughly 160 million American adults and 2.7 billion gamers across the globe in 2020 with the Asia Pacific region as the largest region. In South Korea, video gaming is an obsession and considered by some health officials as a dangerous addiction. "Video games are practically the national pastime, played by the majority of adults and more than 90 percent of adolescents. Rising concerns over the effects of games on mental health have been met with skepticism and disdain by the $13-billion gaming industry" (Kim 2019: A1, A6). The debate over the possible adverse effects of gaming on mental health intensified when the World Health Organization officially added "internet gaming disorder" to the 2022 edition of its *International Classification of Diseases*, which sets global standards for diagnosis (Kim 2019: A6). The American Psychiatric Association's *Diagnostic and Statistical Manual of Mental Disorders (DSM-5)* also recognizes addiction to gaming as a mental disorder (American Psychiatric Association 2020).

Video Gaming and eSports

Video gaming has been a part of the sports world for decades as there are many sports-related video games available to gamers. Every major sport has its own version of video games; so too, do the extreme sports. According to Ranker.com (2020), the most popular sports video games in 2020 were: FIFA 18; NBA 2K20; NBA 2K18; Wii Sports; Madden NFL 20; FIFA 19; Rocket League; Madden NFL 18; Wii Sports Resort; and MLB The Show 18. As the level of technology involved in video gaming is rapidly increasing it is likely that the video games mentioned here have been updated or replaced by new popular video games. The development of technology in video gaming results in highly vivid graphics and a greatly enhanced gaming experience that makes the experience of playing become more realistic.

The relationship between video gaming and sports is most evident with eSports—a general term used to describe video game competitions. The number of global eSports enthusiasts was estimated at 173 million in 2018, with an even larger number of occasional viewers who tune in to watch the bigger events. It is estimated that there will be nearly 650 million eSports followers by 2022 (Gough 2020h). The popularity of eSports has turned many players into celebrities who can earn large sums of money playing in tournaments and via lucrative sponsorship deals. "According to estimates, Johan Sundstein, a player from Denmark, also known as NOtail, earned 6.89 million U.S. dollars throughout his recorded eSports gaming career" (Gough 2020h). It is estimated that worldwide revenues generated in the eSports industry amount to 865 million USD in 2018 and that the market is expected to generate almost 1.8 billion USD by 2020 (Gough 2020h).

The most popularly played game among high schoolers is *Fortnite*. College students enjoy *Fortnite, League of Legends (LoL)* and *Overwatch* (Heilweil 2019; Bomba 2020). Both *LoL* and *Overwatch* have official college leagues sanctioned by the videogamers' publishers. Among college students, 51 percent think being an eSports gamer is a viable career option (Heilweil 2019). This belief is reinforced by a couple of key criteria, the number of viewers and the fact that colleges have been offering eSports scholarships for many years now. As of 2019, there were nearly 200 U.S. colleges offering around $15 million per year in scholarships, with the average eSports scholarship student receiving $4,800 in tuition awards a year; in addition, college teams can earn millions more in tournament prizes (Heilweil 2019). This represents a stark difference from traditional sports wherein college student-athletes are fighting for the right to pay-to-play (see Chapter 7). As for the number of viewers, *Wired* reports that the 2018 League of Legends World Championship attracted more viewers (over 200 million) that the NCAA Final Four (just under 100 million) and the Super Bowl (just over 100 million) combined (Heilweil 2019). Interestingly, while gamers spend about four hours of practice per day (according to a survey of gamers at five universities in 2018) and 24 percent reported that they don't do any sort of exercise, gamers are prone to niche ailments (e.g., eye fatigue, back and neck pain, and wrist and hand injuries) (Heilweil 2019).

The State University of New York (SUNY), the nation's largest comprehensive public university system (64 campuses and over 420,000 students), has embraced eSports, particularly during the pandemic, as a means of offering students a safe way to interact and compete with others. In 2020, SUNY created the SUNY Chancellor eSports Challenge, which included competitors from 46 SUNY schools during the Spring 2020 semester. It is the goal of SUNY to get all 64 member campuses involved in eSports (Bomba 2020). Fortnite is one of the favorite eSports among SUNY students. At some of the campuses eSports is a varsity sport and at others it is a club sport (Bomba 2020).

The vast and ever-growing number of people who view eSports has caught the attention of people outside the college setting as many industries are cashing in on this phenomenon. Casinos have embraced eSports because it helps their bottom lines. Casinos host competitive tournaments because the viewing audience buys hotel rooms, food and drink. "The fast-paced action, vivid graphics, and often violent on-screen action is catnip to millennials, the audience casinos are targeting as their core slot players grow old and die" (Parry 2017: A2). There are an increasing number of platforms offering live eSports coverage as well including Twitch, YouTube, and Hulu TV (Influencer Marketing 2020; Lee 2019). Add to these platforms Video Game Entertainment & News Network (VENN), an upstart network that is aiming to be the MTV of eSports (Lee 2019). A number of eSport events are also aired on ESPN as well.

Initially, eSports were relegated to a club sport designation but with its rise in popularity, a number of colleges have upgraded the designation to varsity sport. The University of Southern California (USC) is among these colleges (Dean 1018). The gamers play against rival schools, draw huge crowds, and avoid the controversy of the inflated salaries that coaches make in sports such as football and basketball.

With eSports, we have institutionalized, structured, sanctioned competitive activities that go beyond the realm of play, and there are relatively complex skills involved (there is even a World Video Game Hall of Fame) but gamers do not engage in athletic activities. This is why games like *Fortnite*, *LoL* and *Overwatch* are described as eSports and not sports. For the hundreds of millions of eSports enthusiasts, this is good enough and represents another reason why so many people love sports, regardless of its designation.

Physical Activity and Sports

At the root of our love for sports is our need and desire for physical activity. Physical activity is also important for overall physical fitness. Physical fitness is one of the best and easiest ways to protect one's health and reduce the risk of nearly every major health problem, including heart disease, cancer, diabetes, and Alzheimer's disease. Unfortunately, there are many people who do not participate in regular physical activity. Just how much physical activity should people get? According to the CDC (2014a) adults need at least 150 minutes of moderate intensity aerobic activity (e.g., walking fast, doing water aerobics, riding a bike on level ground or with few hills, or playing doubles tennis) per week or 75 minutes of vigorous-intensity aerobic activity (e.g., running, swimming laps, riding a bike fast or on hills, or playing basketball) per week. A number of people claim that they don't have time for 150 minutes per week, but if we break it down, all one has to do is workout for 30 minutes per day times five days a week, a figure that equates to less that 1.5 percent of the total minutes in a given week. The typical person spends almost 120 minutes per day on social media so, clearly, we have time to engage in physical activity.

Regular physical activity is very important for children and adolescents as well as it "improves strength and endurance, helps build healthy bones and muscles, helps control weight, reduces anxiety and stress, increases self-esteem, and may improve blood pressure and cholesterol levels" (CDC 2014b). Regular physical activity for young people means at least 60 minutes per day (CDC 2014b). There are three types of physical activity for children: aerobic activity (e.g., running, walking, or anything that makes their hearts beat faster), muscle-strengthening (e.g., climbing or doing push-ups), and bone-strengthening (e.g., jumping or running).

Like the CDC, the authors are firm believers that all schools should require physical education classes or, at the very least, "promote physical activity through comprehensive school physical activity programs, including recess, classroom-based physical activity, intramural physical activity clubs, interscholastic sports, and physical education…. Schools can also work with community organizations to provide out-of-school-time physical activity programs and share physical activity facilities" (CDC 2014b).

According to the CDC (2014b), there are many benefits to regular physical activity including:

- Helps build and maintain healthy bones and muscles.
- Helps reduce the risk of developing obesity and chronic diseases, such as diabetes, cardiovascular disease, and colon cancer.
- Reduces feelings of depression and anxiety and promotes psychological well-being.
- May help improve students' academic performance, including: academic

achievement and grades; academic behavior, such as time on task; and factors that influence academic achievement, such as concentration and attentiveness in the classroom.

Maintaining physical fitness is not only good for our health, it encourages participation in, and a love for, sports. This is why participation in eSports is not a replacement for sport participation. Participation in eSports in addition to regular physical exercise is different; the key is, to maintain a physically-active lifestyle at all ages. The consequences of youth today that are physically unfit, especially compared to past generations, was discussed in Chapter 6 but recall, among other things, that worldwide, children are 15 percent less aerobically fit, making them much slower runners and more susceptible to a *sedentary lifestyle* (a lack of physical activity that leads to someone becoming out of shape or physically unfit that can cause severe health issues).

PHYSICAL ACTIVITY AND PHYSICAL EDUCATION AT SCHOOL AND HOME

The trends of an alarming, growing rate of obesity; an increasing percentage of juveniles and adults who are physically unfit; a general lack of physical activity among youth and adults; and sedentary life habits are alarming and further justify the promotion of physical activity and physical education (PE) in school. Despite warnings for years about the obesity problem in the United States, there had been a disturbing trend among many schools to eliminate mandatory physical education classes taught by certified or licensed educators or to consider recess as a form of physical education. However, "The cornerstone of school-based physical activity programs should be a high-quality physical education program based on national standards" (Basch 2011).

There is great value in offering PE in schools. As Basch (2011) explains, PE can help youth to be active and to learn self-awareness, self-regulation, and other social-emotional skills such as teamwork and cooperation. Basch (2011) points out that physical activity affects metabolism and all major body systems, exerting powerful positive influences on the brain and spinal cord and, consequently, on emotional stability, physical health, and motivation and ability to learn. PE classes will give youth an opportunity to learn the fundamentals of a variety of sports which in turn will give them the confidence to participate in sports. PE also provides kids with a chance to release built-up energy which in turn will help them to focus on their schoolwork. Teachers will concur that PE classes: (1) provide children with opportunities to improve fitness and be active to counter societal trends towards obesity and increased sedentary behaviors; (2) impacts positively on learning and behavior in the classroom; (3) helps children improve social skills and allows some children an opportunity to experience success in a unique learning environment (Morgan and Hansen 2008). Teachers also report that students look forward to gym class as it gives them a mental break from academic work and allows them some time to socialize with peers.

Participating in physical activities is not limited to the school environment. Parents can organize walking, running, or biking groups with their children (as well as with children whose parents are busy working). Adults can also organize physical activities with other adults. It is not necessarily to join a gym or health club to work out, one merely needs to step outside and start walking. Treadmills are reasonably priced and allow people to work out year round despite potential inclement weather outside. Those who can afford to join a health club should take advantage of the facilities and personal trainers available. Dr. Gail Saltz (2005) recommends these five practical tips to help motivate parents and their children to exercise more:

1. *Lead by example.* Children are more likely to be motivated to exercise if there is a positive role model to pattern behavior after.
2. *Take a non-negotiable position.* Just as parents will not put up with children who refuse to brush their teeth or swim without supervision, the same logic applies to keeping children from being sedentary.
3. *Promote the concept of personal best.* Physical exercise is not the same thing as competitive sports. Children can participate in physical activity (e.g., bike riding, dancing, yoga, and aerobics) without the worry of being compared to others. To keep themselves motivated they can attempt to meet and beat their own personal best performances. Parents should give positive feedback to their children who surpass previous performances.
4. *Limit sedentary activities.* Parents must limit the amount of time their children spend in front of the television, computer, and video screen. One hour of physical activity should be the goal for every child and teenager.
5. *Make it "cool."* If the fitness program is viewed as relatively entertaining (e.g., combing music with a workout, promoting diverse activities such as martial arts) it is more likely to be looked upon in favorable terms.

In sum, children and adults should engage in physical activities on a regular basis. Physical exercise along with a proper diet will increase the likelihood of a healthy, long life. Most people who exercise regularly actually find it difficult to miss a workout routine. This is why some people exercise while on vacation while others simply overeat and pursue sedentary activities. Active engagement in physical activity will also encourage participation in sports which, in turn, fosters a further appreciation and love for sports.

Sports for People with Physical Disabilities and Special Needs

There are millions of people who love sports because they provide opportunities for athletic competition among those with physical disabilities and special needs. Sport participation is especially important because physical activity levels are 4.5 times lower for youths with a disability, and the obesity rate is 38 percent higher for these children (Solomon 2020). Participating in sports is important for those with physical challenges and special needs as they are often discriminated against in general society, and organized sports activities help to facilitate an integrative function (Sahlin and Lexell 2015; Wanneberg 2018). The social integration process goes beyond teammates as the benefits of sports participation extends to family members and caregivers as well. Overall, persons with physical needs challenges and special needs benefit from sport participation because of the sense of community created among the athletes and families; the decrease in anxiety and depression among the athletes; the thrill of competition; and, the health benefits of participation.

Sports for People with Special Needs

Stanford Children's Health (SCH) (2020) agrees with our position that "all children can benefit from exercise, energy release, and pure enjoyment of playing sports" and that "this includes children with special needs." *Persons with special needs* are generally those identified as having any sort of difficulty (e.g., physical, emotional, behavioral, or learning disability or impairment) that causes them to require additional or specialized services or accommodations, such as education, recreation, and sports. SCH (2020) states that about 18 percent of U.S. children have a disability or chronic health problem and indicates that special needs children are not always encouraged to exercise as their parents or guardians fear they may get hurt. Nonetheless, physical activity is as important for special needs children as it is for any child. Among the benefits of special needs children participating in sports cited by SCH (2020) are: it boosts self-confidence; improves skills in relationship building and teamwork; and, helps to manage weight. Nearly any sport can be modified for people with special needs to help them with cardiovascular, flexibility, and strength-training benefits. "Children in a wheelchair, for instance, can play basketball or tennis. Children without the use of limbs or those with mental disabilities can enjoy the therapeutic benefits of horseback riding" (SCH 2020). SCH also reminds parents that children should get a complete physical exam prior to starting sports activities and to make sure that the coach understands their child's needs. When all the pieces come together, those with special needs and their parents/guardians will love sports.

Those who promote sport participation for special needs persons do not underestimate the challenges that may occur. Autistic children, for example, often look forward to participating in recreational activities and sports but it is difficult for them because of possible lack of coordination and difficulty understanding what sport entails (e.g., the rules and close contact with others). Playing sports in a structured format in high school scholastic sports presents a difficult challenge for most autistic children. To address this concern, a trend is developing wherein sports leagues consisting entirely of youth with autism are springing up throughout the country. *Autism* is a developmental disability that begins in early childhood and is characterized by marked deficits in communication and social interaction. Successful experiences with organized sport participation have a great deal to do with where a child falls on the autism spectrum, high or low functioning. Nonetheless, recreational activities are important for autistic children. Autistic children can develop motor skills through sport participation. Playing catch within a group setting encourages sharing and communication. Long distance running is beneficial for some autistic people because it is a solitary, repetitive activity that requires determination and stamina, traits that most autistic people have.

As proponents of surfing and saving the oceans from pollution, the authors like to share the story of how surfing can be modified for special needs persons. One might think that autistic kids are afraid of the ocean, but this is not necessarily the case. According to an ESPN report on *SportsCenter* (aired on March 27, 2006), Danielle and Izzy Paskowitz gave birth to an autistic child they named Isaiah. Izzy, a care-free professional surf champion, had a particularly tough time dealing with a son who was autistic. Danielle explains that having an autistic child can be hard on some couples. Initially, it was easier for Izzy to find excuses not to hang out with his often-agitated autistic son. Eventually, Izzy tried surfing with his son. Isaiah loved it. Izzy and Danielle Paskowitz decided to provide a day of surfing for other autistic children. By 2000, Surfers Healing, a non-profit group, was established to give autistic children a free day of surf lessons and fun in the sun and ocean.

Most autistic kids panic upon their initial indoctrination to surfing. A stranger is touching them, they are paddled out (on tandem boards) into the ocean facing seemingly insurmountable waves and they feel helpless. The autistic children often claw at the surf instructors. And then, a major transformation usually occurs. They ride a wave. An instantaneous and unstoppable gigantic grin and smile overwhelms the same children that often don't even speak. The day of surfing is day of bliss for both the autistic children and their parents or guardians. Surfing is not a cure for autism, but it has proven to be highly effective in bringing smiles of acceptance to thousands of children with autism. Every year, dozens of Surfers Healing events, staffed by volunteers, are held on both the east and west coasts. This powerful experience provides a transformative experience (Surfers Healing 2020).

In addition to surfing, autistic children and adults have found comfort in horseback riding. Horse therapy, as it is known, has significant long-term benefits for children with autism spectrum disorders. Research has shown that children participating in a 10-week horse therapy program exhibited improvements in irritability and hyperactivity as well as increased word fluency (Autism Research Institute 2019). Horse Industry News, Welfare and Industry (2020) cites research that shows how brain-building exercises and therapeutic horseback riding improve the motor skills (e.g., dexterity, coordination, and strength) of young people with neurodevelopmental disorders.

SPORTS FOR PEOPLE WITH PHYSICAL DISABILITIES

Adaptive sports can work for people with physical disabilities as well. Sports activities are available for people with developmental disabilities, cerebral palsy, dwarfism, visual impairments and other conditions. These sporting opportunities provide disabled athletes and non-disabled athletes an opportunity to come together in a positive manner. Disabled athletes participate in sport and recreation for the same reasons as nondisabled athletes do. They enjoy interacting with others, they enjoy friendly competition, and they have fun doing it. Participating in sports assists with the physical health of the disabled, who might otherwise lead sedentary lives. In turn, the physical act of playing sports improves the mental health of disabled athletes. In short, sports help the disabled find happiness through participation.

The history of promoting sports for the disabled is rooted in a hospital in England. World War II veterans with injuries were seeking a physical form of rehabilitation. In 1948, Stoke Mandeville Hospital created competitive games for veterans. Before long, sporting events for the disabled sprang up throughout England. In 1967, the National Handicapped Sports (NHS) organization was established by a group of Vietnam veterans to provide physical rehabilitation and sports programs for vets (Jones and Paciorek 1994). Over the years, the NHS has opened chapters throughout the United States and Canada and is open to all people with physical disabilities. The NHS offers such activities as water skiing, other water sports, fitness programs, and a large number of special sporting events. The participants may include persons with visual impairments, amputations, spinal cord injuries, cerebral palsy, head injuries, and other disabilities.

In the tradition of the English seeking to help wounded warriors from the armed forces comes the Invictus Games. (Note: The word "Invictus" means unconquered.) The

Invictus Games, which are championed by Britain's Prince Harry—thus, most assuredly guaranteeing their success—"are about survival in the face of adversity and the strength of the human spirit. They will send a positive message about life beyond disability" (*Invictus Games* 2014). The first Invictus Games took place in London in 2014 and we expect this to be a trending event. "There were over 400 competitors from 13 different nations" who took place in this "international sporting event for the wounded, injured and sick Servicemen and women" (*Invictus Games* 2014). The participants competed in such sports as basketball, cycling, archery, track and field, wheelchair rugby, swimming, and more. The Invictus Games are designed to shed a light on the value of the armed forces but also to provide the competitors an "inspiring and energizing experience in their journey of recovery" (*Invictus Games* 2014).

An increasing number of disabled persons are playing sports today because of technological advancements. For example, biotics is being used to improve the quality of artificial legs and arms. Wheelchairs are specially made for speed, control and stability. There are numerous organizations that provide sporting activities for the physically challenged. They include:

- A variety of Adaptive Ski, Alpine Skiing, Snowboarding, Ski Bike and Cross-Country Ski Programs (see National Sports Center for the Disabled) which provide resources and programs for children with physical disabilities.
- The National Disability Sports Alliance (NDSA), dedicated to providing sporting opportunities for all people with any type of disability.
- The National Handicapped Sports (NHS) program.
- The National Sports Alliance (NSA) program.
- The American with Disabilities Act, designed to help all people with disabilities to work together to solve problems they face.
- The U.S. Association for Blind Athletes (USABA) and the U.S. Cerebral Palsy Athletic Association (USCPAA), which offer chances for all those seeking sporting opportunities.
- The Dwarf Athletic Association of America (DAAA), which is designed to help provide sporting opportunities and competitions for dwarf athletes.
- Kids Enjoy Exercise Now (KEEN), an organization that encourages one on one participation in recreational activities among individuals with disabilities.

Earlier in this chapter, we described how surfing has helped some autistic children find a day on the ocean a blissful experience; now, we want to write about how some blind children have also found bliss in surfing. And, just as there are a number of organizations helping special needs kids through surfing there are a number of organizations such as "Learn to Surf L.A." that have taught blind children how to surf. "Learn to Surf L.A. has been providing year-round surf lessons in the L.A. area since 2002 and started their pro bono Manhattan Beach (CA) camp for the blind at El Porto three years ago" (Dryden 2014: 3). Anyone who has surfed understands the excitement of first learning how to ride waves, especially that first solo wave all the way to shore; and, even if you have not experienced the thrill of surfing imagine the challenges for blind surfers. The surf instructors begin a surf day's instruction with an introductory lesson on how each part of a surfboard works "so that the kids can feel where they'll be lying"; they are then taught about how to put on wetsuits, then "they head right out to the ocean, where volunteers help them find the waves and stand up" (Dryden 2014: 5). Volunteers report that the blind kids often heard the waves coming before they did and after a few practice tries would jump up on the board on their own. The instructors and family members marvel at the sheer, ecstatic joy that the surfers enjoy.

To add to the idea that water sports for people with special needs and physical disabilities is trending comes another example: paddle boarding for wheelchair users. Wheelchair users have joined in the paddleboard craze via a modified paddleboard known as an "ability board." Created by Hawaiian surfer Kawika Watts, who wanted to give wheelchair-bound people a chance to paddleboard, the "Onit" ability board gives people a chance to participate in water sports. Further, as with surfing, being in the water is generally viewed as therapeutic. Wheelchair-bound paddle boarders describe their "Onit" experience as giving them a sense of "normalcy" and as an "emotional" experience to be out on the water (Murray 2014).

The best-known sporting organization for disabled persons is the Special Olympics. The Special Olympics is an international nonprofit organization that is devoted to providing individuals with disabilities (including autism) an opportunity to participate and compete in sports in a "safe" environment. As described in Chapter 6, there were nearly 5.5 million participating athletes from 193 countries competing in over 106,000 competitions, assisted by over 1.1 million volunteers in 2018 (Special Olympics 2020). There are Summer and Winter Special Olympics, similar to the regular Olympics, with many of the same events. The Special Olympics help to unite families and facilitate positive self-esteem in participants. The games were initiated in 1968 by Eunice Kennedy Shriver, sister of the late President John F. Kennedy, in part to honor their sister, Rosemary Kennedy, who was mentally disabled. "On July 19, in 1968, one thousand athletes from 26 states and Canada traveled to Chicago. On July 20th, after breakfast, the athletes got on chartered school buses and were driven to Soldier Field for the Chicago Special Olympics. It was the beginning of a history-making day. Just a couple of years earlier, the idea of people with mental retardation getting together to compete in athletic events seemed incredible. Even in 1968, parents were still being counseled to place their developmentally disabled children into institutions and forget them" (Bueno 1994: 27).

Every four years there are Summer Deaflympics for deaf people and during the two years in between the Winter Deaflympics are held. The first Deaflympics, known as the "International Silent Games," were held in the summer of 1924 in Paris; the Winter Deaflympics were first held in Austria in 1949. The Games were interrupted during World War II (International Committee of Sports for the Deaf 2020). Just prior to being called the Deaflympics, the Games were called the "World Games for the Deaf." Sanctioned by the IOC, deaf athletes compete at an elite level. To qualify for the Games, athletes must have a hearing loss of at least 55 dB in their "better ear." Hearing aids and cochlear implants and the like are not allowed during competition in an effort to place all athletes on the same level (Disabled World 2017). Some examples of the sports played in the summer include: athletics, badminton, basketball, football, judo, shooting, swimming, volleyball, and wrestling. Winter sports include: alpine skiing, cross country skiing, curling, ice hockey and snowboard (Disable World 2017).

As this brief analysis of sports for people with special needs and physical disabilities indicates, nearly everyone can find a sport to enjoy. For those with special needs and challenges, and their family and friends, adaptive sports are another reason why we love sports.

New and Unusual Sports

Another reason people love sports is because new ones are constantly being created. Not a fan of the most traditional sports (e.g., soccer, football, baseball, basketball, hockey, track and field, tennis and golf)? Or, some of the less popular commercialized sports (e.g., lacrosse, equestrian, gymnastics, and handball)? Well, you are in luck, as new and unusual sports are being created all of the time. It seems as though there is a niche sport for nearly everyone. If you still haven't found a sport for you, create one, as many of us have done. Creating ways to entertain ourselves and our friends with made-up games, in some cases with very simple rules and in other cases with well-defined rules established, is a hallmark of human behavior.

One of the authors, Tim Delaney and his brother Tom, created a sport called "roofball" many decades ago. Roofball involves a combination of tennis and volleyball and the use of a ball that is sturdier than a beach ball but softer than a dodgeball. The game can be played as singles or doubles, like tennis, and involves the player(s) alternating hitting the ball, volleyball style, onto a slanted roof with the alternate player or team volleying the ball back onto the roof. If the ball hits the ground during your turn the other player/team receives a point. The game was usually played to 15 but you had to win by 2 points, so the game could go on for a while. For a few summers in the early 1980s the game was so popular with their friends that a recreational league was created. It was fun to play "road games" as other people had different types of roofs, some involving a combination of differently angled roofs and others with longer or steeper roofs. It was very popular with a circle of friends and resembled a summer beer league designed for people to have outdoor fun but involving some athletic skill. We never tried to convert roofball into a sport for others to play; we just had fun with it ourselves.

Other people have created their own new sports too and, for whatever reason, sometimes these new sports would receive publicity and catch on with others. Frisbee golf is a good example. Many people first heard of Frisbee golf on the *Seinfeld* episode "The Summer of George." In this episode, the George Costanza character has recently been terminated from his employment with the New York Yankees. He has received a huge severance package and decides to take the summer off and have fun. A group of people are playing Frisbee golf or "frolf" (as George calls it) and invite him to play along. George is very enthusiastic to join in this sporting activity. Frisbee golf gained in popularity but because "Frisbee" is a brand name this sport is now known as Disc Golf. It even has its own governing body, Professional Disc Golf Association (PDGA), with sanctioned courses across the nation, and outside of the U.S. as well. There are PDGA sponsored tournaments, prize money, and a championship. The more than 100,000 members come from numerous nations.

Hoping to cash in on the idea of disc golf is "foot golf," a combination of soccer and golf, wherein players kick a ball onto a green and try to put the ball into a big golf hole. Foot golf began in the Netherlands in 2009 and has quickly caught on in other parts of the world, including the United States. In the United States, the American FootGolf League (AFGL) was founded in 2011. The AFGL is a member of the Federation for International Foot Golf (FIFG) (American FootGolf League 2020). Another rather obscure, but growing, sport is "Pickleball." "Named after 'Pickles,' a ball-snatching cocker spaniel, Pickleball was invented in 1965 on Bainbridge Island, a short ferry ride from Seattle, by Joel Pritchard, a future Republican Congressman from Washington State" and two of his friends (Tamura 2011). Despite *Tennis* magazine describing Pickleball as "America's newest racket sport" in 1976, it grew slowly but is trending now. The USA Pickleball Association (USAPA) was founded in 1984, "the same year the first rule book was published" (Tamura 2011). The USAPA (2020) describes Pickleball as: (1) a fun sport that combines many elements of tennis, badminton, and ping pong; (2) a sport played both indoors or outdoors on a badminton-sized court and a slightly modified tennis net; (3) played with a paddle and a plastic ball with holes; (4) played as doubles or singles; and, (5) can be enjoyed by all ages and skill levels.

While not a new sport, flag football has been transformed into a competitive, sanctioned sport with leagues for adults and youth. Flag football has grown in popularity due to the concern over concussions associated with tackle football. The American Flag Football League (AFFL), created by founder and CEO Jeff Lewis, is a collective of elite adult athletes hailing from a variety of sports who have speed, agility, and charisma to compete and entertain on the national stage. The AFFL hosts tournaments and culminates with a cash prize championship (American Flag Football League 2020).

If you enjoy skiing but think that hurdling down a mountain is not fast enough for you, how about strapping a paramotor (the generic name for the harness and propulsive portion of a powered paraglider) to your back? Snow paragliding is a growing sport that allows skiers to reach high speeds without the need for a mountain. This is a different sport than ski gliding or ski-paragliding, which usually involves the skier flying like an eagle over mountains. If you prefer a new sport that keeps you mostly grounded sans a motor, how about "breaking"? Breaking, as you might have guessed, comes from breakdancing, a type of dancing that involves a number of athletic skills including airborne tricks. While breakdancing is common at some nightclubs, the International Olympic Committee has recognized breaking as a high-level competitive sport with a network of contests held worldwide. Organizers for the 2024 Summer Games in Paris have proposed adding "breaking" to their program, citing an "unmissable opportunity" to attract young fans (Wharton 2019).

Perhaps none of these new sports ideas appeal to you. No worries, as there are so many new sports in the past decade that there is literally an "A–Z" listing. Robert Wood (2012) compiled an alphabetical listing that begins with numerically-named sports (i.e., 360Ball and 4-Squares), continues with sports starting with the letter "A" (i.e., Aeris, Agball, and Airstrip Tire), and proceeds to include names of sports through the letter "Z" (i.e., Zapball and Zoneball).

Sports Studies and Sports Management Programs

The popularity of the study of sport has led to a trending development of sport studies programs across the United States and throughout the world. In 2013, there were over 880 colleges in the United States that offered a sport studies degree program; there were an additional 115-plus accredited graduate sport studies programs. Tim Delaney researched this because he and a colleague (Chris Mack, associate professor of History) were in the process of developing a sport studies program at the State University of New York at Oswego (there is already an existing degree granting program at Tim Madigan's institution, St. John Fisher College, in Sports Management). At some colleges, sports studies programs offer a major and at others they offer a minor (as does St. John Fisher College's Sports Management program).

The SUNY Oswego Sports Studies program debut in 2016 and offers a minor degree; it was modeled after a review of many other programs across the U.S. The minor incorporates courses from sociology, history, psychology, human development, broadcasting, journalism, health science, and physical education. The sports studies minor is designed to allow people to pursue their interests in sports in a rigorous academic fashion that will have applications in a host of areas that sports touch upon in a variety of occupations, in politics, and in social life. The Oswego program examines sport's cultural relationship with education, the economy, families, the media, psychology, and politics, and considers race/ethnicity, class, and gender differences in the sport experience. As an interdisciplinary program, Sport Studies examines sport in a global context, fosters a spirit of inquiry and calls on students to broaden their perspectives. The program of study emphasizes skills in multi-cultural analysis and critical thinking and offers a focus on the experiences of marginalized groups. The Oswego Sport Studies program is intended to provide an excellent foundation for pursuing careers in sports management, sports broadcasting and journalism, sports information, and for those who want to pursue a graduate degree, or combine their sport studies interest with their major.

The St. John Fisher College program examines common principles in the sport industry such as management, marketing, finance, and law. Students learn to apply what they have learned to the various segments of the industry through internships and practicum. The program is designed to provide students with a broad-based foundation of knowledge in the liberal arts and in business. Classes blend theory with practical examples and require field experiences which provide the tools needed for successful careers in sport.

A degree in sports studies is designed to compliment's a student's major coursework interests. For example, sports broadcasters and journalists benefit from such a degree because it helps to round out their knowledge of sports as they write columns or announce games. Kosiewicz (2016) describes how the reports and comments made by broadcasters and journalists come across in a "common sense" matter among the consuming audience. "Common sense statements contained in the various forms of verbal expressions— for example, statements contained in the journalistic reports and comments on the sports events—often have simply incredible reach and power to influence the audience. They make unimaginable impact on awareness, perceptions and attitudes of spectators, listeners, viewers, and fans. They are influential, value creating, and shape people's reception of the event" (Kosiewicz 2016: 79). Consequently, the more well-rounded the background of the journalist or broadcaster the better as their words have an impact on the audience. The sports management field benefits from having employees with a sports studies degree much in the same manner as the field of communications does. It is important for those in the sports management field to have a background in all the social issues areas covered by a Sports Studies program. As Zervas and Glazzard (2018) explain, it is critical for people in sports management to understand the issues and ethics of the sports field as well as the social backgrounds of athletes and those in the sports field. We have found that many people who pursue a degree in Sports Studies do so not so much for employment purposes but because they want to learn more about a social institution that so deeply affect billions of people. Gaining knowledge of the sports world can only help one as they interact with others.

Combining the interdisciplinary design of Sport Studies programs with America's love affair with sports helps to explain why Sports Studies programs are trending.

Sportsmanship

At SUNY Oswego, the Sport Studies minor involves coursework; opportunities to travel abroad to learn of sports in different countries (currently Ireland and Spain); and, an opportunity to present a paper on the topic of sportsmanship at the co-sponsored Sociology Department and Sports Studies annual Sportsmanship Day Symposium (SDS). The purpose of the Sportsmanship Day Symposium is to provide a multi-disciplinary look at sportsmanship. Faculty, students (including some who are student-athletes and some who are not), and sports administrators from multiple academic disciplines provide a description of sportsmanship from their academic and sporting perspective and then give examples of either good sportsmanship or poor sportsmanship. Such a broad perspective on sportsmanship is quite enlightening as we soon discover that, while everyone seems to assume to know what "sportsmanship" means, not everyone agrees on its parameters. (Note: We provided our definition of sportsmanship in Chapter 6.) Before addressing the parameters of sportsmanship, it is important to note that the SDS was created to coincide with the annual "National Sportsmanship Day."

National Sportsmanship Day (NSD) was established in 1991 by the Institute for International Sport (IIS), which in turn, was founded in 1986 by Daniel E. Doyle, Jr. In addition to creating NSD, the Institute has also established a number of programs including the "Scholar-Athlete Games" and the "World Peace Summit" (*Institute for International Sport* 2014a). As for National Sportsmanship Day itself, the program has several important objectives:

- To promote ethics, honesty, and fair play in athletics and society through education and sport.
- To designate a day each year during which student-athletes, coaches, administrators and parents engage in thoughtful and reasoned discussion about the role of sportsmanship [in sport].
- To provide participating schools, clubs and athletic organizations a template to successfully celebrate the day with sportsmanship themed activities, discussion topics, etc.
- To make participation in National Sportsmanship Day an anchor event that fosters good sportsmanship on a year-round basis [ISS 2014b].

As a sport sociologist, and a professor who has regularly taught sport sociology courses, Delaney became concerned by how few people, especially student-athletes, and coaches, are aware of National Sportsmanship Day. Furthermore, given that ESPN has multiple networks of 24-hour-a-day sports coverage, why don't they make a big deal of National Sportsmanship Day? As a result of this, in 2009, Delaney decided to create the Sportsmanship Day Symposium (SDS) (held on the first Thursday of March) at SUNY Oswego to help draw attention to this day reserved to promote sportsmanship. In 2019, IIS finally chose a specific day—the first Tuesday of March—to recognize National Sportsmanship Day—prior to 2019 the event was not held on a specific day, although always in early March. On March 5, 2020, the 12th annual SDS was held just days before all SUNY colleges were closed due to COVID-19. The March 4, 2021, 13th annual SDS was held via Zoom.

In light of all the problems, big and small in society in general, and in sports specifically; sportsmanship is not promoted nearly enough and certainly not as much as it

Fans from rival teams demonstrate good sportsmanship by peacefully leaving a hurling playoff match between Tipperary and Cork, in Thurles, Ireland.

should be. Many people in the sports world will say that they promote sportsmanship and yet the behaviors of parents and coaches at the youth sports level, the deviant behaviors discussed in Chapter 8, and, all the violent incidents discussed in Chapter 9, seem to suggest otherwise. There are also all the countless small examples of poor sportsmanship, like taunting, refusing to shake the hand of the opponent, disrespecting a referee or game official, and so on. Once again, this is why we promote sportsmanship. And, let's be fair, there are, in fact, many examples of good sportsmanship in the sports world. As we shall see in "Connecting Sports and Popular Culture: Box 16," there are also a number of entities (e.g., sports media, social media, and sports leagues) that acknowledge and award specific persons for their acts of sportsmanship by naming them their "Sportsperson of the Year." Perhaps you the reader have your own stories of good sportsmanship. If you do have a story about good sportsmanship share it with others; ideally, on your college campus at a sportsmanship symposium, at an academic conference, or while hanging out with your friends. Either way, promote good sportsmanship!

As hinted in the second edition of this text, Tim Delaney did release a book on sportsmanship, *Sportsmanship: Multidisciplinary Perspectives* (2016). *Sportsmanship* (McFarland) represents a compilation of the most comprehensive essays on the meaning of sportsmanship in existence. The twenty-seven total contributing scholars (including Delaney and Madigan who contributed their own original articles) represent dozens of unique academic disciplines and reside from five different countries. You can learn much more about sportsmanship in this highly acclaimed book.

Connecting Sports and Popular Culture

Box 16: "Sportsperson of the Year" Awards

There are many examples of good sportsmanship. Some go mostly unnoticed and others draw the attention of a viewing audience. One of the authors attended his nephew's youth baseball game; one of the teams did not have juice boxes or snacks and the other team shared their refreshments. A simple gesture that was met with great thanks; nonetheless this act of sportsmanship did not make the national news or "SportsCenter." Those involved were not surprised or disappointed that this act went mostly unnoticed; after all, deeds of sportsmanship are not done for the glory but because they are the right thing to do. Sports competitors at all levels (youth, high school, college, amateur, or professional) often display simple acts of good sportsmanship and they do it because it's a part of their personality to do good deeds.

While many acts of good sportsmanship go unnoticed, others receive public acknowledgment and a large viewing audience. Both traditional and social media are responsible for providing articles, images, and videos of good sportsmanship. Social media can transform an act of good sportsmanship that might have otherwise gone mostly unnoticed if it was recorded and shared on social media platforms. Sometimes such content will receive a large number of "likes" and "shares" and it may go viral. We can use social media platforms to seek examples of good sportsmanship behaviors; for example, on Instagram you can do a search with #sportsmanship and you will find many images and videos of sportsmanship. The same thing is true with Facebook, that is, you can click the search icon, type sportsmanship, and volumes of articles, images, and videos of sportsmanship will be made available.

Traditional media outlets have long acknowledged individuals whose acts of sportsmanship are considered so grand that they are transformed to hero status when described as "Sportsperson of the Year." Many organizations enjoy promoting someone as a good sportsperson. Among the entities with a sportsperson award is ESPN who named world champion shuttler P.V. Sindhu (badminton) the 2020 "Female Sportsperson of the Year" (for the third consecutive year) while young shooter Saurabh Chaudhary (pistol shooting sports) won the honor for "Male Sportsperson of the Year." Manasi Joshi (badminton) won the "Differently-abled Athlete of the Year/Para-athlete of the year Award" (Negi 2020). In 2019, *Sports Illustrated* named Megan Rapinoe (soccer) as the "Sportsperson of the Year." Serena Williams (tennis) won the BET award for "Sportsperson of the Year" in 2019. In 2020, *The Sporting News* named co-winners, Lionel Messi (soccer) and Lewis Hamilton (Formula One driver), as the Laureus "World Sportsman of the Year" award. *Press Box* named Mo Gaba, a 14 year old who bravely fought cancer and became a darling of the Baltimore Orioles (MLB) was their 2019 "Sportsperson of the Year." He passed on July 28, 2020 (Ordine 2020). Chances are, you have not heard of some of these sportspersons so it is a good idea to broaden your scope of sports knowledge and learn more about them.

In addition to these media awards, most major sports leagues, conferences, and individual teams name an athlete(s) as their "Sportsperson of the Year." Two examples are provided here. The ACC named Syracuse Women's basketball star and cancer survivor Tiana Mangakahia as their 2019 "Sportsperson of the Year" award winner. Tiana is an all-American point guard who courageously fought breast cancer while a member of the

Orange's basketball team (Kramer 2019). The Big 12 conference named Andrew Jones as the conference's "Male Sportsperson of the Year" for the 2019–20 academic year. Jones, a basketball player at the University of Texas fought leukemia and like Mangakahia served as an inspiration to other cancer patients.

The criteria for such an acknowledgment as "Sportsperson of the Year" varies but, as you might imagine, involves doing something honorable, courageous, or inspirational. Who would you name as your "sportsperson of the year" and why?

SUMMARY

Billions of people around the world love sports and we love sports for a number of reasons beyond the joy of playing games, the competitive design of sports, the bonding opportunities, and the cultural importance of sports.

In this chapter, we described some of the other reasons people love sports including: the enjoyment of participating in fantasy sports and video gaming; the need and desire for physical activity; the realization that sports help people, including youth, with special needs and physical disabilities; and, the fun of participating in new and unusual sports. The love that people have for sports has led to the creation of sports studies programs with a degree program at many colleges that incorporates a multi-disciplinary approach to the study of sport and in many cases, provides opportunities for students to travel to foreign countries to learn about the cultural significance of their sports.

We also love sports because they provide us with opportunities to promote good sportsmanship, something that is increasingly important in this era of great socio-political divide and a general lack of civility. In an attempt to publicize the acts of good sportsmanship that so many from the sports world do, sports media outlets and sports leagues acknowledge specific persons as their "Sportsperson of the Year."

Sports mirror society; they are not bigger than life or separate from life, they are a significant aspect of the lives of billions of people.

KEY TERMS

Autism A developmental disability that begins in early childhood, characterized by marked deficits in communication and social interaction.

Fantasy Sports Sports wherein participants act as "owners" by choosing ("drafting") "players" (real athletes) and compete against other "owners" to determine winners and losers by using real-life statistics generated by the actual athletes who play real sports.

Invictus Games Founded in 2014, an international Paralympic-style competitive multi-sporting event for wounded members of the armed services.

National Sportsmanship Day An annual event designed to promote ethics, honesty, and fair play in athletics and society through education and sport.

Persons with Special Needs People with any sort of difficulty (e.g., physical, emotional, behavioral, or learning disability or impairment) that causes them to require additional or specialized services or accommodations, such as education, recreation, and sports.

Physical Activity An important aspect of overall physical fitness that involves aerobic activity, muscle-strengthening, and bone-strengthening.

Sedentary Lifestyle A lack of physical activity that leads to someone becoming out of shape or physically unfit that can cause severe health issues.

Sports Studies Programs Academic programs that offer a degree (major or minor) and that incorporates a multi-disciplinary approach to the study of sport, and in many cases provide opportunities for students to travel to foreign countries to learn about the cultural significance of their sports.

Video Gaming The act of playing video games wherein a player(s) uses a specialized electronic gaming device or a computer or mobile device and display screen, along with the means to control graphic images.

DISCUSSION QUESTIONS

- Is video gaming a "real" sport? Why or why not?
- In your opinion, are video game competitions sporting events? Why or why not?
- Do you agree or disagree with the claim that participating in sports is basically a positive experience?
- Why do you think fantasy sports are so popular? Do you prefer real sports or fantasy sports? Explain.
- Explain how sports can help people with special needs and physical disabilities.
- Do you think that physical education should be mandatory in school and at home? Why or why not? How might such a policy be implemented?
- What is "sportsmanship" and how can it best be promoted?
- What sort of topics do you think a Sports Studies program should address?
- Who would you name as your "sportsperson of the year" and why?

Bibliography

Abend, Gabrel. 2008. "The Meaning of 'Theory.'" *Sociological Theory*, 26(2): 173–199.

Aboulafia, Mitchell. 1986. *The Mediating Self: Mead, Sartre and Self-Determination*. New Haven: Yale University Press.

Abrams, Olivia. 2019. "Why Female Athletes Earn Less Than Men Across Most Sports." *Forbes*, June 23. Available: https://www.forbes.com/sites/oliviaabrams/2019/06/23/why-female-athletes-earn-less-than-men-across-most-sports/#6c8989ee40fb.

Adams, Dwight. 2018. "Victims Share What Larry Nassar Did to Them Under the Guise of Medical Treatment." *Indy Star*, January 25. Available: https://www.indystar.com/story/news/2018/01/25/heres-what-larry-nassar-actually-did-his-patients/1065165001/.

Adelman, Melvin. 1997. "The Early Years of Baseball, 1845–60," pp. 58–87 in *The New American Sport History*, edited by S.W. Pope. Chicago: University of Illinois Press.

Adelson, Andrea. 2020. "Colorado State Suspends Football Activities to Investigate Racism, Verbal Abuse Allegations." *ESPN.com*, August 7. Available: https://www.espn.com/college-football/story/_/id/29617569/colorado-state-suspends-football-activities-investigate-racism-verbal-abuse-allegations.

Adorno, Theodor W. 1981. *Prisms*, translated by Samuel and Shierry Weber. Cambridge, MA: MIT Press.

Afghanistan Culture. 2020. "Kite Flying in Afghanistan." Available: http://www.afghanistan-culture.com/kite-flying-in-afghanistan.html.

African Sky. 2014. "Trophy Hunting Zebra." Available: http://www.africanskyhunting.co.za/trophies/zebra-hunting.html.

Alamri, Abeer Ahmed. 2015. "How Australian Female Students Interpret Challenges in High School Sports." *Journal of Muslim Minority Affairs*, 35(2): 215–229.

Albom, Mitch. 2015. "Hit Somebody (The Hockey Song)." Mitch Albom Website. Available: http://mitchalbom.com/d/4228/hit-somebody-hockey-song-recorded-warren-zevon.

Alcantara, Denise. 2017. "3 Ancient Sports Found in Africa." *Lux Afrique*, December 22. Available: http://luxafrique.net/3-ancient-sports-found-africa/.

Alcohol.org. 2019. "Specific Groups More Prone to Alcoholism." Available: https://www.alcohol.org/faq/who-is-most-prone-to-alcoholism/.

Alexander, Elton. 2005. "When It Comes to Shoes, Athletes Know Best." *The Cleveland Plain Dealer*. October 23: C2.

Ali, Lorraine. 2019. "Boos All Part of the Game." *Los Angeles Times*, October 29: E1, E5.

All-American Girls Professional Baseball League (AAGPBL). 2014. "League History." Available: http://www.aagpbl.org/index.cfm/pages/league/12/league-history.

Allardt, E. 1970. "Basic Approaches in Comparative Sociological Research and the Study of Sport," pp. 14–30 in *Cross-Cultural Analysis of Sport and Games*, edited by Günther Luschen. Champaign, IL: Stipes.

Allyn, Bobby. 2019. "'Lock Him Up': Trump Greeted With Boos and Jeers at World Series Game 5." *NPR*, October 28. Available: https://www.npr.org/2019/10/28/774044200/lock-him-up-trump-greeted-with-boos-and-jeers-at-world-series-game.

Amen, Daniel G., Andrew Newberg, Robert Thatcher, Yi Jin, and Joseph Wu. 2011 (Winter). "Impact of Playing American Professional Football on Long-Term Brain Function." *The Journal of Neuropsychiatry and Clinical Neurosciences*, 23(1): 98–106.

American Film Institute. 2014. "AFI's 100 Greatest Movie Quotes of All Time." Available: http://www.afi.com/100years/quotes.aspx.

American Flag Football League (AFFL). 2020. "We are the Future of Flag." Available: https://www.affl.com/about/.

American FootGolf League (AFGL). 2020. "About AFGL." Available: https://www.footgolfusa.org/about.

American Psychiatric Association. 2020. "Internet Gaming." Available: https://www.psychiatry.org/patients-families/internet-gaming.

American Psychological Association. 2014. "College Athletes with Abusive Coaches More Willing to Cheat." July 7. Available: http://www.apa.org/news/press/releases/2014/07/abusive-coaches.aspx.

American Society for the Prevention of

Cruelty to Animals (ASPCA). 2020. "Cockfighting." Available: https://www.aspca.org/animal-cruelty/other-animal-issues/cockfighting.

American Sociological Association. 2005. "Reflecting on ASA's Centennial Year, 2005." May/June: 1.

American Tailgater Association. 2014. "History of Tailgating: A Time-Honored Tradition." May 10. Available: http://americantailgaterassociation.org/news/history-tailgating-time-honored-tradition/.

American Youth Soccer Organization (AYSO). 2020. "About AYSO." Available: https://ayso.org/about-us/about/.

Anderson, Matt. 2019. "Where is Lacrosse The Most Popular?" Lacrosse All-Stars. Available: https://laxallstars.com/where-is-lacrosse-the-most-popular/.

Anderson, R.J. 2020. "Minor League Baseball Cancels 2020 Season; Here's What It Means for Prospects and Teams." *CBS Sports,* July 1. Available: https://www.cbssports.com/mlb/news/minor-league-baseball-cancels-2020-season-heres-what-it-means-for-prospects-and-teams/.

Andrews, Malika. 2017. "How Should High Schools Define Sexes for Transgender Athletes?" *The New York Times,* November 8. Available: https://www.nytimes.com/2017/11/08/sports/transgender-athletes.html?searchResultPosition=5.

Angst, Frank. 2019. "What Does a Sports Agent Do?" *The Balance Careers,* August 9. Available: https://www.thebalancecareers.com/job-profile-sports-agent-3113312.

Anshel, Mark. 1994. *Sport Psychology,* 2nd edition. Scottsdale, AZ: Gorsuch Scarisbrick.

Anti-Defamation League. 2020. "Prayer in Public Schools." Available: https://www.adl.org/education/resources/tools-and-strategies/religion-in-public-schools/prayer#:~:text=Organized%20prayer%20in%20the%20public%20school%20setting%2C%20whether,does%20not%20interfere%20with%20the%20school%27s%20educational%20mission.

Antonen, Mel. 2000. "A-Rod Gets $252 Million and a New Address in Texas." *USA Today.* December 12: 1C.

Apel, Therese. 2015. "School Mascots: What's In a Name?" *The Clarion-Ledger,* April 22. Available: https://www.clarionledger.com/story/news/2015/04/22/school-mascots-name/26218987/.

Aran, K., and M. Sangiacomo. 1993. "Sockalexis Kin Say He Likes Team Name." *Cleveland Plain Dealer.* June 12: 2B.

Arnold, Brandon. 2006. "History of Snowboarding." Available: http://snowboarding.about.com/65/basics1/a/history.html.

Arnold, Serena. 1980. "The Dilemma of Meaning," pp. 5–18 in *Recreation and Leisure: Issues in an Era of Change,* edited by Thomas Goodale and Peter Witt. State College, PA: Venture.

Ashe-Edmunds, Sam. 2017. "What are the Health Benefits of Playing Youth Sports?" *Healthfully,* August 14. Available: https://healthfully.com/349788-what-are-the-health-benefits-of-playing-youth-sports.html.

The Aspen Institute. 2020. "Youth Sports Facts: Sports Participation and Physical Activity Rates." Available: https://www.aspenprojectplay.org/youth-sports-facts/participation-rates.

Associated Press. 2006. "Sports Fan Names Newborn Son ESPN." Available: http://www.foxnews.com/story/2006/10/07/sports-fan-names-newborn-son-espn/.

_____. 2014a. "NFL Says Abdullah Should Not Have Been Penalized for Conduct." *The Citizen,* October 1: B2.

_____. 2014b. "NCAA Loses Landmark O'Bannon Case." *The Citizen,* August 9: B2.

_____. 2015. "Quick Thinking May Have Averted Massacre at Paris Stadium." *The Citizen,* November 17: B3.

_____. 2016. "Report: Russian Doping Program Involved More than 1,000 Athletes in 30 Sports." *The Citizen,* December 10; B2.

_____. 2017a. "Ultimate Frisbee Now Recognized as Varsity Sport in Vermont." Available: https://www.masslive.com/sports/2017/11/ultimate_frisbee_now_recognize.html.

_____. 2017b. "Blockbuster Arrests Not Shocking to College Hoops Followers." *The Citizen,* October 10: B5.

_____. 2017c. "Dogsledding Engulfed in Scandal." *The Citizen,* October 25: B3.

_____. 2017d. "Looking Back at Rio One Year Later." *The Citizen,* July 29: B2.

_____. 2018. "Criticize the Russian Team? Pay Up." *The Post-Standard,* June 19: B5.

_____. 2019a. "Timeline of Russia's Doping Cases and Cover-ups." *NBC Sports,* December 9. Available: https://olympics.nbcsports.com/2019/12/09/russia-doping-history/.

_____. 2019b. "AP Poll: U.S. Divided on Betting College vs. Pros." *The Citizen,* March 21: B4.

_____. 2019c. "Betting Revenues Miss Estimates." *The Citizen,* April 3: B2.

_____. 2019d. "Players Hope Success Leads to More Support." *The Citizen,* July 9: B2.

_____. 2019e. "Transgender High School Athletes Spark Controversy, Debate in Connecticut," February 25. Available: https://www.foxnews.com/sports/transgender-high-school-athletes-spark-controversy-debate-in-connecticut.

_____. 2020a. "WNBA, Players Reach Tentative Eight-Year Labor Deal," January 14. Available: https://www.si.com/wnba/2020/01/14/wnba-cba-deal-salary-raise.

_____. 2020b. "K-State Players Announce Boycott for Tweet." *The Citizen,* June 30: B3.

_____. 2020c. "Oklahoma State's Gundy Takes Pay Cut In Wake of Criticism." *The Post-Standard,* July 5: C7.

_____. 2020d. "Politics and Olympics Intertwined." *Los Angeles Times,* January 21: D5.

Atlanta American Journal Constitution (AJC). com. "Will the *Sports Illustrated* Cover Jinx Strike Again?" Available: http://www.

ajc.com/gallery/sports/college/college-football-sports-illustrated-cover-jinx/g6Y3/#2891502.

Atlanta Braves History. 2000. "All Dressed up in History." Available: www.atlantabraves.com.

Auer, Holly. 2003. "Betting Against All Odds." *Buffalo News.* April 21: A-1.

Autism Research Institute. 2019. "Lasting Benefits Seen from Horse Therapy." Available: https://www.autism.org/horse-therapy-autism/.

Axe, Brent. 2020. "Could Syracuse Fans Find Their Loyalty Being Tested?" *The Post-Standard,* August 4: B1.

Babe Ruth League. 2020. "History of the Babe Ruth Program. Available: https://www.baberuthleague.org/about-babe-ruth-league.aspx.

Baca, Mindy. 2017. "Why is Regular Exercise Important for Children?" *Healthfully,* June 13. Available: https://healthfully.com/349788-what-are-the-health-benefits-of-playing-youth-sports.html.

Badenhausen, Kurt. 2011. "The Business of Michael Jordan Is Booming." *Forbes,* September 22. Available: http://www.forbes.com/sites/kurtbadenhausen/2011/09/22/the-business-of-michael-jordan-is-booming/2/.

_____. 2019. "The 20 Highest-Paid Coaches in American Sports 2019." *Forbes,* December 5. Available: https://www.forbes.com/sites/kurtbadenhausen/2019/12/05/the-20-highest-paid-coaches-in-american-sports/#7c9f42c64fae.

_____. 2020. "Highest-Paid Athletes in the World." *Forbes,* May 21. Available: https://www.forbes.com/athletes/#14a4bcc455ae.

Badenhausen, Kurt, Mike Ozanian and Christina Settimi. 2014. "Knicks, Lakers are NBA's Richest Teams." *Forbes,* January 22. Available: http://www.forbes.com/nba-valuations/.

Bagnall, Janet. 2005. "Hazing Rituals Should Not Be Tolerated." *The Gazette.* September 23: A27.

Bailey, Darlene. 2006. "J-Mac: The Story Behind The Kid in the Highlights." *The Post-Standard* (originally printed in the *Daily Messenger* of Canandaigua, New York). February 24: A-1, A-6.

Bailey, Stephen. 2017. "Cupping Method Catches on with Orange Players." *The Post Standard,* August 20: C5.

Bain-Selbo, Eric and D. Gregory Sapp. 2016. *Understanding Sport as a Religious Phenomenon: An Introduction* (Kindle version). London: Bloomsbury Publishing.

Baird, Woody. 2007. "Pregnant Athlete Loses Her Funding." *The Post-Standard,* May 13: A-16.

Bairner, Alan. 2001. *Sport, Nationalism, and Globalization.* Albany: State University of New York Press.

Baker, W. J. 1982. *Sports in the Western World.* Totowa, NJ: Rowan & Littlefield.

Balko, Radley. 2014. "Mass Shooting Hysteria and the Death of John Crawford." *The Washington Post,* September 25. Available: http://www.washingtonpost.com/news/the-watch/wp/2014/09/25/mass-shooting-hysteria-and-the-death-of-john-crawford/.

Balsamo, Michael. 2019. "Ten Former Players Charged with Fraud." *The Citizen,* December 13: B1.

Barber, Nicholas. 2016. "How Leni Riefenstahl Shaped How We See the Olympics." *BBC.com,* August 10. Available: https://www.bbc.com/culture/article/20160810-how-leni-riefenstahl-shaped-the-way-we-see-the-olympics.

Barnes, Katie. 2020. "'Bring It On': From Spirit Fingers to Appropriation, the Cult Sports Film is Much More than a Teen Rom-Com." *ESPN.com,* August 25. Available: https://www.espn.com/espn/story/_/id/29731506/bring-spirit-fingers-appropriation-cult-sports-film-much-more-teen-rom-com.

Barrabi, Thomas. 2014. "Top 10 Sports Endorsement Deals: Michael Jordan Still the Richest Athlete Endorser After Kevin Durant Offer?" *International Business Times,* August 21. Available: http://www.ibtimes.com/top-10-sports-endorsements-deals-michael-jordan-still-no-1-richest-athlete-endorser-after-1665548.

Bartollas, Clemens. 1985. *Correctional Treatment Theory and Practice.* Englewood Cliffs, NJ: Prentice Hall.

Barton, Chris. 2020. "ESPN, But No Sports." *Los Angeles Times,* March 21: E1, E4.

Basch, Charles E. 2011. "Physical Activity and the Achievement Gap Among Urban Minority Youth." *Journal of School Health,* 81(10): 626–634.

Battista, Judy. 2020. "NFL Reveals 2019 Injury Data, Hopeful Rule Changes are Working." *NFL.com,* January 23. Available: https://www.nfl.com/news/nfl-reveals-2019-injury-data-hopeful-rule-changes-are-working-0ap3000001098679.

Baudrillard, Jean. 2006. *The System of Objects.* Brooklyn, NY: Verso.

Baumeister, R. F. 1991. *Meanings of Life.* New York: Guilford Press.

Bawan, Ofelia M., Marilou P. Pascual, and Arneil G. Gabriel. 2017. "Hazing and Organization Tradition in a Higher Education Institution in the Philippines: What Has the Law Got to Do with It?" *Open Journal of Social Sciences,* 5(12): 110–125.

Baxter, Kevin. 2018. "Rule-breaking Fans are Costing Mexico, Serbia." *Los Angeles Times,* June 21: D2.

_____. 2020a. "Two Charged in Alleged Bribes for World Cup Rights." *Los Angeles Times,* April 7: B6.

_____. 2020b. "U.S. Soccer President Steps Down." *Los Angeles Times,* May 13: D6.

_____. 2020c. "MLB Contract Perks Are Strange But True." *Los Angeles Times,* June 1: B7.

Bazzano, Carmelo. 1994. "The Italian-American Sporting Experience," pp. 103–116 in *Ethnicity and Sport in North American History and Culture,* edited by George Eisen and David K. Wiggins. Westport, CT: Greenwood Press.

BBC News. 2000. "Jumbo Race a 'Big Success.'" July 16. Available: http://news.bbc.co.uk.

_____. 2015. "High Court Rules Bridge Is Not a Sport." October 15. Available: https://www.bbc.com/news/uk-34537024.

_____. 2019. "Russia Banned for Four Years to Include 2020 Olympics and 2022 World Cup," December 9. Available: https://www.bbc.com/sport/olympics/50710598.

Beam, Adam. 2019. "Calif. to let College Athletes Sign Endorsement Deals." *The Post-Standard,* October 1: B2.

Beard, Aaron. 2020. "Title IX Major Factor for Program Cuts." *The Citizen,* May 28: B1.

Beaton, Rod. 2002. "Age May Be Off for Hundreds in Baseball." *USA Today.* February 26: C1.

Bechtel, Mark. 2005. "The Right Way to Cheat: Pulling a Fast One is Sometimes Part of the Game." *Sports Illustrated,* August 24. Available: http://sportsillustrated.cnn.com.

Beck, Daniel, and Louis Bosshart. 2003 (Winter). "Sports, Media, Politics, and National Identity." *Communication Research Trends.* 22(4): 10–15.

Bedingfield, Gary. 2014. "Baseball in World War II." *Baseball in Wartime.* Available: http://www.baseballinwartime.com/baseball_in_wwii/baseball_in_wwii.htm.

Beebe, Eileen, Claire Marsh, Lauren Riemann, Tianyu Ying, and Margaret D. Condrasky. 2010. "The Culinary and Nutritional Aspects Surrounding the Newfound Sport of Tailgating." *Journal of Culinary Science & Technology,* 8(1): 50–56.

Beezley, William H., and Joseph P. Hobbs. 1989. "Nice Girls Don't Sweat: Women in American Sport," pp. 337–349 in *Sport in Contemporary Society,* 3rd edition, edited by D. Stanley Eitzen. New York: St. Martin's.

Belkin, Douglas. 2014. "Liberal Education: At This College, Video Games Are a Varsity Sport." *The Wall Street Journal,* September 1. Available: http://www.wsj.com/articles/a-college-offers-videogame-scholarships-for-league-of-legends-1409625331.

Bell, Daryl. 2017. "The NHL's First Black Player, Willie O'Ree, Had a Short but Pathbreaking Stint with the Boston Bruins." *The Undefeated,* February 14: https://theundefeated.com/features/nhl-first-black-player-willie-oree/.

Bell, J. Bowyer. 1987. *To Play the Game.* New Brunswick, NJ: Transaction.

Bell, Jarrett. 2005. "Progress Would Have Pleased Pollard, Grandson Says." *USA Today.* August 8: 8C.

Bell, Richard C. 2008. "A History of Women in Sport Prior to Title IX." *The Sport Journal,* March. Available: http://thesportjournal.org/article/a-history-of-women-in-sport-prior-to-title-ix/.

Bellamy, Robert V., Jr., and James R. Walker. 2005. "Whatever Happened to Synergy?" *Nine,* 13(2): 19–31.

Bellucci Basketball Academy. 2014. "Home Page." Available: http://www.belluccibasketballacademy.com/.

Bender, Thomas. 1991. *Community and Social Change in America.* Baltimore: Johns Hopkins University Press.

Beneke, Chris, and Arthur Remillard. 2014. "Is Religion Losing Ground to Sports?" *The Washington Post,* December 17. Available: http://www.washingtonpost.com/opinions/is-religion-losing-ground-to-sports/2014/01/31/6faa4d64-82bd-11e3-9dd4-e7278db80d86_story.html.

Berger, Peter. 1963. *Invitation to Sociology: A Humanistic Perspective.* New York: Doubleday (Anchor edition).

Berkowitz, Steve. 2020. "New Name, Images, Likeness Lawsuit Against NCAA Could Put Hundreds of Millions of Dollars at Stake." *USA Today,* June 15. Available: https://www.usatoday.com/story/sports/college/2020/06/15/ncaa-lawsuit-over-athletes-images-likeness-puts-big-money-stake/3189283001/.

Bertram, Colin. 2020. "Aaron Hernandez: Timeline of His Football Career, Murder Trials, and Death." *Biography,* January 15. Available: https://www.biography.com/news/aaron-hernandez-timeline#:~:text=%20Aaron%20Hernandez%3A%20Timeline%20of%20His%20Football%20Career%2C,drafted%20by%20the%20New%20England%20Patriots...%20More%20.

Best, Joel, and David F. Luckenbill. 1994. *Organizing Deviance.* Englewood Cliffs, NJ: Prentice Hall.

Bhalerao, Sarang. 2014. "PICS: 14 Cricketers Turned Politicians." *India Times,* March 9. Available: https://www.indiatimes.com/sports/cricket/pics-14-cricketers-turned-politicians-133329.html

Binns, Melissa. 2019. "10 Richest Sports Team Owners in America (And How Much They're Worth). *The Richest,* August 2. Available: https://www.therichest.com/sports-entertainment/richest-sports-team-owners-how-much-theyre-worth/.

Biography.com. 2014. "Jim Thorpe Biography." Available: http://www.biography.com/people/jim-thorpe-9507017#synopsis.

Birnbaum, Justin. 2020. "What a Lost College Football Season Would Mean to the College Sports Economy." *CNBC,* July 18. Available: https://www.cnbc.com/2020/07/18/will-college-football-happen-what-a-lost-season-means-for-ncaa-economy.html.

Birrell, Susan. 1981. "Sport as Ritual: Interpretations from Durkheim to Goffman." *Social Forces,* 62(2): 354–376.

Bjarkman, Peter C. 1996. *Baseball with a Latin Beat.* Jefferson, NC: McFarland.

Black, Lewis. 2008. *Me of Little Faith.* New York: Riverhead Books.

Blackwell, Liam. 2015. "The Power of Superstitions and Rituals in Sport." Believe and Perform. Available: https://believeperform.com/the-power-of-superstitions-and-rituals-in-sport/.

Blackwell, Tom. 2014. "MMA Fighters Suffer Traumatic Brain Injury in Almost a Third of Professional Bouts: Study." *National Post,* March 26. Available: http://news.nationalpost.com/2014/03/26/mma-fighters-suffer-traumatic-brain-injury-in-almost-a-third-of-professional-bouts-study/.

Blakemore, Erin. 2016. "Leni Riefenstahl's Nazi Olympics." *Arts and Culture,* August 12. Available: https://daily.jstor.org/leni-riefenstahls-nazi-olympics/.

Bleak, Jared L., and Christina M. Frederick. 1998.

"Superstitious Behavior in Sport: Levels of Effectiveness and Determinants of Use in Three Collegiate Sports." *Journal of Sport Behavior*. Vol. 21 (March), No. 1: 1–15.

Bledsoe, Gregory H., Edbert B. Hsu, Jurek George Grabowski, Justin D. Brill, and Guohua Li. 2006. "Incidence of Injury in Professional Mixed Martial Arts Competition." *Journal of Sports Science and Medicine*, 1: 136–142.

Blidner, Rachelle. 2014. "Hot Dog Eaters Weigh in for Eat-Off." *Daily Breeze*, July 4: A3.

Block, David, and Tim Wiles. 2006. *Baseball Before We Knew It: A Search for the Roots of the Game*." Lincoln, NE: University of Nebraska Press.

Bloom, Deborah E., and Jareen Imam. 2014. "New York Man Dies after Chokehold by Police." *CNN. com*, December 8. Available: http://www.cnn.com/2014/07/20/justice/ny-chokehold-death/.

Blum, Matt. 2007. "Big-League Wallets Bursting with Cash." *The Post-Standard*. April 3: D-4.

Blum, Ronald. 2006. "Life of Luxury Costly for Yanks." *The Post-Standard*. December 23: D-2.

Blum, Ronald, and Jimmy Golen. 2020. "MLB Punishes Red Sox." *The Citizen*, April 23: B1.

Blumer, Herbert. 1969. *Symbolic Interaction*. Englewood Cliffs, NJ: Prentice Hall.

Bodet, Guillaume. 2009. "Sport Participation and Consumption and Post-modern Society: From Apollo to Dionysus?" *Loisir et Société*, 32(2): 223–241.

Boeheim, Jim, with Jack McCallum. 2014. *Bleeding Orange: Fifty Years of Blind Referees, Screaming Fans, Beasts of the East, and Syracuse Basketball*. New York: HarperCollins.

Bolch, Ben. 2020. "Under Armour Plans to End UCLA Deal." *Los Angeles Times*, June 28: B9.

Bomba, Jared. 2020. "SUNY eSports Program Growing." *The Citizen*, October 2: B1.

Bonesteel, Matt. 2020. "Kentucky Fires Cheerleading Coaches After Investigation." *The Post Standard*, May 19: B3.

Booker, Brakkton. 2020a. "NFL Announces New Rules to Tackle Lack of Diversity In Its Coaching, Executive Ranks." *NPR*, May 19. Available: https://www.npr.org/2020/05/19/858702029/nfl-announces-new-rules-to-tackle-lack-of-diversity-in-its-coaching-executive-ra.

_____. 2020b. "NASCAR Reinstates Racer Kyle Larson After Suspending Him for Using the N-Word." *NPR*, October 20. Available: https://www.npr.org/sections/live-updates-protests-for-racial-justice/2020/10/20/925741441/nascar-reinstates-racer-kyle-larson-after-suspending-him-for-using-n-word.

Boren, Cindy. 2020. "A Timeline of Colin Kaepernick's Protests Against Police Brutality." *The Washington Post*, June 1. Available: https://www.washingtonpost.com/sports/2020/06/01/colin-kaepernick-kneeling-history/.

Borte, Jason. 2000. "George Freeth." Available: http://www.surfing.com/surfa2/freeth_george.cfm.

Boston University Alzheimer's Disease Center (BUADC). 2014. "What is CTE?" Available: http://www.bu.edu/cte/about/what-is-cte/.

Bowen, William G., and Sarah A. Levin. 2003. *Reclaiming the Game: College Sports and Educational Values*. Princeton, NJ: Princeton University Press.

Bowman, John, and Joel Zoss. 1989. *Diamonds in the Rough: The Untold Story of Baseball*. New York: Macmillan.

Bradley, Steven. 2012 (Sept). "Tigers Focused on 'Task at Hand' for Furman." *My Orange Update*. Available: http://www.myorangeupdate.com/2012/09/tigers-focused-on-task-at-hand-for-furman-game/.

Brady, Erik. 2002a. "Cheerleading in the USA: A Sport and an Industry." *USA Today*. April 26–28: 1A.

_____. 2002b. "Title IX Hits Middle America." *USA Today*. June 13: 1A, 2A.

_____. 2014. "NFL Eases Its Pot Rules, Leaving No One Satisfied." *USA Today*, October 24: 1A-2A.

Branch, John. 2016. "Brandi Chastain to Donate Her Brain for C.T.E. Research." *The New York Times*, March 3. Available: https://www.nytimes.com/2016/03/04/sports/soccer/brandi-chastain-to-donate-her-brain-for-cte-research.html?searchResultPosition=1.

Brandt, David. 2019. "Report: Astros Stole Signs, Broke Rules." *The Citizen*, November 13: B1, B3.

Brayshaw, R.D. 1974. "Leisure Counseling for People in Correctional Institutions." *Leisurability*, Vol. 1: 10–14.

_____. 1978. "Reducing Recidivism: A Community Responsibility." *Leisurability*, Vol. 5: 30–32.

_____. 1981. "The Future of Correctional Recreation." *Journal of Physical Education, Recreation and Dance*, Vol. 52: 53.

Brennan, Christine. 2013. "Report: Colleges Doing Poorly at Hiring Women Coaches." *USA Today*, December 19. Available: http://www.usatoday.com/story/sports/college/2013/12/18/christine-brennan-women-college-coaches/4118067/.

Brohm, Jean-Marie. 1976. *Sport—A Prison of Measured Time*, translated by Ian Fraser. London: Ink Links.

Brookes, Rod. 2002. *Representing Sport*. New York: Oxford University Press.

Brooks, Bradley. 2014. "Nutty Would Cup Flips Brazil's Expectations." *The Post-Standard*, July 15: C-1.

Brott, Armin. 2018. "Title IX: A Good Thing Gone Bad." *The Citizen*, November 17: B4.

_____. 2019. "Slow Children Playing." *The Citizen*, December 21: B4.

Brown, Ethan, ed. 2009. "Athletics and Title IX of the 1972 Education Amendments." *Journal of Gender and Law*, 10(2): 505–531.

Brown, Kevin. 2019. *The HERO Effect: Being Your Best When It Matters the Most*. Dallas: Corner Stone Leadership Institute.

Brown, Peter Jensen. 2016. "Early Sports and Pop Culture History Blog." *ESPN Blogspot*, September 5. Available: https://esnpc.blogspot.com/2016/09/a-stand-up-history-and-origin-of.

html#:~:text=Popular%20history%20 places%20the%20origin%20of%20the%20 tradition,inning%20stretch%20%E2%80%9D%20 of%20game%20one%20in%20Boston.

Bryner, Jeanna. 2013. "What Is Blood Doping?" *Live Science,* January 3. Available: https://www. livescience.com/32388-what-is-blood-doping. html.

Bueno, Ana. 1994. *Special Olympics: The First 25 Years.* San Francisco, CA: Foghorn Press.

Bumbaca, Chris. 2020. "'We're Products': Michael Phelps, Other Olympians Call on USOPC to Help Athletes in Mental Health Battle." *USA Today,* July 29. Available: https://www.usatoday.com/ story/sports/olympics/2020/07/29/michael-phelps-weight-of-gold-olympics-mental-health-shaun-white/5537713002/.

Bureau of Labor Statistics (BLS). 2017. "American Time Use Survey: Leisure Time On Average Day." Available: https://www.bls.gov/TUS/CHARTS/ LEISURE.HTM.

Burhan, Nik Ahmad Sufian, Yohan Kurniawan, Abdul Halim Sidek, and Mohd Rosli Mohamad. 2014. "Crimes and the Bell Curve: The Role of People with High, Average, and Low Intelligence." *Intelligence,* 47: 12–32.

Cahn, Susan K. 2003. *Coming on Strong: Gender and Sexuality in Twentieth Century Women's Sports.* Cambridge, MA: Harvard University Press.

Calhoun, Donald W. 1987. *Sport, Culture and Personality.* Champaign, IL: Human Kinetics.

California Community College Athletic Association (CCCAA). 2014. "Welcome to the CCCAA." Available: http://www.cccaasports.org/about/ about.

Campa, Andrew J. 2020. "Serra Statues to Be Removed." *Los Angeles Times,* July 7: B2.

Campbell, Dave. 2020. "Stadiums Need Clean Air." *The Citizen,* June 2: B2.

Campbell, Richard M., Jr., Damon Aiken, and Aubrey Kent. 2004. "Beyond BIRGing and CORFing: Continuing the Exploration of Fan Behavior." *Sport Marketing Quarterly,* 13(3): 151–157.

Cannella, Stephen. 2005. "Can You Tell the Difference?" *Sports Illustrated.* Available: https://vault.si.com/ vault/2005/07/04/can-you-tell-the-difference.

Cannizzaro, Mark. 2014. "Black Hockey Players Feel Sting of Sterling Race Fiasco." *New York Post,* April 20. Available: http://nypost. com/2014/04/29/black-hockey-players-feel-sting-of-sterling-race-fiasco/.

Caponi-Tabery, Gena. 2002. "Jump for Joy: Jump Blues, Dance, and Basketball in 1930s African America," pp. 39–74 in *Sports Matters: Race, Recreation and Culture,* edited by John Bloom and Michael Nevin Willard. New York: New York University Press.

Career Explorer. 2020. "What Does a Sports Broadcaster Do?' Available: https:// www.careerexplorer.com/careers/sports-broadcaster/#:~:text=What%20is%20a%20

Sports%20Broadcaster%3F%0A%20sports%20 broadcaster,a%20sports%20broadcaster%20 can%20vary%20quite%20a%20bit.

Carlson, Chris. 2016. "The Question in Syracuse: What About Penalties Against Tar Heels?" *The Post Standard,* January 10: C4.

Carlson, Jenni. 2011. "Why Do They Sing the National Anthem before Sporting Events?" *NewsOK,* March 24. Available: http://newsok.com/why-do-they-sing-the-national-anthem-at-sporting-events/ article/3551560.

Carroll, Charlotte. 2019. "Kansas to 'Fiercely Dispute' Charges In Notice of Allegations" *Sports Illustrated,* September 23. Available: https:// www.si.com/college/2019/09/23/kansas-ncaa-violations-bill-self-recruiting-adidas.

Carroll, John. 1999. *Red Grange and the Rise of Modern Football.* Chicago: University of Illinois Press.

Castillo, Jorge. 2020a. "MLB Ruling Leads to Astros Firing G.M. and Manager." *Los Angeles Times,* January 14: D1, D2.

_____. 2020b. "Bellinger: Astros 'Stole the Ring.'" *Los Angeles Times,* February 15: D1, D6.

Cauchon, Dennis. 2005. "Childhood Pastimes Are Increasingly Moving Indoors." *USA Today.* July 12: A1, A2.

Cazentre, Don. 2020. "For the First Time, Pro Sports Bets are Legal in New York." *The Post Standard,* January 30: A1.

CBS News. 2015. "Ringleader in FAMU Hazing Death Sentenced to 6 Years," January 9. Available: https://www.cbsnews.com/news/dante-martin-ringleader-in-famu-hazing-death-sentenced-to-6-years/.

_____. 2018. "Claims in NFL Concussion Settlement Hit $500 Million In Less Than 2 Years," July 30. Available: https://www.cbsnews.com/news/nfl-concussion-claims-hit-500-million-less-than-2-years/.

_____. 2019. "Lawrence Cherono Wins Men's Boston Marathon in Sprint to Tape; Worknesh Degefa Wins Women's Race." Available: https://www.cbsnews.com/news/2019-boston-marathon-results-winners-times-lawrence-cherono-worknesh-degefa-victories/.

CBS This Morning. 2014. "Driving Change: Saudi Women Fight for Equality Behind the Wheel." Original airdate, December 3.

_____. 2017. "More Surfers Brave Frostbite to Ride Arctic Waves in Lofoten Islands." Original air date, October 18. Available: https://www.cbsnews. com/news/surfing-arctic-circle-lofoten-islands-search-of-beauty-and-adventure/.

Centers for Disease Control and Prevention (CDC). 2002. "Injury Fact Book: 2001–2002." Available: http://www.cdc.gov/fact-book.

_____. 2007. "Obesity and Overweight: Introduction." Available: http://www.cdc.gov.

_____. 2014a. "How Much Physical Activity Do Adults Need?" Available: http://www.cdc.gov/ physicalactivity/everyone/guidelines/adults. html.

_____. 2014b. "Physical Activity Facts."

Available: http://www.cdc.gov/healthyyouth/physicalactivity/facts.htm.

_____. 2017. "Body Measurements." Available: https://www.cdc.gov/nchs/fastats/body-measurements.htm.

_____. 2019a. "Protect the Ones You Love: Child Injuries are Preventable." U.S. Department of Health & Human Services. Available: https://www.cdc.gov/safechild/sports_injuries/index.html.

_____. 2019b. "Answering Questions About Chronic Traumatic Encephalopathy (CTE)." Available: https://www.cdc.gov/traumaticbraininjury/pdf/CDC-CTE-FactSheet-508.pdf.

_____. 2019c. "Prevalence of Childhood Obesity in the United States." Available: https://www.cdc.gov/obesity/data/childhood.html.

_____. 2019d. "Adult Obesity Facts." Available: https://www.cdc.gov/obesity/data/adult.html.

_____. 2020. "Alcohol and Public Health." U.S. Department of Health & Human Services. Available: https://www.cdc.gov/alcohol/fact-sheets/underage-drinking.htm.

Chalip, Laurence, and B. Christine Green. 1998. "Establishing and Maintaining a Modified Youth Sport Program: Lessons from Hotelling's Location Game." *Sociology of Sport Journal.* 15: 326– 342.

Chandler, Joan M. 1992. "Sport Is Not a Religion," pp. 55–61 in *Sport and Religion,* edited by Shirl J. Hoffman. Champaign, IL: Human Kinetics.

Chanen, David, and David Shaffer. 2005. "Culpepper, 3 Others Charged in Boat Party." *Minneapolis Star Tribune* (as appeared in *The Post-Standard*). December 16: C-1.

Charles River Editors. 2017. *Francis Scott Key: The Life and Legacy of the Man Who Wrote America's National Anthem.* CreateSpace Independent Publishing.

Chavira, R. 1977. "Three to Cheer." *Nuestro,* 1 (August): 34–35.

Chen, Chen-Yueh, Yi-Hsiu Lin, Chen-Yin Lee, Yen-Kuang Lin, Min-Chieh Min, and Kuan-Nan Lee. 2019. "Reflective or Impulsive Buying or Both? Evidence from the Sport Merchandise Consumption Context." *Social Behavior and Personality: An International Journal,* 47(11): 1–8.

Chen, Grace. 2018. "Hello Budget Cuts, Goodbye Sports: The Threat to Athletics." Public School Review, March 7. Available: https://www.publicschoolreview.com/blog/hello-budget-cuts-goodbye-sports-the-threat-to-athletics.

Cherwa, John. 2020. "27 Indicted on Charges of Alleged Horse Doping." *Los Angeles Times,* March 10: D3.

Christiano, Kevin J., William H. Swatos, Jr., and Peter Kivisto. 2016. *The Sociology of Religion: Contemporary Developments, Third Edition.* Lanham, MD: Rowman & Littlefield.

Christopher, Daron. 2020. "Hazing in High School." The Recovery Village. Available: https://www.therecoveryvillage.com/teen-addiction/related/hazing-in-high-school/.

Chronicle of Higher Education. 1988. "Sidelines." Vol. 34 (May 11): A32.

Church, Ben. 2019. "Shelly-Ann Fraser-Pryce Crowned the Fastest Woman In the World... Not that Many Fans Saw It." *CNN,* September 30. Available: https://edition.cnn.com/2019/09/30/sport/doha-world-championships-shelly-ann-fraser-pryce-spt-intl/index.html.

Cialdini, Robert, Richard Borden, Arril Thorne, Marcus Walker, Stephen Freeman, and Lloyd Sloan. 1976. "Basking in Reflected Glory: Three (Football) Field Studies." *Journal of Personality and Social Psychology,* 34: 366–375.

Cineas, Fabiola. 2020. "These Protests Feel Different Because They're Shifting Public Opinion." Vox.com, June 26. Available: https://www.vox.com/2020/6/26/21301066/public-opinion-shift-black-lives-matter.

Cipriani, Roberto. 2012. "Sport as (Spi)rituality." *Implicit Religion,* 15(2):139–151.

The Citizen. 2014a. "Phelps Suspended for Six Months." October 7: B2.

_____. 2014b. "HGH Blood-testing Setup Has Flaws." November 7: B2.

Clark, Michael A. 2000. "Who's Coaching the Coaches?" pp. 55–65 in *Sports in School: The Future of an Institution,* edited by John R. Gerdy. New York: Teacher's College, Columbia University.

Clement, J. 2019. "Twitter: Number of Monthly Active Users: 2010–2019." Statista, August 14. Available: https://www.statista.com/statistics/282087/number-of-monthly-active-twitter-users/#:~:text=As%20of%20the%20first%20quarter%20of%202019%2C%20Twitter,reporting%20metric%20to%20monetizable%20daily%20active%20users%20%28mDAU%29.

_____. 2020a. "Number of Monthly Active Facebook Users Worldwide, 2008–2020." *Statista,* April 30. Available: https://www.statista.com/statistics/264810/number-of-monthly-active-facebook-users-worldwide/#:~:text=How%20many%20users%20does%20Facebook%20have%3F%20With%20over,the%20first%20social%20network%20ever%20to%20do%20so.

_____. 2020b. "Most Popular Facebook Fan Pages 2020." *Statista,* June 16. Available: https://www.statista.com/statistics/269304/international-brands-on-facebook-by-number-of-fans/.

_____. 2020c. "Athletes with the Most Instagram Followers Worldwide 2020." *Statista,* June 18. Available: https://www.statista.com/statistics/647392/most-followers-instagram-athletes/.

Clinton, Bill. 2005. "We Must Act Now." *Parade.* September 25: 4–5.

CNN.com. 2003. "High School's Sports Participation at Record Level." Available: http://cnnfyi.printthis.clickability.com.

_____. 2005. "Then & Now: Bethany Hamilton—June 22, 2005." Available at: http://cnn.worldnews.print this.clickability.com.

Coakley, Jay. 2006. *Sports in Society,* 9th edition. Boston: McGraw-Hill.

Cockerham, William. 1995. *The Global Society.* New York: McGraw-Hill.

Coe, Sebastian, with Nicholas Mason. 1996. *The Olympians: A Century of Gold.* London: Pavilion.

College Sports Information Directors of America (CoSIDA). 2020. "Staff Directory." Available: https://cosida.com/staff.aspx.

Complete Concussion Management. 2018. "Concussion Rates: What Sport Has the Most Concussions?" Available: https://completeconcussions.com/2018/12/05/concussion-rates-what-sport-most-concussions/.

Congress.gov. 2000. "H.R. 1832—Muhammad Ali Boxing Reform Act." Available: https://www.congress.gov/bill/106th-congress/house-bill/1832.

Connley, Courtney. 2019. "The US Open Awards Men and Women Equal Prize Money—but Tennis Still Has a Pay Gap." *CNBC,* September 11. Available: https://www.cnbc.com/2019/09/11/despite-equal-grand-slam-tournament-prizes-tennis-still-has-a-pay-gap.html.

Conservative Tribune. 2014. "11 Facts about the Eric Garner Case That the Media Are Trying to Hide." December 5. Available: http://conservativetribune.com/11-garner-facts-media-ignoring/.

Cook, Bob. 2019. "High School Football Participation Is On a Decade-Long Decline." *Forbes,* August 29. Available: https://www.forbes.com/sites/bobcook/2019/08/29/high-school-football-participation-is-on-a-decade-long-decline/#26973b0533de.

Cooley, Charles. 1909. *Social Organization.* New York: Scribners.

Cox, Karli. 2016. "Olympic Hero Jesse Owens Couldn't Outrun Racism in Sports Film." *Young Post Discovery,* April 30. Available: https://www.scmp.com/yp/discover/entertainment/movies/article/3066365/olympic-hero-jesse-owens-couldnt-outrun-racism.

Craig, Steve. 2002. *Sports and Games of the Ancients.* Westport, CT: Greenwood Press.

Crepeau, Richard. 1985. "Where Have You Gone, Frank Merriwell? The Decline of the American Sports Hero," pp. 76–82 in *American Sport Culture,* edited by Wiley Lee Umphlett. Lewisburg: Bucknell University Press.

Crow, R. Brian, and Scott R. Rosner. 2004. "Hazing and Sport and the Law," pp. 200–223 in *The Hazing Reader,* edited by Hank Nuwer. Bloomington, IN: Indiana University Press.

Csiszar, John. 2020. "Biggest Pro Athlete Endorsement Deals of the Last Decade." *MSN.com,* June 5. Available: https://www.msn.com/en-us/sports/more-sports/biggest-pro-athlete-endorsement-deals/ss-BB11MFIn#image=1.

Cunningham, Michael. 2020. "Michael Cunningham: New League to Pay College Players, Provide Alternative to NCAA's 'Cartel.'" *The Atlanta Journal-Constitution,* June 21. Available: https://tylerpaper.com/ap/sports/michael-cunningham-new-league-to-pay-college-players-provide-alternative-to-ncaa-s-cartel/article_703adb2b-3372-5cfc-bd87-70b279782918.html.

Curran-Sills, Gwynn and Tasnima Abedin. 2018. "Risk Factors Associated with Injury and Concussion in Sanctioned Amateur and Professional Mixed Martial Arts Bouts in Calgary, Alberta." *Sport and Exercise Medicine,* 4(1). Available: https://www.ncbi.nlm.nih.gov/pmc/articles/PMC6045699/.

Curry, Tim. 1991. "Fraternal Bonding in the Locker Room: A Pro Feminist Analysis of Talk About Competition and Women." *Sociology of Sport Journal.* 8: 119–135.

Curry, Timothy J., and Robert M. Jiobu. 1984. *Sports: A Social Perspective.* Englewood Cliffs, NJ: Prentice Hall.

Curtis, Michael. 2017. "Why Kids Should Play More Than One Sport." Available: https://www.michaelcurtispt.com/early-sport-specialization-drawbacks/.

Czech, Daniel R., Craig A. Wrisberg, Leslee A. Fisher, Charles L. Thompson, and Gene Hayes. 2004. "The Experience of Christian Prayer in Sport: An Existential Phenomenological Investigation." *Journal of Psychology and Christianity.* 25(1): 3–11.

Da Costa, Cassie. 2020. "Inside the Game-Fixing Scandal that Rocked the NBA." *Daily Beast,* August 30. Available: https://www.thedailybeast.com/inside-the-game-fixing-scandal-that-rocked-the-nba.

Dahlberg, Tim. 2012. "Concussions in Boxing: Study Looks for Answers About Head Injuries and Fighting." *Huffington Post Sports,* February 16. Available: http://www.huffingtonpost.com/2012/02/16/boxing-concussions-new-study-effects-head-trauma_n_1281909.html.

_____. 2020. "Endangered: Minority Coaching Hires Still At Dismal Level in NFL." *The Citizen,* January 9: B2.

Daily Mail.com. 2020. "Soccer Violence 'Worst' for Years,'" July 9. Available: https://www.dailymail.co.uk/news/article-196906/Soccer-violence-worst-years.html.

Dan, Major. "Andrew Jackson, President, Patriot, War Hero, Racist?" *History & Headlines,* May 28. Available: https://www.historyandheadlines.com/andrew-jackson-president-patriot-war-hero-racist/.

Dangerous Minds. 2014. "George Orwell's Special Olympic Message: Sports are Bunk." Available: http://dangerousminds.net/comments/george_orwells_special_olympics_message_sports_are_bunk.

Daniels, Stephen. 2005. "How to Talk to Your Kids about Weight." *Parade.* September 25: 6.

Danielson, Bill. 2020. "Speaking of Nature: The Hanson Brothers." *Greenfield Recorder,* August 24. Available: https://www.recorder.com/Speaking-of-Nature-35852268.

Das, Sourav. 2020. "Top 10 Most Popular Sports

in the World [Updated 2020]." *SportsShow.net,* January 21. Available: https://sportsshow.net/top-10-most-popular-sports-in-the-world/.

Daymont, Thomas N. 1981. "The Effects of Monopolistic Procedures on Equality of Competition in Professional Sport Leagues," pp. 241–250 in *Sport, Culture, and Society,* 2nd edition, edited by John W. Loy, Jr., Gerald S. Kenyon and Barry D. McPherson. Philadelphia: Lea & Febiger.

Dean, Sam. 2018. "USC's New Varsity eSports Team is Set to Fight On, Online." *Los Angeles Times,* November 16: C1, C4.

Deffenbacher, Chelsea. 2019. "2 Teens Cited in Locker Room 'Hazing Incident' of Cottage Grove HS Student." *The Register-Guard,* October 21. Available: https://www.registerguard.com/news/20191021/2-teens-cited-in-locker-room-hazing-incident-of-cottage-grove-hs-student.

Delaney, Tim. 2001. *Community, Sport and Leisure.* Auburn, NY: Legend Books.

_____. 2002. "Sport Violence," pp. 1560–1563 in the *Encyclopedia of Crime and Punishment,* Vol. 4, edited by David Levinson. Thousand Oaks, CA: Sage.

_____. 2004. *Classical Social Theory: Investigation and Application.* Upper Saddle River, NJ: Prentice Hall.

_____. 2005. *Contemporary Social Theory: Investigation and Application.* Upper Saddle River, NJ: Prentice Hall.

_____. 2006a. *Seinology: The Sociology of Seinfeld.* Amherst, NY: Prometheus Books.

_____. 2006b. *American Street Gangs.* Upper Saddle River, NJ: Prentice Hall.

_____. 2007. "Basic Concepts of Sports Gambling: An Exploratory Review." *New York Sociologist,* 2: 93–102.

_____. 2012. *Connecting Sociology to Our Lives: An Introduction to Sociology.* Boulder, CO: Paradigm.

_____. 2014. *Classical and Contemporary Social Theory: Investigation and Application.* Upper Saddle River, NJ: Prentice-Hall/Pearson.

_____, editor. 2016. *Sportsmanship: Multidisciplinary Perspectives.* Jefferson, NC: McFarland.

_____. 2018. "The Functionalist Perspective on Sport," pp. 18–28 in *Routledge Sociology of Sport Handbook* (paperback edition) edited by Richard Giulianotti. Oxford, UK: Routlege.

_____. 2021. *Darkened Enlightenment: The Deterioration of Democracy, Human Rights, and Rational Thought in the Twenty-First Century.* London: Routledge.

Delaney, Tim, and Allene Wilcox. 2002. "Sports and the Role of the Media," pp. 199–215 in *Values, Society & Evolution,* edited by H. James Birx and Tim Delaney. Auburn, NY: Legend Books.

Delaney, Tim, and Tim Madigan. 2009. *Sports: Why People Love Them!* Lanham, MD: University Press of America.

_____. 2017. *Friendship and Happiness and the Connection Between the Two.* Jefferson, MD: McFarland.

_____. 2021. *Beyond Sustainability, Second Edition.* Jefferson, NC: McFarland.

DeLessio, Joe. 2014. "9 NFL Players Who Wouldn't Let Their Sons Play Football." *Intelligencer,* November 14. Available: https://nymag.com/intelligencer/2014/11/9-nflers-who-wont-let-their-sons-play-football.html#:~:text=LeBron%20James%20made%20headlines%20this%20week%20when%20he,sons%20play%20football%20because%20of%20the%20health%20risks.

Delfattore, Joan. 2004. *The Fourth R.* New Haven, CT: Yale University Press.

Denzin, Norman. 1969. "Symbolic Interaction and Ethnomethodology: A Proposed Synthesis." *American Sociological Review,* 34(6): 922–934.

Deol, Nishan Singh and Davinder Singh. 2017. "Superstitious Behavior: The Invincible and Invisible Phenomenon in Basketball Sports." *European Journal of Physical Education and Sport Science,* 3(10): 217–224.

Desta, Yohana. 2020. "Colin Kaepernick, Burgeoning Media Mogul, Lands First-Look Deal With Disney." *Vanity Fair,* July 6. Available: https://www.vanityfair.com/hollywood/2020/07/colin-kaepernick-disney-deal.

Devereaux, E. 1976. "Backyard Versus Little League Baseball: The Impoverishment of Children's Games," pp. 37–50 in *Social Problems in Athletics,* edited by D. Landers. Urbana, IL: University of Illinois Press.

Dey, Anindita. 2016. "Wrestling—The Oldest Combat Sport in the World." Go.Unesco, May 30. Available: https://www.gounesco.com/wrestling-oldest-combat-sport/.

Dhonde, B.M., and V.N. Patil. 2012. "Role of Mass Media in Progress of Physical Education and Sports." *Indian Streams Research Journal,* 2(8): 1–3.

Dickerson, John. 2016. "The Locker Room Talk." *CBS News,* October 11. Available: https://www.cbsnews.com/news/the-locker-room-talk-donald-trump/.

Didinger, Ray, and Glen Macnow. 2009. *The Ultimate Book of Sports Movies.* Philadelphia, PA: Running Press Books.

Didtler, Mark. 2020. "Judge: Astros Title Not Earned." *The Citizen,* February 19: B1, B3.

Disabled World. 2017. "Deaflympics: International Games for the Deaf." Available: https://www.disabled-world.com/sports/deaflympics/.

Dobie, Michael. 2004. "Frequently Asked Questions." *Newsday.com* July 11. Available: http://www.newsday.com/sports/ny-pris/-side4,0,3111317.

Dobnik, Verena. 2019. "New York Discusses Banning Tackling." *The Citizen,* October 30: B1, B2.

Dodd, Mike. 2005. "Last Cookie Cutter Crumbles." *USA Today.* September 21: 1C–2C.

_____. 2014. "Baseball's New Palaces: Yankee Stadium and Mets' Citi Field." *USA Today,* April 6. Available: http://usatoday30.usatoday.com/sports/baseball/2009-04-02-baseball-palaces_N.htm.

Domotor, Zsuzsanna, Roberto Ruiz-Barquin, and Attila Szabo. 2016. "Superstitious Behavior in

Sport: A Literature Review." *Scandinavian Journal of Psychology,* 57(4): 368–382.

Dorfman, H.A. 2003. *Coaching the Mental Game.* New York: Taylor.

Dorinson, Joseph. 1997. "Black Heroes in Sport: From Jack Johnson to Muhammad Ali." *Journal of Popular Culture,* 31 (Winter): 115–135.

The Doug Flutie, Jr., Foundation for Autism. 2006. "Homesite." Available: www. dougflutiejrfoundation.org.

Douglas, Mary. 1966. *Purity and Danger.* London: Routledge & Kegan Paul.

Douglas, Steve. 2020. "Players Unite to Protest." *The Citizen,* June 3: B1.

Dowd, Katie. 2016. "Police: Former Raiders QB Todd Marinovich Found Naked In a Stranger's Backyard." *SF Gate,* August 23. Available: https://www.sfgate.com/sports/article/Todd-Marinovich-found-naked-arrest-Irvine-Raiders-9178012.php.

Downward, Paul, and Alistair Dawson. 2000. *The Economics of Professional Team Sports.* New York: Routledge.

Doyle, Paul. 2015. "Patriots and Belichick: Spygate, Deflategame…And More." *Hartford Courant,* January 20. Available: http://www.courant.com/sports/football/hc-patriots-controversies-through-the-years-0121-20150120-story.html.

Drahota, Jo Anne Tremaine, and D. Stanley Eitzen. 1998. "The Role Exit of Professional Athletes." *Sociology of Sport Journal.* 15: 263–278.

Dream Africa. 2017. "Top 7 Traditional African Sports." Available: https://www.thedreamafrica.com/top-7-traditional-african-sports/.

Dryden, Carley. 2014. "Blind Children Catch a Wave off MB El Porto." *Daily Breeze,* July 4: 3, 5.

Dubbert, J.L. 1979. *A Man's Place.* Englewood Cliffs, NJ: Prentice Hall.

Duderstadt, James J. 2003. *Intercollegiate Athletics and the American University: A President's Perspective.* Ann Arbor: University of Michigan Press.

Duncan, Margaret Carlisle, and B. Brummett. 1987. "The Mediation of Spectator Sport." *Research Quarterly,* 38: 168–177.

Dunning, Eric. 1999. *Sport Matters: Sociological Study of Sport, Deviance, Violence and Civilization.* New York: Routledge.

Durkheim, Emile. 1965 [1912]. *The Elementary Forms of Religious Life.* New York: Free Press.

Dyar, Jennifer. 2003 (Summer). "Fatal Attraction: The White Obsession with Indianness." *The Historian,* 6594): 817–836.

Dzhanova, Yelena. 2019. "Wrestling Referee Warned Rep. Jim Jordan about Ohio State's Doctor's Sex Misconduct, New Lawsuit Says." *CNBC,* November 8. Available: https://www.cnbc.com/2019/11/08/referee-told-rep-jim-jordan-about-ohio-state-dr-richard-strauss-sex-abuse-suit-says.html.

Easterbrook, Gregg. 1999. "College Athletes Should Receive Scholarship Extensions," pp. 78–81 in *Sports and Athletes,* edited by Laura Egendorf. San Diego, CA: Greenhaven.

Ebert, Roger. 2005. "Game of Life is Soul of 'Coach Carter." RobertEbert.com, January 13. Available: https://www.rogerebert.com/reviews/coach-carter-2005.

_____. 2009. "2–4–6–8! Who Do We Eviscerate? Fired Up! Fired Up! Yaaaaaaaay!" RobertEbert.com, February 18. Available: https://www.rogerebert.com/reviews/fired-up-2009.

Eden, Scott. 2014. "No One Walks Off the Island." *ESPN The Magazine,* April 17. Available: http://espn.go.com/espn/feature/story/_/id/10781144/no-one-walks-island-los-angeles-dodgers-yasiel-puig-journey-cuba.

_____. 2020. "How Former Ref Tim Donaghy Conspired to Fix NBA Games." *ESPN The Magazine,* July 9. Available: https://www.espn.com/nba/story/_/id/25980368/how-former-ref-tim-donaghy-conspired-fix-nba-games.

Edmondson, Catie. 2018. "Jim Jordan is Defiant as Allegations Mount, and Supporters Point to 'Deep State.'" *The New York Times,* July 8. Available: https://www.nytimes.com/2018/07/06/us/politics/jim-jordan-sexual-misconduct.html?searchResultPosition=1.

Edwards, Harry. 1969. *The Revolt of the Black Athlete.* New York: Free Press.

_____. 1973. *Sociology of Sport.* Homewood, IL: Dorsey.

Eitel, Joseph. 2018. "The Basketball Hoop: A History." *SportsRec,* November 16. Available: https://www.sportsrec.com/6542805/the-basketball-hoop-a-history.

Eitzen, D. Stanley, and George H. Sage. 1989. *Sociology of North American Sport,* 4th edition. Dubuque, IA: Wm. C. Brown.

Eitzen, D. Stanley, editor. 2015. *Sport in Contemporary Society: An Anthology, Tenth Edition.* New York: Oxford University Press.

Elfrink, Tim, and Gus Garcia-Roberts. 2014. "Value Enhanced." *Sports Illustrated,* July 7: 27.

Encyclopedia Britannica. 2020. "Field Hockey." Available: https://www.britannica.com/sports/field-hockey.

Englander, Elizabeth Kandel. 2013. *Bullying and Cyberbullying: What Every Educator Needs To Know.* Cambridge, MA: Harvard Education Press.

Entine, Jon. 2000. *Taboo: Why Black Athletes Dominate Sports and Why We're Afraid to Talk About It.* New York: Public Affairs/Perseus.

Erie County Interscholastic Conference. 2001. "Appendix A: Academic Eligibility." New York State Public High School Athletic Association and the Erie County Interscholastic Conference (E.D.I.C.).

Erlinger, Catherine. 2018. "Childhood Obesity." The Heart Foundation, February 9. Available: https://theheartfoundation.org/2018/02/09/childhood-obesity/.

Ernst, Douglas. 2014. "Russia Wins Sochi Gold for Corruption? IOC Official Cites $18B in Embezzlement." *The Washington Times,* January 10. Available: http://www.washingtontimes.com/

news/2014/jan/10/russia-wins-sochi-gold-corruption-ioc-official-cit/.

ESPN Page 2. 2005. "Page 2's Top 20 Sports Movies of All-Time." July 30. Available: http://espn.go.com/page2/movies/s/top20/fulllist.html.

ESPN.com. 2014a. "NFL: Husain Abdullah Penalty Wrong." September 30. Available: http://espn.go.com/nfl/story/_/id/11616422/nfl-says-husain-abdullah-kansas-city-chiefs-penalized-praying-celebration.

_____. 2014b. "Sleeping Fan Files $10M Lawsuit." July 8. Available: http://espn.go.com/new-york/mlb/story/_/id/11190576/sleeping-fan-files-10-million-defamation-lawsuit-espn-announcers.

Ethical Journalism Network. 2020. "The 5 Principles of Ethical Journalism." Available: https://ethicaljournalismnetwork.org/who-we-are/5-principles-of-journalism.

Euchner, C.C. 1993. *Playing the Field: Why Sports Teams Move and Cities Fight to Keep Them.* Baltimore: Johns Hopkins University Press.

Evans, Jace. 2020. "Happy Birthday, Michael Phelps! The Most Decorated Olympian Ever Turns 35." *USA Today,* June 30. Available: https://www.usatoday.com/story/sports/olympics/2020/06/30/michael-phelps-celebrates-35th-birthday/3283315001/.

Evans-Brown, Michael, and Jim McVeigh. 2009 (October). "Injecting Human Growth Hormone as a Performance-enhancing Drug—Perspectives from the United Kingdom." *Journal of Substance Use,* 14(5): 267–288.

Everard, Harry Stirling Crawford. 2011 [1923]. *History of the Royal and Ancient Golf Club, St. Andrews From 1754–1900.* Charleston, NC: Nabu Press.

Falkener, Edward. 1961. *Games, Ancient and Oriental and How to Play Them.* New York: Dover.

Fallstrom, R.B. 2014. "'Hands Up' Players to Attend Ferguson Christmas Party." *Tucson News,* December 19. Available: http://www.tucsonnewsnow.com/story/27664200/hands-up-players-to-attend-ferguson-christmas-party.

Fantasy Sports & Gaming Association. 2020. "About the FSGA." Available: https://thefsga.org/.

Fantz, Ashley. 2014. "Police Angry at 'Hands Up' Gesture by St. Louis Rams Players." *CNN.com* December 1. Available: http://www.cnn.com/2014/12/01/us/ferguson-nfl-st-louis-rams/.

Farber, Michael. 2005. "Scorecard: Cold Warriors." *Sports Illustrated.* July 4: 16–17.

Farrell, Brendan. 2019. "Stick Fighting and the Origins of the Shillelagh." *Irish Central,* July 22. Available: https://www.irishcentral.com/roots/shillelagh-history.

Federal Bureau of Investigation (FBI). 2020. "Illegal Sports Betting." Available: https://www.fbi.gov/scams-and-safety/common-scams-and-crimes/illegal-sports-betting.

Federation International Football Association (FIFA). 2018. "More Than Half the World Watched Record-breaking 2018 World Cup." Available: https://www.fifa.com/worldcup/news/more-than-half-the-world-watched-record-breaking-2018-world-cup.

Feinberg, Doug. 2006. "Poor Sportsmanship or Good Shooting: Should Epiphanny Prince Have Stayed in to Score 113 Points Against a Helpless Team?" *The Post-Standard.* February 3: C-9

Feldman, Jay. 1993. "Roberto Clemente Went to Bat for Latino Ballplayers." *Smithsonian,* Vol. 24: 128.

Fendrich, Howard. 2002. "NBA Inks New Six-Year, $4.6 Billion Deals with ESPN, ABC, TNT." *The Buffalo News.* January 24: C-5.

Fernas, Rob. 1994. "World Cup USA '94: Semifinals: Spotlight: ROBO-Kicker." *Los Angeles Times,* July 14. Available: https://www.latimes.com/archives/la-xpm-1994-07-14-sp-15318-story.html,

Ferris, Marc. 2014. *Star-Spangled Banner: The Unlikely Story of America's National Anthem.* Baltimore, MD: Johns Hopkins University Press.

FIFA World Football Museum. 2019. *The Official History of the FIFA World Cup, second edition.* London: Carlton Books.

Figler, Stephen, and Gail Whitaker. 1991. *Sport and Play in American Life,* 2nd edition. Dubuque, IA: Wm. C. Brown.

_____. 1995. *Sport and Play in American Life,* 3rd edition. Chicago: Brown and Benchmark.

Finkbeiner, Nathan W.B., Jeffrey E. Max, Stewart Longman, Chantel Debert. 2016. "Knowing What We Don't Know: Long-Term Psychiatric Outcomes Following Adult Concussion in Sports." *The Canadian Journal of Psychiatry,* 61(5): 270–276.

Fischer, Claude E., and C. Ann Stueve. 1977. "Authentic Community: The Role of Place in Modern Life," pp. 163–186 in *Networks and Places,* edited by Claude S. Fischer. New York: Free Press.

Fisher, Donald M. 2001. "Chief Bill Orange and the Saltine Warrior: A Cultural History of Indian Symbols and Imagery at Syracuse University," pp. 25–45 in *Team Spirits: The Native American Mascots Controversy.* Lincoln: University of Nebraska Press.

Fisher, Mike. 2014. "Inside NFL's Wonderlic Test—And Why It Matters." *Fox Sports,* April 12. Available: http://www.foxsports.com/southwest/story/inside-nfl-s-wonderlic-test-and-why-it-matters-041214.

Fitness Revolution. 2015. "Top 10 Health Benefits of Youth Sports." Available: https://www.healthfitnessrevolution.com/top-10-health-benefits-youth-sports/.

Fitzgerald, Jim. 2001. "Iona-Mississippi 'Rivalry' has a History." *Buffalo News.* March 15: B11.

500 Nations. 2020. "Indian Casinos." Available: https://500nations.com/Indian_Casinos.asp#:~:text=Ten%20Largest%20Indian%20Casinos.%201%20WinStar%20World%20Casino,140%20table%20games%2C%2046%20poker%20tables.%20More%20items.

Fleisher Arthur A., III, Brian L. Goff, and Robert D. Tollison. 1992. *The National Collegiate Athletic Association: A Study in Cartel Behavior.* Chicago: University of Chicago Press.

Florio, Mike. 2020. "New Report from Washington Post Points Finger Directly at Daniel Snyder." *Washington Post,* August 26. Available: https://sports.yahoo.com/report-washington-post-points-finger-160730351.html.

Food and Drug Administration (FDA). 2017. "Teens and Steroids: A Dangerous Combo." Available: https://www.fda.gov/consumers/consumer-updates/teens-and-steroids-dangerous-combo.

Football 'N' America. 2020. "About." Available: https://playfna.com/.

Football Unites Racism Divides (FURD). 2014. "Football Against Racism in Europe (FARE)." Available: http://www.furd.org/default.asp?intPageID=55.

Forbes. 2006. "What is Your Team Worth?" (As appearing in *The Post-Standard.*) September 5: D-8.

_____. 2020a. "Sports Money: 2019 NFL Valuations." Available: https://www.forbes.com/nfl-valuations/list/#tab:overall.

_____. 2020b. "The Business of Baseball." Available: https://www.forbes.com/mlb-valuations/list/#tab:overall.

_____. 2020c. "The Business of Basketball." Available: https://www.forbes.com/nba-valuations/list/#tab:overall.

_____. 2020d. "The Business of Hockey." Available: https://www.forbes.com/nhl-valuations/list/#tab:overall.

_____. 2020e. "25 Richest Sports Teams in the World in 2019." Available: https://www.thestreet.com/lifestyle/sports/richest-sports-teams-in-the-world-15109120#:~:text=Here%27s%20a%20look%20at%20the%2025%20richest%20sports,the%20World%20in%202019%201.%20Dallas%20Cowboys%20%28NFL%29.

_____. 2020f. "Sports Agents." Available: https://www.forbes.com/sports-agents/list/#tab:overall.

Fortes, Meyer. 1936. "Ritual Festivals and Social Cohesion in the Hinterland of the Gold Coast." *American Anthropologist,* 38: 602.

Fowler, Clay. 2014. "Sports Team Owners, Venues React to Byran Stow Verdict." *Daily Breeze,* July 10: A7.

Fowler, Linda L. 1996. "Who Runs for Congress?" *PS: Political Science and Politics.* Vol. 29, No. 3 (Sept.): 430–434.

Francis, Leslie. 2001. "Title IX: Equality for Women's Sports?" pp. 247–266 in *Ethics in Sport,* edited by William J. Morgan, Klaus V. Meier, and Angela J. Schneider. Champaign, IL: Human Kinetics.

Freeman, William. 1997. *Physical Education and Sport in a Changing Society.* Boston: Allyn and Bacon.

Frey, James H. 1978. "The Organization of Amateur Sport: Efficiency to Entropy." *American Behavioral Scientist.* 21: 361–378.

_____. 2020. "Personal Email Correspondences." June 15–16.

Frey, James H., and D. Stanley Eitzen. 1991. "Sport and Society." *Annual Review of Sociology,* 17: 503–522.

Frey, James H., and David R. Dickens. 1990. "Leisure as a Primary Institution." *Sociological Inquiry.* 60 (3): 264–273.

Frey, James H., and Tim Delaney. 1996. "The Role of Leisure Participation in Prison: A Report from Consumers." *Journal of Offender Rehabilitation,* Vol. 23 (1/2):79–89.

Frith, David. 2001. *Silence of the Heart: Cricket Suicides.* Edinburgh: Mainstream Publishing.

Fryer, Jenna. 2005. "Four Networks Flag NASCAR." *The Post-Standard.* December 8: D-2.

_____. 2020. "Ganassi Racing Fires Larson." *The Citizen,* April 15: B1.

Funk, Daniel, Daniel Mahony, Makoto Nakazawa, Sumiko Hirakawa. 2001. "Development of the Sport Interest Inventory (SII): Implications for Measuring Unique Consumer Motives at Team Sporting Events (Research Paper)." *International Journal of Sports Marketing and Sponsorships,* 3(3): 291–316.

Garcia, Sandra E. 2020. "Charges against Former Michigan State President are Dismissed." *The New York Times,* May 13. Available: https://www.nytimes.com/2020/05/13/us/michigan-state-university-president-charges.html?searchResultPosition=2.

Garcia-Roberts, Gus. 2014. "Baseball's Scariest Hotel." *American Way,* June: 124.

Gardiner, E. Norman. 1930. *Athletes of the Ancient World.* Oxford: Clarendon Press.

Garfinkel, Harold. 1956. "Conditions of Successful Degradation Ceremonies." *American Journal of Sociology.* 61: 420–424.

Geertz, Clifford. 1965. "Religion as a Cultural System," in *Anthropological Approaches to the Study of Religion,* edited by Michael Banton. London: Tavistock.

Geist, Willie. 2019. "Sunday Today With Willie Geist." NBC, original air date November 3.

Gelston, Dan. 2020. "NASCAR Bans Confederate Flag." *The Citizen,* June 11: B1.

Gerbi, Gemechu B., Tsegaye Habtemariam, Berhanu Tameru, David Nganwa, and Vinaida Robnet. 2009. "The Correlation Between Alcohol Consumption and Risky Sexual Behaviors Among People Living with HIV/AIDS." *Journal of Substance Use,* 14(2): 90–100.

Getlen, Larry. 2014. "How Dock Ellis Dropped Acid and Threw a No-hitter." *New York Post,* August 21. Available: http://nypost.com/2014/08/31/pitcher-dock-ellis-dropped-acid-then-threw-a-no-hitter/.

Giesen, Bernhard. 2005. "Performing Transcendence in Politics: Sovereignty, Deviance and the Void of Meaning." *Sociological Theory,* 23(3): 275–285.

Gifford, Aaron. 2004. "Many Ex-Players Find Life After Pros Difficult." *The Post-Standard.* October 2: A-5.

Gilbert, Kimutai. 2017. "Average Working Time By Country." *World Atlas.* Available: https://www.worldatlas.com/articles/average-working-time-by-country.html.

Gilligan, Carol. 1993. *In a Different Voice.* Cambridge, MA: Harvard University Press.

Glaser, Kyle. 2020. "How Each MLB Team Plans to Pay Minor Leaguers in 2020." *Baseball America,* June 30. Available: https://www.baseballamerica.com/stories/how-each-mlb-team-plans-to-pay-minor-leaguers-in-2020/.

Glass, Alana. 2019. "FIFA Women's World Cup Breaks Viewership Records." *Forbes,* October 21. Available: https://www.forbes.com/sites/alanaglass/2019/10/21/fifa-womens-world-cup-breaks-viewership-records/#5533d9721884.

Gleiber, Michael. 2020. "4 Common Injuries in MMA and UFC Fighters." Concierge Spine Surgery. Available: https://www.michaelgleibermd.com/news/4-common-injuries-mma-ufc-fighters/#:~:text=It%E2%80%99s%20no%20secret%20that%20injuries%20are%20common%20in,ligament%20tears%2C%20and%20head%20injuries%20are%20also%20common.

Glyn, Andrew. 2006. *Capitalism Unleashed: Finance Globalization and Welfare.* New York: Oxford University Press.

Gmelch, George. 1994. "Ritual and Magic in American Baseball," pp. 351–361 in *Conformity & Conflict: Readings in Cultural Anthropology,* 8th edition, edited by James P. Spradley and David W. McCurdy. New York: HarperCollins.

Goldman, Adam. 2014. "CIA Hatched Plan to Make Demon Toy to Counter Osama bin Laden's Influence." *The Washington Post,* June 19. Available: http://www.washingtonpost.com/world/national-security/cia-hatched-plan-to-make-demon-toy-to-counter-bin-laden-influence/2014/06/19/cb3d571c-f0d0–11e3-914c-1fbd0614e2d4_story.html.

Goldman, Chelena. 2018. "The 16 Most Ejected Managers in MLB History." *Sportscasting,* July 22. Available: https://www.sportscasting.com/the-16-most-ejected-managers-in-mlb-history/.

Goldman, Tom. 2008. "Ex-Referee Says 2002 Playoff Was Rigged." *National Public Radio,* June 12. Available: http://www.npr.org/templates/story/story.php?storyId=91415111.

Goldstein, Richard, 1993. *Ivy League Autumns: An Illustrated History of College Football's Grand Old Rivalries.* New York: St. Martin's Press.

Gorman, Fitzalan. 2017. "A High School Athlete's GPA Vs. Average High School Student's GPA." *The Classroom,* September 26. Available: https://www.theclassroom.com/high-school-athletes-gpa-vs-average-high-school-students-gpa-3702.html.

Gottfredson, Linda S. 1998. "Jensen, Jensenism, and the Sociology of Intelligence." *Intelligence,* 26(3): 291–299.

Gough, Christina. 2018. "Running & Jogging—Statistics & Facts." *Statista,* October 18. https://www.statista.com/topics/1743/running-and-jogging/.

_____. 2019a. "Average Playing Career Length in the National Football League." Statista, September 10. Available: https://www.statista.com/statistics/240102/average-player-career-length-in-the-national-football-league/.

_____. 2019b. "The North America Sports Market Size 2009–2023. *Statista,* December 10. Available: https://www.statista.com/statistics/214960/revenue-of-the-north-american-sports-market/.

_____. 2019c. "Number of Participants in Golf In the United States from 2006 to 2018 (in millions)." *Statista.* Available: https://www.statista.com/statistics/191907/participants-in-golf-in-the-us-since-2006/.

_____. 2020h. "Leading eSports Players Worldwide 2020, by Overall Earnings." *Statista,* March 25. Available: https://www.statista.com/statistics/518010/leading-esports-players-worldwide-by-earnings/.

_____. 2020a. "Number of Participants in Snowboarding in the U.S. 2007–2017." *Statista,* January 24. Available: https://www.statista.com/statistics/191319/participants-in-snowboarding-in-the-us-since-2007/

_____. 2020b. "Average Player Salary in the Sports Industry by League 2019/20." *Statista,* May 25. Available: https://www.statista.com/statistics/675120/average-sports-salaries-by-league/.

_____. 2020c. "Share of Sports Fans in the United States as of June 2020." *Statista,* June 18. Available: https://www.statista.com/statistics/300148/interest-nfl-football-age-canada/

_____. 2020d. "Fan Cost Index of MLB Teams 2019." *Statista,* June 19. Available: https://www.statista.com/statistics/202611/fan-cost-index-of-the-major-league-baseball/.

_____. 2020e. "Fan Cost Index of National Football League Teams in 2019." *Statista,* July 30. Available: https://www.statista.com/statistics/202584/nfl—fan-cost-index/.

_____. 2020g. "Age of U.S. Video Game Players in 2020." *Statista,* July 24. Available: https://www.statista.com/statistics/189582/age-of-us-video-game-players-since-2010/.

Grabianowski, Ed. 2020. "How Competitive Eating Works." *HowStuffWorks.* Available: https://entertainment.howstuffworks.com/competitive-eating.htm.

Graham, Bryan Armen. 2020. "The Same People Who Put Trump In Office Run the NFL. No Wonder It's Not Diverse." *The Guardian,* May 22. Available: https://www.theguardian.com/sport/blog/2020/may/22/nfl-rooney-rule-diversity-draft-pick-incentives.

Grange, Pippa, and John H. Kerr. 2011. "Do Elite Athletes Renowned for Their Aggressive Play Transfer Aggression to Nonsport Settings? A Qualitative Exploratory Study." *Journal of Aggression, Maltreatment & Trauma,* 20(4): 359–375.

Green, Dave. 2003. "Fishing in Early Medieval Times." Regia Anglorum. Available: https://regia.org/research/life/fishing.htm.

Green, Lee. 2019."Impact of Competitive Cheer Laws, Regulations on Title IX Compliance." National Federation of State High School

Associations, April 16. Available: https://www. nfhs.org/articles/impact-of-competitive-cheer-laws-regulations-on-title-ix-compliance/.

Green, Tim. 1996. *The Dark Side of the Game: My Life in the NFL*. New York: Warner Books.

_____. 1997. "Cheating to Win Is Rule of Thumb for Teams' Survival." *USA Today*. November 6: 4C.

Green Sports Alliance. 2020. "About: Who We Are & What We Do." Available: https:// greensportsalliance.org/about/.

Greenawalt, Kent. 2005. *Does God Belong in Public Schools?* Princeton: Princeton University Press.

Greenspan, Stanley I., and Serena Wieder. 2006. *Engaging Autism*. New York: Da Capo Press.

Gregory, Sean. 2017. "How Kids' Sports Became a $15 Billion Industry." *Time*, August 24. Available: https://time.com/4913687/how-kids-sports-became-15-billion-industry/.

Greif, Andrew. 2020. "Environmental Report for Clippers Arena Approved By Inglewood City Council." *Los Angeles Times*, July 21. Available: https://www.latimes.com/sports/clippers/ story/2020–07–21/environmental-report-clippers -arena-approved-inglewood-city-council.

Griffin, Pat. 1998. *Strong Women, Deep Closets: Lesbians and Homophobia in Sport*. Champaign, IL: Human Kinetics.

Griffin, Robert S. 1998. *Sports in the Lives of Children and Adolescents: Success on the Field and in Life*. Westport, CT: Praeger.

Griffin, Tim. 2016. "New NFL Rules Czar Jon Runyan was Known for Bending Them During Playing Career." MySanAntonio.com, May 17. Available: https://www.mysanantonio. com/sports/nfl/article/:~:text=Maybe%20 Runyan's%20political%20career%20might%20 have%20changed%20him.,over%20the%20 government%20shutdown%20before%20the%20 2014%20elections.

Grose, Justin P. 2011. "Time to Bury the Tomahawk Chop: An Attempt to Reconcile the Differing Viewpoints of Native Americans and Sports Fans." *American Indian Law Review*, 35(2): 695–728.

Grossman, Hallie. 2019. "Bills Mafia Blends Ketchup, Mustard and, This NFL Season, A Shot of Hope." ESPN, November 5. Available: https://www.espn. com/nfl/story/_/id/27973780/bills-mafia-blends-ketchup-mustard-nfl-season-shot-hope.

Gruneau, R. S. 1975. "Sport, Social Differentiation, and Social Inequality," pp. 117–184 in *Sport and Social Order*, edited by D. Ball and J. Loy. Reading, MA: Addison-Wesley.

Gurko, Miriam. 1974. *The Ladies of Seneca Falls*. New York: Schocken Books.

Guttmann, Allen. 1978. *From Ritual to Record: The Nature of Modern Sports*. New York: Columbia University Press.

_____. 1988. *A Whole New Ball Game*. Chapel Hill, NC: University of North Carolina Press.

_____. 2002. *The Olympics: A History of the Modern Games*, 2nd Edition. Urbana, IL: University of Illinois Press.

_____. 2004. *Sports: The First Five Millennia*. Amherst and Boston: University of Massachusetts Press.

Hadden, Richard. 1997. *Sociological Theory*. Orchard Park, NY: Broadview.

Halpern, Orly. 2008. "For Palestinian Swimmers, It's a Chance to Swim." *The Globe and Mail* (Vancouver, BC). July 7: A3.

Hamilton, Brian. 2005. "How to Operate a 'Whizzinator'—and Its History." *The Mercury News*. May 11. Available: http://www.mercurynews.com/ mld/mercurymnews/sports/11623290.htm.

Hamilton, E.L. 2018. "Lawn Jockeys Dating Back to the Revolutionary War Were Emblematic of Their Era." *The Vintage News*, April 16. Available: https://www.thevintagenews. com/2018/04/16/lawn-jockeys/.

Hanson, Mary Ellen. 1995. *Go! Fight! Win!: Cheerleading in American Culture*. Bowling Green, OH: Bowling Green State University Popular Press.

Hardin, Marie, Julie Dodd, Jean Chance, and Kristie Walsdorf. 2004. "Sporting Image in Black and White: Race and Newspaper Coverage of the 2000 Olympic Games." *The Howard Journal of Communications*, 15: 211–227.

Harris, Jack. 2020. "College Athletes Finding Their Voices for Change." *Los Angeles Times*, June 16: B6.

Harris, Marvin. 2004. "How Our Skins Got their Color," pp. 7–9 in *Rethinking the Color Line: Readings in Race and Ethnicity, 2nd edition*, edited by Charles A. Gallagher. Boston: McGraw-Hill.

Harrison, Todd. 2016. "Emphasizing Sportsmanship in Youth Sport," pp. 87–99 in *Sportsmanship: Multidisciplinary Perspectives*, edited by Tim Delaney. Jefferson, NC: McFarland.

Hartmann, Susan. 1998. "Feminism and Women's Movement," pp. 41–45 in *Reading Women's Lives*, edited by Mary Margaret Fonow. Needham Heights, MA: Simon & Schuster.

Hayward, Paul. 2012. "Bradley Wiggins: Reluctant Hero of the Masses." *The Telegraph*, December 14. Available: http://www.telegraph.co.uk/sport/ sports-personality-of-the-year/9746833/Bradley-Wiggins-reluctant-hero-of-the-masses.html.

Heilweil, Rebecca. 2019. "Infoporn: College Esports Players Are Cashing in Big." *Wired*, January 21. Available: https://www.wired.com/story/ infoporn-college-esports-players-cashing-in-big/#:~:text=Though%20Fortnite%20is%20the%20 most%20played%20game%20among,official%20 college%20leagues%20sanctioned%20by%20 the%20videogames%E2%80%99%20publishers.

Heisler, Mark. 2011. "Marinovich Breaks Family Mold." *The New York Times*, September 15. Available: http://www.nytimes.com/2011/09/16/ sports/ncaafootball/syracuse-player-breaks-the-marinovich-mold.html?pagewanted=all&_r=0.

Helin, Kurt. 2013. "It's Gotta Be the Shoes: How Nike Bet on Jordan, Jordan Bet on Nike, and Both Won, Big." *NBC Sports*, February 15. Available: http:// probasketballtalk.nbcsports.com/2013/02/15/its-gotta-be-the-shoes-how-nike-bet-on-jordan-jordan-bet-on-nike-and-both-won-big/.

Hellendoorn, Joop, Rimmert van der Kooij, and Brian Sutton-Smith. 1994. *Play and Intervention*. Albany, NY: State University of New York Press.

Hellison, D. 1995. *Teaching Responsibility Through Physical Activity*. Champaign, IL: Human Kinetics.

Hernandez, Dylan. 2020. "MLB Team Owners Willing to Let Players Shoulder the Blame If Season Doesn't Start." *Los Angeles Times*, May 12. Available: https://www.latimes.com/sports/story/2020–05–12/mlb-owners-players-proposal-season-coronavirus-negotiations-talks.

Heywood, Leslie. 1998. *Pretty Good for a Girl*. New York: Free Press.

Heywood, Leslie, and Shari L. Dworkin. 2003. *Built to Win: The Female Athlete as Cultural Icon*. Minneapolis: University of Minnesota Press.

Hill, Christopher. 1992. *Olympic Politics*. New York: Manchester University Press.

Hilliard, Dan C. 1996. "Televised Sport and the (Anti) Sociological Imagination," pp. 115–125 in *Sport in Contemporary Society: An Anthology*, 5th edition, edited by D. Stanley Eitzen. New York: St. Martin's Press.

Hiltzik, Michael. 2015. "The NFL's Dropping Its Tax Exemption Isn't a Good Thing. Here's Why." *The Los Angeles Times*, April 28. Available: http://www.latimes.com/business/hiltzik/la-fi-mh-heres-why-the-nfls-dropping-its-taxexemption-20150428-column.html.

History.com. 2020. "Columbus Sets Sail." Available: https://www.history.com/this-day-in-history/columbus-sets-sail#:~:text=From%20the%20Spanish%20port%20of%20Palos%2C%20Italian%20explorer,the%20fabled%20gold%20and%20spice%20islands%20of%20Asia.

Hoberman, John. 2001. "Listening to Steroids," pp. 107–118 in *Ethics in Sport*, edited by William Morgan, Klaus Meier, and Angela Schneider. Champaign, IL: Human Kinetics.

_____. 2005. *Testosterone Dreams: Rejuvenation, Aphrodisia, Doping*. Berkeley, CA: University of California Press.

Hoch, Paul. 1972. *Rip Off the Big Game: The Exploitation of Sports by the Power Elite*. Garden City, NY: Anchor.

Hockey Fights. 2020. "NHL Fight Stats." Available: https://www.hockeyfights.com/stats.

Hoffer, Richard. 2006. "Scorecard: Goodbye, Mr. Chips." *Sports Illustrated*. May 15: 18–19.

Hoffman, Roy. 1996. "It's a Bird, It's a Plane, It's a Flying Anvil." *The Post Standard*. November 7: A-18.

Hoffman, Shirl, editor. 1992. *Sport and Religion*. Champaign, IL: Human Kinetics.

Hole, Christina. 1969. *Encyclopedia of Superstitions*. Chester Springs, PA: Dufour.

Homans, George. 1961. *Social Behavior: Its Elementary Forms*. New York: Harcourt, Brace and World.

Hook, Sidney. 1943. *The Hero in History*. Boston: Beacon Press.

Horn, J.C. 1977. "Parent Egos Take the Fun out of Little League." *Psychology Today*, 11(9): 18, 22.

Horse Industry News, Welfare and Industry. 2020. "Study: Horseback Riding Helps Kids with Autism, ADHD." TheHorse.com, January 31. Available: https://thehorse.com/184472/study-horseback-riding-helps-kids-with-autism-adhd/.

Houlihan, Barrie. 1999. *Dying to Win*. Strasbourg, Germany: Council of Europe Publishing.

Howe, Connor. 2020. "The Real Story Behind 'The Blind Side.'" *TieBreaker*, January 1. Available: https://www.tiebreaker.com/the-real-story-behind-the-blind-side/.

Howell, R. 1982. "Generalizations on Women and Sport, Games and Play in the United States from Settlement to 1860," pp. 87–95 in *Her Story in Sport: A Historical Anthropology of Women in Sports*, edited by R. Howell. West Point, NY: Leisure Press.

Hudak, Stephen. 2014. "State, Defense Rest in FAMU Hazing Trial." *Orlando Sentinel*, October 30. Available: http://www.orlandosentinel.com/features/education/higher-education/os-famu-hazing-robert-champion-trial-defense-20141030-story.html.

Humanitarian Hall of Fame. 2006. "Mission Statement." Available: http://www.sportshumanitarian.com/quick_facts/quick_facts.html.

Hunt, Kristin. 2019. "How Sports Stadiums Are Becoming More Sustainable." Green Matters. Available: https://www.greenmatters.com/travel/2018/07/31/2f5fvD/sports-stadiums-sustainable-design.

Hussaini, Azmatullah and Jules Lipoff. 2020. "COVID-19 and Exploitation of NCAA Student-Athletes." *Los Angeles Times*, June 23: A11.

Hutchins, Carol, Edniesha Curry, and Meredith Flaherty. 2019. "Where Are All the Women Coaches?" *The New York Times*, December 31. Available: https://www.nytimes.com/2019/12/31/opinion/Women-coaching-sports-title-ix.html?searchResultPosition=1.

Hutslar, J. 1985. *Beyond Xs and Os*. Welcome, NC: Wooten.

In Sports. 2018. "Top 10 Most Popular Youth Sports in America." Available: http://insportscenters.com/most-popular-youth-sports/.

Influencer Marketing. 2020. "The Incredible Growth of eSports." Available: https://influencermarketinghub.com/growth-of-esports-stats/.

Inside Hazing. "High School Hazing." Available: http://www.insidehazing.com/statistics_25_high.php.

Institute for International Sport. 2014a. "About IIS." Available: http://www.internationalsport.org/about-iis.cfm.

_____. 2014b. "National Sportsmanship Day." Available: http://www.internationalsport.org/nsd/overview.cfm.

Insurance Information Institute (III). 2020. "Facts + Statistics: Sports Injuries." Available: https://www.iii.org/fact-statistic/facts-statistics-sports-injuries.

International Committee of Sports for the Deaf.

2020. "Brazil Declares Host for the Summer Deaflympics in 2021." Available: https://www.deaflympics.com/news/brazil-declares-host-for-the-summer-deaflympics-in-2021.

Invictus Games. 2014. "About the Invictus Games." Available: http://invictusgames.org/about-invictus/.

Jackman, Spencer. 2018. "The World Cup and Olympics Are in a League of Their Own When It Comes to TV Ratings." *The18.com,* June 12. Available: https://the18.com/soccer-learning/world-cup-vs-olympics-tv-ratings.

Jackson, Dan. 2020. "Why 'Cops' Finally Got Canceled After 32 Seasons." *Thrillist.com,* June 10. Available: https://www.thrillist.com/entertainment/nation/cops-tv-show-cancelled-explained.

James, LeBron. 2014. "I'm Coming Home." *Sports Illustrated,* July 21: 41.

James, Meg. 2020. "Coronavirus Could Wipe Out $10 Billion in TV Ad Spending." *Los Angeles Times,* April 21: A9.

James, William. 1897. *The Will to Believe and Other Essays.* London: Longmans, Green, and Co.

Jamieson, Katherine M. 1998. "Reading Nancy Lopez: Decoding Representations of Race, Class, and Sexuality." *Sociology of Sport Journal.* 15: 343–358.

Jay, Kathryn. 2004. *More Than Just a Game.* New York: Columbia University Press.

Jewell, Mark. 2005. "Don't Ignore Genetics, Say Drug Researchers." *The Post-Standard,* July 15: A-3.

Jewell, R. Todd, Afsheen Moti, and Dennis Coates. 2012. "A Brief History of Violence and Aggression in Spectator Sports," pp. 11–25 in *Violence and Aggression in Sporting Contests: Economics, History and Politics,* edited by R. Todd Jewell. New York: Springer.

Johnson, Arthur T. 1983. "Municipal Administration and the Sports Franchise Relocation Issue." *Public Administration Review.* Nov/Dec: 519–527.

Johnson, Patricia Altenbernd. 2000. *On Wollstonecraft.* New York: Wadsworth.

Jonas, Jeff. 2017. "Hazing in High School Athletics." National Federation of State High Schools. Available: https://www.nfhs.org/articles/hazing-in-high-school-athletics/

Jones, Charisse. 2020. "For Faces Behind Aunt Jemima, Uncle Ben's and Cream of Wheat, Life Transcended Stereotype." *USA Today,* July 10. Available: https://www.usatoday.com/story/money/2020/07/10/real-people-behind-aunt-jemima-uncle-ben-cream-of-wheat/3285054001/.

Jones, Jeffery A., and Michael J. Paciorek. 1994. *Sports and Recreation for the Disabled.* Indianapolis, IN: Master Press.

Kammerer, R. Craig. 2001. "What Is Doping and How Is It Detected?" pp. 3–28 in *Doping in Elite Sport,* edited by Wayne Wilson and Edward Derse. Champaign, IL: Human Kinetics.

Karsten, Matthew. 2019. "Volcano Boarding Is Just Slightly Insane." Expert Vagabond, September 25. Available: https://expertvagabond.com/volcano-boarding/.

Kassimeris, Christos. 2009. *European Football in Black and White: Tackling Racism in Football.* Lanham, MD: Lexington.

Katz, B. 1994. "Seize Every Team!" *The Nation.* September 26: 259, 297.

Keating, Thomas. 1994. *Intimacy with God.* New York: Crossroad.

_____. 1995. *Open Mind, Open Heart.* New York: Continuum.

Kedmey, Dan. 2014. "Native American Group Mounts $9B Lawsuit Against Cleveland Indians." *TIME,* June 25. Available: http://time.com/2921995/cleveland-indians-lawsuit-native-americans/.

Kelley, Bruce, and Carl Carchia. 2013. "Hey, Data, Data—Swing!" *ESPN Magazine,* July 11. Available: http://espn.go.com/espn/story/_/id/9469252/hidden-demographics-youth-sports-espn-magazine.

Kellison, Timothy B. Sylvia Trendafilova, and Brian P. McCullough. 2015. "Considering the Social Impact of Sustainable Stadium Design." *International Journal of Event Management Research,* 10(1): 63–83.

Kendellen, Kelsey and Martin Camire. 2017. "Examining the Life Skill Development and Transfer Experiences of Former High School Athletes." *International Journal of Sport and Exercise Psychology,* 15(4): 395–408.

Kennard, Jerry. 2019. "The Dangers of Boxing Injuries." *Very Well Fit,* November 28. Available: https://www.verywellfit.com/boxing-injuries-2328909.

Kenyon, Gerald S., and Barry D. McPherson. 1981. "Becoming Involved in Physical Activity and Sport: A Process of Socialization," pp. 217–234 in *Sport, Culture and Society,* edited by John W. Loy, Gerald Kenyon and Barry McPherson. Philadelphia: Lea & Febiger.

Kenyon, Gerald S., and John W. Loy. 1965. "Toward Sociology of Sport." *Journal of Health, Physical Education, and Recreation,* 36(5): 24–25, 68–69.

Kerr, John H. 2005. *Rethinking Aggression and Violence in Sport.* New York: Routledge.

Kessel, Anna. 2011. "Caster Semenya, the Athlete Who Became a Reluctant Hero." *The Guardian,* June 11. Available: http://www.theguardian.com/sport/2011/jun/12/caster-semenya-athletics.

Kessler, Glenn, Salvador Rizzo, and Meg Ryan. 2020. "President Trump Has Made More Than 20,000 False or Misleading Claims." *The Washington Post,* July 13. Available: https://www.washingtonpost.com/politics/2020/07/13/president-trump-has-made-more-than-20000-false-or-misleading-claims/.

Khomami, Nadia. 2017. "#MeToo: How a Hashtag Became a Rallying Cry Against Sexual Harassment." *The Guardian,* October 20. Available: https://www.theguardian.com/world/2017/oct/20/women-worldwide-use-hashtag-metoo-against-sexual-harassment.

Kidd, Bruce. 1995. "Inequality in Sport, the Corporation and the State: An Arena for Social

Scientists." *Journal of Sport and Social Issues.* Vol. 19 (Aug.), No. 3: 232–248.

Kim, Victoria. 2019. "South Korea Wrestles with Inability to Unplug." *Los Angeles Times*, October 20: A1, A6.

King, C. Richard, and Charles Fruehling Springwood. 2001. *Team Spirits: The Native American Mascots Controversy.* Lincoln: University of Nebraska Press.

King, Peter. 2010. "The Hits That Are Changing Football." *Sports Illustrated*, November 1.

Kiprop, Victor. 2019. "FIFA Women's World Cup Wins by Country." *World Atlas*, June 17. Available: https://www.worldatlas.com/articles/fifa-women-s-world-cup-wins-by-country.html.

Kirka, Danica. 2006. "Threat of Worldwide Childhood Obesity Looms, New Study Warns." *The Post-Standard.* March 6: A-5.

Kirst, Sean. 2004. "Violence in Sports Included a Riot in Syracuse." *The Post-Standard.* November 29: B-1.

_____. 2014. "Stop Anthem Celebrating Violence Against Women." *The Post-Standard*, December 4: A-2.

_____. 2015. "We Owe Earl Lloyd, And the Ones Who Come Next." *The Post-Standard*, March 31: A-2.

Klein, Jeff Z. 2014. "Study Finds Changes in Brains of Hockey Players Who Had Concussions." *The New York Times*, February 4. Available: http://www.nytimes.com/2014/02/04/sports/hockey/study-finds-changes-in-brains-of-hockey-players-who-had-concussions.html?_r=0.

Knoppers, Annelies, and Mary McDonald. 2010. "Scholarship on Gender and Sport in *Sex Roles* and Beyond." *Sex Roles*, 63(5–6): 311–323.

Koc, Yakup. 2017. "Relationships Between the Physical Education Course Sportsmanship Behaviors with Tendency to Violence and Empathetic Ability (Note 1)." *Journal of Education and Learning*, 6(3): 169–180.

Koch, James V., and Wilbert M. Leonard. 1981. "The NCAA: A Socio-economic Analysis: The Development of the College Sports Cartel from Social Movement to Formal Organization," pp. 251–258 in *Sport, Culture and Society: A Reader on the Sociology of Sport*, edited by John W. Loy, Gerald S. Kenyon and Barry D. McPherson. Philadelphia: Lea & Febiger.

Kooper, Al. 2020. "Bob Dylan: American Musician." *Encyclopedia Britannica*, May 20. Available: https://www.britannica.com/biography/Bob-Dylan-American-musician.

Kosiewicz, Jerzy. 2016. "Considerations on Relation Between Philosophy of Sport and Common Sense Thinking." *Physical Culture and Sport, Studies and Research*, 70(1): 79–87.

Kraft, Dina. 2000. "DNA Study Genetically Links Jews and Arabs: Research Backs Biblical Account of Abraham as Common Ancestor." *Buffalo News*, May 5: A10.

Kramer, Lindsay. 2019. "2019 Sportsperson of the Year: Syracuse Basketball Star and Cancer Warrior Tiana Mangakahia." *Syracuse.com*, December 19. Available: https://www.syracuse.com/sports/2019/12/2019-sportsperson-of-the-year-syracuse-basketball-star-and-cancer-warrior-tiana-mangakahia.html.

Kuhn, Cynthia, Scott Swartzwelder, and Wilkie Wilson. 2000. *Pumped: Straight Facts for Athletes about Drugs, Supplements, and Training.* New York: Norton.

Kupper, Mike. 2015. "Barrier Breaker." *Los Angeles Times*, February 5: B7.

LaCapria, Kim. 2019. "Did the Confederate Flag's Designer Call It a Symbol of White Supremacy, Not Southern Heritage?" *Truth or Fiction. com*, September 26. Available: https://www.truthorfiction.com/did-the-confederate-flags-designer-call-it-a-symbol-of-white-supremacy-not-southern-heritage/.

LaFeber, Walter. 1999. *Michael Jordan and the New Global Capitalism.* New York: Norton.

Lapchick, Richard. 2003. "Sports and Public Behavior," pp. 71–79 in *Public Discourse in America*, edited by Judith Rodin and Stephen P. Steinberg. Philadelphia: University of Pennsylvania Press.

_____. 2013a. "The 2013 Racial and Gender Report Card: National Basketball Association." UCF College of Business Administration, June 25. Available: http://www.tidesport.org/RGRC/2013/2013_NBA_RGRC.pdf.

_____. 2013b. "The 2013 National Racial and Gender Report Card: National Football League." UCF College of Business Administration, October 22. Available: http://www.tidesport.org/RGRC/2013/2013_NFL_RGRC.pdf.

_____. 2014. "The 2014 Racial and Gender Report Card: Major League Baseball." UCF College of Business Administration, May 7. Available: http://www.tidesport.org/MLB%20RGRC%202014%20Revised.pdf.

_____. 2019. "NBA's Racial and Gender Report Card." *ESPN.com*, June 17. Available: https://www.espn.com/nba/story/_/id/26995581/nba-racial-gender-report-card.

Lawrence, Andrew. 2014. "The Drive for Five." *Sports Illustrated*, September 15: 51–55.

Lawrence, Shawn A., Thomas Hall, and Patrice Lancey. 2012. "The Relationship Among Alcohol Consumption, Tailgating, and Negative Consequences." *Journal of Child & Adolescent Substance Abuse*, 21(3): 222–237.

Laxarus, David. 2020. "How Uncle Ben, Aunt Jemima Reinforce Racism." *Los Angeles Times*, June 19: A8.

Le Bon, Gustave. 1952. *The Crowd.* London: Benn.

Learn.org. 2020. "What Is Multimedia Technology?" Available: https://learn.org/articles/What_is_Multimedia_Technology.html#:~:text=The%20definition%20of%20multimedia%20technology%20includes%20interactive%2C%-20computer-based,to%20develop%20and%20manage%20online%20graphics%20and%20content.

LeBron, Steven. 2014. "Did Mo'ne Davis Fall Victim

to the 'Sports Illustrated' Jinx? A Sports Psychologist Explains." Mic.com August 25. Available: http://mic.com/articles/97162/did-mo-ne-davis-fall-victim-to-the-sports-illustrated-jinx-a-sports-psychologist-explains.

Lee, Alicia. 2020. "Why Christopher Columbus Wasn't the Hero We Learned About In School." CNN.com, June 12. Available: https://www.cnn.com/2020/06/12/us/christopher-columbus-slavery-disease-trnd/index.html.

Lee, Wendy. 2019. "Aiming to Create the MTV of eSports." Los Angeles Times, September 18: C3.

Lee, Yueh Ting. 1993. "In Group Preference and Homogeneity Among African American and Chinese American Students." Journal of Social Psychology. 133: 225–235.

Legal Sports Betting. 2020. "U.S. States with Legal Sports Betting," June 18. Available: https://www.legalsportsbetting.com/states-with-legal-sports-betting/.

Legare, Andrew. 2020. "Nation Seeking Mascot Changes." The Citizen, August 28: B1.

Leitch, Will. 2005. "On the Financial Gridiron." PRIMEDIA, February 1. Available: https://www.wealthmanagement.com/opinions/financial-gridiron

LeMay, Michael C. 2005. The Perennial Struggle: Race, Ethnicity and Minority Group Relations in the United States. Upper Saddle River, NJ: Pearson/Prentice Hall.

Lemyre, L., and P.M. Smith. 1985. "Inter-group Discrimination and Self-Esteem in the Minimal Group Paradigm." Journal of Personality and Social Psychology. 49: 660–670.

Lenskyj, Helen Jefferson. 2000. Inside the Olympic Industry. Albany: State University of New York Press.

Leonard, Wilbert M., III. 1988. A Sociological Perspective of Sport. New York: Macmillan.

Leslie, Tim, and Cristen Tilley. 2014. "8 Things to Understand About Gay Rights in Russia and the Sochi Winter Olympics." ABC.net.AU. February 11. Available: http://www.abc.net.au/news/2014–02–06/russia-gay-rights-sochi-explained/5237926.

Let's Move! 2017. "America's Move to Raise a Healthier Generation of Kids." Available: https://letsmove.obamawhitehouse.archives.gov/.

Levin, Susanna. 1996. "The Spoils of Victory: Who Gets Big Money from Sponsors, and Why," pp. 367–372 in Sport in Contemporary Society: An Anthology. New York: St. Martin's Press.

Levin, William. 1991. Sociological Ideas, 3rd edition. Belmont, CA: Wadsworth.

Levitt, Daniel. 2018. "State of Pay: Tennis Has Huge Gender Gap In Earning Power." The Guardian, July 14. Available: https://www.theguardian.com/sport/ng-interactive/2018/jul/14/tennis-pay-gap-shouldnt-be-gender-based.

Lewis, Sophie. 2020. "Lady Antebellum Decides to Keep New Name, Despite Speaking with Blues Singer Lady A." CBS News, June 16. Available: https://www.cbsnews.com/news/lady-antebellum-keeping-new-name-despite-apology-lady-a/.

Lin, Yi-Hsiu and Chen-Yueh Chen. 2012. "Adolescents' Impulse Buying: Susceptibility to Interpersonal Influence and Fear of Negative Evaluation." Social Behavior and Personality: An International Journal, 4093): 353–358.

Lipkins, Susan. 2009. Preventing Hazing. New York: Jossey-Bass.

Lisa, Andrew. 2020. "23 Athletes Who Love Giving Their Money Away." Yahoo! Finance, March 2. Available: https://finance.yahoo.com/news/23-athletes-love-giving-money-181008428.html.

Listerious.com. 2019. "Top Ten Most Popular Sports in the World by Participation." Available: https://www.listerious.com/most-popular-sports-in-the-world-by-participation/.

Litke, Jim. 2020. "Goodell Takes Hard Stance." The Citizen, June 9: B1.

Little League. 2020a. "2020 Season Update." Available: https://www.littleleague.org/.

_____. 2020b. "League Age Determination." Available: https://www.littleleague.org/play-little-league/determine-league-age/.

Lock, S. 2020. "Number of Participates in Bowling in the United States from 2006 to 2017 (in millions)." Statista, February 13. Available: https://www.statista.com/statistics/191898/participants-in-bowling-in-the-us-since-2006/.

Lockwood, Joel, Liam Frape, Steve Lin and Alun Ackery. 2017. "Traumatic Brain Injuries in Mixed Martial Arts: A Systematic Review." Trauma, 20(4): 245–254.

Lockwood, Sean. 2020. "List of 100 Extreme Sports (Ultimate List for 2020). Available: https://www.extremesportslab.com/list-of-100-extreme-sports/.

Lomax, Michael. 2004. "Major League Baseball's Separate-and-Unequal Doctrine," pp. 59–94 in Race and Sport: The Struggle for Inequality On and Off the Field, edited by Charles K. Ross. Jackson, MS: University Press of Mississippi.

Los Angeles Times. 1992. "Politics and the Olympics." July 14: C8.

Loy, John, and Alan Ingham. 1981. "Play, Games, and Sport in the Psychological Development of Children and Youth," pp. 189–216 in Sport, Culture and Society, edited by John Loy, Gerald Kenyon and Barry McPherson. Philadelphia: Lea & Febiger.

Lumpkin, Angela. 1994. Physical Education and Sport, 3rd edition. St. Louis: Mosby.

Lundquist Wanneberg, Pia. 2018. "Sport, Disability and Women: A Study of Organized Swedish Disability Sport in 1969–2012." Polish Journal of Sport and Tourism, 24(4): 213–220.

Luschen, Günther. 1967. "The Sociology of Sport: A Trend Report and Bibliography." Current Sociology, 15(3): 5–140.

_____. 1970a. The Cross-Cultural Analysis of Sports and Games. Champaign, IL: Stipes.

_____. 1970b. "Cooperation, Association and Contest." Journal of Conflict Resolution. 14(1): 21–34.

_____. 1981. "The Interdependence of Sport and

Culture," pp. 287–295 in *Sport, Culture and Society,* edited by John W. Loy, Gerald Kenyon and Barry McPherson. Philadelphia: Lea & Febiger.

Ly, Laura, and Jason Hanna. 2014. "Cleveland Police's Fatal Shooting of Tamir Rice Ruled a Homicide." *CNN.com* December 12. Available: http://www.cnn.com/2014/12/12/justice/cleveland-tamir-rice/.

Maaddi, Rob. 2020. "Jackson Sorry For Anti-Semitic Post." *The Citizen,* July 8: B2.

Mac Donald, Heather. 2020. "There Is No Epidemic of Fatal Police Shooting Against Unarmed Black Americans." *USA Today,* July 3. Available: https://www.usatoday.com/story/opinion/2020/07/03/police-black-killings-homicide-rates-race-injustice-column/3235072001/.

Macionis, John. 2010. *Social Problems, Fourth Edition.* Boston: Prentice Hall/Pearson.

Maddison, Stephen. 2000. *Fags, Hags, and Queer Sisters: Gender Dissent and Heterosocial Bonds in Gay Culture.* New York: St. Martin's Press.

Maesam, T-Abdul-Razak, Mohd Sofian Omar-Fauzee, and Abd-Latif Rozita. "The Perspective of Arabic Muslim Women Toward Sport Participation." *Journal of Asia Pacific Studies,* 1.

Magicians Magazine. 2017. "Types of Magic: From Simple to Advance, Here's a List of 10 Types of Magic." Available: https://magiciansmag.com/magic-tricks/10-different-types-of-magic/.

Magoun, Francis Peabody. 1966 [1938]. *History of Football.* New York: Johnson. Mahon, M.J., and C.C. Bullock. 1991. "Recreation and Corrections: A Review of the Literature over the Past Two Years." *Correctional Recreation Today,* Vol. 5: 7–15.

Mahoney, Ryan. 2014. "Silver: NBA Will Review Domestic Violence Policies." *Aiken Standard,* September 21. Available: https://www.postandcourier.com/aikenstandard/sports/silver-nba-will-review-domestic-violence-policies/article_a8da9cea-3245-5f27-8ea9-b92ed8f80fb9.html.

Mai, H.J. 2020. "NFL Commissioner Gives Up His $40 Million Salary and Will Cut League Employees' Pay." *NPR,* April 29. Available: https://www.npr.org/sections/coronavirus-live-updates/2020/04/29/848083541/nfl-commissioner-gives-up-his-40-million-salary-and-will-cut-league-employees-pa.

Major League Baseball (MLB). 2016. "Anti-Hazing & Anti-Bullying Policy." Available: http://content.mlb.com/documents/1/9/0/296982190/Anti_Hazing_Anti_Bullying_Policy_Major_League_Players.pdf.

Malinowski, Bronislaw. 1927. *Coral Gardens and Their Magic.* London: Routledge & Kegan Paul.

Malm, Christer, Johan Jakobsson, and Andreas Isaksson. 2019. "Physical Activity and Sports—Real Health Benefits: A Review with Insight Into the Public Health of Sweden." *Sports,* 7(5): 127–169. Available: https://www.ncbi.nlm.nih.gov/pmc/articles/PMC6572041/.

Mandel, Richard. 1984. *Sport: A Cultural History.* New York: Columbia University Press.

Mandelaro, Jim. 2014. "Hazing Continues Despite Efforts to Change." *Democrat and Chronicle,* January 12. Available: http://www.democratandchronicle.com/story/sports/2014/01/11/hazing-continues-despite-efforts-to-change/4430677/.

Mandell, Richard. 1984. *Sport: A Cultural History.* New York: Columbia University Press.

Mann, L. 1979. "Sports Crowds Viewed from the Perspective of Collective Behavior," pp. 337–368 in *Sports, Games and Play,* edited by J.H. Goldstein. Hillsdale, NJ: Erlbaum.

Marger, Martin. 2006. *Race and Ethnic Relations: American and Global Perspectives,* 7th edition. Belmont, CA: Wadsworth.

Margolis, Jeffrey A. 1999. *Violence in Sports.* Berkeley Heights, NJ: Enslow.

Martens, Rainer. 1988. "Helping Children Become Independent, Responsible Adults Through Sports," pp. 297–307 in *Competitive Sports for Children and Youth: An Overview of Research and Issues,* edited by E.W. Brown & C.F. Branta. Champaign, IL: Human Kinetics.

Martens, Rainer, and Vern Seefeldt, eds. 1979. *Guidelines for Children's Sports.* Washington, D.C.: National Association for Sport & Physical Education.

Martzke, Rudy, and Reid Cherner. 2004. "Channeling How to View Sports: ESPN's 25th Anniversary Seen in Changing TV Sports Patterns." *USA Today.* August 17: C1, C2.

Maryville University. 2020. "Understanding the Me Too Movement: A Sexual Harassment Awareness Guide." Available: https://online.maryville.edu/blog/understanding-the-me-too-movement-a-sexual-harassment-awareness-guide/.

Mathis-Lilley, Ben. 2016. "Trump Was Recorded in 2005 Bragging About Grabby Women 'By the Pussy.'" *Slate,* October 7. Available: http://www.slate.com/blogs/the_slatest/2016/10/07/donald_trump_2005_tape_i_grab_women_by_the_pussy.html.

Mayo Clinic. 2014. "Healthy Lifestyle: Fitness." Available: http://www.mayoclinic.org/healthy-living/fitness/in-depth/performance-enhancing-drugs/art-20046134.

_____. 2019."Chronic Traumatic Encephalopathy." Available: https://www.mayoclinic.org/diseases-conditions/chronic-traumatic-encephalopathy/symptoms-causes/syc-20370921.

_____. 2020a. "Performance-enhancing Drugs and Teen Athletes." Available: https://www.mayoclinic.org/healthy-lifestyle/tween-and-teen-health/in-depth/performance-enhancing-drugs/art-20046620.

_____. 2020b. "Healthy Aging." Available: https://www.mayoclinic.org/healthy-lifestyle/healthy-aging/in-depth/growth-hormone/art-20045735.

_____. 2020c. "Chronic Traumatic Encephalopathy." Available: https://www.mayoclinic.org/diseases-conditions/chronic-traumatic-encephalopathy/symptoms-causes/syc-20370921.

McAlpine, Kat J. 2019. "How Does CTE Impact Women? Former Soccer Stars Join the First All-Female CTE Study at BU." Boston

University, July 3. Available: http://www.bu.edu/articles/2019/former-soccer-stars-join-first-all-female-cte-study/.

McCann, Michael. 2014. "The Case for ... The NFL's Tax Exemption." *Sports Illustrated,* September 29: 28.

McCauley, Kevin. 2014. "Serbia vs. Albania Abandoned After Flag-Flying Drone Incites Brawl." *SB Nation,* October 14. Available: http://www.sbnation.com/soccer/2014/10/14/6977779/serbia-vs-albania-suspended-euro-2016-kosovo.

McChesney, Robert W. 1989. "Media Made Sport: A History of Sports Coverage in the USA," in *Media Sports and Society,* edited by L. Wenner. London: Sage.

McCutcheon, Chuck. 2006. "Feeling the Strain." *The Post-Standard.* September 18: D-2.

McGreevy, Patrick. 2020. "Lawmakers Postpone Effort to Legalize Sports Betting." *Los Angeles Times,* June 25: B3.

McIntosh, Peter. 1993. "The Sociology of Sport in the Ancient World," pp. 19–38 in *The Sports Process,* edited by Eric Dunning, Joseph Maguire, and Robert Pearton. Champaign, IL: Human Kinetics.

McKee, Ann C., Robert C. Cantu, Christopher J. Nowinski, Tessa Hedley-Whyte, Brandon E. Gavett, Andres E. Budson, Veronica E. Santini, Hyo-Soon Lee, Caroline A. Kubilus, and Robert A. Stern. 2009. "Chronic Traumatic Encephalopathy in Athletes: Progressive Tauopathy Following Repetitive Head Injury." *Journal Neuropathology & Experimental Neurology,* 68(7): 709–735.

McKibben, Dave. 2006. "Tennis, Anyone? Anyone??" *The Los Angeles Times.* January 6: A21.

McLellan, David. 1987. *Marxism and Religion.* New York: Harper and Row.

McPherson, Barry D. 1981. "Past, Present and Future Perspectives for Research in Sport Sociology," pp. 10–20 in *Sport, Culture and Society,* 2nd edition, edited by John W. Loy, Gerald S. Kenyon, and Barry D. McPherson. Philadelphia: Leatfebiger. Reprinted from *International Review of Sport Sociology,* 10(1): 55–72, 1975.

Mead, George Herbert. 1934. *Mind, Self & Society,* edited by Charles W. Morris. Chicago: University of Chicago Press.

Melnick, Merrill, and Donald Sabo. 1994. "Sport and Social Mobility among African American and Hispanic Athletes," pp, 221–241 in *Ethnicity and Sport in North American History and Culture,* edited by George Eisen and David K. Wiggins. Westport, CT: Greenwood Press.

Merrill, Christopher. 1993. *The Grass of Another Country: A Journey Through the World of Soccer.* New York: Henry Holt.

Merton, Robert. 1938. "Social Structure and Anomie," *American Sociological Review,* 3: 672–682.

_____. 1968 [1949]. *Social Theory and Social Structure.* New York: Free Press.

Messner, Michael. 2002. "Sports and Male Domination: The Female as Contested Ideological Terrain," pp. 267–284 in *Ethics in Sport,* edited by

William J. Morgan, Klaus Meier, and Angela J. Schneider. Champaign, IL: Human Kinetics.

Messner, Michael, and Donald Sabo. 1990. "Toward a Critical Feminist Reappraisal of Sport, Men, and the Gender Order," pp. 1–15 in *Sport, Men, and the Gender Order,* edited by Michael Messner and Donald Sabo. Champaign, IL: Human Kinetics.

Metzenbaum, Howard. 1996. "Baseball's Antitrust Immunity Should Be Repealed," pp. 275–277 in *Sport in Contemporary Society: An Anthology,* 5th edition, edited by D. Stanly Eitzen. New York: St. Martin's Press.

Michael, Matt. 2007. "Study: Fewest Blacks in Baseball Since '80s." *The Post-Standard.* April 3: D-3.

Mill, John Stuart. 1996 [1859]. *On Liberty,* edited by Currin V. Shields. Upper Saddle River, NJ: Prentice Hall.

Miller, David. 1973. *George Herbert Mead: Self, Language, and the World.* Austin: University of Texas Press.

Miller, Joshua Rhett. 2019. "High School Football Players Violated with Sticks in Alleged Hazing: Report." The New York Post, November 1. Available: https://nypost.com/2019/11/01/high-school-football-players-violated-with-sticks-in-alleged-hazing-.report/#:~:text=High%20school%20football%20players%20violated%20with%20sticks%20in,sticks%20in%20a%20sexual%20manner%20during%20alleged%20

Miller, Korin. 2020. "The Dixie Chicks Changed Their Name Because the Word 'Dixie' Is Problematic." *Women's Health,* June 25. Available: https://www.womenshealthmag.com/life/a32971828/dixie-chicks-name-change/.

Miller, Randy. 2020. "Giambi: Fan Forgiveness Helps Him 'Sleep Great.'" *The Post-Standard,* May 3: C4.

Miller, Rhett. 2019. "High School Football Players Violated with Sticks in Alleged Hazing: Report." *New York Post,* November 1. Available: https://nypost.com/2019/11/01/high-school-football-players-violated-with-sticks-in-alleged-hazing-report/.

Miller, Walter B. 1958. "Lower Class Culture as a Generating Milieu of Gang Delinquency." *Journal of Social Issues,* 14(3): 5–19.

Mills, C. Wright. 1959. *The Sociological Imagination.* New York: Oxford University Press.

Miner, Julianna W. 2016. "Why 70 Percent of Kids Quit Sports by Age 13." *The Washington Post,* June 1. Available: https://www.washingtonpost.com/news/parenting/wp/2016/06/01/why-70-percent-of-kids-quit-sports-by-age-13/.

Mitchell, Wesley C., editor. 1964. *What Veblen Taught: Selected Writings of Thorstein Veblen.* New York: Kelley.

Miyazaki, Anthony D., and Angela G. Morgan. 2001 (Jan). "Assessing Market Value of Event Sponsoring: Corporate Olympic Sponsorships." *Journal of Advertising Research.* Vol. 41: 11–20.

Mobley, Tanyika. 2016. "Sport Participation and Sportsmanship in Youth Sport," pp. 77- 86 in *Sportsmanship: Multidisciplinary Perspectives,* edited by Tim Delaney. Jefferson, NC: McFarland.

Moffatt, Gregory K. 2002. *Violent Heart: Understanding Aggressive Individuals*. Westport, CT: Praeger.

Moffi, Larry, and Jonathan Kronstadt. 1994. *Crossing the Line: Black Major Leaguers, 1947–1959*. Jefferson, NC: McFarland.

Moital, Miguel, Amy Bain, and Harriet Thomas. 2019 (Nov.). "Summary of Cognitive, Affective, and Behavioral Outcomes of Consuming Prestigious Sports Events." *Sport Management Review*, 22(5): 652–666.

Mooney, Carol Garhart. 2009. *Theories of Attachment: An Introduction to Bowlby, Ainsworth, Gerber, Brazelton, Kennel and Klaus*. St. Paul, MN: Redleaf.

Moran, Barbara. 2017. "CTE Found in 99 Percent of Former NFL Players Studied." Boston University, July 26. Available: https://www.bu.edu/articles/2017/cte-former-nfl-players/.

Morgan, Philip J. and Vibeke Hansen. 2008. "Physical Education in Primary Schools: Classroom Teachers' Perceptions of Benefits and Outcomes." *Health Education Journal*, 67(3): 196–207.

Morgan, William, Klaus Meier, and Angela Schneider. 2002. *Ethics in Sport*. Champaign IL: Human Kinetics.

Morrison, L. Leotus. 1993. "The AIAW: Governance by Women for Women," pp. 59–66 in *Women in Sport: Issues and Controversies*, edited by Greta L. Cohen. Newbury Park, CA: Sage.

Moses, Sarah. 2006. "Native Athletes to Compete in Denver." *The Post-Standard*. April 7: B-3.

Mosier, Chris. 2020. "Policies." TransAthlete.com. Available: https://www.transathlete.com/policies.

Mounk, Yascha. 2014. "Why the US Is the Only Country in the World to Have Elections So Often." *Quartz*, November 5. Available: https://qz.com/291933/why-the-us-is-the-only-country-in-the-world-to-have-elections-so-often/.

MSN. 2020. "Trump Has Played Golf 248 Days of His Presidency, Twice As Often As Obama." May 28. Available: https://www.msn.com/en-us/news/politics/trump-has-played-golf-248-days-of-his-presidency-twice-as-often-as-obama/ar-BB14GOnF.

Muller, Jordan. 2020. "Princeton Removes Woodrow Wilson's Name from School, Citing His 'Racist Thinking and Policies.'" *Yahoo! News*, June 27. Available: https://news.yahoo.com/princeton-removes-woodrow-wilsons-name-173624187.html.

Murray, Elizabeth. 2014. "Hawaiian Surfer Creates Opportunity for Wheelchair-bound to Paddleboard." *NBC Today*, October 12. Available: http://www.today.com/health/hawaiian-surfer-creates-opportunity-wheelchair-bound-paddleboard-2D80210822.

Museum of Appalachia. 2005. "July 4th Celebration and Anvil Shoot." Available: www.museumofappalachia.com.

Nadworny, Elissa. 2019. "College Completion Rates Are Up, But the Numbers Will Surprise You." *NPR*, March 13. Available: https://www.npr.org/2019/03/13/681621047/college-completion-rates-are-up-but-the-numbers-will-still-surprise-you.

Nafziger, James A., and Andrew Strenk. 1978. "The Political Uses and Abuses of Sports." *Connecticut Law Review*. 10: 280–89.

National Association of Collegiate Directors of Athletics (NACDA). 2020. "What is NACDA and What Does it Do?" Available: https://nacda.com/sports/2018/7/17/nacda-nacda-overview-html.aspx.

National Association of Intercollegiate Athletics (NAIA). 2014c. "NAIA Eligibility." Available: http://www.playnaia.org/page/eligibility.php.

_____. 2020. "Why Choose the NAIA?" Available: https://www.naia.org/why-naia/index.

National Athletic Trainers Association (NATA). 2019a. "What is Athletic Training?" Available: https://www.nata.org/about/athletic-training.

_____. 2019b. "NATA Fact Sheet." Available: https://www.nata.org/nata-quick-facts.

National Center for Sports Safety. 2008. "Sports Injuries Facts." Available: http://www.sportsafety.org/sports-injury-facts/.

National Collegiate Athletic Association (NCAA). 2011. "NCAA Participation Rates Going Up: At Least 444,000 Student-Athletes Playing on 18,000 Teams." Available: http://www.ncaa.com/news/ncaa/article/2011-11-02/ncaa-participation-rates-going.

_____. 2013. *2013–14 NCAA Division I Manual*. Indianapolis, IN: The National Collegiate Athletic Association. Available: http://grfx.cstv.com/photos/schools/usc/genrel/auto_pdf/2013–14/misc_non_event/ncaa-manual.pdf.

_____. 2014a. "Staying on Track to Graduate." Available.

_____. 2016. "Addressing Student-Athlete Hazing." Available: http://www.ncaa.org/sport-science-institute/addressing-student-athlete-hazing.

_____. 2018. "NCAA Recruiting Facts." Available: http://www.ncaa.org/sites/default/files/Recruiting%20Fact%20Sheet%20WEB.pdf.

_____. 2020a. "Estimated Probability of Competing in Professional Athletics." Available: http://www.ncaa.org/about/resources/research/estimated-probability-competing-professional-athletics.

_____. 2020b. "NCAA 2019–20 Division I Manual." Available: https://web3.ncaa.org/lsdbi/reports/getReport/90008.

_____. 2020c. "Grade-Point Average." Available: http://www.ncaa.org/student-athletes/future/grade-point-average.

_____. 2020d. "LGBTQ Resources." Available: http://www.ncaa.org/about/resources/inclusion/lgbtq-resources.

National Federation of State High School Associations (NFHS). 2018. "High School Sports Participation Increases for 29th Consecutive Year." *NFHS News*, September 11. Available: https://www.nfhs.org/articles/high-school-sports-participation-increases-for-29th-consecutive-year/.

_____. 2020. "Coaches." Available: https://nfhslearn.com/home/coaches.

National Heart, Lung, and Blood Institute (NIH). 2020. "Calculate Your Body Mass Index." Available: https://www.nhlbi.nih.gov/health/educational/lose_wt/BMI/bmicalc.htm.

National Human Genome Research Institute. 2014. "A Brief Guide to Genomics: DNA, Genes and Genomes." Available: http://www.genome.gov/18016863.

National Junior College Athletic Association (NJCAA). 2020. "About the NJCAA: Mission." Available: https://www.njcaa.org/about/mission/Mission_statement.

Nature. 2009. "Commentary: Should Scientists Study Race and IQ?" Volume 457(12): 786–789.

NCAA News. 2001. "2001 NCAA Drug Use Survey." October 13: 1, 17. Available: www.ncaa.org.

Negi, Laxmi. 2020. "ESPN Sportsperson of the Year Award: Meet the Winners." Available: https://www.rediff.com/sports/report/sportsperson-of-the-year-award-meet-the-winners-sindhu-sourabh/20200220.htm.

Nesmith, Jeff. 2007. "Frontier of Sports Cheating: Genomics." *The Post-Standard.* October 23: D-7.

Neurological Wellness Institute (NWI). 2016. "An Analysis of Concussion In Soccer." Available: https://neurologicwellnessinstitute.com/concussions-in-soccer/.

Newberry, Christina. 2019. "37 Instagram Stats That Matter to Marketers in 2020." *Hootsuite.com,* October 22. Available: https://blog.hootsuite.com/instagram-statistics/#:~:text=Of%20Instagram%E2%80%99s%20one%20billion%20users%2C%20only%20110%20million,Insta-gram%2C%20and%20what%20kind%20of%20content%20to%20create.

Newberry, Paul. 2019a. "NCAA Takes Half Measure for Paying Athletes." *The Citizen,* October 30: B2.

_____. 2019b. "Patriots Bring Us a New Scandal." *The Citizen,* December 11: B1.

Newman, Timothy, Jason Frederick Peck, Charles Harris, and Brendan Wilhide. 2017. *Social Media in Sport Marketing.* New York: Routledge.

NFL.com. 2010. "New NFL Rules Designed to Limit Head Injuries." Available: https://www.nfl.com/news/new-nfl-rules-designed-to-limit-head-injuries-09000d5d81990bdf.

NHL.com. 2016. "NHL Begins Domestic Violence and Sexual Assault Training." Available: https://www.nhl.com/news/nhl-begins-domestic-violence-and-sexual-assault-training/c-797688.

Nixon, Howard L., II. 1984. *Sport and the American Dream.* New York: Leisure Press.

Nixon, Howard L., II, and James H. Frey. 1996. *A Sociology of Sport.* Belmont, CA: Wadsworth.

Norlander, Matt. 2017. "NCAA Ruling in North Carolina Academic Investigation: No Penalties for UNC." *CBS Sports,* October 13. Available: https://www.cbssports.com/college-basketball/news/ncaa-ruling-in-north-carolina-academic-investigation-no-penalties-for-unc/.

Novak, Michael. 1993. "The Joy of Sport," pp. 151–172 in *Religion and Sport,* edited by Charles S. Prebish. Westport, CT: Greenwood Press.

Nuwer, Hank. 1999. *Wrongs of Passage.* Bloomington, IN: Indiana University Press.

_____, ed. 2004. *The Hazing Reader.* Bloomington, IN: Indiana University Press.

_____, ed. 2018. *Hazing: Destroying Young Lives.* Bloomington, IN: Indiana University Press.

O'Bannon, Ed, with Michael McCann. 2018. *Court Justice: The Inside Story of My Battle Against the NCAA.* New York: Diversion Books.

O'Toole, Thomas. 2002. "Crisis on Campus: Fan Disturbances After Sports Events More Common, Destructive." *USA Today.* April 9: 1C.

Oakes, P. J., and J. C. Turner. 1980. "Social Categorization and Inter-Group Behavior: Does Minimal Inter-Group Discrimination Make Social Identity More Positive?" *European Journal of Social Psychology,* 10: 295–301.

Oakley, J. Ronald. 1994. *Baseball's Last Golden Age, 1946–1960: The National Pastime in a Time of Glory and Change.* Jefferson, NC: McFarland.

Official NFL Playing Rules. 2014. "Rule 12: Player Conduct." Available: http://www.nfl.com/static/content/public/image/rulebook/pdfs/15_Rule12_Player_Conduct.pdf.

Oher, Michael. 2014. "Biography." *Biography.com.* Available: http://www.biography.com/people/michael-oher-547478#synopsis.

Ohlemacher, Stephen. 2005. "Fewer Got Game: More Watching, Less Playing." *New York Post.* December 22: 32.

Olson, Eric. 2020. "Number of Eliminated College Sports Programs Nearing 100." *APNews,* May 30. Available: https://apnews.com/1c7202d94f1e4e64353b75920dda9dd3.

Ordine, Bill. 2020. "Sportsperson of the Year: Mo Gaba." *Press Box,* July 28. Available: https://pressboxonline.com/2020/07/28/bestof2019-sportsperson-mo-gaba/.

Organization for Economic Co-Operation and Development (OECD). 2020. "Average Annual Hours Actually Worked Per Worker." *OECD. Stat.* Available: https://stats.oecd.org/Index.aspx?DataSetCode=ANHRS.

Ormseth, Matthew. 2019. "In College Scandal, Rowing Was Rowing Was the Ideal Sport for Stowaways, Cheating." *Los Angeles Times,* April 12. Available: https://www.latimes.com/local/california/la-me-college-admissions-scandal-lori-loughlin-olivia-jade-crew-rowing-20190412-story.html.

Orr, Scott. 2005. "Teen Steroid Use on the Rise: Web Feeds Demand for Drugs." *The Post-Standard.* April 3: A-17.

Orwell, George. 1945. "The Sporting Spirit." *Tribune,* December. Available: http://www.orwell.ru/library/articles/spirit/english/e_spirit.

_____. 1949. *Nineteen Eighty-four.* London: Warburg.

Pampel, Fred. 2000. *Sociological Lines and Ideas.* New York: Worth.

Pappas, Nick T., Patrick C. McKenry and Beth Skilen Catlett. 2004. "Athlete Aggression on the Rink and Off the Ice: Athlete Violence and Aggression in Hockey and Interpersonal Relationships." *Men and Masculinities,* 6: 291–312.

Park, Michael Alan. 2008. *Biological Anthropology, Fifth Edition.* New York: McGraw-Hill

Parry, Wayne. 2017. "Casinos Embrace Esports Even as They Work to Understand It." *The Citizen,* August 9: A2.

Parsons, Talcott. 1949 [1937]. *The Structure of Social Action.* Glencoe, IL: Free Press.

_____. 1951. *The Social System.* Glencoe, IL: Free Press.

Passer, Michael. 1986. "When Should Children Begin Competing? A Psychological Perspective," pp. 55–58 in *Sport for Children and Youths,* edited by Maureen Weiss and Daniel Gould. Champaign, IL: Human Kinetics.

Patra, Kevin. 2014. "Denver Broncos Not Signing Incognito After Workout." NFL.com November 11. Available: http://www.nfl.com/news/story/0ap3000000426621/article/richie-incognito-meeting-with-denver-broncos.

Patriots Wire. 2020. "NFL Slams Patriots with Stern Punishment for Illegal Videotaping," June 29. Available: https://patriotswire.usatoday.com/2020/06/28/spygate-2-patriots-bill-belichick-bengals-punishment/#:~:text=The%20NFL%20will%20hand%20down%20a%20stern%20punishment,Week%2014%20of%20the%202019%20NFL%20regular%20season.

Patterson, John. 2010. "*Gladiator:* No. 21 Best Action and War Film of All Time." *The Guardian.* October 19. Available: http://www.theguardian.com/film/2010/oct/19/gladiator-scott-action.

Peluso, Alessandro M., Cristian Rizzo, and Giovanni Pino. 2019 (May). "Controversial Sports Sponsorships: Effects of Sponsor Moral Appropriateness and Self-team Connection on Sponsored Teams and External Benefit Perceptions." *Journal of Business Research,* 98: 339–351.

Penn Live. 2019. "Horse Racing's Uncomfortable Truth: Horses Die—87 Last Year Alone in Pa," May 29. Available: https://www.pennlive.com/news/2019/05/horse-racings-uncomfortable-truth-horses-die-at-a-rate-of-more-than-one-per-week-in-pa.html.

Penner, Mike. 2001. "*Brian's Song* Remake Goes Flat." *Los Angeles Times.* December 2. Available: http://articles.latimes.com/2001/dec/02/sports/sp-10768.

Perez, Chris. 2014. "Shocking Footage Surfaces on Ray Rice Punching Wife." *New York Post,* September 8. Available: http://nypost.com/2014/09/08/shocking-footage-surfaces-of-ray-rice-punching-his-fiancee/.

Petchesky, Andy. 2014. "Andy Reid: 'When You Go to Mecca, You Should be Able to Slide Wherever.'" Deadspin.com. September 30. Available: http://deadspin.com/andy-reid-when-you-go-to-mecca-you-should-be-able-to-1640709438.

Peterson, Anne M. and Ronald Blum. 2020. "Women Lose Equal Pay Bid; Other Claims Awaiting Trial." *The Post-Standard,* May 3: C3.

Peterson, Robert. 1984. *Only the Ball Was White: A History of Legendary Black Players and All-Black Professional Teams.* New York: McGraw-Hill.

Petite, Steven and Rick Marshall. 2020. "The History of the Madden Curse." Digital Trends, April 21. Available: https://www.digitaltrends.com/gaming/what-is-the-madden-curse/.

Petrie, J., and Trent Anderson. 1996. "Gender Differences in the Perception of College Student-Athletes' Academic Performance." *College of Student Affairs Journal,* 61(1): 62–69.

Pew Research. 2019. "In U.S., Decline of Christianity Continues at Rapid Pace," October 17. Available: https://www.pewforum.org/2019/10/17/in-u-s-decline-of-christianity-continues-at-rapid-pace/#:~:text=In%20Pew%20Research%20Center%20telephone%20surveys%20conducted%20in,down%2012%20percentage%20points%20over%20the%20past%20decade.

Pfeiffer, Ronald P., and Brent C. Mangus. 2002. *Concepts of Athletic Training,* 3rd edition. Boston: Jones and Bartlett.

Pfister, Gertrud, and Susan J. Bandy. 2015. "Gender and Sport," pp. 220–230 in *Routledge Handbook of the Sociology of Sport,* edited by Richard Giulianotti. London: Routledge.

Pfuetze, Paul. 1954. *Self, Society and Existence: Human Nature and Dialogue in the Thoughts of George Herbert Mead and Martin Buber.* New York: Harper Torch.

Phillips, John. 1993. *Sociology of Sport.* Boston: Allyn & Bacon.

Pickering, Evan. 2014. "The 10 Worst Wonderlic Scores in NFL History." *The Richest,* May 31. Available: http://www.therichest.com/sports/football-sports/10-worst-wonderlic-scores-in-nfl-history/.

Pike, Alicia, Riana R. Pryor, Lesley W. Vandermark, Stephanie M. Mazerolle, and Douglas J. Casa. 2017. "Athletic Trainer Services in Public and Private Secondary Schools." *Journal of Athletic Training,* 52(1): 5–11.

Pilcher, Tom. 2011. "Charismatic 'People's Champion' Steve Ballesteros." *Reuters,* May 7. Available: http://blogs.reuters.com/sport/2011/05/07/charismatic-peoples-champion-seve-ballesteros-dies/.

Piscotty, Marc. 2015. "NCAA Report: Lacrosse Is Fastest-Growing College Sport." *Lauderdale Lacrosse,* November 16. Available: http://lauderdalelacrosse.com/ncaa-report-lacrosse-is-fastest-growing-college-sport/.

Pittman, Genevra. 2012. "One in 20 Youths Has Used Steroids to Bulk Up: Study." *Reuters,* November 19. Available: http://www.reuters.com/article/2012/11/19/us-youth-steroids-idUSBRE8AI06L20121119.

The Plain Dealer. 2000. "Massillon Fans Arrested." November 5: 19C.

Plaschke, Bill. 2020. "Dodgers Officially Robbed of 2017 Title." *Los Angeles Times,* January 14: A1, A7.

Playboy. 1992 (May). "Interview with Michael Jordan." Vol. 39, No. 5.

Poliakoff, Michael. 1987. *Combat Sports in the Ancient World.* New Haven, CT: Yale University Press.

Poliquin, Bud. 2005. "Mantle: Flawed Hero." *The Post-Standard.* July 18: C-2.

_____. 2005. "Sex Appeal, True Talent an Exciting Combination." *The Post-Standard.* June 16: D-1.

Pond, Neil. 2020. "Must-Watch Sports Docs." *Parade,* September 6: 10.

The Pop History Dig. 2020. "Celebrity Sell." Available: https://www.pophistorydig.com/topics/tag/honus-wagner-louisville-slugger/.

Pop Warner. 2020. "Benefits of Pop Warner." Available: https://www.popwarner.com/Default.aspx?tabid=1463862.

Popper, Ben. 2013. "Field of Streams: How Twitch Made Video Games a Spectator Sport." *The Verge,* September 30. Available: http://www.theverge.com/2013/9/30/4719766/twitch-raises-20-million-esports-market-booming.

Porter, Cody. 2018. "Hazing, Bullying Prevention—Collaborative Effort for Schools, Communities." National Federation of State High School Associations. Available: https://www.nfhs.org/articles/hazing-bullying-prevention-collaborative-effort-for-schools-communities/.

Porto, Brian. 2003. *A New Season: Using Title IX to Reform College Sports.* Westport, CT: Praeger.

The Post-Standard. 2004. "1791 Ban on Baseball Rewrites History." May 12: A-2.

_____. 2005. "Vikings' 'Whiz' Kid Tries to Put One Past Airport Security." May 12: D-1.

_____. 2015. "Liked SU Enough to Name Kid 'Cuse." January 15: C-2.

Potrikus, Alaina. 2006. "Tribe's Living Heritage." *The Post-Standard.* March 23: B-3.

Potter, Dena. 2008. "Study: Winning in Sports Really Does Bring Universities More Students." *The Post-Standard.* March 8: B-5.

Poverty USA. 2020. "Who Lives in Poverty USA?" Available: https://www.povertyusa.org/facts#:~:text=According%20to%202018%20US%20Census%20Data%2C%20the%20highest,while%20Asians%20had%20a%20poverty%20rate%20at%2010.1%25.

Powell, Robert Andrew. 2003. *We Own This Game.* New York: Atlantic Monthly Press.

Powers, Shad. 2018. "Todd Marinovich Back In Jail After Arrest in Orange County; Ex-football Star Had Been Rehabbing in Desert." *Desert Sun,* April 1. Available: https://www.desertsun.com/story/sports/football/2018/04/01/todd-marinovich-back-jail-after-arrest-orange-county-ex-football-star-had-been-rehabbing-desert/476691002/.

Prebish, Charles. 1984. "Heavenly Father, Divinec-Goalie: Sport and Religion." *The Antioch Review,* 42 (Summer): 306–318.

Probasco, Jim. 2014. "5 Biggest Athlete Endorsement Deals Ever—Under Armour, Inc. (NYSE:UA), Nike, Inc. (NYSE:NKE)." Benzinga.com August 12. Available: http://www.benzinga.com/news/14/08/4774964/5-biggest-athlete-endorsement-deals-ever.

Professional Disc Golf Association (PDGA). 2014. "Homepage." Available: http://www.pdga.com/.

Proffitt, Jennifer M., and Thomas F. Corrigan. 2012. "Penn State's 'Success with Honor': How Institutional Structure and Brand Logic Disincentivized Disclosure." *Cultural Studies and Critical Methodologies,* 12(4): 322–325.

Putnam, Douglas T. 1999. *Controversies of the Sports World.* Westport, CT: Greenwood Press.

Qiu, Linda. 2020. "Trump's Falsehoods on Police Shootings, Biden, Coronavirus and China." *The New York Times,* July 14. Available: https://www.nytimes.com/2020/07/14/us/politics/trump-fact-check-biden-police-coronavirus-china.html?searchResultPosition=1.

Quintanilla, Michael. 1998. "Surf's Up, Big Kahuna." *Los Angeles Times.* June 3: D1.

Rada, A., and K. Tim Wulfemeyer. 2005 (March). "Color Coded: Racial Descriptions in Television Coverage of Intercollegiate Sports." *Journal of Broadcasting & Electronic Media.* 49(1): 65–86.

Rader, Benjamin. 1984. *In Its Own Image: How Television Has Transformed Sports.* New York: Free Press.

_____. 2004. *American Sports,* 5th edition. Upper Saddle River, NJ: Prentice Hall.

Ramachandra, K., S. Narendranath, H.S. Somashekar, Navin A. Patil, S.R. Reshma, and A. Veena. 2012. "Drug Abuse in Sports." *Journal of Pharmacy Research,* 5(1): 593–603.

Rank, Otto. 2004 [1909]. *The Myth of the Birth of the Hero: A Psychological Exploration of Myth.* Baltimore, MD: Johns Hopkins University Press.

Ranker.com 2020. "The Most Popular Sports Video Games Right Now." Available: https://www.ranker.com/list/most-popular-sports-video-games-today/ranker-games.

Ravitch, Frank S. 1999. *School Prayer and Discrimination: The Civil Rights of Religious Minorities and Dissenters.* Boston: Northeastern University Press.

Rawjee, Veena P., Nisha Ramlutchman, and Nereshnee Govender. 2011. "Missing in Action: The Portrayal of Women in Sport in the Print Media." *Loyola Journal of Social Sciences,* 25(2): 177–190.

Real, Michael R. 1996. *Exploring Media Culture: A Guide.* Thousand Oaks, CA: Sage.

Rechtshaffen, Michael. 2019. "Smart Money's on 'Inside Game,' a Fact-Based Tale of Friends and NBA Betting Scandal. *Los Angeles Times,* October 30. Available: https://www.latimes.com/entertainment-arts/movies/story/2019-10-30/inside-game-review-will-sasso-scott-wolf.

Redondo Beach Chamber. 2005. "George Freeth Memorial." Available at: http://www.redondochamber.com/visitors/freeth_memorial.htm.

Reeds, Greg. 2004. "Winning and Losing: A Case Study for Fair Play," pp. 87–90 in *Social Diseases:*

Mafia, Terrorism, Totalitarianism, edited by Tim Delaney, Valeri Kuvakin, and Tim Madigan. Moscow, Russia: Russian Humanist Society.

Reeser, J. C. 2005. "Gender Identity and Sport: Is the Playing Field Level?" *British Journal of Sports Medicine.* Vol. 39: 695–699.

Rego, Anoushka. 2020. "How Much of *Moneyball* Is True?" *TheCinemaholic,* September 2. Available: https://www.thecinemaholic.com/how-much-of-moneyball-is-true/.

Republicans Buy Shoes. 2014. "About *Republicans Buy Shoes.*" Available: http://www.republicansbuyshoes.com/about/.

Reuters. 2011. "Sports-related Brain Injuries in Youngsters Soar, CDC Says." October 6. Available: http://www.reuters.com/article/2011/10/06/us-brain-idUSTRE7955R320111006.

Reynolds, Larry. 1993. *Interactionism: Exposition and Critique,* 3rd edition. Dix Hills, NY: General Hall.

Richer, Alanna Durkin. 2020. "Ex-Texas Coach Gets 6 Months in College Scam, Runs from Courthouse." *Associated Press,* February 24. Available: https://www.post-gazette.com/news/crime-courts/2020/02/24/Michael-Center-University-of-Texas-Austin-college-admissions-scam-Boston-tennis/stories/202002240123.

The Richest. 2020. "Tip 100 Richest Athletes." Available: https://www.therichest.com/top-lists/top-100-richest-athletes/.

Riess, Steven. 1989. *City Games.* Chicago: University of Illinois Press.

_____. 1995. *Sport in Industrial America 1850–1920.* Wheeling, IL: Harlan Davidson.

Risman, Barbara. 1998. *Gender Vertigo: American Families in Transition.* New Haven, CT: Yale University Press.

Ritzer, George. 2000. *Classical Social Theory,* 3rd edition. Boston: McGraw-Hill.

Robert, Scott. 2019. "Transgender Athletes Are Banned From Competition by USA Powerlifting." *JBH News,* February 1. Available: https://jbhnews.com/transgender-athletes-banned-competition-usa-powerlifting/21948/.

Roberts, Andrea L., Alvaro Pascual-Leone, Frank Speizer, Ross D. Zafonte, et al. 2019. "Exposure to American Football and Neuropsychiatric Health in Former National Football League Players: Findings From the Football Players Health Study." *The American Journal of Sports,* 47(12): 2871–2880.

Robinson, Jackie. 1995. *The Autobiography of Jackie Robinson,* with an introduction by Hank Aaron and foreword by Cornel West. Hopewater, NJ: Ecco Press.

Robinson, Tara Rodden and Lisa Cushman Spock. 2020. *Genetics for Dummies, 3rd edition.* Hoboken, NJ: John Wiley & Sons, Inc.

Roby, Erin. 2018. "Band Director Resigns, Band on Probation Amid Hazing Investigation at Bowie State." WUSA9, November 30. Available: https://www.wusa9.com/article/news/local/bowie/band-director-resigns-amid-hazing-investigation-at-bowie-state/65–619086940.

Rojek, Chris. 1985. *Capitalism and Leisure Theory.* New York: Tavistock.

Rollyson, Carl. 2007. "Leni Riefenstahl on Trial." *The New York Sun,* March 7. Available: https://www.nysun.com/arts/leni-riefenstahl-on-trial/49944/.

Rosemond, John. 2000. "A Rough Time with Sports." *Buffalo News.* April 17: C3.

Rosen, L., D.B. McKeon, and D.O. Hough. 1986. "Pathogenic Weight-Control Behavior in Female Athletes." *The Physician and Sports Medicine.* 16 (Jan.): 79–86.

Rosenberg, Matt. 2020. "The 5 Sectors of the Economy." *ThoughtCo.com,* January 29. Available: https://www.thoughtco.com/sectors-of-the-economy-1435795.

Rosenfeld, Isadore. 2005. "Heart Health Should Start Early." *Parade.* September 25: 6–7.

Rosson, Philip. 2001. "Football Shirt Sponsorships: SEGA Europe and Arsenal FC." *International Journal of Sports Marketing & Sponsorship* (June-July), 3(2): 157–183.

Runner's World. 2014. "2014 Boston Marathon Results." Available: http://www.runnersworld.com/print/152631.

_____. 2020. "Everything You Need to Know About the Boston Marathon." Available: https://www.runnersworld.com/races-places/a19605700/boston-marathon-faq/.

Russo, Ralph D. 2020. "NCAA Takes Aim at Confederate Flag." *The Citizen,* June 20: B3.

Ryan, John, and William M. Wentworth. 1999. *Media and Society.* Boston: Allyn and Bacon.

Ryckman, Richard, and Jane Hamel. 1992. "Female Adolescents' Motives Related to Involvement in Organized Team Sports." *International Journal of Sport Psychology.* 23: 147–160.

Sabo, Don. 1985. "Sport, Patriarchy and Male Identity: New Questions about Men and Sport." *Arena Review,* 9: 2.

Sack, Allen L., and Ellen J. Staurowsky. 1998. *College Athletes for Hire: The Evolution and Legacy of the NCAA's Amateur Myth.* Westport, CT: Praeger.

Sage, George H. and D. Stanley Eitzen. 2013. *Sociology of North American Sport.* New York: Oxford University Press.

Sage, George H., ed. 1970. *Sport and American Society: Selected Readings.* Reading, MA: Addison-Wesley.

_____. 1979. "Sport and the Social Sciences." *The Annals of the American Academy of Political and Social Sciences,* 445: 1–14.

Sahlin, Barbara K. and Jan Lexell. 2015. "Impact of Organized Sports on Activity, Participation, and Quality of Life in People with Neurological Disabilities." *PM&R,* 7(10): 1081–1088.

Salazar, Miguel. 2018. "Soccer and Domestic Violence: When the Beautiful Game Turns Ugly." *The Nation,* September 26. Available: https://www.thenation.com/article/archive/soccer-and-domestic-violence-when-the-beautiful-game-turns-ugly/.

Salinger, Tobias. 2015. "Sleeping Yankees Fan's $10M Lawsuit Dismissed: Report." *New York Daily News,* September 30. Available: https://www.nydailynews.com/sports/baseball/yankees/sleeping-yankees-fan-10m-lawsuit-dismissed-article-1.2379498.

Saltz, Gail. 2005. "5 Ways to Get Your Child Moving." *Parade.* September 25: 8.

Sanchez, Raul, and Dominic Malcolm. 2010. "Decivilizing, Civilizing or Informalizing? The International Development of Mixed Martial Arts." *International Review for the Sociology of Sport,* 45(1): 39–58.

Sansone, David. 1998. *Greek Athletics and the Genesis of Sport.* Berkeley: University of California Press.

Saunders, Jim. 2018. "Hazing Conviction Upheld in Death of FAMU Band Member in Orlando." *Orlando Sentinel,* December 13. Available: https://www.orlandosentinel.com/news/os-ne-famu-hazing-conviction-appeal-20181213-story.html.

Schaaf, Phil. 2005. *Sports, Inc.: 100 Years of Sports Business.* Amherst, NY: Prometheus.

Schippers, Michaela C. and Paul A. M. Van Lange. 2006. "The Psychological Benefits of Superstitious Rituals in Top Sport: A Study Among Top Sportspersons." *Journal of Applied Social Psychological,* 36)10): 2532–2553.

Schmitz, Melanie. 2017. "How the NFL Sold Patriotism to the U.S. Military for Millions." *Think Progress,* September 25. Available: https://archive.thinkprogress.org/nfl-dod-national-anthem-6f682cebc7cd/.

School House Connection. 2020. "Press Release: Public Schools Report Record High of Over 1.5 Million Homeless Children and Youth, January 30. Available: https://www.schoolhouseconnection.org/public-schools-report-record-high-of-over-1–5-million-homeless-children-and-youth/.

Schreiber, Lee. 1990. *The Parent's Guide to Kids' Sports.* Boston: Little, Brown.

Schwarb, Amy Wimmer. 2018. "Number of NCAA College Athletes Reaches All-time High." NCAA, October 10. Available: http://www.ncaa.org/about/resources/media-center/news/number-ncaa-college-athletes-reaches-all-time-high.

Schwartz, Nick. 2014. "Floyd Mayweather Tops the List of the Highest Paid Athletes in the World." *USA Today,* June 11. Available: http://ftw.usatoday.com/2014/06/forbes-highest-paid-athletes-mayweather-lebron-ronaldo.

Scott, Jason. 2016. "IOC Announces New Policies for Transgender Athletes." *Athletic Business.* Available: https://www.athleticbusiness.com/rules-regulations/ioc-announces-new-policies-for-transgender-athletes.html#:~:text=IOC%20Announces%20New%20Policies%20for%20Transgender%20Athletes.%20Transgender,updated%20guidelines%20regarding%20transgender%20athletes%20earlier%20this%20week.

Seattle Post-Intelligencer. 2005. "Elma School Officials Ban Short Cheerleader Skirts." September 9. Available: http://seattlepi.nwsource.com.

Seinfeld. 1993. "The Lip Reader." Original airdate: October 28, 1993.

_____. 1997. "The Summer of George." Original airdate: May 15, 1997.

Semyonov, M., and M. Farbstein. 1989. "Ecology of Sports Violence: The Case of Israeli Soccer." *Sociology of Sport Journal,* Vol. 6: 50–59.

Senn, Alfred Erich. 1999. *Power, Politics, and the Olympic Games.* Champaign, IL: Human Kinetics.

Shaikin, Bill. 2019. "Good Luck Getting a Family of Four Into a Professional Sport for $100—Not in Good Seats, But Any Seats." *Los Angeles Times,* December 26. Available: https://www.latimes.com/sports/story/2019-12-26/most-affordable-tickets-prices-dodgers-lakers-clippers-rams-chargers.

Sheridan, Chris. 2004. "Artest Suspended for Season." *Buffalo News.* November 22: D7.

Sheu, Yahtyng, Li-Hui Chen, and Holly Hedegaard. 2016. "Sports- and Recreation-related Injury Episodes in the United States, 2011–2014." National Health Statistics Reports, 99. U.S. Department of Health and Human Services, CDC. Available: https://www.cdc.gov/nchs/data/nhsr/nhsr099.pdf.

Shields, David Light and Brenda Light Bredemeier. 1995. *Character Development and Physical Activity.* Champaign, IL: Human Kinetics.

Shropshire, Kenneth L. 1996. *In Black and White: Race and Sports in America.* New York: New York University Press.

Shulman, James L., and William G. Bowen. 2001. *The Game of Life.* Princeton, NJ: Princeton University Press.

SI.com 2014. "The Madden Cover Curse." June 9. Available: http://www.si.com/more-sports/photos/2014/06/09/madden-cover-curse#2.

Signorini, Renatta. 2020. "Charges Filed in Greater Latrobe Junior High Hazing Incidents." *Trib Live,* May 13. Available: https://triblive.com/local/westmoreland/charges-filed-in-greater-latrobe-junior-high-hazing-incidents/.

Silby, Caroline, with Shelley Smith. 2000. *Games Girls Play: Understanding and Guiding Young Female Athletes.* New York: St. Martin's Press.

Silveira, Jason M. and Michael W. Hudson. 2015. "Hazing in the College Marching Band." *Journal of Research in Music Education,* 63(1): 5–27.

Silver, Adam. 2014. "Legalize and Regulate Sports Betting." *The New York Times,* November 13. Available: http://www.nytimes.com/2014/11/14/opinion/nba-commissioner-adam-silver-legalize-sports-betting.html?_r=0.

Simon, Robert L. 1985. *Sports and Social Values.* Englewood Cliffs, NJ: Prentice Hall.

_____. 1991. *Fair Play.* Boulder, CO: Westview.

The Simpsons. 1997. "Bart Star." Original airdate: November 9, 1997.

_____. 2008. "Any Given Sundance." Original airdate: May 4, 2008.

Sirak, Ron. 2008. "The Rich Get Richer." *Golf Digest.* February: 96–100.

Siu, Antoinette. 2014. "SU Grad who Broke Gender Barriers for Female Runners Returns to CNY Today." *The Post-Standard,* October 19: A-13.

Skinner, B.F. 1948. "Superstition in the Pigeon." *Journal of Experimental Psychology,* 38: 168–172.

Skrbina, Paul. 2018. "When Pro Athletes Are Accused of Abuse, How Often Does Punishment Follow?" *Nashville Tennessean,* September 19. Available: https://www.tennessean.com/story/sports/nhl/predators/2018/09/19/nfl-domestic-violence-sexual-assault-child-abuse-nba-mlb-nhl/1335799002/.

Slusher, Howard. 1993. "Sport and the Religious," pp. 173–196 in *Religion and Sport,* edited by Charles S. Prebish. Westport, CT: Greenwood Press.

Small, Eric, with Linda Spear. 2002. *Kids & Sports.* New York: New Market Press.

Smelser, Neil. 1966. *Social Structure and Mobility in Economic Development.* Chicago: Aldine.

Smith, Adam. 2018. :Here are Five American Cities Which Rioted After Sporting Success and Defeat." *Metro.co.uk,* February 5. Available: https://metro.co.uk/2018/02/05/here-are-five-american-cities-which-rioted-after-sporting-success-and-defeat-7289493/.

Smith, Alexander. 2019. "Italian Soccer Condemned for Using Monkey Paintings in Anti-racism Campaign.'" *NBCNews.com,* December 17. Available: https://www.nbcnews.com/news/nbcblk/italian-soccer-condemned-using-monkey-paintings-anti-racism-campaign-n1103076.

Smith, Alexander, and Ghazi Balkiz. 2014. "Who Are the Circassians, And Why Are They Outraged at Sochi?" NBCNews.com Available: http://www.nbcnews.com/storyline/sochi-olympics/who-are-circassians-why-are-they-outraged-sochi-n23716.

Smith, Claire. 1999. "Pee Wee Reese: A Down-to-Earth, Generous Hero in Life and Baseball." *Philadelphia Inquirer.* August 16: T11.

Smith, Lynn. 2011. "'Robo Dad' Marinovich: He Raises 'Trophy Kids.'" *Los Angeles Times,* September 11. Available: https://www.latimes.com/sports/la-xpm-2011-sep-18-la-sp-marinovich-archives-story.html.

Smith, Michael D. 1974. "Significant Others' Influence on Assaultive Behavior of Young Hockey Players." *International Review of Sport Sociology,* 3–4: 45–56.

_____. 1983. *Violence and Sport.* Toronto: Butterworths.

_____. 1996. "A Typology of Sports Violence," pp. 161–172 in *Sport in Contemporary Society,* 5th edition, edited by D. Stanley Eitzen. New York: St. Martin's Press.

Smith, Rodney K. 1987. *Public Prayer and the Constitution: A Case Study in Constitutional Interpretation.* Wilmington, Delaware: Scholarly Resources.

Smith, Ronald E. 1988. *Sports and Freedom: The Rise of Big-Time College Athletics.* New York: Oxford University Press.

Smithsonian National Museum of Natural History. 2020. "What Does It Mean to Be Human?" Available: https://humanorigins.si.edu/evidence/genetics/human-skin-color-variation/modern-human-diversity-skin-color.

Smolianov, Peter and Joseph F. Aiyeku. 2009. "Corporate Marketing Objectives and Evaluation Measures for Integrated Television Advertising and Sports Event Sponsorships." *Journal of Promotion Management,* 15(1–2): 74–89.

Snyder, C. R., M.A. Lassagard and C.E. Ford. 1986. "Distancing After Group Success and Failure: Basking in Reflected Glory and Cutting off Reflected Failure." *Journal of Personality and Social Psychology,* 51: 382–388.

Snyder, Eldon E., and Elmer Spreitzer. 1978. *Social Aspects of Sport.* Englewood Cliffs, NJ: Prentice Hall.

Snyder, John. 2001. *Soccer's Most Wanted: The Top 10 Book of Clumsy Keepers, Clever Crosses, and Outlandish Oddities.* Washington, D.C.: Brassey.

Social Media Defined. 2014. "What Is Social Media?" Available: http://www.socialmediadefined.com/what-is-social-media/.

Solomon, Jon. 2020. "For Kids with Disabilities, Sports Will Return Much More Cautiously." The Aspen Institute, June 15. Available: https://www.aspenprojectplay.org/coronavirus-and-youth-sports/reports/2020/6/15/for-kids-with-disabilities-sports-will-return-much-more-cautiously.

Somaskekhar, Sandhya and Kimbriell Kelly. 2014. "Was Michael Brown Surrendering or Advancing to Attack Officer Darren Wilson?" *The Washington Post,* November 29. Available: http://www.washingtonpost.com/politics/2014/11/29/b99ef7a8–75d3–11e4-a755-e32227229e7b_story.html.

Spacey, John. 2019. "8 Types of Economic Sector." *Simplicable.com,* February 26. Available: https://simplicable.com/new/economic-sector.

Special Olympics. 2020. "About." Available: https://www.specialolympics.org/about.

Sperber, Murray. 1990. *College Sports Inc.* New York: Henry Holt.

Spitznagel, Eric. 2020. "How a Grifter Persuaded Wealthy Parents to Risk It All—Just to Get Their Kids in College." *New York Post,* July 25. Available: https://nypost.com/2020/07/25/how-the-college-admissions-grifter-got-parents-to-risk-it-all/.

Sport England. 2020. "Economic Development." Available: https://www.sportengland.org/why-were-here/economic-development.

Sports Illustrated. 2006. "Sign of the Apocalypse." September 11: 28.

_____. 2008. "Getting Belichicky." June 23: 28.

_____. 2014. "Go Figure: 50." November 10: 15.

SportsIllustrated.com. 2005. "Going for the Jugular?" October 31. Available: http://sportsillustrated.cnn.com/2005/football/ncaa.

Stanford Children's Health (SCH). 2020. "Sports and Children with Special Needs." Available: https://www.stanfordchildrens.org/en/topic/default?id=sports-and-children-with-special-needs-160–20.

Stanley, Gregory Kent. 1996. *The Rise and Fall of the Sportswoman: Women's Health, Fitness, and Athletics 1860–1940*. New York: Peter Lang.

Staurowsky, Ellen. 1998. "An Act of Honor or Exploitation? The Cleveland Indians: Use of the Louis Francis Sockalexis Story." *Sociology of Sport Journal*. 15: 299–316.

Stearns, Peter N. 2001. *Consumerism in World History: The Global Transformation of Desire*. New York: Routledge.

Stein, Rob. 2005. "Physical Fitness Study Confirms Fears on Health of Many Americans." *Buffalo News* (originally published in the *Washington Post*). December 21: A1, A6.

Stevenson, C. L., and J. E. Nixon. 1972. "A Conceptual Scheme of the Social Functions of Sports." *Sportwis senschaft*, 2: 119–132.

Stewart, Larry. 2002. "'Chickisms' Include Mustard and Everything Else in the Refrigerator." *Los Angeles Times*. August 6: D3.

Stewart, Tilghman, Fox, Bianchi & Cain. 2020. "Nationwide Hazing Laws." Available: https://www.stfblaw.com/hazing-lawyers/nationwide-hazing-laws/.

Stiehm, Jamie. 2018. "'The Star-Spangled Banner's' Racist Lyrics Reflect its Slave Owner Author, Francis Scott Key." The Undefeated, September 6. Available: https://theundefeated.com/features/the-star-spangled-banners-racist-lyrics-reflect-its-slaveowner-author-francis-scott-key/.

Stinchfield, Randy, and Ken C. Winters. 1988. "Gambling and Problem Gambling Among Youths," pp. 172–185 in *The Annals*, edited by James H. Frey. Thousand Oaks, CA: Sage.

Stoll, Sharon, and Jennifer Beller. 2000. "Do Sports Build Character?" pp. 18–30 in *Sports in School: The Future of an Institution*, edited by John Gerdy. New York: Teachers College Press.

Strauss, Lawrence. 1998. "Does Money Tilt the Playing Field?: When Covering Becomes Marketing." *Columbia Journalism Review*. Vol. 37 (Sept./Oct.), Issue 3: 16–17.

Stubbs, Dave. 2020. "Hanson Brothers Halt Appearances Because of Coronavirus." *NHL Insider*, April 7. Available: https://www.nhl.com/news/hanson-brothers-halt-appearances-coronavirus/c-316520410.

Surfers Healing. 2020. "About Us." Available: https://www.surfershealing.org/about-us.

Sutherland, Edwin, and Donald R. Cressey. 1978. *Criminology*, 10th edition. Philadelphia: Lippincott.

Swaddling, Judith. 1980. *The Ancient Olympic Games*. Austin: University of Texas Press.

Swartz, Jon. 2004. "Behind Fun Façade, Professional Wrestling Sees 65 Deaths in 7 Years." *USA Today*. March 12: 1A.

Szymanski, Stefan, and Andrew Zimbalist. 2005. *National Pastime*. Washington, D.C.: Brookings Institution Press.

Tackle ALS. "Don't Be Sorry. Let's Beat This. Available: tackals.com.

Tahirali, Jesse. 2015. "Concussions in the NHL: By the Numbers." *CTV News*, November 30. Available: https://www.ctvnews.ca/w5/concussions-in-the-nhl-by-the-numbers-1.2680486#:~:text=With%20averages%20ranging%20from%204.6%20to%207.7%20concussions,can%20symptoms%20experienced%20by%20those%20who%20experience%20them..

Taino Museum. 2020. "Genocide." Available: https://tainomuseum.org/taino/genocide/.

Tajfel, Henri. 1978. "The Achievement of Inner-group Differentiation," pp. 77–100 in *Differentiation Between Social Groups*, edited by Henri. Jajfel. London: Academic Press.

Tajfel, Henri. and John .C. Turner. 1979. "An Integrative Theory of Inter-group Conflict," pp. 33–47 in *The Social Psychology of Inter-group Relations*, edited by W.G. Austin and S. Worchel. Monterey, CA: Brooks/Cole.

Tamura, Leslie. 2011. "Pickleball, A Tennis-Badminton-Table-Tennis Hybrid, Moves Outdoors in Arlington." *The Washington Post*, June 27. Available: http://www.washingtonpost.com/national/pickleball-a-tennis-badminton-table-tennis-hybrid-moves-outdoors-in-arlington/2011/04/29/AGNnkvnH_story.html.

Telander, Rick. 1988. "Sports Behind the Walls." *Sports Illustrated*, October 17: 82–88.

Tennessee Titans. 2014. "Official Website: Michael Oher." Available: http://www.titansonline.com/team/roster/Michael-Oher/57085330–6700–428c-8669-bd79b37001ed.

Texas Hunt Lodge. 2014. "Zebra Hunts." Available: http://www.texashuntlodge.com/zebra_hunt_package.asp.

Theberge, N. 1981. "A Critique of Critiques: Radical and Feminist Writings on Sport." *Social Forces*, 60(2): 341–353.

Thelin, John R. 1994. *Games Colleges Play: Scandal and Reform in Intercollegiate Athletics*. Baltimore, MD: Johns Hopkins University Press.

Themner, Anders and Roxanna Sjostedt. 2019. "Buying Them Off or Scaring Them Straight: Explaining Warlord Democrats' Electoral Rhetoric." *Security Studies*, 29(1): 1–33.

Thomas, Katie. 2011. "Colleges Cut Men's Programs to Satisfy Title IX." *The New York Times*, May 1. Available: http://www.nytimes.com/2011/05/02/sports/02gender.html?_r=0.

Thomsen, Geoff. 2006. "Top 25 Most Popular Sports/Recreational Activities in the U.S." Available: http://www.doubledonut.com/2006/08/14/top-25-most-popular-sportsrecreational-activities-in-the-us.

Tim Green Books. 2020. Available: Timgreenbooks.com.

Time Toast. 2014. "Intercollegiate Sports: First Women's Collegiate Game." Available: http://www.timetoast.com/timelines/intercollegiate-sports.

Todd, Melissa, and Chris Brown. 2003. "Characteristics Associated with Superstitious Behavior in Track and Field Athletes: Are There NCAA Divisional Level Differences?" *Journal of Sport Behavior*. 26(2): 168– 179.

Todhunter, Andrew. 2000. *Dangerous Games.* New York: Doubleday.

Toglia, Jessica M. and Othello Harris. 2014. "Alumni Perceptions of a University's Decision to Remove Native American Imagery from Its Athletic Program: A Case Study." *Journal of Sport and Social Issues,* 38(4): 291–321.

Tomlinson, Alan, and Christopher Young. 2006. "Culture, Politics, and Spectacle in the Global Sports Event—An Introduction," pp. 1–14 in *National Identity and Global Sports Events,* edited by Alan Tomlinson and Christopher Young. Albany: State University of New York Press.

Torres, Maria. 2020. "Minor Leaguers Say Angels Failed to Pay." *Los Angeles Times,* September 3: B8.

Townsend, Mark. 2014. "Former Major Leaguer Mark Gilbert Approved as U.S. Ambassador." Sports.Yahoo.com. December 13. Available: http://sports.yahoo.com/blogs/mlb-big-league-stew/former-major-leaguer-mark-gilbert-approved-as-us-ambassador-092419675.html.

Trister, Noah. 2015. "Asking for a Game of Tolerance." *The Post-Standard,* December 17: B7.

Tuley, Dave. 2005. "Old Friend or Two-Faced Acquaintance?" July 21. Available: http://www.lexisnexis.com/unworse/document.

Turner, Jonathan. 1975. "A Strategy for Reformulating the Dialectical and Functional Theories of Conflict." *Social Forces,* 53 (3): 433–444.

_____. 2006. *Handbook of Sociological Theory.* New York: Springer.

Turner, Victor. 1967. *The Forest of Symbols.* Ithaca, NY: Cornell University Press.

The TV Shield. 2020. "The Top 10 Largest Football Stadiums in America." Available: https://www.thetvshield.com/blog/the-top-10-largest-football-stadiums-in-america/.

Twitter. 2014. "Top 10 Twitter Athletes." Available: http://twitter-athletes.com/TopAthletes.cfm.

Ullirch-French, Sarah and Alan L. Smith. 2006. "Perceptions of Relationships with Parents and Peers in Youth Sport: Impendent and Combined Prediction Motivational Outcomes." *Psychology of Sport and Exercise,* 7(2): 193–214.

Underwood, John. 1989. "What's Wrong with Organized Youth Sports and What We Should Do About It," pp. 120–132 in *Sport in Contemporary Society,* 3rd edition. New York: St. Martin's Press.

United States Olympic Committee. 2014. "Athlete Bio: Thorpe, Jim." Available: https://web.archive.org/web/20070930201621/http://www.usoc.org/26_37888.htm.

United States Specialty Sports Association (USSSA). 2020. "About USSSA: Our Philosophy." Available: http://www.usssabaseball.org/about-usssa.

United States Sports Academy (USSA). 2014a. "USSA: About Us." Available: http://ussa.edu/about/.

_____. 2014b. "USSA: Certification Programs: National Coaching." Available: http://old.nfhs.org/Activity3.aspx?id=3260.

United States Tennis Association (USTA). "For Young Tennis Players: USTA Junior Tournaments." Available: https://www.usta.com/en/home/play/youth-tennis/programs/national/about-junior-tournaments.html.

University of Utah. 2020. "Memorandum of Understanding Between the Ute Indian Tribe and the University of Utah.," March 3. Available: https://admin.utah.edu/ute-mou/.

U.S. Bureau of Labor Statistics. 2014. "Usual Weekly Earnings.Summary." October 24. Available: http://www.bls.gov/news.release/wkyeng.nr0.htm.

U.S. Census Bureau. 1999. "Current Business Reports BS/98, Service Annual Survey: 1998. Washington, D.C.: USGPO.

_____. 2004. "Historical Income Tables." October 3. Available: www.uscensus.gov.

_____. 2004. "Official Statistics." Available: www.uscensus.gov.

_____. 2012. "2010 Census Shows Nearly Half of All American Indians and Alaska Natives Report Multiple Races." January 25. Available: https://www.census.gov/newsroom/releases/archives/2010_census/cb12-cn06.html.

USA Pickleball Association. 2020. "What is Pickleball?" Available: https://usapickleball.org/what-is-pickleball/.

USA Today. 1999. "New Deal." June 7: C1.

_____. 1999. "Women's Marathon Times." December 30: 1C.

_____. 2000. "Marinovich Back at Work Today." April 27: 17C.

_____. 2019. "NHL Suspends Slava Voynov For 2019–20 Season for Domestic Violence," April 9. Available: https://www.usatoday.com/story/sports/nhl/2019/04/09/nhl-suspends-voynov-for-2019-20-season-for-domestic-violence/39322211/.

Uzoma, Kay. 2018. "How Many Youth Participate in Sports in the U.S.?" *SportsRec,* December 5. Available: https://www.sportsrec.com/6542508/how-many-youth-participate-in-sports-in-the-us.

Vandy Sports. 2005. "Monday Morning Coffee." October 3. Available: http://vanderbilt.rivals.com/content.asp?sid+1087&cid+247065.

Van Keuren, K. 1992. "Title IX 20 Years Later: Has Sport Actually Changed?" *CSSS Digest.* Summer: 9.

Varsity.com. 2014. "Being a Cheerleader—History of Cheerleading." Available: https://www.varsity.com/news/cheerleader-history-cheerleading/#:~:text=Being%20a%20Cheerleader%20%E2%80%93%20History%20of%20Cheerleading.%201,on%20a%20Budget.%204%20Spirit%20Connects%20Everyone.

_____. 2018. "What Is Competitive Cheerleading." Available: https://www.varsity.com/news/what-is-competitive-cheerleading/#:~:text=Competitive%20cheerleading%20is%20when%20cheer%20squads%20compete%20against,each%20division%20gets%20a%20trophy%20and%20bragging%20rights.

Veblen, Thorstein. 1934 [1899]. *The Theory of the Leisure Class: An Economic Study of Institution.* New York: Random House.

Verducci, Tom. 2020. "MLB Reveals Red Sox' Cheating Scandal, Tainting Yet Another Championship Team." *Sports Illustrated,* April 22. Available: https://www.si.com/mlb/2020/04/22/red-sox-sign-stealing-scandal.

Veroff, J. 1969. "Social Comparison and the Development of Achievement Motivation," pp. 46–101 in *Achievement-Related Motives in Children,* edited by C.P. Smith. New York: Russell Sage Foundation.

Vertinsky, Patricia A. *The Eternally Wounded Woman.* Urbana and Chicago: University of Illinois Press.

Vogel, Steve. 2020. "What You Didn't Know About Francis Scott Key." *History News Network.* Available: https://historynewsnetwork.org/article/156907.

Vogler, Conrad, and Stephen Schwartz. 1993. *The Sociology of Sport: An Introduction.* Englewood Cliffs, NJ: Prentice Hall.

vos Savant, Marilyn. 2005. "Ask Marilyn." *Parade,* August 23: 18.

Voy, Robert. 1991. *Drugs, Sport and Politics.* Champaign, IL: Leisure Press.

Wahl, Grant. 2005. "Yes, Hard Feelings." *Sports Illustrated.* March 28: 54–57.

Walker, Ben. 2020. "Astros, MLB Brace for Scandal Fallout." *The Citizen,* January 22: B3.

Walpole, Elinor. 2016. "*Race* and How Sports Movies Can Illustrate Wider Historical Contexts." IntoFilm.org, June 3. Available: https://www.intofilm.org/news-and-views/articles/race-feature.

Walton, Bill. 2005. "Good Sportsmanship Is Losing out to Winning." *USA Today.* December 21: 13A.

Wann, Daniel, and Nyla Branscombe. 1990. "Die-Hard and Fair-Weather Fans: Effects of Identification on BIRGing and CORFing Tendencies." *Journal of Sport and Social Issues.* 14(2): 103–117.

_____. 1993. "Sports Fans: Measuring Degree of Identification with Their Team." *International Journal of Sport Psychology,* 24: 1–17.

Wann, Daniel L. and Mary E. Goeke. 2018. "Sport Fan Superstition: The Importance of Team Identification, Sport Fandom, and Fan Dysfunction. *Journal of Sport Behavior,* 41(2): 227–235.

Wann, Daniel L., Merrill J. Melnick, Gordon W. Russell, and Dale G. Pease. 2001. *Sport Fans.* New York: Routledge.

Warren, William E. 1997. *Coaching & Control.* Paramus, NJ: Prentice Hall.

Watts, Marina. 2020. "Why Did Lady Antebellum Just Change Their Name to Lady A?" *Newsweek,* June 11. Available: https://www.newsweek.com/why-did-lady-antebellum-just-change-their-name-lady-1510271.

Waxman, Olivia B. 2017. "Here's How Standing for the National Anthem Became Part of U.S. Sports Tradition." *Time,* September 25. Available: https://time.com/4955623/history-national-anthem-sports-nfl/.

Webb, Donnie. 2007. "The Money Game." December 5. Available: www.syracuse.com.

Weber, Sam. 2020. "The Top 100 Athletes on Social Media: 2019." Opendorse.com, January 28. Available: https://opendorse.com/blog/the-top-100-athletes-on-social-media-2019/.

Wedgwood, Nikki. 2004. "Kicking Like a Boy: School Girl Australian Rules Football and Bi-Gendered Female Embodiment." *Sociology of Sport Journal.* 21: 140–162.

Weiner, Richard. 1999. "Marinovich Attempts Carve out Comeback," *USA Today.* May 12: 8C.

Weir, Tom. 2004. "Online Sports Betting Spins out of Control." *USA Today.* August 22: A-1.

Weiss, Zeev. 2014. *Public Spectacles in Roman and Late Antique Palestine.* Cambridge, MA: Harvard University Press.

Weissmann, Jordan. 2014. "Big Bucks or Bogus Betting Baloney?" *Slate,* November 21. Available: https://slate.com/business/2014/11/adam-silver-says-theres-400-billion-per-year-of-illegal-sports-betting-in-the-u-s-alone-seriously.html.

Werner, Erica. 2005. "Indian Casinos See Rapid Growth." *The Post-Standard.* February 16: A-6.

Wertheim, L. Jon. 2002. *Venus Envy.* New York: Perennial.

WESH.com 2014. "Former Florida A&M Band Member Convicted of Manslaughter in Drum Major's Hazing Death." October 31. Available: http://www.wesh.com/news/closing-arguments-set-to-begin-in-famu-hazing-trial/29451642.

West, Jenna. 2020. "Lawmakers Introduce Bill to Block College Coronavirus Liability Waivers." *Sports Illustrated,* June 30. Available: https://www.si.com/college/2020/06/30/coronavirus-liability-waivers-legislation-student-athletes

Whannel, Garry. 2002. *Media Sport Stars.* New York; Routledge.

Wharton, David. 2019. "Don't Call It Breakdancing: 'Breaking' Tries to Bust Into the Olympics." *Los Angeles Times,* May 11: A1, A8.

_____. 2020. "Tradition is Under Review." *Los Angeles Times,* July 5: B8.

White, Caroline. 2007. "Mixed Martial Arts and Boxing Should be Banned, says BMA." *British Medical Journal,* 335(7618): 469.

White, G. Edward. 1996. *Creating the National Pastime: Baseball Transforms Itself 1903–1953.* Princeton, NJ: Princeton University Press.

Whithers, Tom. 2018. "Cleveland Dropping Chief Wahoo Logo from Uniforms." *The Post-Standard,* January 30: B2.

_____. 2020. "Attention Shifts to 'Indians' Nickname." *The Citizen,* July 14: B2.

Whitmire, Tim. 1999. "Reese Was the Man of Boys of Summer." *Buffalo News.* August 19: F1.

Wiebe, Robert H. 2003. "Primary Tensions in American Public Life," pp. 35–49 in *Public Discourse in America,* edited by Judith Rodin and Stephen P. Steinberg. Philadelphia: University of Pennsylvania Press.

Wilcox, Ralph C. 1994. "The Shamrock and the Eagle: Irish Americans and Sport in the Nineteenth Century," pp. 55–74 in *Ethnicity and Sport in North American History And Culture,* edited by

George Eisen and David K. Wiggins. Westport, CT: Greenwood Press.

Will, George. 2000. "Sports Gambling Bill a Bad Bet." *Buffalo News.* March 13: B3.

Williams, Dana M. 2007. "No Past, No Respect, and No Power: An Anarchist Evaluation of Native Americans as Sports Nicknames, Logos, and Mascots." *Anarchist Studies,* 15(1): 31–54.

Williams, Henry. 1895. "The Educational and Health Giving Value of Athletics." *Harper's Weekly.* February 16: 166.

Williams, Larry R. 1981 (Apr.). "Women's Correctional Recreation Services." *Journal of Physical Education, Recreation and Dance,* Vol. 52 (4): 56.

Williams, Randy. 2006. *Sports Cinema—100 Movies.* Pompton Plain, NJ: Limelight Editions.

Winderman, Ira. 2014. "Unlike LeBron, No Need for Wade Football Ban for Sons." *Sun Sentinel,* November 17. Available: http://www.sun-sentinel.com/sports/miami-heat/sfl-miami-heat-dwyane-wade-football-s111714-story.html.

Winik, Lyric Wallwork. 2005. "U.S. Olympians Need YOU!" *Parade.* November 20: 27.

Winter, Bud. 1981. *Relax & Win.* San Diego: A. S. Barnes.

Witz, Billy. 2020. "Ohio State Pays $41 Million to Settle Claims From Doctor's Abuse." *The New York Times,* May 8. Available: https://www.nytimes.com/2020/05/08/sports/ohio-state-strauss-settlement.html?searchResultPosition=2.

WKYC. 2019. "Ohio University Investigating Hazing Allegations Made Against Marching Band Members," October 10. Available: https://www.wkyc.com/article/news/local/ohio/ohio-university-investigating-hazing-allegations-made-against-marching-band-members/95-a154f358-37a0-4af5-9652-3296a2a50cc8.

Wober, Mallory. 1971. "Race and Intelligence." *Transition,* 40 (December): 16–26.

Wohl, A. 1970. "Competitive Sport and Its Social Function." *International Review of Sport,* 5: 117– 125.

Wolff, Alexander. 2014. "Scorecard: Members Only." *Sports Illustrated,* August 18: 14–15.

Womack, Mari. 1992. "Why Athletes Need Ritual: A Study of Magic Among Professional Athletes," pp. 191–202 in *Sport and Religion,* edited by Shirl J. Hoffman. Champaign, IL: Human Kinetics.

Women's Sports Foundation. 2004. "27 Year Study Shows Progression of Women in College Athletics." Available: http://www.womenssportsfoundation.org.

Wood, Robert. 2012. "New and Unique Sports List." Topend Sports. Available: https://www.topendsports.com/sport/new/list.htm.

Wood, Ruth. 2019. "The Testosterone Tangent." *Los Angeles Times,* May 6: A11.

World Anti-Doping Agency (WADA). 2020. "What We Do." Available: https://www.wada-ama.org/en/what-we-do/.

World Sport Stacking Association. 2008. "WSSA Mission Statement." WSSA homepage: Available: http://www.worldsportsstackingassociation.org/about.htm.

Wright, Branson. 2012. "Remembering Cleveland's Muhammad Ali Summit, 45 Years Later." *The Plain Dealer,* June 3. Available: http://www.cleveland.com/sports/index.ssf/2012/06/gathering_of_stars.html.

Wright, Perry B. and Kristi J. Erdal. 2009. "Sport Superstition as a Function of Skill Level and Task Difficulty." *Journal of Sport Behavior,* 32(2): 187–199.

Yesalis, Charles, and Virginia Cowart. 1998. *The Steroids Game.* Champaign, IL: Human Kinetics.

Yiannakis, Andrew, Thomas McIntyre, Merrill Melnick, and Dale Hart. 1978. *Sport Sociology: Contemporary Themes.* Dubuque, IA: Kendall Hunt.

YMCA. 2020. "History—Founding." Available: https://www.ymca.net/history/founding.html.

York, Heather. 2013. "7 Pro Athletes Who Spend Their Money on More than Bling." *Take Part,* January 7. Available: http://www.takepart.com/photos/most-generous-athletes/serena-williams.

Young, Jabari. 2019. "With Football Ratings On the Rise, NFL Officials Look to Raise TV Broadcast Fees on Multiyear Media Deals." *CNBC,* December 30. Available: https://www.cnbc.com/2019/12/30/nfl-ratings-recovering-new-media-deals-could-be-on-the-2020-agenda.html.

Youth Hockey. 2019."Homepage." Available: https://www.youthhockey.com/.

Zarum, Lara. 2020. "The Joy and Heartbreak of 'Cheer.'" *Rolling Stone,* January 27. Available: https://www.rollingstone.com/tv/tv-features/netflix-docuseries-cheer-944012/.

Zax, Tayla. 2020. "The Wonderful, Horrible Afterlife of Leni Riefenstahl." *Forward,* February 21. Available: https://forward.com/culture/440207/leni-riefenstahl-legacy-afterlife-nazi-propaganda-or-great-filmmaker/.

Zeigler, Cyd. 2016. "Mexico National Soccer Players Team Up Against Homophobic 'Puto' Chant." *Outsports.com,* April 3. Available: https://www.outsports.com/2016/4/3/11359340/mexico-soccer-gay-puto-chant.

Zervas, Kostas, and Jonathan Glazzard. 2018. "Sport Management Student as Producer: Embedding Critical Management Studies in Sport through Contemporary Pedagogy." *Sport Education and Society,* 23(9): 928–937.

Zillmann, Dolf, Bryant Jennings, and Barry Sapolsky. 1979. "The Enjoyment of Watching Sport Contests," pp. 297–335 in *Sport, Games and Play,* edited by Jeffrey H. Goldstein. Hillsdale, NJ: Laurence Earlbaum.

Zimbalist, Andrew. 1999. *Unpaid Professionals.* Princeton, NJ: Princeton University Press.

Zirin, David. 2005. "When the Arm Breaks: John Chaney and the Rules of Violence." *PoliticalAffairs.net.* Available: http://www.politicalaffairs.net/article/view/729/1/80/.

Zwerman, G. 1995. *Martina Navratilova: Lives of Notable Gay Men and Lesbians.* New York: Chelsea House.

Index